19-24

W9-ANM-132

WITHDRAWN
NDSU

John Milton at the Age of Ten, 1618

THE NEW CAMBRIDGE EDITION

A Revision of the Cambridge Edition
Edited by William Vaughn Moody

The Complete Poetical Works of

JOHN MILTON 1608-1674.

A NEW TEXT EDITED WITH
INTRODUCTION AND NOTES
BY

HARRIS FRANCIS FLETCHER
THE UNIVERSITY OF ILLINOIS

HOUGHTON MIFFLIN COMPANY
BOSTON · NEW YORK · CHICAGO · DALLAS · ATLANTA · SAN FRANCISCO
The Riverside Press Cambridge

821
M64co

Copyright, 1941

HARRIS FRANCIS FLETCHER

All rights reserved

41-1497/3

PR
3551
F5

The Riverside Press
CAMBRIDGE · MASSACHUSETTS
PRINTED IN THE U.S.A.

CONTENTS

Poems Written in School and at College, 1620–1632

Poems Written at Horton, 1632–1638

63862

The English Sonnets, 1630–1660

Paradise Lost

Paradise Regained

Samson Agonistes

Italian, Latin, and Greek Poems and Translations

Miscellaneous English Metrical Pieces and the Psalm Paraphrases

The Psalm Paraphrases

EDITOR'S NOTE

WILLIAM VAUGHN MOODY edited the Cambridge Edition of *The Complete Poetical Works of John Milton* in 1899. His edition soon became the most widely known and used American edition of Milton's poetry. It was published without change until 1924, when Professor E. K. Rand revised the text and Moody's translations of the Latin poems. Otherwise, the edition has been without modifications to the present time. Moody was almost ideally fitted to edit Milton's poetry, and the combination of poetry and editor was a most happy one for both. The appreciation and study of Milton's poetry in this country during the present century are largely due to Moody's remarkably successful and stimulating introductions to the individual poems and groups of poems in his edition.

The task confronting the reviser of his edition is a difficult one. There has been a greater change in attitude towards Milton and his works during the past generation than towards any other great English literary figure. Moody anticipated and brought about some of this change; but it was impossible for him to anticipate all of it. He wrote and lived at the end of an era that completed the fullest and most adequate study and conception of Milton that had ever been made. That study and the conception of the poet which grew out of it centered largely in the labors of one man, David Masson (1822–1907), from 1860 to 1896. His contributions to the knowledge and understanding of Milton are the greatest that one man ever made. His work completely dominated the appreciation and study of Milton and his writings until about 1920. Other men of the late nineteenth century, especially Pattison, Brooke, Raleigh, Trent, Moody, Garnett, Stephen, Saintsbury, and Bailey, although demurring over Masson's indubitable laboriousness, were more or less forced to accept not only Masson's facts but likewise his interpretations of Milton. Moody was anxious to offset some of Masson's prejudices, and depended a great deal on Pattison's little book to do this. But both Masson and Pattison were fundamentally apologists for the poet who, they insisted, was a great national hero, and who, therefore, according to Victorian principles, must at any cost be represented as spotless.

A reaction to Masson and to the whole attitude of the latter half of the nineteenth century toward Milton set in about 1910. A new order of Miltonic scholarship was clearly discernible by 1920. Smart was saying that it had become necessary to 'de-Massonize' Milton. Hanford was turning to Milton's own words on himself and to his recorded readings. Grierson was outlining his theology in a way that made it impossible to ignore any longer the plain sense of certain lines in *Paradise Lost* in the light of reasoned statement in the hitherto neglected *De Doctrina*. Then came the Continentals, especially Saurat, the Frenchman, who insisted that vast areas of Milton's life and activities had been overlooked. Abortive attempts were made to psychoanalyze Milton. All phases of him and of his work were studied intensively. His learning and his studies, his sources and his poetic and literary theories, his life and activities in the light of his times, were reconsidered, and gradually a new conception of him and of his works arose. From all this study, many new facts emerged along with new emphases on old ones. He came to be seen, not as an omniscient, omnipotent, multiform genius as the Victorians had pictured him, but as a great poet who also indulged, however remarkably or unremarkably, in other activities. His life and works can be approached today from a different and more detached point of view than Moody found possible, because of the new scholarship of the past twenty years.

The editor of Milton's poetry today must take into account this mass of new material, and, uniting it with the old, produce an edition that not only does justice to Miltonic scholarship, but also and chiefly to Milton and his poetry in the light of that scholarship.

Moody succeeded in producing an edition which admirably fulfilled such conditions for his generation. The present editor has humbly tried to produce an edition that will serve a later generation as well as Moody's edition served his.

The general plan of the earlier edition has been retained, as it has been found too useful a scheme to abandon. Moody first printed a short account of Milton's life and times; and then printed introductions to a group of poems, each introduction followed by the texts of the poems introduced. Each of the more important poems was preceded by its own separate introduction. The present editor found it impossible to rewrite or rearrange the work of so gifted a genius as Moody, and consequently has written new introductions. New facts or new emphases on old ones virtually forced such a procedure, as much of Moody's most effective writing on Milton can no longer be accepted without great modification. New footnotes have been written and put at the bottom of the proper pages. These notes are selected to help the reader rather than to be elaborate, exhaustive, or forbidding. Hume, Newton, Warton, Todd, and Verity must always be available to the scholar.

The Latin poems are printed apart from the English in the arrangement and order in which Milton printed them, and are published with a minimum of critical apparatus and commentary. Such apparatus is of little value to persons unable to read Latin, and to the classicist, the relatively small amount of it that could be printed in an edition intended for the general reader would be unsatisfactory and insufficient. The Latin poems are therefore very sparsely annotated. Professor William Abbott Oldfather has carefully and generously scrutinized the few added translations of Latin and Greek poems and the Greek text. The responsibility for the final form in which these poems and their translations have been printed is the author's alone. The Italian sonnets are also printed apart from the English sonnets. The English poems are printed in chronological groups; but within the groups, the individual poems, except *Lycidas* and the *Sonnets*, are printed in the order in which Milton printed them. *Lycidas* follows *Comus*, and the English *Sonnets* are collected after it. Poems which Milton failed to print are inserted at such points as he would probably have chosen. Each poem or group of poems is dated if possible, with explanations of the date assigned whenever they seem necessary.

THE TEXT

THE text published herein is a completely new one, based on certain definite principles of text-making that have never been used before by an editor of Milton's poetry. The present editor accepts the principle laid down by the editor of the Columbia edition, Professor Patterson, that the last edition printed by Milton himself should be used as a base text. But that principle alone is not enough. The editor who stops with it will save himself much labor; but his text will soon be suspect. Due to peculiarities of bookmaking in seventeenth-century England, no two copies of the same edition of a book printed then are exactly alike. It is therefore necessary to collate many copies of the same edition with each other in order to arrive at a text that fairly represents what Milton wanted printed. The present text is a modernized result of the collation of many copies of the last editions of the various poems printed in Milton's lifetime, with each other and with many copies of earlier editions if they exist, as well as with manuscript readings. Libraries and individuals in England, France, and in this country have responded generously to requests for photographs or loans of their copies of Milton's poems. The originals, of which a great many were used, or the photographs, chiefly on film, have been collated with each other and with earlier editions and manuscript copies. The reading of a first or other edition, or of a manuscript, has been used, if, as is sometimes the case, every available copy of the final edition is obviously in error. This text is the result of that collation, with modernized spelling. It is not intended to be a basic, completely adequate text with full textual apparatus for scholarly use. Such a text, with its apparatus, would be out of place in an edition intended as this one is for general use.

Spellings are modernized according to *Webster's New International Dictionary*. Capitalization has been modernized, which means that most of Milton's capitals, and those of his printers, have disappeared. Except in the Psalm paraphrases, no italic type is used in the text itself, as it is impossible to follow Milton's usage without becoming inconsistent and arbitrary. The punctuation is Milton's, or his printers'. His punctuation is so essentially a part of his metrics, in so far as he could get his printers to follow it, that it is of great aid in reading his poetry. It has a different meaning from any modern system. Every system of punctuation changes; but in his poems, most of Milton's metrical punctuation is as useful today as it was three centuries ago.

Only those poems generally accepted as Milton's are included. The reader is referred to the Columbia edition for other poems that have been ascribed to him at various times.

LIST OF PORTRAITS

The Life and Times of John Milton
1608–1674

MILTON lived in one of the most revolutionary and exciting centuries in all British history. His life spanned the reigns of three kings, two protectors, and a parliamentary interlude, not to mention the brief operation of the Committee of Safety. He lived through the first three revolutions of the century; and the latter end of his lifetime included the great London fire, which destroyed the old city of London almost completely.

The writing of his biography is beset with difficulties. It is easy to lose him in the background of the great and important events taking place during his lifetime. It is equally easy to make large generalizations about him and his work that are too opinionated and biased to be worth much; but which are all too easy to formulate. Perhaps the greatest difficulty confronting his biographer, regardless of the large or small extent of the biography, is to keep the figure of Milton intact. He seems to break up into several individuals, or to be a different man at different times. But there is a unity in him and in his work that, however difficult it may be to preserve, must not be allowed to disappear or even to fade. In addition to preserving his identity as a man, his biographer must also keep him intact as a poet and man of letters. It is too easy to make him out as primarily a statesman, a scholar, or a social reformer, for he was all of these in varying degrees. But the most important of all facts about John Milton is that he became and remained a great poet.

Every student or persistent reader of Milton should, and ultimately must, study the facts of his life, the nature and contents of his works, prose and verse, and then try to create his own conception of the poet and of the man, Milton.

The biography of John Milton the poet is easy to sketch in its main outlines, but difficult to explain in many of its details. He came from a little-known family which produced no one before or after him particularly known to fame. He lived a fairly simple, almost commonplace existence, accepting good fortune and misfortune as they came to him. His father's prosperity enabled the son to receive an education usually accorded only to the sons of the landed gentry, and for his first fifty years to live as a person of means. The poet early allied himself with the forces supporting the Parliament in the struggle with King Charles I, and made himself so useful to that party as a writer that for about ten years he held a public office under the Commonwealth and the Protectorate. His prose writings made him their foremost mouthpiece and the most effective champion of liberty known to English letters. The Restoration of King Charles II to the English throne found Milton greatly impoverished and totally blind; but neither entirely a pauper nor unable to continue his writing.   He died after having become one of the greatest poets Western Europe ever produced.

The task confronting his biographer is that of telling the story of Milton's life, making as clear as possible the relationships between that life and his writings, especially his poetry.   Sometimes these relationships are obvious; but frequently they are obscure, and in a few instances they seem to be entirely lacking.

The source materials for Milton's biography are numerous and full.[1]   They are of three different kinds.   The first is made up of the official records of his birth, marriage, and various officially recorded transactions in which he was involved, or similar records for his own or his father's family.   The second is made up of autobiographical statements found in his works, prose or verse, the more important of which are contained respectively in the Latin prose *Defensio Secunda* (1654), in the English prose *Apology* (1642), in the English prose *Doctrine and Discipline of Divorce* (1643, 1644, 1645), and in *The Reason of Church Government* (1641/42).   The third kind of source material for his life consists of contemporary accounts of him written by men who knew him, some of them intimately, or who knew members of his family.   He was one of the first Englishmen to be accorded the distinction of a systematic biography, and the first man of letters for whom there are several source biographies.   These contemporary biographies were written because, by accident of time, he lived in the age in which the writing of biography in a modern sense was beginning to appear in Europe; and because, after the Restoration, Milton was a relic of the defeated and discredited Commonwealth and Protectorate party and thus something of a curiosity.

Eleven early biographies of Milton have claims to being source biographies; four having been written by persons who saw and knew him personally, and seven by persons who talked or corresponded with his friends or relatives.   In 1681, John Aubrey (1626–97) sent to Anthony Wood (1632–95) the few untidy pages of notes he called 'Minutes of the Life of Mr. John Milton.'   Aubrey knew Milton, or at least had talked with him; but most of his information came from Milton's third wife, Betty (born, Elizabeth Minshull); from the brother, Christopher Milton; and from the elder nephew, Edward Phillips.   Wood, who may or may not have seen Milton, included a biography of him in his biographies of men connected with Oxford University, because Milton told Aubrey that in 1635 Oxford had granted him the M.A. degree.   Wood used Aubrey's minutes as a basis for the biography of Milton he printed in 1691.[2]   In addition to the minutes by Aubrey, Wood also had before him another manuscript that went unpublished until 1902.[3]   This document, known as *The Anonymous Life of Milton* because no one has dis-

---

[1] Biographical source material is material produced during a person's lifetime, by himself or by persons that knew him, that deals directly with any phase of his individual existence.   It includes contemporary records of all kinds that involve the particular individual concerned.

[2] Wood has some claim to being the first English biographer of note.   His great work is *Athenae Oxonienses* (London, 1691–92, 3 vols.).   Milton's life is in the *Fasti*.   Best edition, *Athenae Oxonienses*, Philip Bliss, editor (London, 1813–20, 4 vols.).   Milton, vol. II.   *Fasti*, cols. 480–86, or under the year 1635.

[3] First published by E. S. Parsons, 'The Earliest Life of Milton,' *English Historical Review*, vol. XVII (1902), pp. 95–110.

covered exactly who wrote it, is, unlike Aubrey's sprawling minutes, a formally written, systematic biography, by someone who knew and talked with Milton or with persons intimately connected with him.[1] The next biography to appear in print was written and published by Edward Phillips (1630?–96?), the elder of the two nephews, as a preface to his edition of an English translation of the Latin letters Milton had written for the Commonwealth and Protectorate. As Edward had lived with the poet, and was virtually under his uncle's tutelage from the time he was ten years old, this biography, except for its more obvious prejudices and the limitations of its author, contains more authentic information concerning Milton than any other of the early biographies. All these, by Aubrey, Wood, the Anonymous, and Phillips, were written by men who knew Milton directly or through his immediate family.

In addition to these four biographies, there are seven others, written by men who did not know Milton directly, but who knew and talked or corresponded with persons who did know him. Probably the earliest of these seven was written in French by a Frenchman, Pierre Bayle (1647–1706). Bayle published *Projets et fragmens d'un Diction-naire critique* at Rotterdam in 1692. Then in 1697 appeared his great *Dictionnaire historique et critique*, also printed at Rotterdam in four volumes. He wrote a long account of Milton, apparently securing his information from a correspondent in England who either knew Milton well or someone connected with him. Bayle could not read English very well, but had read and was very much impressed with Milton's Latin works. John Toland (1670–1722) edited and published Milton's prose works in 1698, and printed a biography written by himself as a preface. Toland had apparently never seen Milton, but had talked with several persons then living who had known the poet. Toland based his biography on his conversations with those persons, some correspondence, and on Aubrey, Wood, and Phillips. He corresponded with Bayle, and out of this correspondence grew some additional remarks in Bayle's second and third editions of the *Dictionnaire*.

The first edition of a biography of Milton by Elijah Fenton (1683–1730) appeared in 1725, prefixed to an edition of *Paradise Lost*. This was the first of what Samuel Johnson called the 'honeysuckle lives' of Milton. Fenton's biography has probably been re-printed more frequently than any biography of him ever written.

Jonathan Richardson (1665–1745), the painter, printed his *Explanatory Notes and Re-marks on Paradise Lost* (London, 1734), with a rambling biography which reflected its author's eccentricity and charm.

Thomas Birch (1705–66), after translating, or helping to translate Bayle, edited Mil-ton's prose works, and printed them with a biography in 1738. Francis Peck (1692–1743) published his *New Memoirs of the Life and Poetical Works of Mr. John Milton* in 1740. Bishop

---

[1] The manuscript was found among Wood's papers, and was probably written by Andrew Allam, one of Wood's helpers, who is known to have written a number of the biographies of literary men in Wood's collection. Aubrey says in his minutes that Allam wrote a life of Milton, and it is most likely that the actual document dis-covered among Wood's papers is the biography by Allam to which Aubrey refers. Miss Helen Darbishire, in the introduction to her useful edition of *The Early Lives of Milton* (London: Constable, 1932) is at great but uncon-vincing pains to prove that John Phillips, the younger of the two nephews, wrote the document. Her proof rests chiefly on handwriting; but, unfortunately for her case, the handwriting is in a formal hand or character, and nothing about authorship can be proved from it. See E. S. Parsons, 'The Authorship of the Anonymous Life of Milton,' *PMLA*, vol. L (1935), pp. 1057–63. Parsons rejects Miss Darbishire's alleged proofs.

Thomas Newton (1704–82) also found it necessary to preface his edition of the poetry (1749–52) with a biography. Each of these seven biographers was able to collect a few new facts, and every one of them was able to talk or correspond with friends or relatives of the poet. Even Birch and Newton talked with Elizabeth Clarke, Milton's granddaughter, daughter of Deborah Milton Clarke, his third daughter. Newton's biography was the last based on any personal contact with Milton or with his friends or immediate relatives.

There is, therefore, a large amount of source material dealing directly with Milton's life, the general outlines of which are well known. But the information we possess is very unevenly distributed at different periods of his life; many details of his existence are obscure or unknown, and some of them will always remain so.[1]

MILTON'S ANCESTRY AND HIS FATHER AND MOTHER

Milton was a Londoner born and bred. Except for the years he spent at Cambridge University and for a Continental journey of about fifteen months, his life was entirely spent in London and its immediate environs. Thanks to Wood and Aubrey, the information about his birth is full and exact. Early in the morning of December 9, 1608, there was born to John Milton, scrivener, and Sarah his wife, in Bread Street, London, a son, who, according to the registers of Allhallows Church, also in Bread Street, was christened John on the twentieth of the same month. The father, John the scrivener, was from a family named Milton that had early settled in Oxfordshire. His father, the poet's grandfather, was Richard Milton, a forest yeoman of a family of forest yeomen. Richard's name occurs on the Recusant Rolls, a fact that probably means that he was a Roman Catholic. Aubrey stated that Richard was a papist. He added that John, the poet's father, went to Christ Church College at Oxford University until such time as Richard, his father, visiting the boy's room unexpectedly, found therein certain dangerous and forbidden books (probably a copy of the Genevan Bible) and thereupon disinherited him. John Milton, senior, was born about the same year as Shakespeare, or in 1564 or 1565. He probably was at Oxford about 1582 or 1583. Upon being disinherited, he went to London, and about 1600 became an active member of the Scriveners' Company [2] and married. What he did between the time he left Oxford and 1600 is not

---

[1] The most scholarly, complete, and important biography of Milton was written by David Masson (1822–1907), the first volume of which appeared in 1859, and the final volume, the index, in 1894. The biography is in six volumes, the first three having been revised. Only the 1881 edition of the first volume should be used. The index is a seventh volume. The work is entitled *The Life of John Milton; Narrated in Connection with the Political, Ecclesiastical, and Literary History of His Times* (London: Macmillan, 1859–96, 6 vols. and index). More recent scholarship, especially since 1920, has discovered a few facts of biographical significance, most of them being *minutiae*. See D. H. Stevens, *Reference Guide to Milton* (Chicago: University of Chicago, 1930); and Harris Fletcher, *Contributions to a Milton Bibliography* (Urbana, Illinois: University of Illinois, 1931.)

[2] The scriveners were public writers or scribes similar to notary publics. They were designated as 'scriveners, or writers of the Court Letters of the city of London.' From the fifteenth to the eighteenth century their services were in great demand, and they were very well paid for their work, as new social adjustments were being made and various forms of new wealth were being absorbed and invested in England. During that period the scriveners also became a very profitable enterprise for conveyancing and financing. A succession of able and enterprising men were attracted to the work because of its highly lucrative nature. Milton's father was one of these, and after his time appeared Sir Robert Clayton (1629–1707), who inherited the fortune and business of his uncle, Robert

known. He married Sarah Jefferies, daughter of Paul and Helen Jefferies of London. Not much more is known of her, except from a bare remark or two casually let drop by her son.

The registers of Allhallows Church in Bread Street contain birth notices of all but one, Anne, of the children known to have been born to John and Sarah Milton. They were, except Anne's, as follows:

> 1601, May 12, burial of a 'crysome childe' (i.e., one under one month old).
> [1603–1607] Anne was born; no record of her birth or baptism is known.
> 1608, [December 9] John, baptized December 20.
> 1612, July 15, Sarah baptized; buried, August 6, of same year.
> 1613, January 30, Tabitha baptized.
> 1615, August 3, Tabitha buried.
> 1615, December 3, Christopher baptized.

The three children, Anne, John, and Christopher, all grew up and outlived both their parents. The family in which John Milton the poet slowly matured consisted, therefore, of the father and mother, an older sister, Anne, John the poet, and Christopher, a younger brother.

MILTON'S YOUTH

There are almost no definite facts known about Milton's youth from the record of his birth in 1608 to his matriculation and entrance into Christ's College, Cambridge, in 1625.[1] Milton mentioned this period in the *Defensio Secunda* (1654):

> I was born in London, of respectable parents. My father was a man of highest integrity; my mother, a fine woman, particularly known in our neighborhood for her charity. I was destined from a child for the pursuits of learning, which I prosecuted with such eagerness that after I was twelve years old I seldom retired to bed from my studies until midnight. Study was the first ruination of my eyesight, and to my eye troubles were added frequent headaches. But these could not diminish my instinctive zeal for study, and my father provided me with masters and tutors to give me daily lessons at home, in addition to the regular instruction of grammar school.[2]

Abbot. Abbot monopolized a large share of the scrivener business in the time of James I. By the time Milton's father entered the Scriveners' Company, the original duties of the scriveners, writing and drawing up conveyances and deeds, had come to include the duties, responsibilities, and opportunities of a banker and a financial agent. Their original duties gradually brought them into contact with persons of property, and they became agents for persons with money to invest or mortgages to offer for loans. Soon, the scriveners themselves were in a position to make loans or to buy property offered for sale to collect mortgages. Great tact and discretion were needed in the individual scrivener if he was to make more than a moderate success of his business. John Milton, the poet's father, was one of these few. Clayton became a financier and banker on the largest scale, at one time being reputed to be the richest man in England. Milton's father anticipated Clayton's success on a much smaller but nevertheless highly lucrative scale. In his day, the scriveners made out or certified accounts of record and were also responsible for official translation into English of charters and other documents originally written in other languages. By the nineteenth century, the scrivener had returned to his former and more limited duties, chiefly those of a notary, and the importance of the craft had greatly declined, probably beginning about 1700.

[1] It has been partly reconstructed by Masson (*Life*, vol. I); by E. K. Rand ('Milton in Rustication,' *Studies in Philology*, vol. XIX [1922], pp. 109–35); and by J. H. Hanford ('The Youth of Milton,' *University of Michigan Publications, Language and Literature*, vol. I [1925], pp. 89–163).

[2] *Col.* VIII:118.

In addition, there is the account of the early education written by his nephew, Edward Phillips:

John our author, who was destined to be the ornament and glory of his country, was sent, together with his brother, to Paul's school, whereof Dr. Gill the elder was then chief master; where he was entered into the first rudiments of learning, and advanced therein with that admirable success, not more by the discipline of the school and good instructions of his masters, (for that he had another master possibly at his father's house, appears by the *Fourth Elegy* of his Latin poems written in his eighteenth year to Thomas Young pastor of the English Company of Merchants at Hamburg, wherein he owns and styles him his master) than by his own happy genius, prompt wit and apprehension, and insuperable industry; for he generally sat up half the night, as well in voluntary improvements of his own choice, as the exact perfecting of his school exercises.   So that at the age of fifteen he was full ripe for academic learning, and accordingly was sent to the University of Cambridge.[1]

Both accounts agree in their main outlines.   Milton was early put under private tutors at home, and later sent to Saint Paul's Grammar School.   Almost no definite information is available for the period before he went to grammar school.   But we know something of his relations during that early period with at least two persons, his father and Thomas Young, the only one of his private tutors we know by name.

Milton's father was perhaps the most important of all influences on his son's education, not only because, as the son informs us, he very early planned that education on a most generous scale, but also because as long as he lived he took a keen and active interest in his son's whole intellectual and artistic development.   John Milton the elder also contributed directly to his son's education.   The father was an accomplished musician, performing and composing music; and it was to his father that the poet owed those musical interests and capacities which exhibit themselves so remarkably throughout his poetry.   Milton played the organ and probably other musical instruments throughout his lifetime.   He was also an accomplished vocalist, as we may discover in the many references to song and singing in his poems.   His father was the principal master of the poet's remarkable musical development.[2]

John Milton the elder, so far as we know, after his disinheritance was a member of the orthodox English or Anglican Church the rest of his life.   However, he is known to have associated with persons opposed to that church, although he seems never to have taken an active part in any of the church quarrels or disputes of the time.   He was, however, directly responsible for bringing his son into contact with the whole church controversy of the age by selecting Thomas Young as the boy's tutor.

So important was this controversy in the lives of most Englishmen of the time, and particularly so in the life of John Milton the poet, that a brief explanation of the church situation in England during his earlier life is necessary.   Every church difficulty encountered during the seventeenth century in England was rooted in the break with the Roman Catholic Church by Henry VIII, about 1534.   When the Princess Elizabeth in

---

[1] [Edward Phillips], *Letters of State Written by Mr. John Milton* (London, 1694), p. viii, and Helen Darbishire, *The Early Lives of Milton* (London: Constable, 1932), p. 53.

[2] For the father's musical accomplishments, see Ernest Brennecke, *John Milton the Elder and His Music* (New York: Columbia University Press, 1938).   For an account of the poet and music see S. G. Spaeth, *Milton's Knowledge of Music* (Princeton, 1913).

1558 came to the English throne, no more difficult problem confronted the English people than that of the church. Under Henry VIII, Elizabeth's father, the break with Rome had resulted in the establishment of the English or Anglican State Church, as universal and all-important for the English as the Roman Church maintained itself to be for the entire world. This Anglican Church was continued under the regency of Henry's son, Edward VI, from 1547 to 1553. After Edward's death and the successful *coup d'état* that put his half sister Mary, a staunch Roman Catholic, on the throne, England returned to the Roman Church. Each of these changes had had immense social and economic consequences of as grave a nature as the ecclesiastical consequences. Five years later, Protestant Elizabeth came to the throne.

The Protestant party was determined that, so far as it was humanly possible, there should be no recurrence of such vacillation between Romanism and Anglicanism. Indeed, all parties in England were anxious to settle the church question as quickly and as permanently as possible. This determination brought about the Elizabethan Settlement of the whole church question, a workable solution, but one filled with compromises, through a temporary union that could not remain unified. So anxious were the English people for ecclesiastical, economic, and social stability that all partisanship was momentarily waived to secure it.

All non-Roman Catholic Englishmen feared Rome. But even during the beginnings of the Anglican Church under Henry VIII and Edward VI, many people in England wanted the new church to be as much like the Roman Church as possible. Others wanted it to be as different as it could be made. The group that wanted the early Anglican Church to be like the Roman became the basis for the High Church party that later developed in the English Church; and the group that wanted it to differ radically from the Roman became the basis for the Low Church party. This latter group also contained many men who wanted the established Anglican Church to be purified of all Roman practices, especially of those most easily subject to abuse. These purifiers gradually became a party within the Anglican Church, and, after the Elizabethan Settlement to which as a party they agreed, became known as the Puritans. As a group, they became more and more powerful within the church, although the officers of church and state did everything in their power to suppress them. By the end of the sixteenth century, the Puritans had begun to insist that in England the Reformation of the Christian Church was incomplete, because the Anglican Church still remained so much like the Roman Church it was supposed to have superseded.

Gradually withdrawing from the English Church, although to do so was a form of treason, the Puritans broke up into sects. The most prominent of these sects in Milton's youth, or during the reign of James I, was the Presbyterian, a form of church organization very much like that of John Calvin's church in Geneva, Switzerland. Presbyterianism had been very successfully established in Scotland by John Knox (1505–72), and the Kirk (Church) of Scotland, essentially a Presbyterian Church, had been established as the state church of that country. In it, Englishmen found a fully developed church organization and practice that differed radically from Roman Catholic organization and practice, and hence from the Anglican.

As Elizabeth's reign came to an end, Englishmen, even many Roman Catholic Englishmen, became almost unitedly concerned over the continuance of the Protestant succession to the throne, as Elizabeth had no direct heirs. All parties in the Anglican Church including the Puritans were almost completely united in asking King James VI of Scotland to become also King James I of England, principally to keep other, equally legitimate Roman Catholic descendants of Henry VIII from claiming and then mounting to the English throne. Another factor that operated to James's advantage was that the Roman Catholics themselves were not certain that he would remain Protestant. Their hope was that James could be won over to Rome.

After James was coronated as king of the English, the Puritans became very sensitive and then alarmed over any practice in the Anglican Church that in any way reminded them of Rome, and over every move that James made which seemed to show tolerance toward Rome or toward the Anglican party in the English Church. They became in James's reign an embattled and fiercely dissenting party that withdrew from the Anglican Church and began to establish sects and even churches of their own, principally Presbyterian and Baptist. They especially attacked the episcopal [1] basis of organization employed in the Anglican Church, and the king and his bishops and prelates resisted and fought them to the utmost of their powers. James succeeded in dominating them in his reign; but his son, Charles I, was not so successful after he came to the throne.

This anti-episcopalian or anti-prelatical group was made up largely of men from the social class that was coming into power in England, especially in London, through its increasing wealth. The English merchants, who were recruited principally from the middle classes of citizenry, were now coming into the position of dominance in England that they still occupy to this day. This class, together with the classes it represented, set itself firmly against the bishops or prelates, the king and the nobles who surrounded him.

At the death of James, in 1625, his son, Charles I, sponsored the extraordinary career in the Anglican Church of William Laud (1573–1645), one of the most capable and powerful individuals ever to appear in the priesthood of the Anglican Church. Laud, because of his activity and desire for uniformity in the English Church, was constantly accused of attempting to bring about the return of England to the Roman faith, and all his plans and actions were greeted with suspicion, distrust, and active resistance by the Puritans or dissenting party. The fact that Laud was a brilliant, forceful man of vision and ambition created and crystallized opposition to him and to the Anglican Church which he so strongly championed. Men whose opinions and attitudes before Laud appeared had been vague and frequently opposed to each other quickly became united in their opposition to him. Their opposition and antagonism flared almost into open rebellion when in 1633 Laud was made Archbishop of Canterbury, the position that is the ecclesiastical headship of the Anglican Church. In 1645 the infuriated and united dissenters overwhelmed the king, the nobles, and the prelates, and forced the execution of Laud, as they less than four years later were to force the execution of the king himself.

[1] From the Greek *episkopos*, meaning *bishop* and the word from which the word *bishop* is derived.

Milton was probably brought early into contact with the Puritan or dissenting position in his father's house, although the family into which he was born was Anglican as the registrations of the births, baptisms, and deaths of the children in an Anglican church testify. But his father's place of business was in his home; and the business of the scrivener brought all kinds of people into his shop. Until the death of James, men talked, argued, and planned matters connected with the reform of the Anglican Church, being especially concerned with keeping it from becoming in any way papistic. The reign of James saw the rise of fiercely dissenting small groups such as the Pilgrims, who deliberately left England for Holland, and ultimately for the bleak shores of New England in North America (1620). But in James's reign, most Englishmen of the middle and upper social classes, like the elder Milton, kept to the middle of the controversial road. They talked and planned as much as they dared, but acted little, and even the talk and the plans were dangerous if discovered by the king or the churchmen.

The young Milton's direct contacts with ideas of church reform came before and during his attendance at Saint Paul's School. He probably first encountered various phases of the controversy by listening to the conversations of his father's friends and clients. These indirect influences were early supplanted by a direct and powerful force, for which his father was primarily responsible. According to Milton's statement, sometime before he began to attend Saint Paul's School, his father procured tutors for him. The only one of these tutors whose name we know was Thomas Young. Young was a Scot who had come to London after receiving the degree of master of arts at Saint Andrew's University in 1606. He had apparently been ordained as a minister in the Kirk (Church) of Scotland, and was a strong Presbyterian with marked Puritanical tendencies so far as the Anglican Church was concerned. Young was a very learned man, who, with his zealous Presbyterian partisanship, exercised a great influence on the young Milton. Milton's gratitude to Young is to be found in the surviving Latin letters which Milton wrote to him when he was in Hamburg, Germany, as pastor to the church of the English merchants there, and in the Latin elegy, virtually a metrical epistle, which Milton also addressed to his former tutor. Milton chiefly praises his learning and his fine character. We can be no more certain of the date at which Milton first came in contact with Young than we can be certain of the date at which Milton first entered Saint Paul's School. It is safest to say with Masson that both events took place sometime before 1620.[1]

[1] The difficulties with the whole problem of Milton's connections with Saint Paul's School arise from the fact that the records of the school disappeared after the great London fire of 1666, and thus the exact date at which Milton began to attend is not known. The date usually selected is 1620, or when Milton was about twelve years old. This date may be correct, but is not very satisfactory, as boys entered grammar school in those days as young as five or six years old. Milton states that he had an early eagerness for study, and that he was daily instructed in the grammar school and by other tutors at home, as if the two forms of instruction went on simultaneously. His statement argues for an earlier date than 1620 at which he entered Saint Paul's; but the matter cannot be definitely settled unless the records of the school have somehow been preserved and some day actually appear. Phillips says that Milton was fifteen when he went to Cambridge, the event that definitely terminated the attendance at Saint Paul's. But the date of his admission to Christ's College, Cambridge, in the record books of that college is, according to Masson, February 12, 1625, or about two months after his sixteenth birthday, in his seventeenth year. Why did he wait until he was over sixteen years old before going to the university? The matriculation in either of the universities of boys as early as their eleventh or twelfth years, noticeable under Elizabeth, to escape taking the Oath of Allegiance to the crown, was no longer necessary. But most lads of Milton's day arrived at either university when they were about fifteen or a little younger.

The curriculum of Saint Paul's School at the time Milton was there has not survived.[1] Nevertheless, by comparison with the curricula of other London grammar schools of the time, and by Milton's own statements, the general scheme of his studies can be closely approximated. Saint Paul's School in his day was undergoing the same kind of changes that were then taking place in all English grammar schools. But the general pattern of the curriculum was still that derived from the Schoolmen of the Middle Ages.

This curriculum had long before Milton's day come to be the seven liberal arts, divided into the Trivium, consisting of grammar, rhetoric, and logic, and the Quadrivium, consisting of arithmetic, geometry, astronomy, and music, both the subjects and the division deriving ultimately from Plato's famous Academy in ancient Athens. The Trivium concerned itself exclusively with Latin. That is, the grammar and rhetoric were Latin grammar and rhetoric, and logic was taught entirely through Latin forms. Since the impetus provided by Erasmus, Colet, More, Cheke, and others during the reign of Henry VIII, Greek had come in for some attention in the universities, and even in the grammar schools. The controversies of the Reformation had likewise forced much attention on the Semitic languages of Scripture, Hebrew, 'Chaldee' or Aramaic, Syriac, and even Arabic. The linguistic work of the grammar schools was almost entirely made up of drill in grammar, vocabulary, and composition, principally in Latin, but increasingly in Greek and even in the Semitic languages. The training in mathematics and astronomy was necessarily pre-Newtonian and principally pre-Copernican.[2] Euclid was used for geometry, the Schoolmen chiefly for arithmetic, and Sacrobosco, or Holywood, was very popular as a textbook of astronomy.[3]

Milton encountered at least three persons at Saint Paul's School who exerted permanent effects on him. When he attended the school, probably as a day scholar, for the school was only two or three blocks from the house in Bread Street, the head master was Alexander Gill the elder. The elder Gill was a remarkable person, and must have exercised considerable influence upon the young Milton. Gill had been appointed head master of the school on March 10, 1607/8 in succession to Richard Mulcaster. Milton was among his pupils some ten years later. Wood said that Gill had 'such an excellent way of training up youth that none in his time went beyond him; whence 'twas that many noted persons in church and state did deem it the greatest of their happiness that they had been educated under him.'[4] He was not only famous as a schoolmaster, but also 'was esteemed by most persons to be a learned man, a noted Latinist, critic, and divine.'[5]

---

[1] There are two manuscript curricula of Saint Paul's School extant in the Trinity College Library, Cambridge (MS. 0.1.42. and MS. 0.10.22.), believed to have been written ca. 1600. Each of these manuscripts has the title 'The Constant Method of Teaching in Saint Paul's School, London.'

[2] The theories of Copernicus (1473–1543), which held that the sun was the center of the solar system, were very slowly accepted by the schools. Cf. the recent studies of the subject by F. R. Johnson, *Astronomical Thought in Renaissance England* (Baltimore: Johns Hopkins Press, 1937), and Grant McColley, 'Milton's Dialogue on Astronomy: The Principal Immediate Sources,' *PMLA*, vol. LII (1937), pp. 728–62.

[3] Johannes Sacrobosco (*fl.* A.D. 1230) was the author of the well-known treatise on the spheres, *Sphera Mundi*. He also wrote an arithmetic much used in English grammar schools. Cf. Robert Steele, editor, *The Earliest Arithmetics in English*, Early English Text Society, no. CXVIII, extra series (Oxford, 1922).

[4] Anthony Wood, *Athenae Oxonienses*, art. 'Gill.'   [5] *Ibid.*

Gill published two or three books that have survived, one of great interest in connection with Milton being entitled *Logonomia Anglica, qua gentis sermo facilius addiscitur*, first printed at London in 1619, and in a second edition in 1621. Dedicated to James I, the book, written in Latin, opens with suggestions for a phonetic system of English spelling. In the section on grammatical and rhetorical figures, Gill quoted freely from Spenser, Wither, Daniel, and other English poets, and showed an intimate acquaintance with their poetry. He was especially fond of Spenser, preferring him to Homer, and many of his examples of English usage were taken from the *Faerie Queene*. He was greatly concerned with the development and use of the English language. His emphasis in this book on the use of English as a literary language is the earliest definite and certain influence that led Milton ultimately to give up the writing of Latin poetry and turn entirely to the English language as the vehicle for his poetic expression.

His son, Alexander Gill the younger, serving in Milton's time as an under-usher of Saint Paul's, was definitely anti-Laudian, if not anti-Anglican. He was later in trouble with the crown for having publicly drunk the health of Felton, slayer of the Duke of Buckingham, and for his unbridled tongue. He and the young Milton became friends, at least three letters written to him by Milton being extant. These letters display the friendly relations that existed between the young poet and a man who was his teacher and only eleven years his senior.

The most beloved friend encountered at Saint Paul's School was young Charles Diodati, son of John Diodati, an Italian physician who had fled Italy because of his Protestant convictions and settled in London. Charles Diodati was the only intimate friend of his own age Milton ever had. He was born about 1610, being 'thirteen years old' when he left Saint Paul's in 1623 for Oxford. He remained at Oxford until 1628, receiving the B.A. degree on December 10, 1625, and the M.A. degree on July 8, 1628.[1] He left Oxford to enter the hospitals in order to study medicine. Thus, in 1623 the direct and intimate contact between Diodati and Milton was broken up, although they continued to see each other intermittently in London, and carried on what must have been a voluminous correspondence. Milton never forgot this friendship, which, as was so frequently the case after he was thirty in his intimate, human relations, resulted in tragedy. For Charles died suddenly in 1638 while Milton was in Italy, and he learned of the death months after his friend had been buried. The surviving letters and two or three Latin poems, virtually metrical epistles, and the Italian poems, largely addressed to Diodati, will repay a good deal of study not only to provide a realization of the friendship, regard, and affection in which the two young men held each other, but also to provide an understanding of Milton's capacity for such relationships and his deep and stirring reactions to them.

The training Milton received at Saint Paul's School, together with that from 'other masters at home,' equipped him with the tools necessary for beginning an illustrious scholarly career. These tools included languages, especially the classical; English readings and study; his interest in music and mathematics and in the peculiar budding science of the day; as well as the inevitable beginnings in theology and church history, with a

---

[1] Cf. R. B. Gardiner, *The Admission Registers of St. Paul's School, 1748–1876* (London: Bell, 1884), p. 34, and Joseph Foster, *Alumni Oxonienses, 1500–1714* (Oxford: Parker, 1891, 4 vols.), vol. I, p. 405.

good start at the mastery of the original texts of the Bible. The early period is, therefore, a most fruitful one for study and consideration because of its later manifestations.

AT CAMBRIDGE (1625-32)

Probably about the time of his sixteenth birthday, Milton began to make preparations to enter Christ's College, Cambridge. Nothing is known of the reasons for selecting that particular college; but he was now bringing to a close his work in grammar school and with private tutors. It was with the equipment and training already described that he left his home in London and set out for Cambridge. He probably first took residence there after the Lenten term; but he was admitted to Christ's College on February 12, 1625.[1] Entering residence at the beginning of the next term, he matriculated in the university on April 9, 1625. He probably had in mind graduation from Christ's College in order to become a priest in the Anglican Church, or, within a year or two, of entering the law as a profession. It was usual at that time for young men intending to enter the legal profession to leave Oxford or Cambridge after a year or two and enter one of the Inns of Court, establishments maintained by professional lawyers in which they lived and, among other activities, trained young men to become lawyers. The fact that Milton remained at Cambridge after 1626 or 1627 may be taken to mean that he decided that early not to become a lawyer, although his express statement that he had so decided was written probably after he left Cambridge.[2]

In Christ's College, he was at first put under the tutelage of William Chappell, a strongly Laudian Anglican divine. During his first year, he apparently quarreled with Chappell, was punished, perhaps whipped, and certainly sent home, or rusticated, for a specified period. Upon his return to the university, he was placed under the tutelage of Nathaniel Tovey.

His career at the university was described by Milton himself and by John Aubrey. Milton's statement occurs in the *Defensio Secunda* (1654):

> Having been taught various languages and acquired a strong taste of the sweetness of philosophy, he [his father] sent me to Cambridge, one of the two national universities. There, away from all unbecoming conduct and being commended by all my respectable colleagues, I spent seven years in the regular course of study, securing, with distinction, the master's degree.[3]

Aubrey's rambling account added little to this:

> Was a very hard student in the university, and performed all his exercises there with very good applause. His first tutor there was Mr. Chappell, from whom receiving some unkindness [whipped him], he was afterwards (though it seemed opposite to the rules of the college) transferred to the tuition of one Mr. Tovell [Tovey], who died parson of Lutterworth....

---

[1] Masson (*Life*, vol. I [1881], p. 112) quotes from the admission registers, 'Johannes Milton, Londoniensis, filius Johannis, institutus fuit in literarum elementis sub Mro Gill, Gymnasii Paulini praefecto; admissus est pensionarius minor Feb. 12, 1624[/25], sub Mro Chappell, solvitque pro ingressu 10s.' 'John Milton, of London, son of John, grounded in the elements of letters under Master Gill, head master of Paul's School; is admitted minor pensioner Feb. 12, 1624[/25], under Master Chappell, and has paid 10s. for being enrolled.' A 'lesser pensioner' was a student, not of one of the great families, who paid for his own board and room.

[2] In the *Letter to an Unknown Friend*, see pp. 45-47. See *Sonnet VII, infra*, p. 125.   [3] *Col.* VIII:118-20.

He was scarce so tall as I am — *quaere*, quot feet I am high: *resp.* of middle stature. He had auburn hair. His complexion exceeding fair — he was so fair that they called him the Lady of Christ College —. Oval face, his eye a dark gray.... His widow has his picture drawn very well and like when a Cambridge scholar. She has his picture when a Cambridge scholar, which ought to be engraven; for the pictures before his books are not at all like him.[1]

The quarrel with Chappell; the production of a number of Latin verses, probably of the Italian songs and sonnets; of a number of the early English poems, notably the *Nativity Ode*; and perhaps, as a growing chorus of voices, noticeably those of Professors Parker and Tillyard, have recently insisted, *L'Allegro* and *Il Penseroso* — all belong to this period. We know also that he maintained some correspondence with Thomas Young, with the younger Gill, and with Diodati. His work in the university was made up largely of extended readings and discussions. He won some fame as an orator, in the technical sense of that term, and was called on to write an occasional work for official performance as well as being called on himself to perform. He remained at the university long enough to proceed to the Master of Arts degree. This was at the time unusual for a man not intending to enter the Anglican priesthood. The whole pattern of his education in grammar school and college is unusual only because in perspective it seems as if by collusion with his father it was planned deliberately with a literary career as its goal. Indeed, such an aim and plan are so apparent to us as we look back at what took place that we are in danger of forgetting that such a plan was much more accidental than real, as the whole of his formal education was that of any young Englishman preparing to take orders in the Anglican Church.[2]

He received the degree of B.A. on March 26, 1629, and the degree of M.A. on July 3, 1632. To receive these degrees, he had signed the three Articles of Religion, on the subscription to which King James had insisted since 1603. These articles acknowledged: (1) that the king was supreme in all spiritual or ecclesiastical as well as temporal 'causes'; (2) that the *Book of Common Prayer* and the 'ordering' of bishops were not contrary to the Word of God; and (3) that the Thirty-Nine Articles of the Anglican Church were not contrary to the Word of God.

The poems written during the Cambridge period reflect his interests and activities, his adventures with his colleagues, tutors, and friends. The Latin poems especially express his thoughts and feelings on the life he was living. They, much more than the English poems of this period, display a love of nature, an enjoyment of entertainments, eager friendships, an active interest in young women with particular attention to at least one, and reactions to other literary and esthetic experiences.

[1] John Aubrey, *Brief Lives, Chiefly of Contemporaries, set down by John Aubrey, between the years 1669 and 1696* (Andrew Clark, editor, Oxford: Clarendon Press, 1898, 2 vols.), vol. II: 60–72.

[2] There is a possibility that Milton's decision against becoming an Anglican priest partly resulted from his failure to secure a fellowship in his college. In 1630, a year in which Milton would have been eligible for a fellowship, Edward King (*Lycidas*) though Milton's junior, received one, and it has been hinted that Milton had unsuccessfully sought a fellowship that year.

HORTON

Milton's father decided to retire from London and move the family to Horton at about the time when the younger brother, Christopher, was preparing to leave home for Christ's College, Cambridge,[1] headed ultimately for the Inns of Court and the law as a profession. Milton speaks of 'my father's country house to which he had retired to pass the remainder of his days.' Evidently the family had moved to Horton before Milton left the university.

Horton was then and is now a very small hamlet, on the north bank of the Thames River, about twenty miles west of London. The move reflected the increasing prosperity of the scrivener, who had already, according to tradition, twice refused the mastership of the Scriveners' Company, although he was later (1634) nominally to accept that honor without apparently doing much of the work connected with the office. The fortunes of the elder Milton were following those of the Scriveners' Company, now in full flood.

The house in which the Milton family lived at Horton is no longer known, although up to the present century tradition pointed to one certain dwelling with its grounds as the one they occupied.

Milton joined his father's family at Horton as a young man about twenty-four years old, who had passed a more or less conventional seven-year period at Christ's College; who had written a good deal of poetry both in Latin and in English, if principally the former, some of which he saw fit to preserve; who had taken part in the various activities of the college and of the university; who had made a number of friends, if few intimates, during his stay there; and who now, for lack of any definite career, announced his need of a period for undisturbed study and meditation. In 1654 he said of his leaving college:

> I... went home, leaving an affectionate regret in most of the college fellows.... At our suburban home, to which my father had retired, at my leisure, I spent my time reading the Greek and Latin writers, sometimes leaving the country for the town to purchase books or to learn of what was new in music or mathematics which amused me at that time. After five years passed in this manner, my mother died... [2]

His biographers generally have made of the whole Horton period a sort of idyllic pastoral. Over these years they have drawn a rosy-colored cloud of happiness, contentment, and idle and idyllic ease. Such a picture of the period is, however, altogether too one-sided and distorted. It was actually a period in which something happened that completely changed Milton's life, but which cannot be exactly determined except by its results. What did Milton actually accomplish during this period, and what did he himself say he was doing? In the extract quoted from the *Defensio Secunda*, he refers to protracted readings and a life of leisure. The loveliness and charm of Horton itself, coupled with the reference to books, leisure, study, and freedom have misled most of

---

[1] Masson (*Life*, vol. I [1881], p. 243) says that Christopher Milton was admitted as a 'lesser pensioner' February 15, 1630/31, under 'Mr. Tovey,' John's tutor.

[2] *Col.* VIII:120.

his biographers. Horton is just across the river from old Windsor, and anyone who visits it today or who visited it during the past three centuries has been entranced by the surroundings of the highly cultivated English countryside.

But what was actually taking place during the Horton period in Milton's life and development? At the beginning of the period he wrote a letter that yields an idea of his state of mind when he wrote it. This is *A Letter to an Unknown Friend* which so far as can be determined was written at Horton and soon after he took up residence there.[1] The *Letter* expresses the uncertainties, misgivings, discouragements, and general discontents of the young Milton, then about twenty-five years old.[2] He had completed his formal education, as so many of our young men and women do today, without having discovered any particular purpose in, or for, his own life, and was also devoid of any urge to enter a profession. He is on the verge of deciding in favor of a literary career; but for this decision he had no precedent. John Milton the poet was the first Englishman who deliberately decided to become a man of letters, principally a poet, and who then succeeded in becoming one of any magnitude. But the *Letter* is chiefly remarkable for its expression of post-adolescent despair and discouragement. It is a youthful performance and typical of the state of mind of a sensitive young man sufficiently gifted to express his disillusionment with what in his childhood and adolescence he had built up as a set of concepts of himself, the world about him, and his relations to it. The *Letter* is essentially the expression of a despair over reality as actually discovered by a young man on the brink of manhood, that might have been written, though not so effectively, by almost any human being passing through the same circumstances and period of development.

Another letter, in Latin, written or dated September 3, 1637, to Charles Diodati, provides another glimpse of Milton later in the Horton period. He says to Diodati, 'Where I now am, you know, I am living meanly and in a constricted fashion.' This letter was penned in London after the death of his mother. It may refer only to temporary quarters in town; but the old conception of the Horton period as one of idyllic ease is not enhanced by it.

Milton was possessed always of unusual sensitivity and ability, but he was not especially precocious. In many instances, he seems the reverse of precocious. His development, particularly his poetic development, was very slow. The production of his poetry, of 'long choosing, and beginning late' as he said of *Paradise Lost* (IX:26), is characterized by two different but concomitant aspects. These are, respectively, a reluctance to publish a poem, and, at the same time, a frequent demand from circumstances to complete and publish it. It is the latter of these two aspects that has led some students of Milton to state that practically all his early poetry was occasional. A fairer

[1] See p. 45. Professor Parker thinks that the letter was addressed to Thomas Young, his former tutor. Cf. *London Times Literary Supplement*, May 16, 1936.

[2] Two slightly different drafts of the *Letter* occur in the *Trinity College Manuscript*, sometimes called the *Cambridge Manuscript*. This manuscript, much of it in Milton's hand, contains many of the poems written between 1630 and 1660, but none of the earliest poems and none of the long poems appear therein. It has been reproduced and printed. Cf. *Facsimile of the Manuscript of Milton's Minor Poems in the Library of Trinity College, Cambridge* (Cambridge: Cambridge University Press, 1899).

statement would be that the occasion usually forced the completion or at least the revelation of an incomplete poem; and what can be learned of Milton's actual methods of poetic composition supports this idea. Such a forcing of poems to completion or revelation is noticeable in the verse written during the Horton period, a period introduced by the note of mingled *Weltschmerz* and personal despair found in the *Letter to an Unknown Friend*.

The outstanding development in Milton's life during the Horton period turned out to be a false development. Too little is known of the friendships he formed at Cambridge; but somehow or other, by 1632, he had become acquainted with the Egerton family of Harefield. The Egertons were one of the great families of England at this time, old Sir Thomas, for whom John Donne had served as secretary, having been Lord Chancellor from 1603 till his death in 1617. His son, Sir John, first Earl of Bridgewater, was the head of the family when Milton knew them, and the old Countess Dowager of Derby, widow of Sir Thomas and mother of Sir John, was still living. The first intimation afforded us of this acquaintance with the Egertons is the statement Milton makes about his songs and declamation entitled the *Arcades*, a fragment of an entertainment that took place at Harefield in 1632 or 1633. This was followed in 1634 by Milton writing the verses for the mask *Comus*, performed by and for the same family at Ludlow Castle in that year to celebrate Sir John's inauguration into the lord presidency of Wales. We should like to know a great deal more about Milton's connections with the Egertons, for while his father had greatly prospered, he was far from having attained a position that would have enabled his son to mingle freely with persons of their social rank and station. Social lines were much more loosely drawn three hundred years ago in England than they are today, and the relations between the Egertons and the handsome young writer of lovely verses would have been at once easy and cordial.

But how did he first meet them, and why did the connection terminate so suddenly with the writing of *Comus*? The Egertons were Royalists and Anglicans; and, while Milton had as yet exhibited none of the intense resentment of priests and prelates, do his associations with the Egertons mean that the bitter attack on the corruptions of the clergy, found in the next poem he wrote after *Comus*, grew out of an unfortunate experience with the Egertons?

Lycidas, so far as we know, was written about three years after the performance of *Comus* in 1634. The poem contains two digressions, the first being on fame and very reminiscent of the mood of personal despair displayed in the *Letter to an Unknown Friend*. Though the second digression is perfectly controlled, it is the most savage attack Milton ever made in a serious poem. Except for poetic characteristics, there is nothing in common between the tone of *Lycidas* (1637), and the tone of the *Epitaph on the Marchioness of Winchester* (1631), *Arcades* (1632 or 1633), and *Comus* (1634). What happened in the latter end of the Horton period that led to the bitter self-recriminations, to the ferocious attack on the corruptions of the clergy, and to the general position, ecclesiastical and political, that Milton exhibits in *Lycidas*? We can only surmise. Certainly the whole Horton period built itself up into some kind of climax, not only for Milton, but for the entire family. The family climax came with the not unexpected death of his mother in the spring of 1637. She must have been about sixty-five years old when she died. We know little or nothing about the circumstances of her death except that she was buried on April 3, 1637. Milton spoke later of her death as that which terminated the Horton period.

He further informs us, years later, that it was during the Horton period that he became much interested in history, reading the Greek and Latin historians, the principal European, and paying special attention to Italian history and to chronicles and romances dealing with British history. Geoffrey of Monmouth, William of Huntington, the Anglo-Saxon chroniclers, Matthew of Florence, Holinshed, Camden, and many others were read systematically. He had also set himself to read church history at Horton, but gave it up after apparently reading much in the Byzantine historians.

Horton had provided the opportunity for Milton to become a very learned man. By the end of the period, he had become filled with the spirit and substance of the ancient classics and of the Bible; of the Italian and other vernacular literatures; of the art, particularly the music and architecture, of the Renaissance; of the scholastic disciplines, especially as represented by Aquinas and Bonaventura, and the theology of the Schoolmen; and of the writings of the reformers, especially Luther, Calvin, Servetus, Zwingli, Paraeus, Ames, Wollebius, and others. He had acquired an unusual knowledge of all phases of Biblical study, including both Christian and rabbinical commentators. He had also absorbed most of the scholarship of his day and earlier, including the work of Erasmus, Colet, Beza, Fagius, Tremellius, Junius, Buxtorf, and many other scholars. But, aside from the outbursts in *Lycidas* and puzzling statements here and there in a few letters, there is no indication whatever in 1638 of the position he was almost immediately to assume on his return from Italy late in 1639.

Seventeen years later in the *Defensio Secunda* (1654), Milton wrote of the end of the Horton period as if, after his mother's death, he had then been able to carry out a plan that he had been forming for some time.

THE ITALIAN JOURNEY (1638–39)

As was customary with the sons of wealthy men — and Milton's father was now a relatively wealthy man — plans for the poet's education had come to include the Grand Tour. This was a journey to the Continent, especially to France and Italy, and in Milton's case intended to include Greece and Sicily. We do not know how long he had actually planned on the journey; but we do know that sometime in the summer of 1638 [1] he set out for Italy with a male companion. He was then just under thirty years old, still young in mind and action; eager, passionate, though self-restrained; possessed of a wide range of interests, intellectual and otherwise; intelligent, and exhibiting a recognized wit.[2] Comparisons of himself with colleagues of his own age were making him con-

---

[1] He reached Florence by September 10, 1638. Cf. signature to *Epistle 8, Col.* XII:38.

[2] Professor Parker ('Milton's Hobson Poems,' *Modern Language Review*, XXXI [1936], pp. 395-402) discovered that the Hobson poems had been printed in Archie Armstrong's *Banquet of Jests* (London, 1640). It is startling, in view of the older conception of Milton, to discover a poem or two of his in one of the jestbooks of the century.

ceited.   Unless the journey was a flight from some unknown experience, he had no cares at this time that we know of, and was something of an intellectual swashbuckler.   He was just beginning to appear as a striking individualist, as in *Lycidas,* and was about ready to amplify the conception of the kind of poet he intended to be, begun in the Latin *Elegy VI* (1629), and continued in the prose tracts of 1641 and 1642.

He left us a relatively detailed account of his travels.[1]   He went overland through France, stopping at Paris long enough to meet the famous Hugo Grotius, at that time ambassador from the Queen of Sweden to the Court of France.   He sailed from Nice and landed in Italy at Genoa, then visited most of the principal towns in the Peninsula, Venice, and then passed into Switzerland to Geneva.   His plans to visit Greece and Sicily were interrupted by news from England, and he returned home from Geneva through France, having been gone about fifteen months.

His experiences in Italy were largely responsible for his decision to write his projected great literary works in English rather than in Latin.   He says in 1641 that, almost as a direct result of the Italian experiences, and in imitation of Ariosto and Tasso, he decided that his great literary pieces, whatever else they were to be, would be written in English, his 'mother dialect':

> For which cause, and not only for that I knew it would be hard to arrive at the second rank among the Latins, I applied myself to that resolution which Ariosto followed against the persuasions of Bembo, to fix all the industry and art I could unite to the adorning of my native tongue; not to make verbal curiosities the end, that were a toilsome vanity, but to be an interpreter and relater of the best and sagest things among mine own citizens throughout this island in the mother dialect.   That what the greatest and choicest wits of Athens, Rome, or modern Italy, and those Hebrews of old did for their country, I in my proportion with this over and above of being a Christian, might do for mine: not caring to be once named abroad, though perhaps I could attain to that, but content with these British islands as my world, whose fortune hath hitherto been, that if the Athenians, as some say, made their small deeds great and renowned by their eloquent writers, England hath had her noble achievements made small by the unskillful handling of monks and mechanics.[2]

Milton's experiences on this journey left a permanent impression on his mind and sensibilities.   He was more proud of the journey and of his reception in Italy than he was of almost any other aspect of his life or fortune.   It seemed to mark his utmost in accomplishment and recognition.   He carefully preserved the laudatory verses written to him by certain Italians, and printed them at the head of his poems in both printings, 1645 and 1673.   Many references to his reception in Italy stud the pages of his English and Latin prose works; and one Latin poem, *Mansus,* addressed to his host in Naples, was the direct outcome of the journey.   Almost everything he wrote in prose or verse after the visit that could in any way be termed autobiographical contains references to, or a suggestion of, the Italian journey.   The friends he made and the places he visited are an interesting study in themselves.

[1] *Defensio Secunda,* 1654, *Col.* VIII:120–26.
[2] *The Reason of Church Government, Col.* III:1:236.

John Milton at the Age of
Twenty-One, 1629

John Milton at About the
Age of Forty-Eight, 1656

Gul. Faithorne ad Vivum

Delin. et sculpsit

Ioannis Miltoni Effigies Ætat: 62.
1670.

JOHN MILTON AT THE AGE OF SIXTY-TWO, 1670

LONDON (1640–49)

Upon his return to London, he took temporary quarters of his own in Saint Bride's Churchyard, off Fleet Street.[1] He took permanent quarters in Aldersgate Street probably a few weeks or months after this, sometime in 1640. Even before these permanent quarters were ready for his occupancy, he had begun his work as a tutor and schoolmaster, at first to his two nephews, Edward and John Phillips, then respectively about ten and nine years old, who came to live with him. Edward Phillips said of this move:

Soon after his return [from Italy], and visits paid to his father and other friends, he took him a lodging in St. Bride's Churchyard, at the house of one Russel a tailor, where he first undertook the education and instruction of his sister's two sons, the younger [John] whereof had been wholly committed to his charge and care... he never set up for a public school to teach all the young fry of a parish, but only was willing to impart his learning and knowledge to relations, and the sons of gentlemen that were his intimate friends.[2]

For ten years or perhaps longer Milton continued to act as schoolmaster to 'relations, and the sons of gentlemen that were his intimate friends' or to as many boys as his living quarters could accommodate.

Milton's reluctance to enter any profession or recognized vocation persisted until he was more than thirty-two years old. He had received a long and relatively expensive education, and then passed through a long period of private study, culminating in the Grand Tour. Until 1640, he seemed deliberately to refuse to settle down to any vocation and to publish anything he had written and acknowledge it. But in the following year, 1641, he suddenly began to take an active part in the attack on the Anglican bishops. It is impossible today for us to discover all the experiences through which he had passed that led to this seemingly sudden decision early in 1641 to participate eagerly in what was then taking place in England.

MILTON AND THE KINGDOM OF THE SAINTS ON EARTH

The death of James I and the succession of his son, Charles I, to the throne in 1625 had far-reaching consequences for the English people. James had almost completely misunderstood the temper and tenor of the times in which he lived. He was called, not unjustly, the 'most learned fool in Christendom,' and throughout his reign showed cause for such a judgment of him. But also throughout his reign he had waged a vigorous and successful defense of the theory of the divine right of kings and of Anglican bishops; had played a much less adroit game of waiting and inaction than had Elizabeth; and by virtue of the united fears of his ununited people and of his own severe measures against

[1] Masson (vol. II [1894], p. 102) located his temporary quarters 'between Fleet Lane and Stonecutters Street and Farrington Street.' He apparently thought that these quarters were north of Fleet Street. But it is more likely that they were south of Fleet Street, as is shown by John Norden's map of London in 1593, showing the church and churchyard of Saint Bridget's properly located south of Fleet Street, as the map of Faithorne and Newcourt of 1658 also shows.

[2] [Edward Phillips], *Letters of State Written by Mr. John Milton* (London, 1694), pp. xvi–xvii and xxviii, and Helen Darbishire, *Early Lives*, pp. 60 and 67.

any opposition to state or church, had succeeded in living out his life span and staying on his throne.

His son, Charles, was neither so fortunate nor so learned a fool. The rise to power of Laud in both church and state brought with it a fierce opposition that grew more rapidly than Laud's power itself. Laud was made head (Archbishop of Canterbury) of the Anglican Church in 1633. Immediately, all the critics and opponents of church and state with real or fancied grievances centered their animosities and dissatisfactions in Laud. It was a time of change, and Laud, who had changes of his own in mind, only succeeded in unifying those forces in England that were opposed to him. Opposition to the bishops began to mount, not only because many people thought that the bishops were a Roman Catholic type of church officer, but also because of the corruption of the Anglican clergy and its palpable neglect of the pastoral care of the English people. The literature of the Continental Reformation, especially that of Germany and Switzerland, was drawn on for the basis of the attack. Most of the charges made by Luther and Calvin against the Roman Catholic priesthood were revived, turned into English, and poured forth against the Anglican priesthood. The king and the church united in their efforts to suppress or entirely choke off these attacks; but, unlike his father in similar circumstances, Charles only succeeded in driving the perpetrators underground for a time.

Careful plans were laid, and, in 1640, about the time Milton returned from Italy, the first and greatest revolution of the century began. Like most movements of vast import, the revolution started slowly, and gave almost no early signs either of its seriousness or of its strength. Its beginning cannot even be given a definite date. Hatred of Laud and all his works, combined with a growing distrust of the king and his short-sighted and uninformed favorites, seemed to be the immediate cause of the revolution.

But behind these immediate irritations lay the accumulated troubles of several centuries arising from slow changes that had taken place but which had not been properly absorbed by the English people. Economically, by or even before 1600, the merchant had supplanted the great landowner or manufacturer as the representative of the wealthiest class in England. But no one, not even the merchant himself, was aware that this had happened. Such a displacement of wealth had brought about social changes that were still less known. The reign of James has been called the wealthiest and most crassly vulgar period in British history. Men from social classes which never before had produced persons of wealth began to amass fortunes and to dominate all affairs, including church and state, that depended on wealth in any form for their existence.[1]

The social and economic forces that were gathering slowly, first coalesced in attacks on the Anglican Church and its royal supporters. The English revolutions of the seventeenth century, especially the first one, were great social movements; but in its own day, the revolution that took place between 1640 and 1650 was looked on by those who participated in it as chiefly a movement of church reform. When the king stood in the way of the attack on the English Church, he, too, was swept away by the force and momentum of the onslaught. So entirely was church organization looked on as the chief phase of

[1] Milton's father was as good an example of this process on a small scale as his contemporary Robert Abbot was on a large scale. Cf. p. 4, note 2.

the struggle that when the Puritan Party actually came into power, it was very little aware of problems of statecraft. The party thought of itself primarily as an ecclesiastical one, and was certain that, if the church it wanted was properly organized, the state would inevitably flourish apace. A Parliament that had never functioned as a political or governmental agency tried to operate on the model of a church synod or general assembly; and ultimately only succeeded in producing anarchy. The Parliamentary Party was led by men whose first concern was church organization or discipline. Many of these leaders were ministers of Presbyterian, Baptist, or other sectarian groups who knew nothing of political government. They were sure that, by changing church conditions in England, they could change the nature of Englishmen, and, if allowed to carry their church reforms far enough, they could change the nature of all mankind. So certain were they of the God-given foundation of their position that they were ready to fight any who opposed their will and to annihilate them.

On November 3, 1640, Charles assembled the Parliament that was to be known as the Long Parliament, so called because it continued to sit until its dissolution by Cromwell in 1653. The events and circumstances which had led to the calling of this Parliament were complicated and involved. In the main, they were made up of the virtual bankruptcy of the king, the struggle for reform in church and state, and the fears engendered by the recent happenings in Scotland. Taken as a whole, it was the news of these events that caused Milton to abandon his plans to be away from England for three or four years, and to hasten home much sooner than he had expected to return. The Long Parliament was split definitely into two main camps which accounted for nearly nine-tenths of its total membership. The roll-call for August, 1642, totaled 505 members, 202 of which were Effective Royalists, and 245, Parliamentarians. The leader of the Royalists was Sir Thomas Wentworth, first Earl of Strafford (1593–1641), who had become Charles's chief adviser in 1638.

Almost immediately after the Parliament opened its sessions, various forces were set in motion that could be neither controlled nor terminated. Attacks were made on Laud and his system; upon the king and his favorites; upon the queen, Henrietta Maria, because she was French and a Roman Catholic; and upon the Anglican Church, even by Royalists such as Sir Benjamin Rudyerd[1] as well as by the anti-Anglican group. Grievances voiced in Parliament became so numerous that Strafford determined to act at once against the Parliamentary leaders. He decided to use the army to seize and guard these leaders. But his plan was betrayed to Parliament, and on November 11, 1640, a committee was named to prepare material for a conference, and 'the charge against the Earl of Strafford.' The report was called for in a few minutes, and Strafford was ordered impeached. His impeachment trial began on the twenty-fourth, his imprisonment having begun perhaps before that; and on May 12, 1641, he was executed for high treason.

Having successfully dealt with Strafford, the aroused Parliamentarians next turned to Laud himself, and on December 18, 1640, impeached him of treason. But Parliament

---

[1] Rudyerd spoke in the debate of November 7, 1640. He said that the oppressive exactions imposed on the people of England by church and state had nearly ruined the Anglican Church and bankrupted the state. He proposed a thorough reformation.

was not yet ready to deal with the system that Laud represented.   On December 11, 1640, a petition signed by fifteen thousand Londoners was presented to the Parliament.   This petition in violent terms demanded thorough church reform and the complete abolition of episcopacy or of all bishops in the Anglican Church.   The Parliament actually voted to consider the petition on the seventeenth, but when that day came, other business prevented its consideration.   But if Parliament was not yet ready to face the problem of church organization, the petition furthered the arrest and impeachment of Laud.   Then in early February, 1641, the whole church question was taken up in earnest; a bill to abolish bishops known as the Root-and-Branch Bill was introduced; and the fierce struggle over episcopacy was begun.

Milton's connections with the sessions of the Long Parliament in 1640 and 1641 can never be fully determined.   The events of that period are almost hopelessly lost in the excitement with which they were surrounded and the rapidity with which they took place.   The student of the period must guard against all tendencies to make the events themselves and Milton's connections with them too simple.   We can be certain that men acted from the same mixed and confused motives as those which cause them to act today. Many men tried to sound a note of high seriousness and to insist that they and they alone were in the right because they possessed a noble and God-given plan for England's future. Groups within and without Parliament sprang up in great numbers, each of which insisted that it had the only true solution to England's problems.   Certainly, many individuals connected with such groups were honest, God-fearing men who looked on themselves as chosen by God to bring His kingdom into earthly being in England.   But it is equally certain that to many of their contemporaries as well as to us today, there was a great deal of fanaticism in these groups.   Much of it was honest fanaticism, but fanaticism nevertheless; and it was ultimately to cause England almost as much trouble as the evils against which it was launched.

The effects of the whole church reform movement upon Milton led directly to the appearance of his first public utterances.   The Root-and-Branch Bill with its attendant attacks on the bishops and the whole idea of episcopacy seemed to stimulate him into action.   Soon after the actual introduction of the bill into Parliament, Milton's first pamphlet appeared, without its author's name, in May or June, 1641, under the title, *Of Reformation Touching Church Discipline in England*.   The theme of this work was that the Reformation begun by Luther had in England stopped far short of the point which it had reached in other countries.   Consequently, England was now suffering and struggling under the load of outmoded ecclesiastical and theological baggage which both politically and spiritually was slowly strangling the country.   Shortly after this, his second pamphlet, *Of Prelatical Episcopacy*, appeared, also dated 1641, and again with no author's name. It was a much slighter pamphlet than the first, and in substance was an attack on, and reply to, a particular form of the argument favoring episcopacy.   It answered and attacked that argument step by step and citation by citation in a fashion to which the student of the controversies of the period must become accustomed.   At almost the same time that the second of Milton's pamphlets appeared, the third pamphlet was printed.   Its title was *Animadversions upon the Remonstrant's Defence, Against Smectymnuus*.   The Smectymnuuan group of dissenting and Presbyterian ministers, the initials of whose names were selected to make the name 'Smectymnuus,' had been battling valiantly against the bishops and the idea of episcopacy.   Their leader, or one of their leaders, was Thomas Young, Milton's former tutor, who supplied the 'ty' in the name of the group.   They had published a tract against episcopacy which had been answered by Bishop Joseph Hall.   Milton's pamphlet was directed against Hall's.

Milton's fourth pamphlet appeared early in 1641/42 with the title *The Reason of Church Government Urged Against Prelaty*, and bore its author's name on its title-page.   It differs in its aim and scope from its predecessors.   In his first and second pamphlets Milton had used the historical method, and in the third, in dialogue form, he had been critical and personal; but in the fourth he argues against episcopacy on rational grounds.   About three months after the fourth pamphlet appeared, another pamphlet, the fifth, appeared in 1642.   This one was titled *An Apology Against a Pamphlet Called a Modest Confutation of the Animadversions upon the Remonstrant against Smectymnuus*.   Bishop Hall and his son had replied to Milton's *Animadversions* with attacks on Milton's character.   His fifth pamphlet took pains to refute these charges and to launch an attack against the Halls.   It is in some ways the most important autobiographical work in English Milton ever wrote.

By the spring of 1642, Milton was well committed to a semi-public career as a pamphleteer.   In several of his pamphlets he tells of the reluctance with which he entered into the episcopalian controversies; but this reluctance was probably more retrospective than it was real.   These pamphlets were the direct result of Milton unreservedly throwing himself into the struggle for revolution in the English church and state, as a Puritan or dissenter, as a Presbyterian, and as a Parliamentarian.   In the works themselves, he seemed possessed by a vision that carried him away.[1]   The vision was that of a new heaven on earth, to be brought about principally by doing away with bishops.   Others of his time were even more strangely moved by similar visions, and they wrote, spoke, and acted in much more violent ways than Milton did.   Nevertheless, his actions and writings from 1640 to 1658 belie Wordsworth's famous line to him, 'Thy soul was like a star and dwelt apart.'   For twenty mad years Milton did not dwell apart from all that was going on in England.

In these early pamphlets, and in his later ones, he wrote, as he himself put it, 'as if with his left hand,' meaning that prose was uncongenial to him, But there is a more important and significant difference between his prose and his verse than that one.   His restraint in the mechanics of his verse and his control of its substance that are so noticeable in his poetry are lacking in his prose.   In prose, he wrote as his Rebel Angels talk, heatedly, eagerly, and almost without reserve.

In the spring of 1642, he was living in a 'pretty garden-house' in Aldersgate Street,

---

[1] The best expression of his vision, as it came to include the establishment in England of the new Jerusalem, is in *Areopagitica*. 'Methinks I see in my mind a noble and puissant nation rousing herself like a strong man after sleep, and shaking her invincible locks: Methinks I see her as an eagle mewing her mighty youth, and kindling her undazzled eyes at the full midday beam; purging and unscaling her long abused sight at the fountain itself of heavenly radiance; while the whole noise of timorous and flocking birds, with those also that love the twilight, flutter about, amazed at what she means, and in their envious gabble would prognosticate a year of sects and schisms.' *Col.* IV: 344.

teaching and tutoring his two young nephews and probably a few other boys from the neighborhood; and he was in the midst of the controversy between the bishops and the Root-and-Branch party, or between the party of the bishops and the king, and the party of the Parliamentarians and dissenters or Puritans.   As a party man and as a Presbyterian, he was taking part in the beginning of the first revolution, using his talents in a way that apparently delighted him at the time,[1] even if it was only the delight arising from seeing his writings and name in print, and from the applause of the highly partisan group surrounding him.   He was learning to become a great controversalist, perhaps the greatest who ever wrote in English.   The ferocious manner in which controversy was conducted in those days was one that has since undergone great changes, and, at least on the surface, is no longer used.   But there is no need to apologize, as too many writers on Milton have apologized, for Milton entering into these controversies, any more than there is need to apologize for the way he conducted himself in them.   These early tracts display a nature in him that could be highly pugnacious and ruthless; and these characteristics grew on him as he continued to engage in controversy.

He seemed at this time to be well advanced toward becoming the leading mouthpiece for the Presbyterian branch of the Parliamentarians.   Then, after the fifth pamphlet, the *Apology*, a change came over him, and he wrote no more Presbyterian tracts.   It seems as if he stopped writing tracts suddenly, and also as if his break with the Presbyterians was equally sudden.   But, as a matter of fact, that break grew directly out of certain of his private affairs and their consequences.   About six months after his thirty-third birthday, Milton, apparently of his own volition, took a step that changed his whole life.

MILTON'S FIRST MARRIAGE

Except for the death of his mother in 1637 and the tragic loss of his friend, Charles Diodati, Milton's almost commonplace private life before 1640 contained scarcely a single setback or disappointment that we know of.   He had been able up to this time, partly through his native abilities and partly through his father's easy circumstances, to do almost anything he wanted to do.   His life had been filled with intense study and the kind of activity which most appealed to him.   He had, it is true, paid some attention to women; but whatever affairs of the heart had engaged him have passed into oblivion from which, save for the experiences recorded in some of the Latin and Italian poems, they cannot be recovered.   Bishop Hall and his son had accused Milton of certain loose dallyings, which charge he took care to refute in the *Apology* (1642).   In that same tract, Milton stated his own attitude toward marriage and thereby either exhibited a sort of naïve idealism or announced an intention already formed and about to be consummated. Was he actually thinking of his own impending marriage when he wrote this tract, and did he have a definite young woman in mind in the following curious statement?

---

[1] His delight and his high hope were expressed in the *Areopagitica* in the fine passage: 'heads there, sitting by their studious lamps, musing, searching, revolving new notions and ideas wherewith to present, as with their homage and their fealty the approaching reformation: others as fast reading, trying all things, assenting to the force of reason and convincement.   What could a man require more from a nation so pliant and prone to seek after knowledge?'   *Col.* IV: 341.

I think with them who both in prudence and elegance of spirit would choose a virgin of mean fortunes honestly bred, before the wealthiest widow.[1]

At all events, Milton's first marriage was the most disastrous act, beginning the most disastrous series of events in his entire life, and is, both figuratively and literally, one of the dark spots in his biography. Its details are not known with certainty, although Phillips gave a long account of it, and all subsequent accounts have been based on his statements:

During the time also of his continuance in this house, there fell out several occasions of the increasing of his family. His father, who till the taking of Reading by the Earl of Essex his forces, had lived with his other son at his house there, was upon that son's dissettlement necessitated to betake himself to this his eldest son, with whom he lived for some years, even to his dying day. In the next place he had an addition of some scholars; to which may be added, his entering into matrimony; but he had his wife's company so small a time, that he may well be said to have become a single man again soon after. About Whitsuntide it was, or a little after, that he took a journey into the country; nobody about him certainly knowing the reason, or that it was any more than a journey of recreation: after a month's stay, home he returns a married-man, that went out a bachelor; his wife being Mary the eldest daughter of Mr. Richard Powell, then a justice of peace, of Forresthill, near Shotover in Oxfordshire; some few of her nearest relations accompanying the bride to her new habitation; which by reason of the father nor anybody else were yet come, was able to receive them; where the feasting held for some days in celebration of the nuptials, and for entertainment of the bride's friends. At length they took their leave, and returning to Forresthill, left the sister behind; probably not much to her satisfaction; as appeared by the sequel; by that time she had for a month or thereabout led a philosophical life (after having been used to a great house, and much company and joviality). Her friends, possibly incited by her own desire, made earnest suit by letter, to have her company the remaining part of the summer, which was granted, on condition of her return at the time appointed, Michaelmas, or thereabout: In the meantime came his father, and some of the forementioned disciples. And now the studies went on with so much the more vigor, as there were more hands and heads employed; the old gentleman living wholly retired to his rest and devotion, without the least trouble imaginable. Our author, now as it were a single man again, made it his chief diversion now and then in an evening to visit the Lady Margaret Lee, daughter to the — Lee, Earl of Marlborough, Lord High Treasurer of England, and President of the Privy Council to King James I. This Lady being a woman of great wit and ingenuity, had a particular honor for him, and took much delight in his company, as likewise her husband Captain Hobson, a very accomplished gentleman; and what esteem he at the same time had for her, appears by a sonnet he made in praise of her, to be seen among his other sonnets in his extant poems. Michaelmas being come, and no news of his wife's return, he sent for her by letter, and receiving no answer, sent several other letters, which were also unanswered; so that at last he dispatched down a foot messenger with a letter, desiring her return; but the messenger came back not only without an answer, at least a satisfactory one, but to the best of my remembrance, reported that he was dismissed with some sort of contempt; this proceeding, in all probability, was grounded upon no other cause but this, namely, that the family being generally addicted to the Cavalier Party, as they called it, and some of them possibly engaged in the King's service, who by this time had his headquarters at Oxford, and was in some prospect of success, they began to repent them of having matched the eldest daughter of the family to a person so contrary to them in opinion; and thought it

[1] *Col.* III: 1: 342.

would be a blot in their escutcheon, whenever that court should come to flourish again; however, it so incensed our author, that he thought it would be dishonorable ever to receive her again, after such a repulse...[1]

It is impossible to understand exactly what Phillips meant by all he wrote of the marriage; and it is equally impossible to discover much of anything about any phase of it he failed to mention. He was so inexact or careless about the year in which the marriage took place that most subsequent, including some of the contemporary, biographers, if they give the exact year at all, have stated that Milton was married in 1643. It is all but certain, however, that the marriage occurred in June, 1642.[2] Phillips gave the name of the bride, the name and residence of her father, then provided no information at all about any arrangements, acquaintanceships, or anything else that would explain why Milton married Mary Powell. He states unequivocally that no one knew that Milton intended to be married until he returned home with his bride. This may actually have been true; but the statement may also mean that no one had told the eleven- or twelve-year-old boy, and that his uncle did not then or later see fit to discuss the marriage with him.[3]

Phillips seems to hint at some reason for the marriage without actually mentioning any. He mentions none of the connections known to exist between the Powells and the Miltons.[4] Richard Powell and William Herne on June 11, 1627, 'did acknowledge themselves to owe unto John Milton, then of Cambridge University, gentleman, son of John Milton, scrivener citizen and scrivener of London, the sum of £500 [about $2500] of lawful money of England' unless before December 12, 1627, they paid to the poet the sum of £312. The latter sum was not paid, and the poet had been in the possession of a claim of £500 on the lands and goods of Richard Powell since that time. Powell was deeply in debt by 1641. It is possible that Milton married Mary Powell expecting to secure a settlement of this old debt; a marriage settlement of some kind;[5] and a handsome young

---

[1] [Edward Phillips,] *Letters of State*, pp. xxi–xxiv, and Helen Darbishire, *Early Lives*, pp. 63–65.

[2] B. A. Wright, 'Milton's First Marriage,' *Modern Language Review*, vol. XXVI (1931), pp. 383–400.

[3] Phillips was probably confused about the date. Aubrey talked with him, probably after Milton's death; Phillips wrote his biography and published it in 1694, twenty years after Milton's death, and over fifty years after the marriage. Phillips was about twelve years old at the time of the marriage, and could scarcely be expected fifty years later to be exact about the date. The marriage ceremony and its date were not important to him; the subsequent separation was uppermost in his mind as he wrote the account. He mentioned one definite event that can be dated. He says that Milton's father came to live with him after Reading, before that having been living 'with his other son [Christopher], at his house there.' Christopher had married the second daughter of the 'widow Webber...many years before.' Reading fell to the Earl of Essex on April 27, 1643. It must have been sometime in May, 1643, that his father came to live with the poet. Phillips also says that Milton returned about July 1 with his bride to his house, and that his father was not yet come. It was, therefore, the year before the fall of Reading that Milton was married, or in 1642.

[4] For a full account of the relations between the Powells and the Miltons that would have had some bearing on the marriage, see Masson, vols. II (1894 revised edition), pp. 491–508, and III (1896 revised edition), pp. 42–79; W. D. Hamilton, 'Original Papers Illustrative of the Life and Writings of John Milton,' *Camden Society Transactions*, vol. LXXV (London, 1859), pp. 75–134; and J. M. French, *Milton in Chancery* (New York: Modern Language Association, 1939), pp. 71–107 and 291–96.

[5] Cf. Henry Todd, editor, *The Poetical Works of John Milton* (London, 1809, 7 vols.), vol. I, pp. 165 ff., for the court proceedings in which testimony about Milton's will was collected. His brother, Christopher, testified that the poet had said to him, 'Brother, the portion due to me from Mr. Powell, my former wife's father, I leave to the unkind children I had by her; but I received no part of it, and my will and meaning is, they shall have no other benefit of my estate, than the said portion.'

bride.   The marriage settlement,[1] if there was one agreed on, and the old debt were never paid, and the handsome, young bride turned out to be a source of great trouble to him for the rest of his life.

Little is known of Mary Powell.   Masson discovered that the parish registers of Forest Hill, Oxford, contain the following entry, 'Marie Powell, daughter of Richard Powell, baptized the XXIVth day of January, 1625.'   If this date is old style,[2] she would have been only six months beyond her sixteenth birthday at the time of her marriage; if the date is new style, she would have been about six months past her seventeenth birthday. Milton, in June, 1642, was six months under thirty-four years old, or about twice as old as his bride.

The early biographers all tell of Mary leaving Milton about a month after the couple returned to London, and refusing to return to him, though he spent at least a year trying to get her to do so.   There seems to have been originally little if any compatibility of temperament between the two, and none seems to have developed during the ten years Mary lived after marriage.   She was gone for three years after the wedding, five as some of the early biographers state, and the couple actually lived together only six or seven years before her death in 1652.

The direct outcome of Mary's desertion of her husband was his formulation of a plan for a legal divorce and remarriage to another woman.   Characteristically he prepared a written plea addressed to Parliament for the reform of the divorce laws of England. In 1643 he published a tract entitled *The Doctrine and Discipline of Divorce*, and twice revised it in 1644 and once in 1645.   He also published two or three other pamphlets on the subject.   These tracts have been a scandal to orthodox Anglicans for three hundred years, and will continue to rankle with conservatives.   When examined, however, these tracts are found to be the first in English that exhibit a present-day attitude towards divorce. Milton's chief plea is for divorce based on incompatibility of temperament.   So strongly does he urge this point and with such a wealth of details that the reader catches echoes of the mental torture through which he passed in order to reconcile himself to the estrangement.   He almost tells us why the marriage took place.   He says:

for all the wariness [that] can be used, it may yet befall a discreet man to be mistaken in his choice, and we have plenty of examples.   The soberest and best governed men are least practised in these affairs; and who knows not that the bashful muteness of a maiden may ofttimes hide all the unliveliness and natural sloth which is really unfit for conversation; nor is there that freedom of access granted or presumed, as may suffice to a perfect discerning till too late: and where any indisposition is suspected, what more usual than the persuasion of friends, that acquaintance, as it increases, will amend all.   And lastly, it is not strange though many who have spent their youth chastely, are in some things not so quick-sighted, while they haste too eagerly to light the nuptial torch; nor is it therefore that for a modest error a man should forfeit so great a happiness, and no charitable means to release.... Whenas the sober man honoring the appearance of modesty, and hoping well of every social virtue under that veil, may easily chance to meet, if not with a body impenetrable, yet often with a mind to

---

[1] Cf. D. H. Stevens, 'Mary Powell's Lost Dowry,' *Milton Papers* (Chicago: Chicago University Press, 1927), pp. 7–13.

[2] The year was formerly begun on March 25, and dates before 1752 from January 1 to March 25 may be found written 1625 or 1626, or herein as 1625/26.

all other due conversation inaccessible, and to all the more estimable and superior purposes of matrimony useless and almost lifeless: and what a solace, what a fit help such a consort would be through the whole life of a man, is less pain to conjecture than to have experience.[1]

Poor Milton — and poor Mary! There was no adequate answer forthcoming to their problem. We know little about Mary's reaction to the situation; and it is pointless to try to assess blame on either party to the marriage. Milton's bitter disappointment over its outcome and his chagrin at being deserted are manifest in every later mention of the affair.

The marriage and its train of unhappy and unfortunate events constitute the great catastrophe of Milton's private life. The relations between the husband and wife were strained beyond repair by the separation. There is nothing attractive or pleasant about the Milton-Powell marriage. It was the union of a physically and mentally mature man, who knew almost nothing about women and even less about marriage, with a young woman, little more than a girl, probably attractive enough, but who brought little to the marriage except her youth and physical endowments. It cannot be adequately explained, and the more one tries to understand it the less comprehensible it becomes. It was apparently a hasty move on Milton's part; but its consequences never left him. All phases of it are almost equally unhappy. But the permanently unfortunate result of the marriage was to exclude him forever from a normal, contented, and happy domestic existence.

Milton's last published tract before his marriage, the *Apology*, supporting Presbyterianism and attacking the bishops, had appeared in the spring of 1642. Later that same spring he married, and for months was overwhelmed by the immediate consequences of that marriage. His next publication was the *Doctrine* which appeared about August 1, 1643. This pamphlet was attacked at once as a blasphemous and shameful performance, especially by Milton's Presbyterian friends, most of whom were ministers. He was attacked in print in a reply to the *Doctrine*; in turn he tried to defend himself in print, then became embittered by the reception accorded his honest effort at one much-needed phase of social reform. His bitterness was expressed in *Sonnets XI* and *XII*, and *On the New Forcers of Conscience*, this latter containing the famous line 'New presbyter is but old priest writ large.' These poems were written sometime between 1645 and 1647 and mark the definite end of his affiliations with the Presbyterians. The direct result of Milton's writings on divorce was to force the break with the Presbyterians.

In 1644, Milton published the first of his two most famous prose works in English, the little pamphlet in the form of a letter addressed to Samuel Hartlib entitled *Of Education*.[2] In it Milton developed briefly his ideal form of education. His statement of edu-

---

[1] *D. & D., Col.* III:2:394-95.

[2] It probably appeared on June 5, 1644. Dates as exact as this can frequently be supplied from the dates on actual copies owned by George Thomason (died in 1666). Thomason was a London bookseller who lived near and knew Milton very well. (See *Sonnet XIV*.) Aside from his connections with the poet, Thomason is best known for his vast collection of books, pamphlets, and other printed materials printed and published in London between 1641 and 1662. He tried to collect everything published in London during those years. The remains of this collection, smaller in bulk than it was at the time Thomason died but a remarkably well preserved and still very large collection, is now in the British Museum. Almost everything published by Milton between 1640 and 1662 is to be found in the collection, many pieces bearing an inscription from Milton to Thomason and practically every one of them bearing Thomason's date.

cational principles and procedures has been greatly misunderstood, but stands as one of the most stimulating schemes of its kind ever written. It cannot be accepted as an educational plan, however, without understanding exactly what Milton was aiming at in it. He proposed to train selected young men for leadership in an ideal commonwealth, the government of which was to be completely aristocratic. As such a scheme, it has many attractive features. Attacks on it, or objections to it, have chiefly stressed the impossibility of carrying it out on a democratic basis; but that was not Milton's intention.

In the same year, 1644, appeared the *Areopagitica*,[1] an impassioned plea for liberty of the press and for liberty in general. This work is the best-known prose piece Milton ever wrote in English. It has been used over and over again in pleas for the liberty of the press, and has been translated into most European languages. As Professor Haller has shown,[2] there is little in it that was strictly new material at the time it was written. Most of the ideas and principles Milton announces had been previously expressed by other men; but his magic of style, rhetoric, and vocabulary forever place the *Areopagitica* among the greatest appeals for liberty and toleration ever written.

Beginning in the year 1641 and continuing through 1645, Milton published pamphlets connected with some of the most controversial issues of the time in much the same fashion and at about the same rate that we would expect today of a professional journalist. These pamphlets were all on subjects close to his heart and concerning which he apparently had thought systematically. But every pamphlet he published was in one way or another a 'tract for the times,' although each one grew out of a personal experience or conviction. Professor Grierson observed that Milton made his personal attitudes and reactions to experiences into high ideals, and that 'the cause for which he fought was always in his eyes the cause of humanity, the great cause of liberty.'[3] But all that such a statement means is that Milton wrote from a sense of deep personal conviction. He described his pamphleteering activities of this period (1641–45) about ten years later.

> Looking about me for some place in which I might take up my abode, if any was to be found in this troubled and fluctuating state of affairs, I hired, for me and my books, a sufficiently spacious house in the city. Here I returned with no little delight to my interrupted studies.... I first wrote *Of Reformation of the English Church*, in two books, to a friend. Next, as there were two bishops of reputation above the rest ... to one of them I replied in two books, one of which was entitled *Of Prelatical Episcopacy*, the other *The Reason of Church Government*; to the other, in some *Animadversions*, and soon after, in an *Apology* ... When the bishops, at whom every man aimed his arrow, had at length fallen ... I began to turn my thoughts to other subjects. Reflecting, therefore, that there are in all three species of liberty, without which it is scarcely possible to pass any life with comfort, namely, ecclesiastical, domestic or private, and civil; that I had already written on the first species, and saw the magistrate diligently employed about the third, I undertook the domestic, which was the one that remained. But as this also appeared to be three-fold, namely, whether the affair of marriage was rightly managed; whether the education of children was properly conducted; whether, lastly, we were to be allowed freedom of opinion — I explained my sentiments not only on the proper mode of contracting

[1] Thomason dated it November 24, 1644.

[2] W. O. Haller, 'Before *Areopagitica*,' *PMLA*, vol. XLII (1927), pp. 875–900.

[3] Sir Herbert (H. J. C.) Grierson, *Cross Currents in the English Literature of the Seventeenth Century* (London: Chatto and Windus, 1929), p. 237.

marriage, but also of dissolving it, should that be found necessary: ... I next treated in one little work, of the education of children, briefly it is true, but at sufficient length, I conceived, for those who apply themselves to the subject with all that earnestness and diligence which it demands — a subject than which there can be none of greater moment to imbue the minds of men with virtue, from which springs that true liberty which is felt within; none for the wise administration of a commonwealth, and for giving it its utmost possible duration. ... Lastly, I wrote, after the model of a regular speech, *Areopagitica*, on the liberty of printing, that the determination of true and false, of what ought to be published and what suppressed, might not be in the hands of the few who may be charged with the inspection of books, men commonly without learning and of vulgar judgment, and by whose licence and pleasure, no one is suffered to publish any thing which may be above vulgar apprehension. The civil species of liberty, the last which remained, I had not touched, as I perceived it drew sufficient attention from the magistrate.[1]

There is, of course, every possibility that Milton systematized his writings after the fact, as the statements quoted were written in 1654, and that he was describing his activities of 1641–45 only in retrospect. However, the headings in the *Commonplace Book* would belie the completely retrospective systematizing of his work in 1654. But one is almost forced to conclude, upon an examination of the statements in the *Defensio Secunda*, the headings in the *Commonplace Book*, and the pamphlets themselves, that he was working according to a definite scheme and pattern. His prose writings came to a temporary end in 1645, and in that year he turned to his first publication of any poetry under his own name.

Sometime late in December of 1645, appeared a slim volume in two parts entitled *Poems of Mr. John Milton, Both English and Latin, Composed at Several Times*, printed by Ruth Raworth for Humphrey Moseley. The English poems were printed first, and then the Latin, each group with a separate title-page and separate pagination. The probability is that the work was sold in two parts, and also with the English and Latin poems bound together. In a letter to Charles Dati of Florence, dated April 21, 1647, Milton said that he had published:

not a few things in our native tongue; which, were they not written in English, I would gladly send you, my friends in Florence, whose opinion I value so highly. I will send you soon that part which is in Latin, if you really want it. I would have sent these Latin poems at once, if it were not for the fact that they contain some severe strictures against the pope, and I was afraid they would be obnoxious to you.[2]

This book contained practically every poem Milton had written up to this time which he saw fit to preserve for posterity.

During the next two or three years after the appearance of this volume of poetry, he settled back into his studies. He says:

Having dispatched these things, and thinking that, for the future, I should now have abundance of leisure, I undertook a history of the nation from its remotest origin; intending to bring it down, if I could, in one unbroken thread to our own times.[3]

His plans to divorce Mary and contract a marriage with another young woman came to naught. Sometime in 1645, Mary successfully sued for a reconciliation and returned

---

[1] *Def. Sec., Col.* VIII:126 ff.   [2] *Fam. Ep. 10, Col.* XII:50.   [3] *Def. Sec., Col.* VIII:136.

to him. The fortunes of the Powell family had suffered greatly in the decline of the Royalist Party, and not only Mary but many of her immediate relatives came to live with Milton. He was forced to take a larger house in the Barbican, only a short distance from the one in Aldersgate Street. His first child, Anne, was born there on July 29, 1646, according to Phillips, 'born within a year after' Mary's return to him. After his wife's return, Milton passed through the course of many domestic events, which included the birth of Anne; the misfortunes of the Powell family; the death of his father-in-law, who was living with him, in January, 1647; the death of his own father, the scrivener, in March of the same year; and the birth of another daughter, Mary, on October 25, 1648. During these years he published nothing, and the only literary pieces he completed were a few sonnets and the Latin *Ode to John Rous*. One or two of the sonnets were addressed to particular persons, the first of the so-called heroic sonnets; and he also then wrote those bitterly ferocious replies in verse to attacks being made on his divorce pamphlets.

FROM THE APPOINTMENT AS LATIN SECRETARY UNTIL HIS DEATH (1649–74)

After the final revision and publication in 1645 of the *Doctrine*, Milton wrote no more tracts of any kind for a time. He was no longer acceptable as a writer, and probably now equally unacceptable as a person, to his former friends, the Presbyterian ministers, because of his open advocacy of divorce. However, the political and administrative group of men, containing few ministers of any sect, making up the Council of State that tried to guide the Parliament, found Milton too effective a writer and too useful a mouth-piece to neglect for long. Political affairs were rapidly coming to a head, and sometime late in 1648, Milton began his long-continued defense of the proposition that the crown was beholden to the citizenry, and his attack on the idea of the divine right of kings. He published his first pamphlet on these subjects, *The Tenure of Kings and Magistrates*, early in 1649.[1] He later stated that he undertook this work

> when certain Presbyterian ministers, at first the bitterest foes to Charles, unable to endure that the Independent Party should now be preferred to them, and that it should have greater influence in the Parliament, began to clamor against the sentence pronounced upon the King (though in no wise angry at the deed, but only that they themselves had not the execution of it).[2]

The *Tenure* was an attack on the position of the king, and also a support of the action of the Parliament in incarcerating their king, then trying him for treason, finding him guilty of the charge, and then executing him.[3] Phillips states that Milton was 'obliged' to write it. Milton was now being selected and sought out as the mouthpiece for the 'Independent' Party, another group among the Parliamentarians, less sectarian if just as religious as the Presbyterians.

He had first stepped into public notice with his anti-prelatical pamphlets, which were little short of sensational. The divorce tracts were completely sensational, and reactions to them appeared, not only in England, but on the Continent. The Parliament was greatly in need of someone who could present their position, and then defend it as de-

[1] Thomason dated it February 13, 1648/49. [2] *Col.* VIII:134.
[3] Charles I was beheaded on January 30, 1649.

fense became necessary. Shortly before the publication of Milton's *Tenure*, there had appeared on February 9, 1648/49, one of the most famous books ever written in England. This was the *Eikon Basilike, the Portraiture of His Sacred Majesty in His Solitudes and Sufferings*, a book of two hundred and sixty-nine pages, purporting to have been written by the king himself. It was a sentimental, pious, and completely appealing work that had an immediate and far-reaching success. It is difficult to understand how Parliament had allowed the book to be printed; but probably no one foresaw the ready acceptance the book was to receive from the English reading public. Certainly the Parliamentarians had paid no attention to it before publication, and were entirely unprepared for its immediate and astonishing success.

Sometime in February, 1648/49, Milton was made foreign correspondent for the Council of State. His own statement is:

> The Council of State, as it is called, now first constituted by authority of Parliament, invited me to lend them my services in the department more particularly of foreign affairs, an event which had never entered my thoughts. Not long after, the book attributed to the King appeared, written certainly with the bitterest malice against the Parliament.[1]

If Milton's chronology can be completely trusted, sometime before the ninth of February, 1648/49, he was asked to become secretary of foreign affairs charged with foreign correspondence, most of which was carried on in Latin.[2] No doubt he was asked to publish and had prepared the *Tenure* as a defense of his own position and that of the government of which he was already or about to become a part.

By the spring of 1649, the furor occasioned by the *Eikon* had grown to huge proportions. Milton 'being ordered to prepare an answer to it... endeavored in the introduction and in other places so far as it was proper, to ward off the reproach.' The result was his book entitled *Eikonoklastes*, which Thomason dated October 6, 1649, and whose only distinction consisted in having been the most powerful of several Parliamentarian attempts to reply to the *Eikon*. But Milton was arguing against sentiments and emotions; and the case for the Parliamentarians was hopeless. The king had been executed. That was a fact and not a theory. Until the time of his actual execution, the national sympathies were increasingly with the Parliamentarians; from the moment of the king's execution, however, many who had advocated it turned against it, and Charles's martyrolatry began, which has scarcely ceased to this day. The actual execution was a tactical error on the part of the Parliamentarians, and yet, from the standpoint of their day and of the position in which they found themselves, there was little else they could do except execute Charles. For Milton's vision of the English people expressed in the *Areopagitica* as a youthful, fledgling people was truly inspired. The Parliamentarians found it impossible to unite public opinion entirely for them or entirely against them, because it had never hitherto existed. Thereupon the peculiar genius of the English people for self-government by disagreement exhibited itself in a more remarkable fashion than in any other period of their history.

[1] *Col.* VIII: 136–38.

[2] A great many of Milton's official letters for the Parliament, Cromwell, and his son have been preserved. They were first published in 1676, as *Literae Pseudo-Senatus Anglicani, Cromwellii*. They are usually referred to as the *Letters of State*.

Milton plunged into the work of the Council with such fervor that he nearly killed himself. But he published nothing after the *Eikonoklastes* in October, 1649, until early in 1651. He had tried his best to refute the *Eikon*; but no one's best could have stemmed the tide of popular feeling and opinion rolling up behind that book. The damage had been done with its publication. The work spoke for itself.

On May 11, 1649,[1] there appeared another work that the Council saw fit to answer almost at once. This book was written in Latin by a French scholar, Claude de Saumaise, or Salmasius in Latin, entitled *Defensio regia pro Carolo I*. It was a long, very scholarly and pedantic defense of the king, attacking the Parliamentarians as regicides. According to Milton's statement, the Council took this work much more seriously than they had at first taken the much more important *Eikon*. He says of it:

> Next came forward Salmasius; and no long time was lost in looking about for some person to answer him, so that all, of their own accord, instantly nominated me, who was then present in the Council.[2]

Milton's reply to Salmasius appeared on April 6, 1651, according to Thomason.[3] He had been ordered by the Council to prepare 'something in answer to the book of Salmasius and when he had done it to bring it to the Council.' The date of this order was January 8, 1650. He worked about a year over his reply, and the book is entered 'both in Latin and in English' in the Stationers' Registers as of December 31, 1650.

This reply was produced by its author under great pressure at a time when his health was poor, and he attributed directly to it the complete loss of his eyesight.[4] He was probably right about this so far as the time was concerned; but, according to his own statements, his eyes had begun to fail him very early in life.[5] Doubtless he would have retained a part of his sight for a few years longer if it had not been for the long hours of reading and writing he put in on his reply to Salmasius; but it is almost equally certain that his eyes would have failed him completely in a few years regardless of what he did with them.

The book that cost him so much in energy and eyesight was entitled *Joannis Miltoni pro Populo Anglicano Defensio contra Claudii Anonymi, alias Salmasii, Defensionem Regiam*. It found immediate readers both in England and on the Continent. If we can judge by

[1] This date is Thomason's, or that of the Thomason *Catalogue*, cf. I:743. Masson was dubious of this date; see Masson, *Life*, IV:151 note. The first mention of the *Defensio Regia* in the Orders in Council (cf. *Calendar of State Papers, Domestic* [Mary A. E. Green, editor, London: Longmans, 1875], I, 411) is under date of November 29, 1649. The Council had been disturbed by the appearance of the book in England and ordered customs officials to search all vessels for it and to seize all copies.

[2] *Def. Sec., Col.* VIII:138.

[3] Again the date is confusing, as the Council on March 5, 1651, had ordered a conference with Milton about 'reprinting' the *Pro Populo*. See *Calendar* (*op. cit.*, vol. III [1877], p. 70).

[4] For a full account of Milton's blindness, see the sensitive study of it by Eleanor Gertrude Brown, *Milton's Blindness* (New York: Columbia University Press, 1934). The book contains an excellent bibliography on the whole subject.

[5] Milton wrote a full account of his blindness in the letter to Philaras dated from Westminster, September 28, 1654. The letter is a pathetic response to Philaras's suggestion that Milton should not abandon all hope of ever seeing again. He was asked to submit a full account of his blindness in order that it might be laid before the great French physician, Thevenot. Milton's description of his blindness, detailed as it is, lacks certain elements that a modern ophthalmologist needs to determine exactly what was wrong with his eyes. See *Col.* XII:54.

the number of different printings, it was more widely read on the Continent than it was in England. So popular did it become that the Council's intention to have it published in both Latin and English was abandoned, as the book circulated in Latin alone sufficiently to make an English translation unnecessary. The book has been almost completely neglected since the seventeenth century. It is, however, of great value in understanding Milton's full intellectual development, for it was written at the height of his powers.

By the time the *Pro Populo* was actually published, Milton was hard put to it, because of the loss of his eyesight and much illness, to carry on his official work for the Council. It was necessary to provide him some assistance. His health was dangerously bad for three or four years. Many domestic difficulties were added to his poor health, including the death of Mary Powell soon after the birth of the third daughter, Deborah, on May 2, 1652.[1] He wrote of his difficulties at this time:

> At that time in an especial manner, I was oppressed with concerns of a far different nature. My health was infirm; I was mourning the recent loss of two relatives; the light had now utterly left my eyes.[2]

He had also prepared himself for a return attack from Salmasius, which failed to materialize only because of Salmasius' death in 1653.

Meanwhile the Commonwealth under the Parliament was finding itself in difficulty. The government lacked a good many things, but chiefly money. There was as yet no provision in England for a regular income to the government. The most pressing financial difficulty was the army's pay. In 1653, Oliver Cromwell (1599–1658), the most successful of all the Parliamentarian generals in the field, with the army urging him on, set himself up as Protector in a virtual dictatorship, by abolishing Parliament. However, he continued the Council. Milton was a good friend of Cromwell, and in 1652 (cf. *Sonnet XVI*) believed with many another Englishman that Cromwell was, or could be, England's savior. After the Protectorate was established, Milton was as dismayed as any man could be who had hoped, planned, and recklessly spent his money and energies to establish a tolerant, free, and stable government.[3] But he made the best of it, and continued to serve the Council and Cromwell as well as his blindness and poor health would permit.

He seems to have recovered his health about 1655; but his sight was completely gone, and it had become increasingly necessary for him to have assistance in his secretaryship. The Council had insisted that he take lodgings in Scotland Yard, and, according to Phillips, he had written the *Pro Populo* in the house of 'one Thomson's next door to the

---

[1] Milton's first child, Anne, was born in the house in the Barbican on July 29, 1646. She was probably named after his sister. The second child, Mary, was born in the house in Holborn on October 25, 1648, and was named after her mother. The third child was a son, John, born in the house in Scotland Yard on March 16, 1650, and named after his father. The son lived over two years, but, says Phillips, 'through the ill usage or bad constitution of an ill-chosen nurse, died an infant.' Cf. the entries in Mary Powell's Bible, as described by Birch in his *Life*, p. lxi; Joseph Hunter, *A Sheaf of Gleanings* (London: Smith, 1850), p. 34; Masson, *Life*, vol. III, p. 483, and vol. IV, p. 385; W. E. Baxter, 'Milton's Bibles,' *Notes and Queries*, ser. 11, vol. III (1911), pp. 109 ff.; and *Facsimiles of Autographs and Documents in the British Museum, Milton, 1608–1674* ([London]: British Museum, 1908).

[2] *Pro Se Defensio, Col.* IX:12.

[3] But see his defense and praise of Cromwell in *Defensio Secunda*, 1654. *Col.* VIII:212 ff.

Bull Head Tavern at Charing-Cross, opening into the spring garden, which seems to have been only a lodging taken, till his designed apartment in Scotland Yard was prepared for him.'¹

He continued to live in Westminster, serving as foreign secretary to Cromwell and the Council, and carrying on the blasting controversy arising from the quarrel with Salmasius, even after the latter's death. The massacre of the Piedmontese in May, 1655, called forth letters of protest from Cromwell; but the student of Milton is much more interested in the sonnet he wrote on the same bloody event. He probably took less and less part in the affairs of the government, as the records of the Council after 1655 indicate. His now total blindness made almost any activity difficult. In a letter dated 1656, he was negotiating for books from the Continent; and on November 12 of the same year he married his second wife, Katherine Woodcock. Little is known of her, except from Phillips; but for the brief span of their married life they were happy, and Milton was deeply in love with her (cf. *Sonnet XXIII*). The burial records of Saint Margaret's parish, Westminster, contain the two entries: 'Feb. 10, 1657[/58]. Mrs. Katherin Milton. Mar. 20, 1657[/58]. Mrs. Katherin Milton.' Only Phillips's statement tells which was mother and which was daughter. 'By his second wife Catharine the daughter of Captain Woodcock of Hackney, he had only one daughter, of which the mother the first year after her marriage died in childbed, and the child also within a month after.' ² This is not strictly true. The child was born October 29, 1657.

In 1658, he issued a second edition of the *Pro Populo*. He made very few changes in it, but concluded it with a new paragraph that contains a statement of interest here. After accounting for the reissue of the work and a statement about the revision, he goes on to say that he is very proud of the work and the attention it has received, both at home and abroad. He concludes with this statement:

> This my zealous labor's fruit — the highest that I for my part have set before me in this life — I gratefull enjoy; yet therewith too consider chief how I may bear witness — not only to my own country, to which I have paid the highest I possessed, but even to men of whatever nation, and to the cause of Christendom above all — that I am still pursuing after yet greater things if my strength suffice (nay, it will if God grant), and for their sake meanwhile am taking thought and studying to make ready.³

He seems here to have been referring to *Paradise Lost*.⁴

Oliver Cromwell died on September 3, 1658, and the army and Council put his son Richard in the Protectorship. But in a few weeks Richard fled London, and England

---

¹ [Edward Phillips], *Letters of State*, p. xxxiii, and Helen Darbishire, *Early Lives*, p. 71.
² Phillips, *op. cit.*, p. xli.   ³ *Col.* VII: 558.
⁴ He had probably finished or compiled sufficiently for purposes of revision, which never ended, his theological system by this time. Cf. J. H. Hanford, 'The Date of Milton's *De Doctrina Christiana*,' *Studies in Philology*, vol. XVII (1920), pp. 309–19. Also, A. Sewell, *Milton's Christian Doctrine* (London: Oxford University Press, 1939). This work, existing then only in manuscript, disappeared toward the latter end of the seventeenth century and did not reappear until 1823 when it was found in the Public Record Office in London. It was first published in 1825 in its original Latin, and in the same year in English translation. The Bohn revised edition of 1858 (*The Prose Works of John Milton* [J. A. St. John, editor, London: Bohn, 1848–53, 5 vols.]; vols. IV and V contain *The Christian Doctrine* as revised by Sumner) or the Columbia edition is recommended for those who wish to use it. The companion list of books and references for it which Milton mentioned has completely disappeared.

was almost without a government.   The Committee of Safety that was nominally in charge of the country was little more than a name.

During the remaining months of the Protectorate and of the Committee of Safety, Milton was still in the Latin secretaryship, at least as late as October, 1659; but there is no trace of his actual service to the Committee of Safety, although he wrote a few official letters in the name of Richard.

In 1660, the country submitted almost gladly to the re-establishment of the monarchy with the son of Charles I on the throne as Charles II.   Upon the Restoration, as Charles II's return is called, Milton went into hiding, being put under sentence of death.   The sentence was never executed for reasons that are not very clear.   It has been variously conjectured that he was saved by Sir William Davenant, by Andrew Marvel, or by some other person with whom he was intimately connected who had the ear and favor of the court.   However, his life was probably never in much danger, as he continued to see and use as amanuenses his two nephews, Edward and John Phillips, and certainly Edward was apparently never wholly out of favor with the easygoing Charles II.   The period of hiding could have been for only a few months, as Charles II reached London on May 29, 1660, and on August 29 of the same year passed the Act of Indemnity and Oblivion that pardoned all except certain specified persons.   Milton was not so specified and was thereafter free from danger.

He had now met and survived all the reversals life had to give him.   He had met and somehow managed to overcome an unsuccessful and disgraceful marriage; blindness and serious illness; the death of a wife he could scarcely have loved, and the loss of a second wife whom he deeply loved; and then, to fill his cup of bitterness to the brim, the collapse of the whole revolutionary movement with which he had identified himself.   Only an extraordinarily well-balanced personality could have withstood such a succession of personal catastrophes.   Milton not only withstood them, but refused to allow them to keep him permanently from his lifetime ambition to complete his major literary plans.[1]

Milton married a third time on February 24, 1663, taking to wife Elizabeth Minshull, who was then about twenty-four years old, while he was in his fifty-fifth year.   She is described by Aubrey as 'a gent. person a peaceful and agreeable humor.'   She was probably fairly well educated, and in those records containing her signatures, she writes very well.   Tradition has preserved several evidences of Milton's affection for her and the fact that her husband thought she sang with a good voice, but no ear.

Milton's eldest daughter, Anne, at this time was about seventeen, Mary was about thirteen, and Deborah, the youngest, was about eleven.   The troubles of the Mary Powell union were reflected in the upbringing of these three daughters.   They were apparently given very little education, although such a neglect of the education of girls at that time was not at all unusual.   The contemporary biographers state that Milton had taught these daughters to read to him in several different languages, and probably write for him, although they did not understand what they read.   The direct line of the family died out

---

[1] As stated in the text, we know very little about Milton's life in detail after 1660.   It has been reconstructed, with fine imagination, by J. H. Hanford, 'Samson Agonistes and Milton in Old Age,' University of Michigan Publications, Language and Literature, vol. I (1925), pp. 167-89.

completely in another generation, although at least two of the daughters were married, and one of them had children. But before 1800, the last direct line through and from John Milton the poet had ceased to be.

Few exact records exist for Milton's life from the date of his third marriage until his burial. It is usually held that he finished *Paradise Lost* by 1665, at the latest. He published it in 1667. *Paradise Regained* and *Samson Agonistes* appeared together in 1671. He had published *The History of Britain* (1670), but his intention (1654) to bring it down to his own day was not carried out, and the *History* stops with the Norman Conquest (1066). He had completed the first four of its six books by 1649. He published two or three other prose works, including a logic and a grammar; then in 1673, another edition of his *Poems*; and in 1674 a second edition of *Paradise Lost*.

He died on November 8, 1674, 'of the gout struck in,' exactly a month before his sixty-sixth birthday, and was buried in Saint Giles, Cripplegate. He did not, as was formerly supposed, die a pauper. He left an estate composed of some money, perhaps fifteen hundred to two thousand pounds (seventy-five hundred to ten thousand dollars), household furnishings, and books. His main income throughout his life was from his own and his father's investments. He lost as much as two or three thousand pounds (ten or fifteen thousand dollars) in Commonwealth securities at the Restoration. The only money he ever earned other than by investment came from various pieces of work and writing he did for the Council of State, and from a salary settled on him late in the Protectorate that was to have been for life, but which could have been paid for only two or three years at the most. Aside from economies made necessary by reduction of income from investments, the household continued to exist about as usual during the last fifteen years of his life. His widow and three daughters survived him, and there was some difficulty in the disposal of the property. It was clearly his intention through his oral will to leave all his estate to his widow. After much dispute, she received most of it. The library was broken up and disposed of; but a few books that formerly belonged to Milton still survive.[1]

He had become a famous man on the Continent largely through his *Letters of State*, the publication of the divorce tracts which led many Englishmen and Continentals to think of him as infamous, and by his reply to Salmasius. Both Phillips and Aubrey speak of many visitors to London seeking him out and enjoying his conversation and company. He is said to have grumbled during his Restoration years of too much company; but this grumbling was only the reaction of a blind and greatly chastened man to a situation which he actually enjoyed.

His fame as a poet was not entirely posthumous, as for many years it was thought to have been. Even his earliest poems were received with warm appreciation and understanding. Sir Henry Wotton, one of the greatest literary patrons and men of letters of his day, had sounded a note of sincerest praise for *Comus* at least as early as 1637. The 1645 *Poems* found that 'fit audience, though few,' to whom he addressed *Paradise Lost*. *Lycidas*, *Comus*, and the *Epitaphium Damonis* circulated early in separate printings of their own or in a collection published by someone other than Milton. He saw fit to republish the *Poems*, and added a few that the 1645 edition had not contained. *Paradise Lost* early

[1] See Hanford, *Handbook*, pp. 386-89.

gained admirers, and by the end of the seventeenth century had begun to become popular. The eighteenth century accorded a rising tide of popularity to his poetry of exactly the kind that would have been least pleasing to him. He became a popular poet during that century in every sense of the word. He was imitated, quoted, translated, parodied, sung, and referred to as the ruling god of English poetry. The nineteenth century tempered this attitude a little, but continued the sound appreciation of him that the previous century almost concealed beneath its idolatry. There has been no period from the time Milton went up to Cambridge to the present day in which his work has been neglected or treated in any fashion which it does not deserve, except for the idolatry of the eighteenth century.

Except for the *Areopagitica* and the *Of Education*, very little of his prose has been read since his day. On occasion, men have gone to other portions of it and have been greatly stimulated thereby. But on the whole, his prose has had its influence through what a few men have said about it rather than by its effects on large numbers of readers. During the eighteenth and nineteenth centuries, the most extravagant claims were made for Milton's importance in the development of English political and social theories. But it is chiefly as a poet that succeeding ages have known him; and it is chiefly as a poet that his life and work must be judged. In his poetry, he is among the great poets of the western world. Perhaps due to his thorough knowledge of music, perhaps due to some other element in him, the most remarkable phase of his poetry is its metrical precision and purity. The reader of his verse inevitably becomes aware of the operation in it of one of the subtlest and most accurate ears that have ever sensed metrical quantities and qualities in any language. Each reader will prefer some lines of Milton's verse to others; but there is no metrically poor line extant from his pen.

BIBLIOGRAPHY

Anonymous Biography. See Darbishire, Parsons.

Aubrey, John, *Brief Lives, Chiefly of Contemporaries, set down by John Aubrey, between the Years 1669 and 1696.* Edited by Andrew Clark (Oxford: Clarendon Press, 1898, 2 vols.), II: 60–72. Also, Helen Darbishire, *The Early Lives of Milton* (London: Constable, 1932), pp. 49–82.

Bailey, John C., *Milton.* Home University Library, vol. CIII. London: Williams and Norgate, 1915.

Bayle, Pierre, *Dictionnaire historique et critique.* Rotterdam: R. Leers, 1697. 2 vols. in 4.

Bayle, Pierre, *A General Dictionary, Historical and Critical . . .* by John Peter Bernard, Thomas Birch, John Lockman (London: Bettenham, 1734–41, 10 vols.), vol. VII (1738), pp. 567–88.

Birch, Thomas, *A Complete Collection of the . . . [Prose] . . . Works of John Milton* (London: Millar, 1738. 2 vols.), vol. I, pp. i–xcvii. The biography occupies pp. i–lxiii, an appendix to it occupying pp. lxiv–xcvii. The second edition appeared at London. Millar, 1753. 2 vols.

Brooke, Stopford, *Milton.* London: Macmillan, 1879. References are to New York: Appleton, 1892.

Darbishire, Helen, *The Early Lives of Milton.* London: Constable, 1932. Contains the *Anonymous Biography*, and those by Aubrey, Phillips, Richardson, Toland, Wood.

Diekhoff, John S., *Milton On Himself.* New York: Oxford University Press, 1939.

Dietz, Frederick C., *A Political and Social History of England* (third edition; New York: Macmillan, 1937), chapters XII, XIII, XIV, XV.

[Fenton, Elijah], *Paradise Lost.* London: Tonson, 1725. *Life* occurs on pp. v–xxviii and postscript. First signed in edition of 1727.

Gardiner, Samuel Rawson, *History of England, 1603–1660*.   London: Longmans, Green, 1863–1903, 17 or 18 vols.

Garnett, Richard, *Life of John Milton*.   London: Scott, 1890.

Hamilton, W. Douglas, *Original Papers Illustrative of the Life and Writings of John Milton*.   Camden Society [vol. LXXV].   [London, 1859.]

Hunter, Joseph, *Milton.   A Sheaf of Gleanings*.   London: Smith, 1850.

Masson, David, *The Life of John Milton*.   London: Macmillan, 1859–96.   6 vols.   Separate index vol. issued in 1894.   Vol. I revised, 1881, and it, not the 1859 volume, should always be used; vol. II revised, 1894; vol. III revised, 1896.

Morand, Paul Phelps, *De Comus à Satan*.   Paris: Didier, 1939.

Newton, Thomas, *Paradise Lost* (London: Tonson and Draper, 1749.   2 vols.), vol. I, pp. i–lxi.

Parsons, E. S., 'The Earliest Life of Milton,' *English Historical Review*, vol. XVII (1902), pp. 95 ff. First publication of *Anonymous Biography*.

Pattison, Mark, *Milton*.   English Men of Letters Series.   London: Macmillan, 1879.

Peck, Francis, *New Memoirs of the Life and Poetical Works of Mr. John Milton*.   London, 1740.

[Phillips, Edward], *Letters of State Written by Mr. John Milton*.   London, 1694.   The biography occupies pp. i–xliv.

Richardson, Jonathan, *Explanatory Notes and Remarks on Paradise Lost.   With the Life of the Author. By J. R., Sen*.   London: Knapton, 1734.   The biography occupies pp. i–clxxxii.

Saintsbury, George, 'Milton,' *Cambridge History of English Literature*.   A. W. Ward and A. R. Waller, editors.   Cambridge: University Press, 1907 ss. 14 vols.   Vol. VII, chapter V, pp. 95–141.

Stephen, Leslie, 'Milton,' *Dictionary of National Biography*.   Sir Sidney Lee, editor.   63 vols.   Vol. XXXVIII (1894), pp. 24–41.   Also issued in 21 vols.   Vol. XIII, pp. 471–88.

Stern, Alred, *Milton und seine Zeit*.   Leipzig: Duncker und Humblot, 1877–79.   2 vols.

Toland, John, *A Complete Collection of the . . . [Prose] Works of John Milton*.   Amsterdam [London], 1698, 3 vols.   The biography occupies pp. 5–47 of vol. I.   Separately printed at London: Darby, 1699.

Trevelyan, G. M., *England Under the Stuarts*.   London: Methuen, 1904.   Revised, 1925.

Wood, Anthony, *Athenae Oxonienses*.   London, 1691–92.   3 vols.   Vol. I, *Fasti*, pp. 880–84.   Also, Philip Bliss, editor.   London, 1813–20.   4 vols.   Vol. II, *Fasti*, cols. 480–86.

Poems Written in School and at College
1620–1632

AUBREY stated that Milton was already a poet when he was ten years old, and the poet remarks that while yet a boy, some of his written exercises, prose and verse, were recognized by those about him as being worthy of preservation. His father must have been early aware that his son was more than ordinarily gifted as a writer to have ' destined [him] from a child for the pursuits' of literature. But Milton was very slow to publish or definitely acknowledge any of his English poetry. He kept most of it in manuscript, changing and correcting it, for years before publishing it, now and then submitting a piece to his friends. He seems to have taken literally Horace's injunction to hold back his poetry from publication 'till the ninth year.'[1] He allowed other men to publish one or another of his poems now and then, at most, with his initials, or else unsigned. But he himself published none of his poems until 1645 when he was over thirty-seven years old. Few of the poems in the little 1645 volume were less than five years old when they were published. Many of the English poems, however, are known in much earlier texts than those printed. Beginning early in the Horton period, perhaps as early as 1632, Milton compiled fair copies of some English poems and preserved rough drafts of others. These copies and drafts are found today in what is called the *Trinity College Manuscript*, now one of the greatest treasures of the Trinity College Library, Cambridge.[2] The *Manuscript* contains a large number of poems in Milton's own handwriting, with some of the late entries in other hands. It is a document of great importance for serious study of any of the poems contained in it. It was probably kept as a repository for fair copies and rough drafts of English poems from about 1632 until after his blindness set in, or for a period of about twenty-five years. It contains no poem written before Horton and no actual verses from any of the three long poems, *Paradise Lost*, *Paradise Regained*, or *Samson Agonistes*, although there are lists of subjects for poems, and several different outlines of what became *Paradise Lost*. The *Manuscript* contains only what Milton saw fit to preserve, and there are some indications that not all of it has survived. None of the Latin poems is in it.

The poems of the period 1620–32 are of two distinct kinds, the English and the Latin. The differences between the two amount to more than the differences between the poetic canons of the two languages. The Latin poetry is polished, highly effective, and some of it ranks with the very best neo-Latin verse. The *Elegies* especially exhibit a uniform excellence that has won admiring comments of all critics from Milton's day to the present. His contemporary friends in England and Italy, as well as the later critics Warton (1785), Todd (1801), Masson (1874), Jerram (1890), and Rand (1922–24), hailed the *Elegies* as re-

---

[1] Cf. Horace (65–8 B.C.), *Ars Poetica*, ll. 388–90, '... nonumque prematur in annum,' etc., 'then put your parchment in the closet and keep it back till the ninth year. What you have not published you can destroy; the word once sent forth can never come back.'

[2] Cf. p. 15, note.

markable. They show the influence of the young Milton's favorite Latin poet, Ovid, of Horace, and of the neo-classic Latinists, especially of the Renaissance. Ovid had brought a perfection of form to Latin elegiac verse (dactylic hexameter and pentameter) that few later poets have equaled. All through the late Middle Ages and the Renaissance Ovid's elegiac poetry had been enjoyed, imitated, and almost worshiped. By Milton's day it had come to be a poetic convention to imitate Ovid in Latin verse in which poets could develop their abilities and at the same time include as much confession of their personal, intimate experiences as the sophisticated, artificial, and essentially unnatural conventions would permit. These conventions called for an 'assumed lightness and well-bred indifference which the cultured but naïve youth wore like a borrowed garment.' Coleridge called the elegy 'the form of poetry natural to the reflective mind,' and Milton was naturally attracted to it. His early Latin poems not only exhibit mastery of the conventions, but also display a glowing poetic imagination, restrained fervor, and sureness in accomplishment that are unusual. He used Latin verse to express many of his most intimate and vivid experiences and moods. We must turn to the Latin rather than to the English poetry of the early period for a realization of Milton's spiritual and esthetic development. In the Latin elegy he found a poetic form that satisfied him, and he used it over and over again. He could readily find and follow in Latin verse accepted forms for almost any poetic expression, on which he put his own stamp. His Latin poems are in the conventional forms and modes of late classical and neo-classic poetry, ranging from the lightly lyrical elegy to the statelier epic form, as *In Quintum Novembris*. In English poetry, such a wide range of conventions did not yet exist. De Quincey found *Paradise Lost* a 'force among forces' in the development of English poetry. But Milton had no English model for it.

Moody rightly contended that Milton's success as an English poet derived from his intensive knowledge of Latin poetry. But, although his English verse is greatly indebted to his literary and scholarly study of classical literature, particularly poetry, who would contend that, without this knowledge, Milton would not have written English? None of his English poems is precisely a Latin model poem in English; and indeed all efforts to resolve any of his English poems into a classical original have failed.

In the English poems of the early period, Milton was not yet at ease poetically. The form of no English poem of the period, except the sonnet, was later repeated. From the early period he preserved only two complete stanzaic poems in English, and, except in some inconsequential psalm paraphrases, never again used the stanza form. Apparently he found it too restricted or otherwise unsuited to his poetic genius. The English forms of the early period, even *L'Allegro* and *Il Penseroso*, are all experimental and juvenile. The fact that he never used them again would seem to indicate that this was Milton's judgment of them. He preserved only 'best examples' of his poetic apprenticeship in English verse in various forms, including modifications of the Spenserian stanza, the heroic couplet, the octosyllabic couplet, and the sonnet.

In English verse, he had perforce to create form, mood, and meter; tone and overtone. But in Latin, adequate poetic conventions and forms already existed, ready at hand. Thus, his Latin poems flowed easily and relatively quickly, and they were probably printed about as they came originally from his pen. He showed little reluctance to use them, or even to allow them to be published, as the *Naturam non Pati Senium*, probably printed in 1628, testifies. But his English poems were another matter. He himself published none of them until 1645. He kept them by him for a long Horatian interval, and the *Manu-*

script shows us how he worked over them. And with all the changes made in the *Manuscript*, even then not a single poem printed from it in 1645 reads exactly like the *Manuscript* copy.

Probably the time will never come when the close student of Milton will be certain of the exact chronological order in which Milton's early poems were written. The exact dates of composition of these poems, Latin or English, are from one point of view impossible to determine. But from another point of view, their general chronological relationships are easy to determine and to understand, and were broadly outlined by Milton himself. We know, within a few years or even a few months or weeks, the dates at which many of them were written. But if we try to be utterly exact, only those poems connected with some definite event whose date we know can be definitely dated. Milton himself was responsible for many of the difficulties that arise in attempting to date his poems exactly. He published the *Minor Poems* twice, the first time in 1645, and the second time in 1673. The arrangement of the English and Latin poems is the same in both editions, the English poems followed by the Latin with their separate title-pages and pagination. In both editions, he classified the poems by poetic forms, following the custom of the poets of the Renaissance. The classification is more noticeable in the case of the Latin poems, these being divided into two books, the first called *Elegiarum Liber*, and the second, *Sylvarum Liber*. Within these two books, he then takes account both of the poetic forms and of the chronological sequence of the poems as he prints them. For a few of the English poems and for many of the Latin, he supplied an indirect approximation of the year in which the individual poem was composed. As a result, the careful student is set a very complex problem, for in several cases Milton's indirect datings are wrong and in others, very confusing. His attempts at dating his poems are best explained in connection with the discussion of each poem.

These early poems were completed in the period during which Milton lived in London as a boy in the house in Bread Street; received instruction from private tutors at home; attended Saint Paul's School; and completed his residence and work at Christ's College, Cambridge. Probably the earliest poems which survive are the two *Psalm Paraphrases* in English, as a heading to which Milton printed 'This and the following *Psalm* were done by the author at fifteen years old.' We know nothing about the exact date of composition of these two paraphrases, except that they probably were written by 1623 or 1624 at the latest. Are they surviving evidence that, as Aubrey says of him, at 'ten years old ... [he] was then a poet'? Milton's statement that they were 'done by the author at fifteen years old' may certainly be taken to mean that they were written at any time before he was sixteen, or between 1620 and 1624.

The next earliest surviving poems are Latin *Elegy I*, and, possibly, Latin *Elegy IV*. The latter poem seems to be referred to in the Latin letter to Thomas Young dated March 26, 1625.[1] *Elegy I* contains a reference to what was probably his rustication from his college quarters, that occurred during his first year at Cambridge.

The following year, 1626, he wrote the Latin poems, *Elegy II* and *Elegy III*, *In Obitum Præsulis Eliensis*, *In Obitum Procancellarii Medici*, *In Quintum Novembris*, and perhaps one of the five others on the same subject. These poems can each be dated by the events they

---

[1] Milton saved thirty-one letters he had written to various individuals and prepared them for the press. They were published in a little volume entitled *Joannis Miltoni, Angli, Epistolarum Familiarium* (London, 1674). The book was licensed for printing and sale for one shilling on July 1, 1674, and was probably in print before Milton's death. It also contains a number of *Prolusiones*, or papers that Milton had written for various official occasions at Cambridge. The collection is almost as important to the student of this period of his life as the poetry.

celebrate. *Elegy II* was printed, as were several other Latin poems after it, with the added heading 'Anno AEtatis 17.' [1]

In 1627 he wrote *Elegy VII*. The following year, 1628, he wrote *Naturam non Pati Senium* and probably *De Idea Platonica*; and the English *On the Death of a Fair Infant*, and *At a Vacation Exercise*, with the prolusion, *VI*, that accompanied it. [2]

The beautiful *On the Morning of Christ's Nativity* was written for the Christmas season of 1629. The poems in Italian were probably written about 1630, and *L'Allegro–Il Penseroso* between 1630 and 1632.

The poetry of the period shows that Milton was chiefly occupied with Latin verse, and for a study of his poetic development, as well as his more intimate thoughts and activities of the time, a knowledge of Latin is essential. On the whole, the Latin poems of the early period are of a much higher order of poetic merit than the English poems of the same period. The Latin poems are available in several translations, some in prose and some in verse. Together with the *Familiar Epistles* and the *Prolusiones*, they form the essential body of material for the study of Milton's development as a man and as a poet during the Cambridge years.

The *Fair Infant* is the first English poem in which elements that are Milton's own begin to appear. There is a certain amount of power in the poem and some of the poetic facility that we later come to expect from him. The promise in this poem is fulfilled in the *Nativity Ode*, written shortly after his twenty-first birthday. The *Ode* is his first great poem in English, although uneven in quality. *L'Allegro–Il Penseroso* are Italianate experiments in the English pastoral lyric, never repeated, surpassing anything of their kind in the language. They show Milton taking up the challenge of Browne's *Britannia's Pastorals* and performing with almost perfect ease two exercises that leave almost nothing more to be done in that particular *genre*.

The poetry, correspondence, and school exercises of this period combine to show us Milton as a young poet beginning to find his wings, experimenting with various verse forms, sometimes with high success and sometimes with mediocre results, who finds his surest poetic medium in Latin. In English verse, he is at this time essentially a polished Elizabethan with the influences of Spenser, Donne, Jonson, Shakespeare, and the Italians permeating his poems. In neither his Latin nor his English poetry does he yet show much concern about producing a new or different type of verse, either in form or substance. He succeeds in some of his early poems in attaining a very high degree of achievement.

REFERENCES

Hanford, J. H., 'The Youth of Milton,' *University of Michigan Publications, Language and Literature*, vol. I (1925), pp. 89–163. *Handbook* (third edition, 1939), pp. 132–56.

[1] This is the first occurrence of this way of dating a Latin poem, and occurs with many other Latin poems. It seems to mean 'in the seventeenth year of his age.' This would mean in the year after his sixteenth birthday. But in all poems with such a superscription that can be dated, he has made himself a year too young, and in at least one instance, two years too young. No explanation of this apparent error has ever been satisfactory. The reason for such superscriptions seems to be that they were the common way of referring to the age of boys in school records. Thus, the brother, Christopher, was admitted to Christ's College, Cambridge, 'anno aetatis 15' on February 15, 1631, although he had celebrated his fifteenth birthday by December, 1630, and consequently was in his sixteenth year.

[2] John Milton, *Private Correspondence and Academic Exercises* (translated from the Latin by Phyllis B. Tillyard, Cambridge: University Press, 1932), pp. xxx–xxxi, 85–104, and 139–42.

Masson, David, *The Poetical Works of John Milton* (London: Macmillan, 1890, 3 vols.), vol. I, pp. 77–136.

Milton, John, *Private Correspondence and Academic Exercises.* Translated from the Latin by Phyllis B. Tillyard, Cambridge: University Press, 1932.

Parker, W. R., 'Some Problems in the Chronology of Milton's Early Poems,' *Review of English Studies,* vol. XI (1935), pp. 276–83. 'On Milton's Early Literary Program,' *Modern Philology,* vol. XXXIII (1935), pp. 49–53.

Patterson, F. A., *et al., The Works of John Milton.* New York: Columbia University Press, 1930–38, 18 vols. in 21. The *Minor Poems* are in vol. I.

Rand, E. K., 'Milton in Rustication,' *Studies in Philology,* vol. XIX (1922), pp. 109–25.

Verity, A. W., *Milton's Ode on the Morning of Christ's Nativity, L'Allegro, Il Penseroso, and Lycidas.* Pitt Press Series. Cambridge: University Press, 1891. Frequently reprinted.

Warton, Thomas, *Poems Upon Several Occasions, English, Italian, and Latin, By John Milton.* Second edition; London: Robinson, 1791.

[LETTER TO A FRIEND]

(ca. 1632)

First Draft

Sir, (besides that in sundry respects I must acknowledge me to profit by you whenever we meet), you are often to me and were yesterday especially as a good watchman to admonish that the hours of the night pass on (for so I call my life as yet obscure & unserviceable to mankind) & that the day is at hand wherein Christ commands all to labor while there is light. which because I am persuaded you do to no other purpose than out of a true desire 5 that God should be honored in every one, I am ever ready, you know, when occasion is, to give you account, as I ought though unasked, of my tardy moving according to the precept of my conscience, which I firmly trust is not without God. yet now I will not strain for any set apology, but will only refer myself to what my mind shall have at any time to declare herself at her best ease.   yet if you think, as you said, that too much love of learn- 10 ing is in fault, & that I have given up myself to dream away my years in the arms of studious retirement, like Endymion with the moon on Latmus hill, yet consider that if it were no more but this to overcome this, there is on the other side both ill more bewitchful, to entice away, & natural cares more swaying & good more available, to withdraw to that which you wish me as first all the fond hopes which forward youth & vanity are fledge 15 with, none of which can sort with this Pluto's helmet, as Homer calls it, of obscurity & would soon cause me to throw it off if there were nothing else in it but an affected & fruitless curiosity of knowing, and then a natural desire of honor & repute, which I think possesses the breast of every scholar as well of him that shall as of him that shall never obtain it (if this be altogether bad) which would quickly oversway this phlegm & melan- 20 choly of bashfulness, or that other humor, & prevail with me to prefer a life that had at least some credit in it, some place given it before a manner of living much disregarded, & discountenanced, there is besides this, as all well know, about this time of a man's life a strong inclination, be it good or no, to build up a house & family of his own in the best manner he may, to which nothing is more helpful than the early entering into some credi- 25 ble employment, & nothing more cross than my way, which my wasting youth would presently bethink her of & kill one love with another, if that were all; but what delight or what peculiar conceit may you in charity think, could hold out against the long knowledge of a contrary command from above, & the terrible seizure of him that hid his

talent, therefore commit grace to grace or nature to nature, there will be found on the 30
other way more obvious temptations to bad as gain, preferment ambition more winning
presentments of good, & more prone affections of nature to incline & dispose not counting
outward causes as expectations & murmurs of friends scandals taken & such like, than the
bare love of notions could resist, so that if it be that which you suppose, it had by this
been round about begirt, & overmastered whether it had proceeded from virtue, vice, or na- 35
ture in me, yet that you may see that I am sometime suspicious of myself, & do take notice
of a certain belatedness in me, I am the bolder to send you some of my nightward thoughts
somewhile since since they come in fitly made up in a Petrarchian stanza.

> How soon hath time the subtle thief of youth
>   stolen on his wing my three & twentieth year
>   my hasting days fly on with full career
>   but my late spring no bud or blossom showeth
> Perhaps my semblance might deceive the truth   5
>   that I to manhood am arrived so near
>   & inward ripeness doth much less appear
>   that some more timely-happy spirits endueth
> Yet be it less or more, or soon or slow
>   it shall be still in strictest measure even   10
>   to that same lot however mean or high
> toward which time leads me, & the will of heaven
>   all is if I have grace to use it so
>   as ever in my great task-master's eye

Second Draft

Sir, besides that in sundry other respects I must acknowledge me to profit by you whenever we meet, you are often to me, & were yesterday especially, as a good watchman to
admonish that the hours of the night pass on (for so I call my life as yet obscure, & unserviceable to mankind) & that the day with me is at hand wherein Christ commands all to
labor while there is light. which because I am persuaded you do to no other purpose than 5
out of a true desire that God should be honored in everyone; I therefore think myself
bound though unasked, to give you account, as oft as occasion is, of this my tardy moving; according to the precept of my conscience, which I firmly trust is not without God.
yet now I will not strain for any set apology, but only refer myself to what my mind shall
have at any time to declare herself at her best ease.   But if you think, as you said, that 10
too much love of learning is in fault, & that I have given up myself to dream away my
years in the arms of studious retirement like Endymion with the moon as the tale of Latmus goes, yet consider that if it were no more but the mere love of learning, whether it
proceed from a principle bad, good, or natural it could not have held out thus long against
so strong opposition on the other side of every kind, for if it be bad why should not all 15
the fond hopes that forward youth and vanity are fledge with together with gain, pride,
& ambition call me forward more powerfully, then a poor regardless & unprofitable sin of
curiosity should be able to withhold me, whereby a man cuts himself off from all action
& becomes the most helpless, pusilanimous & unweaponed creature in the wor[l]d, the
most unfit & unable to do that which all mortals most aspire to either to defend & be 20
useful to his friends, or to offend his enemies.   Or if it be to be thought a natural prone-

ness there is against that a much more potent inclination & inbred which about this time
of a man's life solicits most, the desire of house & family of his own to which nothing is
esteemed more helpful than the early entering into credible employment, & nothing more
hindering than this affected solitariness and though this were enough yet there is to this 25
another act if not of pure yet of refined nature no less available to dissuade prolonged obscurity, a desire of honor & repute & immortal fame seated in the breast of every true
scholar which all make haste to by the readiest ways of publishing & divulging conceived
merits as well those that shall as those that never shall obtain it, nature therefore would
presently work the more prevalent way if there were nothing but this inferior bent of her- 30
self to restrain her. lastly if the love of learning as it is [be] the pursuit of something
good, it would sooner follow the more excellent & supreme good known & presented and
so be quickly diverted from the empty & fantastic chase of shadows & notions to the solid
good flowing from due & timely obedience to that command in the gospel set out by the
terrible seizing of him that hid the talent. it is more probable therefore that not the end- 35
less delight of speculation but this very consideration of that great commandment does
not press forward as soon as maybe to undergo but keeps off with a sacred reverence, &
religious advisement how best to undergo not taking thought of being late so it give advantage to be more fit, for those that were latest lost nothing when the master of the
vineyard came to give each one his hire. & here I am come to a stream head copious enough 40
to disburden itself like Nilus at seven mouths into an ocean, but then I should also run
into a reciprocal contradiction of ebbing & flowing at once & do that which I excuse
myself for not doing preach and not preach. yet that you may see that I am something
suspicious of myself, & do take notice of a certain belatedness in me I am the bolder to
send you some of my nightward thoughts somewhile since because they come in not alto- 45
gether unfitly, made up in a Petrachian stanza which I told you of

after the stanza

by this I believe you may well repent of having made mention at all of this matter, for if I
have not all this while won you to this, I have certainly wearied you to it. this therefore
alone may be a sufficient reason for me to keep me as I am lest having thus tired you singly, 50
I should deal worse with a whole congregation, & and spoil the patience of a parish. for I
myself do not only see my own tediousness but now grow offended with it that has hindered m[e] thus long from coming to the last & best period of my letter, & that which
must now chiefly work my pardon that I am

Your true and unfeigned friend.   55

On the Morning of Christ's Nativity

(Composed 1629)

This is the first poem in the 1645 *Poems*, and the date, 'Composed 1629,'
is part of the title therein. It is also the first poem in the 1673 *Poems*,
though there without the date; but is not found in the *Manuscript*. Aside
from a few minor differences, there is only one notable change in text between the two editions, occurring in lines 143-44. Milton referred to this
poem in two other poems, *Elegy VI*, lines 79-90; and again, fleetingly, in *The
Passion*, lines 1-4. According to the *Elegy*, it was begun in the early morn-

ing of Christmas Day. Milton was then twenty-one years old, and still a student at Cambridge. It is a poem written for the most important of all the Christian holy days, Christmas.

The first four introductory stanzas differ from those of the *Hymn*. For these first four stanzas Milton varied the rhyme royal (a stanza of seven verses in pentameter), used by Chaucer in *Troilus and Cressida* and several of the *Canterbury Tales* and by Spenser in *Foure Hymnes*, by introducing as the last line an alexandrine (six-foot line) instead of the usual five-foot line. He probably took the idea from the *Faerie Queene*, indeed the nine-line stanza of that poem with lines six and seven omitted is practically identical with Milton's seven-line stanza here. In the *Hymn* proper, the eight-line stanza with lines of four different lengths, *a6a6b10c6c6b10d8d12*, so far as is known, was Milton's invention.

The poem has no particular sources. The student should note Virgil's *Eclogue IV*, Tasso's poem on the nativity, and English poems by Robert Southwell (1560–95); parts of Edmund Spenser's (1552–99) *Hymne of Heavenly Love*, lines 134–287; and other poems by John Donne, Joshua Sylvester, Ben Jonson, John and Joseph Beaumont, Edmund Bolton, Henry Constable, William Dunbar, William Drummond, Giles Fletcher, Charles Fitzgeffrey, Joseph Hall, George Herbert, Richard Crashaw, and Thomas Pestel. All these poets of Milton's time or earlier had written poems celebrating the nativity of Jesus.

The *Nativity Ode* has been accorded much praise since its first publication. It is a great Christmas poem, perhaps the greatest such poem in English. But it is the work of a young and immature genius. It is artificial, in both Milton's sense of that word and ours, and was influenced by what Milton was later to call 'our late fantastics' or the metaphysical strain of Donne and his followers. Some of the imagery is almost grotesque, and the leaning toward affectation is unmistakable. But in a young poet, such borrowings are readily understood and allowed for, and on the whole, the poem has come in for a great deal of praise, Hallam calling it 'perhaps the finest in the English language.' Certainly, the poem contains more than a suggestion of the mighty lines that were to follow it from the same pen, if it is not accorded so high a place as some of them. The poem unmistakably sounds for the first time the 'organ tone' we associate with so much of Milton's later poetry. The full erudition is especially noticeable to the classicist; and the poem reveals, as Verity puts it, 'the elevation and inspired enthusiasm of tone:... the happy device of weaving in the narrative names that raise in us a vague thrill of awe, a sense of things remote and great and mysterious: above all, the absolute grandeur of style... the command over great effects of harmony... of all the early poems none displays [all these elements] so conspicuously as the Nativity Ode.'

REFERENCES

Cook, A. S., 'Notes on Milton's *Ode on the Morning of Christ's Nativity*,' *Transactions of the Connecticut Academy of Arts and Sciences*, vol. XV (1909), pp. 307–68.

Hanford, J. H., *Handbook* (third edition, 1939), pp. 141–44.

Verity, A. W., *Milton's Ode on the Morning of Christ's Nativity*, etc., pp. xxiv–xxvii.

I

This is the month, and this the happy morn
Wherein the son of heaven's eternal king,
Of wedded maid, and virgin mother born,
Our great redemption from above did bring;
For so the holy sages once did sing,   5
    That he our deadly forfeit should release,
And with his father work us a perpetual peace.

II

That glorious form, that light unsufferable,
And that far-beaming blaze of majesty,
Wherewith he wont at heaven's high council-table,   10
To sit the midst of trinal unity,
He laid aside; and here with us to be,
    Forsook the courts of everlasting day,
And chose with us a darksome house of mortal clay.

III

Say heavenly muse, shall not thy sacred vein   15
Afford a present to the infant God?
Hast thou no verse, no hymn, or solemn strain,
To welcome him to this his new abode,
Now while the heaven by the sun's team untrod,
    Hath took no print of the approaching light,   20
And all the spangled host keep watch in squadrons bright?

IV

See how from far upon the eastern road
The star-led wizards haste with odors sweet,
O run, prevent them with thy humble ode,
And lay it lowly at his blessed feet;   25
Have thou the honor first, thy Lord to greet,
    And join thy voice unto the angel choir,
From out his secret altar touched with hallowed fire.

The Hymn

I

        It was the winter wild,
        While the heaven-born child,
    All meanly wrapt in the rude manger lies;   30
        Nature in awe to him
        Had doffed her gaudy trim,
    With her great master so to sympathize:
    It was no season then for her
    To wanton with the sun her lusty paramour.

23. **wizards:** the Magi, wise men or sages, the word's former meaning.

II

Only with speeches fair
She woos the gentle air
To hide her guilty front with innocent snow,
And on her naked shame,
Pollute with sinful blame,   40
The saintly veil of maiden white to throw,
Confounded, that her maker's eyes
Should look so near upon her foul deformities.

III

But he her fears to cease,   45
Sent down the meek-eyed peace,
She crowned with olive green, came softly sliding
Down through the turning sphere
His ready harbinger,
With turtle wing the amorous clouds dividing,   50
And waving wide her myrtle wand,
She strikes a universal peace through sea and land.

IV

No war, or battle's sound
Was heard the world around
The idle spear and shield were high uphung,   55
The hooked chariot stood
Unstained with hostile blood,
The trumpet spake not to the armed throng,
And kings sat still with awful eye,
As if they surely knew their sovereign Lord was by.   60

V

But peaceful was the night
Wherein the prince of light
His reign of peace upon the earth began:
The winds with wonder whist,
Smoothly the waters kissed,   65
Whispering new joys to the mild ocean,
Who now hath quite forgot to rave,
While birds of calm sit brooding on the charmed wave.

VI

The stars with deep amaze
Stand fixed in steadfast gaze,   70

50. **with turtle wing**: on the wings of a dove, a 'turtle' meaning 'turtledove.'

56. **hooked chariot**: with hooks or knives protruding from the axles beyond the wheels or on the wheels themselves.

60. **sovereign**: this word, which M. usually spelled 'sovran,' is almost always a two-syllable word in his poetry, as it is here.   64. **whist**: hushed.

68. **birds of calm**: halcyons. 'Halcyon days' are the seven days before and the seven days after the shortest day of the year. While the halcyon breeds, there is fair weather at sea.

Bending one way their precious influence,
    And will not take their flight,
    For all the morning light,
Or Lucifer that often warned them thence;
But in their glimmering orbs did glow,   75
Until their Lord himself bespake, and bid them go.

VII

And though the shady gloom
    Had given day her room,
The sun himself withheld his wonted speed,
    And hid his head for shame,   80
    As his inferior flame,
The new enlightened world no more should need;
He saw a greater sun appear
Than his bright throne, or burning axletree could bear.

VIII

The shepherds on the lawn,   85
    Or ere the point of dawn,
Sat simply chatting in a rustic row;
    Full little thought they then,
    That the mighty Pan
Was kindly come to live with them below;   90
Perhaps their loves, or else their sheep,
Was all that did their silly thoughts so busy keep.

IX

When such music sweet
    Their hearts and ears did greet,
As never was by mortal finger struck,   95
    Divinely-warbled voice
    Answering the stringed noise,
As all their souls in blissful rapture took:
The air such pleasure loath to lose,
With thousand echoes still prolongs each heavenly close.   100

X

Nature that heard such sound
    Beneath the hollow round
Of Cynthia's seat, the airy region thrilling,
    Now was almost won
    To think her part was done,   105
And that her reign had here its last fulfilling;
She knew such harmony alone
Could hold all heaven and earth in happier union.

71. **precious influence**: the astrological power of the stars.

92. **silly**: simple; originally, 'happy.' Few words have changed so completely in meaning in three hundred years.   100. **close**: the conclusion of a strain in music.

102. **the hollow round**: the moon.   103. **Cynthia's seat**: the moon was Diana's, or Cynthia's.

106. **its**: occurs only three times in all the poetry; *PL* I:254; IV:813.

XI

At last surrounds their sight
A globe of circular light,   110
That with long beams the shamefaced night arrayed,
The helmed cherubim
And sworded seraphim,
Are seen in glittering ranks with wings displayed,
Harping in loud and solemn choir,   115
With unexpressive notes to heaven's new-born heir.

XII

Such music (as 'tis said)
Before was never made,
But when of old the sons of morning sung,
While the creator great   120
His constellations set,
And the well-balanced world on hinges hung,
And cast the dark foundations deep,
And bid the weltering waves their oozy channel keep.

XIII

Ring out ye crystal spheres,   125
Once bless our human ears,
(If ye have power to touch our senses so)
And let your silver chime
Move in melodious time;
And let the bass of heaven's deep organ blow,   130
And with your ninefold harmony
Make up full consort to the angelic symphony.

XIV

For if such holy song
Enwrap our fancy long,
Time will run back, and fetch the age of gold,   135
And speckled vanity
Will sicken soon and die,
And leprous sin will melt from earthly mold,
And hell itself will pass away,
And leave her dolorous mansions to the peering day.   140

XV

Yea truth, and justice then
Will down return to men,

110. **globe:** round mass or body; a military term.
116. **unexpressive notes:** inexpressible music; cf. *Lycidas* 176; *Arcades* 72–73.
119. **sons of morning:** *Job* 38:7, 'when the morning stars sang together,' at creation.
125. **crystal spheres:** the spheres of the Ptolemaic system of astronomy.
131. **ninefold:** the nine other spheres of the ten-sphere system, the earth, apparently, being sung to.
132. **consort:** accompaniment.   **symphony:** the full choir song of the angels.

    Orbed in a rainbow; and like glories wearing
      Mercy will sit between,
      Throned in celestial sheen,   145
    With radiant feet the tissued clouds down steering,
And heaven as at some festival,
Will open wide the gates of her high palace hall.

XVI

    But wisest fate says no,
      This must not yet be so,   150
    The babe yet lies in smiling infancy,
      That on the bitter cross
      Must redeem our loss;
    So both himself and us to glorify:
Yet first to those ychained in sleep,   155
The wakeful trump of doom must thunder through the deep.

XVII

    With such a horrid clang
      As on Mount Sinai rang
    While the red fire, and smoldering clouds outbrake:
      The aged earth aghast   160
      With terror of that blast,
    Shall from the surface to the center shake;
When at the world's last session,
The dreadful judge in middle air shall spread his throne.

XVIII

    And then at last our bliss   165
      Full and perfect is
    But now begins; for from this happy day
      The old dragon under ground
      In straiter limits bound,
    Not half so far casts his usurped sway,   170
And wroth to see his kingdom fail,
Swinges the scaly horror of his folded tail.

XIX

    The oracles are dumb,
      No voice or hideous hum
    Runs through the arched roof in words deceiving.   175
      Apollo from his shrine
      Can no more divine,
    With hollow shriek the steep of Delphos leaving.
No nightly trance, or breathed spell,
Inspires the pale-eyed priest from the prophetic cell.   180

143–44. 1645 edition has 'The enameled arras of the rainbow wearing, And mercy set between.'
155. **ychained**: the old preterit prefix *ge* as in German.
168. **the old dragon**: Satan.   172. **swinges**: lashes about.
176 ff. **Apollo . . .**: the most famous oracle was at Delphi.

XX

The lonely mountains o'er,
And the resounding shore,
A voice of weeping heard, and loud lament;
From haunted spring, and dale
Edged with poplar pale,
The parting genius is with sighing sent,   185
With flower-inwoven tresses torn
The nymphs in twilight shade of tangled thickets mourn.

XXI

In consecrated earth,
And on the holy hearth,   190
The lars, and lemures moan with midnight plaint,
In urns, and altars round,
A drear and dying sound
Affrights the flamens at their service quaint;
And the chill marble seems to sweat,   195
While each peculiar power forgoes his wonted seat.

XXII

Peor, and Baalim,
Forsake their temples dim,
With that twice battered god of Palestine,
And mooned Ashtaroth,   200
Heaven's queen and mother both,
Now sits not girt with tapers' holy shine,
The Libyc Hammon shrinks his horn,
In vain the Tyrian maids their wounded Thammuz mourn.

XXIII

And sullen Moloch fled,   205
Hath left in shadows dread,
His burning idol all of blackest hue;
In vain with cymbals' ring,
They call the grisly king,
In dismal dance about the furnace blue;   210
The brutish gods of Nile as fast,
Isis and Orus, and the dog Anubis haste.

181 ff. The cessation of the oracles was related by Plutarch, and by many writers since.

186. **genius:** Milton uses this word almost constantly for the generic name of the spirit of any locality or place.   191. **lars and lemures:** the first, Roman household gods; the second, ghosts.

194. **flamens:** pagan priests.   197. **Peor and Baalim:** famous gods of the Philistines in Palestine.

199. **twice battered god:** Dagon, another god of the Philistines. Cf. *I Samuel* 5.

200. **Ashtaroth:** the moon goddess, Astarte.

201. **Heaven's queen and mother both:** it is interesting to note that Sin, the personification, occupies exactly this same position in hell; that is, Astarte, Ashtaroth is really Sin.

203. **Libyc Hammon:** an Egyptian god.   204. **Thammuz:** a Syrian deity.

205. **Moloch:** the god of the Ammonites, to whom children were sacrificed.

211–14. Gods of Egypt.

XXIV

Nor is Osiris seen
In Memphian grove, or green,
Trampling the unshowered grass with lowings loud: 215
Nor can he be at rest
Within his sacred chest,
Nought but profoundest hell can be his shroud,
In vain with timbreled anthems dark
The sable-stoled sorcerers bear his worshiped ark.   220

XXV

He feels from Judah's land
The dreaded infant's hand,
The rays of Bethlehem blind his dusky eyn;
Nor all the gods beside,
Longer dare abide,   225
Not Typhon huge ending in snaky twine:
Our babe to show his Godhead true,
Can in his swaddling bands control the damned crew.

XXVI

So when the sun in bed,
Curtained with cloudy red,   230
Pillows his chin upon an orient wave,
The flocking shadows pale,
Troop to the infernal jail,
Each fettered ghost slips to his several grave,
And the yellow-skirted fays,   235
Fly after the night-steeds, leaving their moon-loved maze.

XXVII

But see the virgin blest,
Hath laid her babe to rest.
Time is our tedious song should here have ending:
Heaven's youngest teemed star,   240
Hath fixed her polished car,
Her sleeping Lord with handmaid lamp attending:
And all about the courtly stable,
Bright-harnessed angels sit in order serviceable.

219. **timbreled anthems:** songs accompanied by playing on small tambourines.
220. **sable-stoled:** dark-robed.
226. **Typhon:** a crocodile god of Egypt.
227–28. Like the young Hercules.
235. **yellow-skirted fays:** yellow-skirted fairies. See Hesiod, *Theogony*, 273, 358.
240. **youngest teemed:** youngest born.

On the Death of a Fair Infant Dying of a Cough

(1628)

Anno aetatis 17

There is only one text for this poem, that appearing in the 1673 *Poems*. It was not included in the 1645 *Poems*, nor does it occur in the *Manuscript*.

In it, Milton used the same seven-line stanza he had employed in the introduction of the *Nativity Ode*, and which he used once more in *The Passion*. This stanza had been used by Phineas Fletcher, and derives from the Spenserians, although Mr. Tillyard insists that the poem is in the tradition of the Elizabethans imitating Ovid rather than in the Spenserian tradition, which seems a distinction without a difference. The *Fair Infant* seems to be the practice piece for the successful *Ode* written perhaps a year and a half later.

The poem was an epitaph, one of the most widely used and common forms of poetry in Western Europe. Epitaphs were written as late as the nineteenth century by poets in all countries. The theme of death was common in England, especially in plague-ridden London, throughout the centuries. No particular sources have been noted for Milton's poem.

According to the registers for the parish of Saint Martins-in-the-Fields, London, the child whose death must have been commemorated in this poem was Anne, daughter of Milton's sister, Anne Milton, who had married Edward Phillips. Mr. Hanford pointed out that they were married in November 1623.[1] According to the register of births, Anne was baptized on January 12, 1625. She was buried in the church on January 22, 1628. The poem was written to console the mother, lines 71–77. Phillips mentioned the poem as written for a relative. The child died in the winter, line 4, and was a little girl, line 49 and line 72. The poem seems to have been written during the summer or spring, lines 3 and 68, following the death. It was at once an epitaph and a poem to console the grief-stricken mother, and thus a poem for the family which Milton did not see fit to print until nearly fifty years after it was written.

REFERENCES

Hanford, J. H., *Handbook* (third edition), 1939, pp. 138–40.
Masson, David, *The Poetical Works of John Milton*, I:116–18.
Parker, W. R., 'Milton's *Fair Infant*,' *London Times Literary Supplement*, December 17, 1938, p. 802.

I

> O fairest flower no sooner blown but blasted,
> Soft silken primrose fading timelessly,
> Summer's chief honor if thou hadst outlasted,
> Bleak Winter's force that made thy blossom dry;

---

[1] Hanford, *Handbook*, p. 138. Cf. also W. R. Parker, 'Milton's *Fair Infant*,' *London Times Literary Supplement*, December 17, 1938.

For he being amorous on that lovely dye 5
  That did thy cheek envermeil, thought to kiss
But killed alas, and then bewailed his fatal bliss.

II

For since grim Aquilo his charioteer
By boisterous rape the Athenian damsel got,
He thought it touched his deity full near, 10
If likewise he some fair one wedded not,
Thereby to wipe away the infamous blot,
  Of long uncoupled bed, and childless eld,
Which 'mongst the wanton gods a foul reproach was held.

III

So mounting up in icy-pearled car, 15
Through middle empire of the freezing air
He wandered long, till thee he spied from far,
There ended was his quest, there ceased his care.
Down he descended from his snow soft chair,
  But all unwares with his cold-kind embrace 20
Unhoused thy virgin soul from her fair biding place.

IV

Yet art thou not inglorious in thy fate;
For so Apollo, with unwitting hand
Whilom did slay his dearly-loved mate
Young Hyacinth born on Eurotas' strand 25
Young Hyacinth the pride of Spartan land;
  But then transformed him to a purple flower
Alack that so to change thee winter had no power.

V

Yet can I not persuade me thou art dead
Or that thy corpse corrupts in earth's dark womb, 30
Or that thy beauties lie in wormy bed,
Hid from the world in a low delved tomb;
Could heaven for pity thee so strictly doom?
  Oh no! for something in thy face did shine
Above mortality that showed thou wast divine. 35

VI

Resolve me then O soul most surely blest
(If so it be that thou these plaints dost hear)
Tell me bright spirit where'er thou hoverest
Whether above that high first-moving sphere
Or in the Elysian fields (if such there were). 40
  Oh say me true if thou wert mortal wight
And why from us so quickly thou didst take thy flight.

8–9. **Aquilo** . . . : Boreas, or Aquilo, the north wind.   13. **eld**: old age.
15. **icy-pearled**: pearled with ice.   23 ff. **For so Apollo** . . . : cf. Ovid, *Metamorphoses* X:6.
40. **Elysian fields**: the fields of the blessed.   41. **wight**: animate being.

VII

Wert thou some star which from the ruined roof
Of shaked Olympus by mischance didst fall;
Which careful Jove in nature's true behoof   45
Took up, and in fit place did reinstall?
Or did of late earth's sons besiege the wall
    Of sheeny heaven, and thou some goddess fled
Amongst us here below to hide thy nectared head.

VIII

Or wert thou that just maid who once before   50
Forsook the hated earth, O tell me sooth
And camest again to visit us once more?
Or wert thou [mercy] that sweet smiling youth!
Or that crowned matron sage white-robed truth?
    Or any other of that heavenly brood   55
Let down in cloudy throne to do the world some good.

IX

Or wert thou of the golden-winged host,
Who having clad thyself in human weed,
To earth from thy prefixed seat didst post,
And after short abode fly back with speed,   60
As if to show what creatures heaven doth breed,
    Thereby to set the hearts of men on fire
To scorn the sordid world, and unto heaven aspire.

X

But oh why didst thou not stay here below
To bless us with thy heaven-loved innocence,   65
To slake his wrath whom sin hath made our foe
To turn swift-rushing black perdition hence,
Or drive away the slaughtering pestilence,
    To stand 'twixt us and our deserved smart
But thou canst best perform that office where thou art.   70

XI

Then thou the mother of so sweet a child
Her false imagined loss cease to lament,
And wisely learn to curb thy sorrows wild;
Think what a present thou to God hast sent,
And render him with patience what he lent;   75
    This if thou do he will an offspring give,
That till the world's last end shall make thy name to live.

53. **mercy:** omitted in 1673. Most editors supply it for meter.
67–68. The plague.

At a Vacation Exercise in the College, Part Latin, Part English

(*1628*)

Anno aetatis 19

The only text is that of the edition of 1673. The meter is loosely heroic verse (pentameter or five feet), more nearly like some of Ben Jonson's than the more tightly constructed heroics favored later in the seventeenth century. This is part of a college 'exercise' or what we could call a 'performance' with Milton acting as master of ceremonies. The remainder of his contribution was in Latin, and Milton preserved it also, it being the Sixth Academic Latin Exercise. His English verses form the third part of the performance, the first part being a Latin Oration, the second the Latin *Prolusion*, and there was probably a fourth part in prose following the English verses. The remains of this activity are chiefly of biographical interest to us today, except for lines 33–39 and the list of 'subjects for poetry' in lines 47–52 which is made up of heroic themes. The two parts, Latin and English, if read together, provide us with a picture of Milton at play in college, and show us his sharp, slightly ironic, but very real wit, together with an early capacity for broad, even coarse humor.

REFERENCES

Hanford, J. H., *Handbook* (third edition, 1939), pp. 140–41.
Masson, David, *The Poetical Works of John Milton*, I: 118–24.
Milton, John, *Private Correspondence and Academic Exercises* (translated by Phyllis B. Tillyard; Cambridge: University Press, 1932), pp. xxx–xxxi, 85–104, and 139–42.

The Latin Speeches ended, the English thus began.
Hail native language, that by sinews weak
Didst move my first endeavoring tongue to speak,
And madest imperfect words with childish trips,
Half unpronounced, slide through my infant lips,
Driving dumb silence from the portal door,   5
Where he had mutely sat two years before:
Here I salute thee and thy pardon ask,
That now I use thee in my latter task:
Small loss it is that thence can come unto thee,
I know my tongue but little grace can do thee: 10
Thou needest not be ambitious to be first,
Believe me I have thither packed the worst:
And, if it happen as I did forecast,
The daintiest dishes shall be served up last.
I pray thee then deny me not thy aid   15
For this same small neglect that I have made:
But haste thee straight to do me once a pleasure,
And from thy wardrobe bring thy chiefest treasure;
Not those new-fangled toys, and trimming slight
Which takes our late fantastics with delight,   20

But cull those richest robes, and gayest attire
Which deepest spirits, and choicest wits desire:
I have some naked thoughts that rove about
And loudly knock to have their passage out;
And weary of their place do only stay   25
Till thou hast decked them in thy best array;
That so they may without suspect or fears
Fly swiftly to this fair assembly's ears;
Yet I had rather, if I were to choose,
Thy service in some graver subject use,   30
Such as may make thee search thy coffers round,
Before thou clothe my fancy in fit sound:
Such where the deep transported mind may soar
Above the wheeling poles, and at heaven's door
Look in, and see each blissful deity   35
How he before the thunderous throne doth lie,
Listening to what unshorn Apollo sings
To the touch of golden wires, while Hebe brings
Immortal nectar to her kingly sire:
Then passing through the spheres of watchful fire,   40
And misty regions of wide air next under,
And hills of snow and lofts of piled thunder,
May tell at length how green-eyed Neptune raves,
In heaven's defiance mustering all his waves;
Then sing of secret things that came to pass   45
When beldam nature in her cradle was;
And last of kings and queens and heroes old,
Such as the wise Demodocus once told
In solemn songs at king Alcinous' feast,
While sad Ulysses' soul and all the rest   50
Are held with his melodious harmony
In willing chains and sweet captivity.
But fie my wandering muse how thou dost stray!
Expectance calls thee now another way,
Thou knowest it must be now thy only bent   55
To keep in compass of thy predicament:
Then quick about thy purposed business come,
That to the next I may resign my room.

Then ENS *is represented as Father of the Predicaments his ten Sons,*
whereof the eldest stood for SUBSTANCE *with his Canons, which* ENS
thus speaking, explains.

Good luck befriend thee son; for at thy birth
The faery ladies danced upon the hearth;   60
The drowsy nurse hath sworn she did them spy
Come tripping to the room where thou didst lie;
And sweetly singing round about thy bed

37. **unshorn Apollo:** the 'intonsus Cynthius' of Horace, *Odes* I:21:2.
38. **golden wires:** the harp.   **Hebe:** goddess of youth, cup-bearer to the gods.
43. **Neptune:** god of the sea.
48 ff. **Demodocus . . . :** in Homer, *Odyssey*, the blind bard of King Alcinous of the Phaeacians.
56. **thy predicament:** as leader of the exercise.

Strew all their blessings on thy sleeping head.
She heard them give thee this, that thou shouldst still 65
From eyes of mortals walk invisible,
Yet there is something that doth force my fear,
For once it was my dismal hap to hear
A sibyl old, bow-bent with crooked age,
That far events full wisely could presage, 70
And in time's long and dark prospective glass
Foresaw what future days should bring to pass,
'Your son,' said she, '(nor can you it prevent)
Shall subject be to many an accident.
O'er all his brethren he shall reign as king, 75
Yet everyone shall make him underling,
And those that cannot live from him asunder
Ungratefully shall strive to keep him under,
In worth and excellence he shall outgo them,
Yet being above them, he shall be below them; 80
From others he shall stand in need of nothing,
Yet on his brothers shall depend for clothing.
To find a foe it shall not be his hap,
And peace shall lull him in her flowery lap;
Yet shall he live in strife, and at his door 85
Devouring war shall never cease to roar:
Yea it shall be his natural property
To harbor those that are at enmity.'
What power, what force, what mighty spell, if not
Your learned hands, can loose this Gordian knot? 90

The next QUANTITY *and* QUALITY, *spake in prose, then* RELATION *was called by his name.*

Rivers arise; whether thou be the son,
Of utmost Tweed, or Ouse, or gulfy Dun,
Or Trent, who like some earth-born giant spreads
His thirty arms along the indented meads,
Or sullen Mole that runneth underneath, 95
Or Severn swift, guilty of maiden's death,
Or rocky Avon, or of sedgy Lea,
Or coaly Tyne, or ancient hallowed Dee,
Or Humber loud that keeps the Scythian's name,
Or Medway smooth, or royal towered Thame. 100

The rest was prose.

66. **walk invisible:** the substance of anything, its abstraction, is invisible.

74. **accident:** a modifying condition.

90. **Gordian knot:** the knot no one could untie, not even Alexander the Great, who undid it by cutting through it with his sword. Milton is referring to the riddle he has set forth in the preceding lines.

91. **Rivers:** the name of the boy addressed.

96. **maiden's death:** Sabrina. See *Comus* 824 ff. and note.

98. **hallowed Dee:** See *Lycidas* 55 (Deva), Spenser, *Faerie Queene* IV:2:39. Browne, *Britannia's Pastorals* II:5.

99. **keeps the Scythian's name:** Drayton, *Polyolbion* VIII:43 ff., relates the story of how the river derived its name from a Scythian king Humber, who invaded Britain and was drowned after having been defeated by the Britons.

The Passion

(1630)

This poem appeared in the 1645 *Poems*, and also in the 1673 *Poems*, but is not found in the *Manuscript*. It was apparently written for the Passion week of 1630, the spring following the Christmas season of 1629 and the writing of the *Nativity Ode*. *The Passion* employs a meter and stanzaic form identical with those in the introduction of the *Ode*. It is a fragment, and was to have been one of the three poems Milton wrote for different Christian holy days. This one celebrates the sufferings of Jesus through his betrayal, trial, and death on the cross. The author's poor opinion of it is indicated by his refusal to finish it. Perhaps it marks his last surviving attempt at stanzaic poetry, except in the *Psalm Paraphrases*.

I

Erewhile of music, and ethereal mirth,
Wherewith the stage of air and earth did ring,
And joyous news of heavenly infant's birth,
My muse with angels did divide to sing;
But headlong joy is ever on the wing,   5
   In wintry solstice like the shortened light
Soon swallowed up in dark and long outliving night.

II

For now to sorrow must I tune my song,
And set my harp to notes of saddest woe,
Which on our dearest Lord did seize erelong,   10
Dangers, and snares, and wrongs, and worse than so,
Which he for us did freely undergo.
   Most perfect hero, tried in heaviest plight
Of labors huge and hard, too hard for human wight.

III

He sovereign priest stooping his regal head   15
That dropped with odorous oil down his fair eyes,
Poor fleshly tabernacle entered,
His starry front low-roofed beneath the skies;
O what a mask was there, what a disguise!
   Yet more; the stroke of death he must abide,   20
Then lies him meekly down fast by his brethren's side.

IV

These latest scenes confine my roving verse,
To this horizon is my Phoebus bound,
His godlike acts; and his temptations fierce,

22. **latest**: 1645 reads 'latter.'   24 ff. Others have sung of these matters.

And former sufferings otherwhere are found;   25
Loud o'er the rest Cremona's trump doth sound;
 Me softer airs befit, and softer strings
Of lute, or viol still, more apt for mournful things.

V

Befriend me night best patroness of grief,
Over the pole thy thickest mantle throw,   30
And work my flattered fancy to belief,
That heaven and earth are colored with my woe;
My sorrows are too dark for day to know:
 The leaves should all be black whereon I write,
And letters where my tears have washed a wannish white.   35

VI

See see the chariot, and those rushing wheels,
That whirled the prophet up at Chebar flood,
My spirit some transporting cherub feels,
To bear me where the towers of Salem stood,
Once glorious towers, now sunk in guiltless blood;   40
 There doth my soul in holy vision sit
In pensive trance, and anguish, and ecstatic fit.

VII

Mine eye hath found that sad sepulchral rock
That was the casket of heaven's richest store,
And here though grief my feeble hands uplock,   45
Yet on the softened quarry would I score
My plaining verse as lively as before;
 For sure so well instructed are my tears,
That they would fitly fall in ordered characters.

VIII

Or should I thence hurried on viewless wing,
Take up a weeping on the mountains wild,   50
The gentle neighborhood of grove and spring
Would soon unbosom all their echoes mild,
And I (for grief is easily beguiled)
 Might think the infection of my sorrows loud,   55
Had got a race of mourners on some pregnant cloud.

*This subject the author finding to be above the years he had, when he wrote it,
and nothing satisfied with what was begun, left it unfinished.*

26. **Cremona's trump:** Vida (1485-1566), a native of Cremona, Italy, wrote the *Christiad.*
36-37. Cf. *Ezekiel* 1:1.

On Time

(1630–1633)

This poem occurs in the 1645 *Poems*, in the 1673 *Poems*, and in the *Manuscript*. Professor Grierson dated it 1632–33. We really know nothing of its exact time of composition. In the *Manuscript*, struck out, is the explanatory sub-title ['to be] set on a clock case.' The companion piece, *At a Solemn Music*, *Upon the Circumcision*, and this poem are written in iambic lines of varying lengths, irregularly joined in rhyming pairs, but opening in alternate rhymes. But, more important than this, the poems are throughout their lengths sustained outbursts with no real break or heavy pause from first to last. In English, they are the earliest experiments with the single non-stanzaic 'verse paragraph' as a complete poem that Milton has left us.

REFERENCES

Hanford, J. H., *Handbook* (third edition, 1939), pp. 153–54.
Masson, David, *The Poetical Works of John Milton*, I:153.

Fly envious time, till thou run out thy race,
Call on the lazy leaden-stepping hours,
Whose speed is but the heavy plummet's pace;
And glut thyself with what thy womb devours,
Which is no more than what is false and vain, 5
And merely mortal dross;
So little is our loss,
So little is thy gain.
For whenas each thing bad thou hast entombed,
And last of all thy greedy self consumed, 10
Then long eternity shall greet our bliss
With an individual kiss;
And joy shall overtake us as a flood,
When everything that is sincerely good
And perfectly divine, 15
With truth, and peace, and love shall ever shine
About the supreme throne
Of him, to whose happy-making sight alone,
When once our heavenly-guided soul shall climb,
Then all this earthly grossness quit, 20
Attired with stars, we shall forever sit,
    Triumphing over death, and chance, and thee O time.

Upon the Circumcision

(1630–1634?)

This poem was first printed in 1645, again in 1673, and is the fifth poem in the *Manuscript*. Metrically it belongs with *At a Solemn Music* and *On Time*, all three employing an irregular rhyme scheme and varying length of line. These three poems are the only surviving experiments with this type of metrical structure, which culminated in the metrics of *Lycidas*.

Many Christian poets have written poems to celebrate the holy days of the Christian calendar, both in the classical and in the vernacular languages of Europe. Donne and Herbert were the most notable English poets who had written such poems in English before 1630.

It is a poem written to commemorate the performance of the rite of circumcision on the infant Jesus. In the Greek, Roman, and Anglican churches, the celebration of the occurrence of the rite takes place on January 1, in the exact middle of the 'twelve days of Christmas,' six days after the Christ Mass, and six days before Epiphany, or the manifestation of Jesus, on January 6, in the same churches. Because of this time scheme, most, but not all editors have dated the poem immediately following the Christmas of 1629 when Milton wrote the *Nativity Ode*. Professor Grierson thinks that, because of its position and appearance in the *Manuscript*, it may have been written as late as 1634. Whatever its date, it belongs with the *Nativity Oae* and *The Passion* as one of the three poems Milton wrote, each dealing with a Christian feast day. Perhaps they were written for the three succeeding holy days in 1629-30.

> Ye flaming powers, and winged warriors bright,
> That erst with music, and triumphant song
> First heard by happy watchful shepherds' ear,
> So sweetly sung your joy the clouds along
> Through the soft silence of the listening night; 5
> Now mourn, and if sad share with us to bear
> Your fiery essence can distill no tear,
> Burn in your sighs, and borrow
> Seas wept from our deep sorrow,
> He who with all heaven's heraldry whilere 10
> Entered the world, now bleeds to give us ease;
> Alas, how soon our sin
> Sore doth begin
>   His infancy to seize!
> O more exceeding love or law more just? 15
> Just law indeed, but more exceeding love!
> For we by rightful doom remediless
> Were lost in death, till he that dwelt above
> High throned in secret bliss, for us frail dust
> Emptied his glory, even to nakedness; 20
> And that great covenant which we still transgress
> Entirely satisfied,

And the full wrath beside
Of vengeful justice bore for our excess,
And seals obedience first with wounding smart　　25
This day, but O erelong
　　Huge pangs and strong
　　　Will pierce more near his heart..

At a Solemn Music

(1630–1633)

This poem is contained in the 1645 *Poems*, in the 1673 *Poems*, and no less than four different drafts of it occur in the *Manuscript*. Like *On Time*, it is an experiment, twenty-eight lines long, with the verse paragraph type of poem. It is similar in meter, but longer, and the rhyme scheme is about the same. We would today write the title as 'On a Concert of Sacred Music.' The poem becomes in Milton's hands a union of the poetry with the music of the concert to form a short, symphonic harmony of praise addressed, of course, to God.

Blest pair of sirens, pledges of heaven's joy,
Sphere-born harmonious sisters, voice, and verse,
Wed your divine sounds, and mixed power employ
Dead things with inbreathed sense able to pierce,
And to our high-raised phantasy present,　　5
That undisturbed song of pure concent,
Aye sung before the sapphire-colored throne
To him that sits thereon
With saintly shout, and solemn jubilee,
Where the bright seraphim in burning row　　10
Their loud uplifted angel trumpets blow,
And the cherubic host in thousand choirs
Touch their immortal harps of golden wires,
With those just spirits that wear victorious palms,
Hymns devout and holy psalms　　15
Singing everlastingly;
That we on earth with undiscording voice
May rightly answer that melodious noise;
As once we did, till disproportioned sin
Jarred against nature's chime, and with harsh din　　20
Broke the fair music that all creatures made
To their great Lord, whose love their motion swayed
In perfect diapason, whilst they stood
In first obedience, and their state of good.
O may we soon again renew that song,　　25
And keep in tune with heaven, till God erelong
To his celestial consort us unite,
To live with him, and sing in endless morn of light.

6. **concent**: 'agreement of parts in music.' Phillips, *Dict.* (1706). But see *Il Penseroso*, l. 95. 1645 has 'content,' although *MS.* reads 'concent' in all three drafts.

An Epitaph on the Marchioness of Winchester

(1631)

This poem was printed by Milton in 1645 and again in 1673. Warton says that it first appeared at Cambridge in a collection of verses commemorating her death; but that he had never seen the volume.[1] Later scholars have been equally unsuccessful, and if such a volume actually appeared, it has long since disappeared. There is no copy of the poem in the *Manuscript*; but a copy of it occurs, in manuscript, in a collection of poetry in the British Museum.[2] The poem is an epitaph for Jane, wife of John Paulet, fifth Marquis of Winchester. She died when she was only twenty-three years old, on April 15, 1631, in consequence of an infection. The approximate date of her death and its cause are found in a letter dated April 21, 1631.[3] Her death called forth a number of commemorative poems besides Milton's, one of them by Ben Jonson. The letter states that this was because 'she was inclining [just before she died] to become a Protestant.' Just why Milton wrote a poem on her death is not known. He was still at Cambridge, and may have written an epitaph along with several of his fellow students. Perhaps he knew her and her husband; and this possibility is especially noteworthy because John, Marquis of Winchester, was a staunch Roman Catholic and remained so until his death in 1674.

The couplets in which the poem is written anticipate those in *L'Allegro* and *Il Penseroso*, and the irregularity of the meter is characteristic of Milton's verse at this time and later. The lines contain from six to eight syllables, usually eight, and, less frequently, seven, and, rarely, six.

REFERENCES

Masson, David, *The Poetical Works of John Milton*, I: 128–31. *The Life of John Milton*, I:244–46.

> This rich marble doth inter
> The honored wife of Winchester,
> A viscount's daughter, an earl's heir,
> Besides what her virtues fair
> Added to her noble birth,   5
> More than she could own from earth.
> Summers three times eight save one
> She had told, alas too soon,
> After so short time of breath,
> To house with darkness, and with death.   10

[1] Thomas Warton, *Poems Upon Several Occasions, English, Italian, and Latin, By John Milton* (second edition; London: Robinson, 1791), p. 303.

[2] See *Columbia*, I: 2: 425. British Museum MS. Sloane 1446, beginning on p. 72. The *Manuscript* says she died on April 15.

[3] [Thomas Birch, compiler.] *The Court and Times of Charles I* (London, 1848, 2 vols.), II: 106.

Yet had the number of her days
Been as complete as was her praise,
Nature and fate had had no strife
In giving limit to her life.
Her high birth, and her graces sweet,   15
Quickly found a lover meet;
The virgin choir for her request
The god that sits at marriage-feast;
He at their invoking came
But with a scarce-well-lighted flame;   20
And in his garland as he stood,
Ye might discern a cypress bud.
Once had the early matrons run
To greet her of a lovely son,
And now with second hope she goes,   25
And calls Lucina to her throes;
But whether by mischance or blame
Atropos for Lucina came;
And with remorseless cruelty,
Spoiled at once both fruit and tree: 30
The hapless babe before his birth
Had burial, not yet laid in earth,
And the languished mother's womb
Was not long a living tomb.
So have I seen some tender slip   35
Saved with care from winter's nip,
The pride of her carnation train,
Plucked up by some unheedy swain,
Who only thought to crop the flower
New shot up from vernal shower;   40
But the fair blossom hangs the head
Sideways as on a dying bed,
And those pearls of dew she wears,
Prove to be presaging tears
Which the sad morn had let fall   45
On her hastening funeral.
Gentle lady may thy grave
Peace and quiet ever have;
After this thy travail sore
Sweet rest seize thee evermore,   50
That to give the world increase,
Shortened hast thy own life's lease;
Here, besides the sorrowing
That thy noble house doth bring,
Here be tears of perfect moan   55
Wept for thee in Helicon,

22. **cypress bud**: omen of death.   26. **Lucina**: goddess of childbirth.

28. **Atropos**: the fate who cuts the thread of life.

56. **wept**: Milton wanted a long *e* sound here apparently, for he printed 'weept' in 1645 and 1673. **Helicon**: the mountain sacred to the muses, tears wept there being poems commemorating death.

And some flowers, and some bays,
For thy hearse to strew the ways,
Sent thee from the banks of Came,
Devoted to thy virtuous name;   60
Whilst thou bright saint high sittest in glory.
Next her much like to thee in story,
That fair Syrian shepherdess,
Who after years of barrenness,
The highly favored Joseph bore   65
To him that served for her before,
And at her next birth much like thee,
Through pangs fled to felicity,
Far within the bosom bright
Of blazing majesty and light,   70
There with thee, new welcome saint,
Like fortunes may her soul acquaint,
With thee there clad in radiant sheen,
No marchioness, but now a queen.

Song

On May Morning

(1630)

This poem appears in the 1645 *Poems* and again in the 1673 *Poems*. Because it is not in the *Manuscript* and almost wholly for that reason, it has been traditionally assigned to 1630. It may have been written earlier or later than that date. The reader should note its form as an 'apocopated sonnet' with the octet of two quatrains each made up of two pairs of couplets. The first quatrain is in pentameters, and the second quatrain is in the octosyllabic couplets of *L'Allegro–Il Penseroso*. The additional couplet, returning to pentameter, may be thought of as the first two lines of the sestet. The form is never used again by Milton.

Now the bright morning star, day's harbinger,
Comes dancing from the east, and leads with her
The flowery May, who from her green lap throws
The yellow cowslip, and the pale primrose.
  Hail bounteous May that dost inspire   5
  Mirth and youth and warm desire,
  Woods and groves are of thy dressing,
  Hill and dale doth boast thy blessing.
Thus we salute thee with our early song,
And welcome thee, and wish thee long.   10

Winch. 59. **Came**: Cam River, from which Cambridge took its name.
63. Rachel. Cf. *Genesis* 29:9, and 35:18.

On Shakespeare

1630(−1632)

This poem was first printed in the second Shakespeare folio in 1632. It also appeared in the 1640 edition of Shakespeare's *Poems*; in Milton's *Poems*, 1645; in the third Shakespeare folio, 1663–64; and in Milton's *Poems*, 1673. Milton himself dated it 1630, and most editors have accepted this date. Masson conjectured that it had appeared on the flyleaf of Milton's own copy of the first Shakespeare folio. The poem may have been written any time between 1630 and 1632, Milton's date, 1630, being his approximation of the date of the second Shakespeare folio.

It is a sixteen-line epigram in heroic couplets.

In it Milton elaborates an idea expressed by Ben Jonson in his lines on Shakespeare in the first folio (1623): 'Thou art a monument without a tomb.' William Browne, in his elegy on the death of the Countess of Pembroke (1629), anticipated Milton's conceit that Shakespeare by turning his readers or admirers to stone thus creates a monument for himself.

REFERENCE

 Smith, R. M., 'The Variant Issues of Shakespeare's Second Folio and Milton's first Published English Poem,' *Lehigh University Publications*, vol. II (1928), no. 3.

> What needs my Shakespeare for his honored bones,
> The labor of an age in piled stones,
> Or that his hallowed relics should be hid
> Under a star-ypointing pyramid?
> Dear son of memory, great heir of fame,   5
> What needest thou such weak witness of thy name?
> Thou in our wonder and astonishment
> Hast built thyself a livelong monument.
> For whilst to the shame of slow-endeavoring art,
> Thy easy numbers flow, and that each heart   10
> Hath from the leaves of thy unvalued book,
> Those Delphic lines with deep impression took,
> Then thou our fancy of itself bereaving,
> Dost make us marble with too much conceiving;
> And so sepulchered in such pomp dost lie,   15
> That kings for such a tomb would wish to die.

 10. **heart**: so both 1645 and 1673; but the second Shakespeare folio, 1632, reads 'part,' and some recent editors and commentators have preferred this reading. But the Shakespeare *Poems*, 1640, and Milton's two printings point to 'heart' as his choice.

 11. **unvalued**: not to be valued, beyond value, invaluable.

On the University Carrier

(1631)

Who sickened in the time of his Vacancy, being
forbid to go to London, by reason of the Plague.

The second of these two poems, so far as we know, was, as Professor Parker has recently pointed out, first printed anonymously in Archie Armstrong's *Banquet of Jests* in 1640. Milton printed both poems in the 1645 *Poems* and again in 1673. They were both printed anonymously and not by Milton in *Wit Restored*, 1658. Metrically, the two poems are epigrams in the same heroic couplets as the lines *On Shakespeare*.

They were written in connection with the death of Thomas Hobson on January 1, 1631. Hobson was a very successful business man in Cambridge, his business being to drive his horses and conveyances once each week from Cambridge to London and back again carrying letters, parcels, and passengers. He also rented out horses to the townspeople and students of Cambridge. He was doubtless a 'character' to every Cambridge student for sixty years or more, as he lived from 1544 to 1630, or for eighty-six years, and began his carrier business early. No doubt Milton had made the trip with Hobson from Cambridge to London many times. He was a very well-known figure in certain quarters in London.

Many verses besides Milton's were written in commemoration of his death, most of them comic or at least witty. The reader should note that these two poems appeared in at least two jestbooks of the century. Both poems are a succession of quips, puns, and 'metaphysical' conceits. They are, to quote Professor Parker, 'proof incontrovertible that, at least in 1631, [Milton] was capable of humour without moroseness or acrimony.'

REFERENCES

Masson, David, *The Poetical Works of John Milton*, I:126–28.
Parker, W. R., 'Milton's Hobson Poems,' *Modern Language Review*, vol. XXXI (1936), pp. 395–402.

Here lies old Hobson, death hath broke his girt,
And here alas, hath laid him in the dirt,
Or else the ways being foul, twenty to one,
He's here stuck in a slough, and overthrown.
'Twas such a shifter, that if truth were known,　　　　5
Death was half glad when he had got him down;
For he had any time this ten years full,
Dodged with him, betwixt Cambridge and The Bull.
And surely, death could never have prevailed,
Had not his weekly course of carriage failed;　　　　10
But lately finding him so long at home,
And thinking now his journey's end was come,

And that he had taken up his latest inn,
In the kind office of a chamberlain
Showed him his room where he must lodge that night,   15
Pulled off his boots, and took away the light:
If any ask for him, it shall be said,
'Hobson has supped, and's newly gone to bed.'

Another on the Same

Here lieth one who did most truly prove,
That he could never die while he could move,
So hung his destiny never to rot
While he might still jog on and keep his trot,
Made of sphere-metal, never to decay   5
Until his revolution was at stay.
Time numbers motion, yet (without a crime
'Gainst old truth) motion numbered out his time:
And like an engine moved with wheel and weight,
His principles being ceased, he ended straight,   10
Rest that gives all men life, gave him his death,
And too much breathing put him out of breath;
Nor were it contradiction to affirm
Too long vacation hastened on his term.
Merely to drive the time away he sickened,   15
Fainted, and died, nor would with ale be quickened,
'Nay,' quoth he, on his swooning bed outstretched,
'If I may not carry, sure I'll ne'er be fetched,
But vow though the cross doctors all stood hearers,
For one carrier put down to make six bearers.'   20
Ease was his chief disease, and to judge right,
He died for heaviness that his cart went light,
His leisure told him that his time was come,
And lack of load, made his life burdensome,
That even to his last breath (there be that say't)   25
As he were pressed to death, he cried 'more weight;'
But had his doings lasted as they were,
He had been an immortal carrier.
Obedient to the moon he spent his date
In course reciprocal, and had his fate   30
Linked to the mutual flowing of the seas,
Yet (strange to think) his wain was his increase:
His letters are delivered all and gone,
Only remains this superscription.

L'Allegro and Il Penseroso
1630–1632

THESE poems, almost always found together since their first printed appearance, are
contained in both the *Poems* of 1645 and of 1673, but are not in the *Manuscript*.

The date of their composition has come in for much discussion recently. Both
Mr. Tillyard and Professor Parker are convincing in their claims that these poems were
written during the summer of one of Milton's last years at Cambridge. They may have
been written during any one of the summers from 1630 to 1632. Formerly, they were
unanimously assigned to the Horton period.

The metrical patterns of the two poems are identical. After a ten-line introduction
made up of alternate trimeters (three feet) and pentameters (five feet), rhyming *abbacddeec*,
the remainder of each poem is in octosyllabic couplets.

They have no very definite sources. The Italians of the Renaissance had written many
poems in the same vein, and William Browne (1591–1643) in his *Britannia's Pastorals*
(1616) had almost risen to the heights Milton later achieved. Milton knew the work of
the Italian pastoralists, as well as he knew Browne's work, a copy of which he owned
and which has survived.

Probably no other poetry he ever wrote has pleased as many generations of English
readers as have these two poems. They are not the greatest poems he ever wrote; but
no other can lay claim to as universal an appeal to readers as can these two. They are
pastoral lyrics, more successfully lyric and more successfully domiciled and naturalized
to the English country scene than any other poems in the language. The glimpses of
English country life found in them are a constant delight. There is a fresh, crisp, authentic, and yet charming tone to the poems that no other English poet except Housman
has succeeded in catching; and unlike Housman, with his basic note of infinite, nostalgic
sadness over the fleetingness of youth and life, Milton achieves his effects in these poems
entirely without reference to anything outside the poems themselves and the moods they
evoke.

Much has been written about what the two poems represent. Some writers have
stated that *L'Allegro* is a day poem and *Il Penseroso* is a night poem; others have said that
the first represents the gay and active man, and the second the contemplative, thoughtful
man. Still others insist that the two poems represent two different ways of life between
which Milton felt he must choose, and that, because *Il Penseroso* is the latter of the two,
its mood represents Milton's final choice of the kind of life he deliberately chose to live.
But all these attempts to make more of the poems than actually appears in them are of

little real value in so far as our appreciation and enjoyment of them are concerned.   Milton makes almost identical statements in both poems concerning the attractiveness of different moods, the first poem ending with the statement, 'Mirth, with thee I mean to live.'   The second poem ends on exactly the same note, 'And I with thee [Melancholy] will choose to live.'   It is better to take them as two completely disarming and charming attempts to portray different yet complementary moods that occur at different times in all of us.

REFERENCES

Hanford, J. H., *Handbook* (third edition, 1939), pp. 148–55.
Masson, David, *The Poetical Works of John Milton*, I:131–36.
Parker, W. R., 'Some Problems in the Chronology of Milton's Early Poems,' *Review of English Studies*, vol. XI (1935), pp. 276–83.
Verity, A. W., *Milton's Ode on the Morning of Christ's Nativity* ... pp. xxviii–xxxvii.

L'Allegro

Hence loathed melancholy
   Of Cerberus, and blackest midnight born,
In Stygian cave forlorn.
   'Mongst horrid shapes, and shrieks, and sights unholy,
Find out some uncouth cell,   5
   Where brooding darkness spreads his jealous wings,
And the night-raven sings;
   There, under ebon shades, and low-browed rocks,
As ragged as thy locks,
   In dark Cimmerian desert ever dwell.   10
But come thou goddess fair and free,
In heaven yclept Euphrosyne,
And by men, heart-easing mirth,
Whom lovely Venus at a birth
With two sister graces more   15
To ivy-crowned Bacchus bore;
Or whether (as some sager sing)
The frolic wind that breathes the spring.
Zephyr with Aurora playing,
As he met her once a-Maying,   20
There on beds of violets blue,
And fresh-blown roses washed in dew,

2. **Cerberus:** the monstrous fifty- or three-headed dog guarding the entrance to Hades.
3. **Stygian cave:** underworld cave.
5. **uncouth:** strange; here, gloomy.
6. **brooding:** overshadowing.
10. **Cimmerian desert:** the mythical Cimmerii, mentioned by Homer, lived somewhere on the farthest ocean, in a land of constant mists and darkness.   The 'Cimmerian desert' means 'dark waste.'
12. **yclept:** called.   **Euphrosyne:** mirth or joy, one of the three graces.

Filled her with thee a daughter fair,
So buxom, blithe, and debonair.
Haste thee nymph, and bring with thee   25
Jest and youthful jollity,
Quips and cranks, and wanton wiles,
Nods, and becks, and wreathed smiles,
Such as hang on Hebe's cheek,
And love to live in dimple sleek;   30
Sport that wrinkled care derides,
And laughter holding both his sides.
Come, and trip it as you go
On the light fantastic toe,
And in thy right hand lead with thee,   35
The mountain nymph, sweet liberty;
And if I give thee honor due,
Mirth, admit me of thy crew
To live with her, and live with thee,
In unreproved pleasures free;   40
To hear the lark begin his flight,
And singing startle the dull night,
From his watch-tower in the skies,
Till the dappled dawn doth rise;
Then to come in spite of sorrow,   45
And at my window bid good-morrow,
Through the sweet-briar, or the vine,
Or the twisted eglantine.
While the cock with lively din,
Scatters the rear of darkness thin,   50
And to the stack, or the barn-door,
Stoutly struts his dames before,
Oft listening how the hounds and horn
Cheerly rouse the slumbering morn,
From the side of some hoar hill,   55
Through the high wood echoing shrill.
Sometime walking not unseen
By hedgerow elms, on hillocks green,
Right against the eastern gate,
Where the great sun begins his state,   60
Robed in flames, and amber light,
The clouds in thousand liveries dight,
While the plowman near at hand,
Whistles o'er the furrowed land,
And the milkmaid singeth blithe,   65
And the mower whets his scythe,

24. **buxom, blithe:** yielding and gay.   **debonair:** handsome and gentle.
27. **quips and cranks:** smart sayings and odd turns of speech.   **wanton wiles:** loose devices.
28. **becks:** bows.
29. **Hebe:** goddess of youth and cup-bearer to the gods.
55. **hoar hill:** white or gray with hoar frost.
61. **amber light:** yellow light.   62. **dight:** dressed.

And every shepherd tells his tale
Under the hawthorn in the dale.
Straight mine eye hath caught new pleasures
Whilst the landscape round it measures,   70
Russet lawns, and fallows gray,
Where the nibbling flocks do stray,
Mountains on whose barren breast
The laboring clouds do often rest:
Meadows trim with daisies pied,   75
Shallow brooks, and rivers wide.
Towers, and battlements it sees
Bosomed high in tufted trees,
Where perhaps some beauty lies,
The cynosure of neighboring eyes.   80
Hard by, a cottage chimney smokes,
From betwixt two aged oaks,
Where Corydon and Thyrsis met,
Are at their savory dinner set
Of herbs, and other country messes,   85
Which the neat-handed Phillis dresses;
And then in haste her bower she leaves,
With Thestylis to bind the sheaves;
Or if the earlier season lead
To the tanned haycock in the mead,   90
Sometimes with secure delight
The upland hamlets will invite,
When the merry bells ring round,
And jocund rebecs sound
To many a youth, and many a maid,   95
Dancing in the checkered shade;
And young and old come forth to play
On a sunshine holiday,
Till the livelong daylight fail,
Then to the spicy nut-brown ale,   100
With stories told of many a feat,
How Faery Mab the junkets eat,
She was pinched, and pulled she said,
And by the friar's lantern led
Tells how the drudging goblin sweat,   105
To earn his cream-bowl duly set,
When in one night, ere glimpse of morn,
His shadowy flail hath threshed the corn,
That ten day-laborers could not end,
Then lies him down the lubber fiend.   110
And stretched out all the chimney's length,
Basks at the fire his hairy strength;

71. **fallows:** fields plowed, but not planted for a season.
80. **cynosure:** the object of attention of all eyes.
83. **Corydon and Thyrsis:** conventional names in pastoral poetry.
94. **jocund rebecs:** merry fiddles.   104. 1645 edition reads: 'And he by friar's lantern led.'

And crop-full out of doors he flings,
Ere the first cock his matin rings.
Thus done the tales, to bed they creep,   115
By whispering winds soon lulled asleep.
Towered cities please us then,
And the busy hum of men,
Where throngs of knights and barons bold,
In weeds of peace high triumphs hold,   120
With store of ladies, whose bright eyes
Rain influence, and judge the prize,
Of wit, or arms, while both contend
To win her grace, whom all commend,
There let Hymen oft appear   125
In saffron robe, with taper clear,
And pomp, and feast, and revelry,
With mask, and antique pageantry,
Such sights as youthful poets dream
On summer eves by haunted stream.   130
Then to the well-trod stage anon,
If Jonson's learned sock be on,
Or sweetest Shakespeare fancy's child,
Warble his native wood-notes wild,
And ever against eating cares,   135
Lap me in soft Lydian airs,
Married to immortal verse
Such as the meeting soul may pierce
In notes, with many a winding bout
Of linked sweetness long drawn out,   140
With wanton heed, and giddy cunning,
The melting voice through mazes running;
Untwisting all the chains that tie
The hidden soul of harmony.
That Orpheus' self may heave his head   145
From golden slumber on a bed
Of heaped Elysian flowers, and hear
Such strains as would have won the ear
Of Pluto, to have quite set free
His half-regained Eurydice.   150
These delights, if thou canst give,
Mirth, with thee I mean to live.

120. **weeds:** clothes.
125. **Hymen:** god of marriage.
136. **Lydian airs:** tender, effeminate, voluptuous music.
145. **Orpheus:** most skilled of ancient singers.

Il Penseroso

Hence vain deluding joys,
   The brood of folly without father bred,
How little you bested,
   Or fill the fixed mind with all your toys;
Dwell in some idle brain,   5
   And fancies fond with gaudy shapes possess,
As thick and numberless
   As the gay motes that people the sunbeams,
Or likest hovering dreams
   The fickle pensioners of Morpheus' train.   10
But hail thou goddess, sage and holy,
Hail divinest melancholy,
Whose saintly visage is too bright
To hit the sense of human sight;
And therefore to our weaker view,   15
O'erlaid with black staid wisdom's hue.
Black, but such as in esteem,
Prince Memnon's sister might beseem,
Or that starred Ethiop queen that strove
To set her beauty's praise above   20
The sea-nymphs, and their powers offended,
Yet thou art higher far descended,
Thee bright-haired Vesta long of yore,
To solitary Saturn bore;
His daughter she (in Saturn's reign,   25
Such mixture was not held a stain)
Oft in glimmering bowers, and glades
He met her, and in secret shades
Of woody Ida's inmost grove,
Whilst yet there was no fear of Jove.   30
Come pensive nun, devout and pure,
Sober, steadfast, and demure,
All in a robe of darkest grain,
Flowing with majestic train,
And sable stole of cypress lawn,   35
Over thy decent shoulders drawn.
Come, but keep thy wonted state,
With even step, and musing gait,
And looks commercing with the skies,
Thy rapt soul sitting in thine eyes: 40
There held in holy passion still,
Forget thyself to marble, till
With a sad leaden downward cast,
Thou fix them on the earth as fast.

10. **Morpheus:** god of sleep.
19. **Ethiop queen:** Cassiopea.
35. **stole:** gown or robe.
18. **Prince Memnon's sister:** cf. Homer, *Odyssey* XI: 552.
23. **Vesta:** the Roman goddess of the hearth.

And join with thee calm peace, and quiet,   45
Spare fast, that oft with gods doth diet,
And hears the muses in a ring,
Aye round about Jove's altar sing.
And add to these retired leisure;
That in trim gardens takes his pleasure;   50
But first, and chiefest, with thee bring,
Him that yon soars on golden wing,
Guiding the fiery-wheeled throne,
The cherub contemplation,
And the mute silence hist along,   55
'Less Philomel will deign a song,
In her sweetest, saddest plight,
Smoothing the rugged brow of night,
While Cynthia checks her dragon yoke,
Gently o'er the accustomed oak;   60
Sweet bird that shunnest the noise of folly,
Most musical, most melancholy!
Thee chantress oft the woods among,
I woo to hear thy even-song;
And missing thee, I walk unseen   65
On the dry smooth-shaven green,
To behold the wandering moon,
Riding near her highest noon,
Like one that had been led astray
Through the heaven's wide pathless way;   70
And oft, as if her head she bowed,
Stooping through a fleecy cloud.
Oft on a plat of rising ground,
I hear the far-off curfew sound,
Over some wide-watered shore,   75
Swinging slow with sullen roar;
Or if the air will not permit,
Some still removed place will fit,
Where glowing embers through the room
Teach light to counterfeit a gloom,   80
Far from all resort of mirth.
Save the cricket on the hearth,
Or the bellman's drowsy charm,
To bless the doors from nightly harm:
Or let my lamp at midnight hour,   85
Be seen in some high lonely tower,
Where I may oft outwatch the bear,
With thrice great Hermes, or unsphere.
The spirit of Plato to unfold
What worlds, or what vast regions hold   90
The immortal mind that hath forsook
Her mansion in this fleshly nook:

56. **Philomel:** the nightingale.   59. **Cynthia:** the moon.   60. **accustomed oak:** Cf. *Ep. Dam.* 15.
87. **outwatch the bear:** outwatch the stars, the bear being the constellation.
88. **thrice great Hermes:** Hermes Trismegistus.

And of those demons that are found
In fire, air, flood, or underground,
Whose power hath a true consent   95
With planet, or with element.
Sometime let gorgeous tragedy
In sceptered pall come sweeping by,
Presenting Thebes, or Pelops' line,
Or the tale of Troy divine.   100
Or what (though rare) of later age,
Ennobled hath the buskined stage.
But, O sad virgin, that thy power
Might raise Musaeus from his bower,
Or bid the soul of Orpheus sing   105
Such notes as warbled to the string,
Drew iron tears down Pluto's cheek,
And made hell grant what love did seek.
Or call up him that left half told
The story of Cambuscan bold,   110
Of Camball, and of Algarsife,
And who had Canace to wife,
That owned the virtuous ring and glass,
And of the wondrous horse of brass,
On which the Tartar king did ride;   115
And if aught else, great bards beside,
In sage and solemn tunes have sung,
Of tourneys and of trophies hung;
Of forests, and enchantments drear,
Where more is meant than meets the ear,   120
Thus night oft see me in thy pale career,
Till civil-suited morn appear,
Not tricked and frounced as she was wont,
With the Attic boy to hunt,
But kerchieft in a comely cloud,   125
While rocking winds are piping loud,
Or ushered with a shower still,
When the gust hath blown his fill,
Ending on the rustling leaves,
With minute drops from off the eaves.   130
And when the sun begins to fling
His flaring beams, me goddess bring
To arched walks of twilight groves,
And shadows brown that Sylvan loves
Of pine, or monumental oak,   135
Where the rude axe with heaved stroke,
Was never heard the nymphs to daunt,
Or fright them from their hallowed haunt.
There in close covert by some brook,
Where no profaner eye may look,   140

109 ff. **him that left half told**: Chaucer.

134. **brown**: dark, dun, black. Cf. *Lycidas* 2; *PL* IX: 1088; *PR* II: 293; III: 326.   **Sylvan**: god of woods and fields. Cf. *Comus* 268; *PL* IV: 707; *PR* II: 191. Milton usually spelled it *Silvan*.

Hide me from day's garish eye,
While the bee with honeyed thigh,
That at her flowery work doth sing,
And the waters murmuring
With such consort as they keep,   145
Entice the dewy-feathered sleep;
And let some strange mysterious dream,
Wave at his wings in airy stream,
Of lively portraiture displayed,
Softly on my eyelids laid.   150
And as I wake, sweet music breathe
Above, about, or underneath,
Sent by some spirit to mortals good,
Or the unseen genius of the wood.
But let my due feet never fail,   155
To walk the studious cloisters pale,
And love the high embowed roof,
With antique pillars massy proof,
And storied windows richly dight,
Casting a dim religious light.   160
There let the pealing organ blow,
To the full voiced choir below,
In service high, and anthems clear,
As may with sweetness, through mine ear,
Dissolve me into ecstasies,   165
And bring all heaven before mine eyes.
And may at last my weary age
Find out the peaceful hermitage,
The hairy gown and mossy cell,
Where I may sit and rightly spell   170
Of every star that heaven doth show,
And every herb that sips the dew;
Till old experience do attain
To something like prophetic strain.
These pleasures melancholy give,   175
And I with thee will choose to live.

Poems Written at Horton
1632–1638

Arcades and Comus

IN 1632 Milton left his rooms at Cambridge and joined his family, which, probably as early as 1630, had moved outside of London to the little hamlet of Horton, where they remained until 1637 or 1638. During this period, he wrote only three poems that we can be sure of. Perhaps even before he left Cambridge, Milton had begun to write verses for that short-lived semi-dramatic form, the English mask. Sometime about 1632, perhaps earlier, he wrote the fragment known as the *Arcades* (The Arcadians or dwellers in Arcadia). According to the statement he prefixed when he printed it, this was a fragment, 'part of an entertainment presented to the Countess Dowager of Derby at Harefield, by some noble persons of her family, who appear on the scene in pastoral habit, moving toward the seat of state with this song.' The fragment consists of three songs and a recitative in pentameter (five feet) couplets. It is wholly in the tradition of the Jonsonian mask tradition, and is written in Milton's best Elizabethan vein. No specific source for it can be determined. The nature of the entertainment can be guessed at from the surviving fragments. The short poem entitled *At a Solemn Music*, written at about the same time, is similar in tone and character and may have been spoken or sung at the same entertainment, together with other verses that have disappeared.

The *Arcades* is chiefly important because it proves Milton's contacts with the Egerton family in the early sixteen-thirties, and because it was followed up by his production of the mask which since 1738 — that is, not until more than a century after its composition — has been known as *Comus*.

The association with the Egerton family, perhaps begun while Milton was at Cambridge, continued for several years. In 1637, without its author's name, but with his protest at its publication,[1] appeared a thin book entitled 'A Masque Presented at Ludlow Castle, 1634: on Michaelmass night, before the Right Honorable, John Earl of Bridgewater, Viscount Brackley, and one of his Majesty's most honorable Privy Council.' This work, probably the third of Milton's to appear in print,[2] was published by the musician, Henry Lawes,[3] who had been in charge of various entertainments engaged in by the Egerton family.

The study of the metrics of *Comus* is an interesting and valuable investigation in itself.

---

[1] On the title-page is the motto 'Eheu quid volui misero mihi! floribus austrum Perditus —' (Alas! what have I done, miserable me, for my own loss, in allowing the south wind to blow upon my flowers —)

[2] The first was probably the Latin poem *Naturam non Pati Senium* in 1628(?), and the second was certainly the lines *On Shakespeare* (1632).

[3] Cf. *Sonnet XIII*. Lawes was, at this time, musical tutor to the Egertons.

It is only possible here to point out some of the more striking metrical characteristics of the piece. All the speeches or recitatives except one are in iambic pentameter (five feet) blank verse, Milton's first sustained effort in this metrical form. Comus's speech or recitation (ll. 93–144) is in octosyllabic or irregular couplets, the octosyllabic being much like those in *L'Allegro–Il Penseroso*. The five songs are metrically irregular, but use many octosyllabic couplets, and are otherwise irregularly rhymed.[1]

The sources of *Comus* are probably very numerous, although most of those pointed out by various writers rest on parallels. The principal source was the Elizabethan and Italian mask tradition. The mythological story of animal-like monsters who were formerly human beings comes ultimately from the tenth book of Homer's *Odyssey*. As allegory, the story must have been known to Milton in the *Allegoriae* of Heraclides Ponticus, a copy of which he owned, and in Spenser's *Faerie Queene*, Book II, canto XII. William Browne's *Inner Temple Mask* (1915) employed an anti-mask, or parade and dance, of men transformed to bestial monsters. Jonson's *Pleasure Reconciled to Virtue* (1618) uses Comus as a glutton. The *Comus* of Hendrick van der Putten (1608) offers a number of parallels with Milton's work. George Peele's *Old Wives Tale* (1595) may have supplied the plot of the two brothers in search of a lost sister. John Fletcher's *Faithful Shepherdess* almost certainly influenced Milton in writing *Comus*. But, though he took much from the Renaissance and the Elizabethans, Milton went back to the ancient classics for many of his dramatic details.

A number of writers have recently pointed out that the style and tone of *Comus* are largely Elizabethan and non-Miltonic.[2] Mr. Hanford rightly insists that the paramount influence on *Comus* was Spenser.

As a mask, or as a spectacular performance involving music and dancing performed by highborn amateurs, *Comus* lies very largely in the Ben Jonson tradition of such works. Jonson, the poet, and Inigo Jones, architect and stage manager for James I, had collaborated in the production of many court masks, and they quarreled. Jonson insisted on the value of the verse spoken and sung in the masks; but Jones, who had the last word, naturally wanted to play up the pageantry and settings. He wanted the verse to be completely subservient to the spectacle. Jonson openly rebelled against this idea; but he could do little about it, as it was Jones who actually produced the masks, not Jonson. Milton in *Comus* shows himself entirely in sympathy with Jonson, as its poetry is the finest ever written for any mask in English. Nevertheless, *Comus* was written primarily for actual performance, and not as poetry to be read. Except for an occasional production by amateurs, it has seldom been performed on the professional stage since the eighteenth century, and it is today thought of almost entirely as poetry. It is therefore salutary to go back to its origins and realize that so far as Milton was concerned, he was writing not for publication, but for a performance that took place in a definite castle early in the fall of 1634.

Comus offers difficulties to the present-day reader. It is wholly in the Renaissance mask tradition which stemmed from Italy and the canons of which no longer operate on the English-speaking stage. The mask was a dramatic form that depended chiefly for its effects on music, dancing, and spectacle. In England, it was almost entirely a form of

---

[1] The music for the songs survives and has been printed. Cf. *The Mask of Comus*, edited by E. H. Visiak, the music edited by H. J. Foss (London: Nonesuch Press, 1937).

[2] E. M. W. Tillyard, *Milton* (London: Constable, 1930), p. 67; J. H. Hanford, 'The Youth of Milton,' *University of Michigan Publications, Language and Literature*, vol. I (1925), p. 142.

amusement for the court and wealthy nobles, in which handsome if untrained young amateurs, the sons and daughters of the nobles, took the various parts. In no work of today do we find anything that much resembles the kind of task that Milton was called on to produce for the Egerton children. Readers today are therefore more or less shut off from an understanding and hence appreciation of *Comus* as a mask. It is chiefly studied and read today as a poem, because it is in verse of a very high quality. But it should be read in the same way in which we read such plays of Shakespeare as *The Tempest* or *A Midsummer Night's Dream*; not that *Comus* is like or closely resembles either, but it is akin to them in its nature, which is dramatic.

The theme of *Comus* and Milton's treatment of it are both highly conventionalized. Most masks used the personification of a virtue as a central figure. Milton selected feminine chastity and personified that virtue in the Lady, a choice that many critics have thought was unfortunate. His choice was not unusual, and the same virtue had been similarly used before. Whatever faults as a mask *Comus* may have arise, not from Milton's choice of virtues, but from his inability to subordinate the ardor and fervor of his poetic spirit to the spectacle and slight action of his first and only complete mask.

Unable to judge his performance by mask standards, posterity has accepted the work as a long poem in quasi-dramatic form. The action of the piece is slight, as was customary in all masks. There is some dramatic tension arising from the predicament in which the Lady finds herself, through no fault of her own, after she comes under Comus's power. But the whole episode depends on accident, and the reader is never in doubt of the outcome. This lack of dramatic tension and constant announcement of how plots will be resolved is a characteristic of Milton's dramatic and narrative method found in all his work. He informs the reader that the outcome is predetermined, thus eliminating almost entirely the element of narrative or dramatic suspense as we know it. He does this deliberately over and over again in the later long poems. His theory of dramatic construction, as used but never stated by Milton, can only be understood by a study of his elimination of dramatic suspense in all his works, beginning with *Comus* and continuing through the rest. He was thus agreeing with classic, not Renaissance, canons of dramatic construction. In classic drama, the audience knew exactly what was going to happen, and was interested only in how the dramatist worked out the well-known theme.

The study of *Comus* will well repay the student of the period as well as the student of Milton. It offers an excellent approach to the whole study of the mask in Elizabethan, Jacobean, and Caroline England. It is not necessary to account for the title by which we know it, as Milton did not give it that title; but the name 'Comus' is of some interest. It occurs in the form 'komos' in Greek literature, meaning a comic and uncouth spirit, the spirit of revelry or comedy, the two words having the same root.

Lawes's music for the five songs has survived, but like the songs of Campion, none of these is sung today in its own right. Various eighteenth-century musicians, including Arne and Handel, also set these songs to music, and they belong among the most beautiful lyrics in the language.

REFERENCES

Axon, W. E. A., 'Milton's *Comus* and Fletcher's *Faithful Shepherdess*,' *Manchester Quarterly*, July, 1882. Reprinted separately.

Badt, Bertha, 'Milton's *Comus* and Peele's *Old Wives Tale*,' *Archiv für das Studium der Neueren Sprachen und Literaturen*, N.S., vol. CXXIII (1909), pp. 305–09.

Diekhoff, J. S., 'The Text of *Comus*,' *PMLA*, vol. LII (1937), pp. 705-27.

Egerton, Lady Alix, *Milton's Comus, Being the Bridgewater Manuscript*. London: Dent, 1910.

Hall, E. A., '*Comus, Old Wives Tale*, and Drury's *Alvredus*,' *Manly Anniversary Studies* (Chicago: University Press, 1923), pp. 104-44.

Hanford, J. H., 'The Youth of Milton,' *University of Michigan Publications, Language and Literature*, vol. I (1925), pp. 89-163.

Masson, David, *The Poetical Works of John Milton*, III:154-86.

Stevens, D. H., 'The Bridgewater Manuscript of *Comus*,' *Modern Philology*, vol. XXIV (1927), pp. 315-20.

Tillyard, E. M. W., *Milton* (London: Constable, 1930), pp. 66-75.

Todd, H. J., *Milton's Comus*. Canterbury: Bristow, 1798.

Verity, A. W., *Comus*. Cambridge: University Press, 1909. Frequently reprinted.

Visiak, E. H., *The Mask of Comus*. London: Nonesuch Press, 1937. Contains Lawes's music for the five songs edited by H. J. Foss.

Warton, Thomas, *Poems . . . By John Milton*, pp. 117-36.

Welsford, Enid, *The Court Mask in England*. Cambridge: University Press, 1927.

Arcades

(1631–1634)

The fragments of this poem occur in Milton's handwriting in the *Trinity College Manuscript*, and were printed in 1645, and again in 1673.

Part of an Entertainment presented to the Countess Dowager of Derby at Harefield, by some noble persons of her family, who appear on the scene in pastoral habit, moving toward the seat of state, with this song.

I. SONG

Look nymphs, and shepherds look,
What sudden blaze of majesty
Is that which we from hence descry
Too divine to be mistook:
  This this is she
To whom our vows and wishes bend,   5
Here our solemn search hath end.

Fame that her high worth to raise,
Seemed erst so lavish and profuse,
We may justly now accuse
Of detraction from her praise,   10
  Less than half we find expressed,
  Envy bid conceal the rest.

Mark what radiant state she spreads,
In circle round her shining throne,
Shooting her beams like silver threads,   15
This this is she alone,
  Sitting like a goddess bright,
  In the center of her light.

Arcades: The title means the 'Arcadians' or dwellers in Arcadia.

Might she the wise Latona be,   20
Or the towered Cybele,
Mother of a hundred gods;
Juno dares not give her odds;
   Who had thought this clime had held
   A deity so unparalleled?   25

As they come forward, THE GENIUS OF THE WOOD *appears, and turning
   toward them, speaks.*

    Gen. Stay gentle swains, for though in this disguise,
I see bright honor sparkle through your eyes,
Of famous Arcady ye are, and sprung
Of that renowned flood, so often sung,
Divine Alpheus, who by secret sluice,   30
Stole under seas to meet his Arethuse;
And ye the breathing roses of the wood,
Fair silver-buskined nymphs as great and good,
I know this quest of yours, and free intent
Was all in honor and devotion meant   35
To the great mistress of yon princely shrine,
Whom with low reverence I adore as mine,
And with all helpful service will comply
To further this night's glad solemnity;
And lead ye where ye may more near behold   40
What shallow-searching fame hath left untold;
Which I full oft amidst these shades alone
Have sat to wonder at, and gaze upon:
For know by lot from Jove I am the power
Of this fair wood, and live in oaken bower,   45
To nurse the saplings tall, and curl the grove
With ringlets quaint; and wanton windings wove.
And all my plants I save from nightly ill,
Of noisome winds, and blasting vapors chill.
And from the boughs brush off the evil dew,   50
And heal the harms of thwarting thunder blue,
Or what the cross dire-looking planet smites,
Or hurtful worm with cankered venom bites.
When evening gray doth rise, I fetch my round
Over the mount, and all this hallowed ground,   55

20. **Latona:** from Greek mythology; Leto, mother of Apollo and Artemis.

21. **towered Cybele:** Cybele or Rhea was the wife of Saturn and mother of Jupiter, Juno, Neptune, and other gods. 'Towered' refers to the 'turreted' portion of the crown on her head.

23. **Juno:** queen of heaven in the Roman pantheon.

26. **gentle:** genteel, well born.

28. **Arcady:** Arcadia, the ideal land of pastoral poetry.

30–31. **Alpheus . . . Arethuse:** legend says that a hunter, Alpheus, fell in love with Arethusa, one of Diana's virgin nymphs. To escape from him, she was changed into a fountain, and he was changed into a river, to unite with her in the fountain Arethusa.

33. **silver-buskined:** a buskin was a 'legging' wound about the leg from knee to ankle and was the sign of tragic drama, as the sock was the sign of comedy. Cf. *L'Allegro* 132; *Il Penseroso* 102.

46. **curl:** in its earlier meaning, 'to adorn.'   **grove:** grove, in 1673.   47. **quaint:** dainty, pretty.

And early ere the odorous breath of morn
Awakes the slumbering leaves, or tasseled horn
Shakes the high thicket, haste I all about,
Number my ranks, and visit every sprout
With puissant words, and murmurs made to bless,   60
But else in deep of night when drowsiness
Hath locked up mortal sense, then listen I
To the celestial sirens' harmony,
That sit upon the nine infolded spheres,
And sing to those that hold the vital shears,   65
And turn the adamantine spindle round,
On which the fate of gods and men is wound.
Such sweet compulsion doth in music lie,
To lull the daughters of necessity,
And keep unsteady nature to her law,   70
And the low world in measured motion draw
After the heavenly tune, which none can hear
Of human mold with gross unpurged ear;
And yet such music worthiest were to blaze
The peerless height of her immortal praise,   75
Whose luster leads us, and for her most fit,
If my inferior hand or voice could hit
Inimitable sounds, yet as we go,
Whate'er the skill of lesser gods can show,
I will assay, her worth to celebrate,   80
And so attend ye toward her glittering state;
Where ye may all that are of noble stem
Approach, and kiss her sacred vesture's hem.

II. SONG

O'er the smooth enameled green
Where no print of step hath been,   85
    Follow me as I sing,
    And touch the warbled string.
Under the shady roof
Of branching elm star-proof.
    Follow me,   90
I will bring you where she sits
Clad in splendor as befits
    Her deity.
Such a rural Queen
All Arcadia hath not seen.   95

III. SONG

Nymphs and Shepherds dance no more
By sandy Ladon's lilied banks,

62–71. For these lines, cf. Plato, *Republic* X:616–17.
64. **the nine infolded spheres**: the spheres of the Ptolemaic system.
74. **blaze**: proclaim. Cf. *Lycidas* 74.   77. Did Milton take the part of the Genius?
82. **stem**: stock, here meaning 'family.'   97. **sandy Ladon**: a river in Arcadia.

On old Lycaeus or Cyllene hoar,
   Trip no more in twilight ranks,
Though Erymanth your loss deplore,   100
   A better soil shall give ye thanks.
From the stony Maenalus,
Bring your flocks, and live with us,
Here ye shall have greater grace,
To serve the Lady of this place.   105
   Though Syrinx your Pan's mistress were,
   Yet Syrinx well might wait on her.
      Such a rural Queen
      All Arcadia hath not seen.

Comus

(1634)

A Masque Presented at Ludlow Castle, 1634, &c.

The composition of the poem is dated by the event for which it was written, which took place on September 29, 1634, at Ludlow Castle. The text of *Comus* is the most difficult of all Milton texts to deal with properly because there are so many primary texts that must be taken into account. There is a much-worked-over text in Milton's hand in the *Trinity College Manuscript*. It contains some lines never incorporated or printed in any edition of Milton's lifetime. There is also the manuscript still in the possession of the Egerton family, known as the *Bridgewater Manuscript*. Henry Lawes, the musician, printed the mask, without music, in 1637, probably but not certainly from the *Trinity College Manuscript*, or from a transcript of it. Most editors have assumed that the *Trinity College Manuscript* is the oldest form of the text extant, but no one knows with certainty. Some editors have assumed that the *Bridgewater Manuscript* is older than the 1637 printing; but again this is a conjecture, not a certainty. There are also at least two different manuscript copies of the five songs with their music. One of these is a manuscript Lawes himself wrote in autograph, 'signing his work on every page in unmistakable hand,' as H. J. Foss remarked. This manuscript is apparently the property of the Misses Church of Beaconsfield, England. Its history is clearly known for three hundred years. The other manuscript of the songs is a copy in the British Museum (*Add. MSS.* 11518) written in an unknown hand; inaccurate, not entirely legible, but complete. Both of these manuscripts must be taken into account because of the words of the songs they contain.

Milton printed the 1645 text, perhaps from the corrected *Trinity College Manuscript* copy, but perhaps from some other, as Lawes's 1637 text is much more like the *Manuscript* than is Milton's 1645 text. Milton again in 1673 printed the text with a few changes. The most notable of these occurs in line 167 and in the two lines following it. He deleted line 167 com-

98 ff. **Lycaeus, Cyllene, Erymanthus, Maenalus**: mountains in Arcadia.

pletely, and transposed the next two lines. Most editors have treated
these lines as if Milton or his printer had inadvertently omitted line 167,
and somehow transposed the other two lines. But there are corrections
called for in the errata of the 1673 volume that change the sense of line 169.
It is scarcely reasonable to suppose that changes of so minute a nature could
have been made and the lines allowed to stand in any way other than as
Milton wished.

THE PERSONS

The attendant Spirit afterwards in the habit of THYRSIS.
COMUS with his Crew.
The Lady.
1st Brother.
2d Brother.
SABRINA the Nymph.

The chief persons which presented, were
     The Lord Brackley.
     Mr. Thomas Egerton his Brother.
     The Lady Alice Egerton.

[This list of the Persons, &c., appeared in the Edition of 1645, but was omitted in that of 1673.]

The first scene discovers a wild wood.

The attendant Spirit descends or enters

Before the starry threshold of Jove's court
My mansion is, where those immortal shapes
Of bright aerial spirits live insphered
In regions mild of calm and serene air,
Above the smoke and stir of this dim spot,   5
Which men call earth, and with low-thoughted care

4. In the *Trinity College Manuscript*, Milton crossed out a passage that followed line 4, and which
was in turn followed by line 5. The passage contains several corrections, but finally read:

          Amidst the Hesperian gardens, on whose banks
          Bedewed with nectar, and celestial songs
          Eternal roses grow, and hyacinth
          And fruits of golden rind, on whose fair tree
          The scaly harnest dragon ever keeps
          His unenchanted eye, and round the verge
          And sacred limits of this blissful isle
          The jealous ocean that old river winds
          His far extended arms till with steep fall
          Half his waste flood the wide Atlantic fills
          And half the slow unfathomed Stygian pool
          But soft I was not sent to court your wonder
          With distant worlds, and strange removed clim[es]
          Yet thence I come and oft from thence behold

Confined, and pestered in this pinfold here,
Strive to keep up a frail, and feverish being
Unmindful of the crown that virtue gives
After this mortal change, to her true servants   10
Amongst the enthroned gods on sainted seats.
Yet some there be that by due steps aspire
To lay their just hands on that golden key
That opes the palace of eternity:
To such my errand is, and but for such,   15
I would not soil these pure ambrosial weeds,
With the rank vapors of this sin-worn mold.
    But to my task.   Neptune besides the sway
Of every salt flood, and each ebbing stream,
Took in by lot 'twixt high, and nether Jove,   20
Imperial rule of all the sea-girt isles
That like to rich, and various gems inlay
The unadorned bosom of the deep,
Which he to grace his tributary gods
By course commits to several government,   25
And gives them leave to wear their sapphire crowns,
And wield their little tridents, but this isle
The greatest, and the best of all the main
He quarters to his blue-haired deities,
And all this tract that fronts the falling sun   30
A noble peer of mickle trust, and power
Has in his charge, with tempered awe to guide
An old, and haughty nation proud in arms:
Where his fair offspring nursed in princely lore,
Are coming to attend their father's state,   35
And new-entrusted scepter, but their way
Lies through the perplexed paths of this drear wood,
The nodding horror of whose shady brows
Threats the forlorn and wandering passenger.
And here their tender age might suffer peril,   40
But that by quick command from sovereign Jove
I was despatched for their defense, and guard;
And listen why, for I will tell you now
What never yet was heard in tale or song
From old, or modern bard in hall, or bower.   45
    Bacchus that first from out the purple grape,
Crushed the sweet poison of misused wine
After the Tuscan mariners transformed
Coasting the Tyrrhene shore, as the winds listed,
On Circe's island fell (who knows not Circe   50

7. **pinfold:** a pound in which animals are shut up.   13. **golden key:** *Lysidas* 110-11; *PL* V:255, VII:207.
   29. **blue-haired deities:** Poseidon (Neptune) had blue hair. Cf. Homer, *Odyssey* IX:528-536; *Iliad* I:528 (of Zeus, in a different connection; but a 'blue-haired deity'; XX:144). For a more remote possibility, see Masson's note.
   31. **mickle:** much.   39. **passenger:** traveler, one who passes by.
   48. **Tuscan mariners:** Etruscan sailors.   49. **Tyrrhene shore:** the southwest coast of Italy.
   50. **Circe:** a famous sorceress described by Homer, *Odyssey* X.

The daughter of the sun?   Whose charmed cup
Whoever tasted, lost his upright shape,
And downward fell into a groveling swine)
This nymph that gazed upon his clustering locks,
With ivy berries wreathed, and his blithe youth,   55
Had by him, ere he parted thence, a son
Much like his father, but his mother more,
Whom therefore she brought up and Comus named,
Who ripe, and frolic of his full grown age,
Roving the Celtic, and Iberian fields,   60
At last betakes him to this ominous wood,
And in thick shelter of black shades imbowered,
Excels his mother at her mighty art,
Offering to every weary traveler,
His orient liquor in a crystal glass,   65
To quench the drought of Phoebus, which as they taste
(For most do taste through fond intemperate thirst)
Soon as the potion works, their human countenance,
The express resemblance of the gods, is changed
Into some brutish form of wolf, or bear,   70
Or ounce, or tiger, hog, or bearded goat,
All other parts remaining as they were,
And they, so perfect is their misery,
Not once perceive their foul disfigurement,
But boast themselves more comely than before   75
And all their friends, and native home forget
To roll with pleasure in a sensual sty.
Therefore when any favored of high Jove,
Chances to pass through this adventurous glade,
Swift as the sparkle of a glancing star,   80
I shoot from heaven to give him safe convoy,
As now I do: But first I must put off
These my sky robes spun out of Iris' woof,
And take the weeds and likeness of a swain,
That to the service of this house belongs,   85
Who with his soft pipe, and smooth dittied song
Well knows to still the wild winds when they roar,
And hush the waving woods, nor of less faith,
And in this office of his mountain watch,
Likeliest, and nearest to the present aid   90
Of this occasion.   But I hear the tread
Of hateful steps, I must be viewless now.

58. **Comus:** the name means 'reveling.'
60. **Celtic and Iberian fields:** France and Spain.
66. **the drought of Phoebus:** thirst caused by the sun.
71. **ounce:** lynx.
83. **Iris' woof:** the rainbow's texture.   84. **weeds:** clothes.   86. **song:** song, in 1673.
Following line 92, the 'rout of monsters' following Comus is the first anti-mask, or dance of the maskers.
The second occurs after line 657, and a third, after line 956.

COMUS *enters with a charming-rod in one hand, his glass in the other, with him a rout of monsters, headed like sundry sorts of wild beasts, but otherwise like men and women, their apparel glistering, they come in making a riotous and unruly noise, with torches in their hands.*

Comus. The star that bids the shepherd fold,
Now the top of heaven doth hold,
And the gilded car of day,   95
His glowing axle doth allay
In the steep Atlantic stream,
And the slope sun his upward beam
Shoots against the dusky pole,
Pacing toward the other goal   100
Of his chamber in the east.
Meanwhile welcome joy, and feast,
Midnight shout, and revelry,
Tipsy dance, and jollity.
Braid your locks with rosy twine   105
Dropping odors, dropping wine.
Rigor now is gone to bed,
And Advice with scrupulous head,
Strict Age, and sour Severity,
With their grave saws in slumber lie.   110
We that are of purer fire
Imitate the starry choir,
Who in their nightly watchful spheres,
Lead in swift round the months and years.
The sounds, and seas with all their finny drove   115
Now to the moon in wavering morris move,
And on the tawny sands and shelves,
Trip the pert fairies and the dapper elves;
By dimpled brook, and fountain brim,
The wood-nymphs decked with daisies trim,   120
Their merry wakes and pastimes keep:
What hath night to do with sleep?
Night hath better sweets to prove,
Venus now wakes, and wakens love.
Come let us our rites begin,   125
'Tis only daylight that makes sin
Which these dun shades will ne'er report,
Hail goddess of nocturnal sport
Dark veiled Cotytto, to whom the secret flame
Of midnight torches burns; mysterious dame   130
That ne'er art called, but when the dragon womb
Of Stygian darkness spits her thickest gloom,

---

93. **fold**: fold, in 1673.   116. **morris**: morris dance, 'Moors' dance.
117. **tawny**: in the *MS.*, 'yellow' is crossed out.
121. **wakes**: revels.   Originally, the feast of dedication of a church at which people kept awake all night.
129. **Cotytto**: a Thracian goddess whose celebration took place at night.   Cf. Juvenal, *Satire* II: 91-92.
132. **Stygian**: the river that flows about Hades, the Styx, hence gloomiest.

And makes one blot of all the air,
Stay thy cloudy ebon chair,
Wherein thou ridest with Hecat', and befriend   135
Us thy vowed priests, till utmost end
Of all thy dues be done, and none left out,
Ere the blabbing eastern scout,
The nice morn on the Indian steep
From her cabined loop-hole peep,   140
And to the tell-tale sun descry
Our concealed solemnity.
Come, knit hands, and beat the ground,
In a light fantastic round.

The Measure
Break off, break off, I feel the different pace,
Of some chaste footing near about this ground.   145
Run to your shrouds, within these brakes and trees,
Our number may affright: Some virgin sure
(For so I can distinguish by mine art)
Benighted in these woods.   Now to my charms,
And to my wily trains, I shall ere long   150
Be well stocked with as fair a herd as grazed
About my mother Circe.   Thus I hurl
My dazzling spells into the spongy air,
Of power to cheat the eye with blear illusion,
And give it false presentments, lest the place   155
And my quaint habits breed astonishment,
And put the damsel to suspicious flight,
Which must not be, for that's against my course;
I under fair pretense of friendly ends,
And well-placed words of glozing courtesy   160
Baited with reasons not unplausible
Wind me into the easy-hearted man,
And hug him into snares.   When once her eye
Hath met the virtue of this magic dust,
I shall appear some harmless villager   165
And hearken, if I may her business hear.
But here she comes, I fairly step aside

THE LADY *enters*
[*Lady.*] This way the noise was, if mine ear be true,
My best guide now, methought it was the sound   170
Of riot, and ill managed merriment,
Such as the jocund flute, or gamesome pipe

134. **ebon**: black, ebony.
139. **nice**: fastidious, too fastidious to enjoy the rites mentioned.   **Indian steep**: eastern hill.
147. **brakes**: thickets.   'Canebrake' is about the only well-known usage today of this word.
161. **glozing**: flattering.   165. **dust**: dust, in 1673.
167–68. 1645 edition and *MS.* read as follows:

> Whom thrift keeps up about his country gear,
> But here she comes, I fairly step aside
> And hearken, if I may her business hear.

Stirs up among the loose unlettered hinds,
When for their teeming flocks, and granges full
In wanton dance they praise the bounteous Pan,   175
And thank the gods amiss.   I should be loath
To meet the rudeness, and swilled insolence
Of such late wassailers; yet O where else
Shall I inform my unacquainted feet
In the blind mazes of this tangled wood?   180
My brothers when they saw me wearied out
With this long way, resolving here to lodge
Under the spreading favor of these pines,
Stepped as they said to the next thicket side
To bring me berries, or such cooling fruit   185
As the kind hospitable woods provide.
They left me then, when the gray-hooded even
Like a sad votarist in palmer's weed
Rose from the hindmost wheels of Phoebus' wain.
But where they are, and why they came not back,   190
Is now the labor of my thoughts, 'tis likeliest
They had engaged their wandering steps too far,
And envious darkness, ere they could return,
Had stole them from me, else O thievish night
Why shouldst thou, but for some felonious end,   195
In thy dark lantern thus close up the stars,
That nature hung in heaven, and filled their lamps
With everlasting oil, to give due light
To the misled and lonely traveler?
This is the place, as well as I may guess,   200
Whence even now the tumult of loud mirth
Was rife, and perfect in my listening ear,
Yet nought but single darkness do I find.
What might this be?   A thousand fantasies
Begin to throng into my memory   205
Of calling shapes, and beckoning shadows dire,
And airy tongues, that syllable men's names
On sands, and shores, and desert wildernesses.
These thoughts may startle well, but not astound
The virtuous mind, that ever walks attended   210
By a strong siding champion conscience.
O welcome pure-eyed faith, white-handed hope,
Thou hovering angel girt with golden wings,
And thou unblemished form of chastity,
I see ye visibly, and now believe   215
That he, the supreme good, to whom all things ill
Are but as slavish officers of vengeance,
Would send a glistering guardian if need were
To keep my life and honor unassailed.

---

174. **granges:** granaries.   178. **wassailers:** drinkers.
188. **sad votarist:** sober pilgrim in palmer's dress.
189. Just as the sun was setting.   **Phoebus:** the sun.   **wain:** wagon.

Was I deceived, or did a sable cloud   220
Turn forth her silver lining on the night?
I did not err, there does a sable cloud
Turn forth her silver lining on the night,
And casts a gleam over this tufted grove.
I cannot hallo to my brothers, but   225
Such noise as I can make to be heard farthest
I'll venture, for my new enlivened spirits
Prompt me; and they perhaps are not far off.

SONG

Sweet Echo, sweetest nymph that livest unseen
    Within thy airy shell   230
      By slow Meander's margent green,
And in the violet embroidered vale
    Where the love-lorn nightingale
Nightly to thee her sad song mourneth well.
Canst thou not tell me of a gentle pair   235
    That likest thy Narcissus are?
      O if thou have
    Hid them in some flowery cave,
      Tell me but where
    Sweet queen of parley, daughter of the sphere,   240
    So mayest thou be translated to the skies,
And give resounding grace to all heaven's harmonies.
    Comus. Can any mortal mixture of earth's mold
Breathe such divine enchanting ravishment?
Sure something holy lodges in that breast,   245
And with these raptures moves the vocal air
To testify his hidden residence;
How sweetly did they float upon the wings
Of silence, through the empty-vaulted night
At every fall smoothing the raven down   250
Of darkness till it smiled: I have oft heard
My mother Circe with the sirens three,
Amidst the flowery-kirtled naiades
Culling their potent herbs, and baleful drugs,
Who as they sung, would take the prisoned soul,   255
And lap it in Elysium, Scylla wept,
And chid her barking waves into attention,
And fell Charybdis murmured soft applause:
Yet they in pleasing slumber lulled the sense,
And in sweet madness robbed it of itself,   260
But such a sacred, and home-felt delight,
Such sober certainty of waking bliss
I never heard till now.   I'll speak to her
And she shall be my queen.   Hail foreign wonder
Whom certain these rough shades did never breed   265

231. **margent:** margin.   253. **naiades:** fresh-water nymphs.
256–58. **Scylla . . . Charybdis:** the names of two rocks between Sicily and Italy.

Unless the goddess that in rural shrine
Dwellest here with Pan, or Sylvan, by blest song
Forbidding every bleak unkindly fog
To touch the prosperous growth of this tall wood.
 Lady. Nay gentle shepherd ill is lost that praise   270
That is addressed to unattending ears,
Not any boast of skill, but extreme shift
How to regain my severed company
Compelled me to awake the courteous Echo
To give me answer from her mossy couch.   275
 Comus. What chance good lady hath bereft you thus?
 Lady. Dim darkness, and this leafy labyrinth.
 Comus. Could that divide you from near-ushering guides?
 Lady. They left me weary on a grassy turf.
 Comus. By falsehood, or discourtesy, or why?   280
 Lady. To seek in the valley some cool friendly spring.
 Comus. And left your fair side all unguarded lady?
 Lady. They were but twain, and purposed quick return.
 Comus. Perhaps forestalling night prevented them.
 Lady. How easy my misfortune is to hit!   285
 Comus. Imports their loss, beside the present need?
 Lady. No less than if I should my brothers lose.
 Comus. Were they of manly prime, or youthful bloom?
 Lady. As smooth as Hebe's their unrazored lips.
 Comus. Two such I saw, what time the labored ox   290
In his loose traces from the furrow came,
And the swinked hedger at his supper sat;
I saw them under a green mantling vine
That crawls along the side of yon small hill,
Plucking ripe clusters from the tender shoots,   295
Their port was more than human, as they stood;
I took it for a faëry vision
Of some gay creatures of the element
That in the colors of the rainbow live
And play in the plighted clouds. I was awe-struck,   300
And as I passed, I worshiped; if those you seek
It were a journey like the path to heaven,
To help you find them.
 Lady.   Gentle villager
What readiest way would bring me to that place?
 Comus. Due west it rises from this shrubby point.   305
 Lady. To find out that, good shepherd, I suppose,
In such a scant allowance of star-light,
Would overtask the best land-pilot's art,
Without the sure guess of well-practiced feet.
 Comus. I know each lane, and every alley green   310
Dingle, or bushy dell of this wild wood,
And every bosky bourn from side to side
My daily walks and ancient neighborhood,

292. **swinked hedger**: hard-worked dweller among the hedgerows, farmer. Cf. *Ep. Dam.* 54.
312. **bosky bourn**: bushy brook.

And if your stray attendance be yet lodged,
Or shroud within these limits, I shall know   315
Ere morrow wake, or the low roosted lark
From her thatched pallet rouse, if otherwise
I can conduct you lady to a low
But loyal cottage, where you may be safe
Till further quest.
    Lady.   Shepherd I take thy word,   320
And trust thy honest offered courtesy,
Which oft is sooner found in lowly sheds
With smoky rafters, than in tapestry halls
And courts of princes, where it first was named,
And yet is most pretended: In a place   325
Less warranted than this, or less secure
I cannot be, that I should fear to change it,
Eye me blest Providence, and square my trial
To my proportioned strength.
                         Shepherd lead on.

The Two Brothers

    Eld. Bro. Unmuffle ye faint stars, and thou fair moon   330
That wontest to love the traveler's benison,
Stoop thy pale visage through an amber cloud,
And disinherit chaos, that reigns here
In double night of darkness, and of shades;
Or if your influence be quite dammed up   335
With black usurping mists, some gentle taper
Though a rush candle from the wicker hole
Of some clay habitation visit us
With thy long leveled rule of streaming light,
And thou shalt be our star of Arcady,   340
Or Tyrian Cynosure.
    Sec. Bro.   Or if our eyes
Be barred that happiness, might we but hear
The folded flocks penned in their wattled cotes,
Or sound of pastoral reed with oaten stops,
Or whistle from the lodge, or village cock   345
Count the night watches to his feathery dames,
'Twould be some solace yet some little cheering
In this close dungeon of innumerous boughs.
But O that hapless virgin our lost sister
Where may she wander now, whither betake her   350
From the chill dew, amongst rude burs and thistles?
Perhaps some cold bank is her bolster now
Or 'gainst the rugged bark of some broad elm
Leans her unpillowed head fraught with sad fears,
What if in wild amazement, and affright,   355
Or while we speak within the direful grasp
Of savage hunger, or of savage heat?
    Eld. Bro. Peace brother, be not over-exquisite
To cast the fashion of uncertain evils;

331. **benison:** blessing.

For grant they be so, while they rest unknown,   360
What need a man forestall his date of grief,
And run to meet what he would most avoid?
Or if they be but false alarms of fear,
How bitter is such self-delusion?
I do not think my sister so to seek,   365
Or so unprincipled in virtue's book,
And the sweet peace that goodness bosoms ever,
As that the single want of light and noise
(Not being in danger, as I trust she is not)
Could stir the constant mood of her calm thoughts,   370
And put them into misbecoming plight.
Virtue could see to do what virtue would
By her own radiant light, though sun and moon
Were in the flat sea sunk.   And wisdom's self
Oft seeks to sweet retired solitude,   375
Where with her best nurse contemplation
She plumes her feathers, and lets grow her wings
That in the various bustle of resort
Were all too ruffled, and sometimes impaired.
He that has light within his own clear breast   380
May sit in the center, and enjoy bright day,
But he that hides a dark soul, and foul thoughts
Benighted walks under the midday sun;
Himself is his own dungeon.
   Sec. Bro.   'Tis most true
That musing meditation most affects   385
The pensive secrecy of desert cell,
Far from the cheerful haunt of men, and herds,
And sits as safe as in a senate house,
For who would rob a hermit of his weeds,
His few books, or his beads, or maple dish,   390
Or do his gray hairs any violence?
But beauty like the fair Hesperian tree
Laden with blooming gold, had need the guard
Of dragon watch with unenchanted eye,
To save her blossoms, and defend her fruit   395
From the rash hand of bold Incontinence.
You may as well spread out the unsunned heaps
Of miser's treasure by an outlaw's den,
And tell me it is safe, as bid me hope
Danger will wink on opportunity,   400
And let a single helpless maiden pass
Uninjured in this wild surrounding waste.
Of night, or loneliness it recks me not,
I fear the dread events that dog them both,
Lest some ill greeting touch attempt the person   405
Of our unowned sister.

389. **weeds**: clothes.
392. **Hesperian tree**: the tree bearing the golden apples of the Hesperides.
406. **unowned**: unaccompanied.

Eld. Bro.   I do not, brother,
Infer, as if I thought my sister's state
Secure without all doubt, or controversy:
Yet where an equal poise of hope and fear
Does arbitrate the event, my nature is   410
That I incline to hope, rather than fear,
And gladly banish squint suspicion.
My sister is not so defenseless left
As you imagine, she has a hidden strength
Which you remember not.
      Sec. Bro.   What hidden strength,   415
Unless the strength of heaven, if you mean that?
      Eld. Bro. I mean that too, but yet a hidden strength
Which if heaven gave it, may be termed her own:
'Tis chastity, my brother, chastity:
She that has that, is clad in complete steel,   420
And like a quivered nymph with arrows keen
May trace huge forests, and unharbored heaths,
Infamous hills, and sandy perilous wilds,
Where through the sacred rays of chastity,
No savage fierce, bandit, or mountaineer   425
Will dare to soil her virgin purity,
Yea there, where very desolation dwells
By grots, and caverns shagged with horrid shades,
She may pass on with unblenched majesty,
Be it not done in pride, or in presumption.   430
Some say no evil thing that walks by night
In fog, or fire, by lake, or moorish fen,
Blue meager hag, or stubborn unlaid ghost,
That breaks his magic chains at curfew time,
No goblin, or swart faëry of the mine,   435
Hath hurtful power o'er true virginity.
Do ye believe me yet, or shall I call
Antiquity from the old schools of Greece
To testify the arms of chastity?
Hence had the huntress Dian her dread bow   440
Fair silver-shafted queen forever chaste,
Wherewith she tamed the brinded lioness
And spotted mountain pard, but set at nought
The frivolous bolt of Cupid, gods and men
Feared her stern frown, and she was queen of the woods.   445
What was that snaky-headed Gorgon shield
That wise Minerva wore, unconquered virgin,
Wherewith she freezed her foes to congealed stone?
But rigid looks of chaste austerity,
And noble grace that dashed brute violence   450
With sudden adoration, and blank awe.
So dear to heaven is saintly chastity,
That when a soul is found sincerely so,

410. **arbitrate the event:** decide the issue.   429. **unblenched:** undaunted.

63862

A thousand liveried angels lackey her,
Driving far off each thing of sin and guilt,   455
And in clear dream, and solemn vision
Tell her of things that no gross ear can hear,
Till oft converse with heavenly habitants
Begin to cast a beam on the outward shape,
The unpolluted temple of the mind,   460
And turns it by degrees to the soul's essence,
Till all be made immortal: but when lust
By unchaste looks, loose gestures, and foul talk,
But most by lewd and lavish act of sin,
Lets in defilement to the inward parts,   465
The soul grows clotted by contagion,
Imbodies, and imbrutes, till she quite lose
The divine property of her first being.
Such are those thick and gloomy shadows damp
Oft seen in charnel vaults, and sepulchers   470
Lingering, and sitting by a new made grave,
As loath to leave the body that it loved,
And linked itself by carnal sensuality
To a degenerate and degraded state.
    Sec. Bro. How charming is divine philosophy!   475
Not harsh, and crabbed as dull fools suppose,
But musical as is Apollo's lute,
And a perpetual feast of nectared sweets,
Where no crude surfeit reigns.
    Eld. Bro.   List, list, I hear
Some far off hallo break the silent air.   480
    Sec. Bro. Methought so too; what should it be?
    Eld. Bro.   For certain
Either someone like us night-foundered here,
Or else some neighbor woodman, or at worst,
Some roving robber calling to his fellows.
    Sec. Bro. Heaven keep my sister, again, again, and near,   485
Best draw, and stand upon our guard.
    Eld. Bro.   I'll hallo,
If he be friendly he comes well, if not,
Defense is a good cause, and heaven be for us,

    The ATTENDANT SPIRIT *habited like a shepherd*
That hallo I should know, what are you? speak;
Come not too near, you fall on iron stakes else.   490
    Spir. What voice is that, my young lord? speak again.
    Sec. Bro. O brother, 'tis my father's shepherd sure.
    Eld. Bro. Thyrsis? Whose artful strains have oft delayed
The huddling brook to hear his madrigal,
And sweetened every musk rose of the dale,   495
How camest thou here good swain? hath any ram
Slipped from the fold, or young kid lost his dam,
Or straggling wether the pent flock forsook?
How couldst thou find this dark sequestered nook?

Spir. O my loved master's heir, and his next joy,   500
I came not here on such a trivial toy
As a strayed ewe, or to pursue the stealth
Of pilfering wolf, not all the fleecy wealth
That doth enrich these downs, is worth a thought
To this my errand, and the care it brought.   505
But O my virgin lady, where is she?
How chance she is not in your company?
   Eld. Bro. To tell thee sadly shepherd, without blame,
Or our neglect, we lost her as we came.
   Spir. Ay me unhappy then my fears are true.   510
   Eld. Bro. What fears good Thyrsis?   Prithee briefly show.
   Spir. I'll tell ye, 'tis not vain or fabulous,
(Though so esteemed by shallow ignorance)
What the sage poets taught by the heavenly muse,
Storied of old in high immortal verse   515
Of dire chimeras and enchanted isles,
And rifted rocks whose entrance leads to hell,
For such there be, but unbelief is blind.
   Within the navel of this hideous wood,
Immured in cypress shades a sorcerer dwells   520
Of Bacchus, and of Circe born, great Comus,
Deep skilled in all his mother's witcheries,
And here to every thirsty wanderer,
By sly enticement gives his baneful cup,
With many murmurs mixed, whose pleasing poison   525
The visage quite transforms of him that drinks,
And the inglorious likeness of a beast
Fixes instead, unmolding reason's mintage
Charactered in the face; this have I learned
Tending my flocks hard by in the hilly crofts,   530
That brow this bottom glade, whence night by night
He and his monstrous rout are heard to howl
Like stabled wolves, or tigers at their prey,
Doing abhorred rites to Hecate
In their obscured haunts of inmost bowers,   535
Yet have they many baits, and guileful spells
To inveigle and invite the unwary sense
Of them that pass unwitting by the way.
This evening late by then the chewing flocks
Had taken their supper on the savory herb   540
Of knot-grass dew-besprent, and were in fold,
I sat me down to watch upon a bank
With ivy canopied, and interwove
With flaunting honeysuckle, and began
Wrapt in a pleasing fit of melancholy   545
To meditate my rural minstrelsy,
Till fancy had her fill, but ere a close

546. 1673 edition reads: 'meditate upon,' which makes too many syllables in the line.   This is a famous crux.

547 **close:** a musical interval or rest.

The wonted roar was up amidst the woods,
And filled the air with barbarous dissonance
At which I ceased, and listened them a while,   550
Till an unusual stop of sudden silence
Gave respite to the drowsy frighted steeds
That draw the litter of close curtained sleep;
At last a soft and solemn breathing sound
Rose like a steam of rich distilled perfumes,   555
And stole upon the air, that even silence
Was took ere she was ware, and wished she might
Deny her nature, and be never more
Still to be so displaced.   I was all ear,
And took in strains that might create a soul   560
Under the ribs of death, but O ere long
Too well I did perceive it was the voice
Of my most honored lady, your dear sister.
Amazed I stood, harrowed with grief and fear,
And 'O poor hapless nightingale' thought I,   565
'How sweet thou singest, how near the deadly snare!'
Then down the lawns I ran with headlong haste
Through paths, and turnings often trod by day,
Till guided by mine ear I found the place
Where that damned wizard hid in sly disguise   570
(For so by certain signs I knew) had met
Already, ere my best speed could prevent,
The aidless innocent lady his wished prey,
Who gently asked if he had seen such two,
Supposing him some neighbor villager;   575
Longer I durst not stay, but soon I guessed
Ye were the two she meant, with that I sprung
Into swift flight, till I had found you here,
But further know I not.
   Sec. Bro.   O night and shades,
How are ye joined with hell in triple knot   580
Against the unarmed weakness of one virgin
Alone, and helpless! is this the confidence
You gave me brother?
   Eld. Bro.   Yes, and keep it still,
Lean on it safely, not a period
Shall be unsaid for me: against the threats   585
Of malice or of sorcery, or that power
Which erring men call chance, this I hold firm,
Virtue may be assailed, but never hurt,
Surprised by unjust force, but not enthralled,
Yea even that which mischief meant most harm,   590
Shall in the happy trial prove most glory.
But evil on itself shall back recoil,
And mix no more with goodness, when at last
Gathered like scum, and settled to itself

552. **drowsy frighted**: so 1637, 1645, 1673 editions.   But *MS.* reads 'flighted' and so most editors.
Cf. Verity's note.

It shall be in eternal restless change 595
Self-fed, and self-consumed, if this fail,
The pillared firmament is rottenness,
And earth's base built on stubble.   But come let's on.
Against the opposing will and arm of heaven
May never this just sword be lifted up, 600
But for that damned magician, let him be girt
With all the grisly legions that troop
Under the sooty flag of Acheron,
Harpies and Hydras, or all the monstrous forms
'Twixt Africa and Ind, I'll find him out, 605
And force him to return his purchase back,
Or drag him by the curls, to a foul death,
Cursed as his life.
    Spir.   Alas good venturous youth,
I love thy courage yet, and bold emprise,
But here thy sword can do thee little stead, 610
Far other arms, and other weapons must
Be those that quell the might of hellish charms,
He with his bare wand can unthread thy joints,
And crumble all thy sinews.
    Eld. Bro.   Why prithee shepherd
How durst thou then thyself approach so near 615
As to make this relation?
    Spir.   Care and utmost shifts
How to secure the lady from surprisal,
Brought to my mind a certain shepherd lad
Of small regard to see to, yet well skilled
In every virtuous plant and healing herb 620
That spreads her verdant leaf to the morning ray,
He loved me well, and oft would beg me sing,
Which when I did, he on the tender grass
Would sit, and hearken even to ecstasy,
And in requital ope his leathern scrip, 625
And show me simples of a thousand names
Telling their strange and vigorous faculties;
Amongst the rest a small unsightly root,
But of divine effect, he culled me out;
The leaf was darkish, and had prickles on it, 630
But in another country, as he said,
Bore a bright golden flower, but not in this soil:
Unknown, and like esteemed, and the dull swain
Treads on it daily with his clouted shoon,
And yet more medicinal is it than that moly 635
That Hermes once to wise Ulysses gave;
He called it haemony, and gave it me,
And bade me keep it as of sovereign use
'Gainst all enchantments, mildew blast, or damp
Or ghastly furies' apparition; 640

618 ff. **a certain shepherd lad . . . well skilled in . . . healing herb**: this reference is no doubt to Charles Diodati, who may have witnessed the performance.

I pursed it up, but little reckoning made,
Till now that this extremity compelled,
But now I find it true; for by this means
I knew the foul enchanter though disguised,
Entered the very lime-twigs of his spells,   645
And yet came off: if you have this about you
(As I will give you when we go) you may
Boldly assault the necromancer's hall;
Where if he be, with dauntless hardihood,
And brandished blade rush on him, break his glass,   650
And shed the luscious liquor on the ground,
But seize his wand, though he and his cursed crew
Fierce sign of battle make, and menace high,
Or like the sons of Vulcan vomit smoke,
Yet will they soon retire, if he but shrink.   655
    Eld. Bro. Thyrsis lead on apace, I'll follow thee,
And some good angel bear a shield before us.

*The scene changes to a stately palace, set out with all manner of deliciousness:
soft music, tables spread with all dainties.* COMUS *appears with his
rabble, and* THE LADY *set in an enchanted chair, to whom he offers his
glass, which she puts by, and goes about to rise.*

    Comus. Nay lady sit; if I but wave this wand,
Your nerves are all chained up in alabaster,
And you a statue, or as Daphne was   660
Root-bound, that fled Apollo,
    Lady.   Fool do not boast,
Thou canst not touch the freedom of my mind
With all thy charms, although this corporal rind
Thou hast immanacled, while heaven sees good.
    Comus. Why are you vexed lady? why do you frown?   665
Here dwell no frowns, nor anger, from these gates
Sorrow flies far: See here be all the pleasures
That fancy can beget on youthful thoughts,
When the fresh blood grows lively, and returns
Brisk as the April buds in primrose season.   670
And first behold this cordial julep here
That flames, and dances in his crystal bounds
With spirits of balm, and fragrant syrups mixed.
Not that nepenthes which the wife of Thone,
In Egypt gave to Jove-born Helena   675
Is of such power to stir up joy as this,
To life so friendly, or so cool to thirst.
Why should you be so cruel to yourself,
And to those dainty limbs which Nature lent
For gentle usage, and soft delicacy?   680
But you invert the covenants of her trust,
And harshly deal like an ill borrower
With that which you received on other terms,
Scorning the unexempt condition

Following line 657, the second anti-mask.   674. **nepenthes:** opiate.

By which all mortal frailty must subsist,   685
Refreshment after toil, ease after pain,
That have been tired all day without repast,
And timely rest have wanted, but fair virgin
This will restore all soon.
    Lady.   'Twill not false traitor,
'Twill not restore the truth and honesty   690
That thou hast banished from thy tongue with lies,
Was this the cottage, and the safe abode
Thou toldest me of?   What grim aspects are these,
These ugly-headed monsters?   Mercy guard me!
Hence with thy brewed enchantments, foul deceiver,   695
Hast thou betrayed my credulous innocence
With vizored falsehood, and base forgery,
And wouldst thou seek again to trap me here
With liquorish baits fit to ensnare a brute?
Were it a draught for Juno when she banquets,   700
I would not taste thy treasonous offer; none
But such as are good men can give good things,
And that which is not good, is not delicious
To a well-governed and wise appetite.
    Comus. O foolishness of men! that lend their ears   705
To those budge doctors of the Stoic fur,
And fetch their precepts from the Cynic tub,
Praising the lean and sallow abstinence.
Wherefore did nature pour her bounties forth,
With such a full and unwithdrawing hand,   710
Covering the earth with odors, fruits, and flocks,
Thronging the seas with spawn innumerable,
But all to please, and sate the curious taste?
And set to work millions of spinning worms,
That in their green shops weave the smooth-haired silk   715
To deck her sons, and that no corner might
Be vacant of her plenty, in her own loins
She hutched the all-worshiped ore, and precious gems
To store her children with; if all the world
Should in a pet of temperance feed on pulse,   720
Drink the clear stream, and nothing wear but frieze,
The all-giver would be unthanked, would be unpraised,
Not half his riches known, and yet despised,
And we should serve him as a grudging master,
As a penurious niggard of his wealth,   725
And live like nature's bastards, not her sons,
Who would be quite surcharged with her own weight,
And strangled with her waste fertility;
The earth cumbered, and the winged air darked with plumes,
The herds would over-multitude their lords,   730
The sea o'erfraught would swell, and the unsought diamonds

---

706. **budge doctors of the Stoic fur**: probably 'budge' means 'fur' and 'budge doctors' means 'furred philosophers.'   But *OED* states that the word here means 'stiff, formal.'   Cf. Milton's *Observations on the Articles of Peace*, Columbia VI:261:1.   720. **pulse**: peas, beans, etc.

Would so emblaze the forehead of the deep,
And so bestud with stars, that they below
Would grow inured to light, and come at last
To gaze upon the sun with shameless brows.   735
List lady be not coy, and be not cozened
With that same vaunted name virginity,
Beauty is nature's coin, must not be hoarded,
But must be current, and the good thereof
Consists in mutual and partaken bliss,   740
Unsavory in the enjoyment of itself
If you let slip time, like a neglected rose
It withers on the stalk with languished head.
Beauty is nature's brag, and must be shown
In courts, at feasts, and high solemnities   745
Where most may wonder at the workmanship;
It is for homely features to keep home,
They had their name thence; coarse complexions
And cheeks of sorry grain will serve to ply
The sampler, and to tease the housewife's wool.   750
What need a vermeil-tinctured lip for that
Love-darting eyes, or tresses like the morn?
There was another meaning in these gifts,
Think what, and be advised, you are but young yet.
   Lady. I had not thought to have unlocked my lips   755
In this unhallowed air, but that this juggler
Would think to charm my judgment, as mine eyes
Obtruding false rules pranked in reason's garb.
I hate when vice can bolt her arguments,
And virtue has no tongue to check her pride: 760
Imposter do not charge most innocent nature,
As if she would her children should be riotous
With her abundance she good cateress
Means her provision only to the good
That live according to her sober laws,   765
And holy dictate of spare temperance:
If every just man that now pines with want
Had but a moderate and beseeming share
Of that which lewdly-pampered luxury
Now heaps upon some few with vast excess,   770
Nature's full blessings would be well dispensed
In unsuperfluous even proportion,
And she no whit encumbered with her store,
And then the giver would be better thanked,
His praise due paid, for swinish gluttony   775
Ne'er looks to heaven amidst his gorgeous feast,
But with besotted base ingratitude
Crams, and blasphemes his feeder.   Shall I go on?
Or have I said enow?   To him that dares
Arm his profane tongue with contemptuous **words**   780
Against the sun-clad power of chastity;
Fain would I something say, yet to what end?

Thou hast nor ear, nor soul to apprehend
The sublime notion, and high mystery
That must be uttered to unfold the sage 785
And serious doctrine of virginity,
And thou art worthy that thou shouldst not know
More happiness than this thy present lot.
Enjoy your dear wit, and gay rhetoric
That hath so well been taught her dazzling fence, 790
Thou art not fit to hear thyself convinced;
Yet should I try, the uncontrolled worth
Of this pure cause would kindle my rapt spirits
To such a flame of sacred vehemence,
That dumb things would be moved to sympathize, 795
And the brute Earth would lend her nerves, and shake,
Till all thy magic structures reared so high,
Were shattered into heaps o'er thy false head.
   Comus. She fables not, I feel that I do fear
Her words set off by some superior power; 800
And though not mortal, yet a cold shuddering dew
Dips me all o'er, as when the wrath of Jove
Speaks thunder, and the chains of Erebus
To some of Saturn's crew. I must dissemble,
And try her yet more strongly. Come, no more, 805
This is mere moral babble, and direct
Against the canon laws of our foundation;
I must not suffer this, yet 'tis but the lees
And settlings of a melancholy blood;
But this will cure all straight, one sip of this 810
Will bathe the drooping spirits in delight
Beyond the bliss of dreams. Be wise, and taste. —

THE BROTHERS *rush in with swords drawn, wrest his glass out of his hand,
and break it against the ground; his rout make sign of resistance, but are
all driven in; the* ATTENDANT SPIRIT *comes in.*

   Spir. What, have you let the false enchanter scape?
O ye mistook, ye should have snatched his wand
And bound him fast; without his rod reversed, 815
And backward mutters of dissevering power,
We cannot free the lady that sits here
In stony fetters fixed, and motionless;
Yet stay, be not disturbed, now I bethink me,
Some other means I have which may be used, 820
Which once of Meliboeus old I learned,
The soothest shepherd that e'er piped on plains.
   There is a gentle nymph not far from hence,
That with moist curb sways the smooth Severn stream,
Sabrina is her name, a virgin pure, 825
Whilom she was the daughter of Locrine,

821. **Meliboeus old**: referring to Spenser.

825 ff. **Sabrina**: her story is told in Geoffrey of Monmouth. But Milton is referring to Spenser, *Faerie Queene* II:10:14–19.

That had the scepter from his father Brute.
The guiltless damsel flying the mad pursuit
Of her enraged stepdame Guendolen,
Commended her fair innocence to the flood   830
That stayed her flight with his cross-flowing course,
The water nymphs that in the bottom played,
Held up their pearled wrists and took her in,
Bearing her straight to aged Nereus' hall,
Who piteous of her woes, reared her lank head,   835
And gave her to his daughters to imbathe
In nectared lavers strewed with asphodel,
And through the porch and inlet of each sense
Dropped in ambrosial oils till she revived,
And underwent a quick immortal change   840
Made goddess of the river; still she retains
Her maiden gentleness, and oft at eve
Visits the herds along the twilight meadows,
Helping all urchin blasts, and ill luck signs
That the shrewd meddling elf delights to make,   845
Which she with precious vialed liquors heals.
For which the shepherds at their festivals
Carol her goodness loud in rustic lays,
And throw sweet garland wreaths into her stream
Of pansies, pinks, and gaudy daffodils.   850
And, as the old swain said, she can unlock
The clasping charm, and thaw the numbing spell,
If she be right invoked in warbled song,
For maidenhood she loves, and will be swift
To aid a virgin such as was herself   855
In hard-besetting need, this will I try
And add the power of some adjuring verse.

SONG

Sabrina fair
  Listen where thou art sitting
Under the glassy, cool, translucent wave,   860
  In twisted braids of lilies knitting
The loose train of thy amber-dropping hair,
  Listen for dear honor's sake,
  Goddess of the silver lake,
    Listen and save.   865

Listen and appear to us
In name of great Oceanus,
By the earth-shaking Neptune's mace,
And Tethys' grave majestic pace,
By hoary Nereus' wrinkled look,   870
And the Carpathian wizard's hook,

828. **The guiltless damsel:** 1673 reads thus. The earlier editions read 'She guiltless damsel.'
834. **Nereus:** the father of sea nymphs, dwelling at the bottom of the sea.
871. **the Carpathian wizard's hook:** Proteus, herdsman to Neptune, the hook being his crook. He was a magician.

By scaly Triton's winding shell,
And old soothsaying Glaucus' spell,
By Leucothea's lovely hands,
And her son that rules the strands, 875
By Thetis' tinsel-slippered feet,
And the songs of sirens sweet,
By dead Parthenope's dear tomb,
And fair Ligea's golden comb,
Wherewith she sits on diamond rocks 880
Sleeking her soft alluring locks,
By all the nymphs that nightly dance
Upon thy streams with wily glance,
Rise, rise, and heave thy rosy head
From thy coral-paven bed, 885
And bridle in thy headlong wave,
Till thou our summons answered have.

       Listen and save.

SABRINA *rises, attended by water-nymphs, and sings.*
 By the rushy-fringed bank,
Where grows the willow and the osier dank, 890
 My sliding chariot stays,
Thick set with agate, and the azurn sheen
Of turquoise blue, and emerald green
 That in the channel strays,
Whilst from off the waters fleet 895
Thus I set my printless feet
O'er the cowslip's velvet head,
 That bends not as I tread,
Gentle swain at thy request
  I am here. 900

 Spir. Goddess dear
We implore thy powerful hand
To undo the charmed band
Of true virgin here distressed,
Through the force, and through the wile 905
Of unblessed enchanter vile.
 Sab. Shepherd 'tis my office best
To help ensnared chastity;
Brightest lady look on me,
Thus I sprinkle on thy breast 910
Drops that from my fountain pure,
I have kept of precious cure,
Thrice upon thy finger's tip,
Thrice upon thy rubied lip,
Next this marble venomed seat 915
Smeared with gums of glutinous heat

872. **Triton:** a sea god.
873. **soothsaying Glaucus:** who became a god by accident. He was known as a seer.
874. **Leucothea:** cf. Homer, *Odyssey* V:333-35. 876. **Thetis:** sea goddess, mother of Achilles.
878. **Parthenope:** a siren. 879. **Ligea:** a siren.

I touch with chaste palms moist and cold,
Now the spell hath lost his hold;
And I must haste ere morning hour
To wait in Amphitrite's bower.   920

SABRINA *descends, and* THE LADY *rises out of her seat.*
   Spir. Virgin, daughter of Locrine
Sprung of old Anchises' line
May thy brimmed waves for this
Their full tribute never miss
From a thousand petty rills,   925
That tumble down the snowy hills:
Summer drouth, or singed air
Never scorch thy tresses fair,
Nor wet October's torrent flood
Thy molten crystal fill with mud,   930
May thy billows roll ashore
The beryl, and the golden ore,
May thy lofty head be crowned
With many a tower and terrace round,
And here and there thy banks upon   935
With groves of myrrh, and cinnamon.
Come lady while heaven lends us grace,
Let us fly this cursed place,
Lest the sorcerer us entice
With some other new device.   940
Not a waste, or needless sound
Till we come to holier ground,
I shall be your faithful guide
Through this gloomy covert wide,
And not many furlongs thence   945
Is your father's residence,
Where this night are met in state
Many a friend to gratulate
His wished presence, and beside
All the swains that there abide,   950
With jigs, and rural dance resort,
We shall catch them at their sport,
And our sudden coming there
Will double all their mirth and cheer;
Come let us haste, the stars grow high,   955
But night sits monarch yet in the mid sky.

The scene changes, presenting Ludlow Town and the President's castle, then
come in country dancers, after them the ATTENDANT SPIRIT, *with the two*
BROTHERS *and* THE LADY.
                        SONG
      Spir. Back shepherds, back, enough your play,
Till next sun-shine holiday,

Following line 956, the third anti-mask.

Here be without duck or nod
Other trippings to be trod
Of lighter toes, and such court guise   960
As Mercury did first devise
With the mincing Dryades
On the lawns, and on the leas.

This second song presents them to their father and mother.
Noble lord, and lady bright,
I have brought ye new delight,   965
Here behold so goodly grown
Three fair branches of your own,
Heaven hath timely tried their youth,
Their faith, their patience, and their truth.   970
And sent them here through hard assays
With a crown of deathless praise,
    To triumph in victorious dance
O'er sensual folly, and intemperance.

The dances ended, the SPIRIT *epiloguizes.*
Spir. To the ocean now I fly,   975
And those happy climes that lie
Where day never shuts his eye,
Up in the broad fields of the sky:
There I suck the liquid air
All amidst the gardens fair   980
Of Hesperus, and his daughters three
That sing about the golden tree:
Along the crisped shades and bowers
Revels the spruce and jocund spring,
The graces, and the rosy-bosomed hours,   985
Thither all their bounties bring,
There eternal summer dwells,
And west winds, with musky wing
About the cedarn alleys fling
Nard, and cassia's balmy smells.   990
Iris there with humid bow,
Waters the odorous banks that blow
Flowers of more mingled hue
Than her purfled scarf can show,
And drenches with Elysian dew   995
(List mortals if your ears be true)
Beds of hyacinth, and roses
Where young Adonis oft reposes,
Waxing well of his deep wound
In slumber soft, and on the ground   1000
Sadly sits the Assyrian queen;
But far above in spangled sheen
Celestial Cupid her famed son advanced,
Holds his dear Psyche sweet entranced

After her wandering labors long,   1005
Till free consent the gods among
Make her his eternal bride,
And from her fair unspotted side
Two blissful twins are to be born,
Youth and joy; so Jove hath sworn.   1010
   But now my task is smoothly done,
I can fly, or I can run
Quickly to the green earth's end,
Where the bowed welkin slow doth bend,
And from thence can soar as soon   1015
To the corners of the moon.
   Mortals that would follow me,
Love virtue, she alone is free,
She can teach ye how to climb
Higher than the sphery chime;   1020
Or if virtue feeble were,
Heaven itself would stoop to her.

Lycidas

1638

APPARENTLY Milton wrote no English poetry between 1634 (*Comus*) and 1637. In 1638, there appeared at Cambridge a volume of verses, contributed by various friends and colleagues, written to commemorate the death of the unfortunate Edward King, drowned on August 10, 1637, in the Irish Sea. This book of about fifty pages was divided into two parts, each with a separate title-page. The first part with a Latin title-page contained twenty-three Latin and Greek poems lamenting King's death. The second part, with the title-page *Obsequies to the Memory of Mr. Edward King*, contained thirteen English pieces. The last in the book is entitled *Lycidas*, and is signed with the initials J. M. The poem occurs also in the *Trinity College Manuscript* with many changes and revisions made after the composition. It was the changes in this poem that led Charles Lamb to regret and lament that he had ever seen the *Manuscript*.[1] Milton acknowledged *Lycidas* by printing it in the 1645 *Poems*.

Metrically, *Lycidas* is an almost completely successful consummation of a number of Milton's previous metrical experiments; but it has no exact or particular model. Every metrical device in the poem may be found in at least one of Milton's earlier poems, but never before had he achieved such a completely uniform excellence. Most of the lines are iambic pentameter (five feet), sometimes rhyming in couplets, and sometimes in intricate quasi-stanzaic patterns that never become stanzas. The poem has no stanzas in the conventional sense; but the breaks in the cadences of groups of lines produce rhythmic verse paragraphs that function as stanzas. These verse paragraphs may be set off by, or they may contain, effective trimeters (three feet), or an occasional unrhymed line. The whole poem, with major pauses and transitions but without stanzas, is metrically integrated by the magic of Milton's high harmony of numbers throughout its length.

The only direct connection between Edward King and Milton is this poem.[2] We do not know how well Milton knew him. The poem itself shows him unaware of the true circumstances of the death. In the *Manuscript*, *Lycidas* was originally dated November, 1637; but this date was struck out to make room for the statement that heads the poem

[1] Charles Lamb, 'Oxford in the Vacation,' *London Magazine*, vol. II (1820), pp. 365 ff.; also, *Works* (Oxford: Clarendon Press, 1924), pp. 480 ff. and note p. 839. 'I had thought of *Lycidas* as of a full-grown beauty — as springing up with all its parts absolute — till, in an evil hour, I was shown the original written copy of it, together with the other minor poems of its author, in the library of Trinity, kept like some treasure, to be proud of. I wish they had thrown them in the Cam, or sent them, after the later cantos of Spenser, into the Irish Channel.' For a full account of the changes in the *Manuscript*, see L. E. Lockwood, 'Milton's Corrections to the Minor Poems,' *Modern Language Notes*, vol. XXV (1910), pp. 201–05.

[2] Edward King (1612–37) was the younger son of Sir John King (d. 1637), at one time of Yorkshire, and afterward an active civil officer in Ireland. Edward was born in Ireland, but seems to have been partly educated at the school of Thomas Farnaby in London. He was admitted to Christ's College, Cambridge, Milton's college, on June 9, 1626, at the same time as his elder brother Robert. In 1630, by royal mandate, he was elected to a fellowship at Christ's. During 1633–34 he was praelector of his college. He also was a tutor and looked forward to the life of a parish priest. He sailed for Ireland, but the ship on which he took passage sank. For an account of the shipwreck and drowning, see the statement prefixed to the *Obsequies*. Edward's reputation as a poet, so much commented on in various of the commemorative poems, can scarcely be sustained by his extant poems, most of which were in Latin, and all of which were contributions to various collections of poems by Cambridge scholars.

in the 1645 printing, beginning 'In this monody...' This prose statement was not printed in 1638, but was added in 1645.

The poem is a pastoral epitaph or elegy, a kind of poetry that was most popular throughout the Renaissance and in Milton's day. The pastoral elegy derives ultimately from the Greek and originated apparently in Sicily. All pastoral poetry in the classical period early became artificial although earlier, shepherds and country people doubtless produced real songs that formed the basis for the later conventions. *Comus* and *Arcades*, in addition to being masks, are dramatic pastorals, as *L'Allegro* and *Il Penseroso* are pastoral lyrics. In the pastoral epitaph or lament, a shepherd (a poet) laments the death of another shepherd or poet. This type of lament had been used over and over again, and in Milton's day was very popular. But in English, no one before him had completely succeeded in making a pastoral elegy English. Milton's chief accomplishment in the poem is his success in naturalizing the conventions of the pastoral to England and the English scene. It represents a culmination in English of Milton's epitaph writing, although he wrote more epitaphs in Latin than in English. Yet in spite of the popularity of the form in Milton's day, he left only two full examples of the pastoral epitaph or elegy, *Lycidas* in English and the *Epitaphium Damonis* in Latin. The two poems must be read and studied together. Milton frequently paired his poems, or left two examples of a certain kind of poetry, sometimes leaving a pair in English, sometimes in Latin, and sometimes one in English and the other in Latin. No pair is more noteworthy than *Lycidas* in English and the *Epitaphium Damonis* in Latin.

Lycidas marked the full flowering of Milton's poetic genius in English verse. In contrast with *Comus*, lovely and appealing as is the poetry of that mask, Milton's genius in *Lycidas* was unhampered by any peculiarity of artistic temperament or any restrictions imposed by the verse forms he used. The conventions of the form selected in the case of *Lycidas* were most congenial to him. The result is what Mark Pattison called the greatest touchstone of poetic appreciation in the English language. The ability to appreciate *Lycidas* means that the whole realm of lyric poetry in any and all of the European languages is open to one.

The chief distinction of the poem is its complete success with all pastoral elements employed. Milton owed much to Spenser, the two Fletchers, and William Browne, though even more to the classical and Renaissance pastoral poetry; but whereas those great English poets strove valiantly but without complete success to make the spirit of classical and Continental pastoral poetry become English, Milton far surpasses their efforts and attains complete success. He shows no reluctance whatever to conform to classical and Italian conventions; but when he is finished, the poem is completely English. The very conventions of the pastoral, which he so carefully observed, become for him the unobtrusive means of definitely locating the setting of the poem in the English countryside. The poem more than justified his apparent frugality of poetic production during the Horton period. Almost on the basis of this poem alone, he must be admitted, at the age of twenty-nine, to the company of the immortals. *Lycidas* is his greatest shorter poem, and for complete mastery of form and poetic utterance, stands alone in the language.

Verity called it a 'study in the pastoral style.' It has been compared with Shelley's *Adonais*, Tennyson's *In Memoriam*, and Arnold's *Thyrsis*; but is a more complete poetic triumph than any of those poems, chiefly perhaps because Milton was not so much restricted by personal grief in *Lycidas* as were those other poets in their poems. *Lycidas* is not a poem expressing or attempting to express overwhelming grief over an irreconcilable loss by death of a beloved and intimate friend. Milton is left free in it to remain the poet, and not forced to give way to complete mournfulness and sense of desolation by the poignancy of his grief. Weirdly, the poem anticipated the personal grief Milton was soon to experience through the death of the most intimate friend of his own age he ever had, Charles Diodati. And, although written for a particular occasion, the death of King, surely some of the thought and many of the lines were ready for the occasion. Perhaps between April and November, 1637, Milton had tried to write some verses on the death of his mother. Lines 133–51 and 176–81 would be as much at home in a poem commemorating her death as they are in *Lycidas*. In fact, the conventionalized structure of the poem makes it suitable for lamenting any death. It is difficult to believe that much of the idea and some of the structure of *Lycidas* were not pretty well formed, in Milton's mind at least, before the unfortunate event which led to the publication of the poem.

Lycidas contains two digressions, the first, lines 64–69, being a complaint of the evil times on which poetry had fallen. The second, lines 118–31, deals with the corruption of the clergy. This attack on the corruptions of the clergy is the most striking minor note in the poem. The attack is evidence that a vast change has come over Milton in the short interval, two or three years at the most, between it and *Comus*. *Comus* assumes and expresses friendly and cordial relations between Milton and royalist Anglicans. We are, therefore, completely unprepared for the Root-and-Branch attitude of the second digression. Some moving experience must have been the real basis for the change in attitude, if it was a change, or for the announced attitude appearing with such apparent suddenness in *Lycidas*. But exactly what this experience was, has never come to light.

The reader may note the divisions into which the poem naturally falls. It ends with a stanza-like set of lines in *ottava rima*.[1] Masson insisted that the monody or pastoral elegy proper ends with line 186, and that the last eight lines of the poem constitute the stanzaic epilogue in which Milton speaks directly to the reader. However this may be, Verity found that 'to some extent the close is ideal, and studied from other pastoral poems.' As Stopford Brooke stated it,[2]

> *Lycidas* appeals not only to the imagination, but to the educated imagination. There is no ebb and flow of poetical power as in *Comus*; it is an advance on all his previous work, and it fitly closes the poetic labor of his youth. It is needless to analyze it, and all criticism is weaker than the poem itself. Yet we may say that one of its strange charms is its solemn undertone rising like a religious chant through the elegiac music; the sense of a stern national crisis in the midst of the pastoral mourning; the sense of Milton's grave force of character among the flowers and fancies of the poem; the sense of the Christian religion pervading the classical imagery. We might say that these things are ill-fitted to each other. So they would be, were not the art so fine and the poetry so over-mastering; were they not fused together by genius into a whole so that the unfitness itself becomes fascination.

REFERENCES

Hanford, J. H., 'The Pastoral Elegy and Milton's *Lycidas*,' *PMLA*, vol. XXV (1910), pp. 403–47.
Harrison, T. P., *The Pastoral Elegy* (Austin: University of Texas Press, 1939), pp. 17–19, and 289–93.
Jerram, C. S., *Lycidas and Epitaphium Damonis*. London: Longmans, Green, 1881.
Sandys, J. E., 'The Literary Sources of *Lycidas*,' *Royal Society of Literature, Transactions*, second series, vol. XXXII (1914), pp. 233–64.
Todd, H. J., *The Poetical Works of John Milton* (second edition; London, 1809, 7 vols.), VI:187–234.
Verity, A. W., *Comus and Lycidas*. Cambridge: University Press, 1898. Frequently reprinted.

---

[1] A stanza of eight lines of heroic (pentameter, five feet) verse, with three rhymes, the first six **lines rhyming** alternately, and the last two forming a couplet, *abababcc*.

[2] S. A. Brooke, *Milton* (New York: Appleton, 1892), pp. 26–27.

Lycidas

(1638)

This poem was first printed at Cambridge in 1638. It occurs in the *Manuscript* complete and with portions of it redrafted. The date 'Nov. 1637' is struck out to make room for the prose explanation. Milton printed it in 1645 and again in 1673.

In this monody the author bewails a learned friend, unfortunately drowned in his passage from Chester on the Irish Seas, 1637. And by occasion foretells the ruin of our corrupted clergy then in their height.

Yet once more, O ye laurels, and once more
Ye myrtles brown, with ivy never sere,
I come to pluck your berries harsh and crude,
And with forced fingers rude,
Shatter your leaves before the mellowing year.　　　　　　5
Bitter constraint, and sad occasion dear,
Compels me to disturb your season due:
For Lycidas is dead, dead ere his prime,
Young Lycidas, and hath not left his peer:
Who would not sing for Lycidas? he knew　　　　　　10
Himself to sing, and build the lofty rhyme.
He must not float upon his watery bier
Unwept, and welter to the parching wind,
Without the meed of some melodious tear.
　　Begin then, sisters of the sacred well,　　　　　　15
That from beneath the seat of Jove doth spring,
Begin, and somewhat loudly sweep the string.
Hence with denial vain, and coy excuse,
So may some gentle muse
With lucky words favor my destined urn,　　　　　　20
And as he passes turn,
And bid fair peace be to my sable shroud.
For we were nursed upon the self-same hill,
Fed the same flock; by fountain, shade, and rill.
　　Together both, ere the high lawns appeared　　　　　　25
Under the opening eyelids of the morn,
We drove afield, and both together heard
What time the gray-fly winds her sultry horn,
Battening our flocks with the fresh dews of night,
Oft till the star that rose, at evening, bright,　　　　　　30
Toward heaven's descent had sloped his westering wheel.
Meanwhile the rural ditties were not mute,
Tempered to the oaten flute,

3. **crude:** unripe.
8. **Lycidas:** the name of the shepherd in Theocritus, *Idyl VII*, and one of the speakers in Virgil's ninth *Eclogue.*
10. **he knew:** *MS.* and corrected copy of 1638 edition read, in longhand, 'he well knew.'
15. **sisters of the sacred well:** the muses.

Rough satyrs danced, and fauns with cloven heel,
From the glad sound would not be absent long,   35
And old Damaetas loved to hear our song.
　　But O the heavy change, now thou art gone,
Now thou art gone, and never must return!
Thee shepherd, thee the woods, and desert caves,
With wild thyme and the gadding vine o'ergrown,   40
And all their echoes mourn.
The willows, and the hazel copses green,
Shall now no more be seen,
Fanning their joyous leaves to thy soft lays.
As killing as the canker to the rose,   45
Or taint-worm to the weanling herds that graze,
Or frost to flowers, that their gay wardrobe wear,
When first the white-thorn blows;
Such, Lycidas, thy loss to shepherd's ear.
　　Where were ye nymphs when the remorseless deep   50
Closed o'er the head of your loved Lycidas?
For neither were ye playing on the steep,
Where your old bards, the famous druids, lie,
Nor on the shaggy top of Mona high,
Nor yet where Deva spreads her wizard stream: 55
Ay me, I fondly dream!
'Had ye been there' — for what could that have done?
What could the muse herself that Orpheus bore,
The muse herself for her enchanting son
Whom universal nature did lament,   60
When by the rout that made the hideous roar,
His gory visage down the stream was sent,
Down the swift Hebrus to the Lesbian shore.
　Alas! What boots it with uncessant care
To tend the homely slighted shepherd's trade,   65
And strictly meditate the thankless muse,
Were it not better done as others use,
To sport with Amaryllis in the shade,
Or with the tangles of Neaera's hair?
Fame is the spur that the clear spirit doth raise   70
(That last infirmity of noble mind)
To scorn delights, and live laborious days;
But the fair guerdon when we hope to find,
And think to burst out into sudden blaze,
Comes the blind fury with the abhorred shears,   75

34. **satyrs . . . fauns:** sylvan sprites.
36. **Damaetas:** the name no doubt refers to someone at Cambridge.
54. **Mona:** the isle of Anglesey.　For the whole region, cf. Drayton's *Polyolbion*, ninth song.
55. **Deva:** the river Dee.
61–63. The death of Orpheus, son of the muse Calliope; cf. Virgil, *Georgics* IV:517–27, and Ovid, *Metamorphoses* XI:1–55.
64 ff. The first digression is concerned with the low state of the recognition of letters in general and poetry in particular.　　　　　68–69. Referring to love poetry.
75. **the blind fury:** perhaps Atropos, the fate who cuts the thread of life.

And slits the thin-spun life. 'But not the praise,'
Phoebus replied, and touched my trembling ears;
'Fame is no plant that grows on mortal soil,
Nor in the glistering foil
Set off to the world, nor in broad rumor lies,   80
But lives and spreads aloft by those pure eyes,
And perfect witness of all-judging Jove;
As he pronounces lastly on each deed,
Of so much fame in heaven expect thy meed.'
  O fountain Arethuse, and thou honored flood,   85
Smooth-sliding Mincius, crowned with vocal reeds,
That strain I heard was of a higher mood:
But now my oat proceeds,
And listens to the herald of the sea
That came in Neptune's plea,   90
He asked the waves, and asked the felon winds,
What hard mishap hath doomed this gentle swain?
And questioned every gust of rugged wings
That blows from off each beaked promontory;
They knew not of his story,   95
And sage Hippotades their answer brings,
That not a blast was from his dungeon strayed,
The air was calm, and on the level brine,
Sleek Panope with all her sisters played.
It was that fatal and perfidious bark   100
Built in the eclipse, and rigged with curses dark,
That sunk so low that sacred head of thine.
  Next Camus, reverend sire, went footing slow,
His mantle hairy, and his bonnet sedge,
Inwrought with figures dim, and on the edge   105
Like to that sanguine flower inscribed with woe.
'Ah; Who hath reft' (quoth he) 'my dearest pledge?'
Last came, and last did go,
The pilot of the Galilean Lake,
Two massy keys he bore of metals twain,   110
(The golden opes, the iron shuts amain)
He shook his mitered locks, and stern bespake,
'How well could I have spared for thee, young swain,
Enow of such as for their bellies' sake,
Creep and intrude, and climb into the fold?   115

77. **Phoebus:** Apollo.   85. **fountain Arethuse:** the traditional fountain of pastoral verse in Sicily.

86. **Mincius:** a river in Lombardy, Italy, Virgil having lived at Mantua, near which point this river joins the Po.

89. **the herald of the sea:** Triton.   96. **sage Hippotades:** Aeolus, god of the winds.

99. **sleek Panope:** daughter of Nereus, a sea god.

101. **built in the eclipse:** doomed to be unlucky.

103. **Camus:** the river Cam, symbolizing the university.

106. **sanguine flower . . . :** the hyacinth, said to be marked in such a way as to bear the Greek word meaning 'alas.'

108 ff. The second digression is an attack on the corruption of the clergy. It is spoken by Saint Peter.

109. **pilot of the Galilean Lake:** Saint Peter, the first bishop of Rome.

Of other care they little reckoning make,
Than how to scramble at the shearers' feast,
And shove away the worthy bidden guest;
Blind mouths! that scarce themselves know how to hold
A sheep-hook, or have learned aught else the least   120
That to the faithful herdman's art belongs!
What recks it them? What need they? They are sped;
And when they list, their lean and flashy songs
Grate on their scrannel pipes of wretched straw,
The hungry sheep look up, and are not fed,   125
But swollen with wind, and the rank mist they draw,
Rot inwardly, and foul contagion spread:
Besides what the grim wolf with privy paw
Daily devours apace, and nothing said,
But that two-handed engine at the door,   130
Stands ready to smite once, and smite no more.'
    Return Alpheus, the dread voice is past,
That shrunk thy streams; Return Sicilian muse,
And call the vales, and bid them hither cast
Their bells, and flowerets of a thousand hues.   135
Ye valleys low where the mild whispers use,
Of shades and wanton winds, and gushing brooks,
On whose fresh lap the swart star sparely looks,
Throw hither all your quaint enameled eyes,
That on the green turf suck the honeyed showers,   140
And purple all the ground with vernal flowers.
Bring the rathe primrose that forsaken dies,
The tufted crow-toe, and pale jessamine,
The white pink, and the pansy freaked with jet,
The glowing violet.   145
The musk-rose, and the well-attired woodbine,
With cowslips wan that hang the pensive head,
And every flower that sad embroidery wears:
Bid amaranthus all his beauty shed,
And daffodillies fill their cups with tears,   150
To strew the laureate hearse where Lycid lies.
For so to interpose a little ease,
Let our frail thoughts dally with false surmise.
Ay me! Whilst thee the shores, and sounding seas
Wash far away, where'er thy bones are hurled,   155
Whether beyond the stormy Hebrides
Where thou perhaps under the whelming tide
Visitest the bottom of the monstrous world;

120. **sheep-hook** the pastoral staff of the bishop.   124. **scrannel**: weak.

130-31. The sword of divine justice.

132. **Alpheus**: the lover of Arethusa who also symbolizes pastoral poetry.

138. **swart star**: the dog star.   142. **rathe**: early.

143. **the tufted crow-toe**: in Phillips, the crow foot is the anemone, the crow toe 'a kind of flower.' In Boyer's French-English *Dictionary* (1719) the crow foot is French *renoncule* and the crow toe *hyacinte.* Johnson makes the crow toe 'probably crow foot,' which word he defines as 'buttercup.'

144. **freaked**: freckled, hence spotted.   156. **Hebrides**: islands off the west coast of Scotland.

Or whether thou to our moist vows denied,
Sleepest by the fable of Bellerus old,   160
Where the great vision of the guarded mount
Looks toward Namancos and Bayona's hold;
Look homeward angel now, and melt with ruth.
And, O ye dolphins, waft the hapless youth.
   Weep no more, woeful shepherds weep no more,   165
For Lycidas your sorrow is not dead,
Sunk though he be beneath the watery floor,
So sinks the day-star in the ocean bed,
And yet anon repairs his drooping head,
And tricks his beams, and with new-spangled ore,   170
Flames in the forehead of the morning sky:
So Lycidas sunk low, but mounted high,
Through the dear might of him that walked the waves
Where other groves, and other streams along,
With nectar pure his oozy locks he laves,   175
And hears the unexpressive nuptial song,
In the blest kingdoms meek of joy and love.
There entertain him all the saints above,
In solemn troops, and sweet societies
That sing, and singing in their glory move,   180
And wipe the tears forever from his eyes.
Now Lycidas the shepherds weep no more;
Henceforth thou art the genius of the shore,
In thy large recompense, and shalt be good
To all that wander in that perilous flood.   185
   Thus sang the uncouth swain to the oaks and rills,
While the still morn went out with sandals gray,
He touched the tender stops of various quills,
With eager thought warbling his Doric lay:
And now the sun had stretched out all the hills,   190
And now was dropped into the western bay;
At last he rose, and twitched his mantle blue:
Tomorrow to fresh woods, and pastures new.

160. **Bellerus old:** Milton makes Bellerus a fabled giant who gave his name to modern Land's End (Latin *Bellerium*).

161. **vision of the guarded mount:** St. Michael and Mount St. Michael in Cornwall.

162. **Namancos and Bayona's hold:** districts in Spain, hence the 'great vision' looks south.

173. **him that walked the waves:** Christ.

176. **the unexpressive nuptial song:** inexpressible heavenly music. Cf. *Ode to Nativity* 116; *Arcades* 72–73.

186 ff. In these eight lines, Milton is speaking of himself.

188. **stops of various quills:** the holes in different reeds, or the pipes of Pan.

189. **Doric lay:** pastoral poem.

The Sonnets
1630–1660

THE SONNET as a verse form is purely Italian in origin and development. It first appeared in Italy in the twelfth century; it has continued there in unbroken use to the present time; and there is almost no limit to the amount of Italian poetry in this form. At first, as its name implies, it was a 'little song,' and designed to be sung to a musical accompaniment. But very early it became employed for highly formalized poetic uses, and offered, and was used as, a medium for expressing poetic reflections and moods of a nature for which pure song is inadequate. It thus became a definitely limited poetic vehicle at once intimate and subjective in which the poet could speak in his own person, reveal his own emotions, and take the reader completely into his confidence. From the beginnings, it was the favorite meter of love poetry, and then came to be used for expressing friendship, admiration, and even hatred and hostility. It might be used to express one's compliments to a friend or fellow poet, and on occasion, served as a verse epistle. Individual persons and their actions were praised in sonnets either addressed directly to the person so honored, or written in honor of such a person. It was seized on as a form and greatly used by Petrarch, who made it peculiarly his own verse form. He was in this as well as in other respects greatly imitated. His work in sonnets is chiefly concerned with courtly love, and thus the sonnet is essentially a medieval verse form which in no way derives from antiquity. The sixteenth century found all Italy writing sonnets. Ariosto and Tasso wrote sonnets, Tasso a large number of them. Bembo, Rota, Caro, Michelangelo and hosts of other names could be added to the roster of sonnet-writers of the century.

Every school boy knows how Wyatt and Surrey introduced the form to England at the court of Henry VIII and how greatly the importation flourished in England. On its way from Italy to England the sonnet passed into France, and the French poets began imitating Petrarch. In Ronsard the sonnet found another master, perhaps second only to Petrarch himself, and the real attention to the sonnet in England was concerned perhaps as much with the French sonnet and Ronsard as with the Italian sonnet and Petrarch. For the work of Wyatt and Surrey fell on fertile soil. The great flowering time of the sonnet in England is late in the sixteenth century. Spenser, Sidney, Shakespeare, and Drayton were the great English sonneteers, Sidney excelling all the others — and there were hosts of others — excepting Shakespeare himself. With the printing of Shakespeare's *Sonnets* in 1609, the great Elizabethan tidal wave of sonnet writing subsided as suddenly as it began.

When, about 1630, Milton turned to the sonnet form in English after first producing a handful of experiments with it in Italian, almost no one else in England was writing sonnets, whereas thirty or forty years before that, everyone had been writing them. Milton's contemporaries were ignoring it. In the middle of the seventeenth century, almost no one wrote sonnets in England except Milton, and the sonnets he wrote are notable both for their form and their substance or the purpose for which they were used. In his Italian sonnets and songs, the form is not very remarkable, and, except for the student of Milton, the substance is even less so. They are sonnets principally using the closed octet, with sestets rhyming either *cdedce* or *cdcdee*, very common forms, and their subject is — love.

The two early sonnets in English, *O Nightingale* and *How Soon Hath Time* (I and VII), are equally unremarkable so far as form or substance is concerned. They are an indication that Milton was turning to the sonnet form in English, but of his early efforts in that form, he saw fit to keep only two. They give us only a promise of what he was ultimately to do with the form; indeed, like other 'twin poems' of the early period, the form might have been cast aside and never used again. In *O Nightingale* the bookish theme and imagery came originally from the Italian, through the French, especially Eustache Deschamps, and hence to English; the contrast between the nightingale, the bird of love, and the cuckoo, the bird of hate, was set forth by Clanvowe, a contemporary of Chaucer. Facile and lovely, the two early English sonnets with the Italian merely indicate Milton's interest in the sonnet as encountered in his reading and study. *How Soon Hath Time* is interesting chiefly for the origin of its final theme [1] and its intimate reflection of a disturbing mood in its author.

But after 1640, Milton returned to the sonnet, and in the next sixteen or seventeen years produced about that many sonnets. The nineteenth century made much of Milton's defection from the Petrarchan model for the sonnet, for in his later sonnets Milton frequently refrains from using a heavy pause at the end of the octet, and the thought runs over into the sestet. Too much has been made of this point, as Smart acknowledges. But not even that cautious and temperate Scot entirely succeeded in dismissing the nineteenth-century charges laid against Milton's 'tampering' with the 'rules' of the sonnet. As a matter of fact, the sonnet as developed by the Italians shows an almost infinite variety of forms and experiments with relations between form and substance, but all within narrow limits. Anyone who examines the Italian sonnets of the Renaissance in large quantities and in detail will be struck by the wide variety of usages, all carefully kept within very narrow limits.

Milton's two chief contributions to the sonnet as an English poem are, first, his artful manipulation of the pause between octet and sestet, sometimes neglecting it entirely, and secondly, his development in English of the 'Heroic' sonnet. His manipulation of the main pause was due, at least in part, to his reading of Della Casa's sonnets. In 1846, James Glassford pointed out the resemblance in structure between Milton's sonnets and those of Della Casa. [2] Now we know that in December of 1629, Milton purchased a book in which were bound together a 1529 edition of Dante's *Amoroso Convivio*, a 1563 edition of *Rime e Prose di Giovanni della Casa*, and a 1555 edition of the *Sonnetti di Benedetto Varchi*. He paid tenpence for the volume, which price he recorded together with his signature and the date of purchase. His copy of the book is now in the New York Public Library, and Smart's statement, 'its present possessor being unknown,' is no longer true. From Della Casa, in all probability, came Milton's neglect of the pause at the end of the octet; but not even Smart noticed that such neglect first occurs in the very early Italian sonnet, *IV*, 'Diodati...' The most effective use of the runover from octet to sestet occurs in the *Avenge, O Lord, Thy Slaughtered Saints*.

The heroic sonnet Milton doubtless took over from Torquato Tasso. Among Tasso's sonnets, the heroic sonnet of 'compliment and praise, addressed to Popes, Kings, Cardinals, Princes, Dukes, great ladies of ducal courts,' [3] outnumbers every other kind, whether

---

[1] From Pindar, cf. Lewis Campbell, *Classical Review*, vol. VIII (1894), p. 349.

[2] James Glassford, *Lyrical Compositions from the Italian Poets* (Edinburgh: A. and C. Black, 1846), pp. 587–88.

[3] J. S. Smart, *The Sonnets of Milton*, 1921, p. 41.

love sonnets or sacred and moral, all of which classifications Tasso used. This type of sonnet, complimentary and laudatory, was not unknown in English before Milton (witness Surrey on the death of Wyatt, Jonson to Lady Mary Wroth and others); but Milton was the first in English to make a regular practice of using the sonnet to praise persons whom he completely respected and admired, both men and women. Not less than eleven of Milton's sonnets belong to this general classification. These sonnets are of great value in any attempt to understand Milton's relations with people as reflected in his friendships. The heroic sonnets constitute a basis for compiling a list of his friends, and they are legion. Not everyone he most loved and admired is accorded a sonnet, or at least one that has survived. But these poems tell us much about the wide variety of his associations and friendships. The heroic sonnets are addressed to Cromwell and Vane, Parliamentary and Puritan leaders; Lawes, Royalist musician; the young men, Skinner and Lawrence; and four of them to women, but none of these is a love sonnet in the usual sense. All exhibit Milton's remarkable capacity for friendships for persons of different ranks and stations, ages and accomplishments.

Eleven more, including *Methought I Saw My Late Espoused Saint*, counted here as well as with the heroic sonnets, are personal sonnets. Packed with feeling sometimes of a most intimate nature, they provide us with a true picture of Milton in the years of his full maturity. They show us a man of warm but controlled feeling, cheerful, friendly, and easily approached if less easily moved, and show also, when coupled with the heroic sonnets, a man who was courteous and gentle, very human, but possessed of remarkable self-control and deep understanding both of himself and of others. Smart has well said that 'His hours of social ease and kindness are reflected in his sonnets. His manner is still classical, but with a Horatian tranquillity of tone, and a corresponding lucidity and perfection of style.'[1] We can leave the sonnets on no more adequate plane than the same critic's quietly comprehensive statement, full of wisdom and restraint, that in them, indeed throughout his poetry, 'Milton's touch was Attic and Florentine.'[1]

REFERENCES

Hanford, J. H., *Handbook* (third edition, 1939), pp. 170-73.
Pattison, Mark, *The Sonnets of John Milton*. London: Kegan Paul, Trench, 1883.
Smart, J. S., *The Sonnets of Milton*. Glasgow: Maclehose, Jackson, 1921.
Verity, A. W., *Milton's Sonnets*. Pitt Press Series. Cambridge: University Press, 1895. Frequently reprinted, 'with additions and corrections from time to time.'

The Sonnets

(*1630–1660*)

Milton left us a total of twenty-three sonnets, five of them in Italian and the remainder in English. The texts of many of them are in the *Trinity College Manuscript*. In 1645, he printed ten sonnets, including the five Italian ones. In 1648 was printed the sonnet addressed to Henry Lawes (*XIII*) in *Choice Psalms . . . composed by Henry and William Lawes*. This sonnet also appears in the *Trinity College Manuscript* in a rough draft and two fair copies. *XVII*,

[1] J. S. Smart, *op. cit.*, p. 46.

to Sir Henry Vane, was first printed in *The Life and Death of Sir Henry Vane*, in 1660, but was not included in Milton's publication of the *Minor Poems* in 1673. *XV*, *XVI*, and *XXII* were also omitted from that edition. They were first printed by Edward Phillips in 1694. *VII*, *VIII*, *IX*, *X*, *XI*, *XII*, *XIII*, *XIV*, *XV*, *XVI*, *XVII*, *XXI* (lines 5–14 only), *XXII*, and *XXIII* are contained in the *Manuscript* in various forms.

Milton's earliest preserved employment of the sonnet form dates from about 1628 to 1630. It was then that he wrote *I* (*O Nightingale*), the Italian sonnets, and the lone *Canzone*. *VII* (*On his Being Arrived at the Age of 23*) dates itself as of 1631. But the majority of the sonnets were written between 1640 and 1660.

The numbering adopted here is that of the Columbia edition of Milton's works.

(*1629–1630*)

To the Nightingale

This sonnet was printed as the first of the sonnets in 1645 and again in 1673. It does not occur in the *MS*. The resemblance to *Elegy VII* is worth noting. The nightingale as the bird of love, and the cuckoo as the bird of hate was certainly for Milton a bookish tradition. In the English of an earlier period occurs the poem, *The Cuckoo and the Nightingale*, formerly ascribed to Chaucer and printed in his works, but now assigned to Thomas or John Clanvowe, a contemporary of Chaucer (cf. Welles, *Manual of Middle English Writings*, vol. I: 423). The origin of the idea is lost in the mists of the middle ages.

The title 'To the Nightingale' was first given to the poem in 1713.

> O Nightingale, that on yon bloomy spray
>   Warblest at eve, when all the woods are still,
>   Thou with fresh hope the lover's heart dost fill,
>   While the jolly hours lead on propitious May,
> Thy liquid notes that close the eye of day,   5
>   First heard before the shallow cuckoo's bill
>   Portend success in love; O if Jove's will
>   Have linked that amorous power to thy soft lay,
> Now timely sing, ere the rude bird of hate
>   Foretell my hopeless doom in some grove nigh: 10
>   As thou from year to year hast sung too late
> For my relief; yet hadst no reason why,
>   Whether the muse, or love call thee his mate,
>   Both them I serve, and of their train am I.

I:4. **the jolly hours:** cf. Homer, *Iliad* XXI:450. The hours personified.

VII
(*1629–1632*)

On His Having Arrived at the Age of Twenty-Three

This poem was first printed in the 1645 *Poems*, and next appeared in print in 1673. It also appears, as a 'fair copy' and certainly not composed there, in the *MS.* at the end of the first draft of the *Letter to an Unknown Friend*.[1] We do not know exactly when it was written, any more than we know exactly when the *Letter* was written. Every editor has assumed that it was written after Milton's twenty-third birthday, although there is no warrant for this, the only element connecting it with such a date being the second line. But in that line the reading is 'my three and twentieth year.' If we compare this with Milton's *anno aetatis* phrase and assume these English and Latin phrases mean the same thing, then, since the *anno aetatis* years are always one year too young, the poem should be assigned, with those poems carrying the superscription *anno aetatis*, to the year following the birthday. Thus, 'my three and twentieth year' would really be the year after his twenty-third birthday, or the twenty-fourth year of his age. That year would be any time after December 9, 1631, and before December 9, 1632. But suppose that during the Horatian interval after its composition, the word 'one' was changed to 'three' for transmission to the Unknown Friend, and to bring it up to date. Then a date as early as 1630 or, if we put our own interpretation on 'one and twentieth year,' even 1629 would be possible. It is most likely that the poem was written, according to Milton's usual meaning of the formula *anno aetatis*, during his twenty-fourth year, and was occasioned by his contemplation of his impending or just accomplished graduation from Cambridge. The thought contained in lines 10–14 is to be found in Pindar's *Fourth Nemean Ode*, and Milton's own copy of Pindar was read intensively by him between June 17, 1630, and September 28, the same year, having been purchased on November 15, 1629. Therefore the poem may be dated any time between sometime later in 1629 to sometime in 1632. The title 'On his being arriv'd to his 23ᵈ year' was first added in 1713.

How soon hath time the subtle thief of youth,
    Stolen on his wing my three and twentieth year!
    My hasting days fly on with full career,
    But my late spring no bud or blossom showeth.
Perhaps my semblance might deceive the truth,   5
    That I to manhood am arrived so near,
    And inward ripeness doth much less appear,
    That some more timely-happy spirits endueth.
Yet be it less or more, or soon or slow,
    It shall be still in strictest measure even,   10
    To that same lot, however mean or high,
Toward which time leads me, and the will of heaven;
    All is, if I have grace to use it so,
    As ever in my great task master's eye.

[1] See page 45.

VII:5. **my semblance**: his youthful appearance, which he comments on here and elsewhere in his writings.

VIII

(1642)

When the Assault was Intended to the City

This poem was first printed in the 1645 *Poems*, and reprinted in 1673. It also occurs in the *MS.* with two titles, the first, deleted, reading 'On his dore when the Citty expected an assault' and the second, inserted, reading 'When the assault was intended to the Citty,' both of which titles Milton failed to print. In 1713, the poem bore its first printed title 'To the Soldier, to Spare his Dwelling-place.' The occasion for the poem was the action and movement of the Royalist army after the battle of Edgehill, fought on October 23, 1642. It had been a drawn battle, and Essex, by withdrawing his troops towards Warwick, left open and undefended the road to London, whereupon the Royalist army set out for the capital. Great excitement reigned in the City, heightened by the news of the defeat of a Parliamentary force on November 12, at Brentford, which was taken and sacked. Everyone thought London would fall into the hands of the Royalist troops.

The poem is connected with the excitement of those trying days and weeks when it seemed certain the city must fall, and with a time of anxiety and suspense; but these scarcely reflect themselves in it. Rather, its tone is one of light banter and graceful wit. It is almost humorous. It served no purpose, except perhaps, if written during the period of actual uncertainty, to bring a smile to a few readers; or, if written after the tension was broken, certainly, with its original title, it must have had an anticlimactic, comic appeal to the contemporary readers who saw it.

> Captain or colonel, or knight in arms,
> > Whose chance on these defenseless doors may seize,
> > If deed of honor did thee ever please,
> > Guard them, and him within protect from harms,
> He can requite thee, for he knows the charms   5
> > That call fame on such gentle acts as these,
> > And he can spread thy name o'er lands and seas,
> > Whatever clime the sun's bright circle warms.
> Lift not thy spear against the muses' bower,
> > The great Emathian conqueror bid spare   10
> > The house of Pindarus, when temple and tower
> Went to the ground: And the repeated air
> > Of sad Electra's poet had the power
> > To save the Athenian walls from ruin bare.

VIII:10. **the great Emathian conquerer:** Alexander the Great. In storming Boeotia, the entire city was razed, only the house of Pindar being spared.

13. **sad Electra's poet:** Euripides.

IX

(1642–1645)

To a Virtuous Young Lady

The poem is first printed in the 1645 *Poems*, and appears again in 1673. It is also in the *MS.* We know nothing of its date except what its place in the *MS.* suggests. There, Milton places it after *VIII* (1642), and it was so printed in 1645. It is not a love sonnet, but is apparently addressed to a girl still very young, 'in the prime of earliest youth.' It seems to be Milton's kindly encouraging reply to a girl who complained to him of some reproof offered her for her 'growing virtues.' The girl may have been a daughter of Mrs. Thomason, whose memory is celebrated in *XIV*.

No title was connected with the poem until 1713, when 'To a Lady' was added. In 1752, with no explanation for it, Bishop Newton gave the sonnet the title it usually bears today, 'To a Virtuous Young Lady.'

> Lady that in the prime of earliest youth,
>   Wisely hast shunned the broad way and the green,
>   And with those few art eminently seen,
>   That labor up the hill of heavenly truth,
> The better part with Mary and with Ruth,   5
>   Chosen thou hast, and they that overween,
>   And at thy growing virtues fret their spleen,
>   No anger find in thee, but pity and ruth.
> Thy care is fixed and zealously attends
>   To fill thy odorous lamp with deeds of light,
>   And hope that reaps not shame. Therefore be sure   10
> Thou, when the bridegroom with his feastful friends
>   Passes to bliss at the mid hour of night,
>   Hast gained thy entrance, virgin wise and pure.

X

(1643–1645)

To the Lady Margaret Ley

This sonnet was first printed in the 1645 *Poems*, and was printed again in 1673. It occurs also in the *MS.* Only the *MS.* copy bears the title, 'To the Lady Margaret Ley,' the poem having been first printed with a title in 1713. The poem is addressed to Lady Margaret, elder daughter of James Ley, created Earl of Marlborough by Charles I and successively Lord High Treasurer and President of the Council. In 1641, Lady Margaret, his daughter, married John Hobson of Ningwood in the Isle of Wight. He and his wife lived in Aldersgate Street, thus being near neighbors of Milton. Edward Phillips in his *Life of Milton* mentions the cordial and active friendship with the poet, 'this lady being a woman of great wit and ingenuity, had a particular honor for him, and took much delight in his company, as

likewise her husband, Captain Hobson, a very accomplished gentleman.'[1]
The poem can only be dated sometime between the time when his first wife
left him (1642) and 1645, the year it was first published.

> Daughter to that good earl, once president
>   Of England's council, and her treasury,
>   Who lived in both, unstained with gold or fee,
>   And left them both, more in himself content,
> Till the sad breaking of that parliament   5
>   Broke him, as that dishonest victory
>   At Chaeronea, fatal to liberty
> Killed with report that old man eloquent,
> Though later born, than to have known the days
>   Wherein your father flourished, yet by you,   10
>   Madam, methinks I see him living yet;
> So well your words his noble virtues praise,
>   That all both judge you to relate them true,
>   And to possess them, honored Margaret.

XI

(After 1645)

On the Detraction Which Followed upon My Writing Certain Treatises

This poem was first printed in the 1673 *Poems*. It occurs also in the *MS*.
Because in the *MS*. it follows two drafts of *XII*, the numbering of these two
sonnets has caused trouble. However, in 1673, Milton himself printed and
numbered them as they are here. Both are protests against the reception
of his prose tracts on divorce, published between 1643 and 1645. The title
comes from the *MS*.

> A book was writ of late called *Tetrachordon*;
>   And woven close, both matter, form and style;
>   The subject new: it walked the town a while,
>   Numbering good intellects; now seldom pored on.
> Cries the stall-reader, 'bless us! what a word on   5
>   A title-page is this!' and some in file
>   Stand spelling false, while one might walk to Mile-
> End Green. Why is it harder sirs than Gordon,
> Colkitto, or Macdonnel, or Galasp?

---

[1] *Letters of State*, p. xxiii, and Helen Darbishire, *Early Lives*, p. 64.

X:6. **dishonest:** dishonorable, shameful.
7. **Chaeronea:** the place where the Macedonians defeated the Greeks.
8. **old man eloquent:** Isocrates.

XI:7–8. **Mile-End Green:** originally marked by the first milestone from the heart of London on the
Roman road to Colchester and eastern Britain.
8–9. These are deliberately misspelled Scottish names. Colkitto means left-handed Colin, a name given
to the Macdonalds. Galasp is perhaps a form of Gillespie. Milton is reproaching Londoners for making
such mistakes in names.

Those rugged names to our like mouths grow sleek 10
That would have made Quintilian stare and gasp.
Thy age, like ours, O soul of Sir John Cheek,
Hated not learning worse than toad or asp;
When thou taughtest Cambridge, and King Edward Greek.

XII

On the Same

I did but prompt the age to quit their clogs
By the known rules of ancient liberty,
When straight a barbarous noise environs me
Of owls and cuckoos, asses, apes and dogs.
As when those hinds that were transformed to frogs 5
Railed at Latona's twin-born progeny
Which after held the sun and moon in fee.
But this is got by casting pearl to hogs;
That bawl for freedom in their senseless mood,
And still revolt when truth would set them free. 10
License they mean when they cry liberty;
For who loves that, must first be wise and good;
But from that mark how far they rove we see
For all this waste of wealth, and loss of blood.

XIII

(1646)

To Mr. H. Lawes on His Airs

The earliest of the three different drafts of this sonnet in the *MS.* is dated 'Feb. 9, 1645,' i.e., 1646 N.S. The poem was first printed in 1648, in the *Choice Psalmes* by Henry and William Lawes, published by Humphrey Moseley, the same publisher who issued Milton's *Poems* in 1645. Lawes and Milton met sometime before the production of *Comus* (1634), for which Lawes had written the music, and the friendship continued, although Lawes was a staunch Royalist. He was one of the most famous English musicians and composers of the century. The sonnet appears originally to have been written only a few weeks after the appearance of the *Poems* of 1645 (about January 1, 1646, or at the very end of 1645) in gratitude to Lawes for allowing his name to appear on the title-page as the composer of the music for the songs in that volume.

Harry whose tuneful and well measured song
First taught our English music how to span
Words with just note and accent, not to scan
With Midas' ears, committing short and long;

XII:5. Cf. Ovid, *Metamorphoses* VI:331–81.

Thy worth and skill exempts thee from the throng,   5
    With praise enough for envy to look wan;
    To after age thou shalt be writ the man,
    That with smooth air couldst humor best our tongue.
Thou honorest verse, and verse must send her wing
    To honor thee, the priest of Phoebus' choir   10
    That tunest their happiest lines in hymn, or story.
Dante shall give fame leave to set thee higher
    Than his Casella, whom he wooed to sing
    Met in the milder shades of Purgatory.

XIV

(1646)

On the Religious Memory of Mrs. Catharine Thomason, My Christian Friend, Deceased Dec. 1646

This poem was first printed in the 1673 *Poems*. There are three different drafts of it in the *MS.*, the first two in Milton's handwriting. Until 1921, the poem was supposed to be one addressed to Mrs. Thomson, identity unknown. Reference to the *MS.*, however, led J. S. Smart to note that the letter 'a' is crowded in between the 'm' and the 's' which makes the name Thomason, not Thomson. Now Mrs. Catharine Thomson becomes Mrs. Catharine Thomason, wife of the most famous bookseller of the century, most famous because beginning about 1640, George Thomason tried his best to collect everything printed in London from then until 1662. The remains of his great collection, which has suffered relatively little during the three centuries since its compiling, is today in the library of the British Museum. It was to commemorate the death of his friend's wife, then, that Milton wrote this sonnet. That Thomason and Milton were friends is best attested by the large number of copies of Milton's publications, some inscribed by him, in the Thomason Collection. He was probably the bookseller mentioned by Milton and described as his intimate friend (*mihi familiarissimo*) in his letter of April 21, 1647, to Charles Dati in Italy.

When faith and love which parted from thee never,
    Had ripened thy just soul to dwell with God,
    Meekly thou didst resign this earthy load
    Of death, called life; which us from life doth sever.
Thy works and alms and all thy good endeavor   5
    Stayed not behind, nor in the grave were trod;
    But as faith pointed with her golden rod,
    Followed thee up to joy and bliss forever.
Love led them on, and faith who knew them best
    Thy handmaids, clad them o'er with purple beams   10
    And azure wings, that up they flew so dressed,

XIII:9. **send**: so only in 1673, the three *MS.* drafts and 1648 reading 'lend.'

    11. The original printing of 1648 carries the marginal note 'The story of Ariadne set by him in music.' This is the only footnote of its kind written by Milton.

    13. **Casella**: cf. Dante, *Purgatory* II:76–117.

And speak the truth of thee on glorious themes
Before the judge, who thenceforth bid thee rest
And drink thy fill of pure immortal streams.

XV
(1648)

On the Lord General Fairfax, at the Siege of Colchester

This poem was first printed by Edward Phillips at the end of his *Life of Milton* in his edition of the *Letters of State*, published in 1694. It also appears in the *MS.* It is addressed to Fairfax for what he did at the siege of Colchester, which surrendered to him on August 27, 1648. The sonnet expresses the general feeling of the hour that in Fairfax, England was finding a new and vigorous leader. But Fairfax was later unable to stomach the execution of the King, and his resignation and retirement from active connection with the Commonwealth came in July, 1650.

Fairfax, whose name in arms through Europe rings
    Filling each mouth with envy, or with praise,
    And all her jealous monarchs with amaze,
    And rumors loud, that daunt remotest kings,
Thy firm unshaken virtue ever brings   5
    Victory home, though new rebellions raise
    Their hydra heads, and the false north displays
    Her broken league, to imp their serpent wings,
O yet a nobler task awaits thy hand;
    For what can war, but endless war still breed,   10
    Till truth, and right from violence be freed,
And public faith cleared from the shameful brand
    Of public fraud. In vain doth valor bleed
    While avarice, and rapine share the land.

XVI
(1652)

To the Lord General Cromwell, May 1652,
On the Proposals of certain Ministers at the Committee for Propagation of the Gospel

This poem was first printed by Edward Phillips in the 1694 *Letters of State.* It occurs in the *MS.* with the deleted superscription 'To the Lord Generall Cromwell May 1652 On the proposalls of certaine ministers at the Commtee for Propogation of the Gospell.' Cromwell was not yet Protector, though proposals to make him so were then circulating. He had crowned his other successes of 1650 and 1651 with that of Worcester on September 3, 1651, and had returned, the conquering hero, to spend the winter of 1651–52 in London. On March 29, 1652, proposals were presented to Parliament to perpetuate in the Commonwealth an Established Church, with a State-appropriated, State-paid, and State-regulated Clergy, but on a basis broad enough to admit among its clergy, approved men of all orthodox Protestant denominations.   But the general state of mind in England at the time was greatly opposed to any State Church, and Milton's sonnet in general expressed that state of mind.

Cromwell, our chief of men, who through a cloud
　　Not of war only, but detractions rude,
　　Guided by faith and matchless fortitude
　　To peace and truth thy glorious way hast plowed,
And on the neck of crowned fortune proud   5
　　Hast reared God's trophies and his work pursued,
　　While Darwen stream with blood of Scots imbrued,
　　And Dunbar field resounds thy praises loud,
And Worcester's laureate wreath; yet much remains
　　To conquer still; peace hath her victories   10
　　No less renowned than war, new foes arise
Threatening to bind our souls with secular chains:
　　Help us to save free conscience from the paw
　　Of hireling wolves whose gospel is their maw.

XVII
(1652)

To Sir Henry Vane the Younger

This poem was first printed on page 93 of the [George Sikes], *Life and Death of Sir Henry Vane* (n.p. 1662), and therein dated July 3, 1652.

From the abolition of the monarchy in 1649 until Cromwell made himself Protector in 1653, England was governed by the remnant of the Long Parliament and a Council of State appointed by that body and renewed every month.   Sir Henry Vane was one of the most acute, able, and energetic members of the Parliament and of its Council.   Vane and Milton were thrown together in the Council for several years.

Vane, young in years, but in sage counsel old,
　　Than whom a better senator ne'er held
　　The helm of Rome, when gowns not arms repelled
　　The fierce Epirot and the African bold,
Whether to settle peace or to unfold   5
　　The drift of hollow states hard to be spelled,
　　Then to advise how war may best, upheld,
　　Move by her two main nerves, iron and gold
In all her equipage; besides to know
　　Both spiritual power and civil, what each means   10
What severs each thou hast learned which few have done.
The bounds of either sword to thee we owe.
　　Therefore on thy firm hand religion leans
　　In peace, and reckons thee her eldest son.

XVIII

(1655)

On the Late Massacre in Piedmont

This poem was first printed in the 1673 *Poems*. It does not occur in the MS. It is easily the most powerful sonnet ever written. It refers to the climax of a long religious persecution of the Waldenses or Vaudois, a community half French, half Italian, in the Piedmont. This Protestant community, believed to have kept a primitive form of Christianity from the time of the Apostles, had seen various forms of persecution by Rome because of the many resemblances between its forms of worship and those of the Reformed or Protestant Churches, together with its ready acceptance of many Protestant practices and doctrines. The persecutions of 1655 exceeded all others. By an edict of the Duke of Savoy, who was also Prince of Piedmont, on January 25, 1655, the Waldenses were ordered to become Papists or give up their property and leave the country within twenty days. Upon their resistance, troops were marched in and terrible atrocities followed. Butchery, torture, enslavement, and escape only to the wintry mountain passes were the fate of these people. All Protestantism naturally was greatly stunned and indignant. Cromwell took on himself the task of alleviating the sufferings of the survivors and calling the offenders to account. Money was collected for the relief of this distracted people, and plans were made to send armed forces to Italy. So strong were the protests that the edict was withdrawn, and in August, 1655, the Waldenses were allowed their own form of worship without loss of life or property. Most of Cromwell's correspondence on the subject was written by Milton as Latin Secretary. The sonnet is his own powerful protest against the treatment accorded the Waldenses, so powerful that few persons today except professional historians would probably ever have heard of the affair were it not for this sonnet. It is written in Milton's best manner.

> Avenge O Lord thy slaughtered saints, whose bones
>   Lie scattered on the Alpine mountains cold,
>   Even them who kept thy truth so pure of old
>   When all our fathers worshiped stocks and stones,
> Forget not: in thy book record their groans
>   Who were thy sheep and in their ancient fold
>   Slain by the bloody Piemontese that rolled
>   Mother with infant down the rocks. Their moans
> The vales redoubled to the hills, and they
>   To heaven. Their martyred blood and ashes sow
>   O'er all the Italian fields where still doth sway
> The triple tyrant: that from these may grow
>   A hundredfold, who having learned thy way
>   Early may fly the Babylonian woe.

5

10

XIX

(1655)

On His Blindness

This poem was first printed in the 1673 *Poems*. It does not occur in the *MS*. It received its title from Bishop Newton in 1752, never having been printed before then with a title. Milton lost what remained of his failing eyesight in preparing the reply of the Commonwealth to *The Support of the King* by Salmasius. By 1652, he was totally blind, although he says in a letter (1654) that he could still barely distinguish light from darkness. The nature of his blindness cannot be exactly discovered, although many persons have made the attempt, including a number of physicians. He took this calamity greatly to heart, felt it keenly and lamented it bitterly. His enemies seized on it gleefully, and missed no opportunities to twit both Milton and the Government that continued to employ him on his condition. In some ways, there is nothing more remarkable in the annals of English literature than Milton's successful surmounting of his loss of sight. It came when he was in his prime, but with his life's literary ambitions unfulfilled. Ultimately, he succeeded in accepting it as one of the mysteries of God's will, but it was and remained a bitter blow to him. The reader would do well to compare this sonnet with later references in his poetry to his blindness.

REFERENCE

Brown, Eleanor Gertrude, *Milton's Blindness*.

When I consider how my light is spent,
    Ere half my days, in this dark world and wide,
    And that one talent which is death to hide,
    Lodged with me useless, though my soul more bent
To serve therewith my maker, and present   5
    My true account, lest he returning chide,
    'Doth God exact day-labor, light denied,'
    I fondly ask; But patience to prevent
That murmur, soon replies, 'God doth not need
    Either man's work or his own gifts, who best   10
    Bear his mild yoke, they serve him best, his state
Is kingly. Thousands at his bidding speed
    And post o'er land and ocean without rest:
    They also serve who only stand and wait.'

XIX:3. **talent:** cf. *Reason of Church Government* (1642), *Col.* III:1:232:9-18.

XX

(1655–1656)

To Mr. Lawrence

This sonnet was first printed in the 1673 *Poems*, and does not occur in the *MS.* It first received a title in 1713. The poem is an invitation to 'Lawrence' to join him, indoors, in this winter season, and spend a day by the fire, with eating and drinking, in music and song. If the person addressed is, as Smart all but proves,[1] Edward Lawrence, the poem must have been written in 1655 or 1656, as Edward died in 1657 at the age of twenty-four. No one can read this sonnet without gaining an idea of Milton far removed from any which pictures him a dour, straight-laced, Puritanical kill-joy.

> Lawrence of virtuous father virtuous son,
>> Now that the fields are dank, and ways are mire,
>> Where shall we sometimes meet, and by the fire
>> Help waste a sullen day; what may be won
> From the hard season gaining: time will run   5
>> On smoother, till Favonius re-inspire
>> The frozen earth; and clothe in fresh attire
>> The lily and rose, that neither sowed nor spun.
> What neat repast shall feast us, light and choice,
>> Of Attic taste, with wine, whence we may rise   10
>> To hear the lute well touched, or artful voice
> Warble immortal notes and Tuscan air?
>> He who of those delights can judge, **and spare**
>> To interpose them oft, is not unwise.

XXI

(1655)

To Cyriack Skinner

XXI and *XXII* were not both printed by Milton, only *XXI* appearing in the 1673 *Poems*. *XXII* was first printed by Edward Phillips in 1694. Of *XXI*, lines 5–14 occur in the *MS.*, as does the whole of *XXII*. The poems are much like *XX* in tone, and are both addressed to Cyriack Skinner, son of William Skinner. Cyriack was born in November, 1627, and had been under Milton's care in the school in Aldersgate Street.

> Cyriack, whose grandsire on the royal bench
>> Of British Themis, with no mean applause
>> Pronounced and in his volumes taught our laws,
>> Which others at their bar so often wrench;
> Today deep thoughts resolve with me to drench   5
>> In mirth, that after no repenting draws;

[1] J. S. Smart, *The Sonnets of Milton*, pp. 110–14.

XX:6. **Favonius:** Zephyr, the west wind.   10. **Attic taste:** frugal and simple.
12. **Tuscan:** the language of Petrarch, hence very simple and most musical.
XXI:2. **British Themis:** Themis was goddess of justice. Cf. *Paradise Lost* XI:14.

Let Euclid rest and Archimedes pause,
    And what the Swede intend, and what the French.
To measure life, learn thou betimes, and know
    Toward solid good what leads the nearest way;   10
    For other things mild heaven a time ordains,
And disapproves that care, though wise in show,
    That with superfluous burden loads the day,
    And when God sends a cheerful hour, refrains.

XXII

To the Same

Cyriack, this three years' day these eyes, though clear
    To outward view, of blemish or of spot;
    Bereft of light their seeing have forgot,
    Nor to their idle orbs doth sight appear
Of sun or moon or star throughout the year,   5
    Or man or woman.   Yet I argue not
    Against heaven's hand or will, nor bate a jot
    Of heart or hope; but still bear up and steer
Right onward.   What supports me dost thou ask?
    The conscience, friend, to have lost them overplied   10
    In liberty's defense, my noble task,
Of which all Europe rings from side to side.
    This thought might lead me through the world's vain mask
    Content though blind, had I no better guide.

XXIII

(1658)

On His Deceased Wife

    This poem was first printed in the 1673 *Poems*, and it occurs in the *MS*.
The title was added in 1713. This is the most moving and tender poem
Milton ever wrote. The emotion contained in it is overpowering and
almost insufferable. It is concerned with his recently deceased second wife,
Katherine Woodcock, whom he had married in 1656. She died in February,
1658, having borne a child in October, 1657, and the child survived her
only a few weeks. Her nature may best be judged by the poem itself.
Smart was able to discover that she was born in London in 1628.

Methought I saw my late espoused saint
    Brought to me like Alcestis from the grave,
    Whom Jove's great son to her glad husband gave,
    Rescued from death by force though pale and faint.
Mine as whom washed from spot of child-bed taint,   5
    Purification in the old law did save,
    And such, as yet once more I trust to have
    Full sight of her in heaven without restraint,

XXII:12. **rings**: so 1694; *MS*. has 'talks.'

Came vested all in white, pure as her mind:
    Her face was veiled, yet to my fancied sight,   10
    Love, sweetness, goodness, in her person shined
So clear, as in no face with more delight.
    But O as to embrace me she inclined
    I waked, she fled, and day brought back my night.

The Fifth Ode of Horace, Lib. I.

(1650?–1660?)

Qais multa gracilis te puer in rosa, rendered almost word for word without rhyme according to the Latin measure, as near as the language will permit.

Milton's translation of this ode is one of the finest verse translations in English. Most editors have attempted to claim an early or at least a relatively early date for it. Milton first printed it in 1673, and it is a product of his full poetic maturity, and not an early exercise.

What slender youth bedewed with liquid odors
Courts thee on roses in some pleasant cave,
    Pyrrha for whom bindest thou
    In wreaths thy golden hair,
Plain in thy neatness; O how oft shall he   5
On faith and changed gods complain: and seas
    Rough with black winds and storms
    Unwonted shall admire:
Who now enjoys thee credulous, all gold,
Who always vacant always amiable   10
    Hopes thee; of flattering gales
    Unmindful. Hapless they
To whom thou untried seemest fair. Me in my vowed
Picture the sacred wall declares to have hung
    My dank and dropping weeds   15
    To the stern God of Sea.

Paradise Lost
1640–1665

N<small>O INTRODUCTION</small> to *Paradise Lost* can take the place of reading the poem itself in order to become acquainted with it, understand it, and find out what it is about and what it is like. If the reader enjoys it, is moved by it, or finds it appealing to him in any way, no introduction is necessary. If, on the other hand, the reader finds nothing about it or in it that appeals to him, no preliminary statements can make much difference. It is not a poem that grows on one by reading about it; but it is a poem that makes more and more appeal to, and lays more and more demands on, its reader the more it is read. No one who has really tried to read it needs to apologize for failing to be attracted by the poem, any more than Milton needs to apologize for having written it in the hope that it might 'fit audience find, though few.'

The poem is the consummation of Milton's high literary hopes and aspirations. It is the greatest epic in the English language, perhaps the only original poem in that form that has been successful in English with general readers, and certainly the only English epic known to other nations. It is the result of weaving together almost innumerable elements into a gorgeously rich and varied whole that appeals to any reader almost directly in proportion to what he can bring to its reading. But over and above the elements that compose it, the totality of the result; the numberless reaches of high poetry contained in it; the astonishing facility and ease with which on the whole the work is made and sustained as a poem; these accomplishments today call forth more response and admiration than do the elements assembled to make up its substance. Milton's supreme accomplishment in *Paradise Lost* is in making it become and remain a great poem.

No one would maintain that it is equally successful as poetry throughout its entire length. No poem in any language running to more than ten thousand lines has ever maintained itself constantly and throughout its length on any uniform poetic level, and all long poems descend occasionally to a limping, non-poetic level. Indeed, we probably tend to judge all long poems on some such basis as the poet's ability to keep from so descending as much as possible. If poems like Drayton's *Polyolbion* (1613), Cowley's *Davidies* (1656), Blackmore's *Creation* (1712), or Pollok's *Course of Time* (1827) tend perhaps to remain predominantly on a pedestrian, almost non-poetic level, we fail to accord much poetic merit or worth to them. If a poem in English, dealing with almost the same material as *Paradise Lost* deals with, written and published only a few years before Milton's poem, can, as has Samuel Pordage's *Mundorum Explicatio* (1661), become almost completely forgotten, at least to the extent that it is not even mentioned in the principal history of English literature, then there must be some reason for the vast difference in attention accorded to the two poems. Probably most of this difference is due to the relative ability to maintain a high poetic level in the one poem, and inability to maintain a very high level in the other. It is the relative lack of unpoetic, lifeless, creeping verse that most impresses us in *Paradise Lost*. Even the apocalypse or vision contained in the last two books of the poem, relatively unsuccessful as it is, impresses us, perhaps less than any other sustained episode or happening in the poem, but even this portion is not wholly devoid of poetic appeal. The secret of so overwhelming an amount of poetically successful attainment is locked up in the nature of Milton's poetic genius. We must, therefore, first try to understand the substance of the poem, and then understand what he did with this material artistically that produced a great poem.

Milton deliberately set out to write an epic poem containing an account of the whole situation in which man finds himself and how that situation came to be. The poem opens and for the first three books concerns itself with the rebel angels and their relations to God in order to show how it was the 'infernal serpent' or Satan who through God's 'allowance' was responsible for many of the circumstances in which mankind is now placed. But all that Satan and the rebel angels did was part of God's plan. Satan and his rebellious angels were defeated by heaven's loyal forces, the Son of God finally blasting him and his cohorts from the ramparts of heaven; but even then, Satan refused to cease his assaults on God's 'tyranny.' The poem opens with a short announcement of what the poem is to deal with, and then Milton plunges directly into the midst of the action involving the rebel angels and their decisions and designs after the great defeat by the Messiah and their fall into hell, a place for their 'fit punishment prepared.' There, Satan rallied his forces, and after counsel, decided to attempt God's newest creation, the universe. If heaven was impossible of assault, perhaps the newly created universe of which Satan had heard but a vague rumor might yield to him and so yielding, might embarrass its creator. No human figure appears in the first three books of the poem.

The third book opens with the first major pause in the poem; the muse is reinvoked; and Satan has now successfully completed his enterprise to reach the universe and discover the earth, the alleged abode of God's newest creature, man. Satan then discovers man, and his original aim to secure revenge by perverting this creature is supplemented by the envy aroused in him of the happiness of the innocent human pair. But Satan's enmity is toward God, not man. He now hopes to revenge himself on God through man; but his plans are still vague. Man, generic man, is then introduced in the symbolical and allegorical figures of Adam and Eve. This human pair now become the center of interest in the poem and hold that interest throughout the remainder of the epic, although many necessary or diverting asides and digressions are introduced. Entirely through God's will or tolerance, but not through his active desire, the direct main action of the poem occurs, after proper delay in order to make Adam a knowing and therefore a responsible creature; and Satan, though man was duly warned against him, eventually succeeds in seducing Adam through Eve.

The human pair, miserably aware of their now fallen condition, are then lamentably reduced to a most pitiable condition. But Milton insists that their rehabilitation, in allegorical fashion for all mankind, is not only possible, but is actively willed by God himself, whereas their fall was only passively willed or permitted. Now the Messiah himself offers the first divine comfort to the forlorn human pair; but his comfort only perplexes them, because Adam has not yet attained to a sufficient knowledge of God's ways and plans to understand all that the Christ's statements mean. Only gradually does Adam come to know exactly what has happened to him. The tenth book ends with the necessity still before Milton of securing for Adam, or for mankind, a full understanding of his exact situation and how his restoration to the possibility of again partaking of God's grace will be attained. It is the necessary function of the two final books of the poem to show to Adam and thus to the reader the fullness of God's provisions for the continuance of his original plan.

Milton deliberately selects Adam's reason through knowledge as the means by which he is to be brought to faith in, and then acceptance of, God's great plan for man's salvation. Adam must first realize who his adversary really is, and how irrevocably damned is that adversary. He must also learn how easy it is for man himself to be as irrevocably damned as were Satan and the rebel angels, indeed, that many men will by their own choice, not God's choice, be so damned.

We now see that all that has been told of Adam and his creation and all the gifts and graces showered on him by his creator become the basis of the process that leads to his salvation. His knowledge and reason began with a knowledge of God's 'creatures,' or the physical aspects of the visible universe, augmented through the conversations with God himself and with Raphael by an apprehension of heaven or invisible creation through faith and Raphael's representation of the warfare in heaven and creation of the visible universe. Adam was originally taught to reason by arguing with God himself over the necessity for the creation of Eve. Slowly, all these elements that make up or contribute to the development of Adam, or man, as a completely sentient and therefore responsible creature are worked out.

Then, at the very end of the poem or in the final books, Adam has been endowed with or has arrived at complete rational knowledge, to the full extent needed for a mundane existence, that included an awareness of heaven and hell in addition to a direct knowledge of the visible universe and of himself. He is brought gradually to the capacity to receive and understand the vision or revelation that Michael the archangel shows to him. This vision is the Bible story, from the birth of Cain and Abel to the triumph, as related in the gospels, of the incarnated Christ over Satan, sin, and death. Adam, enabled by God's wish to understand all this, graciously and gratefully accepts it by faith as the ineffable and perfect will of God; gives thanks to Michael and to his creator; and tearfully, but willingly and peacefully leaves Eden, at one with the world about him and with God.

Such was the account of man's condition that Milton endeavored to unfold and set before us, putting into it every resource of his being. We must measure his success or failure by the success or failure of his poetry, or by his way of presenting the overwhelming material with which he chose to work. Some characteristics of his way of working with this material are worth noting. He always and throughout the poem refrains from asking for the suspension of our disbelief, although he insists that his material is only real through its acceptance by faith. He never once asks us to heed an account of the necessity of God's existence; he takes that existence for granted as fundamental, as he does many another similarly fundamental fact, or what for him and his age was accepted as a fact. As a result, he wastes no time or energy in trying to prove anything. He accepts man's situation as he finds it, accepting likewise the belief that God's ways are past our finding out except as man's reason is able to construct analogies for or from them, and that man's reason and power of choice (will) are the instruments God intended man to use principally to bring himself to faith and hence to God's grace.

Although the principal appeal of the poem to modern readers is its high poetic attainment, the careful reader soon discovers also Milton's encyclopedic grasp of the learning and scholarship of his day. For the most part and for most readers, even in the last two books, Milton carried his learning lightly; but casual or minute inspection of it reveals that his learning and scholarship were both profound and wide. He is without doubt the most learned person ever to attain recognition as a supreme poetic genius. In many ways it would seem that he succeeded in becoming a great poet in spite of his scholarship and learning; but to many readers the presence of these two elements in all his poetry and especially in *Paradise Lost* makes a permanent appeal.

The actual sources of the poem are legion. For all three of the long poems, the primary source was the Bible. But the Bible to Milton meant the Bible with all its scholarly apparatus of his day. That is, every phase of Bible study known in his day was employed. The early fathers of the church, the theologians, the Christian and Jewish commentators, St. Augustine and the scholastics generally, together with the secular historians of Biblical times, Josephus, and others, as well as all the apocryphal books available in Milton's day were as much a part of his study and use of the Bible as was the bare text itself. And Milton knew and used that text in all its versions. The ultimate text of Scripture to him was the Hebrew Old Testament and the Greek New Testament.

The form and structure of the poem derive from the poems of Homer, Virgil, and what the Greek and Roman critics said about these poems; from the poems of Dante, Chaucer, Ariosto, Boiardo, Tasso, Camoens, Spenser, Du Bartas, and various others in the vernacular languages of western Europe together with critical opinions of epic poetry ranging from Aristotle to the Scaligers. Add to these most of the literatures in the different languages of the works enumerated, with special reference to secular history, the literature of travel, and a propensity to study atlases and maps, in addition to keeping up with technical and vocational developments such as warfare and agriculture, using the study of music and mathematics as a diversion, and we have a bird's-eye view of Milton's reading. All of it is the source of *Paradise Lost*.

The great contemporary appeal of the general subject matter and style of the poem to its own and immediately succeeding times has been well described by Moody.

It is the only English poem with sufficient largeness of theme and breadth of treatment to deserve the name of epic. It is of course not an epic of the Homeric type, springing spontaneously in an unlettered age from the imaginative life of a whole nation; but granted the age of sophistication in which it was produced, it did in a remarkable way seize and draw together the imaginative elements of English thought. The Bible was in Milton's day the very center and substance of that thought. It was for many years almost the only book accessible to the nation at large, and that too at a time when intellectual curiosity was profoundly stirred by the impulses of the Renaissance. The stories of the Bible, its cosmogony, its chronology, its imagery, had sunk into the tissue of English thought like a rich and somber dye. When Milton adopted the story of Genesis as his subject, he was seizing with true epic instinct upon material genuinely national — much more national than the story of King Arthur or any of the historical British kings could have been, because not only the belief but the passion of the race was engaged by it.

The composition of the poem, according to Milton himself, was of 'long choosing, and beginning late.' (Bk. IX:26.) Much has been written of the history of the poem's inception. But it is best to follow the development of the ideas and aspirations that went to make up the poem as they are found in Milton's earlier works. The more one reads this earlier work, the more one is struck by the presence in it of a soaring and consuming literary ambition that plans great accomplishments.

As early as the *Vacation Exercise* (1628) we find a veiled statement in lines 29–52 of an ambition he then had for the production of a great literary work to be carried out in English. In this passage he lists, in the order of importance maintained throughout his life, the subjects he considered worthy of such an ambition. The first, and highest subject is contained in lines 33–36, which refer to the transport of the poet that carries him 'rapt above the pole' to heaven itself, and leads him to sing of the heavenly host.

> Such where the deep transported mind may soar
> Above the wheeling poles, and at heaven's door
> Look in, and see each blissful deity
> How he before the thunderous throne doth lie,

The second subject in lines 35–39 is more a method of writing than a subject; but the method itself more or less furnishes the subject, which is the investment of the poet's highest thoughts in the garb of classical mythology, principally in that of the Greek pantheon.

> ... each blissful deity
> How he before the thunderous throne doth lie,
> Listening to what unshorn Apollo sings
> To the touch of golden wires, while Hebe brings
> Immortal nectar to her kingly sire:

This is followed by a descent, through the upper skies of our world to the sea, and accounts of it:

> Then passing through the spheres of watchful fire,
> And misty regions of wide air next under,
> And hills of snow and lofts of piled thunder,
> May tell at length how green-eyed Neptune raves,
> In heaven's defiance mustering all his waves;

Then, as subject for high poetry, the beginnings of the cosmos, including all that man knows of cosmic (scientific) secrets:

> Then sing of secret things that came to pass
> When beldam nature in her cradle was;

And last, romance, chivalry, and the deeds of heroes of old:

> And last of kings and queens and heroes old,
> Such as the wise Demodocus once told
> In solemn songs at king Alcinous' feast,
> While sad Ulysses' soul and all the rest
> Are held with his melodious harmony
> In willing chains and sweet captivity.

Heaven, its ruler and his cohorts, classical mythology, nature in her beginnings or science, and heroic romance, are the elements he sets forth in this early poem as the subjects most fit for highest poetry.

In *Elegy VI* (1629) Milton definitely aligned himself with the epic poets as opposed to the makers of lighter verse and set for himself a manner of living which he thought fitting for such an ambition. This resolution is re-encountered later in the *Apology* (1642). *Lycidas* (written in 1637, published in 1638) with its digression on poetic fame and the thought contained in the last eight lines, virtually an epilogue, of 'tomorrow to fresh woods, and pastures new,' is further indication of his concern with a soaring poetic ambition.

In *Mansus* (1639–40) he goes so far as to announce his intention of producing a national epic, perhaps with Arthur or the Knights of the Round Table as the central figure or figures. This ambition is stated again in the *Epitaphium Damonis* (1640) in which he implied that he had already begun an Arthurian epic and further informs us that he intends to sing of the history of the British from the landing of Brutus to the death of Arthur. This is the last we ever hear from him of the Arthurian epic.

In the *Reason of Church Government* (dated 1641 on the title-page but which probably appeared in January or February of 1642) he tells us that he has decided to write a great English poem and elaborates his idea of the nature and function of poetry as he intends to write it. He further states that he is as yet uncertain of the subject matter and of the form this work is to take.

The *Trinity College Manuscript* contains lists of possible literary subjects taken almost entirely from Biblical and British history. Some of these are merely put down as subjects, but others are outlined in varying degrees of completeness. All the plans contained in this manuscript are dramatic; but as Professor Gilbert has pointed out, it is possible that there was a similar list of epic subjects which has not survived. The subject of Adam's Fall occurs in a number of drafts in the *Manuscript*, the fourth being entitled *Adam Unparadised*. The material contained in these four different drafts of the subject is the earliest ground work of *Paradise Lost* that has survived. His nephew, Edward Phillips, stated in his *Life* [1] that he recalls a version of Satan's speech addressed to the sun (*Paradise Lost*, Book IV, lines 30–38) as being in existence sometime between 1640–42.

Milton's early urge toward drama as exhibited in *Elegy I* by his references to the stage in London in 1625–26; to Jonson and Shakespeare in *L'Allegro*; his productions of *Arcades* and *Comus*; and the dramatic plans contained in the *Trinity College Manuscript*; all indicate with what serious consideration he projected his literary plans in a dramatic form. We do not know exactly why he gave up this form, but the statements about epic poetry and the epic poet contained in *Elegy VI* seem to be sufficient grounds on which to rest the ultimate responsibility for his giving up the dramatic in favor of the epic form.

The *Familiar Epistles* (1647–56) also constitute a link in the chain of evidence that he long contemplated what he was about to produce of high literary worth.

Altogether, we can be certain that about 1640 and immediately thereafter, he was ready to embark on the consummation of his great literary plans; but the pamphleteering of 1641–42 and after prevented him from doing so. All his training, instincts, desires, and circumstances point to what should have been the beginning of his supreme literary activity at about this time. Until after his return from Italy, he showed no sign of reaching a decision and almost no interest in publication, only a very few poems having been published and those unacknowledged except one or two which were initialed only. He was now ready and had made great plans to begin, as the cumulative evidence makes clear. In this connection we must not make the mistake of accepting the 1645 *Poems* as satisfying his urge for high literary performance. This volume was more or less an accident and makeshift. The year of his return from Italy was the year of the first sitting of the Long Parliament; and the events before the revolution of 1642 captured him. First the Presbyterians used his pen; then the Parliamentarians, and he became the champion of liberty — the champion of too much liberty to suit his former friends the Presbyterians; and finally the Council dominated him, made him Latin secretary in 1649, and saddled him immediately with the task of replying to the attack of Salmasius. He did not spare himself in any of this work, reading, studying, writing, and rewriting, until his eyesight and health both failed him completely, and he nearly died because of the labors piled on him.

---

[1] *Letters of State*, p. xxxv, and Helen Darbishire, *The Early Lives of Milton*, pp. 72–73.

Another important factor in the delay was his domestic situation. He succeeded in publishing a number of prose tracts and the *Poems* while his first wife remained away from him. During this period, he certainly continued his own literary activity, perhaps subordinating it to his publication of prose tracts, but by no means abandoning it. But after the return of Mary Powell, with her entire immediate family, such continued activity became impossible. On April 21, 1647, he wrote to Charles Dati, of Italy, of his regret that Dati had not received his three previously dispatched letters. He goes on to mention his domestic circumstances at that time.

> that sincere gladness of mine at the receipt of this [letter] began to be infected and troubled with a sad regret, and presently something heavier creeps in upon me, to which I am inured in most frequent sorrowings over my own fortune: the feeling that those thrown in close contact with me through the one necessity of proximity, or something equally as trivial, some by accident and some by legal ties, these are the people in whose company I must daily sit, though they are in no other respect worth mentioning. They bore me, no, by heaven, they all but pester me to death whenever they really feel like doing so. Those persons who by habit, disposition, and common taste had been my friends are shut off from me, either by death or removal, and thus mostly so kept from my sight that I live a very lonely existence.[1]

Then came the government work, increasing in its demands and claims on his time and energy. Surely the recently published correspondence between Milton and Mylius exhibits a weary and distracted man (1652). But from the perpetual darkness itself then descending upon him came relief, though he came to accept his blindness very slowly.

What would he have produced had he continued work on his major literary schemes after 1640? We do not know exactly; but undoubtedly their general outlines had been cast about the time he turned to the combat with the 'adversaries of liberty.'

In 1641/42, Milton stated his literary ambitions and plans in an unmistakable manner.[2] He said that he had determined 'to fix all the industry and art I could unite to the adorning of my native tongue' and to be 'an interpreter and relater of the best and sagest things among mine own citizens throughout this island in the mother dialect.' He was still thinking of using material from British history that 'what the greatest and choicest wits of Athens, Rome, or modern Italy, and those Hebrews of old did for their country, I in my proportion with this over and above of being a Christian, might do for mine.' He then elaborated his full literary plans as follows:

> Time serves not now, and perhaps I might seem too profuse to give any certain account of what the mind at home in the spacious circuits of her musing hath liberty to propose to herself, though of highest hope, and hardest attempting, whether that epic form whereof the two poems of Homer, and those other two of Virgil and Tasso are a diffuse, and the book of Job a brief model: or whether the rules of Aristotle herein are strictly to be kept, or nature followed, which in them that know art, and use judgment is no transgression, but an enriching of art. And lastly what King or knight before the Conquest might be chosen in whom to lay the pattern of a Christian hero. And as Tasso gave to a prince of Italy his choice whether he would command him to write of Godfrey's expedition against the infidels, or Belisarius against the Goths, or Charlemagne against the Lombards; if to the instinct of nature and the emboldening of art ought may be trusted, and that there be nothing adverse in our climate, or the fate of this age, it haply would be no rashness from an equal diligence and inclination to present the like offer in our own ancient stories. Or whether those dramatic constitutions, wherein Sophocles and Euripides reign shall be found more doctrinal and exemplary to a nation, the scripture also affords us a divine pastoral drama in the Song of Solomon consisting of two persons and a double

---

[1] *Familiar Epistle 10, Col.* XII: 47.   [2] *Reason of Church Government*, 1641/42. *Col.* III: 1:236.

chorus, as Origen rightly judges.   And the Apocalypse of Saint John is the majestic image of a
high and stately tragedy, shutting up and intermingling her solemn scenes and acts with a sevenfold chorus of hallelujahs and harping symphonies: and this my opinion the grave authority of
Paraeus commenting that book is sufficient to confirm.   Or if occasion shall lead to imitate those
magnific odes and hymns wherein Pindarus and Callimachus are in most things worthy, some
others in their frame judicious, in their matter most an end faulty: But those frequent songs
throughout the Law and Prophets beyond all these, not in their divine argument alone, but in
the very critical art of composition may be easily made appear over all the kinds of lyric poesy,
to be incomparable.[1]

But, he continues, circumstances now prevented him from carrying out these literary
plans.   He must turn from his personal program and plans 'with small willingness' to
combat the bishops 'now when all men offer their aid to help ease and lighten the difficult
labors of the Church.'   But he would return to his poetry when 'the land had once en-
franchised herself from this impertinent yoke of prelaty.'   He asks the indulgence of
those interested in his literary plans 'that for some few years yet I may go on trust with
him toward the payment of what I am now indebted... till which in some measure be
compassed, at mine own peril and cost I refuse not to sustain this expectation from as
many as are not loath to hazard so much credulity upon the best pledges that I can give
them.'[2]

Paradise Lost is the fulfillment of his promise.   It is his great poem 'of highest hope,
and hardest attempting' in 'that epic form whereof the two poems of Homer and those
other two of Virgil and Tasso are a diffuse... model.'   *Paradise Regained* is the outcome
of his conception of a Christian epic 'whereof... the book of Job [is] a brief model';
and *Samson Agonistes* is his 'best example' of 'those dramatic constitutions, wherein
Sophocles and Euripides reign' that are 'doctrinal and exemplary to a nation.'[3]

Despite all attempts to account for their completion otherwise, we owe *Paradise Lost*,
and subsequently *Paradise Regained* and *Samson Agonistes* more to one factor in Milton's
life than to any other.   When, in 1641, he plunged into controversial pamphleteering
and then became the mouthpiece of the Council and Protectorates, he did so without
regret and wholeheartedly.   Though he felt that he wrote prose 'as with [his] left
hand,' nevertheless, he threw himself, literally body and soul, into the fray, consecrat-
ing himself to the task before him.

He says in the letter of 1647 that the

most turbulent state of our Britain... obliged me to divert my mind... from the prosecution
of my studies to the defence anyhow of life and fortune.[4]

In 1654, his eyesight gone and in the midst of domestic turmoil, he writes to Oldenburg,
who has evidently told him that he should be less engaged in controversy than in his
own work, that

this unexpected contest with the Adversaries of Liberty took me off against my will when I
was intent on far different and altogether pleasanter studies: not that in any way I repent of

---

[1] *Ibid. Col.* III:1:237.   [2] *Ibid.*, p. 241.

[3] Professor W. R. Parker with proper caution argues that this passage must not be taken as an announcement in
1641/42 that Milton then definitely intended to write each of the three long poems, *Paradise Lost, Paradise Regained*, and *Samson Agonistes*.   Such a warning should be carefully heeded by the student of *Paradise Lost*; but the
statement quoted above actually became an important step in the formation of the poet's literary ambitions.   It
is especially notable in retrospect, however little it may have been the outline of a definite program at the time it
was written.   See W. R. Parker, 'On Milton's Early Literary Program,' *Modern Philology*, XXXIII:49–53 (1935).

[4] *Fam. Ep. 10, Col.* XII:51.

what I have done, since it was necessary: [note Satan's plea of necessity in *Paradise Lost*, especially IV:393-94

> So spake the fiend, and with necessity,
> The tyrant's plea, excused his devilish deeds.]

for I am far from thinking that I have spent my toil, as you seem to think, on matters of inferior consequence.[1]

But willingly or unwillingly, regretfully or without regret, once he turned to the work of the Council and to controversy, and his pen became through the *Pro Populo* the most powerful and most feared pen in England against the 'Adversaries of Liberty,' and for what he later, in 1660, called 'the Old Cause,' nothing could have stopped him or caused him to turn back, except that which did stop him. This was his blindness. To it and to the frustrations it brought with it we owe his major poems. For though his blindness remained to him 'a sorer affliction than old age,' it slowly released him from the domestic and public turmoils about him. He felt by 1654 that a return to his own literary activities would be a great relief after the kind of life he had been living.

> To prepare myself, as you suggest, for other labors; — whether nobler or more useful I know not, for what can be nobler or more useful in human affairs than the vindication of Liberty? — truly if my health permit, and this blindness of mine, a sorer affliction than old age, and lastly the 'cries' of such brawlers as there have been about me, I shall be induced to *that* easily enough. An idle ease has never had charms for me ... [2]

In 1658, he found means of issuing a second edition of the *Pro Populo* and, as Professor Hanford surmises,[3] by that year or the year before had completed his 'body of divinity' which we know as the *De Doctrina*. He had been busy after the death of Mary Powell in 1652 with his secretarial duties; but had found time to work on a Latin thesaurus and probably a Greek one; to compile the *De Doctrina*; and to issue a second edition of the *Pro Populo*, having carried on the spirited controversy growing out of the first edition of that work. At the end of that second edition is added a fairly long paragraph. Part of it interests us here. This is the statement that, proud as he is of the *Pro Populo* and the attention that has been accorded it, he is now about to begin an even greater piece of work. This can only refer to *Paradise Lost* or to his decision on its exact form and nature. He worked on it without serious interruption straight through the Restoration and its ensuing turmoils until he finished it sometime between 1663 and 1665. He published it in 1667.

THE VERSE

The verse of *Paradise Lost* is normally an unrhymed line with ten syllables and five accents in rising rhythm or unrhymed iambic pentameter. A normal line begins and continues throughout with an unaccented syllable ahead of an accented syllable.

Examples of such a normal line are: *Paradise Lost* I:56 and I:58. This is the normal line but there are frequent deviations of various kinds.

1. Variations of number of syllables in the line.

    a. Extra syllables, i.e., more than ten syllables. Examples: *Paradise Lost* I:98,

---

[1] *Fam. Ep. 14, Col. XII:65.*   [2] *Ibid.*

[3] J. H. Hanford, 'The Date of Milton's *De Doctrina Christiana*,' *Studies in Philology*, XVII:309-18 (1920).

102; IX:249. The extra syllable or syllables could be introduced at any point in the line.

b. Deficiency of syllables, i.e., less than ten. Some metricists deny the existence of such lines in *Paradise Lost*. Bridges says, 'It must be concluded that Milton rejected this form (i.e., nine syllables) of the line.' [1]

2. Variation in the placing of accent.

The normal accent occurs as in an iamb, but frequently Milton varies this placement by putting the accented syllable ahead of the unaccented syllable. He may do this at the opening of a line, as I:10, 65. He may also put this variation in accent elsewhere in the line, as I:1; VII:543; X:840; VI:472. Such a shift in accent occurring at the end of a line as in the last two instances cited is very rare, but it does occur.

3. Variation in the number of accents.

The normal line of *Paradise Lost* contains five accents, as in I:56. Variations may augment or diminish the number of accents to the line. There are some lines which have only three accents as:

'Immutable, immortal, infinite'

and

'Of happiness and final misery'

Other lines contain four accents, such as I:74:

'As from the center thrice to the utmost pole.'

and I:64:

'Served only to discover sights of woe'

and I:63:

'No light, but rather darkness visible'

Occasionally Milton introduces a line with more than five accents, as II:902:

'Light-armed or heavy, sharp, smooth, swift or slow'

Even more rarely he might introduce a line of more than six accents, as II:621:

'Rocks, caves, lakes, fens, bogs, dens, and shades of death'

4. The position of the caesura or break of the line.

The ordinary position of the caesura in English blank verse is such that the line falls into two balanced parts. In Surrey's blank verse version of the *Aeneid*, the caesura occurs almost exactly in the middle of the line. The Elizabethan dramatists with their freedom in such matters tended to depart from such regularity, although only Shakespeare, perhaps, in his dramatic blank verse succeeded in manipulating it successfully by moving it about from one line to another in complete freedom. Milton completely mastered such control of the caesura and it is characteristic of him to manipulate it in *Paradise Lost* in two ways:

a. He moved it back and forth, in one line and another, using practically every possible position in the line at which a break could occur. That is, the break may occur after any light or heavy accent, depending upon the individual line, or

[1] Robert Bridges, *Milton's Prosody* (Oxford: [Oxford University Press], 1921), p. 5.

early in the line, or late in the line. A very few lines read best with no caesura at all; but this is unusual.

b. Not only does Milton persistently shift the caesura back and forth in the line, but he may introduce in a given line not one but two main breaks as in III:412,

'Hail Son of God, saviour of men, thy name.'

But one needs no technical knowledge of English metrics to appreciate Milton's superb mastery of the architectonics and harmonics of the verse structure of *Paradise Lost*. Picking any five hundred lines of the poem and reading them aloud, anyone will be impressed by the individuality of his metrical practice, of his supreme mastery of English rhythms, and feel himself in the presence of the greatest master of non-dramatic blank verse in the language. *Paradise Lost* is his greatest metrical accomplishment.

Most striking of all Milton's metrical devices is his development of the verse paragraph. His earlier poetry contains many experiments with it, but in *Paradise Lost*, the verse paragraph becomes the principal structural unit of the poem. Unlike the stanza, it permitted a degree of flexibility of both quantity and quality of poetry that exactly suited Milton's peculiar poetic powers. He is the complete master of the device throughout the poem.

To secure as much control of his verse as possible, Milton also adopted another device that became most effective as he used it. This was his system, if it be a system, of punctuation in the poem. He could not completely control it, as the printer had the last word; but in so far as he could use punctuation under control, he intended it to be an integral part of the metrical devices of the poem. That is, when the poem is punctuated as he intended, the punctuation is actually part of the metrical structure and each mark becomes the sign of a pause, heavy or light, in the meter. It is not exactly the type of punctuation used today, as modern punctuation depends on certain conventions and meaning. The punctuation which Milton used is not at all conventional, and depends much more on meter than on meaning in the lines, although these two elements tend to become identical, and in the most successful lines they are identical.

The great danger to the successful reading and appreciation of the poem is that our attention will be drawn too greatly to its cosmology, its theology, its angelology, its verse structure, its use of epic devices and conventions, its punctuation, or to some other element that may easily be allowed to come between the reader and the poem as poetry. Consequently, reading and re-reading of it is necessary and inevitable. Gradually the majestic sweep of the verse like the seas of a great ocean takes hold of us, and we are overwhelmed by the totality of its effects. All the elements that go to make it up gradually merge into the one supreme experience of the poem as a whole.

REFERENCES

Text

Baxter, W. E., 'Milton's *Paradise Lost*,' *Transactions of the Bibliographical Society* (London), VI:152–55 (1902). See also same title in *The Bibliographer* (New York), II:73–91 (1903).
Beeching, H. C., *Poetical Works*. Oxford: Oxford University Press, 1900.
Hammond, J. H., forthcoming article on the first edition of *Paradise Lost*.
Patterson, F. A., *Works*, II:2:485–540.

Commentary

H.[ume], P.[atrick], *Notes on Paradise Lost*. London, 1695.
Masson, David, *Poetical Works*.
Newton, Thomas, *Paradise Lost*.
Todd, H. J., *Poetical Works*.
Verity, A. W., *The Cambridge Milton for Schools*. Cambridge, 1891–96. 10 vols.

Prosody

Bridges, Robert, *Milton's Prosody*. Oxford: [Oxford University Press], 1893. Revised edition, 1921.

THE AGREEMENT BETWEEN MILTON AND SAMUEL SIMMONS FOR THE PUBLICATION OF *PARADISE LOST*

These presents made the 27th day of April 1667 between John Milton gentleman of the one party and Samuel Symons printer of the other party, witness: that the said John Milton in consideration of five pounds to him now paid by the said Samuel Symons and other the consideration herein mentioned hath given granted and assigned, and by these points doth give grant and assign unto the said Samuel Symons his executors and assigns all that book copy or manuscript of a poem entitled *Paradise Lost*, or by whatsoever other title or name the same is or shall be called or distinguished now lately licensed to be printed, together with the full benefit profit and advantage thereof, or which shall or may arise thereby. And the said John Milton for him his executors and administrators, doth covenant with the said Samuel Symons his executors and assigns, that he and they shall at all times hereafter have hold and enjoy the same and all impressions thereof accordingly, without the let or hinderance of him, the said John Milton his executors or assigns or any person or persons by his or their consent or privity. And that the said John Milton his executors or administrators, or any other by his or their means or consent shall not print or cause to be printed, or sell dispose or publish the said book or manuscript or any other book or manuscript of the same tenor or subject without the consent of the said Samuel Symons his executors or assigns. In consideration whereof the said Samuel Symons for him his executors and administrators, doth covenant with the said John Milton his executors and assigns, well and truly to pay unto the said John Milton his executors and administrators, the sum of five pounds of lawful English money at the end of the first impression which the said Samuel Symons, his executors or assigns, shall make and publish of the said copy or manuscript, which impression shall be accounted to be ended when thirteen hundred books of the said whole copy or manuscript imprinted shall be sold and retailed off to particular reading customers: And shall also pay other five pounds unto the said Mr. Milton or his assigns, at the end of the second impression to be accounted as aforesaid, and five pounds more at the end of the third impression to be in like manner accounted; and that the said three impressions shall not exceed fifteen hundred books or volumes of the said whole copy or manuscript apiece. And further, that he the said Samuel Symons, and his executors and assigns, shall be ready to make oath before a master in chancery concerning his or their knowledge and belief of or concerning the truth of the disposing and selling the said books by retail as aforesaid whereby the said Mr. Milton is to be entitled to his said money from time to time upon every reasonable request in that behalf, or in default thereof shall pay the said five pounds agreed to be paid upon each impression as aforesaid as if the same were due, and for and in lieu thereof. In witness whereof the said parties have to this writing indented interchangeably set their hands and seals, the day and year first abovewritten

[Signed] John Milton   [Seal]
[The signature is not Milton's, as he was totally blind at this time. This is Simmons' copy and consequently lacks his signature, which would have been on Milton's copy.]

Sealed and delivered in the
   presence of us,
[Signed] John Fisher
[Signed] Benjamin Greene
   servant to Mr. Milton.

EXTRACTS FROM THE *TRINITY COLLEGE MANUSCRIPT* OF PLANS AND TOPICS FOR LITERARY DEVELOPMENT

I

[Earliest Outline of *Paradise Lost*, from p. 35 of *MS.*, p. 33 of 1899 reproduction]

[All this material to the next heading is struck out.]

The Persons

Michael
Heavenly Love
Chorus of Angels
Lucifer
Adam ⎫
Eve ⎭ with the Serpent
Conscience
Death
Labor ⎫
Sickness ⎬ mutes
Discontent ⎭
Ignorance
with others
Faith
Hope
Charity

other Tragedies
Adam ~~ex~~ in Banishment
The Flood
Abram in Egypt.

The Persons

Moses ~~or~~ ~~(Divine~~ (Wisdom
~~Michael~~ ∧ Justice. Mercy
Heavenly Love
The Evening Star Hesperus
                  2   3   1
Chorus of Angels
Lucifer
Adam
Eve
Conscience
~~Death~~
Labor ⎫
Sickness ⎪
Discontent ⎬ mutes
Ignorance ⎪
Fear ⎪
Death ⎭
Faith
Hope
Charity

II

[Another Outline on same page]

Paradise Lost   The Persons   his

Moses *prologizei* [in Greek] recounting how he assumed ~~a~~ true body, that it corrupts not because of his [abode] with God in the mount declares the like of Enoch and Eliah, besides the purity of the pl[ace] that certain winds, dews, and clouds preserve it from corruption whence ~~Heavenly Love~~ [ex]horts to the sight of God, tells they cannot see Adam in the state of innocence by reason of ~~sin~~ their sin.

Justice ⎫ ~~Mercy~~
Mercy ⎬ debating what should become of man if he fall
Wisdom ⎭
Chorus of Angels sing a (hymn of the creation)

Act 2.
Heavenly Love
Evening star
Chorus sing the marriage song and describe Paradise

Act 3.
Lucifer contriving Adam's ruin
   Chorus fears for Adam and relates Lucifer's rebellion and fall

Act 4.
Adam ⎫
Eve   fallen ⎬
Conscience cites them to God's examination
Chorus bewails and tells the good Adam hath lost

Act 5.
Adam and Eve, driven out of Paradise
  presented by an angel with
  labor, grief, hatred, envy, war, famine, pestilence
  sickness   ⎫ mutes to whom he gives
  discontent ⎪ their names
  ignorance ⎬ likewise winter, heat tempest &c
  fear   ⎭ entered into the world
  death   ／
  Faith   ⎫
  Hope   ⎬ comfort and instruct him
  Charity ⎭
    Chorus briefly concludes

[Topics from the *Manuscript*]

III

[From p. 34 of reproduction]

Samson pursophorus   ·   marriing or
  or Hybristes or   Samson ∧ in Ramath Lechi Jud. 15.
Dagonalia Jud. 16.

IV

[From p. 38 of reproduction]

Christ bound
Christ crucified
Christ risen

V

[From p. 38 of reproduction]
Adam unparadised
Adam~~'s Banishment~~

The angel Gabriel, either descending or entering, showing since this globe was created, his frequency as much on earth, as in heaven, describes Paradise. next ~~first~~ the Chorus showing the reason of his coming to keep his watch in Paradise after Lucifer's rebellion by command from God, & withal expressing his desire to see, & know more concerning this excellent new creature man.   The angel Gabriel as by his name signifying a prince of power tracing Paradise with a more free office ~~comes~~ passes by the station of the chorus & desired by them relates what he knew of man as the creation of Eve with their love, & marriage.   After this Lucifer appears after his overthrow, bemoans himself, seeks revenge on man the Chorus prepare resistance at his first approach at last after discourse of enmity on either side he departs whereat the chorus sings of the battle, & victory in heaven against him & his accomplices, as before after the first act was sung a hymn of the creation.*   Man next & Eve having by this time been seduced by the serpent appears confusedly covered with leaves conscience in a shape accuses him, Justice cites him to the place whither Jehovah called for him in the meanwhile the chorus entertains the stage, & his [sic] informed by some angel the manner of his fall.*   Adam then & Eve return accuse one another but especially Adam lays the blame to his wife, is stubborn in his offence Justice appears reason with him convinces him*   The angel is sent to banish them out of Paradise but before causes to pass before his eyes in shapes a mask of all the evils of this life & world he is humbled relents, despairs.   At last appears mercy comforts him ~~& brings in faith hope and charity~~ promises the Messiah, then calls in faith, hope, and charity, instructs him he repents gives God the glory, submits to his penalty the chorus briefly concludes.   compare this with the former draft.

VI

[Another Topic from p. 41 of *MS*. and p. 39 of reproduction]

Christus patiens

The scene in the garden beginning from the coming thither till Judas betrays and the officers lead him away the rest by message and chorus.   His agony ~~make~~ may receive noble expressions

* here again may appear Lucifer relating, & insulting in what he had done to the destruction of man
* here the Chorus bewails Adam's fall
* the Chorus admonishes Adam, and bids him beware by Lucifer's example of impenitence

Paradise Lost

(*1640–1665*)

A Poem in Twelve Books

Some of the old biographers state that this poem was written piecemeal, and the more the poem is studied, the more the reader's conviction grows that such was actually the case. The poem was doubtless begun in one form or another about 1640. Probably in its early stages, it was projected as a drama. Then, probably by 1650, the dramatic form was abandoned, and work begun on the poem as an epic. It was probably again laid aside, to be taken up again about 1658, and was completed in the third period about 1663–65. It was first printed in 1667.

About fifteen hundred copies, all that were allowed in a single printing, were printed. It was printed in small quarto, and apparently was first sold with text only, which in this edition was in ten books. There are two different title pages bearing the date 1667. The agreement with the first printer or publisher, Samuel Simmons, which is still extant, is dated April 27, 1667. The book was licensed for sale at three shillings during the week of August 20, 1667. Soon after its original appearance, additional preliminary sheets were added which included a statement from the printer to the reader, prose arguments for each book of the poem by the author, a statement about the verse by the author, and a list of errata. There are at least three different states of these preliminary leaves. These leaves were certainly issued with the second 1667 title page, and with any or all subsequent title pages. The edition exists bound with or without various states of the preliminary leaves, and with six different title pages, two dated 1667, two 1668, and two 1669. There are, therefore, twenty-four possible binding combinations. Minor differences in the text are found in different copies; but only one of these, the so-called cancel of the final two leaves in the second 1669 binding, is connected with a particular title page, as the text proper was printed complete and then title pages were printed as needed and bound with the text as sold. There is a manuscript copy extant of the first book only, probably used by the printer for the first edition and certainly used by the licenser. This manuscript is now in the Morgan Library in New York.[1]

Milton published a second edition of the poem in 1674. In it he divided the poem into twelve books instead of ten, which necessitated the addition of a few transitional lines here and there, and distributed the arguments at the beginning of the proper books throughout. This edition was licensed for sale at three shillings during the week of July 6, 1674, by Roger L'Estrange. Less than six months later Milton was dead. This second

---

[1] Helen Darbishire, *The Manuscript of Paradise Lost* (Oxford: Clarendon Press, 1931). The writing is not Milton's. The holograph copy is reproduced and a printed transcript provided.

edition was a smaller book than the first edition, on the whole was more carefully printed, but in much poorer and smaller type.

THE VERSE

The measure is English heroic verse without rhyme, as that of Homer in Greek, and of Virgil in Latin; rhyme being no necessary adjunct or true ornament of poem or good verse, in longer works especially, but the invention of a barbarous age, to set off wretched matter and lame meter; graced indeed since by the use of some famous modern poets, carried away by custom, but much to their own vexation, hindrance, and constraint to express many things otherwise, and for the most part worse than else they would have expressed them. Not without cause therefore some both Italian and Spanish poets of prime note have rejected rhyme both in longer and shorter works, as have also long since our best English tragedies, as a thing of itself, to all judicious ears, trivial and of no true musical delight; which consists only in apt numbers, fit quantity of syllables, and the sense variously drawn out from one verse into another, not in the jingling sound of like endings, a fault avoided by the learned ancients both in poetry and all good oratory. This neglect then of rhyme so little is to be taken for a defect, though it may seem so perhaps to vulgar readers, that it rather is to be esteemed an example set, the first in English, of ancient liberty recovered to heroic poem from the troublesome and modern bondage of rhyming.

BOOK I

THE ARGUMENT

This first book proposes, first in brief, the whole subject, Man's disobedience, and the loss thereupon of Paradise wherein he was placed: Then touches the prime cause of his fall, the serpent, or rather Satan in the serpent; who revolting from God, and drawing to his side many legions of angels, was by the command of God driven out of heaven with all his crew into the great deep. Which action passed over, the poem hastes into the midst of things, presenting Satan with his angels now fallen into hell, described here, not in the center (for heaven and earth may be supposed as yet not made, certainly not yet accursed) but in a place of utter darkness, fitliest called chaos: Here Satan with his angels lying on the burning lake, thunderstruck and astonished, after a certain space recovers, as from confusion, calls up him who next in order and dignity lay by him; they confer of their miserable fall. Satan awakens all his legions, who lay till then in the same manner confounded; They rise, their numbers, array of battle, their chief leaders named, according to the idols known afterwards in Canaan and the countries adjoining. To these Satan directs his speech, comforts them with hope yet of regaining heaven, but tells them lastly of a new world and new kind of creature to be created, according to an ancient prophecy or report in heaven; for that angels were long before this visible creation, was the opinion of many ancient fathers. To find out the truth of this prophecy, and what to determine thereon he refers to a full council. What his associates thence attempt. Pandemonium the palace of Satan rises, suddenly built out of the deep: The infernal peers there sit in council.

> Of man's first disobedience, and the fruit
> Of that forbidden tree, whose mortal taste
> Brought death into the world, and all our woe,
> With loss of Eden, till one greater man

4. **greater man:** referring to the Christ.

Restore us, and regain the blissful seat,   5
Sing heavenly muse, that on the secret top
Of Oreb, or of Sinai, didst inspire
That shepherd, who first taught the chosen seed,
In the beginning how the heavens and earth
Rose out of chaos: Or if Sion hill   10
Delight thee more, and Siloa's brook that flowed
Fast by the oracle of God; I thence
Invoke thy aid to my adventurous song,
That with no middle flight intends to soar
Above the Aonian mount, while it pursues   15
Things unattempted yet in prose or rhyme.
And chiefly thou, O spirit, that dost prefer
Before all temples the upright heart and pure,
Instruct me, for thou knowest; thou from the first
Wast present, and, with mighty wings outspread   20
Dove-like satest brooding on the vast abyss
And madest it pregnant: What in me is dark
Illumine, what is low raise and support;
That to the height of this great argument
I may assert eternal providence,   25
And justify the ways of God to men.
   Say first, for heaven hides nothing from thy view,
Nor the deep tract of hell, say first what cause
Moved our grand parents in that happy state,
Favored of heaven so highly, to fall off   30
From their creator, and transgress his will
For one restraint, lords of the world besides?
Who first seduced them to that foul revolt?
The infernal serpent; he it was, whose guile
Stirred up with envy and revenge, deceived   35
The mother of mankind, what time his pride
Had cast him out from heaven, with all his host
Of rebel angels, by whose aid aspiring
To set himself in glory above his peers,

6–26. **heavenly muse:** the Holy Spirit that inspired the writers of Scripture. Cf. the 'eternal spirit' cited in *Reason of Church Government.*

8. **that shepherd:** Moses.

10 ff. **Sion hill . . . Siloa's brook . . . oracle of God:** Jerusalem and the temple.

13. **adventurous:** in the old editions, the word is printed 'adventrous.' Phillips' *World of Words* (1706) defines *adventurous* as 'hazardous, bold.'

15. **Aonian mount:** a mountain of Boeotia, Helicon, the haunt of the muses. Milton intends to surpass the ancients. Thus, the 'muse' addressed in this opening invocation is a composite made up of the muse of epic poetry, the spirit that inspired the Hebrew prophets, and the Holy Ghost itself.

17. **thou, O spirit:** some copies of 1674 edition read 'thou O spirit,' others have a comma after 'thou' though it is lacking in first edition.   It is lacking in 1678 (third edition), but occurs in 1688–95, only to disappear again until 1727, and was then present through Newton's edition, 1749 *ss.*

21–22. **dove-like, etc.:** cf. *Genesis* 1:2.

25–26. These lines announce one, perhaps the principal, aim of the poem. But other aims are mentioned.

29. **grand parents:** Adam and Eve.

35. **envy and revenge:** Satan's motivation in his whole attitude towards mankind.

He trusted to have equaled the most high, 40
If he opposed; and with ambitious aim
Against the throne and monarchy of God
Raised impious war in heaven and battle proud
With vain attempt. Him the almighty power
Hurled headlong flaming from the ethereal sky 45
With hideous ruin and combustion down
To bottomless perdition, there to dwell
In adamantine chains and penal fire,
Who durst defy the omnipotent to arms.
Nine times the space that measures day and night 50
To mortal men, he with his horrid crew
Lay vanquished, rolling in the fiery gulf
Confounded though immortal: But his doom
Reserved him to more wrath; for now the thought
Both of lost happiness and lasting pain 55
Torments him; round he throws his baleful eyes
That witnessed huge affliction and dismay
Mixed with obdurate pride and steadfast hate:
At once as far as angels' ken he views
The dismal situation waste and wild, 60
A dungeon horrible, on all sides round
As one great furnace flamed, yet from those flames
No light, but rather darkness visible
Served only to discover sights of woe,
Regions of sorrow, doleful shades, where peace 65
And rest can never dwell, hope never comes
That comes to all; but torture without end
Still urges, and a fiery deluge, fed
With ever-burning sulphur unconsumed:
Such place eternal justice had prepared 70
For those rebellious, here their prison ordained
In utter darkness, and their portion set
As far removed from God and light of heaven
As from the center thrice to the utmost pole.
O how unlike the place from whence they fell! 75
There the companions of his fall, o'erwhelmed
With floods and whirlwinds of tempestuous fire,
He soon discerns, and weltering by his side
One next himself in power, and next in crime,

44–47. These famous lines are Milton's rendition of traditional accounts of the fall of the rebel angels. Cf. especially Heywood's *Hierarchy of the Blessed Angels*, Lib. VI.

56. **baleful**: full of sorrow or woe.

59. **ken**: a noun. But many commentators insist it is a verb.

63. **darkness visible**: the first of many oxymorons, imitating Homer.

68. **urges**: to press upon.

72. **utter**: a half-pun, the word meaning originally the same as 'outer' and here partaking of both meanings, outer, and complete.

74. See *D. & D., Col.* III:2:442, 'hell ... that uttermost and bottomless gulf of chaos, deeper from holy bliss than the world's diameter multiplied.' Cf. *infra*, I:91–92; 247; 282.

78. **weltering**: Phillips, 'to wallow, or lie grovelling.'

Long after known in Palestine, and named   80
Beelzebub.   To whom the arch-enemy,
And thence in heaven called Satan, with bold words
Breaking the horrid silence thus began.
       'If thou beest he; but O how fallen! how changed
From him, who in the happy realms of light   85
Clothed with transcendent brightness didst outshine
Myriads though bright: If he whom mutual league,
United thoughts and counsels, equal hope
And hazard in the glorious enterprise,
Joined with me once, now misery hath joined   90
In equal ruin: into what pit thou seest
From what height fallen, so much the stronger proved
He with his thunder: and till then who knew
The force of those dire arms? yet not for those,
Nor what the potent victor in his rage   95
Can else inflict, do I repent or change,
Though changed in outward luster; that fixed mind
And high disdain, from sense of injured merit,
That with the mightiest raised me to contend,
And to the fierce contention brought along   100
Innumerable force of spirits armed
That durst dislike his reign, and me preferring,
His utmost power with adverse power opposed
In dubious battle on the plains of heaven,
And shook his throne. What though the field be lost?   105
All is not lost; the unconquerable will,
And study of revenge, immortal hate,
And courage never to submit or yield;
And what is else not to be overcome?
That glory never shall his wrath or might   110
Extort from me.   To bow and sue for grace
With suppliant knee, and deify his power,
Who from the terror of this arm so late
Doubted his empire, that were low indeed,
That were an ignominy and shame beneath   115
This downfall; since by fate the strength of gods
And this empyreal substance cannot fail,
Since through experience of this great event
In arms not worse, in foresight much advanced,
We may with more successful hope resolve   120
To wage by force or guile eternal war
Irreconcilable, to our grand foe,
Who now triumphs, and in the excess of joy
Sole reigning holds the tyranny of heaven.'

81. **Beelzebub:** from *Matthew* 12:24.   The name in Hebrew means 'Lord of Flies,' but of flies as pests, not as little creatures.

81–82. **arch-enemy . . . Satan:** the word *Satan* in Hebrew means 'adversary' and never occurs in the *OT* without the definite article.

84 ff. Note how the incomplete sentences and general construction reflect the emotional turmoil in the speaker.   117. **empyreal substance:** the angels were non-material essences.

So spake the apostate angel, though in pain,   125
Vaunting aloud, but racked with deep despair:
And him thus answered soon his bold compeer.
    'O prince, O chief of many throned powers,
That led the embattled seraphim to war
Under thy conduct, and in dreadful deeds   130
Fearless, endangered heaven's perpetual king;
And put to proof his high supremacy,
Whether upheld by strength, or chance, or fate,
Too well I see and rue the dire event,
That with sad overthrow and foul defeat   135
Hath lost us heaven, and all this mighty host
In horrible destruction laid thus low,
As far as gods and heavenly essences
Can perish: for the mind and spirit remains
Invincible, and vigor soon returns,   140
Though all our glory extinct, and happy state
Here swallowed up in endless misery.
But what if he our conqueror, (whom I now
Of force believe almighty, since no less
Than such could have o'erpowered such force as ours)   145
Have left us this our spirit and strength entire
Strongly to suffer and support our pains,
That we may so suffice his vengeful ire,
Or do him mightier service as his thralls
By right of war, whate'er his business be   150
Here in the heart of hell to work in fire,
Or do his errands in the gloomy deep;
What can it then avail though yet we feel
Strength undiminished, or eternal being
To undergo eternal punishment?'   155
    Whereto with speedy words the arch-fiend replied.
    'Fallen cherub, to be weak is miserable
Doing or suffering: but of this be sure,
To do aught good never will be our task,
But ever to do ill our sole delight,   160
As being the contrary to his high will
Whom we resist.   If then his providence
Out of our evil seek to bring forth good,
Our labor must be to pervert that end,
And out of good still to find means of evil;   165
Which ofttimes may succeed, so as perhaps
Shall grieve him, if I fail not, and disturb
His inmost counsels from their destined aim.
But see the angry victor hath recalled
His ministers of vengeance and pursuit   170
Back to the gates of heaven: the sulphurous hail

128-29. **powers . . . seraphim:** the angels were early divided into hierarchies, with upper and lower ranks.   Milton recognizes all the ranks, but never clearly intended to discriminate between their relative positions.

167. **if I fail not:** if I am not mistaken.

Shot after us in storm, o'erblown hath laid
The fiery surge, that from the precipice
Of heaven received us falling, and the thunder,
Winged with red lightning and impetuous rage,   175
Perhaps hath spent his shafts, and ceases now
To bellow through the vast and boundless deep.
Let us not slip the occasion, whether scorn,
Or satiate fury yield it from our foe.
Seest thou yon dreary plain, forlorn and wild,   180
The seat of desolation, void of light,
Save what the glimmering of these livid flames
Casts pale and dreadful?   Thither let us tend
From off the tossing of these fiery waves,
There rest, if any rest can harbor there,   185
And reassembling our afflicted powers,
Consult how we may henceforth most offend
Our enemy, our own loss how repair,
How overcome this dire calamity,
What reinforcement we may gain from hope,   190
If not what resolution from despair.
     Thus Satan talking to his nearest mate
With head uplift above the wave, and eyes
That sparkling blazed, his other parts besides
Prone on the flood, extended long and large   195
Lay floating many a rood, in bulk as huge
As whom the fables name of monstrous size,
Titanian, or earth-born, that warred on Jove,
Briareos or Typhon, whom the den
By ancient Tarsus held, or that sea-beast   200
Leviathan, which God of all his works
Created hugest that swim the ocean stream:
Him haply slumbering on the Norway foam
The pilot of some small night-foundered skiff,
Deeming some island, oft, as seamen tell,   205
With fixed anchor in his scaly rind
Moors by his side under the lee, while night
Invests the sea, and wished morn delays:
So stretched out huge in length the arch-fiend lay
Chained on the burning lake, nor ever thence   210
Had risen or heaved his head, but that the will
And high permission of all-ruling heaven
Left him at large to his own dark designs,
That with reiterated crimes he might
Heap on himself damnation, while he sought   215
Evil to others, and enraged might see

199. **Briareos:** in Greek mythology, a son of Uranus, and meant to represent the Titans and later the Giants.   **Typhon:** commonly described as a hundred-headed serpent-monster, who, seeking to seize sovereignty over gods and men, was slain by Zeus with a thunderbolt and buried under Etna.

200. **ancient Tarsus:** Tarsus was the capital of Cilicia.   Pindar and Aeschylus have Typhon living in a 'Cilician den.'

201. **Leviathan, etc.:** a common traveler's tale is that of mistaking a whale for an island.

How all his malice served but to bring forth
Infinite goodness, grace and mercy shown
On man by him seduced, but on himself
Treble confusion, wrath and vengeance poured.   220
Forthwith upright he rears from off the pool
His mighty stature; on each hand the flames
Driven backward slope their pointing spires, and rolled
In billows, leave in the midst a horrid vale.
Then with expanded wings he steers his flight   225
Aloft, incumbent on the dusky air
That felt unusual weight, till on dry land
He lights, if it were land that ever burned
With solid, as the lake with liquid fire;
And such appeared in hue, as when the force   230
Of subterranean wind transports a hill
Torn from Pelorus, or the shattered side
Of thundering Etna, whose combustible
And fueled entrails thence conceiving fire,
Sublimed with mineral fury, aid the winds,   235
And leave a singed bottom all involved
With stench and smoke: Such resting found the sole
Of unblest feet.   Him followed his next mate,
Both glorying to have scaped the Stygian flood
As gods, and by their own recovered strength,   240
Not by the sufferance of supernal power.
   'Is this the region, this the soil, the clime,'
Said then the lost archangel, 'this the seat
That we must change for heaven, this mournful gloom
For that celestial light?   Be it so, since he   245
Who now is sovereign can dispose and bid
What shall be right: farthest from him is best
Whom reason hath equaled, force hath made supreme
Above his equals.   Farewell happy fields
Where joy forever dwells: Hail horrors, hail   250
Infernal world, and thou profoundest hell
Receive thy new possessor: One who brings
A mind not to be changed by place or time.
The mind is its own place, and in itself
Can make a heaven of hell, a hell of heaven.   255
What matter where, if I be still the same,
And what I should be, all but less than he
Whom thunder hath made greater?   Here at least
We shall be free; the almighty hath not built
Here for his envy, will not drive us hence: 260

229–30. So 1667 and 1674 editions.   But *MS.* reads:
                    ... as the lake with liquid fire,
                    And such appeared in hue;
This punctuation is probably to be preferred.

230–31. **the force of subterranean wind transports a hill**: early theories of earthquakes usually relied on internal gases to explain the disturbance of the earth's surface.

232. **Pelorus**: now Cape Fero in Sicily, near Etna.

235. **sublimed**: sublimated.   A term from alchemy.

Here we may reign secure, and in my choice
To reign is worth ambition though in hell:
Better to reign in hell, than serve in heaven.
But wherefore let we then our faithful friends,
The associates and copartners of our loss   265
Lie thus astonished on the oblivious pool,
And call them not to share with us their part
In this unhappy mansion, or once more
With rallied arms to try what may be yet
Regained in heaven, or what more lost in hell?'   270
    So Satan spake, and him Beelzebub
Thus answered.   'Leader of those armies bright,
Which but the omnipotent none could have foiled
If once they hear that voice, their liveliest pledge
Of hope in fears and dangers, heard so oft   275
In worst extremes, and on the perilous edge
Of battle when it raged, in all assaults
Their surest signal, they will soon resume
New courage and revive, though now they lie
Groveling and prostrate on yon lake of fire,   280
As we erewhile, astounded and amazed,
No wonder, fallen such a pernicious height.'
    He scarce had ceased when the superior Fiend
Was moving toward the shore; his ponderous shield
Ethereal temper, massy, large and round,   285
Behind him cast; the broad circumference
Hung on his shoulders like the moon, whose orb
Through optic glass the Tuscan artist views
At evening from the top of Fesole,
Or in Valdarno, to descry new lands,   290
Rivers or mountains in her spotty globe.
His spear, to equal which the tallest pine
Hewn on Norwegian hills, to be the mast
Of some great ammiral, were but a wand,
He walked with to support uneasy steps   295
Over the burning marl, not like those steps
On heaven's azure, and the torrid clime
Smote on him sore besides, vaulted with fire;
Nathless he so endured, till on the beach
Of that inflamed sea, he stood and called   300
His legions, angel forms, who lay entranced
Thick as autumnal leaves that strew the brooks
In Vallombrosa, where the Etrurian shades

288. **optic glass:** the telescope.   **the Tuscan artist:** Galileo.   Milton says (*Areopagitica*) that while in Italy he 'saw and visited' the famous user of telescopes.

289. **Fesole:** Italian *Fiesole*, classical Foesulae, a hill about three miles northeast of Florence.

290. **Valdarno:** the valley of the Arno River, in which lies Florence.

294. **ammiral:** the same word as *admiral*, which meant both the officer and the ship he officered.   Cf. *ameer* from the Arabic.

296. **marl:** Phillips defined it as 'a kind of fat earth.'   It is usually a clay heavy in calcium compounds.

303. **Vallombrosa:** literally 'shady valley,' about eighteen miles from Florence.

High over arched embower; or scattered sedge
Afloat, when with fierce winds Orion armed   305
Hath vexed the Red Sea coast, whose waves o'erthrew
Busiris and his Memphian chivalry,
While with perfidious hatred they pursued
The sojourners of Goshen, who beheld
From the safe shore their floating carcasses   310
And broken chariot wheels, so thick bestrewn
Abject and lost lay these, covering the flood,
Under amazement of their hideous change.
He called so loud, that all the hollow deep
Of Hell resounded. 'Princes, potentates,   315
Warriors, the flower of heaven, once yours, now lost,
If such astonishment as this can seize
Eternal spirits; or have ye chosen this place
After the toil of battle to repose
Your wearied virtue, for the ease you find   320
To slumber here, as in the vales of heaven?
Or in this abject posture have ye sworn
To adore the conqueror? who now beholds
Cherub and seraph rolling in the flood
With scattered arms and ensigns, till anon   325
His swift pursuers from heaven gates discern
The advantage, and descending tread us down
Thus drooping, or with linked thunderbolts
Transfix us to the bottom of this gulf.
Awake, arise, or be forever fallen.'   330
   They heard, and were abashed, and up they sprung
Upon the wing, as when men wont to watch
On duty, sleeping found by whom they dread,
Rouse and bestir themselves ere well awake.
Nor did they not perceive the evil plight   335
In which they were, or the fierce pains not feel;
Yet to their general's voice they soon obeyed
Innumerable.   As when the potent rod
Of Amram's son in Egypt's evil day
Waved round the coast, up called a pitchy cloud   340
Of locusts, warping on the eastern wind,
That o'er the realm of impious Pharoah hung
Like night, and darkened all the land of Nile:
So numberless were those bad angels seen
Hovering on wing under the cope of hell   345
'Twixt upper, nether, and surrounding fires;
Till, as a signal given, the uplifted spear

304. **sedge:** the local name of the Red Sea is the 'Sea of Sedge.'

305. **Orion armed:** referring to the constellation, which, rising in midsummer, sets early in November attended with storms.

306–10. *Exodus* 14.

307. **Busiris:** no one has ever exactly accounted for Milton's use of this name here.

338–43. *Exodus* 10:12–15. Cf. the account of the ten plagues, XII:184–86.

339. **Amram's son:** Moses.

Of their great sultan waving to direct
Their course, in even balance down they light
On the firm brimstone, and fill all the plain;   350
A multitude, like which the populous north
Poured never from her frozen loins, to pass
Rhene or the Danaw, when her barbarous sons
Came like a deluge on the south, and spread
Beneath Gibraltar to the Libyan sands.   355
Forthwith from every squadron and each band
The heads and leaders thither haste where stood
Their great commander; godlike shapes and forms
Excelling human, princely dignities,
And powers that erst in heaven sat on thrones;   360
Though of their names in heavenly records now
Be no memorial blotted out and rased
By their rebellion, from the books of life.
Nor had they yet among the sons of Eve
Got them new names, till wandering o'er the earth,   365
Through God's high sufferance for the trial of man,
By falsities and lies the greatest part
Of mankind they corrupted to forsake
God their creator, and the invisible
Glory of him that made them, to transform   370
Oft to the image of a brute, adorned
With gay religions full of pomp and gold,
And devils to adore for deities:
Then were they known to men by various names,
And various idols through the heathen world.   375
Say, muse, their names then known, who first, who last,
Roused from the slumber, on that fiery couch,
At their great emperor's call, as next in worth
Came singly where he stood on the bare strand,
While the promiscuous crowd stood yet aloof?   380
The chief were those who from the pit of hell
Roaming to seek their prey on earth, durst fix
Their seats long after next the seat of God,
Their altars by his altar, gods adored
Among the nations round, and durst abide   385
Jehovah thundering out of Sion, throned
Between the cherubim; yea, often placed
Within his sanctuary itself their shrines,
Abominations; and with cursed things
His holy rites, and solemn feasts profaned,   390
And with their darkness durst affront his light.
First Moloch, horrid king besmeared with blood

351–55. Alluding to the invasions of Italy by the Goths.

353. **Rhene or the Danaw:** Rhine or the Danube.

361–63. Cf. *Revelation* 3:5. Also *Christ. Doc. Col.* XIV:92–95.

362. memorial: *MS.*, first, third, and fourth editions have a comma after this word.

392. **Moloch:** a sun god, a destroyer. Cf. *I Kings* 11:7; worshiped with human sacrifice. *II Kings* 23:10.

Of human sacrifice, and parents' tears,
Though for the noise of drums and timbrels loud
Their children's cries unheard, that passed through fire   395
To his grim idol.   Him the Ammonite
Worshiped in Rabba and her watery plain,
In Argob and in Basan, to the stream
Of utmost Arnon.   Nor content with such
Audacious neighborhood, the wisest heart   400
Of Solomon he led by fraud to build
His temple right against the temple of God
On that opprobrious hill, and made his grove
The pleasant valley of Hinnom, Tophet thence
And black Gehenna called, the type of hell.   405
Next Chemos, the obscene dread of Moab's sons,
From Aroar to Nebo, and the wild
Of southmost Abarim; in Hesebon
And Horonaim, Seon's realm, beyond
The flowery dale of Sibma clad with vines,   410
And Eleale to the asphaltic pool.
Peor his other name, when he enticed
Israel in Sittim on their march from Nile
To do him wanton rites, which cost them woe.
Yet thence his lustful orgies he enlarged   415
Even to that hill of scandal, by the grove
Of Moloch homicide, lust hard by hate;
Till good Josiah drove them thence to hell.
With these came they, who from the bordering flood
Of old Euphrates to the brook that parts   420
Egypt from Syrian ground, had general names
Of Baalim and Ashtaroth, those male,
These feminine.   For spirits when they please
Can either sex assume, or both; so soft
And uncompounded is their essence pure,   425
Not tied or manacled with joint or limb,
Nor founded on the brittle strength of bones,
Like cumbrous flesh; but in what shape they choose
Dilated or condensed, bright or obscure,
Can execute their airy purposes,   430
And works of love or enmity fulfill.
For those the race of Israel oft forsook
Their living strength, and unfrequented left

396–99. The proper names are Biblical.   398. **Basan:** the ordinary form is *Bashan*.
401–03. Cf. *I Kings* 11:5–7.
404–05. **Hinnom, Tophet . . . Gehenna:** names connected with volcanic ravines near Jerusalem.
406. **Chemos:** sometimes identified with Moloch, and certainly linked with him.   Cf. *I Kings* 11:7.
408. **Abarim:** a mountain range containing Mount Nebo.   **Hesebon:** cf. *Numbers* 21:26.
411. **Eleale to the asphaltic pool:** from a mountain in the Abarim to the Dead Sea.
412. **Peor:** cf. *Numbers* 25:1–5.
422. **Baalim and Ashtaroth:** gods and goddesses of the Canaanites, the first male, the second female.
423–31. Milton's doctrine of angelic essences is stated fully here and frequently used throughout the poem.   Satan takes whatever shape he pleases.   So does Raphael.

His righteous altar, bowing lowly down
To bestial gods; for which their heads as low   435
Bowed down in battle, sunk before the spear
Of despicable foes. With these in troop
Came Astoreth, whom the Phoenicians called
Astarte, queen of heaven, with crescent horns;
To whose bright image nightly by the moon   440
Sidonian virgins paid their vows and songs,
In Sion also not unsung, where stood
Her temple on the offensive mountain, built
By that uxorious king, whose heart though large,
Beguiled by fair idolatresses, fell   445
To idols foul. Thammuz came next behind,
Whose annual wound in Lebanon allured
The Syrian damsels to lament his fate
In amorous ditties all a summer's day,
While smooth Adonis from his native rock   450
Ran purple to the sea, supposed with blood
Of Thammuz yearly wounded: the love-tale
Infected Sion's daughters with like heat,
Whose wanton passions in the sacred porch
Ezekiel saw, when by the vision led   455
His eye surveyed the dark idolatries
Of alienated Judah.   Next came one
Who mourned in earnest, when the captive ark
Maimed his brute image, head and hands lopped off
In his own temple, on the grunsel edge,   460
Where he fell flat, and shamed his worshipers:
Dagon his name, sea monster, upward man
And downward fish: yet had his temple high
Reared in Azotus, dreaded through the coast
Of Palestine, in Gath and Ascalon   465
And Accaron and Gaza's frontier bounds.
Him followed Rimmon, whose delightful seat
Was fair Damascus, on the fertile banks
Of Abbana and Pharphar, lucid streams.
He also against the house of God was bold: 470
A leper once he lost and gained a king,
Ahaz his sottish conqueror, whom he drew
God's altar to disparage and displace
For one of Syrian mode, whereon to burn
His odious offerings, and adore the gods   475

438–39. **Astoreth . . . Astarte:** the queen of heaven, Istar in Assyrian, Aphrodite in Greek, Venus in Latin. Cf. *Nat. Ode* 200.   444. **uxorious:** excessively wife loving.

446. **Thammuz:** identical with the Greek Adonis, whose myths derive from Thammuz. Cf. *Ezekiel* 8:13–14.

451. **purple:** Phillips (1658), 'that color which we commonly call red.'

462. **Dagon:** a god of the Philistines. Cf. the story of these lines in *I Samuel* 5:1–5.

464–66. **Azotus . . . Gath and Ascalon and Accaron and Gaza:** the five chief cities of the Philistines.

467. **Rimmon:** cf. *II Kings* 5:18. Chief deity of ancient Damascus.

471. **A leper once he lost:** cf. *II Kings* 5.   472. **Ahaz:** cf. *II Kings* 16.   **sottish:** foolish.

Whom he had vanquished.   After these appeared
A crew who under names of old renown,
Osiris, Isis, Orus and their train
With monstrous shapes and sorceries abused
Fanatic Egypt and her priests, to seek   480
Their wandering gods disguised in brutish forms
Rather than human.   Nor did Israel scape
The infection when their borrowed gold composed
The calf in Oreb: and the rebel king
Doubled that sin in Bethel and in Dan,   485
Likening his maker to the grazed ox,
Jehovah, who in one night when he passed
From Egypt marching, equaled with one stroke
Both her first born and all her bleating gods.
Belial came last, than whom a spirit more lewd   490
Fell not from heaven, or more gross to love
Vice for itself: To him no temple stood
Or altar smoked; yet who more oft than he
In temples and at altars, when the priest
Turns atheist, as did Eli's sons, who filled   495
With lust and violence the house of God.
In courts and palaces he also reigns
And in luxurious cities, where the noise
Of riot ascends above their loftiest towers,
And injury and outrage: And when night   500
Darkens the streets, then wander forth the sons
Of Belial, flown with insolence and wine.
Witness the streets of Sodom, and that night
In Gibeah, when the hospitable door
Exposed a matron to avoid worse rape.   505
These were the prime in order and in might;
The rest were long to tell, though far renowned,
The Ionian gods, of Javan's issue held
Gods, yet confessed later than heaven and earth
Their boasted parents; Titan Heaven's first born   510
With his enormous brood, and birthright seized
By younger Saturn, he from mightier Jove
His own and Rhea's son like measure found;
So Jove usurping reigned: these first in Crete
And Ida known, thence on the snowy top   515
Of cold Olympus ruled the middle air
Their highest heaven; or on the Delphian cliff,
Or in Dodona, and through all the bounds
Of Doric land; or who with Saturn old

478. **Osiris, Isis, Orus:** Egyptian deities.   484. **The calf in Oreb:** cf. *Exodus* 32.
487–89. Among the most effective poetic lines in the whole poem.

490. **Belial:** a generic term from the *OT* which Milton has personified.   It means utter profligacy, or worthlessness.   The expression is usually 'Sons of Belial,' as in 501–02.

495. **Eli's sons:** cf. *I Samuel* 2:12–17.   503–05. Cf. *Genesis* 19 or *Judges* 19.
508. **Javan's issue:** cf. *Deuteronomy* 32:17 and *Genesis* 10:2.   Also *SA* 715–16.
510–20. Greek mythology and its origins.

Fled over Adria to the Hesperian fields,   520
And o'er the Celtic roamed the utmost isles.
All these and more came flocking; but with looks
Downcast and damp, yet such wherein appeared
Obscure some glimpse of joy, to have found their chief
Not in despair, to have found themselves not lost   525
In loss itself; which on his countenance cast
Like doubtful hue: but he his wonted pride
Soon recollecting, with high words, that bore
Semblance of worth, not substance, gently raised
Their fainting courage, and dispelled their fears.   530
Then straight commands that at the warlike sound
Of trumpets loud and clarions be upreared
His mighty standard; that proud honor claimed
Azazel as his right, a cherub tall:
Who forthwith from the glittering staff unfurled   535
The imperial ensign, which full high advanced
Shone like a meteor streaming to the wind
With gems and golden luster rich emblazed,
Seraphic arms and trophies: all the while
Sonorous metal blowing martial sounds: 540
At which the universal host upsent
A shout that tore hell's concave, and beyond
Frighted the reign of chaos and old night.
All in a moment through the gloom were seen
Ten thousand banners rise into the air   545
With orient colors waving: with them rose
A forest huge of spears: and thronging helms
Appeared, and serried shields in thick array
Of depth immeasurable: Anon they move
In perfect phalanx to the Dorian mood   550
Of flutes and soft recorders; such as raised
To height of noblest temper heroes old
Arming to battle, and instead of rage
Deliberate valor breathed, firm and unmoved
With dread of death to flight or foul retreat,   555
Nor wanting power to mitigate and swage
With solemn touches, troubled thoughts, and chase
Anguish and doubt and fear and sorrow and pain
From mortal or immortal minds.   Thus they
Breathing united force with fixed thought   560
Moved on in silence to soft pipes that charmed
Their painful steps o'er the burnt soil; and now

520. **Hesperian fields:** Italy.   521. **utmost isles:** Britain.

534. **Azazel:** Milton's assignment of this fallen angel is probably from various rabbinical and Christian discussions of the name as it occurs in *Leviticus* 16.

548. **serried:** locked together.

550. **Dorian:** Plato's 'strain of courage' contrasted with the softly effeminate Lydian; cf. *L'Allegro* 136.

551. **recorders:** a recorder was a 'fipple flute,' also called a 'common flute' before the invention of the modern transverse flute.   It was a straight, eight-hole instrument.

556. **swage:** assuage, literally 'to sweeten.'

Advanced in view, they stand, a horrid front
Of dreadful length and dazzling arms, in guise
Of warriors old with ordered spear and shield,   565
Awaiting what command their mighty chief
Had to impose: He through the armed files
Darts his experienced eye, and soon traverse
The whole battalion views, their order due,
Their visages and stature as of gods,   570
Their number last he sums.   And now his heart
Distends with pride, and hardening in his strength
Glories: For never since created man,
Met such embodied force, as named with these
Could merit more than that small infantry   575
Warred on by cranes: though all the giant brood
Of Phlegra with the heroic race were joined
That fought at Thebes and Ilium, on each side
Mixed with auxiliar gods; and what resounds
In fable or romance of Uther's son   580
Begirt with British and Armoric knights;
And all who since, baptized or infidel
Jousted in Aspramont or Montalban,
Damasco, or Morocco, or Trebisond,
Or whom Biserta sent from Afric shore   585
When Charlemain with all his peerage fell
By Fontarabbia.   Thus far these beyond
Compare of mortal prowess, yet observed
Their dread commander: he above the rest
In shape and gesture proudly eminent   590
Stood like a tower; his form had yet not lost
All her original brightness, nor appeared
Less than archangel ruined, and the excess
Of glory obscured: As when the sun new risen
Looks through the horizontal misty air   595
Shorn of his beams, or from behind the moon
In dim eclipse disastrous twilight sheds
On half the nations, and with fear of change
Perplexes monarchs.   Darkened so, yet shone
Above them all the archangel: but his face   600
Deep scars of thunder had intrenched, and care

563. **horrid**: probably as Latin *horridus*, meaning 'bristling.'

575. **small infantry**: the Pigmies.   Cf. Homer, *Iliad* 3:5.

577. **Phlegra**: in Macedonia, where the Giants were born and vanquished by the Gods.

578. **Thebes and Ilium**: there is still magic in these names, the greatest in classical heroics.

580. **Uther's son**: King Arthur was the son of Uther Pendragon.

581. **Armoric**: of Brittany.

583-84. **Aspramont or Montalban, Damasco, or Morocco, or Trebisond**: names of places famous for fighting throughout the Middle Ages and the Renaissance.

587. **Fontarabbia**: the name of this place as that at which Roland was slain has greatly troubled most modern commentators.   But a number of writers contemporary with Milton state that this place was where Roland's last battle and death took place.

597. **disastrous**: ill-starred.   597-99. These lines were objected to by the censor.

Sat on his faded cheek, but under brows
Of dauntless courage, and considerate pride
Waiting revenge: cruel his eye, but cast
Signs of remorse and passion to behold   605
The fellows of his crime, the followers rather
(Far other once beheld in bliss) condemned
Forever now to have their lot in pain,
Millions of spirits for his fault amerced
Of heaven, and from eternal splendors flung   610
For his revolt, yet faithful how they stood,
Their glory withered.   As when heaven's fire
Hath scathed the forest oaks, or mountain pines,
With singed top their stately growth though bare
Stands on the blasted heath.   He now prepared   615
To speak; whereat their doubled ranks they bend
From wing to wing, and half enclose him round
With all his peers: attention held them mute.
Thrice he assayed, and thrice in spite of scorn,
Tears such as angels weep, burst forth: at last   620
Words interwove with sighs found out their way.
    'O myriads of immortal spirits, O powers
Matchless, but with the almighty, and that strife
Was not inglorious, though the event was dire,
As this place testifies, and this dire change   625
Hateful to utter: but what power of mind
Foreseeing or presaging, from the depth
Of knowledge past or present, could have feared,
How such united force of gods, how such
As stood like these, could ever know repulse?   630
For who can yet believe, though after loss,
That all these puissant legions, whose exile
Hath emptied heaven, shall fail to reascend
Self-raised, and repossess their native seat?
For me be witness all the host of heaven,   635
If counsels different, or danger shunned
By me, have lost our hopes.   But he who reigns
Monarch in heaven, till then as one secure
Sat on his throne, upheld by old repute,
Consent or custom, and his regal state   640
Put forth at full, but still his strength concealed,
Which tempted our attempt, and wrought our fall.
Henceforth his might we know, and know our own
So as not either to provoke, or dread
New war, provoked; our better part remains   645
To work in close design, by fraud or guile
What force effected not: that he no less
At length from us may find, who overcomes
By force, hath overcome but half his foe.
Space may produce new worlds; whereof so rife   650

609-10. **amerced of heaven**: penalized by exile from heaven.   611. **how**: should it read 'now.'
650. **Space may produce new worlds**: the idea of a multiplicity of worlds was prevalent in Milton's time.

There went a fame in heaven that he erelong
Intended to create, and therein plant
A generation, whom his choice regard
Should favor equal to the sons of heaven:
Thither, if but to pry, shall be perhaps   655
Our first eruption, thither or elsewhere:
For this infernal pit shall never hold
Celestial spirits in bondage, nor the abyss
Long under darkness cover.   But these thoughts
Full counsel must mature: Peace is despaired,   660
For who can think submission?   War then, war
Open or understood must be resolved.'
    He spake: and to confirm his words, out flew
Millions of flaming swords, drawn from the thighs
Of mighty cherubim; the sudden blaze   665
Far round illumined hell: highly they raged
Against the highest, and fierce with grasped arms
Clashed on their sounding shields the din of war,
Hurling defiance toward the vault of heaven.
    There stood a hill not far whose grisly top   670
Belched fire and rolling smoke; the rest entire
Shone with a glossy scurf, undoubted sign
That in his womb was hid metallic ore,
The work of sulphur.   Thither winged with speed
A numerous brigade hastened.   As when bands   675
Of pioneers with spade and pickaxe armed
Forerun the royal camp, to trench a field,
Or cast a rampart.   Mammon led them on,
Mammon, the least erected spirit that fell
From heaven, for even in heaven his looks and thoughts   680
Were always downward bent, admiring more
The riches of heaven's pavement, trodden gold,
Than aught divine or holy else enjoyed
In vision beatific: by him first
Men also, and by his suggestion taught,   685
Ransacked the center, and with impious hands
Rifled the bowels of their mother earth
For treasures better hid.   Soon had his crew
Opened into the hill a spacious wound
And digged out ribs of gold.   Let none admire   690
That riches grow in hell; that soil may best
Deserve the precious bane.   And here let those
Who boast in mortal things, and wondering tell
Of Babel, and the works of Memphian kings
Learn how their greatest monuments of fame,   695
And strength and art are easily outdone
By spirits reprobate, and in an hour

673–74. Precious metals and minerals were thought to be composed of sulphur and mercury.
676. pioneers: sappers, a military term, usually called *engineers* today.
678. Mammon: like Belial a generic term, not a proper name, meaning 'wealth.'
694. Babel, and the works of Memphian kings: the tower of Babel and the pyramids of Egypt.

What in an age they with incessant toil
And hands innumerable scarce perform.
Nigh on the plain in many cells prepared,   700
That underneath had veins of liquid fire
Sluiced from the lake, a second multitude
With wondrous art found out the massy ore,
Severing each kind, and scummed the bullion dross:
A third as soon had formed within the ground   705
A various mold, and from the boiling cells
By strange conveyance filled each hollow nook,
As in an organ from one blast of wind
To many a row of pipes the soundboard breathes.
Anon out of the earth a fabric huge   710
Rose like an exhalation, with the sound
Of dulcet symphonies and voices sweet,
Built like a temple, where pilasters round
Were set, and Doric pillars overlaid
With golden architrave; nor did there want   715
Cornice or frieze, with bossy sculptures graven,
The roof was fretted gold. Not Babylon,
Nor great Alcairo such magnificence
Equaled in all their glories, to enshrine
Belus or Serapis their gods, or seat   720
Their kings, when Egypt with Assyria strove
In wealth and luxury. The ascending pile
Stood fixed her stately height, and straight the doors
Opening their brazen folds discover wide
Within, her ample spaces, o'er the smooth   725
And level pavement: from the arched roof
Pendent by subtle magic many a row
Of starry lamps and blazing cressets fed
With naphtha and asphaltus yielded light
As from a sky. The hasty multitude   730
Admiring entered, and the work some praise
And some the architect: his hand was known
In heaven by many a towered structure high,

700–09. Note the details in this picture of a metal refinery.

710 ff. Cf. Ovid, *Metamorphoses* II, opening lines which describe the palace of the sun. Also, George Sandys' translation and notes of 1632, pp. 37 [41] and 65.

712. **symphonies:** Milton apparently used the word almost exactly as we do today. Phillips (1706) defines it as a 'consort of instrumental music.'

718. **Alcairo:** Cairo with the Arabic article prefixed, meaning 'Memphis.' This was common practice in Milton's day, and one regularly reads of the Alkoran. Our word *algebra* retains the *al* — prefixed article from the Arabic.

720. **Belus or Serapis:** the first is the famous Bel, god of the Assyrians, the Baal of the *OT*. Serapis was an Egyptian god to whom great temples were built.

722–30. Notice the effect Milton achieves without giving us a single definite detail.

727. **Pendent by subtle magic:** Tennyson said of this line, 'I always like this, it is mystical.' What did he mean?

729. **naphtha and asphaltus:** the first was oil (liquid), used in the lamps, and the second was a solid, used in the cressets. Milton had first-hand experience with both of these lighting devices, as they were employed even after his time.   732. **the architect:** who was he? Critics disagree.

Where sceptered angels held their residence,
And sat as princes, whom the supreme king   735
Exalted to such power, and gave to rule,
Each in his hierarchy, the orders bright.
Nor was his name unheard or unadored
In ancient Greece; and in Ausonian land
Men called him Mulciber; and how he fell   740
From heaven, they fabled, thrown by angry Jove
Sheer o'er the crystal battlements; from morn
To noon he fell, from noon to dewy eve,
A summer's day; and with the setting sun
Dropped from the zenith like a falling star,   745
On Lemnos the Aegaean isle: thus they relate,
Erring; for he with this rebellious rout
Fell long before; nor aught availed him now
To have built in heaven high towers; nor did he scape
By all his engines, but was headlong sent   750
With his industrious crew to build in hell.
Meanwhile the winged heralds by command
Of sovereign power, with awful ceremony
And trumpet's sound throughout the host proclaim
A solemn council forthwith to be held   755
At Pandemonium, the high capital
Of Satan and his peers: their summons called
From every band and squared regiment
By place or choice the worthiest; they anon
With hundreds and with thousands trooping came   760
Attended: all access was thronged, the gates
And porches wide, but chief the spacious hall
(Though like a covered field, where champions bold
Wont ride in armed, and at the soldan's chair
Defied the best of paynim chivalry   765
To mortal combat or career with lance)
Thick swarmed, both on the ground and in the air,
Brushed with the hiss of rustling wings.   As bees
In springtime, when the sun with Taurus rides,
Pour forth their populous youth about the hive   770
In clusters; they among fresh dews and flowers
Fly to and fro, or on the smoothed plank,
The suburb of their straw-built citadel,
New rubbed with balm, expatiate and confer
Their state affairs.   So thick the airy crowd   775
Swarmed and were straitened; till the signal given,

739. **In ancient Greece**: supreme architecture was not uncommon.   **in Ausonian land**: Italy.

740. **Mulciber**: cf. Homer, *Iliad* 1:591 ff.

750. **engines**: Phillips says 'an artifice, device, or contrivance.'

756. **Pandemonium**: one of the few learnedly invented words that has been taken into the language. Milton spelled it *Pandaemonium*, but the language has taken it over.

764. **soldan's**: sultan's.   765. **paynim**: pagan. Also *PR* III:343.

774. **expatiate**: to walk abroad, but this old meaning was only a literary one, even in Milton's day, as Phillips gives only one meaning of the word 'to enlarge on a subject.'

Behold a wonder! they but now who seemed
In bigness to surpass earth's giant sons
Now less than smallest dwarfs, in narrow room
Throng numberless, like that pygmaean race   780
Beyond the Indian mount, or faery elves,
Whose midnight revels, by a forest side
Or fountain some belated peasant sees,
Or dreams he sees, while overhead the moon
Sits arbitress, and nearer to the earth   785
Wheels her pale course, they on their mirth and dance
Intent, with jocund music charm his ear;
At once with joy and fear his heart rebounds.
Thus incorporeal spirits to smallest forms
Reduced their shapes immense, and were at large,   790
Though without number still amidst the hall
Of that infernal court.   But far within
And in their own dimensions like themselves
The great seraphic lords and cherubim
In close recess and secret conclave sat   795
A thousand demi-gods on golden seats,
Frequent and full.   After short silence then
And summons read, the great consult began.

THE END OF THE FIRST BOOK

BOOK II

THE ARGUMENT

The consultation begun, Satan debates whether another battle be to be hazarded for the recovery of heaven: some advise it, others dissuade: A third proposal is preferred, mentioned before by Satan, to search the truth of that prophecy or tradition in heaven concerning another world, and another kind of creature equal or not much inferior to themselves, about this time to be created: Their doubt who shall be sent on this difficult search: Satan their chief undertakes alone the voyage, is honored and applauded.   The council thus ended, the rest betake them several ways and to several employments, as their inclinations lead them, to entertain the time till Satan return.   He passes on his journey to hell gates, finds them shut, and who sat there to guard them, by whom at length they are opened, and discover to him the great gulf between hell and heaven; with what difficulty he passes through, directed by chaos, the power of that place, to the sight of this new world which he sought.

High on a throne of royal state, which far
Outshone the wealth of Ormus and of Ind,

777–92. This passage has been criticized as representing an absurdity.   Not many modern readers will be offended by it, and surely the likening of the throngs of fallen angels to troops of faery elves is pleasing (ll. 781–87).   Milton implies that it only seemed as if the rebels shrank in size.   Later in the poem, he seems to have left most of the rebel hosts on the outside.   Note that the principal rebels regain their original size and forms.   Could Milton here have been mildly satirizing the loss of power by all members of the Long Parliament, except its leaders?

2. **Ormus and of Ind:** Ormus was a city on the Persian Gulf, famous for its precious stones.   'Ind' was India, a fabulous name meaning untold wealth and desirable possessions.

Or where the gorgeous east with richest hand
Showers on her kings barbaric pearl and gold,
Satan exalted sat, by merit raised   5
To that bad eminence; and from despair
Thus high uplifted beyond hope, aspires
Beyond thus high, insatiate to pursue
Vain war with heaven, and by success untaught
His proud imaginations thus displayed.   10
        'Powers and dominions, deities of heaven,
For since no deep within her gulf can hold
Immortal vigor, though oppressed and fallen,
I give not heaven for lost.   From this descent
Celestial virtues rising, will appear   15
More glorious and more dread than from no fall,
And trust themselves to fear no second fate:
Me though just right, and the fixed laws of heaven
Did first create your leader, next free choice,
With what besides, in council or in fight,   20
Hath been achieved of merit, yet this loss
Thus far at least recovered, hath much more
Established in a safe unenvied throne
Yielded with full consent.   The happier state
In heaven, which follows dignity, might draw   25
Envy from each inferior; but who here
Will envy whom the highest place exposes
Foremost to stand against the thunderer's aim
Your bulwark, and condemns to greatest share
Of endless pain? where there is then no good   30
For which to strive, no strife can grow up there
From faction; for none sure will claim in hell
Precedence, none, whose portion is so small
Of present pain, that with ambitious mind
Will covet more.   With this advantage then   35
To union, and firm faith, and firm accord,
More than can be in heaven, we now return
To claim our just inheritance of old,
Surer to prosper than prosperity
Could have assured us; and by what best way,   40
Whether of open war or covert guile,
We now debate; who can advise, may speak.'
    He ceased, and next him Moloch, sceptered king
Stood up, the strongest and the fiercest spirit
That fought in heaven; now fiercer by despair: 45
His trust was with the eternal to be deemed
Equal in strength, and rather than be less
Cared not to be at all; with that care lost
Went all his fear: of God, or hell, or worse
He recked not, and these words thereafter spake.   50
        'My sentence is for open war: Of wiles,

9. **by success untaught:** the word *success* here has its older meaning, 'the issue of a business, either good or bad' (Phillips). We would say 'experience.'   Gradually the word came to mean a happy issue only.

More unexpert, I boast not: them let those
Contrive who need, or when they need, not now.
For while they sit contriving, shall the rest,
Millions that stand in arms, and longing wait   55
The signal to ascend, sit lingering here
Heaven's fugitives, and for their dwelling place
Accept this dark opprobrious den of shame,
The prison of his tyranny who reigns
By our delay? no, let us rather choose   60
Armed with hell flames and fury all at once
O'er heaven's high towers to force resistless way,
Turning our tortures into horrid arms
Against the torturer; when to meet the noise
Of his almighty engine he shall hear   65
Infernal thunder, and for lightning see
Black fire and horror shot with equal rage
Among his angels; and his throne itself
Mixed with Tartarean sulphur, and strange fire,
His own invented torments.   But perhaps   70
The way seems difficult and steep to scale
With upright wing against a higher foe.
Let such bethink them, if the sleepy drench
Of that forgetful lake benumb not still,
That in our proper motion we ascend   75
Up to our native seat: descent and fall
To us is adverse.   Who but felt of late
When the fierce foe hung on our broken rear
Insulting, and pursued us through the deep,
With what compulsion and laborious flight   80
We sunk thus low?   The ascent is easy then;
The event is feared; should we again provoke
Our stronger, some worse way his wrath may find
To our destruction: if there be in hell
Fear to be worse destroyed: what can be worse   85
Than to dwell here, driven out from bliss, condemned
In this abhorred deep to utter woe;
Where pain of unextinguishable fire
Must exercise us without hope of end
The vassals of his anger, when the scourge   90
Inexorably, and the torturing hour
Calls us to penance?   More destroyed than thus
We should be quite abolished and expire.
What fear we then? what doubt we to incense
His utmost ire? which to the height enraged,   95
Will either quite consume us, and reduce
To nothing this essential, happier far
Than miserable to have eternal being:
Or if our substance be indeed divine,

69. **Tartarean sulphur:** infernal sulphur.

73. **sleepy drench:** sleep-producing soaking, received in the burning lake.   There is no need here to make the drench a drink.   The rebel angels fell into the burning lake, they did not drink of it.

And cannot cease to be, we are at worst   100
On this side nothing; and by proof we feel
Our power sufficient to disturb his heaven,
And with perpetual inroads to alarm,
Though inaccessible, his fatal throne:
Which if not victory is yet revenge.'   105
    He ended frowning, and his look denounced
Desperate revenge, and battle dangerous
To less than gods.   On the other side uprose
Belial, in act more graceful and humane;
A fairer person lost not heaven; he seemed   110
For dignity composed and high exploit:
But all was false and hollow; though his tongue
Dropped manna, and could make the worse appear
The better reason, to perplex and dash
Maturest counsels: for his thoughts were low;   115
To vice industrious, but to nobler deeds
Timorous and slothful: yet he pleased the ear,
And with persuasive accent thus began.
    'I should be much for open war, O peers,
As not behind in hate; if what was urged   120
Main reason to persuade immediate war,
Did not dissuade me most, and seem to cast
Ominous conjecture on the whole success:
When he who most excels in fact of arms,
In what he counsels and in what excels   125
Mistrustful, grounds his courage on despair
And utter dissolution, as the scope
Of all his aim, after some dire revenge.
First, what revenge? the towers of heaven are filled
With armed watch, that render all access   130
Impregnable; oft on the bordering deep
Encamp their legions, or with obscure wing
Scout far and wide into the realm of night,
Scorning surprise.   Or could we break our way
By force, and at our heels all hell should rise   135
With blackest insurrection, to confound
Heaven's purest light, yet our great enemy
All incorruptible would on his throne
Sit unpolluted, and the ethereal mold

101–05. Moloch advocates incessant guerilla warfare.   104. **fatal:** decreed by fate.

112–13. **his tongue dropped manna:** sweet words.   Cf. *Exodus* 16:31.

113–15. **make the worse appear the better reason, etc.:** a sophist.

119 ff. Contrast Belial's speech, especially the opening, with Moloch's.

124. **fact:** feat, the words being originally identical.

127. **scope:** mark; cf. Phillips's defining the word as 'prospect, aim, end, purpose.'

129. 'Note the great pauses in Belial's speech.' — Tennyson.

129 ff. Note Belial's easy skill in debate, answering Moloch point by point without apparent design.

130. **render:** a plural because its subject, 'watch,' is a collective.

139. **ethereal mold:** again, the non-substantial substance of which the angels were made.

Incapable of stain would soon expel 140
Her mischief, and purge off the baser fire
Victorious. Thus repulsed, our final hope
Is flat despair: we must exasperate
The almighty victor to spend all his rage,
And that must end us, that must be our cure, 145
To be no more; sad cure; for who would lose,
Though full of pain, this intellectual being,
Those thoughts that wander through eternity,
To perish rather, swallowed up and lost
In the wide womb of uncreated night, 150
Devoid of sense and motion? and who knows,
Let this be good, whether our angry foe
Can give it, or will ever? how he can
Is doubtful; that he never will is sure.
Will he, so wise, let loose at once his ire, 155
Belike through impotence, or unaware,
To give his enemies their wish, and end
Them in his anger, whom his anger saves
To punish endless? "wherefore cease we then?"
Say they who counsel war, "we are decreed, 160
Reserved and destined to eternal woe;
Whatever doing, what can we suffer more,
What can we suffer worse?" is this then worst,
Thus sitting, thus consulting, thus in arms?
What when we fled amain, pursued and struck 165
With heaven's afflicting thunder, and besought
The deep to shelter us? this hell then seemed
A refuge from those wounds: or when we lay
Chained on the burning lake? that sure was worse.
What if the breath that kindled those grim fires 170
Awaked should blow them into sevenfold rage
And plunge us in the flames? or from above
Should intermitted vengeance arm again
His red right hand to plague us? what if all
Her stores were opened, and this firmament 175
Of hell should spout her cataracts of fire,
Impendent horrors, threatening hideous fall
One day upon our heads; while we perhaps
Designing or exhorting glorious war,
Caught in a fiery tempest shall be hurled 180
Each on his rock transfixed, the sport and prey
Of racking whirlwinds, or for ever sunk
Under yon boiling ocean, wrapt in chains;
There to converse with everlasting groans,
Unrespited, unpitied, unreprieved, 185

143. **flat despair:** complete despair. We still speak of a 'flat failure.'
150. **uncreated night:** chaos.   174. **red right hand:** *rubens dextera* of Jupiter. Horace, *Od.* I:2:2:3.
182. **racking:** scudding. 'Racking clouds' are blown, fast-flying clouds.
184. **converse:** live with.   185. Note the effective meter and accent of this line.

Ages of hopeless end; this would be worse.
War therefore, open or concealed, alike
My voice dissuades; for what can force or guile
With him, or who deceive his mind, whose eye
Views all things at one view? he from heaven's height   190
All these our motions vain, sees and derides;
Not more almighty to resist our might
Than wise to frustrate all our plots and wiles.
Shall we then live thus vile, the race of heaven
Thus trampled, thus expelled to suffer here   195
Chains and these torments? better these than worse
By my advice; since fate inevitable
Subdues us, and omnipotent decree,
The victor's will.   To suffer, as to do,
Our strength is equal, nor the law unjust   200
That so ordains: this was at first resolved,
If we were wise, against so great a foe
Contending, and so doubtful what might fall.
I laugh, when those who at the spear are bold
And venturous, if that fail them, shrink and fear   205
What yet they know must follow, to endure
Exile, or ignominy, or bonds, or pain,
The sentence of their conqueror: This is now
Our doom; which if we can sustain and bear,
Our supreme foe in time may much remit   210
His anger, and perhaps thus far removed
Not mind us not offending, satisfied
With what is punished; whence these raging fires
Will slacken, if his breath stir not their flames.
Our purer essence then will overcome   215
Their noxious vapor, or inured not feel,
Or changed at length, and to the place conformed
In temper and in nature, will receive
Familiar the fierce heat, and void of pain;
This horror will grow mild, this darkness light,   220
Besides what hope the never-ending flight
Of future days may bring, what chance, what change
Worth waiting, since our present lot appears
For happy though but ill, for ill not worst,
If we procure not to ourselves more woe.'   225
    Thus Belial with words clothed in reason's garb
Counseled ignoble ease, and peaceful sloth,
Not peace: and after him thus Mammon spake.
    'Either to disenthrone the king of heaven
We war, if war be best, or to regain   230
Our own right lost: him to unthrone we then
May hope when everlasting fate shall yield

191. **derides:** cf. *Psalm* 2:4, 'the Lord shall have them in derision.'

216. **inured:** accustomed to [the flames].   The word *inure* literally means, from the Latin, 'to bring into
use' (*ure*).

226 ff. Milton's conception of peace was always positive, something to strive for and then strive to retain.

To fickle chance, and chaos judge the strife:
The former vain to hope argues as vain
The latter: for what place can be for us   235
Within heaven's bound, unless heaven's lord supreme
We overpower?   Suppose he should relent
And publish grace to all, on promise made
Of new subjection; with what eyes could we
Stand in his presence humble, and receive   240
Strict laws imposed, to celebrate his throne
With warbled hymns, and to his Godhead sing
Forced hallelujahs; while he lordly sits
Our envied sovereign, and his altar breathes
Ambrosial odors and ambrosial flowers,   245
Our servile offerings.   This must be our task
In heaven this our delight; how wearisome
Eternity so spent in worship paid
To whom we hate.   Let us not then pursue
By force impossible, by leave obtained   250
Unacceptable, though in heaven, our state
Of splendid vassalage, but rather seek
Our own good from ourselves, and from our own
Live to ourselves, though in this vast recess,
Free, and to none accountable, preferring   255
Hard liberty before the easy yoke
Of servile pomp.   Our greatness will appear
Then most conspicuous, when great things of small,
Useful of hurtful, prosperous of adverse
We can create, and in what place so e'er   260
Thrive under evil, and work ease out of pain
Through labor and endurance.   This deep world
Of darkness do we dread?   How oft amidst
Thick clouds and dark doth heaven's all-ruling sire
Choose to reside, his glory unobscured,   265
And with the majesty of darkness round
Covers his throne; from whence deep thunders roar
Mustering their rage, and heaven resembles hell?
As he our darkness, cannot we his light
Imitate when we please?   This desert soil   270
Wants not her hidden luster, gems and gold;
Nor want we skill or art, from whence to raise
Magnificence; and what can heaven show more?
Our torments also may in length of time
Become our elements, these piercing fires   275
As soft as now severe, our temper changed
Into their temper; which must needs remove
The sensible of pain.   All things invite
To peaceful counsels, and the settled state
Of order, how in safety best we may   280

251–52. **our state of splendid vassalage**: Milton believed that many, perhaps most, men prefer 'Bondage
with ease [to] strenuous liberty.' *SA* 271.

278. **sensible**: adjective for noun. Sense.

Compose our present evils, with regard
Of what we are and were, dismissing quite
All thoughts of war: ye have what I advise.'
  He scarce had finished, when such murmur filled
The assembly, as when hollow rocks retain   285
The sound of blustering winds, which all night long
Had roused the sea, now with hoarse cadence lull
Seafaring men o'erwatched, whose bark by chance
Or pinnace anchors in a craggy bay
After the tempest: Such applause was heard   290
As Mammon ended, and his sentence pleased,
Advising peace: for such another field
They dreaded worse than hell: so much the fear
Of thunder and the sword of Michael
Wrought still within them; and no less desire   295
To found this nether empire, which might rise
By policy, and long process of time,
In emulation opposite to heaven.
Which when Beelzebub perceived, than whom,
Satan except, none higher sat, with grave   300
Aspect he rose, and in his rising seemed
A pillar of state; deep on his front engraven
Deliberation sat and public care;
And princely counsel in his face yet shone,
Majestic though in ruin: sage he stood   305
With Atlantean shoulders fit to bear
The weight of mightiest monarchies; his look
Drew audience and attention still as night
Or summer's noontide air, while thus he spake.
  'Thrones and imperial powers, offspring of heaven   310
Ethereal virtues; or these titles now
Must we renounce, and changing style be called
Princes of hell? for so the popular vote
Inclines, here to continue, and build up here
A growing empire; doubtless; while we dream,   315
And know not that the king of heaven hath doomed
This place our dungeon, not our safe retreat
Beyond his potent arm, to live exempt
From heaven's high jurisdiction, in new league
Banded against his throne, but to remain   320

281. **Compose:** arrange, hence adjust or adapt.   282. **were:** 1st edition reads 'where.'
288. **o'erwatched:** worn out with too much watching.   292. **field:** battle.
294. **the sword of Michael:** the 'two-handed' sword from the 'armory of God.' Cf. VI:251–52.
290–300. Cf. *Matthew* 12:24.   302. **front:** face.
306. **Atlantean shoulders:** like those of Atlas in the myth who held up the heavens.
  310 ff. Note how well each speech is fitted to the character of the speaker. Beelzebub brushes aside the speeches that have gone before, ignores the 'popular vote' as indicated by the applause accorded Mammon's speech, and cuts through to the heart of the matter. They cannot fight directly, but they may seek revenge, perhaps in other ways.

  312. **style:** title, appellation. We still speak of the 'style' of a business organization, meaning the title by which it is known, but this meaning of the word is disappearing.

In strictest bondage, though thus far removed,
Under the inevitable curb, reserved
His captive multitude: For he, be sure
In height or depth, still first and last will reign
Sole king, and of his kingdom lose no part   325
By our revolt, but over hell extend
His empire, and with iron scepter rule
Us here, as with his golden those in heaven.
What sit we then projecting peace and war?
War hath determined us, and foiled with loss   330
Irreparable; terms of peace yet none
Vouchsafed or sought; for what peace will be given
To us enslaved, but custody severe,
And stripes, and arbitrary punishment
Inflicted? and what peace can we return,   335
But to our power hostility and hate,
Untamed reluctance, and revenge though slow,
Yet ever plotting how the conqueror least
May reap his conquest, and may least rejoice
In doing what we most in suffering feel?   340
Nor will occasion want, nor shall we need
With dangerous expedition to invade
Heaven, whose high walls fear no assault or siege,
Or ambush from the deep.   What if we find
Some easier enterprise?   There is a place   345
(If ancient and prophetic fame in heaven
Err not) another world, the happy seat
Of some new race called man, about this time
To be created like to us, though less
In power and excellence, but favored more   350
Of him who rules above; so was his will
Pronounced among the gods, and by an oath,
That shook heaven's whole circumference, confirmed.
Thither let us bend all our thoughts, to learn
What creatures there inhabit, of what mold,   355
Or substance, how endued, and what their power,
And where their weakness, how attempted best,
By force or subtlety: Though heaven be shut,
And heaven's high arbitrator sit secure
In his own strength, this place may lie exposed   360
The utmost border of his kingdom, left
To their defense who hold it: here perhaps
Some advantageous act may be achieved
By sudden onset, either with hell fire
To waste his whole creation, or possess   365
All as our own, and drive as we were driven,
The puny habitants, or if not drive,

337. **reluctance**: resistance.

344 ff. Milton apparently did not care to make the exact time of creation fit a definite scheme of chronology.   Cf. VII:140 ff.   But all these events took place before time began.

346. **fame**: rumor.   Cf. I:651.

Seduce them to our party, that their God
May prove their foe, and with repenting hand
Abolish his own works.   This would surpass   370
Common revenge, and interrupt his joy
In our confusion, and our joy upraise
In his disturbance; when his darling sons
Hurled headlong to partake with us, shall curse
Their frail original, and faded bliss,   375
Faded so soon.   Advise if this be worth
Attempting, or to sit in darkness here
Hatching vain empires.'   Thus Beelzebub
Pleaded his devilish counsel, first devised
By Satan, and in part proposed: for whence,   380
But from the author of all ill could spring
So deep a malice, to confound the race
Of mankind in one root, and earth with hell
To mingle and involve, done all to spite
The great creator?   But their spite still serves   385
His glory to augment.   The bold design
Pleased highly those infernal states, and joy
Sparkled in all their eyes; with full assent
They vote: whereat his speech he thus renews.
    'Well have ye judged, well ended long debate,   390
Synod of gods, and like to what ye are,
Great things resolved, which from the lowest deep
Will once more lift us up, in spite of fate,
Nearer our ancient seat; perhaps in view
Of those bright confines, whence with neighboring arms 395
And opportune excursion we may chance
Re-enter heaven; or else in some mild zone
Dwell not unvisited of heaven's fair light
Secure, and at the brightening orient beam
Purge off this gloom; the soft delicious air,   400
To heal the scar of these corrosive fires
Shall breathe her balm.   But first whom shall we send
In search of this new world, whom shall we find
Sufficient? who shall tempt with wandering feet
The dark unbottomed infinite abyss   405
And through the palpable obscure find out
His uncouth way, or spread his airy flight
Upborne with indefatigable wings
Over the vast abrupt, ere he arrive
The happy isle; what strength, what art can then   410
Suffice, or what evasion bear him safe
Through the strict sentries and stations thick
Of angels watching round?   Here he had need
All circumspection, and we now no less

387. **states**: parliaments.   391. **Synod**: meeting or assembly.
404. **tempt**: attempt.   406. **palpable obscure**: tangible darkness.
407. **uncouth**: unknown.   412. **stations**: outposts.

Choice in our suffrage; for on whom we send,   415
The weight of all and our last hope relies.'
    This said, he sat; and expectation held
His look suspense, awaiting who appeared
To second, or oppose, or undertake
The perilous attempt: but all sat mute,   420
Pondering the danger with deep thoughts; and each
In other's countenance read his own dismay
Astonished: none among the choice and prime
Of those heaven-warring champions could be found
So hardy as to proffer or accept   425
Alone the dreadful voyage; till at last
Satan, whom now transcendent glory raised
Above his fellows, with monarchal pride
Conscious of highest worth, unmoved thus spake.
   'O progeny of heaven, empyreal thrones,   430
With reason hath deep silence and demur
Seized us, though undismayed: long is the way
And hard, that out of hell leads up to light;
Our prison strong, this huge convex of fire,
Outrageous to devour, immures us round   435
Ninefold, and gates of burning adamant
Barred over us prohibit all egress.
These passed, if any pass, the void profound
Of unessential night receives him next
Wide gaping, and with utter loss of being   440
Threatens him, plunged in that abortive gulf
If thence he scape into whatever world,
Or unknown region, what remains him less
Than unknown dangers and as hard escape.
But I should ill become this throne, O peers,   445
And this imperial sovereignty, adorned
With splendor, armed with power, if aught proposed
And judged of public moment, in the shape
Of difficulty or danger could deter
Me from attempting.   Wherefore do I assume   450
These royalties, and not refuse to reign,
Refusing to accept as great a share
Of hazard as of honor, due alike
To him who reigns, and so much to him due
Of hazard more, as he above the rest   455
High honored sits?   Go therefore mighty powers,
Terror of heaven, though fallen; intend at home,
While here shall be our home, what best may ease
The present misery, and render hell

---

415. **Choice in our suffrage**: care in our election.   435. **immures us**: walls us.

439. **unessential night**: immaterial night, without essence or life.

441. **abortive**: unformed.   457. **intend**: consider.

456–63. Satan enjoins the rebel angels to maintain consideration of their future, keep strict watch for attack from heaven, while he sets out on his perilous enterprise.

More tolerable; if there be cure or charm   460
To respite or deceive, or slack the pain
Of this ill mansion: intermit no watch
Against a wakeful foe, while I abroad
Through all the coasts of dark destruction seek
Deliverance for us all: this enterprise   465
None shall partake with me.'   Thus saying rose
The monarch, and prevented all reply,
Prudent, lest from his resolution raised
Others among the chief might offer now
(Certain to be refused) what erst they feared;   470
And so refused might in opinion stand
His rivals, winning cheap the high repute
Which he through hazard huge must earn.   But they
Dreaded not more the adventure than his voice
Forbidding; and at once with him they rose;   475
Their rising all at once was as the sound
Of thunder heard remote.   Towards him they bend
With awful reverence prone; and as a god
Extol him equal to the highest in heaven:
Nor failed they to express how much they praised,   480
That for the general safety he despised
His own: for neither do the spirits damned
Lose all their virtue; lest bad men should boast
Their specious deeds on earth, which glory excites,
Or close ambition varnished o'er with zeal.   485
Thus they their doubtful consultations dark
Ended rejoicing in their matchless chief:
As when from mountain tops the dusky clouds
Ascending, while the north wind sleeps, o'erspread
Heaven's cheerful face, the louring element   490
Scowls o'er the darkened landscape snow, or shower;
If chance the radiant sun with farewell sweet
Extend his evening beam, the fields revive,
The birds their notes renew, and bleating herds
Attest their joy, that hill and valley rings.   495
O shame to men! Devil with devil damned
Firm concord holds, men only disagree
Of creatures rational, though under hope
Of heavenly grace: and God proclaiming peace,
Yet live in hatred, enmity, and strife   500
Among themselves, and levy cruel wars,
Wasting the earth, each other to destroy:
As if (which might induce us to accord)
Man had not hellish foes enow besides,
That day and night for his destruction wait.   505
    The Stygian council thus dissolved; and forth

467. **prevented**: anticipated.   468. **raised**: encouraged.
478. **awful**: filled with awe.   485. **close**: secret.
506. **Stygian**: hellish, infernal (from the name of the river Styx).

In order came the grand infernal peers,
Midst came their mighty paramount, and seemed
Alone the antagonist of heaven, nor less
Than hell's dread emperor with pomp supreme,   510
And god-like imitated state; him round
A globe of fiery seraphim enclosed
With bright emblazonry, and horrent arms.
Then of their session ended they bid cry
With trumpet's regal sound the great result: 515
Toward the four winds four speedy cherubim
Put to their mouths the sounding alchemy
By herald's voice explained: the hollow abyss
Heard far and wide, and all the host of hell
With deafening shout, returned them loud acclaim.   520
Thence more at ease their minds and somewhat raised
By false presumptuous hope, the ranged powers
Disband, and wandering, each his several way
Pursues, as inclination or sad choice
Leads him perplexed, where he may likeliest find   525
Truce to his restless thoughts, and entertain
The irksome hours, till this great chief return.
Part on the plain, or in the air sublime
Upon the wing, or in swift race contend,
As at the Olympian games or Pythian fields;   530
Part curb their fiery steeds, or shun the goal
With rapid wheels, or fronted brigades form.
As when to warn proud cities war appears
Waged in the troubled sky, and armies rush
To battle in the clouds, before each van   535
Prick forth the airy knights, and couch their spears
Till thickest legions close; with feats of arms
From either end of heaven the welkin burns.
Others with vast Typhoean rage more fell
Rend up both rocks and hills, and ride the air   540
In whirlwind; hell scarce holds the wild uproar.
As when Alcides from Oechalia crowned
With conquest, felt the envenomed robe, and tore
Through pain up by the roots Thessalian pines,
And Lichas from the top of Oeta threw   545
Into the Euboic sea. Others more mild,
Retreated in a silent valley, sing
With notes angelical to many a harp

512. **globe**: a ring of warriors (a military term). Cf. *Nat. Ode* 110; *PR* IV:581.
513. **horrent**: bristling.
516. **four speedy cherubim**: note the parallel ranking of the rebel with the loyal angels.
517. **the sounding alchemy**: trumpets made from the metal alchemy, or any yellow alloy.
526. **entertain**: to pass, or while away time.
527. **this**: second edition reads, 'this'; first edition, 'his'; the pronoun in line 525 calls for 'his.'
528. **sublime**: Latin sense, meaning aloft, or uplifted.
542. **Alcides**: Hercules. Cf. Ovid, *Metamorphoses* IX, for the story.

Their own heroic deeds and hapless fall
By doom of battle; and complain that fate   550
Free virtue should enthrall to force or chance.
Their song was partial, but the harmony
(What could it less when spirits immortal sing?)
Suspended hell, and took with ravishment
The thronging audience. In discourse more sweet   555
(For eloquence the soul, song charms the sense,)
Others apart sat on a hill retired,
In thoughts more elevate, and reasoned high
Of providence, foreknowledge, will and fate,
Fixed fate, free will, foreknowledge absolute,   560
And found no end, in wandering mazes lost.
Of good and evil much they argued then,
Of happiness and final misery,
Passion and apathy, and glory and shame,
Vain wisdom all, and false philosophy: 565
Yet with a pleasing sorcery could charm
Pain for a while or anguish, and excite
Fallacious hope, or arm the obdured breast
With stubborn patience as with triple steel.
Another part in squadrons and gross bands,   570
On bold adventure to discover wide
That dismal world, if any clime perhaps
Might yield them easier habitation, bend
Four ways their flying march, along the banks
Of four infernal rivers that disgorge   575
Into the burning lake their baleful streams;
Abhorred Styx the flood of deadly hate,
Sad Acheron of sorrow, black and deep;
Cocytus, named of lamentation loud
Heard on the rueful stream; fierce Phlegeton   580
Whose waves of torrent fire inflame with rage.
Far off from these a slow and silent stream,
Lethe the river of oblivion rolls
Her watery labyrinth, whereof who drinks,
Forthwith his former state and being forgets,   585
Forgets both joy and grief, pleasure and pain.
Beyond this flood a frozen continent
Lies dark and wild, beat with perpetual storms
Of whirlwind and dire hail, which on firm land
Thaws not, but gathers heap, and ruin seems   590
Of ancient pile; all else deep snow and ice,
A gulf profound as that Serbonian bog

552. **partial**: favoring themselves.

576. **baleful**: woeful.

577 ff. **Styx . . . Acheron . . . Cocytus . . . Lethe**: the four rivers of Hades. Milton lists them in order and description more definitely than any ancient writer, yet separately he has ample authority for each statement he makes. Cf. Dante.

587. **a frozen continent**: hell contains both extremes of temperature.

592. **Serbonian bog**: in Egypt in ancient times.

Betwixt Damiata and Mount Casius old,
Where armies whole have sunk: the parching air
Burns frore, and cold performs the effect of fire.   595
Thither by harpy-footed furies haled,
At certain revolutions all the damned
Are brought: and feel by turns the bitter change
Of fierce extremes, extremes by change more fierce,
From beds of raging fire to starve in ice   600
Their soft ethereal warmth, and there to pine
Immovable, infixed, and frozen round,
Periods of time, thence hurried back to fire.
They ferry over this Lethean sound
Both to and fro, their sorrow to augment,   605
And wish and struggle, as they pass, to reach
The tempting stream, with one small drop to lose
In sweet forgetfulness all pain and woe,
All in one moment, and so near the brink;
But fate withstands, and to oppose the attempt   610
Medusa with Gorgonian terror guards
The ford, and of itself the water flies
All taste of living wight, as once it fled
The lip of Tantalus.   Thus roving on
In confused march forlorn, the adventurous bands   615
With shuddering horror pale, and eyes aghast
Viewed first their lamentable lot, and found
No rest: through many a dark and dreary vale
They passed, and many a region dolorous,
O'er many a frozen, many a fiery alp,   620
Rocks, caves, lakes, fens, bogs, dens, and shades of death,
A universe of death, which God by curse
Created evil, for evil only good,
Where all life dies, death lives, and nature breeds,
Perverse, all monstrous, all prodigious things,   625
Abominable, inutterable, and worse
Than fables yet have feigned, or fear conceived,
Gorgons and hydras, and chimeras dire.
    Meanwhile the adversary of God and man,
Satan with thoughts inflamed of highest design,   630
Puts on swift wings, and towards the gates of hell
Explores his solitary flight; sometimes
He scours the right hand coast, sometimes the left,
Now shaves with level wing the deep, then soars
Up to the fiery concave towering high.   635

595. **Burns frore:** burns cold, another contradiction.
596–603. There are many instances in literature of this idea of hell.
596. **harpy-footed:** talons, claws.
600. **starve:** to perish, the original meaning of the word in Old English.
611. **Medusa:** one of the three gorgons.   612–14. Cf. any classical dictionary for the story.
620. **alp:** a high mountain.   625. **prodigious:** unnatural, monstrous.
634. **shaves:** skims.   635. **concave:** as in I:542, the roof or vaulted 'overhead.'

As when far off at sea a fleet descried
Hangs in the clouds, by equinoctial winds
Close sailing from Bengala, or the isles
Of Ternate and Tidore, whence merchants bring
Their spicy drugs: they on the trading flood   640
Through the wide Ethiopian to the cape
Ply stemming nightly toward the pole.   So seemed
Far off the flying fiend: at last appear
Hell bounds high reaching to the horrid roof,
And thrice threefold the gates; three folds were brass,   645
Three iron, three of adamantine rock,
Impenetrable, impaled with circling fire,
Yet unconsumed.   Before the gates there sat
On either side a formidable shape;
The one seemed woman to the waist, and fair,   650
But ended foul in many a scaly fold
Voluminous and vast, a serpent armed
With mortal sting: about her middle round
A cry of hell hounds never ceasing barked
With wide Cerberean mouths full loud, and rung   655
A hideous peal: yet, when they list, would creep,
If aught disturbed their noise, into her womb,
And kennel there, yet there still barked and howled,
Within unseen.   Far less abhorred than these
Vexed Scylla bathing in the sea that parts   660
Calabria from the hoarse Trinacrian shore:
Nor uglier follow the night-hag, when called
In secret, riding through the air she comes
Lured with the smell of infant blood, to dance
With Lapland witches, while the laboring moon   665
Eclipses at their charms.   The other shape,
If shape it might be called that shape had none
Distinguishable in member, joint, or limb,
Or substance might be called that shadow seemed,
For each seemed either; black it stood as night,   ,   670
Fierce as ten furies, terrible as hell,
And shook a dreadful dart; what seemed his head
The likeness of a kingly crown had on.

641. **the wide Ethiopian**: the Indian Ocean.

644. **horrid roof**: in both senses of the word *horrid*, rugged, juttingly uneven, and terrible.

648 ff. The whole picture is a composite allegory and emblem based on *James* 1:15. Note Milton's 'incorrigible romanticism' breaking through in the introduction of the 'night-hag' in line 662.

650. Such a figure of sin was conventional, and the same statement is equally true of the 'shade' of death in lines 666 ff.

661. **Calabria ... Trinacrian shore**: Italy and Sicily.

662. **night-hag**: Hecate, with a touch of Lilith.

665. **Lapland witches**: as everybody knew, Lapland was the land of witchcraft.

666 ff. It is impossible to visualize this figure, though illustrators have been fascinated by it. Vivid and convincing in its place, nowhere in all his work does Milton succeed so well as in this figure in presenting our minds with a fully rounded figure, not a single detail of which is detailed, definite, or certain. This is a characteristic of his that appears often, but never more effectively than here.

Satan was now at hand, and from his seat
The monster moving onward came as fast   675
With horrid strides, hell trembled as he strode.
The undaunted fiend what this might be admired,
Admired, not feared; God and his Son except,
Created thing naught valued he nor shunned;
And with disdainful look thus first began.   680
   'Whence and what art thou, execrable shape,
That darest, though grim and terrible, advance
Thy miscreated front athwart my way
To yonder gates? through them I mean to pass,
That be assured, without leave asked of thee: 685
Retire, or taste thy folly, and learn by proof,
Hell-born, not to contend with spirits of heaven.'
   To whom the goblin full of wrath replied,
'Art thou that traitor angel, art thou he,
Who first broke peace in heaven and faith, till then   690
Unbroken, and in proud rebellious arms
Drew after him the third part of heaven's sons
Conjured against the highest, for which both thou
And they outcast from God, are here condemned
To waste eternal days in woe and pain?   695
And reckonest thou thyself with spirits of heaven,
Hell-doomed, and breathest defiance here and scorn
Where I reign king, and to enrage thee more,
Thy king and lord?   Back to thy punishment,
False fugitive, and to thy speed add wings,   700
Lest with a whip of scorpions I pursue
Thy lingering, or with one stroke of this dart
Strange horror seize thee, and pangs unfelt before.'
   So spake the grisly terror, and in shape,
So speaking and so threatening, grew tenfold   705
More dreadful and deform: on the other side
Incensed with indignation Satan stood
Unterrified, and like a comet burned,
That fires the length of Ophiuchus huge
In the arctic sky, and from his horrid hair   710
Shakes pestilence and war.   Each at the head
Leveled his deadly aim; their fatal hands
No second stroke intend, and such a frown
Each cast at the other, as when two black clouds
With heaven's artillery fraught, come rattling on   715
Over the Caspian, then stand front to front
Hovering a space, till winds the signal blow
To join their dark encounter in mid-air:

677. **admired**: wondered.   Cf. I:190.

689 ff. We are not told how Death knew all that had taken place, but cf. lines 768–77.   Even there, the action and the chronology are obscure.

708. **like a comet burned**: cf. Virgil, *Aeneid* X:272–73.

709. **Ophiuchus**: a huge constellation.   710–11. Comets were omens, generally of disaster.

So frowned the mighty combatants, that hell
Grew darker at their frown, so matched they stood;   720
For never but once more was either like
To meet so great a foe: and now great deeds
Had been achieved, whereof all hell had rung,
Had not the snaky sorceress that sat
Fast by hell gate, and kept the fatal key,   725
Risen, and with hideous outcry rushed between.
     'O father, what intends thy hand,' she cried,
'Against thy only son?   What fury O son,
Possesses thee to bend that mortal dart
Against thy father's head? and knowest for whom;   730
For him who sits above and laughs the while
At thee ordained his drudge, to execute
Whate'er his wrath, which he calls justice, bids,
His wrath which one day will destroy ye both.'
     She spake, and at her words the hellish pest   735
Forbore, then these to her Satan returned:
     'So strange thy outcry, and thy words so strange
Thou interposest, that my sudden hand
Prevented spares to tell thee yet by deeds
What it intends; till first I know of thee,   740
What thing thou art, thus double-formed, and why
In this infernal vale first met thou callest
Me father, and that phantasm callest my son?
I know thee not, nor ever saw till now
Sight more detestable than him and thee.'   745
     To whom thus the portress of hell gate replied;
'Hast thou forgot me then, and do I seem
Now in thine eye so foul, once deemed so fair
In heaven, when at the assembly, and in sight
Of all the seraphim with thee combined   750
In bold conspiracy against heaven's king,
All on a sudden miserable pain
Surprised thee, dim thine eyes, and dizzy swum
In darkness, while thy head flames thick and fast
Threw forth, till on the left side opening wide,   755
Likest to thee in shape and countenance bright,
Then shining heavenly fair, a goddess armed
Out of thy head I sprung: amazement seized
All the host of heaven; back they recoiled afraid
At first, and called me Sin, and for a sign   760
Portentous held me; but familiar grown,
I pleased, and with attractive graces won
The most averse, thee chiefly, who full oft
Thyself in me thy perfect image viewing

747 ff. The allegory of the birth of sin, engendered alone by Satan and his proud, rebellious thoughts; born, like Minerva; then Satan uniting with sin to beget death, a rapacious monster; breeding other monsters with sin; then devouring all; restrained only from devouring sin herself in order to satiate his appetites — all this was exactly the kind of complicated and terrible allegory admired in the Middle Ages, the Renaissance, and even later.   Cf. *James* 1:15, in *NT*.   See also *Apology Col.* III:1:355–56.

Becamest enamored, and such joy thou tookest   765
With me in secret, that my womb conceived
A growing burden.   Meanwhile war arose,
And fields were fought in heaven; wherein remained
(For what could else) to our almighty foe
Clear victory, to our part loss and rout   770
Through all the empyrean: down they fell
Driven headlong from the pitch of heaven, down
Into this deep, and in the general fall
I also; at which time this powerful key
Into my hand was given, with charge to keep   775
These gates forever shut, which none can pass
Without my opening.   Pensive here I sat
Alone, but long I sat not, till my womb
Pregnant by thee, and now excessive grown
Prodigious motion felt and rueful throes.   780
At last this odious offspring whom thou seest
Thine own begotten, breaking violent way
Tore through my entrails, that with fear and pain
Distorted, all my nether shape thus grew
Transformed: but he my inbred enemy   785
Forth issued, brandishing his fatal dart
Made to destroy: I fled, and cried out "Death;"
Hell trembled at the hideous name, and sighed
From all her caves, and back resounded "Death."
I fled, but he pursued (though more, it seems,   790
Inflamed with lust than rage) and swifter far,
Me overtook his mother all dismayed,
And in embraces forcible and foul
Engendering with me, of that rape begot
These yelling monsters that with ceaseless cry   795
Surround me, as thou sawest, hourly conceived
And hourly born, with sorrow infinite
To me, for when they list into the womb
That bred them they return, and howl and gnaw
My bowels, their repast; then bursting forth   800
Afresh with conscious terrors vex me round,
That rest or intermission none I find.
Before mine eyes in opposition sits
Grim Death my son and foe, who sets them on,
And me his parent would full soon devour   805
For want of other prey, but that he knows
His end with mine involved; and knows that I
Should prove a bitter morsel, and his bane,
Whenever that shall be; so fate pronounced.
But thou O father, I forewarn thee, shun   810
His deadly arrow; neither vainly hope
To be invulnerable in those bright arms,
Though tempered heavenly, for that mortal dint,
Save he who reigns above, none can resist.'

768. **fields were fought**: battles were fought.   Cf. I:105; II:292.
785. **inbred enemy**: a mild pun.   813. **dint**: blow.

She finished, and the subtle fiend his lore   815
Soon learned, now milder, and thus answered smooth.
'Dear daughter, since thou claimest me for thy sire,
And my fair son here showest me, the dear pledge
Of dalliance had with thee in heaven, and joys
Then sweet, now sad to mention, through dire change   820
Befallen us unforeseen, unthought of, know
I come no enemy, but to set free
From out this dark and dismal house of pain,
Both him and thee, and all the heavenly host
Of spirits that in our just pretences armed   825
Fell with us from on high: from them I go
This uncouth errand sole, and one for all
Myself expose, with lonely steps to tread
The unfounded deep, and through the void immense
To search with wandering quest a place foretold   830
Should be, and, by concurring signs, ere now
Created vast and round, a place of bliss
In the purlieus of heaven, and therein placed
A race of upstart creatures, to supply
Perhaps our vacant room, though more removed,   835
Lest heaven surcharged with potent multitude
Might hap to move new broils: Be this or aught
Than this more secret now designed, I haste
To know, and this once known, shall soon return,
And bring ye to the place where thou and death   840
Shall dwell at ease, and up and down unseen
Wing silently the buxom air, embalmed
With odors; there ye shall be fed and filled
Immeasurably, all things shall be your prey.'
He ceased, for both seemed highly pleased, and death   845
Grinned horrible a ghastly smile, to hear
His famine should be filled, and blessed his maw
Destined to that good hour: no less rejoiced
His mother bad, and thus bespake her sire.
'The key of this infernal pit by due,   850
And by command of heaven's all-powerful king
I keep, by him forbidden to unlock
These adamantine gates; against all force
Death ready stands to interpose his dart,
Fearless to be o'ermatched by living might.   855
But what owe I to his commands above
Who hates me, and hath hither thrust me down
Into this gloom of Tartarus profound,
To sit in hateful office here confined,
Inhabitant of heaven, and heavenly-born,   860
Here in perpetual agony and pain,

827. **uncouth**: unknown in the sense of uncertain.
842. **buxom**: yielding and pliant.
853. **adamantine**: made of diamond, the hardest of all substances.

With terrors and with clamors compassed round
Of mine own brood, that on my bowels feed:
Thou art my father, thou my author, thou
My being gavest me; whom should I obey   865
But thee, whom follow? thou wilt bring me soon
To that new world of light and bliss, among
The gods who live at ease, where I shall reign
At thy right hand voluptuous, as beseems
Thy daughter and thy darling, without end.'   870
　　Thus saying, from her side the fatal key,
Sad instrument of all our woe, she took;
And towards the gate rolling her bestial train,
Forthwith the huge portcullis high updrew,
Which but herself not all the Stygian powers   875
Could once have moved; then in the keyhole turns
The intricate wards, and every bolt and bar
Of massy iron or solid rock with ease
Unfastens: on a sudden open fly
With impetuous recoil and jarring sound   880
The infernal doors, and on their hinges grate
Harsh thunder, that the lowest bottom shook
Of Erebus.　She opened, but to shut
Excelled her power; the gates wide open stood,
That with extended wings a bannered host   885
Under spread ensigns marching might pass through
With horse and chariots ranked in loose array;
So wide they stood, and like a furnace mouth
Cast forth redounding smoke and ruddy flame.
Before their eyes in sudden view appear   890
The secrets of the hoary deep, a dark
Illimitable ocean without bound,
Without dimension, where length, breadth, and height,
And time and place are lost; where eldest night
And chaos, ancestors of nature, hold   895
Eternal anarchy, amidst the noise
Of endless wars, and by confusion stand.
For hot, cold, moist, and dry, four champions fierce
Strive here for mastery, and to battle bring
Their embryon atoms; they around the flag   900
Of each his faction, in their several clans,
Light-armed or heavy, sharp, smooth, swift or slow,
Swarm populous, unnumbered as the sands

868–69. Note the sacrilegious mimicry of God and the Christ, his only begotten Son.
874. **the huge portcullis high updrew**: most illustrators have ignored this line, using only lines 881–82.
877. **intricate wards**: tumblers, perhaps, but the word *ward* has a technical meaning in locksmithery.
879–82. Compare with opening of heaven's doors, VII:205–07.
883. **Erebus**: from Greek mythology, used for hell.
891. **the hoary deep**: gray with mists and timelessness.
891 ff. Cf. Ovid, *Metamorphoses* I:5–20, and Lucretius.
903–04. Regions (cities) in North Africa.

Of Barca or Cyrene's torrid soil,
Levied to side with warring winds, and poise   905
Their lighter wings.   To whom these most adhere,
He rules a moment; chaos umpire sits,
And by decision more embroils the fray
By which he reigns: next him high arbiter
Chance governs all.   Into this wild abyss,   910
The womb of nature and perhaps her grave,
Of neither sea, nor shore, nor air, nor fire,
But all these in their pregnant causes mixed
Confusedly, and which thus must ever fight,
Unless the almighty maker them ordain   915
His dark materials to create more worlds,
Into this wild abyss the wary fiend
Stood on the brink of hell and looked a while,
Pondering his voyage; for no narrow frith
He had to cross.   Nor was his ear less pealed   920
With noises loud and ruinous (to compare
Great things with small) than when Bellona storms,
With all her battering engines bent to rase
Some capital city; or less than if this frame
Of heaven were falling, and these elements   925
In mutiny had from her axle torn
The steadfast earth.   At last his sail-broad vanes
He spreads for flight, and in the surging smoke
Uplifted spurns the ground, thence many a league
As in a cloudy chair ascending rides   930
Audacious, but that seat soon failing, meets
A vast vacuity: all unawares
Fluttering his pennons vain plumb down he drops
Ten thousand fathom deep, and to this hour
Down had been falling, had not by ill chance   935
The strong rebuff of some tumultuous cloud
Instinct with fire and niter hurried him
As many miles aloft: that fury stayed,
Quenched in a boggy Syrtis, neither sea,
Nor good dry land: nigh foundered on he fares,   940
Treading the crude consistence, half on foot,
Half flying; behooves him now both oar and sail.
As when a griffin through the wilderness
With winged course o'er hill or moory dale,
Pursues the Arimaspian, who by stealth   945

916. **more worlds:** in Milton's day appeared a number of speculations on the idea of new worlds being made.

919. **frith:** firth, arm of the sea.   922. **Bellona:** war personified.

927. **vanes:** most editors print *vans*, but more people say 'weathervanes' than say 'weathervans,' though the two words have common affiliations with *fan* and *fane*, a sail.   Should line 933 read 'pennons' vane,' 'pennon's vane,' or 'pennons vain'?

932 ff. Does the whole action of the poem depend on this accident?

937. **Instinct:** filled.   939. **Syrtis:** quicksands.

943 ff. Cf. Herodotus, IV:13, 27, and Pliny, *Natural History* VII:2.

Had from his wakeful custody purloined
The guarded gold: So eagerly the fiend
O'er bog or steep, through strait, rough, dense, or rare,
With head, hands, wings or feet pursues his way,
And swims or sinks, or wades, or creeps, or flies: 950
At length a universal hubbub wild
Of stunning sounds and voices all confused
Borne through the hollow dark assaults his ear
With loudest vehemence: thither he plies,
Undaunted to meet there whatever power   955
Or Spirit of the nethermost abyss
Might in that noise reside, of whom to ask
Which way the nearest coast of darkness lies
Bordering on light; when straight behold the throne
Of Chaos, and his dark pavilion spread   960
Wide on the wasteful deep; with him enthroned
Sat sable-vested Night, eldest of things,
The consort of his reign; and by them stood
Orcus and Ades, and the dreaded name
Of Demogorgon; Rumor next and Chance,   965
And Tumult and Confusion all embroiled,
And Discord with a thousand various mouths.
     To whom Satan turning boldly, thus.   'Ye powers
And spirits of this nethermost abyss,
Chaos and ancient Night, I come no spy,   970
With purpose to explore or to disturb
The secrets of your realm, but by constraint
Wandering this darksome desert, as my way,
Lies through your spacious empire up to light,
Alone, and without guide, half lost, I seek   975
What readiest path leads where your gloomy bounds
Confine with heaven; or if some other place
From your dominion won, the ethereal king
Possesses lately, thither to arrive
I travel this profound, direct my course;   980
Directed no mean recompense it brings
To your behoof, if I that region lost,
All usurpation thence expelled, reduce
To her original darkness and your sway
(Which is my present journey) and once more   985
Erect the standard there of ancient night;
Yours be the advantage all, mine the revenge.'
     Thus Satan; and him thus the anarch old
With faltering speech and visage incomposed
Answered.   'I know thee, stranger, who thou art,   990

948. **rare**: thin.
956. **nethermost abyss**: was Satan now below hell?   Note how ambiguous Milton really is concerning definite locations.
960–67. The names are personifications.   964. **Orcus and Ades**: names of Pluto.
965. **Demogorgon**: cf. Spenser, *Faerie Queene* IV:2:47.   972. **constraint**: necessity.
977. **Confine with**: border on.   988. **anarch**: leader of anarchy.

That mighty leading angel, who of late
Made head against heaven's king, though overthrown.
I saw and heard, for such a numerous host
Fled not in silence through the frighted deep
With ruin upon ruin, rout on rout,   995
Confusion worse confounded; and heaven gates
Poured out by millions her victorious bands
Pursuing.   I upon my frontiers here
Keep residence; if all I can will serve,
That little which is left so to defend,   1000
Encroached on still through our intestine broils
Weakening the scepter of old night: first hell
Your dungeon stretching far and wide beneath;
Now lately heaven and earth, another world
Hung o'er my realm, linked in a golden chain   1005
To that side heaven from whence your legions fell:
If that way be your walk, you have not far;
So much the nearer danger; go and speed;
Havoc and spoil and ruin are my gain.'
        He ceased; and Satan stayed not to reply,   1010
But glad that now his sea should find a shore,
With fresh alacrity and force renewed
Springs upward like a pyramid of fire
Into the wild expanse, and through the shock
Of fighting elements, on all sides round   1015
Environed wins his way; harder beset
And more endangered, than when Argo passed
Through Bosporus betwixt the justling rocks:
Or when Ulysses on the larboard shunned
Charybdis, and by the other whirlpool steered.   1020
So he with difficulty and labor hard
Moved on, with difficulty and labor he;
But he once passed, soon after when man fell,
Strange alteration!   Sin and death amain
Following his track, such was the will of heaven,   1025
Paved after him a broad and beaten way
Over the dark abyss, whose boiling gulf
Tamely endured a bridge of wondrous length
From hell continued reaching the utmost orb
Of this frail world; by which the spirits perverse   1030
With easy intercourse pass to and fro
To tempt or punish mortals, except whom

1001. **our:** both first and second editions read 'our,' and though the sense calls for 'your' only Newton (1749) has actually printed it.

1002–03. According to this account, hell was made first, then the universe 'heaven and earth.'   Cf. VII:131 ff.

1017–18. The Argonauts.   1019–20. Cf. Homer, *Odyssey* XII:73 ff.

1024. **amain:** with speed.

1024–30. No real source for this notion has ever been found.   The story is probably Persian in origin and reached Europe through Arabic tales.   Cf. X:293 ff.

1030. **this frail world:** as usual, 'world' denotes the created universe.

God and good angels guard by special grace.
But now at last the sacred influence
Of light appears, and from the walls of heaven   1035
Shoots far into the bosom of dim night
A glimmering dawn; here nature first begins
Her farthest verge, and chaos to retire
As from her outmost works a broked foe
With tumult less and with less hostile din,   1040
That Satan with less toil, and now with ease
Wafts on the calmer wave by dubious light
And like a weather-beaten vessel holds
Gladly the port, though shrouds and tackle torn;
Or in the emptier waste, resembling air,   1045
Weighs his spread wings, at leisure to behold
Far off the empyreal heaven, extended wide
In circuit, undetermined square or round,
With opal towers and battlements adorned
Of living sapphire, once his native seat;   1050
And fast by hanging in a golden chain
This pendent world, in bigness as a star
Of smallest magnitude close by the moon.
Thither full fraught with mischievous revenge,
Accursed, and in a cursed hour he hies.   1055

THE END OF THE SECOND BOOK

BOOK III

THE ARGUMENT

God sitting on his throne sees Satan flying towards this world, then newly created; shows him to the Son who sat at his right hand; foretells the success of Satan in perverting mankind; clears his own justice and wisdom from all imputation, having created man free and able enough to have withstood his tempter; yet declares his purpose of grace towards him, in regard he fell not of his own malice, as did Satan, but by him seduced. The Son of God renders praises to his father for the manifestation of his gracious purpose towards man; but God again declares, that grace cannot be extended towards man without the satisfaction of divine justice; man hath offended the majesty of God by aspiring to Godhead, and therefore with all his progeny devoted to death must die, unless someone can be found sufficient to answer for his offence, and undergo his punishment. The Son of God freely offers himself a ransom for man: the father accepts him, ordains his incarnation, pronounces his exaltation above all names in heaven and earth; commands all the angels to adore him; they obey, and hymning to their harps in full choir, celebrate the Father and the Son. Meanwhile Satan alights upon the bare convex of this

---

1034-35. **influence of light:** here an astrological term, *influence*, meaning 'emanation.' Cf. *Job* 38:31, in *AV*.   1039. **broked:** so second edition; first edition reads 'broken.'

1048. **undetermined square or round:** Milton deliberately refrains from giving a shape to heaven, therefore the next line immediately becomes figurative.

1052. **This pendent world:** the whole created universe, not the earth. Note the magnitude of the conception.   1055. **Accursed, and in a cursed:** a somber pun.

world's outermost orb; where wandering he first finds a place since called the limbo
of vanity; what persons and things fly up thither; thence comes to the gate of
heaven, described ascending by stairs, and the waters above the firmament that
flow about it: His passage thence to the orb of the sun; he finds there Uriel the
regent of that orb, but first changes himself into the shape of a meaner angel; and
pretending a zealous desire to behold the new creation and man whom God had
placed here, inquires of him the place of his habitation, and is directed; alights
first on Mount Niphates.

Hail holy light, offspring of heaven first-born,
Or of the eternal coeternal beam
May I express thee unblamed? since God is light,
And never but in unapproached light
Dwelt from eternity, dwelt then in thee,   5
Bright effluence of bright essence increate.
Or hearest thou rather pure ethereal stream,
Whose fountain who shall tell? before the sun,
Before the heavens thou wert, and at the voice
Of God, as with a mantle didst invest   10
The rising world of waters dark and deep,
Won from the void and formless infinite.
Thee I revisit now with bolder wing,
Escaped the Stygian pool, though long detained
In that obscure sojourn, while in my flight   15
Through utter and through middle darkness borne
With other notes than to the Orphean lyre
I sung of chaos and eternal night,
Taught by the heavenly muse to venture down
The dark descent, and up to reascend,   20
Though hard and rare: thee I revisit safe,
And feel thy sovereign vital lamp; but thou
Revisitest not these eyes, that roll in vain
To find thy piercing ray, and find no dawn;
So thick a drop serene hath quenched their orbs,   25
Or dim suffusion veiled.   Yet not the more
Cease I to wander where the muses haunt
Clear spring, or shady grove, or sunny hill,
Smit with the love of sacred song; but chief
Thee Sion and the flowery brooks beneath   30
That wash thy hallowed feet, and warbling flow,
Nightly I visit: nor sometimes forget
Those other two equaled with me in fate,
So were I equaled with them in renown,
Blind Thamyris and blind Maeonides,   35
And Tiresias and Phineus prophets old.

22 ff. One of the most famous accounts of Milton's blindness.

25. **drop serene:** Latin, *gutta serena,* or complete amaurosis, total blindness.

35. **Thamyris:** cf. Homer, *Iliad* II:595–600; a Thracian poet who was deprived of his eyesight and voice
for boasting he could surpass the muses in song.   **Maeonides:** Homer.

36. **Tiresias:** the blind soothsayer of Thebes celebrated by many poets.   **Phineus:** another blind
prophet-poet.   Cf. Apollonius Rhodius, *Argonautica.*

Then feed on thoughts, that voluntary move
Harmonious numbers; as the wakeful bird
Sings darkling, and in shadiest covert hid
Tunes her nocturnal note.   Thus with the year   40
Seasons return, but not to me returns
Day, or the sweet approach of even or morn,
Or sight of vernal bloom, or summer's rose,
Or flocks, or herds, or human face divine;
But cloud instead, and ever-during dark   45
Surrounds me, from the cheerful ways of men
Cut off, and for the book of knowledge fair
Presented with a universal blank
Of nature's works to me expunged and rased,
And wisdom at one entrance quite shut out.   50
So much the rather thou celestial light
Shine inward, and the mind through all her powers
Irradiate, there plant eyes, all mist from thence
Purge and disperse, that I may see and tell
Of things invisible to mortal sight.   55
   Now had the almighty father from above,
From the pure empyrean where he sits
High throned above all height, bent down his eye,
His own works and their works at once to view:
About him all the sanctities of heaven   60
Stood thick as stars, and from his sight received
Beatitude past utterance; on his right
The radiant image of his glory sat,
His only Son; On earth he first beheld
Our two first parents, yet the only two   65
Of mankind, in the happy garden placed,
Reaping immortal fruits of joy and love,
Uninterrupted joy, unrivaled love
In blissful solitude; he then surveyed
Hell and the gulf between, and Satan there   70
Coasting the wall of heaven on this side night
In the dun air sublime, and ready now
To stoop with wearied wings, and willing feet
On the bare outside of this world, that seemed
Firm land imbosomed without firmament,   75
Uncertain which, in ocean or in air.
Him God beholding from his prospect high,
Wherein past, present, future he beholds,
Thus to his only son foreseeing spake.
   'Only begotten son, seest thou what rage   80
Transports our adversary, whom no bounds

38. **wakeful bird:** the nightingale.

48. **universal blank:** probably *blanc* (meaning 'white') would be better, as in both first and second editions.

61–62. **his sight . . . beatitude:** the beatific vision of the scholastics.   Cf. I:684.   Only pure spirits can see the glory and beauty of God.

72. **dun air:** dusky atmosphere.   73. **stoop:** to alight as a bird alights.

Prescribed, no bars of hell, nor all the chains
Heaped on him there, nor yet the main abyss
Wide interrupt can hold; so bent he seems
On desperate revenge, that shall redound   85
Upon his own rebellious head.   And now
Through all restraint broke loose he wings his way
Not far off heaven, in the precincts of light,
Directly towards the new created world,
And man there placed, with purpose to assay   90
If him by force he can destroy, or worse,
By some false guile pervert; and shall pervert
For man will hearken to his glozing lies,
And easily transgress the sole command,
Sole pledge of his obedience: So will fall,   95
He and his faithless progeny: whose fault?
Whose but his own? ingrate, he had of me
All he could have; I made him just and right,
Sufficient to have stood, though free to fall.
Such I created all the ethereal powers   100
And spirits, both them who stood and them who failed;
Freely they stood who stood, and fell who fell.
Not free, what proof could they have given sincere
Of true allegiance, constant faith or love,
Where only what they needs must do, appeared,   105
Not what they would? what praise could they receive?
What pleasure I from such obedience paid,
When will and reason (reason also is choice)
Useless and vain, of freedom both despoiled,
Made passive both, had served necessity,   110
Not me.   They therefore as to right belonged,
So were created, nor can justly accuse
Their maker, or their making, or their fate,
As if predestination overruled
Their will, disposed by absolute decree   115
Or high foreknowledge; they themselves decreed
Their own revolt, not I: if I foreknew,
Foreknowledge had no influence on their fault,
Which had no less proved certain unforeknown.
So without least impulse or shadow of fate,   120
Or aught by me immutably forseen,
They trespass, authors to themselves in all
Both what they judge and what they choose; for so
I formed them free, and free they must remain,
Till they enthrall themselves: I else must change   125
Their nature, and revoke the high decree
Unchangeable, eternal, which ordained
Their freedom, they themselves ordained their fall.
The first sort by their own suggestion fell,

93. **glozing lies:** flattering or extenuating lies.   Cf. IX:549, 'so glozed the tempter.'

111 ff. Note how carefully Milton denies the Calvinistic position with reference to the non-freedom of the will or predestination.   Other Calvinistic doctrines he accepts, in part, but not this one.

Self-tempted, self-depraved: Man falls deceived   130
By the other first: Man therefore shall find grace,
The other none: in mercy and justice both,
Through heaven and earth, so shall my glory excel,
But mercy first and last shall brightest shine.'
   Thus while God spake, ambrosial fragrance filled   135
All heaven, and in the blessed spirits elect
Sense of new joy ineffable diffused:
Beyond compare the Son of God was seen
Most glorious, in him all his father shone
Substantially expressed, and in his face   140
Divine compassion visibly appeared,
Love without end, and without measure grace,
Which uttering thus he to his father spake.
   'O father, gracious was that word which closed
Thy sovereign sentence, that man should find grace;   145
For which both heaven and earth shall high extol
Thy praises, with the innumerable sound
Of hymns and sacred songs, wherewith thy throne
Encompassed shall resound thee ever blest.
For should man finally be lost, should man   150
Thy creature late so loved, thy youngest son
Fall circumvented thus by fraud, though joined
With his own folly? that be from thee far,
That far be from thee, father, who art judge
Of all things made, and judgest only right.   155
Or shall the adversary thus obtain
His end, and frustrate thine, shall he fulfill
His malice, and thy goodness bring to naught,
Or proud return though to his heavier doom,
Yet with revenge accomplished and to hell   160
Draw after him the whole race of mankind,
By him corrupted? or wilt thou thyself
Abolish thy creation, and unmake,
For him, what for thy glory thou hast made?
So should thy goodness and thy greatness both   165
Be questioned and blasphemed without defense.'
   To whom the great creator thus replied.
'O Son, in whom my soul hath chief delight,
Son of my bosom, Son who art alone
My word, my wisdom, and effectual might,   170
All hast thou spoken as my thoughts are, all
As my eternal purpose hath decreed:
Man shall not quite be lost, but saved who will,
Yet not of will in him, but grace in me
Freely vouchsafed; once more I will renew   175
His lapsed powers, though forfeit and enthralled

---

136. **blessed spirits elect**: both words 'blessed' and 'elect' are adjectives.
156. **the adversary**: an exact translation of the Hebrew 'the satan.'
173–75. Milton's doctrine of salvation.   Salvation herein depends on man's will and God's grace.

By sin to foul exorbitant desires;
Upheld by me, yet once more he shall stand
On even ground against his mortal foe,
By me upheld, that he may know how frail   180
His fallen condition is, and to me owe
All his deliverance, and to none but me.
Some I have chosen of peculiar grace
Elect above the rest; so is my will:
The rest shall hear me call, and oft be warned   185
Their sinful state, and to appease betimes
The incensed Deity, while offered grace
Invites; for I will clear their senses dark,
What may suffice, and soften stony hearts
To pray, repent, and bring obedience due.   190
To prayer, repentance, and obedience due,
Though but endeavored with sincere intent,
Mine ear shall not be slow, mine eye not shut.
And I will place within them as a guide
My umpire conscience, whom if they will hear,   195
Light after light well used they shall attain,
And to the end persisting, safe arrive.
This my long sufferance and my day of grace
They who neglect and scorn, shall never taste;
But hard be hardened, blind be blinded more,   200
That they may stumble on, and deeper fall;
And none but such from mercy I exclude.
But yet all is not done; man disobeying,
Disloyal breaks his fealty, and sins
Against the high supremacy of heaven,   205
Affecting godhead, and so losing all,
To expiate his treason hath naught left,
But to destruction sacred and devote,
He with his whole posterity must die,
Die he or justice must; unless for him   210
Some other able, and as willing, pay
The rigid satisfaction, death for death.
Say heavenly powers, where shall we find such love,
Which of ye will be mortal to redeem
Man's mortal crime, and just the unjust to save,   215
Dwells in all heaven charity so dear?'
    He asked, but all the heavenly choir stood mute,
And silence was in heaven: on man's behalf
Patron or intercessor none appeared,

183–84. Milton's doctrine of the saints, for saints there are in his scheme, but they are saints through their own volition, though God permits them to be so.

195. **whom:** a rare distinction in case form in the seventeenth century.

202. **none but such:** only those who refuse God's precepts and grace are excluded from the elect.

206. **Affecting godhead:** note IX:708 and *Genesis* 3:5.

217 ff. Note similarity to scene in hell when Satan called for volunteers. Everything done in heaven is imitated in hell, but reversed in intent and outcome.

219. **Patron:** defender or advocate.

Much less that durst upon his own head draw   220
The deadly forfeiture, and ransom set.
And now without redemption all mankind
Must have been lost, adjudged to death and hell
By doom severe, had not the Son of God,
In whom the fulness dwells of love divine,   225
His dearest mediation thus renewed.
   'Father, thy word is passed, man shall find grace;
And shall grace not find means, that finds her way,
The speediest of thy winged messengers,
To visit all thy creatures, and to all   230
Comes unprevented, unimplored, unsought,
Happy for man, so coming; he her aid
Can never seek, once dead in sins and lost;
Atonement for himself or offering meet,
Indebted and undone, hath none to bring: 235
Behold me then, me for him, life for life
I offer, on me let thine anger fall;
Account me man; I for his sake will leave
Thy bosom, and this glory next to thee
Freely put off, and for him lastly die   240
Well pleased, on me let death wreak all his rage;
Under his gloomy power I shall not long
Lie vanquished; thou hast given me to possess
Life in myself forever, by thee I live,
Though now to death I yield, and am his due   245
All that of me can die, yet that debt paid,
Thou wilt not leave me in the loathsome grave
His prey, nor suffer my unspotted soul
Forever with corruption there to dwell;
But I shall rise victorious, and subdue   250
My vanquisher, spoiled of his vaunted spoil;
Death his death's wound shall then receive, and stoop
Inglorious, of his mortal sting disarmed.
I through the ample air in triumph high
Shall lead hell captive mauger hell, and show   255
The powers of darkness bound.   Thou at the sight
Pleased, out of heaven shalt look down and smile,
While by thee raised I ruin all my foes,
Death last, and with his carcass glut the grave:
Then with the multitude of my redeemed   260
Shall enter heaven long absent, and return,
Father, to see thy face, wherein no cloud
Of anger shall remain, but peace assured,
And reconcilement; wrath shall be no more
Thenceforth, but in thy presence joy entire.'   265
   His words here ended, but his meek aspect
Silent yet spake, and breathed immortal love

255. **mauger:** in spite of; French *malgré*.

259. **carcass:** many modern editions print 'carcase,' though there is no reason for doing so.   Wright,
Verity, and Hanford 'carcase,' but both first and second editions read 'carcass.'

To mortal men, above which only shone
Filial obedience: as a sacrifice
Glad to be offered, he attends the will   270
Of his great father.   Admiration seized
All heaven, what this might mean, and whither tend
Wondering; but soon the almighty thus replied:
    'O thou in heaven and earth the only peace
Found out for mankind under wrath, O thou   275
My sole complacence! well thou knowest how dear,
To me are all my works, nor man the least
Though last created, that for him I spare
Thee from my bosom and right hand, to save,
By losing thee a while, the whole race lost.   280
Thou therefore whom thou only canst redeem,
Their nature also to thy nature join;
And be thyself man among men on earth,
Made flesh, when time shall be, of virgin seed,
By wondrous birth: Be thou in Adam's room   285
The head of all mankind, though Adam's son.
As in him perish all men, so in thee
As from a second root shall be restored,
As many as are restored, without thee none.
His crime makes guilty all his sons, thy merit   290
Imputed shall absolve them who renounce
Their own both righteous and unrighteous deeds,
And live in thee transplanted, and from thee
Receive new life.   So man, as is most just,
Shall satisfy for man, be judged and die,   295
And dying rise, and rising with him raise
His brethren, ransomed with his own dear life.
So heavenly love shall outdo hellish hate
Giving to death, and dying to redeem,
So dearly to redeem what hellish hate   300
So easily destroyed, and still destroys
In those who, when they may, accept not grace.
Nor shalt thou by descending to assume
Man's nature, lessen or degrade thine own.
Because thou hast, though throned in highest bliss   305
Equal to God, and equally enjoying
God-like fruition, quitted all to save
A world from utter loss, and hast been found
By merit more than birthright Son of God,
Found worthiest to be so by being good,   310
Far more than great or high; because in thee
Love hath abounded more than glory abounds,
Therefore thy humiliation shall exalt

271. **Admiration**: wonder, astonishment.
285. **room**: stead, the two words meaning exactly the same thing.
290 ff. Milton's theory, not original with him, but to which he subscribes, of imputed righteousness.
Cf. XII:407-10.
299. **Giving to death**: yielding to death.

With thee thy manhood also to this throne;
Here shalt thou sit incarnate, here shalt reign
Both God and man, son both of God and man,   315
Anointed universal king; all power
I give thee, reign forever, and assume
Thy merits; under thee as head supreme
Thrones, princedoms, powers, dominions I reduce: 320
All knees to thee shall bow, of them that bide
In heaven, or earth, or under earth in hell;
When thou attended gloriously from heaven
Shalt in the sky appear, and from thee send
The summoning archangels to proclaim   325
Thy dread tribunal: forthwith from all winds
The living, and forthwith the cited dead
Of all past ages to the general doom
Shall hasten, such a peal shall rouse their sleep.
Then all thy saints assembled, thou shalt judge   330
Bad men and angels, they arraigned shall sink
Beneath thy sentence; hell her numbers full,
Thenceforth shall be forever shut.   Meanwhile
The world shall burn, and from her ashes spring
New heaven and earth, wherein the just shall dwell,   335
And after all their tribulations long
See golden days, fruitful of golden deeds,
With joy and love triumphing, and fair truth.
Then thou thy regal scepter shalt lay by,
For regal scepter then no more shall need,   340
God shall be all in all.   But all ye gods,
Adore him, who to compass all this dies,
Adore the Son, and honor him as me.'
    No sooner had the almighty ceased, but all
The multitude of angels with a shout   345
Loud as from numbers without number, sweet
As from blest voices, uttering joy, heaven rung
With jubilee, and loud hosannas filled
The eternal regions: lowly reverent
Towards either throne they bow, and to the ground   350
With solemn adoration down they cast
Their crowns inwove with amarant and gold,
Immortal amarant, a flower which once
In Paradise, fast by the tree of life
Began to bloom, but soon for man's offense   355
To heaven removed where first it grew, there grows,
And flowers aloft shading the fount of life,
And where the river of bliss through midst of heaven
Rolls o'er Elysian flowers her amber stream;
With these that never fade the spirits elect   360
Bind their resplendent locks inwreathed with beams,

317. **king;** *Col.* **king,** but both first and second editions have semicolon.
329. **peal:** from the last trumpet.
333 ff. The world shall end in fire, a theological point here, not a scientific one, based on *II Peter* 3:12, 13.

Now in loose garlands thick thrown off, the bright
Pavement that like a sea of jasper shone
Impurpled with celestial roses smiled.
Then crowned again their golden harps they took,   365
Harps ever tuned, that glittering by their side
Like quivers hung, and with preamble sweet
Of charming symphony they introduce
Their sacred song, and waken raptures high;
No voice exempt, no voice but well could join   370
Melodious part, such concord is in heaven.
   Thee father first they sung omnipotent,
Immutable, immortal, infinite,
Eternal king; thee author of all being,
Fountain of light, thyself invisible   375
Amidst the glorious brightness where thou sittest
Throned inaccessible, but when thou shadest
The full blaze of thy beams, and through a cloud
Drawn round about thee like a radiant shrine,
Dark with excessive bright thy skirts appear,   380
Yet dazzle heaven, that brightest seraphim
Approach not, but with both wings veil their eyes.
Thee next they sang of all creation first,
Begotten Son, divine similitude,
In whose conspicuous countenance, without cloud   385
Made visible, the almighty father shines,
Whom else no creature can behold; on thee
Impressed the effulgence of his glory abides,
Transfused on thee his ample spirit rests.
He heaven of heavens and all the powers therein   390
By thee created, and by thee threw down
The aspiring dominations: thou that day
Thy father's dreadful thunder didst not spare,
Nor stop thy flaming chariot wheels, that shook
Heaven's everlasting frame, while o'er the necks   395
Thou drovest of warring angels disarrayed.
Back from pursuit thy powers with loud acclaim
Thee only extolled, son of thy father's might,
To execute fierce vengeance on his foes,
Not so on man; him through their malice fallen,   400
Father of mercy and grace, thou didst not doom
So strictly, but much more to pity incline:
No sooner did thy dear and only son
Perceive thee purposed not to doom frail man
So strictly, but much more to pity inclined,   405
He to appease thy wrath, and end the strife
Of mercy and justice in thy face discerned,
Regardless of the bliss wherein he sat

---

385. **conspicuous**: eminent.
392–99. This action has taken place, but it has not yet been fully presented to the reader.
402, 405. Did Milton intend to print both of these lines?

Second to thee, offered himself to die
For man's offense.   O unexampled love,   410
Love nowhere to be found less than divine!
Hail Son of God, Saviour of men, thy name
Shall be the copious matter of my song
Henceforth, and never shall my harp thy praise
Forget, nor from thy father's praise disjoin.   415
     Thus they in heaven, above the starry sphere,
Their happy hours in joy and hymning spent.
Meanwhile upon the firm opacous globe
Of this round world, whose first convex divides
The luminous inferior orbs, enclosed   420
From chaos and the inroad of darkness old,
Satan alighted walks: a globe far off
It seemed, now seems a boundless continent
Dark, waste, and wild, under the frown of night
Starless exposed, and ever-threatening storms   425
Of chaos blustering round, inclement sky;
Save on that side which from the wall of heaven
Though distant far some small reflection gains
Of glimmering air less vexed with tempest loud:
Here walked the fiend at large in spacious field.   430
As when a vulture on Imaus bred,
Whose snowy ridge the roving Tartar bounds,
Dislodging from a region scarce of prey
To gorge the flesh of lambs or yeanling kids
On hills where flocks are fed, flies toward the springs   435
Of Ganges or Hydaspes, Indian streams;
But in his way lights on the barren plains
Of Sericana, where Chineses drive
With sails and wind their cany wagons light:
So on this windy sea of land, the fiend   440
Walked up and down alone bent on his prey,
Alone, for other creature in this place
Living or lifeless to be found was none,
None yet, but store hereafter from the earth
Up hither like aerial vapors flew   445
Of all things transitory and vain, when sin
With vanity had filled the works of men:
Both all things vain, and all who in vain things
Built their fond hopes of glory or lasting fame,
Or happiness in this or the other life;   450

413. **copious:** abounding, hence complete.

418. **opacous:** dark, hence not transparent, or not easily penetrated.   Cf. Phillips's definitions.   The outer shell of 'this pendent world' was 'opacous' in order to keep the light in, as the succeeding lines explain.

431–39. For the geography of this elaborate simile, see Gilbert, *A Geographical Dictionary of Milton.*

434. **yeanling:** newly born.

440. **So:** marks the return from the digression of the simile, as always and regularly in Milton.

444–97. The famous, or infamous, limbo of vanities or paradise of fools passage.   It probably should be taken as burlesque, in which case it does not belong in the epic.   Cf. Verity and others on the passage.

All who have their reward on earth, the fruits
Of painful superstition and blind zeal,
Naught seeking but the praise of men, here find
Fit retribution, empty as their deeds;
All the unaccomplished works of nature's hand,   455
Abortive, monstrous, or unkindly mixed,
Dissolved on earth, fleet hither, and in vain,
Till final dissolution, wander here,
Not in the neighboring moon, as some have dreamed;
Those argent fields more likely habitants,   460
Translated saints, or middle spirits hold
Betwixt the angelical and human kind:
Hither of ill-joined sons and daughters born
First from the ancient world those giants came
With many a vain exploit, though then renowned: 465
The builders next to Babel on the plain
Of Sennaar, and still with vain design
New Babels, had they wherewithal, would build:
Others came single; he who to be deemed
A god, leaped fondly into Etna flames,   470
Empedocles, and he who to enjoy
Plato's Elysium, leaped into the sea,
Cleombrotus, and many more too long,
Embryos and idiots, eremites and friars
White, black and gray, with all their trumpery.   475
Here pilgrims roam, that strayed so far to seek
In Golgotha him dead, who lives in heaven;
And they who to be sure of paradise
Dying put on the weeds of Dominic,
Or in Franciscan think to pass disguised;   480
They pass the planets seven, and pass the fixed,
And that crystalline sphere whose balance weighs
The trepidation talked, and that first moved;
And now Saint Peter at heaven's wicket seems
To wait them with his keys, and now at foot   485
Of heaven's ascent they lift their feet, when lo
A violent cross wind from either coast
Blows them transverse ten thousand leagues awry
Into the devious air; then might ye see
Cowls, hoods and habits with their wearers tossed   490
And fluttered into rags, then relics, beads,
Indulgences, dispenses, pardons, bulls,
The sport of winds: all these upwhirled aloft
Fly o'er the backside of the world far off
Into a limbo large and broad, since called   495
The paradise of fools, to few unknown
Long after, now unpeopled, and untrod;
All this dark globe the fiend found as he passed,

457. **in vain**: aimlessly.

463–65. Cf. *Genesis* 6.

460–61. Cf. Wilkins' *New World in the Moon*.

474 ff. This is a satirical attack on religious orders.

And long he wandered, till at last a gleam
Of dawning light turned thitherward in haste   500
His traveled steps; far distant he descries
Ascending by degrees magnificent
Up to the wall of heaven a structure high,
At top whereof, but far more rich appeared
The work as of a kingly palace gate   505
With frontispiece of diamond and gold
Embellished, thick with sparkling orient gems
The portal shone, inimitable on earth
By model, or by shading pencil drawn.
The stairs were such as whereon Jacob saw   510
Angels ascending and descending, bands
Of guardians bright, when he from Esau fled
To Padan-Aram in the field of Luz,
Dreaming by night under the open sky,
And waking cried, 'This is the gate of Heaven.'   515
Each stair mysteriously was meant, nor stood
There always, but drawn up to heaven sometimes
Viewless, and underneath a bright sea flowed
Of jasper, or of liquid pearl, whereon
Who after came from earth, sailing arrived,   520
Wafted by angels, or flew o'er the lake
Rapt in a chariot drawn by fiery steeds.
The stairs were then let down, whether to dare
The fiend by easy ascent, or aggravate
His sad exclusion from the doors of bliss.   525
Direct against which opened from beneath,
Just o'er the blissful seat of Paradise,
A passage down to the earth, a passage wide,
Wider by far than that of aftertimes
Over Mount Sion, and, though that were large,   530
Over the promised land to God so dear,
By which, to visit oft those happy tribes,
On high behests his angels to and fro
Passed frequent, and his eye with choice regard
From Paneas the fount of Jordan's flood   535
To Beersaba, where the Holy Land
Borders on Egypt and the Arabian shore;
So wide the opening seemed, where bounds were set
To darkness, such as bound the ocean wave.
Satan from hence now on the lower stair   540
That scaled by steps of gold to heaven gate
Looks down with wonder at the sudden view
Of all this world at once.   As when a scout

509. This line accounts for much of Milton's lack of precision in detail throughout the entire universe.
516. **mysteriously**: allegorically or symbolically, even mystically.
519. **Of jasper, or of liquid pearl**: the glassy sea.
540. Symbolic of his present state, this bottom step of the golden stairway is as near as he can get to heaven, and never again will he come that close.   He is utterly serene and collected as he stands looking straight through the universe to the earth.

Through dark and desert ways with peril gone
All night; at last by break of cheerful dawn   545
Obtains the brow of some high-climbing hill,
Which to his eye discovers unaware
The goodly prospect of some foreign land
First seen, or some renowned metropolis
With glistering spires and pinnacles adorned,   550
Which now the rising sun gilds with his beams.
Such wonder seized, though after heaven seen,
The spirit malign, but much more envy seized
At sight of all this world beheld so fair.
Round he surveys, and well might, where he stood   555
So high above the circling canopy
Of night's extended shade; from eastern point
Of Libra to the fleecy star that bears
Andromeda far off Atlantic seas
Beyond the horizon; then from pole to pole   560
He views in breadth, and without longer pause
Down right into the world's first region throws
His flight precipitant, and winds with ease
Through the pure marble air his oblique way
Amongst innumerable stars, that shone   565
Stars distant, but nigh hand seemed other worlds,
Or other worlds they seemed, or happy isles,
Like those Hesperian gardens famed of old,
Fortunate fields, and groves and flowery vales,
Thrice happy isles, but who dwelt happy there   570
He stayed not to inquire: above them all
The golden sun in splendor likest heaven
Allured his eye: Thither his course he bends
Through the calm firmament; but up or down
By center, or eccentric, hard to tell,   575
Or longitude, where the great luminary
Aloof the vulgar constellations thick,
That from his lordly eye keep distance due,
Dispenses light from far; they as they move
Their starry dance in numbers that compute   580
Days, months, and years, towards his all-cheering lamp
Turn swift their various motions, or are turned
By his magnetic beam, that gently warms
The universe, and to each inward part
With gentle penetration, though unseen,   585
Shoots invisible virtue even to the deep:

564. **marble**: lucid, clear as marble is bright.

565. **innumerable stars**: this passage gives evidence of Milton's acquaintance with some of the contemporary accounts of the appearance of certain stars and planets as seen through the telescope, as well as with speculation about the possibility of the stars' being other worlds.

571. **above them all**: most of all.

575. **hard to tell**: never do we learn exact positions except on earth.

577. **Aloof**: apart from; very rare as preposition.

579 ff. A brief look at the ancient Ptolemaic theory of the solar system and the universe.

So wondrously was set his station bright.
There lands the fiend, a spot like which perhaps
Astronomer in the sun's lucent orb
Through his glazed optic tube yet never saw.   590
The place he found beyond expression bright,
Compared with aught on earth, metal or stone;
Not all parts like, but all alike informed
With radiant light, as glowing iron with fire;
If metal, part seemed gold, part silver clear;   595
If stone, carbuncle most or chrysolite,
Ruby or topaz, to the twelve that shone
In Aaron's breastplate, and a stone besides
Imagined rather oft than elsewhere seen,
That stone, or like to that which here below   600
Philosophers in vain so long have sought,
In vain, though by their powerful art they bind
Volatile Hermes, and call up unbound
In various shapes old Proteus from the sea,
Drained through a limbec to his native form.   605
What wonder then if fields and regions here
Breathe forth elixir pure, and rivers run
Potable gold, when with one virtuous touch
The arch-chemic sun so far from us remote
Produces with terrestrial humor mixed   610
Here in the dark so many precious things
Of color glorious and effect so rare?
Here matter new to gaze the devil met
Undazzled, far and wide his eye commands,
For sight no obstacle found here, nor shade,   615
But all sunshine, as when his beams at noon
Culminate from the equator, as they now
Shot upward still direct, whence no way round
Shadow from body opaque can fall, and the air,
Nowhere so clear, sharpened his visual ray   620
To objects distant far, whereby he soon
Saw within ken a glorious angel stand,
The same whom John saw also in the sun:
His back was turned, but not his brightness hid;
Of beaming sunny rays, a golden tiar   625
Circled his head, nor less his locks behind
Illustrious on his shoulders fledge with wings
Lay waving round; on some great charge employed
He seemed, or fixed in cogitation deep.
Glad was the spirit impure as now in hope   630
To find who might direct his wandering flight
To Paradise the happy seat of man,

589–90. Looking at the sun through a telescope was relatively unknown when this was written.

592. **metal**: in both first and second editions, the word is printed 'medal,' an obsolete usage, even in Milton's day.

601. The philosopher's stone, or the stone that would turn base metals to gold.

602–05. Alchemical tricks.   623. *Revelation* 19:17.

His journey's end and our beginning woe.
But first he casts to change his proper shape,
Which else might work him danger or delay: 635
And now a stripling cherub he appears,
Not of the prime, yet such as in his face
Youth smiled celestial, and to every limb
Suitable grace diffused, so well he feigned;
Under a coronet his flowing hair   640
In curls on either cheek played, wings he wore
Of many a colored plume sprinkled with gold,
His habit fit for speed succinct, and held
Before his decent steps a silver wand.
He drew not nigh unheard, the Angel bright,   645
Ere he drew nigh, his radiant visage turned,
Admonished by his ear, and straight was known
The archangel Uriel, one of the seven
Who in God's presence, nearest to his throne
Stand ready at command, and are his eyes   650
That run through all the heavens, or down to the earth
Bear his swift errands over moist and dry,
O'er sea and land: him Satan thus accosts;
    'Uriel, for thou of those seven spirits that stand
In sight of God's high throne, gloriously bright,   655
The first art wont his great authentic will
Interpreter through highest heaven to bring,
Where all his sons thy embassy attend;
And here art likeliest by supreme decree
Like honour to obtain, and as his eye   660
To visit oft this new creation round;
Unspeakable desire to see, and know
All these his wondrous works, but chiefly man,
His chief delight and favor, him for whom
All these his works so wondrous he ordained,   665
Hath brought me from the choirs of cherubim
Alone thus wandering. Brightest seraph tell
In which of all these shining orbs hath man
His fixed seat, or fixed seat hath none,
But all these shining orbs his choice to dwell;   670
That I may find him, and with secret gaze,
Or open admiration him behold
On whom the great creator hath bestowed
Worlds, and on whom hath all these graces poured;
That both in him and all things, as is meet,   675
The universal maker we may praise;
Who justly hath driven out his rebel foes
To deepest hell, and to repair that loss
Created this new happy race of men
To serve him better: wise are all his ways.'   680
    So spake the false dissembler unperceived;
For neither man nor angel can discern

648. **Uriel, one of the seven:** *Revelation* 8:2. The name means 'fire of God.'

Hypocrisy, the only evil that walks
Invisible, except to God alone,
By his permissive will, through heaven and earth: 685
And oft though wisdom wake, suspicion sleeps
At wisdom's gate, and to simplicity
Resigns her charge, while goodness thinks no ill
Where no ill seems: Which now for once beguiled
Uriel, though regent of the sun, and held 690
The sharpest sighted spirit of all in heaven;
Who to the fraudulent impostor foul
In his uprightness answer thus returned.
'Fair angel, thy desire which tends to know
The works of God, thereby to glorify 695
The great work-master, leads to no excess
That reaches blame, but rather merits praise
The more it seems excess, that led thee hither
From thy empyreal mansion thus alone,
To witness with thine eyes what some perhaps 700
Contented with report hear only in heaven:
For wonderful indeed are all his works,
Pleasant to know, and worthiest to be all
Had in remembrance always with delight;
But what created mind can comprehend 705
Their number, or the wisdom infinite
That brought them forth, but hid their causes deep.
I saw when at his word the formless mass,
This world's material mold, came to a heap:
Confusion heard his voice, and wild uproar 710
Stood ruled, stood vast infinitude confined;
Till at his second bidding darkness fled,
Light shone, and order from disorder sprung:
Swift to their several quarters hasted then
The cumbrous elements, earth, flood, air, fire, 715
And this ethereal quintessence of heaven
Flew upward, spirited with various forms,
That rolled orbicular, and turned to stars
Numberless, as thou seest, and how they move;
Each had his place appointed, each his course, 720
The rest in circuit walls this universe.
Look downward on that globe whose hither side
With light from hence, though but reflected, shines;
That place is earth the seat of man, that light
His day, which else as the other hemisphere 725
Night would invade, but there the neighboring moon
(So call that opposite fair star) her aid
Timely interposes, and her monthly round
Still ending, still renewing, through mid-heaven;
With borrowed light her countenance triform 730
Hence fills and empties to enlighten the earth,

730. **triform:** we speak of four phases of the moon, but we see only three, the fourth being the 'dark of
the moon.'

And in her pale dominion checks the night.
That spot to which I point is Paradise,
Adam's abode, those lofty shades his bower.
Thy way thou canst not miss, me mine requires.'   735
  Thus said, he turned, and Satan bowing low,
As to superior spirits is wont in heaven,
Where honor due and reverence none neglects,
Took leave, and toward the coast of earth beneath,
Down from the ecliptic, sped with hoped success,   740
Throws his steep flight in many an airy wheel,
Nor staid, till on Niphates' top he lights.

THE END OF THE THIRD BOOK

BOOK IV

THE ARGUMENT

Satan now in prospect of Eden, and nigh the place where he must now attempt the bold enterprise which he undertook alone against God and man, falls into many doubts with himself, and many passions, fear, envy, and despair; but at length confirms himself in evil, journeys on to Paradise, whose outward prospect and situation is described, overleaps the bounds, sits in the shape of a cormorant on the tree of life, as highest in the garden to look about him. The garden described; Satan's first sight of Adam and Eve; his wonder at their excellent form and happy state, but with resolution to work their fall; overhears their discourse, thence gathers that the tree of knowledge was forbidden them to eat of, under penalty of death; and thereon intends to found his temptation, by seducing them to transgress: then leaves them a while, to know further of their state by some other means. Meanwhile Uriel descending on a sunbeam warns Gabriel, who had in charge the gate of Paradise, that some evil spirit had escaped the deep, and passed at noon by his sphere in the shape of a good angel down to Paradise, discovered after by his furious gestures in the mount. Gabriel promises to find him ere morning. Night coming on, Adam and Eve, discourse of going to their rest: their bower described; their evening worship. Gabriel drawing forth his bands of night-watch to walk the round of Paradise, appoints two strong angels to Adam's bower, lest the evil spirit should be there doing some harm to Adam or Eve sleeping; there they find him at the ear of Eve, tempting her in a dream, and bring him, though unwilling, to Gabriel; by whom questioned, he scornfully answers, prepares resistance, but hindered by a sign from heaven, flies out of Paradise.

O for that warning voice, which he who saw
The Apocalypse, heard cry in heaven aloud,
Then when the dragon, put to second rout,
Came furious down to be revenged on men,
'Woe to the inhabitants on earth!' that now,   5
While time was, our first parents had been warned
The coming of their secret foe, and scaped
Haply so scaped his mortal snare; for now
Satan, now first inflamed with rage, came down,

740. **ecliptic:** the sun's orbit.   742. **Niphates:** a mountain of Armenia.
1–2. *Revelation* 12:12.

The tempter ere the accuser of mankind,   10
To wreck on innocent frail man his loss
Of that first battle, and his flight to hell:
Yet not rejoicing in his speed, though bold,
Far off and fearless, nor with cause to boast,
Begins his dire attempt, which nigh the birth   15
Now rolling, boils in his tumultuous breast,
And like a devilish engine back recoils
Upon himself; horror and doubt distract
His troubled thoughts, and from the bottom stir
The hell within him, for within him hell   20
He brings, and round about him, nor from hell
One step no more than from himself can fly
By change of place: Now conscience wakes despair
That slumbered, wakes the bitter memory
Of what he was, what is, and what must be   25
Worse; of worse deeds worse sufferings must ensue.
Sometimes towards Eden which now in his view
Lay pleasant, his grieved look he fixes sad,
Sometimes towards heaven and the full-blazing sun,
Which now sat high in his meridian tower: 30
Then much revolving, thus in sighs began.
 'O thou that with surpassing glory crowned,
Lookest from thy sole dominion like the god
Of this new world; at whose sight all the stars
Hide their diminished heads; to thee I call,   35
But with no friendly voice, and add thy name
O sun, to tell thee how I hate thy beams
That bring to my remembrance from what state
I fell, how glorious once above thy sphere;
Till pride and worse ambition threw me down   40
Warring in heaven against heaven's matchless king:
Ah wherefore! he deserved no such return
From me, whom he created what I was
In that bright eminence, and with his good
Upbraided none; nor was his service hard.   45
What could be less than to afford him praise,
The easiest recompense, and pay him thanks,
How due! yet all his good proved ill in me,
And wrought but malice; lifted up so high
I 'sdained subjection, and thought one step higher   50
Would set me highest, and in a moment quit
The debt immense of endless gratitude,

11–12. Revenge was Satan's first motive in tempting the human pair.

17. **engine**: contrivance.

18 ff. Satan's nature seemingly regained conscience from his contact with the bottom step of the heavenly stairway.   Almost, remorse stops his enterprise.

32–41. These lines, on the statement of Edward Phillips, Milton's nephew, are supposed to have been written as early as 1640–42.   They are essentially a dramatic soliloquy.

40. Satan fell through pride and ambition above his station, and appeal to the same elements in Eve defeated her.

So burdensome still paying, still to owe;
Forgetful what from him I still received,
And understood not that a grateful mind   55
By owing owes not, but still pays, at once
Indebted and discharged; what burden then?
O had his powerful destiny ordained
Me some inferior angel, I had stood
Then happy; no unbounded hope had raised   60
Ambition.   Yet why not? some other power
As great might have aspired, and me though mean
Drawn to his part; but other powers as great
Fell not, but stand unshaken, from within
Or from without, to all temptations armed.   65
Hadst thou the same free will and power to stand?
Thou hadst: whom hast thou then or what to accuse,
But heaven's free love dealt equally to all?
Be then his love accursed, since love or hate,
To me alike, it deals eternal woe.   70
Nay cursed be thou; since against his thy will
Chose freely what it now so justly rues.
Me miserable! which way shall I fly
Infinite wrath, and infinite despair?
Which way I fly is hell; myself am hell;   75
And in the lowest deep a lower deep
Still threatening to devour me opens wide,
To which the hell I suffer seems a heaven.
O then at last relent: is there no place
Left for repentance, none for pardon left?   80
None left but by submission; and that word
Disdain forbids me, and my dread of shame
Among the spirits beneath, whom I seduced
With other promises and other vaunts
Than to submit, boasting I could subdue   85
The omnipotent.   Ay me, they little know
How dearly I abide that boast so vain,
Under what torments inwardly I groan;
While they adore me on the throne of hell,
With diadem and scepter high advanced   90
The lower still I fall, only supreme
In misery; such joy ambition finds.
But say I could repent and could obtain
By act of grace my former state; how soon
Would height recall high thoughts, how soon unsay   95
What feigned submission swore: ease would recant
Vows made in pain, as violent and void.
For never can true reconcilement grow
Where wounds of deadly hate have pierced so deep:
Which would but lead me to a worse relapse   100

73 ff. A famous, much-quoted passage noted for its despair and pathos.
87. **abide**: suffer for.

And heavier fall: so should I purchase dear
Short intermission bought with double smart.
This knows my punisher; therefore as far
From granting he, as I from begging peace:
All hope excluded thus, behold instead   105
Of us outcast, exiled, his new delight,
Mankind created, and for him this world.
So farewell hope, and with hope farewell fear,
Farewell remorse: all good to me is lost;
Evil be thou my good; by thee at least   110
Divided empire with heaven's king I hold
By thee, and more than half perhaps will reign;
As man erelong, and this new world shall know.'
     Thus while he spake, each passion dimmed his face
Thrice changed with pale, ire, envy and despair,   115
Which marred his borrowed visage, and betrayed
Him counterfeit, if any eye beheld.
For heavenly minds from such distempers foul
Are ever clear.   Whereof he soon aware,
Each perturbation smoothed with outward calm,   120
Artificer of fraud; and was the first
That practiced falsehood under saintly show,
Deep malice to conceal, couched with revenge:
Yet not enough had practiced to deceive
Uriel once warned; whose eye pursued him down   125
The way he went, and on the Assyrian mount
Saw him disfigured, more than could befall
Spirit of happy sort: his gestures fierce
He marked and mad demeanor, then alone,
As he supposed, all unobserved, unseen.   130
So on he fares, and to the border comes,
Of Eden, where delicious Paradise,
Now nearer, crowns with her enclosure green,
As with a rural mound the champaign head
Of a steep wilderness, whose hairy sides   135
With thicket overgrown, grotesque and wild,
Access denied; and overhead up grew
Insuperable height of loftiest shade,
Cedar, and pine, and fir, and branching palm,
A sylvan scene, and as the ranks ascend   140
Shade above shade, a woody theater
Of stateliest view.   Yet higher than their tops

110. Note that the Argument states that Satan 'confirms himself in evil.'

115. **ire, envy and despair**: the Argument reads 'fear, envy, and despair.'

126. **the Assyrian mount**: Niphates.

134. **champaign head**: the level summit of the 'rural mound.'

136. **grotesque**: linguistically, this is one of the most interesting words in the poem.   The *OED* lists
only one occurrence before 1600 (1561) of the word in any form or usage in English.   Milton apparently
means here 'attractively unkempt because growing naturally,' a meaning that belongs to the era of the
'picturesque' of more than a century later.   No earlier use of the word in this sense is recorded in the *OED*,
and the word probably lost this meaning by 1800.   It is from the Italian through the French.

The verdurous wall of Paradise up sprung:
Which to our general sire gave prospect large
Into his nether empire neighboring round.   145
And higher than that wall a circling row
Of goodliest trees laden with fairest fruit,
Blossoms and fruits at once of golden hue
Appeared, with gay enameled colors mixed:
On which the sun more glad impressed his beams   150
Than in fair evening cloud, or humid bow,
When God hath showered the earth; so lovely seemed
That landscape: And of pure now purer air
Meets his approach, and to the heart inspires
Vernal delight and joy, able to drive   155
All sadness but despair: now gentle gales
Fanning their odoriferous wings dispense
Native perfumes, and whisper whence they stole
Those balmy spoils.   As when to them who sail
Beyond the Cape of Hope, and now are past   160
Mozambic, off at sea north-east winds blow
Sabean odors from the spicy shore
Of Araby the blest, with such delay
Well pleased they slack their course, and many a league
Cheered with the grateful smell old ocean smiles.   165
So entertained those odorous sweets the fiend
Who came their bane, though with them better pleased
Than Asmodeus with the fishy fume,
That drove him, though enamored, from the spouse
Of Tobit's son, and with a vengeance sent   170
From Media post to Egypt, there fast bound.
   Now to the ascent of that steep savage hill
Satan had journeyed on, pensive and slow;
But further way found none, so thick entwined,
As one continued brake, the undergrowth   175
Of shrubs and tangling bushes had perplexed
All path of man or beast that passed that way:
One gate there only was, and that looked east
On the other side: which when the arch felon saw
Due entrance he disdained, and in contempt,   180
At one slight bound high overleaped all bound
Of hill or highest wall, and sheer within
Lights on his feet.   As when a prowling wolf,
Whom hunger drives to seek new haunt for prey,
Watching where shepherds pen their flocks at eve   185

159 ff. The reader by this time will have noted Milton's willingness to indulge in romantic digression. In this respect, as in other respects, Bach's willingness to do likewise in his music comes to mind.

163. **Araby the blest:** the very name, even today, spells enchantment.   Arabia has always fascinated the European.

168. **Asmodeus:** cf. the *Book of Tobit*, an apocryphal book, and V:221–23, *PR* II:151.

171. **post:** with speed.

172. **savage:** wild or, as some commentators, woody, from Latin *silvaticus*.

181. **bound ... bound:** a pun.

In hurdled cotes amid the field secure,
Leaps o'er the fence with ease into the fold:
Or as a thief bent to unhoard the cash
Of some rich burgher, whose substantial doors,
Cross-barred and bolted fast, fear no assault,   190
In at the window climbs, or o'er the tiles;
So clomb this first grand thief into God's fold:
So since into his church lewd hirelings climb.
Thence up he flew, and on the tree of life
The middle tree and highest there that grew,   195
Sat like a cormorant; yet not true life
Thereby regained, but sat devising death
To them who lived; nor on the virtue thought
Of that life-giving plant, but only used
For prospect, what well used had been the pledge   200
Of immortality.   So little knows
Any, but God alone, to value right
The good before him, but perverts best things
To worst abuse, or to their meanest use.
Beneath him with new wonder now he views   205
To all delight of human sense exposed
In narrow room nature's whole wealth, yea more,
A heaven on earth, for blissful Paradise
Of God the garden was, by him in the east
Of Eden planted; Eden stretched her line   210
From Auran eastward to the royal towers
Of great Seleucia, built by Grecian kings,
Or where the sons of Eden long before
Dwelt in Telassar: in this pleasant soil
His far more pleasant garden God ordained;   215
Out of the fertile ground he caused to grow
All trees of noblest kind for sight, smell, taste;
And all amid them stood the tree of life,
High eminent, blooming ambrosial fruit
Of vegetable gold; and next to life   220
Our death the tree of knowledge grew fast by,
Knowledge of good bought dear by knowing ill.
Southward through Eden went a river large,
Nor changed his course, but through the shaggy hill
Passed underneath ingulfed, for God had thrown   225
That mountain as his garden mold high raised
Upon the rapid current, which through veins
Of porous earth with kindly thirst updrawn,
Rose a fresh fountain, and with many a rill
Watered the garden; thence united fell   230
Down the steep glade, and met the nether flood,
Which from his darksome passage now appears,

192. **clomb:** climbed.   193. **lewd:** base.
196. **cormorant:** in *Isaiah* 34:11, a pelican.   A bird of prey.

205 ff. An old map of the eastern Mediterranean and Near East is really needed to make the location of the region called Eden significant.   The garden, Paradise, is in the eastern part of Eden.

And now divided into four main streams,
Runs diverse, wandering many a famous realm
And country whereof here needs no account,   235
But rather to tell how, if art could tell,
How from that sapphire fount the crisped brooks,
Rolling on orient pearl and sands of gold,
With mazy error under pendent shades
Ran nectar, visiting each plant, and fed   240
Flowers worthy of Paradise which not nice art
In beds and curious knots, but nature boon
Poured forth profuse on hill and dale and plain,
Both where the morning sun first warmly smote
The open field, and where the unpierced shade   245
Imbrowned the noontide bowers: Thus was this place,
A happy rural seat of various view;
Groves whose rich trees wept odorous gums and balm,
Others whose fruit burnished with golden rind
Hung amiable, Hesperian fables true,   250
If true, here only, and of delicious taste:
Betwixt them lawns, or level downs, and flocks
Grazing the tender herb, were interposed,
Or palmy hillock, or the flowery lap
Of some irriguous valley spread her store,   255
Flowers of all hue, and without thorn the rose:
Another side, umbrageous grots and caves
Of cool recess, o'er which the mantling vine
Lays forth her purple grape, and gently creeps
Luxuriant; meanwhile murmuring waters fall   260
Down the slope hills, dispersed, or in a lake,
That to the fringed bank with myrtle crowned,
Her crystal mirror holds, unite their streams.
The birds their choir apply; airs, vernal airs,
Breathing the smell of field and grove, attune   265
The trembling leaves, while universal Pan
Knit with the graces and the hours in dance
Led on the eternal spring.   Not that fair field
Of Enna, where Proserpin gathering flowers
Herself a fairer flower by gloomy Dis   270
Was gathered, which cost Ceres all that pain
To seek her through the world; nor that sweet grove
Of Daphne by Orontes, and the inspired

237. **crisped brooks:** rippling brooks.   239. **error:** wandering, the word's original meaning.
241. **nice:** fastidious.   246. **Imbrowned:** darkened.
255. **irriguous:** irrigated, watered.   257. **umbrageous:** shadowed.
266 ff. Eden had only one 'season' — spring.   See Book V:394-95.
268 ff. The passage that compares all the famous gardens of classical literature with Paradise in order to enhance its beauty and attractiveness.
269. **Enna . . . Proserpin:** cf. Ovid, *Metamorphoses* V:385 ff.   The nature myth involving Proserpine, daughter of Ceres, carried off by Dis (Pluto), is among the best known of all Latin myths.
270. **Dis:** Pluto, god of the underworld.   271. **Ceres:** goddess of growing vegetation.
272-73. **grove of Daphne by Orontes:** a grove sacred to Apollo.

Castalian spring, might with this Paradise
Of Eden strive; nor that Nyseian isle   275
Girt with the river Triton, where old Cham,
Whom Gentiles Ammon call and Libyan Jove,
Hid Amalthea and her florid son
Young Bacchus from his stepdame Rhea's eye;
Nor where Abassin kings their issue guard,   280
Mount Amara, though this by some supposed
True Paradise under the Ethiop line
By Nilus head, enclosed with shining rock,
A whole day's journey high, but wide remote
From this Assyrian garden, where the fiend   285
Saw undelighted all delight, all kind
Of living creatures new to sight and strange:
Two of far nobler shape erect and tall,
God-like erect, with native honor clad
In naked majesty seemed lords of all,   290
And worthy seemed, for in their looks divine
The image of their glorious maker shone,
Truth, wisdom, sanctitude severe and pure,
Severe but in true filial freedom placed;
Whence true authority in men; though both   295
Not equal, as their sex not equal seemed;
For contemplation he and valor formed,
For softness she and sweet attractive grace,
He for God only, she for God in him:
His fair large front and eye sublime declared   300
Absolute rule; and hyacinthine locks
Round from his parted forelock manly hung
Clustering, but not beneath his shoulders broad:
She as a veil down to the slender waist
Her unadorned golden tresses wore   305
Disheveled, but in wanton ringlets waved
As the vine curls her tendrils, which implied
Subjection, but required with gentle sway,
And by her yielded, by him best received,
Yielded with coy submission, modest pride,   310
And sweet reluctant amorous delay.
Nor those mysterious parts were then concealed,
Then was not guilty shame, dishonest shame
Of nature's works, honor dishonorable,
Sin-bred, how have ye troubled all mankind   315

275. **Nyseian isle:** cf. Diodorus Siculus, III:67–70. Milton identifies Jupiter Ammon with Ham, son of Noah.

280. **Abassin:** Abyssinian, Ethiopian.

281. **Mount Amara:** cf. Coleridge, *Kubla Khan,* 'Mount Abora,' a mountain retreat and garden where Abyssinian princes were sent to be educated.

284. **wide remote:** the garden retreat of Mount Amara was not Paradise, as some had held.

296. **Not equal:** the sexes are complementary, not identical in the scheme of creation.

300. **front:** brow, forehead.   301. **hyacinthine locks:** dark hair.

306. **wanton:** unrestrained.

With shows instead, mere shows of seeming pure,
And banished from man's life his happiest life,
Simplicity and spotless innocence.
So passed they naked on, nor shunned the sight
Of God or angel, for they thought no ill: 320
So hand in hand they passed, the loveliest pair
That ever since in love's embraces met,
Adam the goodliest man of men since born
His sons, the fairest of her daughters Eve.
Under a tuft of shade that on a green   325
Stood whispering soft, by a fresh fountain side
They sat them down, and after no more toil
Of their sweet gardening labor than sufficed
To recommend cool zephyr, and make ease
More easy, wholesome thirst and appetite   330
More grateful, to their supper fruits they fell,
Nectarine fruits which the compliant boughs
Yielded them, sidelong as they sat recline
On the soft downy bank damasked with flowers:
The savory pulp they chew, and in the rind   335
Still as they thirsted scoop the brimming stream;
Nor gentle purpose, nor endearing smiles
Wanted, nor youthful dalliance as beseems
Fair couple, linked in happy nuptial league,
Alone as they.   About them frisking played   340
All beasts of the earth, since wild, and of all chase
In wood or wilderness, forest or den;
Sporting the lion ramped, and in his paw
Dandled the kid; bears, tigers, ounces, pards,
Gamboled before them, the unwieldy elephant   345
To make them mirth used all his might, and wreathed
His lithe proboscis; close the serpent sly
Insinuating, wove with Gordian twine
His braided train, and of his fatal guile
Gave proof unheeded; others on the grass   350
Couched, and now filled with pasture gazing sat,
Or bedward ruminating: for the sun
Declined was hastening now with prone career
To the ocean isles, and in the ascending scale
Of heaven the stars that usher evening rose: 355
When Satan still in gaze, as first he stood,
Scarce thus at length failed speech recovered sad.
   'O hell! what do mine eyes with grief behold,
Into our room of bliss thus high advanced
Creatures of other mold, earth-born perhaps,   360
Not spirits, yet to heavenly spirits bright

325 ff. Milton pours into his account of the 'fair couple' all his pent-up idealizations of the marital relationships denied him in his own first marriage.

344. **ounces, pards:** lynxes and leopards.   349. **braided:** twisted.

358 ff. Satan is almost won over to the human pair.   Milton almost infers that only 'envy' kept Satan to his original purpose; cf. lines 502–04.

Little inferior; whom my thoughts pursue
With wonder, and could love, so lively shines
In them divine resemblance, and such grace
The hand that formed them on their shape hath poured.   365
Ah gentle pair, ye little think how nigh
Your change approaches, when all these delights
Will vanish and deliver ye to woe,
More woe, the more your taste is now of joy;
Happy, but for so happy ill secured   370
Long to continue, and this high seat your heaven
Ill fenced for heaven to keep out such a foe
As now is entered; yet no purposed foe
To you whom I could pity thus forlorn
Though I unpitied: League with you I seek,   375
And mutual amity so strait, so close,
That I with you must dwell, or you with me
Henceforth; my dwelling haply may not please
Like this fair Paradise, your sense, yet such
Accept your maker's work; he gave it me,   380
Which I as freely give; hell shall unfold,
To entertain you two, her widest gates,
And send forth all her kings; there will be room,
Not like these narrow limits, to receive
Your numerous offspring; if no better place,   385
Thank him who puts me loath to this revenge
On you who wrong me not for him who wronged.
And should I at your harmless innocence
Melt, as I do, yet public reason just,
Honor and empire with revenge enlarged,   390
By conquering this new world, compels me now
To do what else though damned I should abhor.'
    So spake the fiend, and with necessity,
The tyrant's plea, excused his devilish deeds.
Then from his lofty stand on that high tree   395
Down he alights among the sportful herd
Of those four-footed kinds, himself now one,
Now other, as their shape served best his end
Nearer to view his prey, and unespied
To mark what of their state he more might learn   400
By word or action marked: about them round
A lion now he stalks with fiery glare,
Then as a tiger, who by chance hath spied
In some purlieu two gentle fawns at play,
Straight couches close, then rising changes oft   405
His couchant watch, as one who chose his ground
Whence rushing he might surest seize them both
Gripped in each paw: When Adam first of men

393–94. **necessity, the tyrant's plea:** exactly the same plea Milton himself used for his partisanship and his prose controversial tracts.

404. **purlieu:** edge of a forest; the word has a curious history.

406. **couchant:** lying, the French participle form.

To first of women Eve thus moving speech,
Turned him all ear to hear new utterance flow.   410
'Sole partner and sole part of all these joys,
Dearer thyself than all; needs must the power
That made us, and for us this ample world
Be infinitely good, and of his good
As liberal and free as infinite,   415
That raised us from the dust and placed us here
In all this happiness, who at his hand
Have nothing merited, nor can perform
Aught whereof he hath need, he who requires
From us no other service than to keep   420
This one, this easy charge, of all the trees
In Paradise that bear delicious fruit
So various, not to taste that only tree
Of knowledge, planted by the tree of life,
So near grows death to life, whate'er death is,   425
Some dreadful thing no doubt; for well thou knowest
God hath pronounced it death to taste that tree,
The only sign of our obedience left
Among so many signs of power and rule
Conferred upon us, and dominion given   430
Over all other creatures that possess
Earth, air, and sea.   Then let us not think hard
One easy prohibition, who enjoy
Free leave so large to all things else, and choice
Unlimited of manifold delights: 435
But let us ever praise him, and extol
His bounty, following our delightful task
To prune these growing plants, and tend these flowers,
Which were it toilsome, yet with thee were sweet.'
    To whom thus Eve replied. 'O thou for whom   440
And from whom I was formed flesh of thy flesh,
And without whom am to no end, my guide
And head, what thou hast said is just and right.
For we to him indeed all praises owe,
And daily thanks, I chiefly who enjoy   445
So far the happier lot, enjoying thee
Pre-eminent by so much odds, while thou
Like consort to thyself canst nowhere find.
That day I oft remember, when from sleep
I first awaked, and found myself reposed   450
Under a shade of flowers, much wondering where
And what I was, whence thither brought, and how.
Not distant far from thence a murmuring sound
Of waters issued from a cave and spread
Into a liquid plain, then stood unmoved   455

421 ff. Milton uses the essentially dramatic device of letting Satan and the reader gain information by overhearing a conversation.

425. How do you suppose even the word 'death' came to be known to the human pair by this time?

451. of flowers: the first edition reads 'on flowers' and the second edition reads as printed herein.

Pure as the expanse of heaven; I thither went
With unexperienced thought, and laid me down
On the green bank, to look into the clear
Smooth lake, that to me seemed another sky.
As I bent down to look, just opposite,   460
A shape within the watery gleam appeared
Bending to look on me, I started back,
It started back, but pleased I soon returned,
Pleased it returned as soon with answering looks
Of sympathy and love; there I had fixed   465
Mine eyes till now, and pined with vain desire,
Had not a voice thus warned me, "What thou seest,
What there thou seest fair creature is thyself,
With thee it came and goes: but follow me,
And I will bring thee where no shadow stays   470
Thy coming, and thy soft embraces, he
Whose image thou art, him thou shalt enjoy
Inseparably thine, to him shalt bear
Multitudes like thyself, and thence be called
Mother of human race:" what could I do,   475
But follow straight, invisibly thus led?
Till I espied thee, fair indeed and tall,
Under a platane, yet methought less fair,
Less winning soft, less amiably mild,
Than that smooth watery image; back I turned,   480
Thou following criedst aloud, "Return fair Eve,
Whom fliest thou? whom thou fliest, of him thou art,
His flesh, his bone; to give thee being I lent
Out of my side to thee, nearest my heart
Substantial life, to have thee by my side   485
Henceforth an individual solace dear;
Part of my soul I seek thee, and thee claim
My other half:" with that thy gentle hand
Seized mine, I yielded, and from that time see
How beauty is excelled by manly grace   490
And wisdom, which alone is truly fair.'
    So spake our general mother, and with eyes
Of conjugal attraction unreproved,
And meek surrender, half embracing leaned
On our first father, half her swelling breast   495
Naked met his under the flowing gold
Of her loose tresses hid: he in delight
Both of her beauty and submissive charms
Smiled with superior love, as Jupiter
On Juno smiles, when he impregns the clouds   500
That shed May flowers; and pressed her matron lip
With kisses pure: aside the devil turned
For envy, yet with jealous leer malign
Eyed them askance, and to himself thus plained.

478. **platane**: plane tree.   500. **impregns**: impregnates. Cf. also IX:737.
502–04. Now, and not till now, Satan has a real and direct cause to ruin the human pair. Cf. IX:263–64.

'Sight hateful, sight tormenting! thus these two   505
Imparadised in one another's arms
The happier Eden, shall enjoy their fill
Of bliss on bliss, while I to hell am thrust,
Where neither joy nor love, but fierce desire,
Among our other torments not the least,   510
Still unfulfilled with pain of longing pines;
Yet let me not forget what I have gained
From their own mouths; all is not theirs it seems:
One fatal tree there stands of knowledge called,
Forbidden them to taste: Knowledge forbidden?   515
Suspicious, reasonless.   Why should their Lord
Envy them that? can it be sin to know,
Can it be death? and do they only stand
By ignorance, is that their happy state,
The proof of their obedience and their faith?   520
O fair foundation laid whereon to build
Their ruin!   Hence I will excite their minds
With more desire to know, and to reject
Envious commands, invented with design
To keep them low whom knowledge might exalt   525
Equal with gods; aspiring to be such,
They taste and die: what likelier can ensue?
But first with narrow search I must walk round
This garden, and no corner leave unspied;
A chance but chance may lead where I may meet   530
Some wandering spirit of heaven, by fountainside,
Or in thick shade retired, from him to draw
What further would be learned.   Live while ye may,
Yet happy pair; enjoy, till I return,
Short pleasures, for long woes are to succeed.'   535
    So saying, his proud step he scornful turned,
But with sly circumspection, and began
Through wood, through waste, o'er hill, o'er dale, his roam.
Meanwhile in utmost longitude, where heaven
With earth and ocean meets, the setting sun   540
Slowly descended, and with right aspect
Against the eastern gate of Paradise
Leveled his evening rays: it was a rock
Of alabaster, piled up to the clouds,
Conspicuous far, winding with one ascent   545
Accessible from earth, one entrance high;
The rest was craggy cliff, that overhung
Still as it rose, impossible to climb.

517. **can it be sin to know?**   This was the most important question raised, and answered, by Milton's time.

518 ff.   The first hint of Milton's underlying doctrine of the 'fortunate fall,' that man was really a more admirable creature potentially after the fall than before it.

521 ff.   Satan plans to use the ignorance of the 'fair couple' to their ruin; but to ruin them, he must play on their pride and ambition, the same elements that ruined Satan himself.

530. **A chance but chance:** a pun.

Betwixt these rocky pillars Gabriel sat
Chief of the angelic guards, awaiting night;   550
About him exercised heroic games
The unarmed youth of heaven, but nigh at hand
Celestial armory, shields, helms, and spears,
Hung high with diamond flaming, and with gold.
Thither came Uriel, gliding through the even   555
On a sunbeam, swift as a shooting star
In autumn thwarts the night, when vapors fired
Impress the air, and shows the mariner
From what point of his compass to beware
Impetuous winds: he thus began in haste.   560
　　'Gabriel, to thee thy course by lot hath given
Charge and strict watch that to this happy place
No evil thing approach or enter in;
This day at height of noon came to my sphere
A spirit, zealous, as he seemed, to know   565
More of the almighty's works, and chiefly man
God's latest image: I described his way
Bent all on speed, and marked his airy gait;
But in the mount that lies from Eden north,
Where he first lighted, soon discerned his looks   570
Alien from heaven, with passions foul obscured:
Mine eye pursued him still, but under shade
Lost sight of him; one of the banished crew
I fear, hath ventured from the deep, ro raise
New troubles; him thy care must be to find.'   575
　　To whom the winged warrior thus returned:
'Uriel, no wonder if thy perfect sight,
Amid the sun's bright circle where thou sittest,
See far and wide: in at this gate none pass
The vigilance here placed, but such as come   580
Well known from heaven; and since meridian hour
No creature thence: if spirit of other sort,
So minded, have o'erleaped these earthy bounds
On purpose, hard thou knowest it to exclude
Spiritual substance with corporeal bar.   585
But if within the circuit of these walks,
In whatsoever shape he lurk, of whom
Thou tellest, by morrow dawning I shall know.'
　　So promised he, and Uriel to his charge
Returned on that bright beam, whose point now raised   590
Bore him slope downward to the sun now fallen
Beneath the Azores; whither the prime orb,

567. **described**: probably 'descried,' but *describe* also means 'to mark out.'
568. **airy gait**: printed 'gate,' airy way.
577. **perfect**: Milton, or his printers, usually spelled this word 'perfet.'
592. **whither**: printed 'whether' first in 1719 and followed by most editors since.

592–95. Sunset is due either to the movement of the sun about the earth, the geocentric Ptolemaic hypothesis, or to the revolution of the earth on its axis during its relatively slow progress around the sun, the Copernican theory. Milton presents both ideas here without choosing between them.

Incredible how swift, had thither rolled
Diurnal, or this less volubile earth
By shorter flight to the east, had left him there   595
Arraying with reflected purple and gold
The clouds that on his western throne attend:
Now came still evening on, and twilight gray
Had in her sober livery all things clad;
Silence accompanied, for beast and bird,   600
They to their grassy couch, these to their nests
Were slunk, all but the wakeful nightingale;
She all night long her amorous descant sung;
Silence was pleased: now glowed the firmament
With living sapphires: Hesperus that led   605
The starry host, rode brightest, till the moon
Rising in clouded majesty, at length
Apparent queen unveiled her peerless light,
And o'er the dark her silver mantle threw.
    When Adam thus to Eve: 'Fair consort, the hour   610
Of night, and all things now retired to rest
Mind us of like repose, since God hath set
Labor and rest, as day and night to men
Successive, and the timely dew of sleep
Now falling with soft slumberous weight inclines   615
Our eyelids; other creatures all day long
Rove idle unemployed, and less need rest;
Man hath his daily work of body or mind
Appointed, which declares his dignity,
And the regard of heaven on all his ways;   620
While other animals unactive range,
And of their doings God takes no account.
Tomorrow ere fresh morning streak the east
With first approach of light, we must be risen,
And at our pleasant labor, to reform   625
Yon flowery arbors, yonder alleys green,
Our walk at noon, with branches overgrown,
That mock our scant manuring, and require
More hands than ours to lop their wanton growth:
Those blossoms also, and those dropping gums,   630
That lie bestrewn unsightly and unsmooth,
Ask riddance, if we mean to tread with ease;
Meanwhile, as nature wills, night bids us rest.'
    To whom thus Eve with perfect beauty adorned.
'My author and disposer, what thou biddest   635
Unargued I obey; so God ordains,
God is thy law, thou mine: to know no more
Is woman's happiest knowledge and her praise.

594. **volubile**: turning.   **less volubile**: the earth could turn much more slowly to bring about day and night than the sun would have to move to bring about the same results.

608. **Apparent queen**: obviously the queen of night.

628. **our scant manuring**: our scanty handiwork. 'Manuring' originally meant 'to cultivate by manual (hand) labor,' then to enrich, and now to fertilize.

With thee conversing I forget all time,
All seasons and their change, all please alike.   640
Sweet is the breath of morn, her rising sweet,
With charm of earliest birds; pleasant the sun
When first on this delightful land he spreads
His orient beams, on herb, tree, fruit, and flower,
Glistering with dew; fragrant the fertile earth   645
After soft showers; and sweet the coming on
Of grateful evening mild, then silent night
With this her solemn bird and this fair moon,
And these the gems of heaven, her starry train:
But neither breath of morn when she ascends   650
With charm of earliest birds, nor rising sun
On this delightful land, nor herb, fruit, flower,
Glistering with dew, nor fragrance after showers,
Nor grateful evening mild, nor silent night
With this her solemn bird, nor walk by moon,   655
Or glittering starlight without thee is sweet.
But wherefore all night long shine these, for whom
This glorious sight, when sleep hath shut all eyes?'
   To whom our general ancestor replied.
'Daughter of God and man, accomplished Eve,   660
Those have their course to finish, round the earth,
By morrow evening, and from land to land
In order, though to nations yet unborn,
Ministering light prepared, they set and rise;
Lest total darkness should by night regain   665
Her old possession, and extinguish life
In nature and all things, which these soft fires
Not only enlighten, but with kindly heat
Of various influence foment and warm,
Temper or nourish, or in part shed down   670
Their stellar virtue on all kinds that grow
On earth, made hereby apter to receive
Perfection from the sun's more potent ray.
These then, though unbeheld in deep of night,
Shine not in vain, nor think, though men were none,   675
That heaven would want spectators, God want praise;
Millions of spiritual creatures walk the earth
Unseen, both when we wake, and when we sleep:
All these with ceaseless praise his works behold
Both day and night: how often from the steep   680
Of echoing hill or thicket have we heard
Celestial voices to the midnight air,
Sole, or responsive each to other's note
Singing their great creator: oft in bands

641–66. Note the parallelism in this passage, the first part positive, balanced by 'but neither...' then a parade of negatives reversing the positives.

644. **orient beams**: rising beams.   565. **total darkness**: the darkness of primeval chaos.

667 ff. Milton rather cautiously suggests astrological influences of the stars on the earth and its creatures.

While they keep watch, or nightly rounding walk   685
With heavenly touch of instrumental sounds
In full harmonic number joined, their songs
Divide the night, and lift our thoughts to heaven.'
    Thus talking hand in hand alone they passed
On to their blissful bower; it was a place   690
Chosen by the sovereign planter, when he framed
All things to man's delightful use; the roof
Of thickest covert was inwoven shade
Laurel and myrtle, and what higher grew
Of firm and fragrant leaf; on either side   695
Acanthus, and each odorous bushy shrub
Fenced up the verdant wall; each beauteous flower,
Iris all hues, roses, and jessamine
Reared high their flourished heads between, and wrought
Mosaic; underfoot the violet,   700
Crocus, and hyacinth with rich inlay
Broidered the ground, more colored than with stone
Of costliest emblem: other creature here
Beast, bird, insect, or worm durst enter none;
Such was their awe of man.   In shady bower   705
More sacred and sequestered, though but feigned,
Pan or Sylvanus never slept, nor nymph,
Nor Faunus haunted.   Here in close recess
With flowers, garlands, and sweet-smelling herbs
Espoused Eve decked first her nuptial bed,   710
And heavenly choirs the hymenaean sung,
What day the genial angel to our sire
Brought her in naked beauty more adorned,
More lovely than Pandora, whom the gods
Endowed with all their gifts, and O too like   715
In sad event, when to the unwiser son
Of Japhet brought by Hermes, she ensnared
Mankind with her fair looks, to be avenged
On him who had stole Jove's authentic fire.
    Thus at their shady lodge arrived, both stood   720
Both turned, and under open sky adored
The God that made both sky, air, earth, and heaven
Which they beheld, the moon's resplendent globe
And starry pole: 'Thou also madest the night,
Maker omnipotent, and thou the day,   725

705. **shady:** the first edition read 'shadier,' as do most modern editions.   But the double comparative is not needed, and I have adopted the reading of the second edition, 'In shady bower more sacred . . . Pan . . . never slept.'

711. **hymenaean song:** the marriage song.

714 ff. A myth related by Hesiod.   Pandora (all-gifted) was a woman made of earth to bring misery on mankind at the command of Zeus.   She was then brought to Epimetheus, 'the unwise son of Japhet,' who, forgetting the counsel of his brother, Prometheus, not to accept anything from Zeus, married her.   She brought with her from heaven a box containing all human ills and let them loose.   Another version says the box contained blessings, and Pandora's curiosity finally causing her to open the box, they all escaped save hope.   The whole affair was to secure revenge by Zeus on Prometheus for stealing fire from heaven for mankind.

Which we in our appointed work employed
Have finished happy in our mutual help
And mutual love, the crown of all our bliss
Ordained by thee, and this delicious place
For us too large, where thy abundance wants 730
Partakers, and uncropped falls to the ground.
But thou hast promised from us two a race
To fill the earth, who shall with us extol
Thy goodness infinite, both when we wake,
And when we seek, as now, thy gift of sleep.' 735
   This said unanimous, and other rites
Observing none, but adoration pure
Which God likes best, into their inmost bower
Handed they went; and eased the putting off
These troublesome disguises which we wear, 740
Straight side by side were laid, nor turned I ween
Adam from his fair spouse, nor Eve the rites
Mysterious of connubial love refused:
Whatever hypocrites austerely talk
Of purity and place and innocence, 745
Defaming as impure what God declares
Pure, and commands to some, leaves free to all.
Our maker bids increase, who bids abstain
But our destroyer, foe to God and man?
Hail wedded love, mysterious law, true source 750
Of human offspring, sole propriety,
In Paradise of all things common else.
By thee adulterous lust was driven from men
Among the bestial herds to range, by thee
Founded in reason, loyal, just, and pure, 755
Relations dear, and all the charities
Of father, son, and brother first were known.
Far be it, that I should write thee sin or blame,
Or think thee unbefitting holiest place,
Perpetual fountain of domestic sweets, 760
Whose bed is undefiled and chaste pronounced,
Present, or past, as saints and patriarchs used.
Here love his golden shafts employs, here lights
His constant lamp, and waves his purple wings,
Reigns here and revels; not in the bought smile 765
Of harlots, loveless, joyless, unendeared,
Casual fruition, nor in court amours
Mixed dance, or wanton mask, or midnight ball,
Or serenade, which the starved lover sings
To his proud fair, best quitted with disdain. 770
These lulled by nightingales embracing slept,
And on their naked limbs the flowery roof
Showered roses, which the morn repaired.   Sleep on
Blest pair; and O yet happiest if ye seek
No happier state, and know to know no more. 775

751. **sole propriety:** the one thing exclusively held by Adam and Eve.

Now had night measured with her shadowy cone
Halfway uphill this vast sublunar vault,
And from their ivory port the cherubim
Forth issuing at the accustomed hour stood armed
To their night watches in warlike parade,   780
When Gabriel to his next in power thus spake.
  'Uzziel, half these draw off, and coast the south
With strictest watch; these other wheel the north,
Our circuit meets full west.'   As flame they part
Half wheeling to the shield, half to the spear.   785
From these, two strong and subtle spirits he called
That near him stood, and gave them thus in charge.
  'Ithuriel and Zephon, with winged speed
Search through this garden, leave unsearched no nook,
But chiefly where those two fair creatures lodge,   790
Now laid perhaps asleep secure of harm.
This evening from the sun's decline arrived
Who tells of some infernal spirit seen
Hitherward bent (who could have thought?) escaped
The bars of hell, on errand bad no doubt: 795
Such where ye find, seize fast, and hither bring.'
  So saying, on he led his radiant files,
Dazzling the moon; these to the bower direct
In search of whom they sought: him there they found
Squat like a toad, close at the ear of Eve;   800
Assaying by his devilish art to reach
The organs of her fancy, and with them forge
Illusions as he list, phantasms and dreams,
Or if, inspiring venom, he might taint
The animal spirits that from pure blood arise   805
Like gentle breaths from rivers pure, thence raise
At least distempered, discontented thoughts,
Vain hopes, vain aims, inordinate desires
Blown up with high conceits engendering pride.
Him thus intent Ithuriel with his spear   810
Touched lightly; for no falsehood can endure
Touch of celestial temper, but returns
Of force to its own likeness: up he starts
Discovered and surprised.   As when a spark
Lights on a heap of nitrous powder, laid   815
Fit for the tun some magazine to store
Against a rumored war, the smutty grain
With sudden blaze diffused, inflames the air:

782. **Uzziel:** Phillips, 'the buck-goat of God.'   Strength of God.

785. **shield ... spear:** half to the left (shield), half to the right (spear), or in the directions indicated by the hands that bear respectively the shield and the spear.

788. **Ithuriel and Zephon:** discovery of God, and a lookout.

800. **like a toad:** was Satan actually in the form of a toad here?

801 ff. The whole passage is a reflection of contemporary notions about dreams and 'distempered, discontented thoughts.'

816. **tun:** barrel.   817. **smutty:** like soot or coal.

So started up in his own shape the fiend.
Back stepped those two fair angels half amazed   820
So sudden to behold the grisly king;
Yet thus, unmoved with fear, accost him soon.
  'Which of those rebel spirits adjudged to hell
Comest thou, escaped thy prison, and transformed,
Why sattest thou like an enemy in wait   825
Here watching at the head of these that sleep?'
  'Know ye not then' said Satan, filled with scorn,
'Know ye not me? ye knew me once no mate
For you, there sitting where ye durst not soar;
Not to know me argues yourselves unknown,   830
The lowest of your throng; or if ye know,
Why ask ye, and superfluous begin
Your message, like to end as much in vain?'
To whom thus Zephon, answering scorn with scorn.
'Think not, revolted spirit, thy shape the same,   835
Or undiminished brightness, to be known
As when thou stoodest in heaven upright and pure;
That glory then, when thou no more wast good,
Departed from thee, and thou resemblest now
Thy sin and place of doom obscure and foul.   840
But come, for thou, be sure, shalt give account
To him who sent us, whose charge is to keep
This place inviolable, and these from harm.'
  So spake the cherub, and his grave rebuke
Severe in youthful beauty, added grace   845
Invincible: abashed the devil stood,
And felt how awful goodness is, and saw
Virtue in her shape how lovely, saw, and pined
His loss; but chiefly to find here observed
His luster visibly impaired; yet seemed   850
Undaunted.   'If I must contend,' said he,
'Best with the best, the sender not the sent,
Or all at once; more glory will be won,
Or less be lost.'   'Thy fear,' said Zephon bold,
'Will save us trial what the least can do   855
Single against thee wicked, and thence weak.'
  The fiend replied not, overcome with rage;
But like a proud steed reined, went haughty on,
Champing his iron curb: to strive or fly
He held it vain; awe from above had quelled   860
His heart, not else dismayed.   Now drew they nigh
The western point, where those half-rounding guards
Just met, and closing stood in squadron joined
Awaiting next command.   To whom their chief
Gabriel from the front thus called aloud.   865

821. **grisly**: inspiring horror or fear.

835 ff. Satan's appearance has suffered the same progressive degradation as has his nature, but he is unaware of it.

840. **obscure**: dark, gloomy.

'O friends, I hear the tread of nimble feet
Hasting this way, and now by glimpse discern
Ithuriel and Zephon through the shade,
And with them comes a third of regal port,
But faded splendor wan; who by his gait   870
And fierce demeanor seems the prince of hell,
Not likely to part hence without contest;
Stand firm, for in his look defiance lours.'
   He scarce had ended, when those two approached
And brief related whom they brought, where found,   875
How busied, in what form and posture couched.
   To whom with stern regard thus Gabriel spake.
'Why hast thou, Satan, broke the bounds prescribed
To thy transgressions, and disturbed the charge
Of others, who approve not to transgress   880
By thy example, but have power and right
To question thy bold entrance on this place;
Employed it seems to violate sleep, and those
Whose dwelling God hath planted here in bliss?'
   To whom thus Satan, with contemptuous brow.   885
'Gabriel, thou hadst in heaven the esteem of wise,
And such I held thee; but this question asked
Puts me in doubt.   Lives there who loves his pain?
Who would not, finding way, break loose from hell,
Though thither doomed?   Thou wouldst thyself, no doubt,   890
And boldly venture to whatever place
Farthest from pain, where thou mightest hope to change
Torment with ease, and soonest recompense
Dole with delight, which in this place I sought;
To thee no reason; who knowest only good,   895
But evil hast not tried: and wilt object
His will who bound us? let him surer bar
His iron gates, if he intends our stay
In that dark durance: thus much what was asked.
The rest is true, they found me where they say;   900
But that implies not violence or harm.'
   Thus he in scorn.   The warlike angel moved,
Disdainfully half smiling thus replied.
'O loss of one in heaven to judge of wise,
Since Satan fell, whom folly overthrew,   905
And now returns him from his prison scaped,
Gravely in doubt whether to hold them wise
Or not, who ask what boldness brought him hither
Unlicensed from his bounds in hell prescribed;
So wise he judges it to fly from pain   910

869. **port**: bearing.

870. **gait**: Milton printed the word 'gate' here and elsewhere.   Phillips has an interesting entry under 'gate' (1706).

894. **Dole**: pain.   899. **durance**: imprisonment.

904 ff. Note the irony, satire, and penetration of this speech.   These speeches are really a debate of wit. The humor is intellectual, and depends on wit that bites like acid.   Note lines 907–23.

However, and to scape his punishment.
So judge thou still, presumptuous, till the wrath,
Which thou incurrest by flying, meet thy flight
Sevenfold, and scourge that wisdom back to hell,
Which taught thee yet no better, that no pain   915
Can equal anger infinite provoked.
But wherefore thou alone? wherefore with thee
Came not all hell broke loose? is pain to them
Less pain, less to be fled, or thou than they
Less hardy to endure? courageous chief,   920
The first in flight from pain, hadst thou alleged
To thy deserted host this cause of flight,
Thou surely hadst not come sole fugitive.'
    To which the fiend thus answered frowning stern.
'Not that I less endure, or shrink from pain,   925
Insulting angel, well thou knowest I stood
Thy fiercest, when in battle to thy aid
The blasting volleyed thunder made all speed
And seconded thy else not dreaded spear.
But still thy words at random, as before,   930
Argue thy inexperience what behooves
From hard assays and ill successes past
A faithful leader, not to hazard all
Through ways of danger by himself untried,
I therefore, I alone first undertook   935
To wing the desolate abyss, and spy
This new created world, whereof in hell
Fame is not silent, here in hope to find
Better abode, and my afflicted powers
To settle here on earth, or in mid-air;   940
Though for possession put to try once more
What thou and thy gay legions dare against;
Whose easier business were to serve their lord
High up in heaven, with songs to hymn his throne,
And practiced distances to cringe, not fight.'   945
    To whom the warrior angel, soon replied.
'To say and straight unsay, pretending first
Wise to fly pain, professing next the spy,
Argues no leader but a liar traced,
Satan, and couldst thou "faithful" add?   O name,   950
O sacred name of faithfulness profaned!
Faithful to whom? to thy rebellious crew?
Army of fiends, fit body to fit head;
Was this your discipline and faith engaged,
Your military obedience, to dissolve   955
Allegiance to the acknowledged power supreme?
And thou sly hypocrite, who now wouldst seem
Patron of liberty, who more than thou

938. **Fame**: report.   942. **gay**: fine.
947 ff. Note how **every** statement Satan has made is herein turned to his disadvantage.
958. **Patron**: champion.

Once fawned, and cringed, and servilely adored
Heaven's awful monarch? wherefore but in hope   960
To dispossess him, and thyself to reign?
But mark what I aread thee now, avaunt;
Fly thither whence thou fleddst: if from this hour
Within these hallowed limits thou appear,
Back to the infernal pit I drag thee chained,   965
And seal thee so, as henceforth not to scorn
The facile gates of hell too slightly barred.'
    So threatened he, but Satan to no threats
Gave heed, but waxing more in rage replied.
    'Then when I am thy captive talk of chains,   970
Proud limitary cherub, but ere then
Far heavier load thyself expect to feel
From my prevailing arm, though heaven's king
Ride on thy wings, and thou with thy compeers,
Used to the yoke, drawest his triumphant wheels   975
In progress through the road of heaven star-paved.'
    While thus he spake, the angelic squadron bright
Turned fiery red, sharpening in mooned horns
Their phalanx, and began to hem him round
With ported spears, as thick as when a field   980
Of Ceres ripe for harvest waving bends
Her bearded grove of ears, which way the wind
Sways them; the careful plowman doubting stands
Lest on the threshing floor his hopeful sheaves
Prove chaff. On the other side Satan alarmed   985
Collecting all his might dilated stood,
Like Teneriff or Atlas unremoved:
His stature reached the sky, and on his crest
Sat horror plumed; nor wanted in his grasp
What seemed both spear and shield: now dreadful deeds   990
Might have ensued, nor only Paradise
In this commotion, but the starry cope
Of heaven perhaps, or all the elements
At least had gone to wrack, disturbed and torn
With violence of this conflict, had not soon   995
The eternal to prevent such horrid fray
Hung forth in heaven his golden scales, yet seen
Betwixt Astraea and the Scorpion sign,
Wherein all things created first he weighed,
The pendulous round earth with balanced air   1000
In counterpoise, now ponders all events,

962. **aread**: advise.

971. **limitary**: guarding the frontier, or limits.   But also *limited*, not free.

980. **ported spears**: port arms.

987. **Teneriff or Atlas**: the first, a high peak in the Canary Islands, and the second, the mountains in Africa on whose summits, according to classical mythology, the heavens were supported.

994. **wrack**: wreck, the old form preserved in 'wrack and ruin.'

997. **his golden scales**: a symbolic sign, Satan's side kicking the beam because it flew up, being the lighter of the two.

Battles and realms: in these he put two **weights**
The sequel each of parting and of fight;
The latter quick upflew, and kicked the beam;
Which Gabriel spying, thus bespake the fiend.
'Satan, I know thy strength, and thou knowest mine,   1005
Neither our own but given; what folly then
To boast what arms can do, since thine no more
Than heaven permits, nor mine, though doubled now
To trample thee as mire: for proof look up,   1010
And read thy lot in yon celestial sign
Where thou art weighed, and shown how light, how weak,
If thou resist.' The fiend looked up and knew
His mounted scale aloft: nor more; but fled
Murmuring, and with him fled the shades of night.   1015

THE END OF THE FOURTH BOOK

BOOK V

THE ARGUMENT

Morning approached, Eve relates to Adam her troublesome dream; he likes it
not, yet comforts her: They come forth to their day labors: Their morning hymn
at the door of their bower. God to render man inexcusable sends Raphael to
admonish him of his obedience, of his free estate, of his enemy near at hand; who
he is, and why his enemy, and whatever else may avail Adam to know. Raphael
comes down to Paradise, his appearance described, his coming discerned by Adam
afar off sitting at the door of his bower; he goes out to meet him, brings him to
his lodge, entertains him with the choicest fruits of Paradise got together by Eve;
their discourse at table: Raphael performs his message, minds Adam of his state
and of his enemy; relates at Adam's request who that enemy is, and how he came
to be so, beginning from his first revolt in heaven, and the occasion thereof; how
he drew his legions after him to the parts of the north, and there incited them
to rebel with him, persuading all but only Abdiel a seraph, who in argument
dissuades and opposes him, then forsakes him.

Now morn her rosy steps in the eastern clime
Advancing, sowed the earth with orient pearl,
When Adam waked, so customed, for his sleep
Was airy light from pure digestion bred,
And temperate vapors bland, which the only sound   5
Of leaves and fuming rills, Aurora's fan,
Lightly dispersed, and the shrill matin song
Of birds on every bough; so much the more
His wonder was to find unwakened Eve
With tresses discomposed, and glowing cheek,   10
As through unquiet rest: he on his side
Leaning half raised, with looks of cordial love
Hung over her enamored, and beheld
Beauty, which whether waking or asleep,
Shot forth peculiar graces; then with voice   15

Mild, as when Zephyrus on Flora breathes,
Her hand soft touching, whispered thus. 'Awake
My fairest, my espoused, my latest found,
Heaven's last best gift, my ever new delight,
Awake, the morning shines, and the fresh field   20
Calls us, we lose the prime, to mark how spring
Our tended plants, how blows the citron grove,
What drops the myrrh, and what the balmy reed,
How nature paints her colors, how the bee
Sits on the bloom extracting liquid sweet.'   25
    Such whispering waked her, but with startled eye
On Adam, whom embracing, thus she spake.
    'O sole in whom my thoughts find all repose,
My glory, my perfection, glad I see
Thy face, and morn returned, for I this night,   30
Such night till this I never passed, have dreamed,
If dreamed, not as I oft am wont, of thee,
Works of day past, or morrow's next design,
But of offense and trouble, which my mind
Knew never till this irksome night; methought   35
Close at mine ear one called me forth to walk
With gentle voice, I thought it thine; it said,
"Why sleepest thou Eve? now is the pleasant time,
The cool, the silent, save where silence yields
To the night-warbling bird, that now awake   40
Tunes sweetest his love-labored song; now reigns
Full-orbed the moon, and with more pleasing light
Shadowy sets off the face of things; in vain,
If none regard; heaven wakes with all his eyes,
Whom to behold but thee, nature's desire,   45
In whose sight all things joy, with ravishment
Attracted by thy beauty still to gaze."
I rose as at thy call, but found thee not;
To find thee I directed then my walk;
And on, methought, alone I passed through ways   50
That brought me on a sudden to the tree
Of interdicted knowledge: fair it seemed,
Much fairer to my fancy than by day:
And as I wondering looked, beside it stood
One shaped and winged like one of those from heaven   55
By us oft seen; his dewy locks distilled
Ambrosia; on that tree he also gazed;
And "O fair plant," said he, "with fruit surcharged,
Deigns none to ease thy load and taste thy sweet,
Nor God, nor man; is knowledge so despised?   60
Or envy, or what reserve forbids to taste?
Forbid who will, none shall from me withhold

40. **night-warbling bird**: the nightingale.

50–92. Just as Satan received from Uriel a brief account of Creation (III:708–34), that was to be greatly expanded later in the poem, so in these lines we get a brief anticipation of what is to come.

54–57. The figure seems to have been the same as that in which Satan appeared to Uriel, III:636–44.

Longer thy offered good, why else set here?''
This said he paused not, but with venturous arm
He plucked, he tasted; me damp horror chilled   65
At such bold words vouched with a deed so bold:
But he thus overjoyed, ''O fruit divine,
Sweet of thyself, but much more sweet thus cropped,
Forbidden here, it seems, as only fit
For gods, yet able to make gods of men: 70
And why not gods of men, since good, the more
Communicated, more abundant grows,
The author not impaired, but honored more?
Here, happy creature, fair angelic Eve,
Partake thou also; happy though thou art,   75
Happier thou mayest be, worthier canst not be:
Taste this, and be henceforth among the gods
Thyself a goddess, not to Earth confined,
But sometimes in the air, as we, sometimes
Ascend to heaven, by merit thine, and see   80
What life the gods live there, and such live thou.''
So saying, he drew nigh, and to me held,
Even to my mouth of that same fruit held part
Which he had plucked; the pleasant savory smell
So quickened appetite, that I, methought,   85
Could not but taste.   Forthwith up to the clouds
With him I flew, and underneath beheld
The earth outstretched immense, a prospect wide
And various: wondering at my flight and change
To this high exaltation; suddenly   90
My guide was gone, and I, methought, sunk down,
And fell asleep; but O how glad I waked
To find this but a dream!'   Thus Eve her night
Related, and thus Adam answered sad.
    'Best image of myself and dearer half,   95
The trouble of thy thoughts this night in sleep
Affects me equally; nor can I like
This uncouth dream, of evil sprung I fear;
Yet evil whence? in thee can harbor none,
Created pure.   But know that in the soul   100
Are many lesser faculties that serve
Reason as chief; among these fancy next
Her office holds; of all external things,
Which the five watchful senses represent,
She forms imaginations, airy shapes,   105
Which reason joining or disjoining, frames
All what we affirm or what deny, and call
Our knowledge or opinion; then retires
Into her private cell when nature rests.
Oft in her absence mimic fancy wakes   110
To imitate her; but misjoining shapes,

95 ff. Adam gives Eve a lecture on psychology.   98. uncouth: strange, unknown.
102. fancy: imagination in its loftiest form.   104. represent: give representations of.

Wild work produces oft, and most in dreams,
Ill matching words and deeds long past or late.
Some such resemblances methinks I find
Of our last evening's talk, in this thy dream,   115
But with addition strange: yet be not sad.
Evil into the mind of God or man
May come and go, so unapproved, and leave
No spot or blame behind: Which gives me hope
That what in sleep thou didst abhor to dream,   120
Waking thou never wilt consent to do.
Be not disheartened then, nor cloud those looks
That wont to be more cheerful and serene
Than when fair morning first smiles on the world,
And let us to our fresh employments rise   125
Among the groves, the fountains, and the flowers
That open now their choicest bosomed smells
Reserved from night, and kept for thee in store.'
    So cheered he his fair spouse, and she was cheered,
But silently a gentle tear let fall   130
From either eye, and wiped them with her hair;
Two other precious drops that ready stood,
Each in their crystal sluice, he ere they fell
Kissed as the gracious signs of sweet remorse
And pious awe, that feared to have offended.   135
    So all was cleared, and to the field they haste.
But first from under shady arborous roof,
Soon as they forth were come to open sight
Of day-spring, and the sun, who scarce uprisen
With wheels yet hovering o'er the ocean brim,   140
Shot parallel to the earth his dewy ray,
Discovering in wide landscape all the east
Of Paradise and Eden's happy plains,
Lowly they bowed adoring, and began
Their orisons, each morning duly paid   145
In various style, for neither various style
Nor holy rapture wanted they to praise
Their maker, in fit strains pronounced or sung
Unmeditated, such prompt eloquence
Flowed from their lips, in prose or numerous verse,   150
More tuneable than needed lute or harp
To add more sweetness, and they thus began.
    'These are thy glorious works, parent of good,
Almighty, thine this universal frame,
Thus wondrous fair; thyself how wondrous then!   155
Unspeakable, who sittest above these heavens
To us invisible or dimly seen

117 ff. In this passage, Milton almost takes his stand with the Baconians on the problem of knowledge and how much it is fitting for man to know. Here he says man may know evil so long as he does not approve of it. Later (VIII:167–68) he says there are many matters beyond man's comprehension, hence those matters he should not know. Cf. V:568–70.

150. **numerous:** rhythmical.   153 ff. The morning hymn.

In these thy lowest works, yet these declare
Thy goodness beyond thought, and power divine:
Speak ye who best can tell, ye sons of light,   160
Angels, for ye behold him, and with songs
And choral symphonies, day without night,
Circle his throne rejoicing, ye in heaven,
On earth join all ye creatures to extol
Him first, him last, him midst, and without end.   165
Fairest of stars, last in the train of night,
If better thou belong not to the dawn,
Sure pledge of day, that crownest the smiling morn
With thy bright circlet, praise him in thy sphere
While day arises, that sweet hour of prime.   170
Thou sun, of this great world both eye and soul,
Acknowledge him thy greater, sound his praise
In thy eternal course, both when thou climbest,
And when high noon hast gained, and when thou fallest.
Moon, that now meetest the orient sun, now fliest   175
With the fixed stars, fixed in their orb that flies,
And ye five other wandering fires that move
In mystic dance not without song, resound
His praise, who out of darkness called up light.
Air, and ye elements the eldest birth   180
Of nature's womb, that in quaternion run
Perpetual circle, multiform; and mix
And nourish all things, let your ceaseless change
Vary to our great maker still new praise.
Ye mists and exhalations that now rise   185
From hill or steaming lake, dusky or gray,
Till the sun paint your fleecy skirts with gold,
In honor to the world's great author rise,
Whether to deck with clouds the uncolored sky,
Or wet the thirsty earth with falling showers,   190
Rising or falling still advance his praise.
His praise ye winds, that from four quarters blow,
Breathe soft or loud; and wave your tops, ye pines,
With every plant, in sign of worship wave.
Fountains and ye, that warble, as ye flow,   195
Melodious murmurs, warbling tune his praise.
Join voices all ye living souls, ye birds,
That singing up to heaven gate ascend,
Bear on your wings and in your notes his praise;
Ye that in waters glide, and ye that walk   200
The earth, and stately tread, or lowly creep;

166. **Fairest of stars**: Venus.

175–76. **fliest ... flies**: moves.   The motion is circular.

177. **five other wandering fires**: the planets.

178. **In mystic dance**: mysterious movement.   **song**: the Pythagorean music of the spheres.

181. **quaternion run**: fourfold mixture, there being four elements.   Cf. Cicero, *De Natura Deorum* II:33.

189. **uncolored**: unicolored, one color.

191. **advance**: raise.   197–98. The lark.

Witness if I be silent, morn or even,
To hill, or valley, fountain, or fresh shade
Made vocal by my song, and taught his praise.
Hail universal Lord, be bounteous still   205
To give us only good; and if the night
Have gathered aught of evil or concealed,
Disperse it, as now light dispels the dark.'
    So prayed they innocent, and to their thoughts
Firm peace recovered soon and wonted calm.   210
On to their morning's rural work they haste
Among sweet dews and flowers; where any row
Of fruit-trees over-woody reached too far
Their pampered boughs, and needed hands to check
Fruitless embraces: or they led the vine   215
To wed her elm; she spoused about him twines
Her marriageable arms, and with her brings
Her dower the adopted clusters, to adorn
His barren leaves.   Them thus employed beheld
With pity heaven's high king, and to him called   220
Raphael, the sociable spirit, that deigned
To travel with Tobias, and secured
His marriage with the seven times-wedded maid.
   'Raphael,' said he, 'thou hearest what stir on earth
Satan from hell scaped through the darksome gulf   225
Hath raised in Paradise, and how disturbed
This night the human pair, how he designs
In them at once to ruin all mankind.
Go therefore, half this day as friend with friend
Converse with Adam, in what bower or shade   230
Thou findest him from the heat of noon retired,
To respite his day-labor with repast,
Or with repose; and such discourse bring on,
As may advise him of his happy state,
Happiness in his power left free to will,   235
Left to his own free will, his will though free,
Yet mutable; whence warn him to beware
He swerve not too secure: tell him withal
His danger, and from whom, what enemy
Late fallen himself from heaven, is plotting now   240
The fall of others from like state of bliss;
By violence, no, for that shall be withstood,
But by deceit and lies; this let him know,
Lest willfully transgressing he pretend
Surprisal, unadmonished, unforewarned.'   245
   So spake the eternal father, and fulfilled
All justice: nor delayed the winged saint
After his charge received; but from among
Thousand celestial ardors, where he stood
Veiled with his gorgeous wings, upspringing light   250
Flew through the midst of heaven; the angelic choirs

222. **Tobias:** cf. IV:167–71.

On each hand parting, to his speed gave way
Through all the empyreal road; till at the gate
Of heaven arrived, the gate self-opened wide
On golden hinges turning, as by work
Divine the sovereign architect had framed.   255
From hence, no cloud, or, to obstruct his sight,
Star interposed, however small he sees,
Not unconform to other shining globes,
Earth and the garden of God, with cedars crowned
Above all hills.   As when by night the glass   260
Of Galileo, less assured, observes
Imagined lands and regions in the moon:
Or pilot from amidst the Cyclades
Delos or Samos first appearing kens
A cloudy spot.   Down thither prone in flight   265
He speeds, and through the vast ethereal sky
Sails between worlds and worlds, with steady wing
Now on the polar winds, then with quick fan
Winnows the buxom air; till within soar
Of towering eagles, to all the fowls he seems   270
A phoenix, gazed by all, as that sole bird
When to enshrine his relics in the sun's
Bright temple, to Egyptian Thebes he flies.
At once on the eastern cliff of Paradise
He lights, and to his proper shape returns   275
A seraph winged; six wings he wore, to shade
His lineaments divine; the pair that clad
Each shoulder broad, came mantling o'er his breast
With regal ornament; the middle pair   280
Girt like a starry zone his waist, and round
Skirted his loins and thighs with downy gold
And colors dipped in heaven; the third his feet
Shadowed from either heel with feathered mail
Sky-tinctured grain.   Like Maia's son he stood,   285
And shook his plumes, that heavenly fragrance filled
The circuit wide.   Straight knew him all the bands
Of Angels under watch; and to his state,
And to his message high in honor rise;
For on some message high they guessed him bound.   290
Their glittering tents he passed, and now is come
Into the blissful field, through groves of myrrh,
And flowering odors, cassia, nard, and balm;
A wilderness of sweets; for nature here
Wantoned as in her prime, and played at will   295
Her virgin fancies, pouring forth more sweet,
Wild above rule or art; enormous bliss.
Him through the spicy forest onward come

272 ff. **A phoenix**: cf. Ovid, *Amores* II:6:54.   Only one phoenix bird existed at a time.

285. **Maia's son**: Hermes, son of Zeus and Maia.   Hermes was the winged messenger of the Olympian gods.

292–93. Biblical plants.

Adam discerned, as in the door he sat
Of his cool bower, while now the mounted sun   300
Shot down direct his fervid rays to warm
Earth's inmost womb, more warmth than Adam needs;
And Eve within, due at her hour prepared
For dinner savory fruits, of taste to please
True appetite, and not disrelish thirst   305
Of nectarous draughts between, from milky stream,
Berry or grape: to whom thus Adam called.
    'Haste hither Eve, and worth thy sight behold
Eastward among those trees, what glorious Shape
Comes this way moving; seems another morn   310
Risen on mid-noon; some great behest from heaven
To us perhaps he brings, and will vouchsafe
This day to be our guest.   But go with speed,
And what thy stores contain, bring forth and pour
Abundance, fit to honor and receive   315
Our heavenly stranger; well we may afford
Our givers their own gifts, and large bestow
From large bestowed, where nature multiplies
Her fertile growth, and by disburdening grows
More fruitful, which instructs us not to spare.'   320
    To whom thus Eve. 'Adam, earth's hallowed mold,
Of God inspired, small store will serve, where store,
All seasons, ripe for use hangs on the stalk;
Save what by frugal storing firmness gains
To nourish, and superfluous moist consumes: 325
But I will haste and from each bough and brake,
Each plant and juiciest gourd will pluck such choice
To entertain our angel guest, as he
Beholding shall confess that here on earth
God hath dispensed his bounties as in heaven.'   330
    So saying, with dispatchful looks in haste
She turns, on hospitable thoughts intent
What choice to choose for delicacy best,
What order, so contrived as not to mix
Tastes, not well joined, inelegant, but bring   335
Taste after taste upheld with kindliest change,
Bestirs her then, and from each tender stalk
Whatever earth all-bearing mother yields
In India east or west, or middle shore
In Pontus or the Punic coast, or where   340
Alcinous reigned, fruit of all kinds, in coat,
Rough, or smooth rinded, or bearded husk, or shell
She gathers, tribute large, and on the board

299 ff. *Genesis* 17:1 ff.   Milton follows God's visit to Abraham in setting forth Raphael's visit with Adam.

302. **needs**: Verity says that the first edition reads 'need' and the second edition reads 'needs,' but this is not true, the *s* in the first edition being suppressed in many copies, but still faintly discernible.

333. **choice to choose**: a jingle like this, which the Elizabethans so loved, is very unusual in Milton.

341. **Alcinous**: in Homer, *Odyssey*, king of the Phaeacians, who entertained Odysseus.

Heaps with unsparing hand; for drink the grape
She crushes, inoffensive must, and meaths   345
From many a berry, and from sweet kernels pressed
She tempers dulcet creams, nor these to hold
Wants her fit vessels pure, then strews the ground
With rose and odors from the shrub unfumed.
Meanwhile our primitive great sire, to meet   350
His godlike guest, walks forth, without more train
Accompanied than with his own complete
Perfections, in himself was all his state,
More solemn than the tedious pomp that waits
On princes, when their rich retinue long   355
Of horses led, and grooms besmeared with gold
Dazzles the crowd, and sets them all agape.
Nearer his presence Adam though not awed,
Yet with submiss approach and reverence meek,
As to a superior nature, bowing low,   360
    Thus said.   'Native of heaven, for other place
None can than heaven such glorious shape contain;
Since by descending from the thrones above,
Those happy places thou hast deigned a while
To want, and honor these, vouchsafe with us   365
Two only, who yet by sovereign gift possess
This spacious ground, in yonder shady bower
To rest, and what the garden choicest bears
To sit and taste, till this meridian heat
Be over, and the sun more cool decline.'   370
    Whom thus the angelic virtue answered mild.
'Adam, I therefore came, nor art thou such
Created, or such place hast here to dwell,
As may not oft invite, though spirits of heaven
To visit thee; lead on then where thy bower   375
O'ershades; for these mid-hours, till evening rise
I have at will.'   So to the sylvan lodge
They came, that like Pomona's arbor smiled
With flowerets decked and fragrant smells; but Eve
Undecked, save with herself more lovely fair   380
Than wood-nymph, or the fairest goddess feigned
Of three that in Mount Ida naked strove,
Stood to entertain her guest from heaven; no veil
She needed, virtue-proof, no thought infirm

345. **must:** new wine.   **meaths:** sweet beverages, meads.
349. **unfumed:** unsmoked.
350 ff. One of the many pre-romantic passages in the poem.
378. **Pomona:** Roman goddess of fruits.
381–82. **fairest goddess feigned of three:** the judgment of Paris, who had to choose the most beautiful of the three, Hera (Juno), Athena (Minerva), and Aphrodite (Venus).   He chose Aphrodite, thus incurring the wrath of the other two; Aphrodite gave him Helen, for which rape the Trojan War ensued.   Cf. Tennyson, *Oenone*.
382. **Mount Ida:** a mountain in Asia Minor.
384. **virtue-proof:** of proved virtue.

Altered her cheek.   On whom the angel 'Hail'   385
Bestowed, the holy salutation used
Long after to blest Mary, second Eve.
    'Hail mother of mankind, whose fruitful womb
Shall fill the world more numerous with thy sons
Than with these various fruits the trees of God   390
Have heaped this table.'   Raised of grassy turf
Their table was, and mossy seats had round,
And on her ample square from side to side
All autumn piled, though spring and autumn here
Danced hand in hand.   A while discourse they hold;   395
No fear lest dinner cool; when thus began
Our author.   'Heavenly stranger, please to taste
These bounties which our nourisher, from whom
All perfect good unmeasured out, descends,
To us for food and for delight hath caused   400
The earth to yield; unsavory food perhaps
To spiritual natures; only this I know,
That one celestial father gives to all.'
    To whom the angel.   'Therefore what he gives
(Whose praise be ever sung) to man in part   405
Spiritual, may of purest spirits be found
No ingrateful food: and food alike those pure
Intelligential substances require
As doth your rational; and both contain
Within them every lower faculty   410
Of sense, whereby they hear, see, smell, touch, taste,
Tasting concoct, digest, assimilate,
And corporeal to incorporeal turn.
For know, whatever was created, needs
To be sustained and fed; of elements   415
The grosser feeds the purer, earth the sea,
Earth and the sea feed air, the air those fires
Ethereal, and as lowest first the moon;
Whence in her visage round those spots, unpurged
Vapors not yet into her substance turned.   420
Nor doth the moon no nourishment exhale
From her moist continent to higher orbs.
The sun that light imparts to all, receives
From all his alimental recompense
In humid exhalations, and at even   425
Sups with the ocean: though in heaven the trees

385–87. 'Ave, Maria.'   393. **her**: its.

396. **No fear lest dinner cool**: Addison calls this one of the few colloquialisms in the poem.   Tennyson calls it 'a terrible bathos.'

409–13. One of the many discussions in the poem of the nature of angels.   In general, Milton here is pointing out, as in many other places, that everything on earth has its counterpart in heaven, but on a higher, and incomprehensible, plane.

419–20. Milton says that the spots on the moon are unassimilated vapors, or clouds (cf. VIII:145–46).   This notion is found in Pliny, *Natural History*.   But in I:287–91, it certainly seems as if Milton also knew the 'spots' as heights and depths, mountains and great pits.

Of life ambrosial fruitage bear, and vines
Yield nectar, though from off the boughs each morn
We brush mellifluous dews, and find the ground
Covered with pearly grain: yet God hath here   430
Varied his bounty so with new delights,
As may compare with heaven; and to taste
Think not I shall be nice.'   So down they sat,
And to their viands fell, nor seemingly
The angel, nor in mist, the common gloss   435
Of theologians, but with keen dispatch
Of real hunger, and concoctive heat
To transubstantiate: what redounds, transpires
Through spirits with ease; nor wonder; if by fire
Of sooty coal the empiric alchemist   440
Can turn, or holds it possible to turn
Metals of drossiest ore to perfect gold
As from the mine.   Meanwhile at table Eve
Ministered naked, and their flowing cups
With pleasant liquors crowned: O innocence   445
Deserving Paradise! if ever, then,
Then had the sons of God excuse to have been
Enamored at that sight; but in those hearts
Love unlibidinous reigned, nor jealousy
Was understood, the injured lover's hell.   450
      Thus when with meats and drinks they had sufficed,
Not burdened nature, sudden mind arose
In Adam, not to let the occasion pass
Given him by this great conference to know
Of things above his world, and of their being   455
Who dwell in heaven, whose excellence he saw
Transcend his own so far, whose radiant forms
Divine effulgence, whose high power so far
Exceeded human, and his wary speech
Thus to the empyreal minister he framed.   460
   'Inhabitant with God, now know I well
Thy favor, in this honor done to man,
Under whose lowly roof thou hast vouchsafed
To enter, and these earthly fruits to taste,
Food not of angels, yet accepted so,   465
As that more willingly thou couldst not seem
At heaven's high feasts to have fed: yet what compare?'
   To whom the winged hierarch replied.
'O Adam, one almighty is, from whom
All things proceed, and up to him return,   470
If not depraved from good, created all
Such to perfection, one first matter all,

430. **pearly grain**: dewdrops.   434-36. The angel really ate 'with keen dispatch.'
435. **gloss**: interpretation.   437. **concoctive heat**: cf. V:412 and VI:514.
440. **empiric**: experimenting.
442. The aim of alchemy was to produce gold from baser metals.   446 ff. *Genesis* 6:1–7.
469 ff. One of the most important passages in the poem for its statement of Milton's theology.

Endued with various forms, various degrees
Of substance, and in things that live, of life;
But more refined, more spiritous, and pure,   475
As nearer to him placed or nearer tending
Each in their several active spheres assigned,
Till body up to spirit work, in bounds
Proportioned to each kind.   So from the root
Springs lighter the green stalk, from thence the leaves   480
More airy, last the bright consummate flower
Spirits odorous breathes: flowers and their fruit
Man's nourishment, by gradual scale sublimed
To vital spirits aspire, to animal,
To intellectual, give both life and sense,   485
Fancy and understanding, whence the soul
Reason receives, and reason is her being,
Discursive, or intuitive; discourse
Is oftest yours, the latter most is ours,
Differing but in degree, of kind the same.   490
Wonder not then, what God for you saw good
If I refuse not, but convert, as you,
To proper substance; time may come when men
With angels may participate, and find
No inconvenient diet, nor too light fare: 495
And from these corporal nutriments perhaps
Your bodies may at last turn all to spirit,
Improved by tract of time, and winged ascend
Ethereal, as we, or may at choice
Here or in heavenly paradises dwell;   500
If ye be found obedient, and retain
Unalterably firm his love entire
Whose progeny you are.   Meanwhile enjoy
Your fill what happiness this happy state
Can comprehend, incapable of more.'   505
    To whom the patriarch of mankind replied,
'O favorable spirit, propitious guest,
Well hast thou taught the way that might direct
Our knowledge, and the scale of nature set
From center to circumference, whereon   510
In contemplation of created things
By steps we may ascend to God.   But say,
What meant that caution joined, "if ye be found
Obedient?" can we want obedience then
To him, or possibly his love desert   515
Who formed us from the dust, and placed us here
Full to the utmost measure of what bliss
Human desires can seek or apprehend?'
    To whom the angel. 'Son of heaven and earth,
Attend: That thou art happy, owe to God;   520
That thou continuest such, owe to thyself,

493. **proper:** [my] own.
498–503. If Adam had not sinned, he ultimately would have been translated to heaven.

That is, to thy obedience; therein stand.
This was that caution given thee; be advised.
God made thee perfect, not immutable;
And good he made thee, but to persevere
He left it in thy power, ordained thy will   525
By nature free, not over-ruled by fate
Inextricable, or strict necessity;
Our voluntary service he requires,
Not our necessitated, such with him
Finds no acceptance, nor can find, for how   530
Can hearts, not free, be tried whether they serve
Willing or no, who will but what they must
By destiny, and can no other choose?
Myself and all the angelic host that stand
In sight of God enthroned, our happy state   535
Hold, as you yours, while our obedience holds;
On other surety none; freely we serve,
Because we freely love, as in our will
To love or not; in this we stand or fall:
And some are fallen, to disobedience fallen,   540
And so from heaven to deepest hell; O fall
From what high state of bliss into what woe!'
    To whom our great progenitor. 'Thy words
Attentive, and with more delighted ear,
Divine instructor, I have heard, than when   545
Cherubic songs by night from neighboring hills
Aerial music send: nor knew I not
To be both will and deed created free;
Yet that we never shall forget to love
Our maker, and obey him whose command   550
Single, is yet so just, my constant thoughts
Assured me, and still assure: though what thou tellest
Hath passed in heaven, some doubt within me move,
But more desire to hear, if thou consent,
The full relation, which must needs be strange,   555
Worthy of sacred silence to be heard;
And we have yet large day, for scarce the sun
Hath finished half his journey, and scarce begins
His other half in the great zone of heaven.'   560
    Thus Adam made request, and Raphael
After short pause assenting, thus began.
    'High matter thou enjoinest me, O prime of men,
Sad task and hard, for how shall I relate
To human sense the invisible exploits   565
Of warring spirits; how without remorse
The ruin of so many glorious once
And perfect while they stood; how last unfold
The secrets of another world, perhaps
Not lawful to reveal? yet for thy good   570
This is dispensed, and what surmounts the reach

525-34. A discourse on free will similar to III:96-128.   566. **remorse**: pity.

Of human sense, I shall delineate so,
By likening spiritual to corporal forms,
As may express them best, though what if earth
Be but the shadow of heaven, and things therein   575
Each to other like, more than on earth is thought?
    ' As yet this world was not, and chaos wild
Reigned where these heavens now roll, where earth now rests
Upon her center poised, when on a day
(For time, though in eternity, applied   580
To motion, measures all things durable
By present, past, and future) on such day
As heaven's great year brings forth, the empyreal host
Of angels by imperial summons called,
Innumerable before the almighty's throne   585
Forthwith from all the ends of heaven appeared
Under their hierarchs in orders bright
Ten thousand thousand ensigns high advanced,
Standards, and gonfalons twixt van and rear
Stream in the air, and for distinction serve   590
Of hierarchies, of orders, and degrees;
Or in their glittering tissues bear emblazed
Holy memorials, acts of zeal and love
Recorded eminent.   Thus when in orbs
Of circuit inexpressible they stood,   595
Orb within orb, the father infinite,
By whom in bliss embosomed sat the Son,
Amidst as from a flaming mount, whose top
Brightness had made invisible, thus spake.
    '"Hear all ye angels, progeny of light,   600
Thrones, dominations, princedoms, virtues, powers,
Hear my decree, which unrevoked shall stand.
This day I have begot whom I declare
My only Son, and on this holy hill
Him have anointed, whom ye now behold   605
At my right hand; your head I him appoint;
And by myself have sworn to him shall bow
All knees in heaven, and shall confess him Lord:
Under his great vicegerent reign abide
United as one individual soul   610
Forever happy: him who disobeys
Me disobeys, breaks union, and that day
Cast out from God and blessed vision, falls
Into utter darkness, deep engulfed, his place
Ordained without redemption, without end."   615

578. **these heavens:** the skies above them now, not the empyrean.
583. **heaven's great year:** Plato's great year, sometimes estimated at 36,000 years.
588. **advanced:** uplifted.   589. **gonfalons:** flags.
603–08. Milton here took care only to quote Scripture, though these lines come from different verses.
605. **anointed:** *Messiah* means 'anointed.'
609. **vicegerent:** viceregents have delegated powers.
613. **blessed vision:** the beatific vision again.

'So spake the omnipotent, and with his words
All seemed well pleased, all seemed, but were not all.
That day, as other solemn days, they spent
In song and dance about the sacred hill,
Mystical dance, which yonder starry sphere   620
Of planets and of fixed in all her wheels
Resembles nearest, mazes intricate,
Eccentric, intervolved, yet regular
Then most, when most irregular they seem,
And in their motions harmony divine   625
So smooths her charming tones, that God's own ear
Listens delighted.   Evening now approached
(For we have also our evening and our morn,
We ours for change delectable, not need)
Forthwith from dance to sweet repast they turn   630
Desirous; all in circles as they stood,
Tables are set, and on a sudden piled
With angels' food, and rubied nectar flows
In pearl, in diamond, and massy gold,
Fruit of delicious vines, the growth of heaven.   635
On flowers reposed, and with fresh flowerets crowned,
They eat, they drink, and in communion sweet
Quaff immortality and joy, secure
Of surfeit where full measure only bounds
Excess, before the all bounteous king, who showered   640
With copious hand, rejoicing in their joy.
Now when ambrosial night with clouds exhaled
From that high mount of God, whence light and shade
Spring both, the face of brightest heaven had changed
To grateful twilight (for night comes not there   645
In darker veil) and roseate dews disposed
All but the unsleeping eyes of God to rest,
Wide over all the plain, and wider far
Than all this globous earth in plain outspread,
(Such are the courts of God) the angelic throng   650
Dispersed in bands and files their camp extend
By living streams among the trees of life,
Pavilions numberless, and sudden reared,
Celestial tabernacles, where they slept
Fanned with cool winds, save those who in their course   655
Melodious hymns about the sovereign throne
Alternate all night long: but not so waked
Satan, so call him now, his former name
Is heard no more in heaven; he of the first,
If not the first archangel, great in power,   660
In favor and pre-eminence, yet fraught
With envy against the Son of God, that day

623. **Eccentric**: occurs in III:575; VIII:83, all three astronomical.
625. **harmony divine**: referring again to the music of the spheres.
627. **now**: lacking in first edition.   647. **unsleeping eyes of God**: angels appointed to watch.
658. **his former name**: no longer known because it is forgotten.

Honored by his great father, and proclaimed
Messiah king anointed, could not bear
Through pride that sight, and thought himself impaired.   665
Deep malice thence conceiving and disdain,
Soon as midnight brought on the dusky hour
Friendliest to sleep and silence, he resolved
With all his legions to dislodge, and leave
Unworshiped, unobeyed the throne supreme   670
Contemptuous, and his next subordinate
Awakening, thus to him in secret spake.
        '"Sleepest thou companion dear, what sleep can close
Thy eyelids? and rememberest what decree
Of yesterday, so late hath passed the lips   675
Of heaven's almighty.   Thou to me thy thoughts
Wast wont, I mine to thee was wont to impart;
Both waking we were one; how then can now
Thy sleep dissent? new laws thou seest imposed;
New laws from him who reigns, new minds may raise   680
In us who serve, new counsels, to debate
What doubtful may ensue, more in this place
To utter is not safe.   Assemble thou
Of all those myriads which we lead the chief;
Tell them that by command, ere yet dim night   685
Her shadowy cloud withdraws, I am to haste,
And all who under me their banners wave,
Homeward with flying march where we possess
The quarters of the north, there to prepare
Fit entertainment to receive our king   690
The great Messiah, and his new commands,
Who speedily through all the hierarchies
Intends to pass triumphant, and give laws."
     'So spake the false archangel, and infused
Bad influence into the unwary breast   695
Of his associate; he together calls,
Or several one by one, the regent powers,
Under him regent, tells, as he was taught,
That the most high commanding, now ere night,
Now ere dim night had disencumbered heaven,   700
The great hierarchal standard was to move;
Tells the suggested cause, and casts between
Ambiguous words and jealousies, to sound
Or taint integrity; but all obeyed
The wonted signal, and superior voice   705
Of their great potentate; for great indeed
His name, and high was his degree in heaven;
His countenance, as the morning star that guides

   671. **his next subordinate**: Beelzebub.
   689. **The quarters of the north**: the north has always been the abode of evil.   In the *OT*, the north is the
abode of evil, and throughout Semitic literature it is the north that represents evil.
   704. **but all obeyed**: indicating Satan's power and influence in heaven.
   708. **morning star**: Lucifer.

The starry flock, allured them, and with lies
Drew after him the third part of heaven's host: 710
Meanwhile the eternal eye, whose sight discerns
Abstrusest thoughts, from forth his holy mount
And from within the golden lamps that burn
Nightly before him, saw without their light
Rebellion rising, saw in whom, how spread   715
Among the sons of morn, what multitudes
Were banded to oppose his high decree;
And smiling to his only Son thus said.
  '"Son, thou in whom my glory I behold
In full resplendence, heir of all my might,   720
Nearly it now concerns us to be sure
Of our omnipotence, and with what arms
We mean to hold what anciently we claim
Of deity or empire, such a foe
Is rising, who intends to erect his throne   725
Equal to ours, throughout the spacious north;
Nor so content, hath in his thought to try
In battle, what our power is, or our right.
Let us advise, and to this hazard draw
With speed what force is left, and all employ   730
In our defense, lest unawares we lose
This our high place, our sanctuary, our hill."
  'To whom the Son with calm aspect and clear
Lightning divine, ineffable, serene,
Made answer. "Mighty father, thou thy foes   735
Justly hast in derision, and secure
Laughest at their vain designs and tumults vain,
Matter to me of glory, whom their hate
Illustrates, when they see all regal power
Given me to quell their pride, and in event   740
Know whether I be dextrous to subdue
Thy rebels, or be found the worst in heaven."
  'So spake the Son, but Satan with his powers
Far was advanced on winged speed, an host
Innumerable as the stars of night,   745
Or stars of morning, dewdrops, which the sun
Impearls on every leaf and every flower.
Regions they passed, the mighty regencies
Of seraphim and potentates and thrones
In their triple degrees, regions to which   750
All thy dominion, Adam, is no more
Than what this garden is to all the earth,
And all the sea, from one entire globose
Stretched into longitude; which having passed
At length into the limits of the north   755
They came, and Satan to his royal seat

739. **Illustrates:** makes illustrious.   740. **event:** result.
745–47. Note the incorrigible romantic touch breaking through.
753. **globose:** generally or roughly spherical.

High on a hill, far blazing, as a mount
Raised on a mount, with pyramids and towers
From diamond quarries hewn, and rocks of gold,
The palace of great Lucifer, (so call   760
That structure in the dialect of men
Interpreted) which not long after, he
Affecting all equality with God,
In imitation of that mount whereon
Messiah was declared in sight of heaven,   765
The mountain of the congregation called;
For thither he assembled all his train,
Pretending so commanded to consult
About the great reception of their king,
Thither to come, and with calumnious art   770
Of counterfeited truth thus held their ears
    '"Thrones, dominations, princedoms, virtues, powers,
If these magnific titles yet remain
Not merely titular, since by decree
Another now hath to himself engrossed   775
All power, and us eclipsed under the name
Of king anointed, for whom all this haste
Of midnight march, and hurried meeting here,
This only to consult how we may best
With what may be devised of honors new   780
Receive him coming to receive from us
Knee-tribute yet unpaid, prostration vile,
Too much to one, but double how endured,
To one and to his image now proclaimed?
But what if better counsels might erect   785
Our minds and teach us to cast off this yoke?
Will ye submit your necks, and choose to bend
The supple knee? ye will not, if I trust
To know ye right, or if ye know yourselves
Natives and sons of heaven possessed before   790
By none, and if not equal all, yet free,
Equally free; for orders and degrees
Jar not with liberty, but well consist.
Who can in reason then or right assume
Monarchy over such as live by right   795
His equals, if in power and splendor less,
In freedom equal? or can introduce
Law and edict on us, who without law
Err not, much less for this to be our lord,
And look for adoration to the abuse   800
Of those imperial titles which assert
Our being ordained to govern, not to serve?"
    'Thus far his bold discourse without control
Had audience, when among the seraphim
Abdiel, than whom none with more zeal adored   805
The Deity, and divine commands obeyed,

763. **Affecting:** aiming at.

Stood up, and in a flame of zeal severe
The current of his fury thus opposed.
   '"O argument blasphemous, false and proud!
Words which no ear ever to hear in heaven   810
Expected, least of all from thee, ingrate
In place thyself so high above thy peers.
Canst thou with impious obloquy condemn
The just decree of God, pronounced and sworn,
That to his only Son by right endued   815
With regal scepter, every soul in heaven
Shall bend the knee, and in that honor due
Confess him rightful king? unjust thou sayest
Flatly unjust, to bind with laws the free,
And equal over equals to let reign,   820
One over all with unsucceeded power.
Shalt thou give law to God, shalt thou dispute
With him the points of liberty, who made
Thee what thou art, and formed the powers of heaven
Such as he pleased, and circumscribed their being? 825
Yet by experience taught we know how good,
And of our good, and of our dignity
How provident he is, how far from thought
To make us less, bent rather to exalt
Our happy state under one head more near   830
United.   But to grant it thee unjust,
That equal over equals monarch reign:
Thyself though great and glorious dost thou count,
Or all angelic nature joined in one,
Equal to him begotten Son, by whom   835
As by his word the mighty father made
All things, even thee, and all the spirits of heaven
By him created in their bright degrees,
Crowned them with glory, and to their glory named
Thrones, dominations, princedoms, virtues, powers, 840
Essential powers, nor by his reign obscured,
But more illustrious made, since he the head
One of our number thus reduced becomes,
His laws our laws, all honor to him done
Returns our own. Cease then this impious rage,   845
And tempt not these; but hasten to appease
The incensed father, and the incensed Son,
While pardon may be found in time besought."
   'So spake the fervent angel, but his zeal
None seconded, as out of season judged,   850
Or singular and rash, whereat rejoiced
The apostate, and more haughty thus replied.
"That we were formed then sayest thou? and the work
Of secondary hands, by task transferred
From father to his Son? strange point and new!   855
Doctrine which we would know whence learned: who saw
When this creation was? rememberest thou

Thy making, while the maker gave thee being?
We know no time when we were not as now;
Know none before us, self-begot, self-raised   860
By our own quickening power, when fatal course
Had circled his full orb, the birth mature
Of this our native heaven, ethereal Sons.
Our puissance is our own, our own right hand
Shall teach us highest deeds, by proof to try   865
Who is our equal: then thou shalt behold
Whether by supplication we intend
Address, and to begirt the almighty throne
Beseeching or besieging.   This report,
These tidings carry to the anointed king;   870
And fly, ere evil intercept thy flight."
    'He said, and as the sound of waters deep
Hoarse murmur echoed to his words applause
Through the infinite host, nor less for that
The flaming seraph fearless, though alone   875
Encompassed round with foes, thus answered bold.
    '"O alienate from God, O spirit accursed,
Forsaken of all good; I see thy fall
Determined, and thy hapless crew involved
In this perfidious fraud, contagion spread   880
Both of thy crime and punishment: henceforth
No more be troubled how to quit the yoke
Of God's Messiah; those indulgent laws
Will not be now vouchsafed, other decrees
Against thee are gone forth without recall;   885
That golden scepter which thou didst reject
Is now an iron rod to bruise and break
Thy disobedience.   Well thou didst advise,
Yet not for thy advice or threats I fly
These wicked tents devoted, lest the wrath   890
Impendent, raging into sudden flame
Distinguish not: for soon expect to feel
His thunder on thy head, devouring fire.
Then who created thee lamenting learn,
When who can uncreate thee thou shalt know."   895
    'So spake the seraph Abdiel faithful found,
Among the faithless, faithful only he;
Among innumerable false, unmoved,
Unshaken, unseduced, unterrified
His loyalty he kept, his love, his zeal;   900
Nor number, nor example with him wrought
To swerve from truth, or change his constant mind
Though single.   From amidst them forth he passed,
Long way through hostile scorn, which he sustained
Superior, nor of violence feared aught;   905
And with retorted scorn his back he turned
On those proud towers to swift destruction doomed.'
                THE END OF THE FIFTH BOOK

890. **devoted**: doomed, fated.

BOOK VI

THE ARGUMENT

Raphael continues to relate how Michael and Gabriel were sent forth to battle against Satan and his angels. The first fight described: Satan and his powers retire under night: He calls a council, invents devilish engines, which in the second day's fight put Michael and his angels to some disorder; but they at length pulling up mountains overwhelmed both the force and machines of Satan: Yet the tumult not so ending, God on the third day sends Messiah his son, for whom he had reserved the glory of that victory: He in the power of his father coming to the place, and causing all his legions to stand still on either side, with his chariot and thunder driving into the midst of his enemies, pursues them unable to resist towards the wall of heaven; which opening, they leap down with horror and confusion into the place of punishment prepared for them in the deep: Messiah returns with triumph to his father.

'All night the dreadless angel unpursued
Through heaven's wide champaign held his way, till morn,
Waked by the circling hours, with rosy hand
Unbarred the gates of light.   There is a cave
Within the mount of God, fast by his throne,   5
Where light and darkness in perpetual round
Lodge and dislodge by turns, which makes through heaven
Grateful vicissitude, like day and night;
Light issues forth, and at the other door
Obsequious darkness enters, till her hour   10
To veil the heaven, though darkness there might well
Seem twilight here; and now went forth the morn
Such as in highest heaven, arrayed in gold
Empyreal, from before her vanished night,
Shot through with orient beams: when all the plain   15
Covered with thick embattled squadrons bright,
Chariots and flaming arms, and fiery steeds
Reflecting blaze on blaze, first met his view:
War he perceived, war in procinct, and found
Already known what he for news had thought   20
To have reported: gladly then he mixed
Among those friendly powers who him received
With joy and acclamations loud, that one
That of so many myriads fallen, yet one
Returned not lost: On to the sacred hill   25
They led him high applauded, and present
Before the seat supreme; from whence a voice
From midst a golden cloud thus mild was heard.
   '"Servant of God, well done, well hast thou fought
The better fight, who single hast maintained   30
Against revolted multitudes the cause
Of truth, in word mightier than they in arms;
And for the testimony of truth hast borne

1. **dreadless angel:** Abdiel.   8. **vicissitude:** change.
10. **Obsequious:** obedient, not in its modern sense of 'servile.'   19. **war in procinct:** ready.

Universal reproach, far worse to bear
Than violence: for this was all thy care   35
To stand approved in sight of God, though worlds
Judged thee perverse: the easier conquest now
Remains thee, aided by this host of friends,
Back on thy foes more glorious to return
Than scorned thou didst depart, and to subdue   40
By force, who reason for their law refuse,
Right reason for their law, and for their king
Messiah, who by right of merit reigns.
Go Michael of celestial armies prince,
And thou in military prowess next   45
Gabriel, lead forth to battle these my sons
Invincible, lead forth my armed saints
By thousands and by millions ranged for fight;
Equal in number to that godless crew
Rebellious, them with fire and hostile arms   50
Fearless assault, and to the brow of heaven
Pursuing drive them out from God and bliss,
Into their place of punishment, the gulf
Of Tartarus, which ready opens wide
His fiery chaos to receive their fall."   55
 'So spake the sovereign voice, and clouds began
To darken all the hill, and smoke to roll
In dusky wreaths, reluctant flames, the sign
Of wrath awaked: nor with less dread the loud
Ethereal trumpet from on high gan blow: 60
At which command the powers militant,
That stood for heaven, in mighty quadrate joined
Of union irresistible, moved on
In silence their bright legions, to the sound
Of instrumental harmony that breathed   65
Heroic ardor to adventurous deeds
Under their godlike leaders, in the cause
Of God and his Messiah.   On they move
Indissolubly firm; nor obvious hill,
Nor straitening vale, nor wood, nor stream divides   70
Their perfect ranks; for high above the ground
Their march was, and the passive air upbore
Their nimble tread, as when the total kind
Of birds in orderly array on wing
Came summoned over Eden to receive   75
Their names of thee; so over many a tract
Of heaven they marched, and many a province wide
Tenfold the length of this terrene: at last
Far in the horizon to the north appeared
From skirt to skirt a fiery region, stretched   80

44–55. Cf. *Revelation* 12:7–9.   44. **Michael**: one of the four angels of the presence.
46. **Gabriel**: another of the four principal angels.
53–54. **the gulf of Tartarus**: Phillips, *Dictionary* (1658) 'a deep place in hell often mentioned by the poets.'

Note to English Department Faculty

Corrections on Graduate Adviser List

1. Add Stan Kvinge
   1201 13th Ave. N.
   Fargo
   Adviser: Bonfield

2. New Adviser for Sherry Wieland
   Changed from Cabral to Cosgrove

3. Add Ginger Newton
   1410 12th Ave. N
   Fargo
   Adviser: Cater

Sid, you don't

Hope you & [?] [?]

mind —

[signature] Haskell

In battailous aspect, and nearer view
Bristled with upright beams innumerable
Of rigid spears, and helmets thronged, and shields
Various, with boastful argument portrayed,
The banded powers of Satan hasting on   85
With furious expedition; for they weened
That selfsame day by fight, or by surprise
To win the mount of God, and on his throne
To set the envier of his state, the proud
Aspirer, but their thoughts proved fond and vain   90
In the midway: though strange to us it seemed
At first, that angel should with angel war,
And in fierce hosting meet, who wont to meet
So oft in festivals of joy and love
Unanimous, as sons of one great sire   95
Hymning the eternal father: but the shout
Of battle now began, and rushing sound
Of onset ended soon each milder thought.
High in the midst exalted as a god
The apostate in his sun-bright chariot sat   100
Idol of majesty divine, enclosed
With flaming cherubim, and golden shields;
Then lighted from his gorgeous throne, for now
'Twixt host and host but narrow space was left,
A dreadful interval, and front to front   105
Presented stood in terrible array
Of hideous length: before the cloudy van,
On the rough edge of battle ere it joined,
Satan with vast and haughty strides advanced,
Came towering, armed in adamant and gold;   110
Abdiel that sight endured not, where he stood
Among the mightiest, bent on highest deeds,
And thus his own undaunted heart explores.
    '"O heaven! that such resemblance of the highest
Should yet remain, where faith and realty   115
Remain not; wherefore should not strength and might
There fail where virtue fails, or weakest prove
Where boldest; though to sight unconquerable?
His puissance, trusting in the almighty's aid,
I mean to try, whose reason I have tried   120
Unsound and false; nor is it aught but just,
That he who in debate of truth hath won,
Should win in arms, in both disputes alike
Victor; though brutish that contest and foul,
When reason hath to deal with force, yet so   125
Most reason is that reason overcome."
    'So pondering, and from his armed peers

84. **argument**: design, the same thing, except visual and not in words, as what precedes each book in this poem.

93. **hosting**: a host is an army, hence 'fighting.'   114 ff. A soliloquy.

115. **realty**: loyalty, from the Italian. Truth.

Forth stepping opposite, half way he met
His daring foe, at this prevention more
Incensed, and thus securely him defied.   130
    '"Proud, art thou met? thy hope was to have reached
The height of thy aspiring unopposed,
The throne of God unguarded, and his side
Abandoned at the terror of thy power
Or potent tongue; fool, not to think how vain   135
Against the omnipotent to rise in arms;
Who out of smallest things could without end
Have raised incessant armies to defeat
Thy folly; or with solitary hand
Reaching beyond all limit at one blow   140
Unaided could have finished thee, and whelmed
Thy legions under darkness; but thou seest
All are not of thy train; there be who faith
Prefer, and piety to God, though then
To thee not visible, when I alone   145
Seemed in thy world erroneous to dissent
From all: my sect thou seest, now learn too late
How few sometimes may know, when thousands err."
    'Whom the grand foe with scornful eye askance
Thus answered. "Ill for thee, but in wished hour   150
Of my revenge, first sought for thou returnest
From flight, seditious angel, to receive
Thy merited reward, the first assay
Of this right hand provoked, since first that tongue
Inspired with contradiction durst oppose   155
A third part of the gods, in synod met
Their deities to assert, who while they feel
Vigor divine within them, can allow
Omnipotence to none.   But well thou comest
Before thy fellows, ambitious to win   160
From me some plume, that thy success may show
Destruction to the rest: this pause between
(Unanswered lest thou boast) to let thee know;
At first I thought that liberty and heaven
To heavenly souls had been all one; but now   165
I see that most through sloth had rather serve,
Ministering spirits, trained up in feast and song;
Such hast thou armed, the minstrelsy of heaven,
Servility with freedom to contend,
As both their deeds compared this day shall prove."   170
    'To whom in brief thus Abdiel stern replied.
"Apostate, still thou errest, nor end wilt find
Of erring, from the path of truth remote:
Unjustly thou depravest it with the name
Of servitude to serve whom God ordains,   175

---

129. **prevention**: a coming before, from Latin *praevenire*.   130. **securely**: without anxiety.
147. **sect**: party.   161. **success**: again, outcome.
167–68. **Ministering ... minstrelsy**: contemptuous jingle.

Or nature; God and nature bid the same,
When he who rules is worthiest, and excels
Them whom he governs.   This is servitude,
To serve the unwise, or him who hath rebelled
Against his worthier, as thine now serve thee,   180
Thyself not free, but to thyself enthralled;
Yet lewdly darest our ministering upbraid.
Reign thou in hell thy kingdom, let me serve
In heaven God ever blest, and his divine
Behests obey, worthiest to be obeyed,   185
Yet chains in hell, not realms expect: meanwhile
From me returned, as erst thou saidst, from flight,
This greeting on thy impious crest receive."
    'So saying, a noble stroke he lifted high,
Which hung not, but so swift with tempest fell   190
On the proud crest of Satan, that no sight,
Nor motion of swift thought, less could his shield
Such ruin intercept: ten paces huge
He back recoiled; the tenth on bended knee
His massy spear upstayed; as if on earth   195
Winds under ground or waters forcing way
Sidelong, had pushed a mountain from his seat
Half-sunk with all his pines.   Amazement seized
The rebel thrones, but greater rage to see
Thus foiled their mightiest, ours joy filled, and shout,   200
Presage of victory and fierce desire
Of battle: whereat Michael bid sound
The archangel trumpet; through the vast of heaven
It sounded, and the faithful armies rung
Hosanna to the highest: nor stood at gaze   205
The adverse legions, nor less hideous joined
The horrid shock: now storming fury rose,
And clamor such as heard in heaven till now
Was never, arms on armor clashing brayed
Horrible discord, and the madding wheels   210
Of brazen chariots raged; dire was the noise
Of conflict; overhead the dismal hiss
Of fiery darts in flaming volleys flew,
And flying vaulted either host with fire.
So under fiery cope together rushed   215
Both battles main, with ruinous assault
And inextinguishable rage; all heaven
Resounded, and had earth been then, all earth
Had to her center shook.   What wonder? when
Millions of fierce encountering angels fought   220
On either side, the least of whom could wield
These elements, and arm him with the force
Of all their regions: how much more of power
Army against army numberless to raise
Dreadful combustion warring, and disturb,   225

182. **lewdly**: basely.   215. **cope**: canopy; *cape* is a related word.   216. **battles**: armies.

Though not destroy, their happy native seat;
Had not the eternal king omnipotent
From his stronghold of heaven high overruled
And limited their might; though numbered such
As each divided legion might have seemed   230
A numerous host, in strength each armed hand
A legion, led in fight, yet leader seemed
Each warrior single as in chief, expert
When to advance, or stand, or turn the sway
Of battle, open when, and when to close   235
The ridges of grim war; no thought of flight,
None of retreat, no unbecoming deed
That argued fear; each on himself relied,
As only in his arm the moment lay
Of victory; deeds of eternal fame   240
Were done, but infinite: for wide was spread
That war and various; sometimes on firm ground
A standing fight, then soaring on main wing
Tormented all the air; all air seemed then
Conflicting fire: long time in even scale   245
The battle hung; till Satan, who that day
Prodigious power had shown, and met in arms
No equal, ranging through the dire attack
Of fighting seraphim confused, at length
Saw where the sword of Michael smote, and felled 250
Squadrons at once, with huge two-handed sway
Brandished aloft the horrid edge came down
Wide-wasting; such destruction to withstand
He hasted, and opposed the rocky orb
Of tenfold adamant, his ample shield   255
A vast circumference: At his approach
The great archangel from his warlike toil
Surceased, and glad as hoping here to end
Intestine war in heaven, the arch-foe subdued
Or captive dragged in chains, with hostile frown 260
And visage all inflamed first thus began.
 '"Author of evil, unknown till thy revolt,
Unnamed in heaven, now plenteous, as thou seest
These acts of hateful strife, hateful to all,
Though heaviest by just measure on thyself   265
And thy adherents: how hast thou disturbed
Heaven's blessed peace, and into nature brought
Misery, uncreated till the crime
Of thy rebellion? how hast thou instilled
Thy malice into thousands, once upright   270
And faithful, now proved false.   But think not here
To trouble holy rest; heaven casts thee out
From all her confines.   Heaven the seat of bliss
Brooks not the works of violence and war.
Hence then, and evil go with thee along   275
Thy offspring, to the place of evil, hell,

Thou and thy wicked crew; there mingle broils,
Ere this avenging sword begin thy doom,
Or some more sudden vengeance winged from God
Precipitate thee with augmented pain.''   280
'So spake the prince of angels; to whom thus
The adversary.   ''Nor think thou with wind
Of airy threats to awe whom yet with deeds
Thou canst not.   Hast thou turned the least of these
To flight, or if to fall, but that they rise   285
Unvanquished, easier to transact with me
That thou shouldst hope, imperious, and with threats
To chase me hence? err not that so shall end
The strife which thou callest evil, but we style
The strife of glory: which we mean to win,   290
Or turn this heaven itself into the hell
Thou fablest, here however to dwell free,
If not to reign: meanwhile thy utmost force,
And join him named almighty to thy aid,
I fly not, but have sought thee far and nigh.''   295
'They ended parle, and both addressed for fight
Unspeakable; for who, though with the tongue
Of angels, can relate, or to what things
Liken on earth conspicuous, that may lift
Human imagination to such height   300
Of godlike power: for likest gods they seemed,
Stood they or moved, in stature, motion, arms
Fit to decide the empire of great heaven.
Now waved their fiery swords, and in the air
Made horrid circles; two broad suns their shields   305
Blazed opposite, while expectation stood
In horror; from each hand with speed retired
Where erst was thickest fight, the angelic throng,
And left large field, unsafe within the wind
Of such commotion, such as to set forth   310
Great things by small, if nature's concord broke,
Among the constellations war were sprung,
Two planets rushing from aspect malign
Of fiercest opposition in mid sky,
Should combat, and their jarring spheres confound.   315
Together both with next to almighty arm,
Uplifted imminent one stroke they aimed
That might determine, and not need repeat,
As not of power, at once; nor odds appeared
In might or swift prevention; but the sword   320
Of Michael from the armory of God
Was given him tempered so, that neither keen
Nor solid might resist that edge: it met
The sword of Satan with steep force to smite

291–92. **the hell thou fablest:** hell has been created, but Satan is either unaware of its creation or at
least of its nature.

296. **parle:** speech, French *parler*, English *parley*.

Descending, and in half cut sheer, nor stayed,   325
But with swift wheel reverse, deep entering shared
All his right side; then Satan first knew pain,
And writhed him to and fro convolved; so sore
The griding sword with discontinuous wound
Passed through him, but the ethereal substance closed   330
Not long divisible, and from the gash
A stream of nectarous humor issuing flowed
Sanguine, such as celestial spirits may bleed,
And all his armor stained erewhile so bright.
Forthwith on all sides to his aid was run   335
By angels many and strong, who interposed
Defense, while others bore him on their shields
Back to his chariot; where it stood retired
From off the files of war; there they him laid
Gnashing for anguish and despite and shame   340
To find himself not matchless, and his pride
Humbled by such rebuke, so far beneath
His confidence to equal God in power.
Yet soon he healed; for spirits that live throughout
Vital in every part, not as frail man   345
In entrails, heart or head, liver or reins;
Cannot but by annihilating die;
Nor in their liquid texture mortal wound
Receive, no more than can the fluid air:
All heart they live, all head, all eye, all ear,   350
All intellect, all sense, and as they please,
They limb themselves, and color, shape or size
Assume, as likes them best, condense or rare.
    'Meanwhile in other parts like deeds deserved
Memorial, where the might of Gabriel fought,   355
And with fierce ensigns pierced the deep array
Of Moloch furious king, who him defied,
And at his chariot wheels to drag him bound
Threatened, nor from the holy one of heaven
Refrained his tongue blasphemous; but anon   360
Down cloven to the waist, with shattered arms
And uncouth pain fled bellowing. On each wing
Uriel and Raphael his vaunting foe,
Though huge, and in a rock of diamond armed,
Vanquished Adramelech, and Asmadai,   365
Two potent thrones, that to be less than gods
Disdained, but meaner thoughts learned in their flight,
Mangled with ghastly wounds through plate and mail,
Nor stood unmindful Abdiel to annoy
The atheist crew, but with redoubled blow   370

326. **shared**: cut in two parts.   329. **griding**: cutting.
346. **reins**: first edition reads 'rein.'   362. **uncouth**: unknown, or strange.

363. **Uriel and Raphael**: the other two of the four principal angels. Adam gets an account from an eye-witness.

365. **Adramelech**: cf. *II Kings* 17:31.   **Asmadai**: same as *Asmodeus* from *Tobit*.

Ariel and Arioch, and the violence
Of Ramiel scorched and blasted overthrew.
I might relate of thousands, and their names
Eternize here on earth; but those elect
Angels contented with their fame in heaven 375
Seek not the praise of men: the other sort
In might though wondrous and in acts of war,
Nor of renown less eager, yet by doom
Canceled from heaven and sacred memory,
Nameless in dark oblivion let them dwell. 380
For strength from truth divided and from just,
Illaudable, nought merits but dispraise
And ignominy, yet to glory aspires
Vainglorious, and through infamy seeks fame:
Therefore eternal silence be their doom. 385
  'And now their mightiest quelled, the battle swerved,
With many an inroad gored; deformed rout
Entered, and foul disorder; all the ground
With shivered armor strewn, and on a heap
Chariot and charioteer lay overturned 390
And fiery foaming steeds; what stood, recoiled
O'er-wearied, through the faint Satanic host
Defensive scarce, or with pale fear surprised,
Then first with fear surprised and sense of pain
Fled ignominious, to such evil brought 395
By sin of disobedience, till that hour
Not liable to fear or flight or pain.
Far otherwise the inviolable saints
In cubic phalanx firm advanced entire,
Invulnerable, impenetrably armed: 400
Such high advantages their innocence
Gave them above their foes, not to have sinned,
Not to have disobeyed; in fight they stood
Unwearied, unobnoxious to be pained
By wound, though from their place by violence moved. 405
  'Now night her course began, and over heaven
Inducing darkness, grateful truce imposed,
And silence on the odious din of war:
Under her cloudy covert both retired,
Victor and vanquished: on the foughten field 410
Michael and his angels prevalent
Encamping, placed in guard their watches round,
Cherubic waving fires: on the other part
Satan with his rebellious disappeared,
Far in the dark dislodged, and void of rest, 415
His potentates to council called by night;
And in the midst thus undismayed began.

371. **Ariel**: the name in Hebrew means 'a champion.' It is the rabbinical name of a fierce and evil spirit. **Arioch**: about the same as Ariel.

372. **Ramiel**: God's thunder. For all these names cf. Fletcher, *Milton's Rabbinical Readings, loc. cit.*
374. **Eternize**: make eternal.   404. **unobnoxious to be pained**: not liable or subject to pain.

      '"O now in danger tried, now known in arms
Not to be overpowered, companions dear,
Found worthy not of liberty alone,   420
Too mean pretense, but what we more affect,
Honor, dominion, glory, and renown,
Who have sustained one day in doubtful fight
(And if one day, why not eternal days?)
What heaven's Lord had powerfullest to send   425
Against us from about his throne, and judged
Sufficient to subdue us to his will,
But proves not so: then fallible, it seems,
Of future we may deem him, though till now
Omniscient thought.   True is, less firmly armed,   430
Some disadvantage we endured and pain,
Till now not known, but known as soon contemned,
Since now we find this our empyreal form
Incapable of mortal injury
Imperishable, and though pierced with wound,   435
Soon closing, and by native vigor healed.
Of evil then so small as easy think
The remedy; perhaps more valid arms,
Weapons more violent, when next we meet,
May serve to better us, and worse our foes,   440
Or equal what between us made the odds,
In nature none: if other hidden cause
Left them superior, while we can preserve
Unhurt our minds, and understanding sound,
Due search and consultation will disclose."   445
   'He sat; and in the assembly next upstood
Nisroch, of principalities the prime;
As one he stood escaped from cruel fight,
Sore toiled, his riven arms to havoc hewn,
And cloudy in aspect thus answering spake.   450
"Deliverer from new lords, leader to free
Enjoyment of our right as gods; yet hard
For gods, and too unequal work we find
Against unequal arms to fight in pain,
Against unpained, impassive; from which evil   455
Ruin must needs ensue; for what avails
Valor or strength, though matchless, quelled with pain
Which all subdues, and makes remiss the hands
Of mightiest.   Sense of pleasure we may well
Spare out of life perhaps, and not repine,   460
But live content, which is the calmest life:
But pain is perfect misery, the worst
Of evils, and excessive, overturns
All patience.   He who therefore can invent
With what more forcible we may offend   465
Our yet unwounded enemies, or arm

447. **Nisroch**: cf. *II Kings* 19:37.   The name means *flight* according to Phillips.
458. **remiss**: slack, languid.

Ourselves with like defense, to me deserves
No less than for deliverance what we owe."
　'Whereto with look composed Satan replied.
"Not uninvented that, which thou aright   470
Believest so main to our success, I bring;
Which of us who beholds the bright surface
Of this ethereous mold whereon we stand,
This continent of spacious heaven, adorned
With plant, fruit, flower ambrosial, gems and gold,   475
Whose eye so superficially surveys
These things, as not to mind from whence they grow
Deep under ground, materials dark and crude,
Of spiritous and fiery spume, till touched
With heaven's ray, and tempered they shoot forth   480
So beauteous, opening to the ambient light.
These in their dark nativity the deep
Shall yield us pregnant with infernal flame,
Which into hollow engines long and round
Thick-rammed, at the other bore with touch of fire   485
Dilated and infuriate shall send forth
From far with thundering noise among our foes
Such implements of mischief as shall dash
To pieces, and o'erwhelm whatever stands
Adverse, that they shall fear we have disarmed   490
The thunderer of his only dreaded bolt.
Nor long shall be our labor, yet ere dawn,
Effect shall end our wish.   Meanwhile revive;
Abandon fear; to strength and counsel joined
Think nothing hard, much less to be despaired."   495
He ended, and his words their drooping cheer
Enlightened, and their languished hope revived.
The invention all admired, and each, how he
To be the inventor missed, so easy it seemed
Once found, which yet unfound most would have thought   500
Impossible: yet haply of thy race
In future days, if malice should abound,
Some one intent on mischief, or inspired
With devilish machination might devise
Like instrument to plague the sons of men   505
For sin, on war and mutual slaughter bent.
Forthwith from council to the work they flew,
None arguing stood, innumerable hands
Were ready, in a moment up they turned
Wide the celestial soil, and saw beneath   510
The originals of nature in their crude
Conception; sulphurous and nitrous foam
They found, they mingled, and with subtle art,

　470. Ariosto, Spenser, Drayton, that is, an Italian poet and two English poets, prior to Milton, assigned the invention of cannon to hell.
　481. **ambient:** encompassing, surrounding.
　482. **nativity:** native state.　　　　512. **foam:** pumice.

Concocted and adusted they reduced
To blackest grain, and into store conveyed: 515
Part hidden veins digged up (nor hath this earth
Entrails unlike) of mineral and stone,
Whereof to found their engines and their balls
Of missive ruin; part incentive reed
Provide, pernicious with one touch to fire.   520
So all ere day spring, under conscious night
Secret they finished, and in order set,
With silent circumspection unespied.
Now when fair morn orient in heaven appeared
Up rose the victor angels, and to arms   525
The matin trumpet sung: in arms they stood
Of golden panoply, refulgent host,
Soon banded; others from the dawning hills
Looked round, and scouts each coast light armed scour,
Each quarter, to descry the distant foe,   530
Where lodged, or whither fled, or if for fight,
In motion or in halt: him soon they met
Under spread ensigns moving nigh, in slow
But firm battalion; back with speediest sail
Zophiel, of cherubim the swiftest wing,   535
Came flying, and in mid air aloud thus cried.
  '"Arm, warriors, arm for fight, the foe at hand,
Whom fled we thought, will save us long pursuit
This day, fear not his flight; so thick a cloud
He comes, and settled in his face I see   540
Sad resolution and secure: let each
His adamantine coat gird well, and each
Fit well his helm, grip fast his orbed shield,
Borne even or high, for this day will pour down,
If I conjecture aught, no drizzling shower,   545
But rattling storm of arrows barbed with fire."
So warned he them aware themselves, and soon
In order, quit of all impediment;
Instant without disturb they took alarm,
And onward move embattled; when behold   550
Not distant far with heavy pace the foe
Approaching gross and huge; in hollow cube
Training his devilish enginry, impaled
On every side with shadowing squadrons deep,
To hide the fraud.   At interview both stood   555
A while, but suddenly at head appeared
Satan: And thus was heard commanding loud.
  '"Vanguard, to right and left the front unfold;

514. **Concocted and adusted**: cooked up chemically and dried out by heat.   Cf. XII:635.
518. **engines**: here, cannon as contrivances.   519. **incentive reed**: the fuse.
535. **Zophiel**: spy of God.   541. **Sad**: steadfast.   **secure**: without fear.
548. **impediment**: from Latin *impedimenta*, 'baggage.'

558 ff. and 609 ff.   These speeches are ironic, satiric, and intended to be witty.   Most editors have found
them unworthy of Milton, but they are dramatically fitted to the occasion.   Note that we do not receive
them directly, but as Raphael can remember them.

That all may see who hate us, how we seek
Peace and composure, and with open breast   560
Stand ready to receive them, if they like
Our overture, and turn not back perverse;
But that I doubt, however witness heaven,
Heaven witness thou anon, while we discharge
Freely our part; ye who appointed stand   565
Do as you have in charge, and briefly touch
What we propound, and loud that all may hear."
    'So scoffing in ambiguous words he scarce,
Had ended; when to right and left the front
Divided, and to either flank retired.   570
Which to our eyes discovered new and strange,
A triple mounted row of pillars laid
On wheels (for like to pillars most they seemed
Or hollowed bodies make of oak or fir
With branches lopped, in wood or mountain felled)   575
Brass, iron, stony mold, had not their mouths
With hideous orifice gaped on us wide,
Portending hollow truce; at each behind
A seraph stood, and in his hand a reed
Stood waving tipped with fire; while we suspense,   580
Collected stood within our thoughts amused,
Not long, for sudden all at once their reeds
Put forth, and to a narrow vent applied
With nicest touch.   Immediate in a flame,
But soon obscured with smoke, all heaven appeared,   585
From those deep throated engines belched, whose roar
Emboweled with outrageous noise the air,
And all her entrails tore, disgorging foul
Their devilish glut, chained thunderbolts and hail
Of iron globes, which on the victor host   590
Leveled, with such impetuous fury smote,
That whom they hit, none on their feet might stand,
Though standing else as rocks, but down they fell
By thousands, angel on archangel rolled;
The sooner for their arms, unarmed they might   595
Have easily as spirits evaded swift
By quick contraction or remove; but now
Foul dissipation followed and forced rout;
Nor served it to relax their serried files.
What should they do? if on they rushed, repulse   600
Repeated, and indecent overthrow
Doubled, would render them yet more despised,
And to their foes a laughter; for in view
Stood ranked of seraphim another row
In posture to displode their second tier   605
Of thunder: back defeated to return
They worse abhorred.   Satan beheld their plight,

581. **amused:** musing, wondering, the older meaning of the word.
584. **nicest:** most exact.   587. **Emboweled:** filled.   601. **indecent:** disgraceful.

And to his mates thus in derision called.
  '"O friends, why come not on these victors proud?
Erewhile they fierce were coming, and when we,   610
To entertain them fair with open front
And breast, (what could we more?) propounded terms
Of composition, straight they changed their minds,
Flew off, and into strange vagaries fell,
As they would dance, yet for a dance they seemed   615
Somewhat extravagant and wild, perhaps
For joy of offered peace: but I suppose
If our proposals once again were heard
We should compel them to a quick result."
  'To whom thus Belial in like gamesome mood,   620
"Leader, the terms we sent were terms of weight,
Of hard contents, and full of force urged home,
Such as we might perceive amused them all,
And stumbled many, who receives them right,
Had need from head to foot well understand;   625
Not understood, this gift they have besides,
They show us when our foes walk not upright."
  'So they among themselves in pleasant vein
Stood scoffing, heightened in their thoughts beyond
All doubt of victory, eternal might   630
To match with their inventions they presumed
So easy, and of his thunder made a scorn,
And all his host derided, while they stood
A while in trouble; but they stood not long,
Rage prompted them at length, and found them arms   635
Against such hellish mischief fit to oppose.
Forthwith (behold the excellence, the power
Which God hath in his mighty angels placed)
Their arms away they threw, and to the hills
(For earth hath this variety from heaven   640
Of pleasure situate in hill and dale)
Light as the lightning glimpse they ran, they flew,
From their foundations loosening to and fro
They plucked the seated hills with all their load,
Rocks, waters, woods, and by the shaggy tops   645
Uplifting bore them in their hands: Amaze,
Be sure, and terror seized the rebel host,
When coming towards them so dread they saw
The bottom of the mountains upward turned,
Till on those cursed engines' triple row   650
They saw them whelmed, and all their confidence
Under the weight of mountains buried deep,
Themselves invaded next, and on their heads
Main promontories flung, which in the air
Came shadowing, and oppressed whole legions armed,   655
Their armor helped their harm, crushed in and bruised
Into their substance pent, which wrought them pain
Implacable, and many a dolorous groan,

Long struggling underneath, ere they could wind
Out of such prison, though spirits of purest light, 660
Purest at first, now gross by sinning grown.
The rest in imitation to like arms
Betook them, and the neighboring hills uptore;
So hills amid the air encountered hills
Hurled to and fro with jaculation dire, 665
That underground they fought in dismal shade;
Infernal noise; war seemed a civil game
To this uproar; horrid confusion heaped
Upon confusion rose: and now all heaven
Had gone to wrack, with ruin overspread, 670
Had not the almighty father where he sits
Shrined in his sanctuary of heaven secure,
Consulting on the sum of things, foreseen
This tumult, and permitted all, advised:
That his great purpose he might so fulfill, 675
To honor his anointed Son avenged
Upon his enemies, and to declare
All power on him transferred: whence to his Son
The assessor of his throne he thus began.
    ' "Effulgence of my glory, Son beloved, 680
Son in whose face invisible is beheld
Visibly, what by deity I am,
And in whose hand what by decree I do,
Second omnipotence, two days are past,
Two days, as we compute the days of heaven, 685
Since Michael and his powers went forth to tame
These disobedient; sore hath been their fight,
As likeliest was, when two such foes met armed;
For to themselves I left them, and thou knowest,
Equal in their creation they were formed, 690
Save what sin hath impaired, which yet hath wrought
Insensibly, for I suspend their doom;
Whence in perpetual fight they needs must last
Endless, and no solution will be found:
War wearied hath performed what war can do, 695
And to disordered rage let loose the reins,
With mountains as with weapons armed, which makes
Wild work in heaven, and dangerous to the main.
Two days are therefore passed, the third is thine;
For thee I have ordained it, and thus far 700
Have suffered, that the glory may be thine
Of ending this great war, since none but thou
Can end it.   Into thee such virtue and grace
Immense I have transfused, that all may know

665. **jaculation:** a hurling.
670. The first day's battle was just a lot of noise; the second promised to destroy heaven.
679. **assessor:** literally, one who sits by.
681–82. **invisible is beheld visibly:** an oxymoron, made up of two contradictory terms.
692. **suspend:** hold up, delay.   698. **main:** a broad expanse; here, the mainland.

In heaven and hell thy power above compare,   705
And this perverse commotion governed thus,
To manifest thee worthiest to be heir
Of all things, to be heir and to be king
By sacred unction, thy deserved right.
Go then thou mightiest in thy father's might,   710
Ascend my chariot, guide the rapid wheels
That shake heaven's basis, bring forth all my war,
My bow and thunder, my almighty arms
Gird on, and sword upon thy puissant thigh;
Pursue these sons of darkness, drive them out   715
From all heaven's bounds into the utter deep:
There let them learn, as likes them, to despise
God and Messiah his anointed king."
  'He said, and on his Son with rays direct
Shone full, he all his father full expressed   720
Ineffably into his face received,
And thus the filial Godhead answering spake.
  '"O father, O supreme of heavenly thrones,
First, highest, holiest, best, thou always seekest
To glorify thy son, I always thee,   725
As is most just; this I my glory account,
My exaltation, and my whole delight,
That thou in me well pleased, declarest thy will
Fulfilled, which to fulfill is all my bliss.
Scepter and power, thy giving, I assume,   730
And gladlier shall resign, when in the end
Thou shalt be all in all, and I in thee
Forever, and in me all whom thou lovest:
But whom thou hatest, I hate, and can put on
Thy terrors, as I put thy mildness on,   735
Image of thee in all things: and shall soon,
Armed with thy might, rid heaven of these rebelled,
To their prepared ill mansion driven down
To chains of darkness, and the undying worm,
That from thy just obedience could revolt,   740
Whom to obey is happiness entire.
Then shall thy saints unmixed, and from the impure
Far separate, circling thy holy mount
Unfeigned hallelujahs to thee sing,
Hymns of high praise, and I among them chief."   745
So said, he o'er his scepter bowing, rose
From the right hand of glory where he sat,
And the third sacred morn began to shine
Dawning through heaven: forth rushed with whirlwind sound
The chariot of paternal deity,   750
Flashing thick flames, wheel within wheel undrawn,
Itself instinct with spirit, but convoyed

709. **unction:** the act of anointing with oil.   714. **puissant:** powerful.

716. **utter:** outer.   739. **the undying worm:** Satan, as a snake.

749 ff. **The chariot and the charge of its host; this passage is made up of Scripture texts from the** *OT.*

By four cherubic shapes, four faces each
Had wondrous, as with stars their bodies all
And wings were set with eyes, with eyes the wheels
Of beryl, and careering fires between;   755
Over their heads a crystal firmament,
Whereon a sapphire throne, inlaid with pure
Amber, and colors of the showery arch.
He in celestial panoply all armed
Of radiant urim, work divinely wrought,   760
Ascended, at his right hand victory
Sat eagle-winged, beside him hung his bow
And quiver with three-bolted thunder stored,
And from about him fierce effusion rolled
Of smoke and bickering flame, and sparkles dire;   765
Attended with ten thousand thousand saints,
He onward came, far off his coming shone,
And twenty thousand (I their number heard)
Chariots of God, half on each hand were seen:
He on the wings of cherub rode sublime   770
On the crystalline sky, in sapphire throned.
Illustrious far and wide, but by his own
First seen, them unexpected joy surprised,
When the great ensign of Messiah blazed
Aloft by angels borne, his sign in heaven: 775
Under whose conduct Michael soon reduced
His army, circumfused on either wing,
Under their head embodied all in one.
Before him power divine his way prepared;
At his command the uprooted hills retired   780
Each to his place, they heard his voice and went
Obsequious, heaven his wonted face renewed,
And with fresh flowerets hill and valley smiled.
This saw his hapless foes but stood obdured,
And to rebellious fight rallied their powers   785
Insensate, hope conceiving from despair.
In heavenly spirits could such perverseness dwell?
But to convince the proud what signs avail,
Or wonders move the obdurate to relent?
They hardened more by what might most reclaim,   790
Grieving to see his glory, at the sight
Took envy, and aspiring to his height,
Stood re-embattled fierce, by force or fraud

756. **beryl**: a kind of crystal.   **careering**: darting, a term from tourneys.
760. **panoply**: 'the whole armor of God,' *Ephesians* 6:11.
761. **urim**: the stone of the breastplate in the Hebrew priest's costume.
765. **effusion**: a pouring out.   766. **bickering**: trembling, flashing.
769–70. **twenty thousand . . . chariots of God**: *Psalms* 68:17.
778. **circumfused**: spread around.
783. **Obsequious**: obedient; again no abject servility, but ready compliance.
785. **obdured**: stubbornly wicked.   787. **Insensate**: senseless.
790. **obdurate**: stiff-necked.

Weening to prosper, and at length prevail   795
Against God and Messiah, or to fall
In universal ruin last, and now
To final battle drew, disdaining flight,
Or faint retreat; when the great Son of God
To all his host on either hand thus spake.   800
  '"Stand still in bright array ye saints, here stand
Ye angels armed, this day from battle rest;
Faithful hath been your warfare, and of God
Accepted, fearless in his righteous cause,
And as ye have received, so have ye done   805
Invincibly; but of this cursed crew
The punishment to other hand belongs,
Vengeance is his, or whose he sole appoints;
Number to this day's work is not ordained
Nor multitude, stand only and behold   810
God's indignation on these godless poured
By me, not you but me they have despised,
Yet envied; against me is all their rage,
Because the father, to whom in heaven supreme
Kingdom and power and glory appertains,   815
Hath honored me according to his will.
Therefore to me their doom he hath assigned;
That they may have their wish, to try with me
In battle which the stronger proves, they all,
Or I alone against them, since by strength   820
They measure all, of other excellence
Not emulous, nor care who them excels;
Nor other strife with them do I vouchsafe."
  'So spake the Son, and into terror changed
His countenance too severe to be beheld   825
And full of wrath bent on his enemies.
At once the four spread out their starry wings
With dreadful shade contiguous, and the orbs
Of his fierce chariot rolled, as with the sound
Of torrent floods, or of a numerous host.   830
He on his impious foes right onward drove,
Gloomy as night; under his burning wheels
The steadfast empyrean shook throughout,
All but the throne itself of God.   Full soon
Among them he arrived; in his right hand   835
Grasping ten thousand thunders, which he sent
Before him, such as in their souls infixed
Plagues; they astonished all resistance lost,
All courage; down their idle weapons dropped;
O'er shields and helms, and helmed heads he rode   840
Of thrones and mighty seraphim prostrate,
That wished the mountains now might be again
Thrown on them as a shelter from his ire.
Nor less on either side tempestuous fell

795. **Weening**: thinking.

His arrows, from the fourfold visaged four,   845
Distinct with eyes, and from the living wheels
Distinct alike with multitude of eyes,
One spirit in them ruled, and every eye
Glared lightning, and shot forth pernicious fire
Among the accursed, that withered all their strength,   850
And of their wonted vigor left them drained,
Exhausted, spiritless, afflicted, fallen.
Yet half his strength he put not forth, but checked
His thunder in mid-volley, for he meant
Not to destroy, but root them out of heaven: 855
The overthrown he raised, and as a herd
Of goats or timorous flock together thronged
Drove them before him thunderstruck, pursued
With terrors and with furies to the bounds
And crystal wall of heaven, which opening wide,   860
Rolled inward, and a spacious gap disclosed
Into the wasteful deep; the monstrous sight
Struck them with horror backward, but far worse
Urged them behind; headlong themselves they threw
Down from the verge of heaven, eternal wrath   865
Burnt after them to the bottomless pit.
  'Hell heard the unsufferable noise, hell saw
Heaven ruining from heaven and would have fled
Affrighted; but strict fate had cast too deep
Her dark foundations, and too fast had bound.   870
Nine days they fell; confounded chaos roared,
And felt tenfold confusion in their fall
Through his wild anarchy, so huge a rout
Encumbered him with ruin: Hell at last
Yawning received them whole, and on them closed,   875
Hell their fit habitation fraught with fire
Unquenchable, the house of woe and pain.
Disburdened heaven rejoiced, and soon repaired
Her mural breach, returning whence it rolled.
Sole victor from the expulsion of his foes   880
Messiah his triumphal chariot turned:
To meet him all his saints, who silent stood
Eye witnesses of his almighty acts,
With jubilee advanced; and as they went,
Shaded with branching palm, each order bright,   885
Sung triumph, and him sung victorious king,
Son, heir, and lord, to him dominion given,
Worthiest to reign: he celebrated rode
Triumphant through mid heaven, into the courts
And temple of his mighty father throned   890
On high: who into glory him received,
Where now he sits at the right hand of bliss.
  'Thus measuring things in heaven by things on earth

879. **mural breach**: breach of the wall.   884. **jubilee**: rejoicing with trumpets.
885. **order**: rank and line of angels.

At thy request, and that thou mayest beware
By what is past, to thee I have revealed   895
What might have else to human race been hid;
The discord which befell, and war in heaven
Among the angelic powers, and the deep fall
Of those too high aspiring, who rebelled
With Satan, he who envies now thy state,   900
Who now is plotting how he may seduce
Thee also from obedience, that with him
Bereaved of happiness thou mayest partake
His punishment, eternal misery;
Which would be all his solace and revenge,   905
As a despite done against the most high,
Thee once to gain companion of his woe.
But listen not to his temptations, warn
Thy weaker; let it profit thee to have heard
By terrible example the reward   910
Of disobedience; firm they might have stood,
Yet fell; remember, and fear to transgress.'

THE END OF THE SIXTH BOOK

BOOK VII

THE ARGUMENT

Raphael at the request of Adam relates how and wherefore this world was first created; that God, after the expelling of Satan and his angels out of heaven, declared his pleasure to create another world and other creatures to dwell therein; sends his Son with glory and attendance of angels to perform the work of creation in six days: the angels celebrate with hymns the performance thereof, and his reascension into heaven.

Descend from heaven Urania, by that name
If rightly thou art called, whose voice divine
Following, above the Olympian hill I soar,
Above the flight of Pegasean wing.
The meaning, not the name I call: for thou   5
Nor of the muses nine, nor on the top
Of old Olympus dwellest, but heavenly born,
Before the hills appeared, or fountain flowed,
Thou with eternal wisdom didst converse,
Wisdom thy sister, and with her didst play   10

909. **Thy weaker:** Eve.
1–40. Invocation to his muse, Urania, to sustain him.   This is the main pause in the poem, at almost its exact middle.   The two minor pauses occur at III: 1–55 and IX: 1–47.
1. **Urania:** goddess of the heavens.
2. **If rightly thou art called:** he acknowledges that he is not using the name *Urania* in the usual fashion.
4. **Pegasean wing:** Pegasus was the winged horse on which poets soared — to poetry.
7–12. *Proverbs* 8:23–30.

In presence of the almighty father, pleased
With thy celestial song.   Upled by thee
Into the heaven of heavens I have presumed,
An earthly guest, and drawn empyreal air,
Thy tempering; with like safety guided down   15
Return me to my native element:
Lest from this flying steed unreined, (as once
Bellerophon, though from a lower clime)
Dismounted, on the Aleian field I fall
Erroneous there to wander and forlorn.   20
Half yet remains unsung, but narrower bound
Within the visible diurnal sphere;
Standing on earth, not rapt above the pole,
More safe I sing with mortal voice, unchanged
To hoarse or mute, though fallen on evil days,   25
On evil days though fallen, and evil tongues;
In darkness, and with dangers compassed round,
And solitude; yet not alone, while thou
Visitest my slumbers nightly, or when morn
Purples the east: still govern thou my song,   30
Urania, and fit audience find, though few.
But drive far off the barbarous dissonance
Of Bacchus and his revelers, the race
Of that wild rout that tore the Thracian bard
In Rhodope, where woods and rocks had ears   35
To rapture, till the savage clamor drowned
Both harp and voice; nor could the muse defend
Her son.   So fail not thou, who thee implores:
For thou art heavenly, she an empty dream.
  Say Goddess, what ensued when Raphael,   40
The affable archangel, had forewarned
Adam by dire example to beware
Apostasy, by what befell in heaven
To those apostates, lest the like befall
In Paradise to Adam or his race,   45
Charged not to touch the interdicted tree,
If they transgress, and slight that sole command,
So easily obeyed amid the choice
Of all tastes else to please their appetite,
Though wandering.   He with his consorted Eve   50
The story heard attentive, and was filled
With admiration, and deep muse to hear
Of things so high and strange, things to their thought
So unimaginable as hate in heaven,
And war so near the peace of God in bliss   55

17–20. The story of Bellerophon is mentioned by Homer, *Iliad* VI:200–02.
20. **Erroneous**: straying.   23. **rapt**: caught up.
24–28. Referring to his own situation, probably after 1660.
33. Cf. *Lycidas* 58–63 also for the legend of Orpheus being torn to pieces by Thracian women in bacchanalian orgies. Ovid, *Metamorphoses* XI:1–55. But see also *Reas. of Ch. Govt. Col.* III:1:239.
35. **Rhodope**: a mountain range in Thrace.

With such confusion: but the evil soon
Driven back redounded as a flood on those
From whom it sprung, impossible to mix
With blessedness.   Whence Adam soon repealed
The doubts that in his heart arose: and now   60
Led on, yet sinless, with desire to know
What nearer might concern him, how this world
Of heaven and earth conspicuous first began,
When, and whereof created, for what cause,
What within Eden or without was done   65
Before his memory, as one whose drouth
Yet scarce allayed still eyes the current stream,
Whose liquid murmur heard new thirst excites,
Proceeded thus to ask his heavenly guest.
    'Great things, and full of wonder in our ears,   70
Far differing from this world, thou hast revealed
Divine interpreter, by favor sent
Down from the empyrean to forewarn
Us timely of what might else have been our loss,
Unknown, which human knowledge could not reach: 75
For which to the infinitely good we owe
Immortal thanks, and his admonishment
Receive with solemn purpose to observe
Immutably his sovereign will, the end
Of what we are.   But since thou hast vouchsafed   80
Gently for our instruction to impart
Things above earthly thought, which yet concerned
Our knowing, as to highest wisdom seemed,
Deign to descend now lower, and relate
What may no less perhaps avail us known,   85
How first began this heaven which we behold
Distant so high, with moving fires adorned
Innumerable, and this which yields or fills
All space, the ambient air wide interfused
Embracing round this florid earth, what cause   90
Moved the creator in his holy rest
Through all eternity so late to build
In chaos, and the work begun, how soon
Absolved, if unforbid thou mayest unfold
What we, not to explore the secrets ask   95
Of his eternal empire, but the more
To magnify his works, the more we know.
And the great light of day yet wants to run
Much of his race though steep, suspense in heaven
Held by thy voice, thy potent voice he hears,   100
And longer will delay to hear thee tell
His generation, and the rising birth
Of nature from the unapparent deep:

59. **repealed**: called back.   94. **Absolved**: was completed.
98. **wants**: lacks.   102. **generation**: how he was made.
103. **unapparent**: invisible.

Or if the star of evening and the moon
Haste to thy audience, night with her will bring   105
Silence, and sleep listening to thee will watch,
Or we can bid his absence, till thy song
End, and dismiss thee ere the morning shine.'
　　Thus Adam his illustrious guest besought:
　　And thus the godlike angel answered mild.   110
'This also thy request with caution asked
Obtain: though to recount almighty works
What words or tongue of seraph can suffice,
Or heart of man suffice to comprehend?
Yet what thou canst attain, which best may serve   115
To glorify the maker, and infer
Thee also happier, shall not be withheld
Thy hearing, such commission from above
I have received, to answer thy desire
Of knowledge within bounds; beyond abstain   120
To ask, nor let thine own inventions hope
Things not revealed, which the invisible king,
Only omniscient, hath suppressed in night,
To none communicable in earth or heaven:
Enough is left besides to search and know.   125
But knowledge is as food, and needs no less
Her temperance over appetite, to know
In measure what the mind may well contain,
Oppresses else with surfeit, and soon turns
Wisdom to folly, as nourishment to wind.   130
　'Know then, that after Lucifer from heaven
(So call him, brighter once amidst the host
Of angels, than that star the stars among)
Fell with his flaming legions through the deep
Into his place, and the great Son returned   135
Victorious with his saints, the omnipotent
Eternal father from his throne beheld
Their multitude, and to his Son thus spake.
　'"At least our envious foe hath failed, who thought
All like himself rebellious, by whose aid   140
This inaccessible high strength, the seat
Of deity supreme, us dispossessed,
He trusted to have seized, and into fraud
Drew many, whom their place knows here no more;
Yet far the greater part have kept, I see,   145
Their station, heaven yet populous retains
Number sufficient to possess her realms
Though wide, and this high temple to frequent
With ministeries due and solemn rites:
But lest his heart exalt him in the harm   150

104. **star of evening**: Hesperus; Venus to us.　　116. **infer**: show, prove.
121. **inventions**: foolish imaginations. Cf. *Psalms* 106:29; *Proverbs* 8:12; *Ecclesiastes* 7:29.
131. **Lucifer**: meaning (Greek) 'light bringer.' Cf. *Isaiah* 14:12.
143. **fraud**: crime, sin.

Already done, to have dispeopled heaven
My damage fondly deemed, I can repair
That detriment, if such it be to lose
Self-lost, and in a moment will create
Another world, out of one man a race   155
Of men innumerable, there to dwell,
Not here, till by degrees of merit raised
They open to themselves at length the way
Up hither, under long obedience tried,
And earth be changed to heaven, and heaven to earth,   160
One kingdom, joy and union without end.
Meanwhile inhabit lax, ye powers of heaven,
And thou my word, begotten Son, by thee
This I perform, speak thou, and be it done:
My overshadowing spirit and might with thee   165
I send along, ride forth, and bid the deep
Within appointed bounds be heaven and earth,
Boundless the deep, because I am who fill
Infinitude, nor vacuous the space.
Though I uncircumscribed myself retire,   170
And put not forth my goodness, which is free
To act or not, necessity and chance
Approach not me, and what I will is fate."
    'So spake the almighty, and to what he spake
His word, the filial Godhead, gave effect.   175
Immediate are the acts of God, more swift
Than time or motion, but to human ears
Cannot without process of speech be told,
So told as earthly notion can receive.
Great triumph and rejoicing was in heaven   180
When such was heard declared the almighty's will;
Glory they sung to the most high, good will
To future men, and in their dwellings peace:
Glory to him whose just avenging ire
Had driven out the ungodly from his sight   185
And the habitations of the just; to him
Glory and praise, whose wisdom had ordained
Good out of evil to create, instead
Of spirits malign a better race to bring
Into their vacant room, and thence diffuse   190
His good to worlds and ages infinite.
So sang the hierarchies: Meanwhile the Son
On his great expedition now appeared,
Girt with omnipotence, with radiance crowned
Of majesty divine, sapience and love   195
Immense, and all his father in him shone.
About his chariot numberless were poured
Cherub and seraph, potentates and thrones,
And virtues, winged spirits, and chariots winged,
From the armory of God, where stand of old   200

162. **inhabit lax:** dwell at ease.   168-73. Apparently a Thomistic conception of God.

Myriads between two brazen mountains lodged
Against a solemn day, harnessed at hand,
Celestial equipage; and now came forth
Spontaneous, for within them spirit lived,
Attendant on their Lord: Heaven opened wide   205
Her ever during gates, harmonious sound
On golden hinges moving, to let forth
The king of glory in his powerful word
And spirit coming to create new worlds.
On heavenly ground they stood, and from the shore   210
They viewed the vast immeasurable abyss
Outrageous as a sea, dark, wasteful, wild,
Up from the bottom turned by furious winds
And surging waves, as mountains to assault
Heaven's height, and with the center mix the pole.   215
     '"Silence, ye troubled waves, and thou deep, peace,"
Said then the omnific word, "your discord end:"
     'Nor stayed, but on the wings of cherubim
Uplifted, in paternal glory rode
Far into chaos, and the world unborn;   220
For chaos heard his voice: him all his train
Followed in bright procession to behold
Creation, and the wonders of his might.
Then stayed the fervid wheels, and in his hand
He took the golden compasses, prepared   225
In God's eternal store, to circumscribe
This universe, and all created things:
One foot he centered, and the other turned
Round through the vast profundity obscure,
And said, "thus far extend, thus far thy bounds,   230
This be thy just circumference, O world."
Thus God the heaven created, thus the earth,
Matter unformed and void: Darkness profound
Covered the abyss: but on the watery calm
His brooding wings the spirit of God outspread,   235
And vital virtue infused, and vital warmth
Throughout the fluid mass, but downward purged
The black tartareous cold infernal dregs
Adverse to life: then founded, then conglobed
Like things to like, the rest to several place   240
Disparted, and between spun out the air,
And earth self balanced on her center hung.
     '"Let there be light," said God, and forthwith light
Ethereal, first of things, quintessence pure

---

201. Cf. *Zachariah* 6:1.   217. **omnific**: all-making, all-powerful.
224. **fervid**: glowing.   225 ff. Cf. Fletcher, *Milton's Rabbinical Readings*, pp. 100 ff.
228. **One foot**: of the compasses.

234. **on the watery calm**: the whole idea is contained in commentaries to the opening verses of *Genesis* in the Hebrew, Greek, and Latin Bibles.

243 ff. The remainder of this book follows the account of creation in *Genesis*, amplifies and embroiders it, then adds bits from *Job* and one or two other books of the *OT* that mention the subject.

Sprung from the deep, and from her native east   245
To journey through the airy gloom began,
Sphered in a radiant cloud, for yet the sun
Was not; she in a cloudy tabernacle
Sojourned the while.   God saw the light was good;   250
And light from darkness by the hemisphere
Divided: light the day, and darkness night
He named.   Thus was the first day even and morn:
Nor passed uncelebrated, nor unsung
By the celestial choirs, when orient light
Exhaling first from darkness they beheld;   255
Birthday of heaven and earth; with joy and shout
The hollow universal orb they filled,
And touched their golden harps, and hymning praised
God and his works, creator him they sung,
Both when first evening was, and when first morn.   260
    'Again, God said, "let there be firmament
Amid the waters, and let it divide
The waters from the waters:" and God made
The firmament, expanse of liquid, pure,
Transparent, elemental air, diffused   265
In circuit to the uttermost convex
Of this great round: partition firm and sure,
The waters underneath from those above
Dividing: for as earth, so he the world
Built on circumfluous waters calm, in wide   270
Crystalline ocean, and the loud misrule
Of chaos far removed, lest fierce extremes
Contiguous might distemper the whole frame:
And heaven he named the firmament: So even
And morning chorus sung the second day.   275
    'The earth was formed, but in the womb as yet
Of waters, embryon immature involved,
Appeared not: over all the face of earth
Main ocean flowed, not idle, but with warm
Prolific humor softening all her globe,   280
Fermented the great mother to conceive,
Satiate with genial moisture, when God said
"Be gathered now ye waters under heaven
Into one place, and let dry land appear."
Immediately the mountains huge appear   285
Emergent, and their broad bare backs upheave
Into the clouds, their tops ascend the sky:
So high as heaved the tumid hills, so low
Down sunk a hollow bottom broad and deep,
Capacious bed of waters: thither they   290
Hasted with glad precipitance, uprolled
As drops on dust conglobing from the dry;
Part rise in crystal wall, or ridge direct,

271. **misrule:** wild anarchy referred to in VI:871–73.
277. **involved:** wrapped.   282. **genial:** fertilizing, generating.

For haste; such flight the great command impressed
On the swift floods: as armies at the call   295
Of trumpet (for of armies thou hast heard)
Troop to their standard, so the watery throng,
Wave rolling after wave, where way they found,
If steep, with torrent rapture, if through plain,
Soft-ebbing; nor withstood them rock or hill,   300
But they, or underground, or circuit wide
With serpent error wandering, found their way,
And on the washy ooze deep channels wore;
Easy, ere God had bid the ground be dry,
All but within those banks, where rivers now   305
Stream, and perpetual draw their humid train.
The dry land, earth, and the great receptacle
Of congregated waters he called seas:
And saw that it was good, and said, "Let the earth
Put forth the verdant grass, herb yielding seed,   310
And fruit tree yielding fruit after her kind;
Whose seed is in herself upon the earth."
He scarce had said, when the bare earth, till then
Desert and bare, unsightly, unadorned,
Brought forth the tender grass, whose verdure clad   315
Her universal face with pleasant green,
Then herbs of every leaf, that sudden flowered
Opening their various colors, and made gay
Her bosom smelling sweet: and these scarce blown,
Forth flourished thick the clustering vine, forth crept   320
The smelling gourd, up stood the corny reed
Embattled in her field: and the humble shrub,
And bush with frizzled hair implicit: last
Rose as in dance the stately trees, and spread
Their branches hung with copious fruit; or gemmed   325
Their blossoms: with high woods the hills were crowned,
With tufts the valleys and each fountainside,
With borders long the rivers.   That earth now
Seemed like to heaven, a seat where gods might dwell,
Or wander with delight, and love to haunt   330
Her sacred shades: though God had yet not rained
Upon the earth, and man to till the ground
None was, but from the earth a dewy mist
Went up and watered all the ground, and each
Plant of the field, which ere it was in the earth   335
God made, and every herb, before it grew
On the green stem; God saw that it was good.
So even and morn recorded the third day.
    'Again the almighty spake: "Let there be lights
High in the expanse of heaven to divide   340

302. **serpent error**: serpentine wandering.

322. **and the humble shrub**: first edition reads 'add' and Verity speaks of 'and' as a modern corruption; 'and' is printed here because it is in the second edition.

325. **gemmed**: put forth, usually 'put forth buds.'

The day from night; and let them be for signs,
For seasons, and for days, and circling years,
And let them be for lights as I ordain
Their office in the firmament of heaven
To give light on the earth;" and it was so.   345
And God made two great lights, great for their use
To man, the greater to have rule by day,
The less by night altern: and made the stars,
And set them in the firmament of heaven
To illuminate the earth, and rule the day   350
In their vicissitude, and rule the night,
And light from darkness to divide.   God saw,
Surveying his great work, that it was good:
For of celestial bodies first the sun
A mighty sphere he framed, unlightsome first,   355
Though of ethereal mold: then formed the moon
Globose, and every magnitude of stars,
And sowed with stars the heaven thick as a field:
Of light by far the greater part he took,
Transplanted from her cloudy shrine, and placed   360
In the sun's orb, made porous to receive
And drink the liquid light, firm to retain
Her gathered beams, great palace now of light.
Hither as to their fountain other stars
Repairing, in their golden urns draw light,   365
And hence the morning planet gilds her horns;
By tincture or reflection they augment
Their small peculiar, though from human sight
So far remote, with diminution seen.
First in his east the glorious lamp was seen,   370
Regent of day, and all the horizon round
Invested with bright rays, jocund to run
His longitude through heaven's high road: the gray
Dawn, and the Pleiades before him danced
Shedding sweet influence: less bright the moon,   375
But opposite in leveled west was set
His mirror, with full face borrowing her light
From him, for other light she needed none
In that aspect, and still that distance keeps
Till night, then in the east her turn she shines,   380
Revolved on heaven's great axle, and her reign

354-55. **the sun . . . unlightsome first:** this is a little difficult for the modern.   Milton must follow the first and second chapters of *Genesis* very exactly.   To do this he had to tell of the creation of the two great lights (ll. 346-48), then create the sun, then set the sun in heaven, 'transplanted from her cloudy shrine,' then put light in the sun, 'made porous to receive and drink the liquid light.'

366. **the morning planet gilds her horns:** the planet is Venus, and her phases were unknown until after the invention of the telescope.

367. **tincture:** tint of 'their small peculiar,' i.e., their own small light.

372. **Invested:** arrayed.   **jocund:** cheerful, lively.

373. **longitude:** straight distance from east to west.

376. **leveled:** due west.

With thousand lesser lights dividual holds,
With thousand thousand stars, that then appeared
Spangling the hemisphere: then first adorned
With her bright luminaries that set and rose,   385
Glad evening and glad morn crowned the fourth day.
  'And God said, "let the waters generate
Reptile with spawn abundant, living soul:
And let fowl fly above the earth, with wings
Displayed on the open firmament of heaven."   390
And God created the great whales, and each
Soul living, each that crept, which plenteously
The waters generated by their kinds,
And every bird of wing after his kind;
And saw that it was good, and blessed them, saying,   395
"Be fruitful, multiply, and in the seas
And lakes and running streams the waters fill;
And let the fowl be multiplied on the earth."
Forthwith the sounds and seas, each creek and bay
With fry innumerable swarm, and shoals   400
Of fish that with their fins and shining scales
Glide under the green wave, in sculls that oft
Bank the midsea: part single or with mate
Graze the seaweed their pasture, and through groves
Of coral stray, or sporting with quick glance   405
Show to the sun their waved coats dropped with gold,
Or in their pearly shells at ease, attend
Moist nutriment, or under rocks their food
In jointed armor watch: on smooth the seal,
And bended dolphins play: part huge of bulk   410
Wallowing unwieldy, enormous in their gait
Tempest the ocean: there leviathan
Hugest of living creatures, on the deep
Stretched like a promontory sleeps or swims,
And seems a moving land, and at his gills   415
Draws in, and at his trunk spouts out a sea.
Meanwhile the tepid caves, and fens and shores
Their brood as numerous hatch, from the egg that soon
Bursting with kindly rupture forth disclosed
Their callow young, but feathered soon and fledge   420
They summed their pens, and soaring the air sublime
With clang despised the ground, under a cloud
In prospect; there the eagle and the stork
On cliffs and cedar tops their aeries build:
Part loosely wing the region, part more wise   425
In common, ranged in figure wedge their way,
Intelligent of seasons, and set forth
Their airy caravan high over seas
Flying, and over lands with mutual wing

382. **dividual:** divided.
402. **sculls:** schools, shoals; these words originally were probably the same.
412. **leviathan:** cf. I:200–05.   421. **summed their pens:** added their feathers.

Easing their flight; so steers the prudent crane   430
Her annual voyage, borne on winds; the air
Floats, as they pass, fanned with unnumbered plumes:
From branch to branch the smaller birds with song
Solaced the woods, and spread their painted wings
Till even, nor then the solemn nightingale   435
Ceased warbling, but all night tuned her soft lays:
Others on silver lakes and rivers bathed
Their downy breast; the swan with arched neck
Between her white wings mantling proudly, rows
Her state with oary feet: yet oft they quit   440
The dank, and rising on stiff pennons, tower
The mid aerial sky: Others on ground
Walked firm; the crested cock whose clarion sounds
The silent hours, and the other whose gay train
Adorns him, colored with the florid hue   445
Of rainbows and starry eyes.   The waters thus
With fish replenished, and the air with fowl,
Evening and morn solemnized the fifth day.
      'The sixth, and of creation last arose
With evening harps and matin, when God said,   450
"Let the earth bring forth soul living in her kind,
Cattle and creeping things, and beast of the earth,
Each in their kind."   The earth obeyed, and straight
Opening her fertile womb teemed at a birth
Innumerous living creatures, perfect forms,   455
Limbed and full-grown: out of the ground uprose
As from his lair the wild beast where he wons
In forest wild, in thicket, brake, or den;
Among the trees in pairs they rose, they walked:
The cattle in the fields and meadows green: 460
Those rare and solitary, these in flocks
Pasturing at once, and in broad herds upsprung.
The grassy clods now calved, now half appeared
The tawny lion, pawing to get free
His hinder parts, then springs as broke from bonds,   465
And rampant shakes his brinded mane; the ounce,
The libbard, and the tiger, as the mole
Rising, the crumbled earth above them threw
In hillocks; the swift stag from underground
Bore up his branching head: scarce from his mold   470
Behemoth biggest born of earth upheaved
His vastness: Fleeced the flocks and bleating rose,
As plants: ambiguous between sea and land
The river horse and scaly crocodile.
At once came forth whatever creeps the ground,   475

451. **soul**: Hawkey in 1747 seems to be the first editor to follow Bentley (1732) and print 'soul' instead of
'fowl.'   It must be accepted, as 'fowl' had been created on the fifth day.   But cf. V:197.
   457. **wons**: dwells.   The same generic carnivorous wild beast as in XI:187.
   466. **ounce**: lynx.   467. **libbard**: leopard.
   471. **Behemoth**: the elephant.   474. **river horse**: hippopotamus.

Insect or worm; those waved their limber fans
For wings, and smallest lineaments exact
In all the liveries decked of summer's pride
With spots of gold and purple, azure and green:
These as a line their long dimension drew,   480
Streaking the ground with sinuous trace; not all
Minims of nature; some of serpent kind
Wondrous in length and corpulence involved
Their snaky folds, and added wings.   First crept
The parsimonious emmet, provident   485
Of future, in small room large heart enclosed,
Pattern of just equality perhaps
Hereafter, joined in her popular tribes
Of commonalty: swarming next appeared
The female bee that feeds her husband drone   490
Deliciously, and builds her waxen cells
With honey stored: the rest are numberless,
And thou their natures knowest, and gavest them names,
Needless to thee repeated; nor unknown
The serpent subtlest beast of all the field,   495
Of huge extent sometimes, with brazen eyes
And hairy mane terrific, though to thee
Not noxious, but obedient at thy call.
Now heaven in all her glory shone, and rolled
Her motions, as the great first mover's hand   500
First wheeled their course; earth in her rich attire
Consummate lovely smiled; air, water, earth,
By fowl, fish, beast, was flown, was swum, was walked
Frequent; and of the sixth day yet remained;
There wanted yet the master work, the end   505
Of all yet done; a creature who not prone
And brute as other creatures, but endued
With sanctity of reason, might erect
His stature, and upright with front serene
Govern the rest, self-knowing, and from thence   510
Magnanimous to correspond with heaven,
But grateful to acknowledge whence his good
Descends, thither with heart and voice and eyes
Directed in devotion, to adore
And worship God supreme, who made him chief   515
Of all his works: therefore the omnipotent
Eternal father (for where is not he
Present) thus to his Son audibly spake.
        '"Let us make now man in our image, man
In our similitude, and let them rule   520

482. **Minims of nature**: very small or smallest creatures.
484. **and added wings**: does he mean winged dragons?
485. **emmet**: ant.
494. **Needless**: both first and second editions read 'needlest.'
495 ff. The serpent's curse after the fall of man was that it must now crawl on its belly in the dust, the most prone posture possible.   These lines suggest that as created the serpent was much different.

Over the fish and fowl of sea and air,
Beast of the field, and over all the earth,
And every creeping thing that creeps the ground."
This said, he formed thee, Adam, thee O man
Dust of the ground, and in thy nostrils breathed   525
The breath of life; in his own image he
Created thee, in the image of God
Express, and thou becamest a living soul.
Male he created thee, but thy consort
Female for race; then blessed mankind, and said,   530
"Be fruitful, multiply, and fill the earth,
Subdue it, and throughout dominion hold
Over fish of the sea, and fowl of the air,
And every living thing that moves on the earth."
Wherever thus created, for no place   535
Is yet distinct by name, thence, as thou knowest
He brought thee into this delicious grove,
This garden, planted with the trees of God,
Delectable both to behold and taste;
And freely all their pleasant fruit for food   540
Gave thee, all sorts are here that all the earth yields,
Variety without end; but of the tree
Which tasted works knowledge of good and evil,
Thou mayest not; in the day thou eatest, thou diest;
Death is the penalty imposed, beware,   545
And govern well thy appetite, lest sin
Surprise thee, and her black attendant death.
Here finished he, and all that he had made
Viewed, and behold all was entirely good;
So even and morn accomplished the sixth day: 550
Yet not till the creator from his work
Desisting, though unwearied, up returned
Up to the heaven of heavens his high abode,
Thence to behold this new created world
The addition of his empire, how it showed   555
In prospect from his throne, how good, how fair,
Answering his great idea.   Up he rode
Followed with acclamation and the sound
Symphonious of ten thousand harps that tuned
Angelic harmonies: the earth, the air   560
Resounded, (thou rememberest, for thou heardst)
The heavens and all the constellations rung,
The planets in their stations listening stood,
While the bright pomp ascended jubilant.
"Open, ye everlasting gates," they sung,   565
"Open, ye heavens, your living doors; let in
The great creator from his work returned
Magnificent, his six days' work, a world;
Open, and henceforth oft; for God will deign
To visit oft the dwellings of just men   570

563. **stations:** first edition thus, but second reads 'station.'

Delighted, and with frequent intercourse
Thither will send his winged messengers
On errands of supernal grace." So sung
The glorious train ascending: He through heaven,
That opened wide her blazing portals, led   575
To God's eternal house direct the way,
A broad and ample road, whose dust is gold
And pavement stars, as stars to thee appear,
Seen in the galaxy, that milky way
Which nightly as a circling zone thou seest   580
Powdered with stars. And now on earth the seventh
Evening arose in Eden, for the sun
Was set, and twilight from the east came on,
Forerunning night; when at the holy mount
Of heaven's high-seated top, the imperial throne   585
Of Godhead, fixed forever firm and sure,
The filial power arrived, and sat him down
With his great father (for he also went
Invisible, yet stayed such privilege
Hath omnipresence) and the work ordained,   590
Author and end of all things, and from work
Now resting, blessed and hallowed the seventh day,
As resting on that day from all his work,
But not in silence holy kept; the harp
Had work and rested not; the solemn pipe,   595
And dulcimer, all organs of sweet stop,
All sounds on fret by string or golden wire
Tempered soft tunings, intermixed with voice
Choral or unison: of incense clouds
Fuming from golden censers hid the mount.   600
Creation and the six days' acts they sung,
"Great are thy works, Jehovah, infinite
Thy power; what thought can measure thee or tongue
Relate thee; greater now in thy return
Than from the giant angels; thee that day   605
Thy thunders magnified; but to create
Is greater than created to destroy.
Who can impair thee, mighty king, or bound
Thy empire? easily the proud attempt
Of spirits apostate and their counsels vain   610
Thou hast repelled, while impiously they thought
Thee to diminish, and from thee withdraw
The number of thy worshipers. Who seeks
To lessen thee, against his purpose serves
To manifest the more thy might: his evil   615
Thou usest, and from thence createst more good.
Witness this new-made world, another heaven
From heaven gate not far, founded in view
On the clear hyaline, the glassy sea;

596. **dulcimer:** a stringed instrument.
619. **the clear hyaline, the glassy sea:** these are the same.

Of amplitude almost immense, with stars   620
Numerous, and every star perhaps a world
Of destined habitation; but thou knowest
Their seasons: among these the seat of men,
Earth with her nether ocean circumfused,
Their pleasant dwelling place.   Thrice happy men,   625
And sons of men, whom God hath thus advanced,
Created in his image, there to dwell
And worship him, and in reward to rule
Over his works, on earth, in sea, or air,
And multiply a race of worshipers   630
Holy and just: thrice happy if they know
Their happiness, and persevere upright.''
   'So sung they, and the empyrean rung,
With hallelujahs: Thus was Sabbath kept.
And thy request think now fulfilled, that asked   635
How first this world and face of things began,
And what before thy memory was done
From the beginning, that posterity
Informed by thee, might know; if else thou seekest
Aught, not surpassing human measure, say.'   640

THE END OF THE SEVENTH BOOK

BOOK VIII

THE ARGUMENT

Adam inquires concerning celestial motions, is doubtfully answered, and ex-
horted to search rather things more worthy of knowledge: Adam assents, and still
desirous to detain Raphael, relates to him what he remembered since his own
creation, his placing in Paradise, his talk with God concerning solitude and fit
society, his first meeting and nuptials with Eve, his discourse with the angel thereupon; who after admonitions repeated departs.

The angel ended, and in Adam's ear
So charming left his voice, that he a while
Thought him still speaking, still stood fixed to hear;
Then as new-waked thus gratefully replied.
'What thanks sufficient, or what recompense   5
Equal have I to render thee, divine
Historian, who thus largely hast allayed
The thirst I had of knowledge, and vouchsafed
This friendly condescension to relate
Things else by me unsearchable, now heard   10
With wonder, but delight, and, as is due,
With glory attributed to the high
Creator; something yet of doubt remains,
Which only thy solution can resolve.

When I behold this goodly frame, this world   15
Of heaven and earth consisting, and compute,
Their magnitudes, this earth a spot, a grain,
An atom, with the firmament compared
And all her numbered stars, that seem to roll
Spaces incomprehensible (for such   20
Their distance argues and their swift return
Diurnal) merely to officiate light
Round this opacous earth, this punctual spot,
One day and night; in all their vast survey
Useless besides, reasoning I oft admire,   25
How nature wise and frugal could commit
Such disproportions, with superfluous hand
So many nobler bodies to create,
Greater so manifold to this one use,
For aught appears, and on their orbs impose   30
Such restless revolution day by day
Repeated, while the sedentary earth,
That better might with far less compass move,
Served by more noble than herself, attains
Her end without least motion, and receives,   35
As tribute such a sumless journey brought
Of incorporeal speed, her warmth and light;
Speed, to describe whose swiftness number fails.'
   So spake our sire, and by his countenance seemed
Entering on studious thoughts abstruse, which Eve   40
Perceiving where she sat retired in sight,
With lowliness majestic from her seat,
And grace that won who saw to wish her stay,
Rose, and went forth among her fruits and flowers,
To visit how they prospered, bud and bloom,   45
Her nursery; they at her coming sprung
And touched by her fair tendance gladlier grew.
Yet went she not, as not with such discourse
Delighted, or not capable her ear
Of what was high: such pleasure she reserved,   50
Adam relating, she sole auditress;
Her husband the relater she preferred
Before the angel, and of him to ask
Chose rather; he, she knew would intermix
Grateful digressions, and solve high dispute   55
With conjugal caresses, from his lip
Not words alone pleased her.   O when meet now
Such pairs, in love and mutual honor joined?
With goddess-like demeanor forth she went;
Not unattended, for on her as queen   60
A pomp of winning graces waited still,
And from about her shot darts of desire
Into all eyes to wish her still in sight.
And Raphael now to Adam's doubt proposed
Benevolent and facile thus replied.   65

'To ask or search I blame thee not, for heaven
Is as the book of God before thee set,
Wherein to read his wondrous works, and learn
His seasons, hours, or days, or months, or years:
This to attain, whether heaven move or earth,   70
Imports not, if thou reckon right, the rest
From man or angel the great architect
Did wisely to conceal, and not divulge
His secrets to be scanned by them who ought
Rather admire; or if they list to try   75
Conjecture, he his fabric of the heavens
Hath left to their disputes, perhaps to move
His laughter at their quaint opinions wide
Hereafter, when they come to model heaven
And calculate the stars, how they will wield   80
The mighty frame, how build, unbuild, contrive
To save appearances, how gird the sphere
With centric and eccentric scribbled o'er,
Cycle and epicycle, orb in orb:
Already by thy reasoning this I guess,   85
Who art to lead thy offspring, and supposest
That bodies bright and greater should not serve
The less not bright, nor heaven such journeys run,
Earth sitting still, when she alone receives
The benefit: consider first, that great   90
Or bright infers not excellence: the earth
Though, in comparison of heaven, so small,
Nor glistering, may of solid good contain
More plenty than the sun that barren shines,
Whose virtue on itself works no effect,   95
But in the fruitful earth; there first received
His beams, unactive else, their vigor find.
Yet not to earth are those bright luminaries
Officious, but to thee earth's habitant.
And for the heaven's wide circuit, let it speak   100
The maker's high magnificence, who built
So spacious, and his line stretched out so far;
That man may know he dwells not in his own;
An edifice too large for him to fill,
Lodged in a small partition, and the rest   105
Ordained for uses to his Lord best known.
The swiftness of those circles attribute,
Though numberless, to his omnipotence,
That to corporeal substances could add
Speed almost spiritual; me thou thinkest not slow,   110
Who since the morning hour set out from heaven
Where God resides, and ere midday arrived
In Eden, distance inexpressible
By numbers that have name.   But this I urge,

85. **I guess:** from Adam's reasoning, Raphael anticipates the theories and conjectures on cosmic structure that he has just mentioned.

Admitting motion in the heavens, to show 115
Invalid that which thee to doubt it moved;
Not that I so affirm, though so it seem
To thee who hast thy dwelling here on earth.
God to remove his ways from human sense,
Placed heaven from earth so far, that earthly sight, 120
If it presume, might err in things too high,
And no advantage gain. What if the sun
Be center to the world, and other stars
By his attractive virtue and their own
Incited, dance about him various rounds? 125
Their wandering course now high, now low, then hid,
Progressive, retrograde, or standing still,
In six thou seest, and what if seventh to these
The planet earth, so steadfast though she seem,
Insensibly three different motions move? 130
Which else to several spheres thou must ascribe,
Moved contrary with thwart obliquities,
Or save the sun his labor, and that swift
Nocturnal and diurnal rhomb supposed,
Invisible else above all stars, the wheel 135
Of day and night; which needs not thy belief,
If earth industrious of herself fetch day
Traveling east, and with her part averse
From the sun's beam meet night, her other part
Still luminous by his ray. What if that light 140
Sent from her through the wide transpicuous air,
To the terrestrial moon be as a star
Enlightening her by day, as she by night
This earth? reciprocal, if land be there,
Fields and inhabitants: Her spots thou seest 145
As clouds, and clouds may rain, and rain produce
Fruits in her softened soil, for some to eat
Allotted there; and other suns perhaps
With their attendant moons thou wilt descry
Communicating male and female light, 150
Which two great sexes animate the world,
Stored in each orb perhaps with some that live.
For such vast room in nature unpossessed
By living soul, desert and desolate,
Only to shine, yet scarce to contribute 155
Each orb a glimpse of light, conveyed so far
Down to this habitable, which returns
Light back to them, is obvious to dispute.
But whether thus these things, or whether not,
Whether the sun predominant in heaven 160
Rise on the earth, or earth rise on the sun,
He from the east his flaming road begin,

129. **The planet earth**: the most daring idea in the Copernican theory was that the earth was only a planet.
145. **inhabitants**: the possibility that the moon was inhabited. Cf. Wilkins, *A New World in the Moon.*
150. **male and female light**: original and reflected light.

Or she from west her silent course advance
With inoffensive pace that spinning sleeps
On her soft axle, while she paces even,   165
And bears thee soft with the smooth air along,
Solicit not thy thoughts with matters hid,
Leave them to God above, him serve and fear;
Of other creatures, as him pleases best,
Wherever placed, let him dispose: joy thou   170
In what he gives to thee, this Paradise
And thy fair Eve; heaven is for thee too high
To know what passes there; be lowly wise:
Think only what concerns thee and thy being;
Dream not of other worlds, what creatures there   175
Live, in what state, condition or degree,
Contented that thus far hath been revealed
Not of earth only but of highest heaven.'
   To whom thus Adam cleared of doubt, replied.
'How fully hast thou satisfied me, pure   180
Intelligence of heaven, angel serene,
And freed from intricacies, taught to live,
The easiest way, nor with perplexing thoughts
To interrupt the sweet of life, from which
God hath bid dwell far off all anxious cares,   185
And not molest us, unless we ourselves
Seek them with wandering thoughts, and notions vain.
But apt the mind or fancy is to rove
Unchecked, and of her roving is no end;
Till warned, or by experience taught, she learn,   190
That not to know at large of things remote
From use, obscure and subtle, but to know
That which before us lies in daily life,
Is the prime wisdom, what is more, is fume,
Or emptiness, or fond impertinence,   195
And renders us in things that most concern
Unpracticed, unprepared, and still to seek.
Therefore from this high pitch let us descend
A lower flight, and speak of things at hand
Useful, whence haply mention may arise   200
Of something not unseasonable to ask
By sufferance, and thy wonted favor deigned.
Thee I have heard relating what was done
Ere my remembrance: now hear me relate
My story, which perhaps thou hast not heard;   205
And day is yet not spent; till then thou seest
How subtly to detain thee I devise,
Inviting thee to hear while I relate,
Fond, were it not in hope of thy reply:
For while I sit with thee, I seem in heaven,   210
And sweeter thy discourse is to my ear

183–97. Take these lines as a protest against barren speculation, not against modern science. Milton accepted the telescope and many of the new ideas it brought with it.

Than fruits of palm-tree pleasantest to thirst
And hunger both, from labor, at the hour
Of sweet repast; they satiate, and soon fill,
Though pleasant, but thy words with grace divine   215
Imbued, bring to their sweetness no satiety.'
      To whom thus Raphael answered heavenly meek.
'Nor are thy lips ungraceful, sire of men,
Nor tongue ineloquent; for God on thee
Abundantly his gifts hath also poured   220
Inward and outward both, his image fair:
Speaking or mute all comeliness and grace
Attends thee, and each word, each motion forms,
Nor less think we in heaven of thee on earth
Than of our fellow servant, and inquire   225
Gladly into the ways of God with man:
For God we see hath honored thee, and set
On man his equal love: say therefore on;
For I that day was absent, as befell,
Bound on a voyage uncouth and obscure,   230
Far on excursion toward the gates of hell;
Squared in full legion (such command we had)
To see that none thence issued forth a spy,
Or enemy, while God was in his work,
Lest he incensed at such eruption bold,   235
Destruction with creation might have mixed.
Not that they durst without his leave attempt,
But us he sends upon his high behests
For state, as sovereign king, and to inure
Our prompt obedience.   Fast we found, fast shut   240
The dismal gates, and barricadoed strong;
But long ere our approaching heard within
Noise, other than the sound of dance or song,
Torment, and loud lament, and furious rage.
Glad we returned up to the coasts of light   245
Ere Sabbath evening: so we had in charge.
But thy relation now; for I attend,
Pleased with thy words no less than thou with mine.'
      So spake the godlike power, and thus our sire.
'For man to tell how human life began   250
Is hard; for who himself beginning knew?
Desire with thee still longer to converse
Induced me.   As new waked from soundest sleep
Soft on the flowery herb I found me laid
In balmy sweat, which with his beams the sun   255
Soon dried, and on the reeking moisture fed.
Straight toward heaven my wondering eyes I turned,
And gazed a while the ample sky, till raised

212. **palm-tree:** the date palm.
229. **that day:** strictly, the sixth day of creation, the day Adam was created.
230. **uncouth:** unknown, strange, also rough, here.
241. **barricadoed:** barricaded.   247. **relation:** story, report.

By quick instinctive motion up I sprung, 260
As thitherward endeavoring, and upright
Stood on my feet; about me round I saw
Hill, dale, and shady woods, and sunny plains,
And liquid lapse of murmuring streams; by these,
Creatures that lived, and moved, and walked, or flew, 265
Birds on the branches warbling; all things smiled,
With fragrance and with joy my heart o'erflowed.
Myself I then perused, and limb by limb
Surveyed, and sometimes went, and sometimes ran
With supple joints, as lively vigor led: 270
But who I was, or where, or from what cause,
Knew not; to speak I tried, and forthwith spake,
My tongue obeyed and readily could name
Whate'er I saw. "Thou sun," said I, "fair light,
And thou enlightened earth, so fresh and gay, 275
Ye hills and dales, ye rivers, woods, and plains,
And ye that live and move, fair creatures, tell,
Tell, if ye saw, how came I thus, how here?
Not of myself; by some great maker then,
In goodness and in power pre-eminent; 280
Tell me, how may I know him, how adore,
From whom I have that thus I move and live,
And feel that I am happier than I know."
While thus I called, and strayed I knew not whither,
From where I first drew air, and first beheld 285
This happy light, when answer none returned,
On a green shady bank profuse of flowers
Pensive I sat me down; there gentle sleep
First found me, and with soft oppression seized
My drowsed sense, untroubled, though I thought 290
I then was passing to my former state
Insensible, and forthwith to dissolve:
When suddenly stood at my head a dream,
Whose inward apparition gently moved
My fancy to believe I yet had being, 295
And lived: One came, methought, of shape divine,
And said, "thy mansion wants thee, Adam, rise,
First Man, of men innumerable ordained
First father, called by thee I come thy guide
To the garden of bliss, thy seat prepared." 300
So saying, by the hand he took me raised,
And over fields and waters, as in air
Smooth sliding without step, last led me up
A woody mountain; whose high top was plain,
A circuit wide, enclosed, with goodliest trees 305
Planted, with walks, and bowers, that what I saw
Of earth before scarce pleasant seemed. Each tree
Laden with fairest fruit that hung to the eye
Tempting, stirred in me sudden appetite

302-03. **led me up a woody mountain:** Paradise was on a high hill.

To pluck and eat; whereat I waked, and found
Before mine eyes all real, as the dream
Had lively shadowed: Here had new begun   310
My wandering, had not he who was my guide
Up hither, from among the trees appeared
Presence divine.   Rejoicing, but with awe
In adoration at his feet I fell
Submiss: he reared me, and "Whom thou soughtest I am,"   315
Said mildly, "Author of all this thou seest
Above, or round about thee or beneath.
This Paradise I give thee, count it thine
To till and keep, and of the fruit to eat:
Of every tree that in the garden grows   320
Eat freely with glad heart; fear here no dearth:
But of the tree whose operation brings
Knowledge of good and ill, which I have set
The pledge of thy obedience and thy faith,
Amid the garden by the tree of life,   325
Remember what I warn thee, shun to taste,
And shun the bitter consequence: for know,
The day thou eatest thereof, my sole command
Transgressed, inevitably thou shalt die;
From that day mortal, and this happy state   330
Shalt lose, expelled from hence into a world
Of woe and sorrow."   Sternly he pronounced
The rigid interdiction, which resounds
Yet dreadful in mine ear, though in my choice
Not to incur; but soon his clear aspect   335
Returned and gracious purpose thus renewed.
"Not only these fair bounds, but all the earth
To thee and to thy race I give; as lords
Possess it, and all things that therein live,
Or live in sea, or air, beast, fish, and fowl.   340
In sign whereof each bird and beast behold
After their kinds; I bring them to receive
From thee their names, and pay thee fealty
With low subjection; understand the same
Of fish within their watery residence,   345
Not hither summoned, since they cannot change
Their element to draw the thinner air."
As thus he spake, each bird and beast behold
Approaching two and two, these cowering low
With blandishment, each bird stooped on his wing.   350
I named them, as they passed, and understood
Their nature, with such knowledge God endued
My sudden apprehension: but in these
I found not what methought I wanted still;
And to the heavenly vision thus presumed.   355
  "'O by what name, for thou above all these,
Above mankind, or aught than mankind higher,

316. **Submiss:** prostrate.

Surpassest far my naming, how may I
Adore thee, author of this universe,   360
And all this good to man, for whose well being
So amply, and with hands so liberal
Thou hast provided all things: but with me
I see not who partakes.   In solitude
What happiness, who can enjoy alone,   365
Or all enjoying, what contentment find?''
Thus I presumptuous; and the vision bright,
As with a smile more brightened, thus replied.
    '"What callest thou solitude, is not the earth
With various living creatures, and the air   370
Replenished, and all these at thy command
To come and play before thee, knowest thou not
Their language and their ways, they also know,
And reason not contemptibly; with these
Find pastime, and bear rule; thy realm is large."   375
So spake the universal lord, and seemed
So ordering.   I with leave of speech implored,
And humble deprecation thus replied.
    '"Let not my words offend thee, heavenly power,
My maker, be propitious while I speak.   380
Hast thou not made me here thy substitute,
And these inferior far beneath me set?
Among unequals what society
Can sort, what harmony or true delight?
Which must be mutual, in proportion due   385
Given and received; but in disparity
The one intense, the other still remiss
Cannot well suit with either, but soon prove
Tedious alike: Of fellowship I speak
Such as I seek, fit to participate   390
All rational delight, wherein the brute
Cannot be human consort; they rejoice
Each with their kind, lion with lioness;
So fitly them in pairs thou hast combined;
Much less can bird with beast, or fish with fowl   395
So well converse, nor with the ox the ape;
Worse then can man with beast, and least of all."
Whereto the almighty answered, not displeased.
"A nice and subtle happiness I see
Thou to thyself proposest, in the choice   400
Of thy associates, Adam, and wilt taste
No pleasure, though in pleasure, solitary.
What thinkest thou then of me, and this my state,
Seem I to thee sufficiently possessed
Of happiness, or not? who am alone   405
From all eternity, for none I know
Second to me or like, equal much less.
How have I then with whom to hold converse
Save with the creatures which I made, and those

To me inferior, infinite descents   410
Beneath what other creatures are to thee?"
    'He ceased, I lowly answered. "To attain
The height and depth of thy eternal ways
All human thoughts come short, supreme of things;
Thou in thyself art perfect, and in thee   415
Is no deficience found; not so is man,
But in degree, the cause of his desire
By conversation with his like to help,
Or solace his defects.   No need that thou
Shouldst propagate, already infinite;   420
And through all numbers absolute, though one;
But man by number is to manifest
His single imperfection, and beget
Like of his like, his image multiplied,
In unity defective, which requires   425
Collateral love, and dearest amity.
Thou in thy secrecy although alone,
Best with thyself accompanied, seekest not
Social communication, yet so pleased,
Canst raise thy creature to what height thou wilt   430
Of union or communion, deified;
I by conversing cannot these erect
From prone, nor in their ways complacence find."
Thus I emboldened spake, and freedom used
Permissive, and acceptance found, which gained   435
This answer from the gracious voice divine.
    '"Thus far to try thee, Adam, I was pleased,
And find thee knowing not of beasts alone,
Which thou hast rightly named, but of thyself,
Expressing well the spirit within thee free,   440
My image, not imparted to the brute,
Whose fellowship therefore unmeet for thee
Good reason was thou freely shouldst dislike,
And be so minded still; I, ere thou spakest,
Knew it not good for man to be alone,   445
And no such company as then thou sawest
Intended thee, for trial only brought,
To see how thou couldst judge of fit and meet:
What next I bring shall please thee, be assured,
Thy likeness, thy fit help, thy other self,   450
Thy wish exactly to thy heart's desire."
    'He ended, or I heard no more, for now
My earthly by his heavenly overpowered,
Which it had long stood under, strained to the height
In that celestial colloquy sublime,   455
As with an object that excels the sense,
Dazzled and spent, sunk down, and sought repair
Of sleep, which instantly fell on me, called
By nature as in aid, and closed mine eyes.
Mine eyes he closed, but open left the cell   460

Of fancy my internal sight, by which
Abstract as in a trance methought I saw,
Though sleeping, where I lay, and saw the shape
Still glorious before whom awake I stood;
Who stooping opened my left side, and took   465
From thence a rib, with cordial spirits warm;
And life blood streaming fresh; wide was the wound,
But suddenly with flesh filled up and healed:
The rib he formed and fashioned with his hands;
Under his forming hands a creature grew,   470
Manlike, but different sex, so lovely fair,
That what seemed fair in all the world, seemed now
Mean, or in her summed up, in her contained
And in her looks, which from that time infused
Sweetness into my heart, unfelt before,   475
And into all things from her air inspired
The spirit of love and amorous delight.
She disappeared, and left me dark, I waked
To find her, or forever to deplore
Her loss, and other pleasures all abjure: 480
When out of hope, behold her, not far off,
Such as I saw her in my dream, adorned
With what all earth or heaven could bestow
To make her amiable: On she came,
Led by her heavenly maker, though unseen,   485
And guided by his voice, nor uninformed
Of nuptial sanctity and marriage rites:
Grace was in all her steps, heaven in her eye,
In every gesture dignity and love.
I overjoyed could not forbear aloud.   490
    '"This turn hath made amends; thou hast fulfilled
Thy words, creator bounteous and benign,
Giver of all things fair, but fairest this
Of all thy gifts, nor enviest.   I now see
Bone of my bone, flesh of my flesh, myself   495
Before me; woman is her name, of man
Extracted; for this cause he shall forgo
Father and mother, and to his wife adhere;
And they shall be one flesh, one heart, one soul."
    'She heard me thus, and though divinely brought,   500
Yet innocence and virgin modesty,
Her virtue and the conscience of her worth,
That would be wooed, and not unsought be won,
Not obvious, not obtrusive, but retired,
The more desirable, or to say all,   505
Nature herself, though pure of sinful thought,
Wrought in her so, that seeing me, she turned;
I followed her, she what was honor knew,
And with obsequious majesty approved
My pleaded reason.   To the nuptial bower   510
I led her blushing like the morn: all heaven,

And happy constellations on that hour
Shed their selectest influence; the earth
Gave sign of gratulation, and each hill;
Joyous the birds; fresh gales and gentle airs   515
Whispered it to the woods, and from their wings
Flung rose, flung odors from the spicy shrub,
Disporting, till the amorous bird of night
Sung spousal, and bid haste the evening star
On his hilltop to light the bridal lamp.   520
Thus have I told thee all my state, and brought
My story to the sum of earthly bliss
Which I enjoy, and must confess to find
In all things else delight indeed, but such
As used or not, works in the mind no change,   525
Nor vehement desire, these delicacies
I mean of taste, sight, smell, herbs, fruits, and flowers,
Walks, and the melody of birds; but here
Far otherwise, transported I behold,
Transported touch; here passion first I felt,   530
Commotion strange, in all enjoyments else
Superior and unmoved, here only weak
Against the charm of beauty's powerful glance.
Or nature failed in me, and left some part
Not proof enough such object to sustain,   535
Or from my side subducting, took perhaps
More than enough; at least on her bestowed
Too much of ornament, in outward show
Elaborate, of inward less exact.
For well I understand in the prime end   540
Of nature her the inferior, in the mind
And inward faculties, which most excel,
In outward also her resembling less
His image who made both, and less expressing
The character of that dominion given   545
O'er other creatures; yet when I approach
Her loveliness, so absolute she seems
And in herself complete, so well to know
Her own, that what she wills to do or say,
Seems wisest, virtuousest, discreetest, best;   550
All higher knowledge in her presence falls
Degraded, wisdom in discourse with her
Loses discountenanced, and like folly shows;
Authority and reason on her wait,
As one intended first, not after made   555
Occasionally; and to consummate all,
Greatness of mind and nobleness their seat
Build in her loveliest, and create an awe
About her, as a guard angelic placed.'
To whom the angel, with contracted brow.   560
  'Accuse not nature, she hath done her part;
Do thou but thine, and be not diffident

Of wisdom, she deserts thee not, if thou
Dismiss not her, when most thou needest her nigh,
By attributing overmuch to things   565
Less excellent, as thou thyself perceivest.
For what admirest thou, what transports thee so,
An outside? fair no doubt, and worthy well
Thy cherishing, thy honoring, and thy love,
Not thy subjection: weigh with her thyself;   570
Then value: Ofttimes nothing profits more
Than self esteem, grounded on just and right
Well managed; of that skill the more thou knowest,
The more she will acknowledge thee her head,
And to realities yield all her shows: 575
Made so adorn for thy delight the more,
So awful, that with honor thou mayest love
Thy mate, who sees when thou art seen least wise.
But if the sense of touch whereby mankind
Is propagated seem such dear delight   580
Beyond all other, think the same vouchsafed
To cattle and each beast; which would not be
To them made common and divulged, if aught
Therein enjoyed were worthy to subdue
The soul of man, or passion in him move.   585
What higher in her society thou findest
Attractive, human, rational, love still:
In loving thou dost well, in passion not,
Wherein true love consists not; love refines
The thoughts, and heart enlarges, hath his seat   590
In reason, and is judicious, is the scale
By which to heavenly love thou mayest ascend,
Not sunk in carnal pleasure, for which cause
Among the beasts no mate for thee was found.'
    To whom thus half abashed Adam replied.   595
'Neither her outside formed so fair, nor aught
In procreation common to all kinds
(Though higher of the genial bed by far,
And with mysterious reverence I deem)
So much delights me as those graceful acts,   600
Those thousand decencies that daily flow
From all her words and actions mixed with love
And sweet compliance, which declare unfeigned
Union of mind, or in us both one soul;
Harmony to behold in wedded pair   605
More grateful than harmonious sound to the ear.
Yet these subject not; I to thee disclose
What inward thence I feel, not therefore foiled,
Who meet with various objects, from the sense
Variously representing; yet still free   610
Approve the best, and follow what I approve.
To love thou blamest me not, for love thou sayest
Leads up to heaven, is both the way and guide;

Bear with me then, if lawful what I ask;
Love not the heavenly spirits, and how their love   615
Express they, by looks only, or do they mix
Irradiance, virtual or immediate touch?'
    To whom the angel with a smile that glowed
Celestial rosy red, love's proper hue,
Answered.   'Let it suffice thee that thou knowest   620
Us happy, and without love no happiness.
Whatever pure thou in the body enjoyest
(And pure thou wert created) we enjoy
In eminence, and obstacle find none
Of membrane, joint, or limb, exclusive bars: 625
Easier than air with air, if spirits embrace,
Total they mix, union of pure with pure
Desiring; nor restrained conveyance need
As flesh to mix with flesh, or soul with soul.
But I can now no more; the parting sun   630
Beyond the earth's green cape and verdant isles
Hesperean sets, my signal to depart.
Be strong, live happy, and love, but first of all
Him whom to love is to obey, and keep
His great command; take heed lest passion sway   635
Thy judgment to do aught, which else free will
Would not admit; thine and of all thy sons
The weal or woe in thee is placed; beware.
I in thy persevering shall rejoice,
And all the blest: stand fast; to stand or fall   640
Free in thine own arbitrament it lies.
Perfect within, no outward aid require;
And all temptation to transgress repel.'
    So saying, he arose; whom Adam thus
Followed with benediction.   'Since to part,   645
Go heavenly guest, ethereal messenger,
Sent from whose sovereign goodness I adore.
Gentle to me and affable hath been
Thy condescension, and shall be honored ever
With grateful memory: thou to mankind   650
Be good and friendly still, and oft return.'
    So parted they, the angel up to heaven
From the thick shade, and Adam to his bower.

THE END OF THE EIGHTH BOOK

618. Notice how adroitly Adam turns the tables on Raphael after naïvely confessing his own helplessness in the presence of Eve. Raphael, confused, tells him that the angels enjoy all pleasures known to man, then abruptly changes the subject.

631. **earth's green cape:** Cape Verde or Verd.

641. **arbitrament:** power of decision.

BOOK IX

THE ARGUMENT

Satan having compassed the earth, with mediated guile returns as a mist by night into Paradise, enters into the serpent sleeping. Adam and Eve in the morning go forth to their labors, which Eve proposes to divide in several places, each laboring apart: Adam consents not, alleging the danger, lest that enemy, of whom they were forewarned, should attempt her found alone: Eve loath to be thought not circumspect or firm enough, urges her going apart, the rather desirous to make trial of her strength; Adam at last yields: The serpent finds her alone; his subtle approach, first gazing, then speaking, with much flattery extolling Eve above all other creatures. Eve wondering to hear the serpent speak, asks how he attained to human speech and such understanding not till now; the serpent answers, that by tasting of a certain tree in the garden he attained both to speech and reason, till then void of both: Eve requires him to bring her to that tree, and finds it to be the tree of knowledge forbidden: The serpent now grown bolder, with many wiles and arguments induces her at length to eat; she pleased with the taste deliberates a while whether to impart thereof to Adam or not, at last brings him of the fruit, relates what persuaded her to eat thereof: Adam at first amazed, but perceiving her lost, resolves through vehemence of love to perish with her; and extenuating the trespass, eats also of the fruit: The effects thereof in them both; they seek to cover their nakedness; then fall to variance and accusation of one another.

No more of talk where God or angel guest
With man, as with his friend, familiar used
To sit indulgent, and with him partake
Rural repast, permitting him the while
Venial discourse unblamed: I now must change   5
Those notes to tragic; foul distrust, and breach
Disloyal on the part of man, revolt,
And disobedience: On the part of heaven
Now alienated, distance and distaste,
Anger and just rebuke, and judgment given,   10
That brought into this world a world of woe,
Sin and her shadow death, and misery
Death's harbinger: Sad task, yet argument
Not less but more heroic than the wrath
Of stern Achilles on his foe pursued   15
Thrice fugitive about Troy wall; or rage
Of Turnus for Lavinia disespoused,
Or Neptune's ire or Juno's, that so long
Perplexed the Greek and Cytherea's son;
If answerable style I can obtain   20
Of my celestial patroness, who deigns
Her nightly visitation unimplored,
And dictates to me slumbering, or inspires
Easy my unpremeditated verse:

13-19. Milton refers to the *Iliad* in lines 15-16, the *Odyssey* in lines 16-17, and the *Aeneid* of Vergil in lines 18-19 in order to state that this poem, *PL*, is more, not less, heroic than those, and its subject is to be preferred to theirs. He bases this claim on the definite moral purpose this poem of his possesses. Milton felt that the great poet must first of all be a great teacher, then a singer, and then inspired.

19. **Cytherea's son:** [Venus's son] Aeneas.   21. **celestial patroness:** Urania, his muse.

Since first this subject for heroic song
Pleased me long choosing, and beginning late;   25
Not sedulous by nature to indite
Wars, hitherto the only argument
Heroic deemed, chief mastery to dissect
With long and tedious havoc fabled knights
In battles feigned; the better fortitude   30
Of patience and heroic martyrdom
Unsung; or to describe races and games,
Or tilting furniture, emblazoned shields,
Impreses quaint, caparisons and steeds;
Bases and tinsel trappings, gorgeous knights   35
At joust and tournament; then marshaled feast
Served up in hall with sewers, and seneshals;
The skill of artifice or office mean,
Not that which justly gives heroic name
To person or to poem.   Me of these   40
Nor skilled nor studious, higher argument
Remains, sufficient of itself to raise
That name, unless an age too late, or cold
Climate, or years damp my intended wing   45
Depressed, and much they may, if all be mine,
Not hers who brings it nightly to my ear.
    The sun was sunk, and after him the star
Of Hesperus, whose office is to bring
Twilight upon the earth, short arbiter   50
Twixt day and night, and now from end to end
Night's hemisphere had veiled the horizon round:
When Satan who late fled before the threats
Of Gabriel out of Eden, now improved
In meditated fraud and malice, bent   55
On man's destruction, mauger what might hap
Of heavier on himself, fearless returned.
By night he fled, and at midnight returned
From compassing the earth, cautious of day,
Since Uriel regent of the sun descried   60
His entrance, and forewarned the cherubim
That kept their watch; thence full of anguish driven,
The space of seven continued nights he rode
With darkness, thrice the equinoctial line
He circled, four times crossed the car of night   65
From pole to pole, traversing each colure;
On the eighth returned, and on the coast averse
From entrance or cherubic watch, by stealth
Found unsuspected way.   There was a place,

35. **Impreses**: Phillips defines an imprese as an 'emblem or device with a motto.'   Here, devices on shields or armor.   Italian, *impresa*.

56. **mauger**: in spite of.

63–67. Satan spent seven days traveling about the earth, three in circling the earth at the equator from east to west, and four in circling the earth from pole to pole.

66. **colure**: a great circle of the earth passing through the poles.

Now not, though sin, not time, first wrought the change,   70
Where Tigris at the foot of Paradise
Into a gulf shot under ground, till part
Rose up a fountain by the tree of life;
In with the river sunk, and with it rose
Satan involved in rising mist, then sought   75
Where to lie hid; sea he had searched and land
From Eden over Pontus, and the pool
Maeotis, up beyond the river Ob;
Downward as far antarctic; and in length
West from Orontes to the ocean barred   80
At Darien, thence to the land where flows
Ganges and Indus: thus the orb he roamed
With narrow search; and with inspection deep
Considered every creature, which of all
Most opportune might serve his wiles, and found   85
The serpent subtlest beast of all the field.
Him after long debate, irresolute
Of thoughts revolved, his final sentence chose
Fit vessel, fittest imp of fraud, in whom
To enter, and his dark suggestions hide   90
From sharpest sight: for in the wily snake,
Whatever sleights none would suspicious mark,
As from his wit and native subtlety
Proceeding, which in other beasts observed
Doubt might beget of diabolic power   95
Active within beyond the sense of brute.
Thus he resolved, but first from inward grief
His bursting passion into plaints thus poured:
  'O earth, how like to heaven, if not preferred
More justly, seat worthier of gods, as built   100
With second thoughts, reforming what was old!
For what god after better worse would build?
Terrestrial heaven, danced round by other heavens
That shine, yet bear their bright officious lamps,
Light above light, for thee alone, as seems,   105
In thee concentering all their precious beams
Of sacred influence: As God in heaven
Is center, yet extends to all, so thou
Centering receivest from all those orbs; in thee,
Not in themselves, all their known virtue appears   110
Productive in herb, plant, and nobler birth
Of creatures animate with gradual life
Of growth, sense, reason, all summed up in man.

71. **Tigris:** one of the two great rivers of Mesopotamia.
76–82. A geographical account of Satan's travels.   77. **Pontus:** the Black Sea.
77–78. **pool Maeotis:** the Sea of Azof, opening into the Black Sea.
78. **Ob:** a river in western Siberia emptying into the Arctic Ocean.
80. **Orontes:** the chief river of Syria.   81. **Darien:** Isthmus of Panama.
82. **Ganges and Indus:** chief rivers of India.   86. Cf. *Genesis* 3:1.
90. **suggestions:** temptations.

With what delight could I have walked thee round,
If I could joy in aught, sweet interchange   115
Of hill, and valley, rivers, woods and plains,
Now land, now sea, and shores with forest crowned,
Rocks, dens, and caves; but I in none of these
Find place or refuge; and the more I see
Pleasures about me, so much more I feel   120
Torment within me, as from the hateful siege
Of contraries; all good to me becomes
Bane, and in heaven much worse would be my state.
But neither here seek I, no nor in heaven
To dwell, unless by mastering heaven's supreme;   125
Nor hope to be myself less miserable
By what I seek, but others to make such
As I, though thereby worse to me redound:
For only in destroying I find ease
To my relentless thoughts; and him destroyed,   130
Or won to what may work his utter loss,
For whom all this was made, all this will soon
Follow, as to him linked in weal or woe,
In woe then; that destruction wide may range:
To me shall be the glory sole among   135
The infernal powers, in one day to have marred
What he almighty styled, six nights and days
Continued making, and who knows how long
Before had been contriving, though perhaps
Not longer than since I in one night freed   140
From servitude inglorious well-nigh half
The angelic name, and thinner left the throng
Of his adorers: he to be avenged,
And to repair his numbers thus impaired,
Whether such virtue spent of old now failed   145
More angels to create, if they at least
Are his created, or to spite us more,
Determined to advance into our room
A creature formed of earth, and him endow,
Exalted from so base original,   150
With heavenly spoils, our spoils: What he decreed
He effected; man he made, and for him built
Magnificent this world, and earth his seat,
Him Lord pronounced, and, O indignity!
Subjected to his service angel wings,   155
And flaming ministers to watch and tend
Their earthy charge: Of these the vigilance
I dread, and to elude, thus wrapped in mist
Of midnight vapor glide obscure, and pry

119–23. Note that Satan has now progressed so far in moral degradation that he can no longer debate the possibility of remorse or reform. He can only plunge madly on down the road to ruin.

123. **Bane**: curse.

145 ff. The old traditional accounts of the Jewish rabbis that the angels were jealous of man and hated him are all transferred by Milton to Satan and his jealousy of Adam and Eve.

In every bush and brake, where hap may find   160
The serpent sleeping, in whose mazy folds
To hide me, and the dark intent I bring.
O foul descent! that I who erst contended
With gods to sit the highest, am now constrained
Into a beast, and mixed with bestial slime,   165
This essence to incarnate and imbrute,
That to the height of deity aspired;
But what will not ambition and revenge
Descend to? who aspires must down as low
As high he soared, obnoxious first or last   170
To basest things.   Revenge, at first though sweet,
Bitter ere long back on itself recoils;
Let it; I reck not, so it light well aimed,
Since higher I fall short, on him who next
Provokes my envy, this new favorite   175
Of heaven, this man of clay, son of despite,
Whom us the more to spite his maker raised
From dust: spite then with spite is best repaid.'
    So saying, through each thicket dank or dry,
Like a black mist low creeping, he held on   180
His midnight search, where soonest he might find
The serpent: him fast sleeping soon he found
In labyrinth of many a round self rolled,
His head the midst, well stored with subtle wiles:
Not yet in horrid shade or dismal den,   185
Nor nocent yet, but on the grassy herb
Fearless unfeared he slept: in at his mouth
The devil entered, and his brutal sense,
In heart or head, possessing soon inspired
With act intelligential; but his sleep   190
Disturbed not, waiting close the approach of morn.
Now when as sacred light began to dawn
In Eden on the humid flowers, that breathed
Their morning incense, when all things that breathe,
From the earth's great altar send up silent praise   195
To the creator, and his nostrils fill
With grateful smell, forth came the human pair
And joined their vocal worship to the choir
Of creatures wanting voice, that done, partake
The season, prime for sweetest scents and airs: 200
Then commune how that day they best may ply
Their growing work: for much their work outgrew
The hands' dispatch of two gardening so wide.
And Eve first to her husband thus began.
    'Adam, well may we labor still to dress   205
This garden, still to tend plant, herb and flower,
Our pleasant task enjoined, but till more hands
Aid us, the work under our labor grows,
Luxurious by restraint; what we by day

170. **obnoxious:** liable, exposed to.   186. **nocent:** harmful.

Lop overgrown, or prune, or prop, or bind,   210
One night or two with wanton growth derides
Tending to wild.   Thou therefore now advise
Or bear what to my mind first thoughts present,
Let us divide our labors, thou where choice
Leads thee, or where most needs, whether to wind   215
The woodbine round this arbor, or direct
The clasping ivy where to climb, while I
In yonder spring of roses intermixed
With myrtle, find what to redress till noon:
For while so near each other thus all day   220
Our task we choose, what wonder if so near
Looks intervene and smiles, or object new
Casual discourse draw on, which intermits
Our day's work brought to little, though begun
Early, and the hour of supper comes unearned.'   225
   To whom mild answer Adam thus returned.
'Sole Eve, associate sole, to me beyond
Compare above all living creatures dear,
Well hast thou motioned, well thy thoughts employed
How we might best fulfill the work which here   230
God hath assigned us, nor of me shalt pass
Unpraised: for nothing lovelier can be found
In woman, than to study household good,
And good works in her husband to promote.
Yet not so strictly hath our Lord imposed   235
Labor, as to debar us when we need
Refreshment, whether food, or talk between,
Food of the mind, or this sweet intercourse
Of looks and smiles, for smiles from reason flow,
To brute denied, and are of love the food,   240
Love not the lowest end of human life.
For not to irksome toil, but to delight
He made us, and delight to reason joined.
These paths and bowers doubt not but our joint hands
Will keep from wilderness with ease, as wide   245
As we need walk, till younger hands erelong
Assist us: But if much converse perhaps
Thee satiate, to short absence I could yield.
For solitude sometimes is best society,
And short retirement urges sweet return.   250
But other doubt possesses me, lest harm
Befall thee severed from me; for thou knowest
What hath been warned us, what malicious foe
Envying our happiness, and of his own
Despairing, seeks to work us woe and shame   255
By sly assault; and somewhere nigh at hand
Watches, no doubt, with greedy hope to find
His wish and best advantage, us asunder,

213. **bear:** first edition, 'hear.'   218. **spring of roses:** clump of roses; the word was originally 'sprig.'
229. **motioned:** proposed; the same word as that in 'make a motion' in a meeting.

Hopeless to circumvent us joined, where each
To other speedy aid might lend at need;   260
Whether his first design be to withdraw
Our fealty from God, or to disturb
Conjugal love, than which perhaps no bliss
Enjoyed by us excites his envy more;
Or this, or worse, leave not the faithful side   265
That gave thee being, still shades thee and protects.
The wife, where danger or dishonor lurks,
Safest and seemliest by her husband stays,
Who guards her, or with her the worst endures.'
    To whom the virgin majesty of Eve,   270
As one who loves, and some unkindness meets,
With sweet austere composure thus replied,
  'Offspring of heaven and earth, and all earth's lord,
That such an enemy we have, who seeks
Our ruin, both by thee informed I learn,   275
And from the parting angel overheard
As in a shady nook I stood behind,
Just then returned at shut of evening flowers.
But that thou shouldst my firmness therefore doubt
To God or thee, because we have a foe   280
May tempt it, I expected not to hear.
His violence thou fearest not, being such,
As we, not capable of death or pain,
Can either not receive, or can repel.
His fraud is then thy fear, which plain infers   285
Thy equal fear that my firm faith and love
Can by his fraud be shaken or seduced;
Thoughts, which how found they harbor in thy breast
Adam, misthought of her to thee so dear?'
    To whom with healing words Adam replied.   290
'Daughter of God and man, immortal Eve,
For such thou art, from sin and blame entire:
Not diffident of thee do I dissuade
Thy absence from my sight, but to avoid
The attempt itself, intended by our foe.   295
For he who tempts, though in vain, at least asperses
The tempted with dishonor foul, supposed
Not incorruptible of faith, not proof
Against temptation: thou thyself with scorn
And anger wouldst resent the offered wrong,   300
Though ineffectual found: misdeem not then,
If such affront I labor to avert
From thee alone, which on us both at once
The enemy, though bold, will hardly dare,
Or daring, first on me the assault shall light.   305
Nor thou his malice and false guile contemn;
Subtle he needs must be, who could seduce
Angels, nor think superfluous others' aid.

270. virgin majesty: sinless.   **292. entire:** free from, untouched.

I from the influence of thy looks receive
Access in every virtue, in thy sight   310
More wise, more watchful, stronger, if need were
Of outward strength; while shame, thou looking on,
Shame to be overcome or overreached
Would utmost vigor raise, and raised unite.
Why shouldst not thou like sense within thee feel   315
When I am present, and thy trial choose
With me, best witness of thy virtue tried.'
    So spake domestic Adam in his care
And matrimonial love; but Eve, who thought
Less attributed to her faith sincere,   320
Thus her reply with accent sweet renewed.
    'If this be our condition, thus to dwell
In narrow circuit straitened by a foe,
Subtle or violent, we not endued
Single with like defense, wherever met,   325
How are we happy, still in fear of harm?
But harm precedes not sin: only our foe
Tempting affronts us with his foul esteem
Of our integrity: his foul esteem
Sticks no dishonor on our front, but turns   330
Foul on himself; then wherefore shunned or feared
By us? who rather double honor gain
From his surmise proved false, find peace within,
Favor from heaven, our witness from the event.
And what is faith, love, virtue unassayed   335
Alone, without exterior help sustained?
Let us not then suspect our happy state
Left so imperfect by the maker wise,
As not secure to single or combined.
Frail is our happiness, if this be so,   340
And Eden were no Eden thus exposed.'
    To whom thus Adam fervently replied.
'O woman, best are all things as the will
Of God ordained them, his creating hand
Nothing imperfect or deficient left   345
Of all that he created, much less man,
Or aught that might his happy state secure,
Secure from outward force; within himself
The danger lies, yet lies within his power:
Against his will he can receive no harm.   350
But God left free the will, for what obeys
Reason, is free, and reason he made right,
But bid her well beware, and still erect,
Lest by some fair appearing good surprised
She dictate false, and misinform the will   355
To do what God expressly hath forbid,
Not then mistrust, but tender love enjoins,
That I should mind thee oft, and mind thou me.
Firm we subsist, yet possible to swerve,

Since reason not impossibly may meet   360
Some specious object by the foe suborned,
And fall into deception unaware,
Not keeping strictest watch, as she was warned.
Seek not temptation then, which to avoid
Were better, and most likely if from me   365
Thou sever not: Trial will come unsought.
Wouldst thou approve thy constancy, approve
First thy obedience; the other who can know,
Not seeking thee attempted, who attest?
But if thou think, trial unsought may find   370
Us both securer than thus warned thou seemest,
Go; for thy stay, not free, absents thee more;
Go in thy native innocence, rely
On what thou hast of virtue, summon all,
For God towards thee hath done his part, do thine.'   375
   So spake the patriarch of mankind, but Eve
Persisted, yet submiss, though last, replied.
  'With thy permission then, and thus forewarned
Chiefly by what thy own last reasoning words
Touched only, that our trial, when least sought,   380
May find us both perhaps far less prepared,
The willinger I go, nor much expect
A foe so proud will first the weaker seek;
So bent, the more shall shame him his repulse.'
Thus saying, from her husband's hand her hand   385
Soft she withdrew, and like a wood nymph light
Oread or dryad, or of Delia's train,
Betook her to the groves, but Delia's self
In gait surpassed and goddess-like deport,
Though not as she with bow and quiver armed,   390
But with such gardening tools as art yet rude,
Guiltless of fire had formed, or angels brought.
To Pales, or Pomona thus adorned,
Likeliest she seemed, Pomona when she fled
Vertumnus, or to Ceres in her prime,   395
Yet virgin of Proserpina from Jove.
Her long with ardent look his eye pursued
Delighted, but desiring more her stay.
Oft he to her his charge of quick return
Repeated, she to him as oft engaged   400
To be returned by noon amid the bower,
And all things in best order to invite
Noontide repast, or afternoon's repose.

361. **specious**: showy, attractive, but false.   **suborned**: procured unlawfully, or for an evil purpose.
387. **Oread**: mountain nymph in Greek mythology.   **dryad**: wood nymph.
    Delia's train: Artemis or Diana, who hunted with a retinue of nymphs.
393. **Pales**: a Roman divinity of flocks.   **Pomona**: goddess of fruits.
394. **Likeliest**: most like, *likely* formerly meaning 'like.'   Verity's note is wrong.   Compare line 414.
394-95. **Pomona when she fled Vertumnus**: cf. Ovid, *Metamorphoses* XIV:623 ff.
395. **Ceres**: goddess of agriculture.

O much deceived, much failing, hapless Eve,
Of thy presumed return! event perverse!
Thou never from that hour in Paradise   405
Foundest either sweet repast, or sound repose;
Such ambush hid among sweet flowers and shades
Waited with hellish rancor imminent
To intercept thy way, or send thee back   410
Despoiled of innocence, of faith, of bliss.
For now, and since first break of dawn the fiend,
Mere serpent in appearance, forth was come,
And on his quest, where likeliest he might find
The only two of mankind, but in them   415
The whole included race, his purposed prey.
In bower and field he sought, where any tuft
Of grove or garden plot more pleasant lay,
Their tendance or plantation for delight,
By fountain or by shady rivulet   420
He sought them both, but wished his hap might find
Eve separate, he wished, but not with hope
Of what so seldom chanced, when to his wish,
Beyond his hope, Eve separate he spies,
Veiled in a cloud of fragrance, where she stood,   425
Half spied, so thick the roses bushing round
About her glowed, oft stooping to support
Each flower of slender stalk, whose head though gay
Carnation, purple, azure, or specked with gold,
Hung drooping unsustained, them she upstays   430
Gently with myrtle band, mindless the while,
Herself, though fairest unsupported flower,
From her best prop so far, and storm so nigh.
Nearer he drew, and many a walk traversed
Of stateliest covert, cedar, pine, or palm,   435
Then voluble and bold, now hid, now seen
Among thick-woven arborets and flowers
Imbordered on each bank, the hand of Eve:
Spot more delicious than those gardens feigned
Or of revived Adonis, or renowned   440
Alcinous, host of old Laertes' son,
Or that, not mystic, where the sapient king
Held dalliance with his fair Egyptian spouse.
Much he the place admired, the person more.
As one who long in populous city pent,   445

419. **tendance:** that which is tended.   436. **voluble:** rolling.

438. **Imbordered:** planted so as to form a border.

439–40. **those gardens feigned or of revived Adonis:** cf. Spenser, *Faerie Queene* III:6:29–49; also Pliny, *Natural History* XIX:19.   **revived:** or, after he came to life after being slain by the wild boar.

440–41. **renowned Alcinous:** as in V:340–41, King of the Phaeacians, who entertained Odysseus; Homer describes his palace and gardens.

441. **Laertes' son:** Odysseus.

442. **not mystic:** because Biblical.   **the sapient king:** the wise King Solomon in the Bible.

445 ff. Compare this passage with *L'Allegro* and *Elegy VII*.

Where houses thick and sewers annoy the air,
Forth issuing on a summer's morn to breathe
Among the pleasant villages and farms
Adjoined, from each thing met conceives delight,
The smell of grain, or tedded grass, or kine,   450
Or dairy, each rural sight, each rural sound;
If chance with nymphlike step fair virgin pass,
What pleasing seemed, for her now pleases more,
She most, and in her look sums all delight.
Such pleasure took the serpent to behold   455
This flowery plat, the sweet recess of Eve
Thus early, thus alone; her heavenly form
Angelic, but more soft, and feminine,
Her graceful innocence, her every air
Of gesture or least action overawed   460
His malice, and with rapine sweet bereaved
His fierceness of the fierce intent it brought:
That space the evil one abstracted stood
From his own evil, and for the time remained
Stupidly good, of enmity disarmed,   465
Of guile, of hate, of envy, of revenge;
But the hot hell that always in him burns,
Though in mid heaven, soon ended his delight,
And tortures him now more, the more he sees
Of pleasure not for him ordained: then soon   470
Fierce hate he recollects, and all his thoughts
Of mischief, gratulating, thus excites.
    'Thoughts, whither have ye led me, with what sweet
Compulsion thus transported to forget
What hither brought us, hate, not love, nor hope   475
Of Paradise for hell, hope here to taste
Of pleasure, but all pleasure to destroy,
Save what is in destroying, other joy
To me is lost.   Then let me not let pass
Occasion which now smiles, behold alone   480
The woman, opportune to all attempts,
Her husband, for I view far round, not nigh,
Whose higher intellectual more I shun,
And strength, of courage haughty, and of limb
Heroic built, though of terrestrial mold,   485
Foe not informidable, exempt from wound,
I not; so much hath hell debased, and pain
Enfeebled me, to what I was in heaven.
She fair, divinely fair, fit love for gods,
Not terrible, though terror be in love   490
And beauty, not approached by stronger hate,
Hate stronger, under show of love well feigned,
The way which to her ruin now I tend.'
    So spake the enemy of mankind, enclosed
In serpent, inmate bad, and toward Eve   495

446. **annoy**: pollute.

Addressed his way, not with indented wave,
Prone on the ground, as since, but on his rear,
Circular base of rising folds, that towered
Fold above fold a surging maze, his head
Crested aloft, and carbuncle his eyes;   500
With burnished neck of verdant gold, erect
Amidst his circling spires, that on the grass
Floated redundant: pleasing was his shape,
And lovely, never since of serpent kind
Lovelier, not those that in Illyria changed   505
Hermione and Cadmus, or the god
In Epidaurus; nor to which transformed
Ammonian Jove, or Capitoline was seen,
He with Olympias, this with her who bore
Scipio the height of Rome.   With tract oblique   510
At first, as one who sought access, but feared
To interrupt, sidelong he works his way.
As when a ship by skillful steersman wrought
Nigh river's mouth or foreland, where the wind
Veers oft, as oft so steers, and shifts her sail;   515
So varied he, and of his tortuous train
Curled many a wanton wreath in sight of Eve,
To lure her eye; she busied heard the sound
Of rustling leaves, but minded not, as used
To such disport before her through the field,   520
From every beast, more duteous at her call,
Than at Circean call the herd disguised.
He bolder now, uncalled before her stood;
But as in gaze admiring: Oft he bowed
His turret crest, and sleek enameled neck,   525
Fawning, and licked the ground whereon she trod.
His gentle dumb expression turned at length
The eye of Eve to mark his play; he glad
Of her attention gained, with serpent tongue
Organic, or impulse of vocal air,   530
His fraudulent temptation thus began.
   'Wonder not, sovereign mistress, if perhaps
Thou canst, who art sole wonder, much less arm
Thy looks, the heaven of mildness, with disdain,
Displeased that I approach thee thus, and gaze   535
Insatiate, I thus single, nor have feared
Thy awful brow, more awful thus retired.
Fairest resemblance of thy maker fair,
Thee all things living gaze on, all things thine
By gift, and thy celestial beauty adore   540
With ravishment beheld, there best beheld

502. **spires:** coils, spirals.
   506. **Hermione and Cadmus:** Cadmus, King of Thebes, and his wife Harmonia came into Illyria and were changed into serpents.   Cf. Ovid, *Metamorphoses* XV:622 ff.
   508. **Ammonian Jove, or Capitoline:** Jove Ammon or Jove Capitoline.
   521-22. The story of Circe, who turned men into swine.

Where universally admired; but here
In this enclosure wild, these beasts among,
Beholders rude, and shallow to discern
Half what in thee is fair, one man except,   545
Who sees thee? (and what is one?) who shouldst be seen
A goddess among gods, adored and served
By angels numberless, thy daily train.'
   So glozed the tempter, and his proem tuned;
Into the heart of Eve his words made way,   550
Though at the voice much marveling; at length
Not unamazed she thus in answer spake.
'What may this mean?   Language of man pronounced
By tongue of brute, and human sense expressed?
The first at least of these I thought denied   555
To beasts, whom God on their creation-day
Created mute to all articulate sound;
The latter I demur, for in their looks
Much reason, and in their actions oft appears.
Thee, serpent, subtlest beast of all the field   560
I knew, but not with human voice endued;
Redouble then this miracle, and say,
How camest thou speakable of mute, and how
To me so friendly grown above the rest
Of brutal kind, that daily are in sight?   565
Say, for such wonder claims attention due.'
   To whom the guileful tempter thus replied.
'Empress of this fair world, resplendent Eve,
Easy to me it is to tell thee all
What thou commandest, and right thou shouldst be obeyed: 570
I was at first as other beasts that graze
The trodden herb, of abject thoughts and low,
As was my food, nor aught but food discerned
Or sex, and apprehended nothing high:
Till on a day roving the field, I chanced   575
A goodly tree far distant to behold
Laden with fruit of fairest colors mixed,
Ruddy and gold: I nearer drew to gaze;
When from the boughs a savory odor blown,
Grateful to appetite, more pleased my sense   580
Than smell of sweetest fennel or the teats
Of ewe or goat dropping with milk at even,
Unsucked of lamb or kid, that tend their play
To satisfy the sharp desire I had
Of tasting those fair apples, I resolved   585
Not to defer; hunger and thirst at once,
Powerful persuaders, quickened at the scent
Of that alluring fruit, urged me so keen.
About the mossy trunk I wound me soon,

549. **glozed**: flattered.   **proem**: introduction.
581. **fennel**: a plant that greatly attracted snakes.   See Pliny, *Natural History* VIII:41, XIX:56,
XX:95.

For high from ground the branches would require   590
Thy utmost reach or Adam's: Round the tree
All other beasts that saw, with like desire
Longing and envying stood, but could not reach.
Amid the tree now got, where plenty hung
Tempting so nigh, to pluck and eat my fill   595
I spared not, for such pleasure till that hour
At feed or fountain never had I found.
Sated at length, erelong I might perceive
Strange alteration in me, to degree
Of reason in my inward powers, and speech   600
Wanted not long, though to this shape retained.
Thenceforth to speculations high or deep
I turned my thoughts, and with capacious mind
Considered all things visible in heaven,
Or earth, or middle, all things fair and good;   605
But all that fair and good in thy divine
Semblance, and in thy beauty's heavenly ray
United I beheld; no fair to thine
Equivalent or second, which compelled
Me thus, though importune perhaps, to come   610
And gaze, and worship thee of right declared
Sovereign of creatures, universal dame.'
   So talked the spirited sly snake; and Eve
Yet more amazed unwary thus replied.
   'Serpent, thy overpraising leaves in doubt   615
The virtue of that fruit, in thee first proved:
But say, where grows the tree, from hence how far?
For many are the trees of God that grow
In Paradise, and various, yet unknown
To us, in such abundance lies our choice,   620
As leaves a greater store of fruit untouched,
Still hanging incorruptible, till men
Grow up to their provision, and more hands
Help to disburden nature of her birth.'
   To whom the wily adder, blithe and glad.   625
'Empress, the way is ready, and not long,
Beyond a row of myrtles, on a flat,
Fast by a fountain, one small thicket past
Of blowing myrrh and balm; if thou accept
My conduct, I can bring thee thither soon.'   630
   'Lead then,' said Eve.   He leading swiftly rolled
In tangles, and made intricate seem straight,
To mischief swift.   Hope elevates, and joy
Brightens his crest, as when a wandering fire,
Compact of unctuous vapor, which the night   635
Condenses, and the cold environs round,
Kindled through agitation to a flame,
Which oft, they say, some evil spirit attends

602 ff. Signs of intoxication.   624. **birth:** Milton printed 'bearth,' that which is born.
635. **Compact of unctuous vapor:** made of oily mist.

Hovering and blazing with delusive light,
Misleads the amazed night-wanderer from his way   640
To bogs and mires, and oft through pond or pool,
There swallowed up and lost, from succor far.
So glistered the dire snake, and into fraud
Led Eve our credulous mother, to the tree
Of prohibition, root of all our woe;   645
Which when she saw, thus to her guide she spake.
    'Serpent, we might have spared our coming hither,
Fruitless to me, though fruit be here to excess,
The credit of whose virtue rest with thee,
Wondrous indeed, if cause of such effects.   650
But of this tree we may not taste nor touch;
God so commanded, and left that command
Sole daughter of his voice: the rest, we live
Law to ourselves, our reason is our law.'
    To whom the tempter guilefully replied.   655
'Indeed? hath God then said that of the fruit
Of all these garden trees ye shall not eat,
Yet lords declared of all in earth or air?'
    To whom thus Eve yet sinless. 'Of the fruit
Of each tree in the garden we may eat,   660
But of the fruit of this fair tree amidst
The garden, God hath said, "Ye shall not eat
Thereof, nor shall ye touch it, lest ye die."'
    She scarce had said, though brief, when now more bold
The tempter, but with show of zeal and love   665
To man, and indignation at his wrong,
New part puts on, and as to passion moved,
Fluctuates disturbed, yet comely and in act
Raised, as of some great matter to begin.
As when of old some orator renowned   670
In Athens or free Rome, where eloquence
Flourished, since mute, to some great cause addressed,
Stood in himself collected, while each part,
Motion, each act won audience ere the tongue,
Sometimes in height began, as no delay   675
Of preface brooking through his zeal of right.
So standing, moving, or to height upgrown
The tempter all impassioned thus began.
    'O sacred, wise, and wisdom-giving plant,
Mother of science, now I feel thy power   680
Within me clear, not only to discern
Things in their causes, but to trace the ways
Of highest agents, deemed however wise.
Queen of this universe, do not believe
Those rigid threats of death; ye shall not die: 685
How should ye? by the fruit? it gives you life
To knowledge. By the threatener, look on me,

668. **Fluctuates**: moving his body.   680. **science**: *scientia*, 'knowledge.'
685–712. Cf. *Genesis* 3:4, 5.

Me who have touched and tasted, yet both live,
And life more perfect have attained than fate
Meant me, by venturing higher than my lot.   690
Shall that be shut to man, which to the beast
Is open? or will God incense his ire
For such a petty trespass, and not praise
Rather your dauntless virtue, whom the pain
Of death denounced, whatever thing death be,   695
Deterred not from achieving what might lead
To happier life, knowledge of good and evil;
Of good, how just? of evil, if what is evil
Be real, why not known, since easier shunned?
God therefore cannot hurt ye, and be just;   700
Not just, not God; not feared then, nor obeyed:
Your fear itself of death removes the fear.
Why then was this forbid? Why but to awe,
Why but to keep ye low and ignorant,
His worshipers; he knows that in the day   705
Ye eat thereof, your eyes that seem so clear,
Yet are but dim, shall perfectly be then
Opened and cleared, and ye shall be as gods,
Knowing both good and evil as they know.
That ye should be as gods, since I as man,   710
Internal man, is but proportion meet,
I of brute human, ye of human gods.
So ye shall die perhaps, by putting off
Human, to put on gods, death to be wished,
Though threatened, which no worse than this can bring.   715
And what are gods that man may not become
As they, participating godlike food?
The gods are first, and that advantage use
On our belief, that all from them proceeds;
I question it, for this fair earth I see,   720
Warmed by the sun, producing every kind,
Them nothing: If they all things, who enclosed
Knowledge of good and evil in this tree,
That whoso eats thereof, forthwith attains
Wisdom without their leave? and wherein lies   725
The offense, that man should thus attain to know?
What can your knowledge hurt him, or this tree
Impart against his will if all be his?
Or is it envy, and can envy dwell
In heavenly breasts? these, these and many more   730
Causes import your need of this fair fruit.
Goddess humane, reach then, and freely taste.'
    He ended, and his words replete with guile
Into her heart too easy entrance won:
Fixed on the fruit she gazed, which to behold   735
Might tempt alone, and in her ears the sound
Yet rung of his persuasive words, impregned
With reason, to her seeming, and with truth;
Meanwhile the hour of noon drew on, and waked

An eager appetite, raised by the smell   740
So savory of that fruit, which with desire,
Inclinable now grown to touch or taste,
Solicited her longing eye; yet first
Pausing a while, thus to herself she mused.
　'Great are thy virtues, doubtless, best of fruits,   745
Though kept from man, and worthy to be admired,
Whose taste, too long forborne, at first assay
Gave elocution to the mute, and taught
The tongue not made for speech to speak thy praise:
Thy praise he also who forbids thy use,   750
Conceals not from us, naming thee the tree
Of knowledge, knowledge both of good and evil;
Forbids us then to taste, but his forbidding
Commends thee more, while it infers the good
By thee communicated, and our want: 755
For good unknown, sure is not had, or had
And yet unknown, is as not had at all.
In plain then, what forbids he but to know,
Forbids us good, forbids us to be wise?
Such prohibitions bind not. But if death   760
Bind us with after-bands, what profits then
Our inward freedom? In the day we eat
Of this fair fruit, our doom is, we shall die.
How dies the serpent? he hath eaten and lives,
And knows, and speaks, and reasons, and discerns,   765
Irrational till then. For us alone
Was death invented? or to us denied
This intellectual food, for beasts reserved?
For beasts it seems: yet that one beast which first
Hath tasted, envies not, but brings with joy   770
The good befallen him, author unsuspect,
Friendly to man, far from deceit or guile.
What fear I then, rather what know to fear
Under this ignorance of good and evil,
Of God or death, of law or penalty?   775
Here grows the cure of all, this fruit divine,
Fair to the eye, inviting to the taste,
Of virtue to make wise: what hinders then
To reach, and feed at once both body and mind?'
　So saying, her rash hand in evil hour   780
Forth reaching to the fruit, she plucked, she eat:
Earth felt the wound, and nature from her seat
Sighing through all her works gave signs of woe,
That all was lost. Back to the thicket slunk
The guilty serpent, and well might, for Eve   785
Intent now wholly on her taste, naught else

745. fruits: second edition reads 'fruits.'

781. eat: past tense, as frequently in the seventeenth century and earlier.

782–84. Signs and portents are introduced in a classical manner and tradition.

786. wholly: many modern editions (Montgomery, Masson, Wright, Verity, Hanford) print 'only' for no reason, as I cannot find an edition before Montgomery (1843) in which 'only' occurs.

Regarded, such delight till then, as seemed,
In fruit she never tasted, whether true
Or fancied so, through expectation high
Of knowledge, nor was godhead from her thought.   790
Greedily she engorged without restraint,
And knew not eating death: Satiate at length,
And heightened as with wine, jocund and boon,
Thus to herself she pleasingly began.
　　'O sovereign, virtuous, precious of all trees   795
In Paradise, of operation blessed
To sapience, hitherto obscured, infamed,
And thy fair fruit let hang, as to no end
Created; but henceforth my early care,
Not without song, each morning, and due praise   800
Shall tend thee, and the fertile burden ease
Of thy full branches offered free to all;
Till dieted by thee I grow mature
In knowledge, as the gods who all things know;
Though others envy what they cannot give;   805
For had the gift been theirs, it had not here
Thus grown.　Experience, next to thee I owe,
Best guide; not following thee, I had remained
In ignorance, thou openest wisdom's way,
And givest access, though secret she retire.   810
And I perhaps am secret; heaven is high,
High and remote to see from thence distinct
Each thing on earth; and other care perhaps
May have diverted from continual watch
Our great forbidder, safe with all his spies   815
About him.　But to Adam in what sort
Shall I appear? shall I to him make known
As yet my change, and give him to partake
Full happiness with me, or rather not,
But keep the odds of knowledge in my power   820
Without copartner? so to add what wants
In female sex, the more to draw his love,
And render me more equal, and perhaps,
A thing not undesirable, sometime
Superior; for inferior who is free?   825
This may be well: but what if God have seen,
And death ensue? then I shall be no more,
And Adam wedded to another Eve,

790. **nor was godhead from her thought**: perhaps this 'overweening' ambition was the real sin.
793. **boon**: gay, almost the same as *jocund*.
797. **sapience**: wisdom.　　**infamed**: unfamed, unknown.
803–05. She intends to go on eating the fruit until she equals the gods.
811. **secret**: not observed.
816 ff. Eve's soliloquy is at once to set forth the state of her mind after eating of the fruit, and to show that she willfully 'seduced' Adam to eat of it.
827. The real reason for getting Adam to eat of the fruit was another sin, jealousy.　Jewish rabbinical commentators on *Genesis* had made much of this point.

Shall live with her enjoying, I extinct;
A death to think.   Confirmed then I resolve,   830
Adam shall share with me in bliss or woe:
So dear I love him, that with him all deaths
I could endure, without him live no life.'
    So saying, from the tree her step she turned,
But first low reverence done, as to the power   835
That dwelt within, whose presence had infused
Into the plant sciential sap, derived
From nectar, drink of gods.   Adam the while
Waiting desirous her return, had wove
Of choicest flowers a garland to adorn   840
Her tresses, and her rural labors crown,
As reapers oft are wont their harvest queen.
Great joy he promised to his thoughts, and new
Solace in her return, so long delayed;
Yet oft his heart, divine of something ill,   845
Misgave him; he the faltering measure felt;
And forth to meet her went, the way she took
That morn when first they parted; by the tree
Of knowledge he must pass, there he her met,
Scarce from the tree returning; in her hand   850
A bough of fairest fruit that downy smiled,
New gathered, and ambrosial smell diffused.
To him she hasted, in her face excuse
Came prologue, and apology to prompt,
Which with bland words at will she thus addressed.   855
    'Hast thou not wondered, Adam, at my stay?
Thee I have missed, and thought it long, deprived
Thy presence, agony of love till now
Not felt, nor shall be twice, for never more
Mean I to try, what rash untried I sought,   860
The pain of absence from thy sight.   But strange
Hath been the cause, and wonderful to hear:
This tree is not as we are told, a tree
Of danger tasted, nor to evil unknown
Opening the way, but of divine effect   865
To open eyes, and make them gods who taste;
And hath been tasted such: the serpent wise,
Or not restrained as we, or not obeying,
Hath eaten of the fruit, and is become,
Not dead, as we are threatened, but thenceforth   870
Endued with human voice and human sense,
Reasoning to admiration, and with me
Persuasively hath so prevailed, that I
Have also tasted, and have also found
The effects to correspond, opener mine eyes,   875
Dim erst, dilated spirits, ampler heart,

837. **sciential:** conferring knowledge.

856 ff. Note the sketchy nature of Eve's argument and the unimpressive way in which she presents it.
She is intoxicated by the fruit.

And growing up to godhead; which for thee
Chiefly I sought, without thee can despise.
For bliss, as thou hast part, to me is bliss,
Tedious, unshared with thee, and odious soon. 880
Thou therefore also taste, that equal lot
May join us, equal joy, as equal love;
Lest thou not tasting, different degree
Disjoin us, and I then too late renounce
Deity for thee, when fate will not permit.' 885
　　Thus Eve with countenance blithe her story told;
But in her cheek distemper flushing glowed.
On the other side, Adam, soon as he heard
The fatal trespass done by Eve, amazed,
Astonied stood and blank, while horror chill 890
Ran through his veins, and all his joints relaxed;
From his slack hand the garland wreathed for Eve
Down dropped, and all the faded roses shed:
Speechless he stood and pale, till thus at length
First to himself he inward silence broke. 895
　　'O fairest of creation, last and best
Of all God's works, creature in whom excelled
Whatever can to sight or thought be formed,
Holy, divine, good, amiable, or sweet!
How art thou lost, how on a sudden lost, 900
Defaced, deflowered, and now to death devote?
Rather how hast thou yielded to transgress
The strict forbiddance, how to violate
The sacred fruit forbidden! some cursed fraud
Of enemy hath beguiled thee, yet unknown, 905
And me with thee hath ruined, for with thee
Certain my resolution is to die;
How can I live without thee, how forgo
Thy sweet converse and love so dearly joined,
To live again in these wild woods forlorn? 910
Should God create another Eve, and I
Another rib afford, yet loss of thee
Would never from my heart; no no, I feel
The link of nature draw me: Flesh of flesh,
Bone of my bone thou art, and from thy state 915
Mine never shall be parted, bliss or woe.'
　　So having said, as one from sad dismay
Recomforted, and after thoughts disturbed
Submitting to what seemed remediless,
Thus in calm mood his words to Eve he turned. 920
　　'Bold deed thou hast presumed, adventurous Eve,
And peril great provoked, who thus hath dared
Had it been only coveting to eye

877–85. Note how deceitful is this statement compared with lines 817–25 *supra*.

890. **blank:** probably should be spelled 'blanc' as elsewhere. Phillips defines it as 'pale and wan, hence out of countenance.' Cf. French *blanc*, and English *blanch*, which is the same word.

904 ff. **fraud … yet unknown:** neither Adam nor Eve yet know that the serpent was Satan.

That sacred fruit, sacred to abstinence,
Much more to taste it under ban to touch.   925
But past who can recall, or done undo?
Not God omnipotent, nor fate, yet so
Perhaps thou shalt not die, perhaps the fact
Is not so heinous now, foretasted fruit,
Profaned first by the serpent, by him first   930
Made common and unhallowed ere our taste;
Nor yet on him found deadly, he yet lives,
Lives, as thou saidst, and gains to live as man
Higher degree of life, inducement strong
To us, as likely tasting to attain   935
Proportional ascent, which cannot be
But to be gods, or angels demi-gods.
Nor can I think that God, creator wise,
Though threatening, will in earnest so destroy
Us his prime creatures, dignified so high,   940
Set over all his works, which in our fall,
For us created, needs with us must fail,
Dependent made; so God shall uncreate,
Be frustrate, do, undo, and labor lose,
Not well conceived of God, who though his power   945
Creation could repeat, yet would be loath
Us to abolish, lest the adversary
Triumph and say; "Fickle their state whom God
Most favors, who can please him long; me first
He ruined, now mankind; whom will he next?"   950
Matter of scorn, not to be given the foe,
However I with thee have fixed my lot,
Certain to undergo like doom, if death
Consort with thee, death is to me as life;
So forcible within my heart I feel   955
The bond of nature draw me to my own,
My own in thee, for what thou art is mine;
Our state cannot be severed, we are one,
One flesh; to lose thee were to lose myself.'
    So Adam, and thus Eve to him replied.   960
'O glorious trial of exceeding love,
Illustrious evidence, example high!
Engaging me to emulate, but short
Of thy perfection, how shall I attain,
Adam, from whose dear side I boast me sprung,   965
And gladly of our union hear thee speak,
One heart, one soul in both; whereof good proof
This day affords, declaring thee resolved,
Rather than death or aught than death more dread
Shall separate us, linked in love so dear,   970

932 ff. This is exactly the same argument used by the serpent to Eve.
948 ff. This is the antithesis of the whole poem's thesis. It is never completely resolved.
959. This is the same general statement of how Adam felt about Eve that he had made to Raphael.
Raphael's only help offered was to keep reason in control.

To undergo with me one guilt, one crime,
If any be, of tasting this fair fruit,
Whose virtue, for of good still good proceeds,
Direct, or by occasion hath presented
This happy trial of thy love, which else   975
So eminently never had been known.
Were it I thought death menaced would ensue
This my attempt, I would sustain alone
The worst, and not persuade thee rather die
Deserted, than oblige thee with a fact   980
Pernicious to thy peace, chiefly assured
Remarkably so late of thy so true,
So faithful love unequaled; but I feel
Far otherwise the event, not death, but life
Augmented, opened eyes, new hopes, new joys,   985
Taste so divine, that what of sweet before
Hath touched my sense, flat seems to this, and harsh.
On my experience, Adam, freely taste,
And fear of death deliver to the winds.'
    So saying, she embraced him, and for joy   990
Tenderly wept, much won that he his love
Had so ennobled, as of choice to incur
Divine displeasure for her sake, or death.
In recompense (for such compliance bad
Such recompense best merits) from the bough   995
She gave him of that fair enticing fruit
With liberal hand: he scrupled not to eat
Against his better knowledge, not deceived,
But fondly overcome with female charm.
Earth trembled from her entrails, as again   1000
In pangs, and nature gave a second groan,
Sky loured and muttering thunder, some sad drops
Wept at completing of the mortal sin
Original; while Adam took no thought,
Eating his fill, nor Eve to iterate   1005
Her former trespass feared, the more to soothe
Him with her loved society, that now
As with new wine intoxicated both
They swim in mirth, and fancy that they feel
Divinity within them breeding wings   1010
Wherewith to scorn the earth: but that false fruit
Far other operation first displayed,
Carnal desire inflaming, he on Eve
Began to cast lascivious eyes, she him
As wantonly repaid; in lust they burn: 1015

977. Note Eve's attempt at heroics, ending in a plea to eat.
980. **oblige**: lay under obligation, hence under punishment.
1000 ff. More portents and omens.   1005. **iterate**: to repeat.
1007 ff. The debauch of sense; the senses only, not the will, intellect, or love, now being in full control.
The description is of two drunken revelers.
1015. **lust**: to Milton, this meant desire unbridled by reason and out of control of the will.

Till Adam thus 'gan Eve to dalliance move,
  'Eve, now I see thou art exact of taste,
And elegant, of sapience no small part,
Since to each meaning savor we apply,
And palate call judicious; I the praise   1020
Yield thee, so well this day thou hast purveyed.
Much pleasure we have lost, while we abstained
From this delightful fruit, nor known till now
True relish, tasting; if such pleasure be
In things to us forbidden, it might be wished,   1025
For this one tree had been forbidden ten.
But come, so well refreshed, now let us play,
As meet is, after such delicious fare;
For never did thy beauty since the day
I saw thee first and wedded thee, adorned   1030
With all perfections, so inflame my sense
With ardor to enjoy thee, fairer now
Than ever, bounty of this virtuous tree.'
  So said he, and forbore not glance or toy
Of amorous intent, well understood   1035
Of Eve, whose eye darted contagious fire.
Her hand he seized, and to a shady bank,
Thick overhead with verdant roof embowered
He led her nothing loath; flowers were the couch,
Pansies, and violets, and asphodel,   1040
And hyacinth, earth's freshest softest lap.
There they their fill of love and love's disport
Took largely, of their mutual guilt the seal,
The solace of their sin, till dewy sleep
Oppressed them, wearied with their amorous play.   1045
Soon as the force of that fallacious fruit,
That with exhilarating vapor bland
About their spirits had played, and inmost powers
Made err, was now exhaled, and grosser sleep
Bred of unkindly fumes, with conscious dreams   1050
Encumbered, now had left them, up they rose
As from unrest, and each the other viewing,
Soon found their eyes how opened, and their minds
How darkened; innocence, that as a veil
Had shadowed them from knowing ill, was gone,   1055
Just confidence, and native righteousness
And honor from about them, naked left
To guilty shame he covered, but his robe
Uncovered more, so rose the Danite strong
Herculean Samson from the harlot-lap   1060
Of Philistean Dalilah, and waked
Shorn of his strength, they destitute and bare
Of all their virtue: silent, and in face

1018. **sapience:** wisdom, and perhaps a pun, with 'savor' in following line.
1019. **we apply:** 1674 edition reads 'me apply.'   1021. **purveyed:** provided.
1050. **unkindly:** not natural.   1059–60. **Danite . . . Samson:** cf. *Judges* 16:4–20.

Confounded long they sat, as stricken mute,
Till Adam, though not less than Eve abashed,   1065
At length gave utterance to these words constrained.
  'O Eve, in evil hour thou didst give ear
To that false worm, of whomsoever taught
To counterfeit man's voice, true in our fall,
False in our promised rising; since our eyes   1070
Opened we find indeed, and find we know
Both good and evil, good lost, and evil got,
Bad fruit of knowledge, if this be to know,
Which leaves us naked thus, of honor void,
Of innocence, of faith, of purity,   1075
Our wonted ornaments now soiled and stained,
And in our faces evident the signs
Of foul concupiscence; whence evil store;
Even shame, the last of evils; of the first
Be sure then.   How shall I behold the face   1080
Henceforth of God or angel, erst with joy
And rapture so oft beheld? those heavenly shapes
Will dazzle now this earthly, with their blaze
Insufferably bright.   O might I here
In solitude live savage, in some glade   1085
Obscured, where highest woods impenetrable
To star or sunlight, spread their umbrage broad
And brown as evening: Cover me ye pines,
Ye cedars, with innumerable boughs
Hide me, where I may never see them more.   1090
But let us now, as in bad plight, devise
What best may for the present serve to hide
The parts of each from other, that seem most
To shame obnoxious, and unseemliest seen,
Some tree whose broad smooth leaves together sewed,   1095
And girded on our loins, may cover round
Those middle parts, that this new comer, shame,
There sit not, and reproach us as unclean,'
  So counseled he, and both together went
Into the thickest wood, there soon they chose   1100
The fig tree, not that kind for fruit renowned,
But such as at this day to Indians known
In Malabar or Decan spreads her arms
Branching so broad and long, that in the ground
The bended twigs take root, and daughters grow   1105

1068. **false worm**: false serpent, but no connection yet in Adam's mind between the serpent and Satan.

1076. **wonted**: usual.

1078. **concupiscence**: wholly selfish sexual desire.   To understand the exact effects of the fall on the sexual relations of Adam and Eve, the reader needs a knowledge of medieval scholastic ideas of sin and virtue.   In some systems (Bonaventura), love and its nature is all-important; in Aquinas, intellect and control by reason is necessary.   In still others (Scotus), the will is made dominant.   Milton implies that the fall caused Adam and Eve to lose their sense of balance.

1088. **brown**: dark.   1101 ff. The banyan tree.

1103. **Malabar or Decan**: the first, the western coast of Hindustan; the second, the name of the whole Indian peninsula.

About the mother tree, a pillared shade
High overarched, and echoing walks between;
There oft the Indian herdsman shunning heat
Shelters in cool, and tends his pasturing herds
At loopholes cut through thickest shade: Those leaves   1110
They gathered, broad as Amazonian targe,
And with what skill they had, together sewed,
To gird their waist, vain covering if to hide
Their guilt and dreaded shame; O how unlike
To that first naked glory.   Such of late   1115
Columbus found the American so girt
With feathered cincture, naked else and wild
Among the trees on isles and woody shores.
Thus fenced, and as they thought, their shame in part
Covered, but not at rest or ease of mind,   1120
They sat them down to weep, nor only tears
Rained at their eyes, but high winds worse within
Began to rise, high passions, anger, hate,
Mistrust, suspicion, discord, and shook sore
Their inward state of mind, calm region once   1125
And full of peace, now tossed and turbulent:
For understanding ruled not, and the will
Heard not her lore, both in subjection now
To sensual appetite, who from beneath
Usurping over sovereign reason claimed   1130
Superior sway: from thus distempered breast,
Adam, estranged in look and altered style,
Speech intermitted thus to Eve renewed.
    'Would thou hadst hearkened to my words, and stayed
With me, as I besought thee, when that strange   1135
Desire of wandering this unhappy morn,
I know not whence possessed thee; we had then
Remained still happy, not as now, despoiled
Of all our good, shamed, naked, miserable.
Let none henceforth seek needless cause to approve   1140
The faith they owe; when earnestly they seek
Such proof, conclude, they then begin to fail.'
    To whom soon moved with touch of blame thus Eve.
'What words have passed thy lips, Adam severe,
Imputest thou that to my default, or will   1145
Of wandering, as thou callest it, which who knows
But might as ill have happened thou being by,
Or to thyself perhaps: hadst thou been there,
Or here the attempt, thou couldst not have discerned
Fraud in the serpent, speaking as he spake;   1150

1111. **Amazonian targe**: a targe was a shield or target, and 'Amazonian' here refers to the Amazons of antiquity, the famous warrior women.

1116-17. **the American . . . wild**: to Milton and to his age the two words were virtually synonymous.

1123 ff. The effects of the intoxication wearing off, the usual aftermath of it begins.

1127. **understanding ruled not, and the will**: cf. note on lines 1078 ff. *supra*.

1149-50. The worst feature of Eve's argument is — its truth.   Adam could not have discovered the fraud, as Uriel could not in the 'stripling cherub.'

No ground of enmity between us known,
Why he should mean me ill, or seek to harm.
Was I to have never parted from thy side?
As good have grown there still a lifeless rib.
Being as I am, why didst not thou the head   1155
Command me absolutely not to go,
Going into such danger as thou saidst?
Too facile then thou didst not much gainsay,
Nay didst permit, approve, and fair dismiss.
Hadst thou been firm and fixed in thy dissent,   1160
Neither had I transgressed, nor thou with me.'
   To whom then first incensed Adam replied,
'Is this the love, is this the recompense
Of mine to thee, ingrateful Eve, expressed
Immutable when thou wert lost, not I,   1165
Who might have lived and joyed immortal bliss,
Yet willingly chose rather death with thee:
And am I now upbraided, as the cause
Of thy transgressing? not enough severe,
It seems, in thy restraint: what could I more?   1170
I warned thee, I admonished thee, foretold
The danger, and the lurking enemy
That lay in wait; beyond this had been force,
And force upon free will hath here no place.
But confidence then bore thee on, secure   1175
Either to meet no danger, or to find
Matter of glorious trial; and perhaps
I also erred in overmuch admiring
What seemed in thee so perfect, that I thought
No evil durst attempt thee, but I rue   1180
That error now, which is become my crime,
And thou the accuser.   Thus it shall befall
Him who to worth in women overtrusting
Lets her will rule; restraint she will not brook,
And left to herself, if evil thence ensue,   1185
She first his weak indulgence will accuse.
   Thus they in mutual accusation spent
The fruitless hours, but neither self-condemning,
And of their vain contest appeared no end.

THE END OF THE NINTH BOOK

1160 ff. When Eve tells Adam their trouble is all his fault because he did not *order* her to stay with him, it is too much and his first reviling speech follows.

1166. **and joyed:** Milton might have dictated 'enjoyed.'

1182 ff. Perhaps the most completely personal lines in the poem.   Probably exactly the same situation confronted Milton in his relations with his first wife after her return to him.

BOOK X

THE ARGUMENT

Man's transgression known, the guardian angels forsake Paradise, and return up to heaven to approve their vigilance, and are approved, God declaring that the entrance of Satan could not be by them prevented. He sends his Son to judge the transgressors, who descends and gives sentence accordingly; then in pity clothes them both, and reascends. Sin and death sitting till then at the gates of hell, by wondrous sympathy feeling the success of Satan in this new world, and the sin by man there committed, resolve to sit no longer confined in hell, but to follow Satan their sire up to the place of man: To make the way easier from hell to this world to and fro, they pave a broad highway or bridge over chaos, according to the track that Satan first made; then preparing for earth, they meet[1] him proud of his success returning to hell; their mutual gratulation. Satan arrives at Pandemonium, in full of assembly relates with boasting his success against man; instead of applause is entertained with a general hiss by all his audience, transformed with himself also suddenly into serpents, according to his doom given in Paradise; then deluded with a show of the forbidden tree springing up before them, they greedily reaching to take of the fruit, chew dust and bitter ashes. The proceedings of sin and death; God foretells the final victory of his Son over them, and the renewing of all things; but for the present commands his angels to make several alterations in the heavens and elements. Adam more and more perceiving his fallen condition heavily bewails, rejects the condolement of Eve; she persists and at length appeases him: then to evade the curse likely to fall on their offspring, proposes to Adam violent ways which he approves not, but conceiving better hope, puts her in mind of the late promise made them, that her seed should be revenged on the serpent, and exhorts her with him to seek peace of the offended deity, by repentance and supplication.

Meanwhile the heinous and despiteful act
Of Satan done in Paradise, and how
He in the serpent, had perverted Eve,
Her husband she, to taste the fatal fruit,
Was known in heaven; for what can scape the eye   5
Of God all-seeing, or deceive his heart
Omniscient, who in all things wise and just,
Hindered not Satan to attempt the mind
Of man, with strength entire, and free will armed,
Complete to have discovered and repulsed   10
Whatever wiles of foe or seeming friend.
For still they knew, and ought to have still remembered
The high injunction not to taste that fruit,
Whoever tempted; which they not obeying,
Incurred, what could they less, the penalty,   15
And manifold in sin, deserved to fall.
Up into heaven from Paradise in haste
The angelic guards ascended, mute and sad
For man, for of his state by this they knew,
Much wondering how the subtle fiend had stolen   20
Entrance unseen.   Soon as the unwelcome news

---

[1] One copy of second edition reads 'met.'

---

1. heinous: hatefully bad.   **7. Omniscient:** all-knowing.   **16. manifold:** many times.
20 ff. Only the fallen angels were jealous of man, the loyal angels being most friendly towards him.

From earth arrived at heaven gate, displeased
All were who heard, dim sadness did not spare
That time celestial visages, yet mixed
With pity, violated not their bliss.   25
About the new-arrived, in multitudes
The ethereal people ran, to hear and know
How all befell: they towards the throne supreme
Accountable made haste to make appear
With righteous plea, their utmost vigilance,   30
And easily approved; when the most high
Eternal father from his secret cloud,
Amidst in thunder uttered thus his voice.
    'Assembled angels, and ye powers returned
From unsuccessful charge, be not dismayed,   35
Nor troubled at these tidings from the earth,
Which your sincerest care could not prevent,
Foretold so lately what would come to pass,
When first this tempter crossed the gulf from hell.
I told ye then he should prevail and speed   40
On his bad errand, man should be seduced
And flattered out of all, believing lies
Against his maker; no decree of mine
Concurring to necessitate his fall,
Or touch with lightest moment of impulse   45
His free will, to her own inclining left
In even scale.   But fallen he is, and now
What rests but that the mortal sentence pass
On his transgression, death denounced that day,
Which he presumes already vain and void,   50
Because not yet inflicted, as he feared,
By some immediate stroke; but soon shall find
Forbearance no acquittance ere day end.
Justice shall not return as bounty scorned.
But whom send I to judge them? whom but thee   55
Vicegerent Son, to thee I have transferred
All judgment whether in heaven, or earth, or hell.
Easy it may be seen that I intend
Mercy colleague with justice, sending thee
Man's friend, his mediator, his designed   60
Both ransom and redeemer voluntary,
And destined man himself to judge man fallen.'
    So spake the father, and, unfolding bright
Toward the right hand his glory, on the Son
Blazed forth unclouded deity; he full   65
Resplendent all his father manifest
Expressed, and thus divinely answered mild.
    'Father eternal, thine is to decree,
Mine both in heaven and earth to do thy will
Supreme, that thou in me thy son beloved   70
Mayest ever rest well pleased.   I go to judge

46. **her:** its.   59. **colleague:** join, a verb here.

On earth these thy transgressors, but thou knowest,
Whoever judged, the worst on me must light,
When time shall be, for so I undertook
Before thee; and not repenting, this obtain   75
Of right, that I may mitigate their doom
On me derived, yet I shall temper so
Justice with mercy, as may illustrate most
Them fully satisfied, and thee appease.
Attendance none shall need, nor train, where none   80
Are to behold the judgment, but the judged,
Those two; the third best absent is condemned,
Convict by flight, and rebel to all law
Conviction to the serpent none belongs.'
　　Thus saying, from his radiant seat he rose   85
Of high collateral glory: him thrones and powers,
Princedoms, and dominations ministrant
Accompanied to heaven gate, from whence
Eden and all the coast in prospect lay.
Down he descended straight; the speed of gods   90
Time counts not, though with swiftest minutes winged.
Now was the sun in western cadence low
From noon, and gentle airs due at their hour
To fan the earth now waked, and usher in
The evening cool when he from wrath more cool   95
Came the mild judge and intercessor both
To sentence man: the voice of God they heard
Now walking in the garden, by soft winds
Brought to their ears, while day declined, they heard,
And from his presence hid themselves among   100
The thickest trees, both man and wife, till God
Approaching, thus to Adam called aloud.
　　'Where art thou Adam, wont with joy to meet
My coming seen far off? I miss thee here,
Not pleased, thus entertained with solitude,   105
Where obvious duty erewhile appeared unsought:
Or come I less conspicuous, or what change
Absents thee, or what chance detains? Come forth.'
He came, and with him Eve, more loath, though first
To offend, discountenanced both, and discomposed;   110
Love was not in their looks, either to God
Or to each other, but apparent guilt,
And shame, and perturbation, and despair,
Anger, and obstinacy, and hate, and guile.
Whence Adam, faltering long, thus answered brief.   115
　　'I heard thee in the garden, and of thy voice
Afraid, being naked, hid myself.' To whom
The gracious judge without revile replied.
　　'My voice thou oft hast heard, and hast not feared,
But still rejoiced, how is it now become   120
So dreadful to thee? that thou art naked, who

92. **cadence**: falling, a noun.　　　103. **wont**: accustomed.

Hath told thee? hast thou eaten of the tree
Whereof I gave thee charge thou shouldst not eat?'
   To whom thus Adam sore beset replied.
'O heaven! in evil strait this day I stand   125
Before my judge, either to undergo
Myself the total crime, or to accuse
My other self, the partner of my life;
Whose failing, while her faith to me remains,
I should conceal, and not expose to blame   130
By my complaint; but strict necessity
Subdues me, and calamitous constraint
Lest on my head both sin and punishment,
However insupportable, be all
Devolved; though should I hold my peace, yet thou   135
Wouldst easily detect what I conceal.
This woman whom thou madest to be my help,
And gavest me as thy perfect gift, so good,
So fit, so acceptable, so divine,
That from her hand I could suspect no ill,   140
And what she did, whatever in itself,
Her doing seemed to justify the deed;
She gave me of the tree, and I did eat.'
   To whom the sovereign presence thus replied.
'Was she thy God, that her thou didst obey   145
Before his voice, or was she made thy guide,
Superior, or but equal, that to her
Thou didst resign thy manhood, and the place
Wherein God set thee above her made of thee,
And for thee, whose perfection far excelled   150
Hers in all real dignity: Adorned
She was indeed, and lovely to attract
Thy love, not thy subjection, and her gifts
Were such as under government well seemed,
Unseemly to bear rule, which was thy part   155
And person, hadst thou known thyself aright.'
   So having said, he thus to Eve in few:
'Say Woman, what is this which thou hast done?'
   To whom sad Eve with shame nigh overwhelmed,
Confessing soon, yet not before her judge   160
Bold or loquacious, thus abashed replied.
   'The serpent me beguiled and I did eat.'
   Which when the Lord God heard, without delay
To judgment he proceeded on the accused
Serpent though brute, unable to transfer   165
The guilt on him who made him instrument
Of mischief, and polluted from the end
Of his creation; justly then accursed,
As vitiated in nature: more to know
Concerned not man (since he no further knew)   170

168–69. **justly then accursed, as vitiated in nature:** Milton thought of this curse as destroying Satan's power, or, more strictly, as the beginning of its destruction.

Nor altered his offense; yet God at last
To Satan first in sin his doom applied,
Though in mysterious terms, judged as then best:
And on the serpent thus his curse let fall.
   'Because thou hast done this, thou art accursed   175
Above all cattle, each beast of the field;
Upon thy belly groveling thou shalt go,
And dust shalt eat all the days of thy life.
Between thee and the woman I will put
Enmity, and between thine and her seed;   180
Her seed shall bruise thy head, thou bruise his heel.'
   So spake this oracle, then verified
When Jesus son of Mary second Eve,
Saw Satan fall like lightning down from heaven,
Prince of the air; then rising from his grave   185
Spoiled principalities and powers, triumphed
In open show, and with ascension bright
Captivity led captive through the air,
The realm itself of Satan long usurped,
Whom he shall tread at last under our feet;   190
Even he who now foretold his fatal bruise,
And to the woman thus his sentence turned.
   'Thy sorrow I will greatly multiply
By thy conception; children thou shalt bring
In sorrow forth, and to thy husband's will   195
Thine shall submit, he over thee shall rule.'
   On Adam last thus judgment he pronounced.
'Because thou hast hearkened to the voice of thy wife,
And eaten of the tree concerning which
I charged thee, saying: Thou shalt not eat thereof,   200
Cursed is the ground for thy sake, thou in sorrow
Shalt eat thereof all the days of thy life;
Thorns also and thistles it shall bring thee forth
Unbid, and thou shalt eat the herb of the field,
In the sweat of thy face thou shalt eat bread,   205
Till thou return unto the ground, for thou
Out of the ground wast taken, know thy birth,
For dust thou art, and shalt to dust return.'
   So judged he man, both judge and saviour sent,
And the instant stroke of death denounced that day   210
Removed far off; then pitying how they stood
Before him naked to the air, that now
Must suffer change, disdained not to begin
Thenceforth the form of servant to assume,
As when he washed his servants' feet so now   215
As father of his family he clad
Their nakedness with skins of beasts, or slain,
Or as the snake with youthful coat repaid;
And thought not much to clothe his enemies:
Nor he their outward only with the skins   220

173. **mysterious terms:** we are not told exactly what was the curse that was laid on Satan.

Of beasts, but inward nakedness, much more
Opprobrious, with his robe of righteousness,
Arraying covered from his father's sight.
To him with swift ascent he up returned,
Into his blissful bosom reassumed   225
In glory as of old, to him appeased
All, though all-knowing, what had passed with man
Recounted, mixing intercession sweet.
Meanwhile ere thus was sinned and judged on earth,
Within the gates of hell sat sin and death,   230
In counterview within the gates, that now
Stood open wide, belching outrageous flame
Far into chaos, since the fiend passed through,
Sin opening, who thus now to death began.
   'O son, why sit we here each other viewing   235
Idly, while Satan our great author thrives
In other worlds, and happier seat provides
For us his offspring dear? It cannot be
But that success attends him; if mishap,
Ere this he had returned, with fury driven   240
By his avengers, since no place like this
Can fit his punishment, or their revenge.
Methinks I feel new strength within me rise,
Wings growing, and dominion given me large
Beyond this deep; whatever draws me on,   245
Or sympathy, or some connatural force
Powerful at greatest distance to unite
With secret amity things of like kind
By secretest conveyance.   Thou my shade
Inseparable must with me along: 250
For death from sin no power can separate.
But lest the difficulty of passing back
Stay his return perhaps over this gulf
Impassable, impervious, let us try
Adventurous work, yet to thy power and mine   255
Not unagreeable, to found a path
Over this main from hell to that new world
Where Satan now prevails, a monument
Of merit high to all the infernal host,
Easing their passage hence, for intercourse,   260
Of transmigration, as their lot shall lead.
Nor can I miss the way, so strongly drawn
By this new felt attraction and instinct.'
   Whom thus the meager shadow answered soon.
'Go whither fate and inclination strong   265
Leads thee, I shall not lag behind, nor err
The way, thou leading, such a scent I draw
Of carnage, prey innumerable, and taste

241. **avengers:** first edition prints 'avenger' and second edition 'avengers,' which must be adopted to agree with 'their' in next line.

257. **this main:** this expanse [of chaos].

The savor of death from all things there that live:
Nor shall I to the work thou enterprisest　　　　　270
Be wanting, but afford thee equal aid,'
　　So saying, with delight he snuffed the smell
Of mortal change on earth.　As when a flock
Of ravenous fowl, though many a league remote,
Against the day of battle, to a field,　　　　　275
Where armies lie encamped, come flying, lured
With scent of living carcasses designed
For death, the following day, in bloody fight.
So scented the grim feature, and upturned
His nostril wide into the murky air,　　　　　280
Sagacious of his quarry from so far.
Then both from out hell gates into the waste
Wide anarchy of chaos damp and dark
Flew diverse, and with power (their power was great)
Hovering upon the waters; what they met　　　　285
Solid or slimy, as in raging sea
Tossed up and down, together crowded drove
From each side shoaling towards the mouth of hell.
As when two polar winds blowing adverse
Upon the Cronian sea, together drive　　　　　290
Mountains of ice, that stop the imagined way
Beyond Petsora eastward, to the rich
Cathaian coast.　The aggregated soil
Death with his mace petrific, cold and dry,
As with a trident smote, and fixed as firm　　　295
As Delos floating once; the rest his look
Bound with Gorgonian rigor not to move,
And with asphaltic slime; broad as the gate,
Deep to the roots of hell the gathered beach
They fastened, and the mole immense wrought on　　300
Over the foaming deep high arched, a bridge
Of length prodigious joining to the wall
Immovable of this now fenceless world
Forfeit to death; from hence a passage broad,
Smooth, easy, inoffensive down to hell.　　　　305
So, if great things to small may be compared,
Xerxes, the liberty of Greece to yoke,
From Susa his Memnonian palace high
Came to the sea, and over Hellespont

279. **grim feature:** grim shape.
290. **Cronian sea:** Arctic Ocean.
291. **the imagined way:** the northeast passage to China.
292. **Petsora:** a town in northern Russia on the Arctic Ocean.
293. **Cathaian coast:** coast of China.
296. **Delos:** originally one of the Cyclades Islands in the Aegean Sea which tradition said was originally a floating island.
297. **Gorgonian rigor:** petrified rigor, as the Gorgons turned all to stone who beheld their faces.
307. **Xerxes:** the Persian king who warred against Greece.
308. **Susa:** Xerxes' capital.

Bridging his way, Europe with Asia joined,   310
And scourged with many a stroke the indignant waves.
Now had they brought the work by wondrous art
Pontifical, a ridge of pendent rock
Over the vexed abyss, following the track
Of Satan, to the selfsame place where he   315
First lighted from his wing, and landed safe
From out of chaos to the outside bare
Of this round world: with pins of adamant
And chains they made all fast, too fast they made
And durable; and now in little space   320
The confines met of empyrean heaven
And of this world, and on the left hand hell
With long reach interposed; three several ways
In sight, to each of these three places led.
And now their way to earth they had descried,   325
To Paradise first tending, when behold
Satan in likeness of an angel bright
Betwixt the Centaur and the Scorpion steering
His zenith, while the sun in Aries rose:
Disguised he came, but those his children dear   330
Their parent soon discerned, though in disguise.
He after Eve seduced, unminded slunk
Into the wood fast by, and changing shape
To observe the sequel, saw his guileful act
By Eve, though all unwitting, seconded   335
Upon her husband, saw their shame that sought
Vain covertures; but when he saw descend
The Son of God to judge them terrified
He fled, not hoping to escape, but shun
The present, fearing guilty what his wrath   340
Might suddenly inflict; that past, returned
By night, and listening where the hapless pair
Sat in their sad discourse, and various plaint,
Thence gathered his own doom, which understood
Not instant, but of future time. With joy   345
And tidings fraught, to hell he now returned,
And at the brink of chaos, near the foot
Of this new wondrous pontifice, unhoped
Met who to meet him came, his offspring dear.
Great joy was at their meeting, and at sight   350
Of that stupendous bridge his joy increased.
Long he admiring stood, till sin, his fair

310. **Bridging:** the famous bridge of boats mentioned by Herodotus, *History* VII:36.

313. **Pontifical:** Milton probably used this as a double-edged word meaning first 'pertaining to bridges,' and then as a hidden meaning, the cunning art of the Papists, 'wondrous art pontifical.'

322. **and on the left hand hell:** sin and death are now at the same point in the universe at which Satan first stood on the outer shell of 'this pendent world,' the spot at which the golden stairs reached down to this world, and from which the 'quick descent' led, through the spheres, to the earth. Standing there, looking towards the solar system, hell was on their left. The location of hell on the left was probably, as a definite direction, due to the location of hell to the left of the altar in church performances of miracles and moralities, and the later location of the mouth of hell to the actors' left-hand side of the stage.

Enchanting daughter, thus the silence broke.
  'O parent, these are thy magnific deeds,
Thy trophies, which thou viewest as not thine own,   355
Thou art their author and prime architect:
For I no sooner in my heart divined,
My heart, which by a secret harmony
Still moves with thine, joined in connection sweet,
That thou on earth hadst prospered, which thy looks   360
Now also evidence, but straight I felt
Though distant from thee worlds between, yet felt
That I must after thee with this thy son;
Such fatal consequence unites us three:
Hell could no longer hold us in her bounds,   365
Nor this unvoyageable gulf obscure
Detain from following thy illustrious track.
Thou hast achieved our liberty, confined
Within hell gates till now, thou us empowered
To fortify thus far, and overlay   370
With this portentous bridge the dark abyss.
Thine now is all this world, thy virtue hath won
What thy hands builded not, thy wisdom gained
With odds what war hath lost, and fully avenged
Our foil in heaven; here thou shalt monarch reign,   375
There didst not; there let him still victor sway,
As battle hath adjudged, from this new world
Retiring, by his own doom alienated,
And henceforth monarchy with thee divide
Of all things parted by the empyreal bounds,   380
His quadrature, from thy orbicular world,
Or try thee now more dangerous to his throne.'
  Whom thus the prince of darkness answered glad.
'Fair daughter, and thou son and grandchild both,
High proof ye now have given to be the race   385
Of Satan (for I glory in the name,
Antagonist of heaven's almighty king)
Amply have merited of me, of all
The infernal empire, that so near heaven's door
Triumphal with triumphal act have met,   390
Mine with this glorious work, and made one realm
Hell and this world, one realm, one continent
Of easy thoroughfare. Therefore while I
Descend through darkness, on your road with ease
To my associate powers, them to acquaint   395
With these successes, and with them rejoice,
You two this way, among these numerous orbs
All yours, right down to Paradise descend;
There dwell and reign in bliss, thence on the earth
Dominion exercise and in the air,   400
Chiefly on man, sole lord of all declared,

371. **portentous bridge**: monstrous, prodigious, wonderful bridge.
374. **With odds**: with advantage.   381. **quadrature**: a square.

Him first make sure your thrall, and lastly kill.
My substitutes I send ye, and create
Plenipotent on earth, of matchless might
Issuing from me: on your joint vigor now   405
My hold of this new kingdom all depends,
Through sin to death exposed by my exploit.
If your joint power prevails, the affairs of hell
No detriment need fear, go and be strong.'
    So saying he dismissed them, they with speed   410
Their course through thickest constellations held
Spreading their bane; the blasted stars looked wan,
And planets, planet-struck, real eclipse
Then suffered.   The other way Satan went down
The causey to hell-gate; on either side   415
Disparted chaos over built exclaimed,
And with rebounding surge the bars assailed,
That scorned his indignation: through the gate,
Wide open and unguarded, Satan passed,
And all about found desolate; for those   420
Appointed to sit there, had left their charge,
Flown to the upper world; the rest were all
Far to the inland retired, about the walls
Of Pandemonium, city and proud seat
Of Lucifer, so by allusion called,   425
Of that bright star to Satan paragoned.
There kept their watch the legions, while the grand
In council sat, solicitous what chance
Might intercept their emperor sent, so he
Departing gave command, and they observed.   430
As when the Tartar from his Russian foe
By Astracan over the snowy plains
Retires, or Bactrian Sophi from the horns
Of Turkish crescent, leaves all waste beyond
The realm of Aladule, in his retreat   435
To Tauris or Casbeen.   So these the late
Heaven-banished host, left desert utmost hell
Many a dark league, reduced in careful watch
Round their metropolis, and now expecting
Each hour their great adventurer from the search   440
Of foreign worlds: he through the midst unmarked,
In show plebeian angel militant
Of lowest order, passed; and from the door
Of that Plutonian hall, invisible
Ascended his high throne, which under state   445

404. **Plenipotent:** invested with full power.
415. **causey:** raised way; here, the bridge.
426. **paragoned:** compared.   Frequent in Shakespeare.
433. **Bactrian Sophi:** Persian shah.   433–34. **horns of Turkish crescent:** Turkish armies.
435. **Aladule:** greater Armenia.
436. **Tauris or Casbeen:** towns in the north of Persia.
438. **reduced:** led back.   445. **state:** canopy.

Of richest texture spread, at the upper end
Was placed in regal luster.   Down a while
He sat, and round about him saw unseen:
At last as from a cloud his fulgent head
And shape star bright appeared, or brighter, clad   450
With what permissive glory since his fall
Was left him, or false glitter: All amazed
At that so sudden blaze the Stygian throng
Bent their aspect, and whom they wished beheld,
Their mighty chief returned: loud was the acclaim: 455
Forth rushed in haste the great consulting peers,
Raised from their dark divan, and with like joy
Congratulant approached him, who with hand
Silence, and with these words attention won.
   'Thrones, dominations, princedoms, virtues, powers,   460
For in possession such, not only of right,
I call ye and declare ye now, returned
Successful beyond hope, to lead ye forth
Triumphant out of this infernal pit
Abominable, accursed, the house of woe,   465
And dungeon of our tyrant: Now possess,
As lords, a spacious world, to our native heaven
Little inferior, by my adventure hard
With peril great achieved.   Long were to tell
What I have done, what suffered, with what pain   470
Voyaged the unreal, vast, unbounded deep
Of horrible confusion, over which
By sin and death a broad way now is paved
To expedite your glorious march; but I
Toiled out my uncouth passage, forced to ride   475
The untractable abyss, plunged in the womb
Of unoriginal night and chaos wild,
That jealous of their secrets fiercely opposed
My journey strange, with clamorous uproar
Protesting fate supreme; thence how I found   480
The new created world, which fame in heaven
Long had foretold, a fabric wonderful
Of absolute perfection, therein man
Placed in a paradise, by our exile
Made happy: Him by fraud I have seduced   485
From his creator, and the more to increase
Your wonder, with an apple; he thereat
Offended, worth your laughter, hath given up
Both his beloved man and all his world,
To sin and death a prey, and so to us,   490
Without our hazard, labor, or alarm,

449. **fulgent**: shining.

451–52. **what permissive glory since his fall was left him**: Satan has greatly degenerated in appearance
since he left on his mission.

475. **uncouth**: unknown, and also rough.

477. **unoriginal**: having no originator, unoriginated, uncreated.

To range in, and to dwell, and over man
To rule, as over all he should have ruled.
True is, me also he hath judged, or rather
Me not, but the brute serpent in whose shape 495
Man I deceived: that which to me belongs,
Is enmity, which he will put between
Me and mankind; I am to bruise his heel;
His seed, when is not set, shall bruise my head:
A world who would not purchase with a bruise, 500
Or much more grievous pain?   Ye have the account
Of my performance: What remains, ye gods,
But up and enter now into full bliss.'
    So having said, a while he stood, expecting
Their universal shout and high applause 505
To fill his ear, when contrary he hears
On all sides, from innumerable tongues
A dismal universal hiss, the sound
Of public scorn; he wondered, but not long
Had leisure, wondering at himself now more; 510
His visage drawn he felt to sharp and spare,
His arms clung to his ribs, his legs entwining
Each other, till supplanted down he fell
A monstrous serpent on his belly prone,
Reluctant, but in vain, a greater power 515
Now ruled him, punished in the shape he sinned,
According to his doom: he would have spoke,
But hiss for hiss returned with forked tongue
To forked tongue, for now were all transformed
Alike, to serpents all as accessories 520
To his bold riot: dreadful was the din
Of hissing through the hall, thick swarming now
With complicated monsters head and tail,
Scorpion and asp, and Amphisbaena dire,
Cerastes horned, Hydrus, and Ellops drear, 525
And Dipsas (not so thick swarmed once the soil
Bedropped with blood of Gorgon, or the isle
Ophiusa) but still greatest he the midst,
Now dragon grown, larger than whom the sun
Engendered in the Pythian vale on slime, 530
Huge Python, and his power no less he seemed
Above the rest still to retain; they all
Him followed issuing forth to the open field,
Where all yet left of that revolted rout
Heaven-fallen, in station stood or just array, 535
Sublime with expectation when to see
In triumph issuing forth their glorious chief;

521. **his bold riot**: rebellion.
521-28. Note Milton's attempt through the sound of words to secure a sound picture of what was taking place.
524-28. A list of snakes and serpents.
529-31. Referring to Python, born from the slime after the flood.   Cf. Ovid, *Metamorphoses* I:434 ff.

They saw, but other sight instead, a crowd
Of ugly serpents; horror on them fell,
And horrid sympathy; for what they saw, 540
They felt themselves now changing; down their arms,
Down fell both spear and shield, down they as fast,
And the dire hiss renewed, and the dire form
Catched by contagion, like in punishment,
As in their crime. Thus was the applause they meant, 545
Turned to exploding hiss, triumph to shame
Cast on themselves from their own mouths. There stood
A grove hard by, sprung up with this their change,
His will who reigns above, to aggravate
Their penance, laden with fair fruit, like that 550
Which grew in Paradise, the bait of Eve
Used by the tempter: on that prospect strange
Their earnest eyes they fixed, imagining
For one forbidden tree a multitude
Now risen, to work them further woe or shame; 555
Yet parched with scalding thirst and hunger fierce,
Though to delude them sent, could not abstain,
But on they rolled in heaps, and up the trees
Climbing, sat thicker than the snaky locks
That curled Megaera: greedily they plucked 560
The fruitage fair to sight, like that which grew
Near that bituminous lake where Sodom flamed;
This more delusive, not the touch, but taste
Deceived; they fondly thinking to allay
Their appetite with gust, instead of fruit 565
Chewed bitter ashes, which the offended taste
With spattering noise rejected: oft they assayed,
Hunger and thirst constraining, drugged as oft,
With hatefulest disrelish writhed their jaws
With soot and cinders filled; so oft they fell 570
Into the same illusion, not as man
Whom they triumphed once lapsed. Thus were they plagued
And worn with famine, long and ceaseless hiss,
Till their lost shape, permitted, they resumed,
Yearly enjoined, some say, to undergo 575
This annual humbling certain numbered days,
To dash their pride, and joy for man seduced.
However some tradition they dispersed
Among the heathen of their purchase got,
And fabled how the serpent, whom they called 580
Ophion with Eurynome, the wide-

560. **Megaera:** one of the Eumenides or Furies, the punishers of crime, who had serpents twined in her hair.

561–62. The apples of Asphaltis, fair to outward view, were ashes within. They grew by the Lake of Asphalt, the Dead Sea.

581. **Ophion:** one of the Titans and first ruler of Olympus.   **Eurynome:** his wife.

581–82. **the wide-encroaching Eve:** unless this means, as Newton suggested, that Eve 'encroached' when she dominated her husband, I suspect that it is a misprint that can never be understood. Why does

Encroaching Eve perhaps, had first the rule
Of high Olympus, thence by Saturn driven
And Ops, ere yet Dictaean Jove was born.
Meanwhile in Paradise the hellish pair   585
Too soon arrived, sin there in power before,
Once actual, now in body, and to dwell
Habitual habitant; behind her death
Close following pace for pace, not mounted yet
On his pale horse: to whom sin thus began.   590
    'Second of Satan sprung, all conquering death,
What thinkest thou of our empire now, though earned
With travail difficult, not better far
Than still at hell's dark threshold to have sat watch,
Unnamed, undreaded, and thyself half starved?'   595
    Whom thus the sin-born monster answered soon.
'To me, who with eternal famine pine,
Alike is hell, or Paradise, or heaven,
There best, where most with ravin I may meet;
Which here, though plenteous, all too little seems   600
To stuff this maw, this vast unhide-bound corpse.'
    To whom the incestuous mother thus replied.
'Thou therefore on these herbs, and fruits, and flowers
Feed first, on each beast next, and fish, and fowl,
No homely morsels, and whatever thing   605
The scythe of time mows down, devour unspared,
Till I in man residing through the race,
His thoughts, his looks, words, actions all infect,
And season him thy last and sweetest prey.'
    This said, they both betook them several ways,   610
Both to destroy, or unimmortal make
All kinds, and for destruction to mature
Sooner or later; which the almighty seeing,
From his transcendent seat the saints among,
To those bright orders uttered thus his voice.   615
    'See with what heat these dogs of hell advance
To waste and havoc yonder world, which I
So fair and good created, and had still
Kept in that state, had not the folly of man
Let in these wasteful furies, who impute   620
Folly to me, so doth the prince of hell
And his adherents, that with so much ease
I suffer them to enter and possess
A place so heavenly, and conniving seem
To gratify my scornful enemies,   625

it occur here? Milton might have meant that Eurynome was another form of the Eve story, but only speculation is possible here.
    584. **Ops**: wife of Saturn.   **Dictaean Jove**: Cretan Jove.
    590. **his pale horse**: cf. *Revelation* 6:8.   593. **travail**: labor, work, struggle.
    597. **pine**: suffer.   599. **ravin**: rapine, rapacity.   For death's ravages cf. *El.* III:16–30.
    615 ff. The most difficult explanation of God's 'ways to men' in the poem; indeed, the explanation on
whose success or failure rests the success or failure of the poem.

That laugh, as if transported with some fit
Of passion, I to them had quitted all,
At random yielded up to their misrule;
And know not that I called and drew them thither
My hell-hounds, to lick up the draff and filth   630
Which man's polluting sin with taint hath shed
On what was pure, till crammed and gorged, nigh burst
With sucked and glutted offal, at one sling
Of thy victorious arm, well-pleasing Son,
Both sin, and death, and yawning grave at last   635
Through chaos hurled, obstruct the mouth of hell
Forever, and seal up his ravenous jaws.
Then heaven and earth renewed shall be made pure
To sanctity that shall receive no stain:
Till then the curse pronounced on both precedes.'   640
    He ended, and the heavenly audience loud
Sung hallelujah, as the sound of seas,
Through multitude that sung: 'Just are thy ways,
Righteous are thy decrees on all thy works;
Who can extenuate thee?   Next, to the Son,   645
Destined restorer of mankind, by whom
New heaven and earth shall to the ages rise,
Or down from heaven descend.'   Such was their song,
While the creator calling forth by name
His mighty angels gave them several charge,   650
As sorted best with present things.   The sun
Had first his precept so to move, so shine,
As might affect the earth with cold and heat
Scarce tolerable, and from the north to call
Decrepit winter, from the south to bring   655
Solstitial summer's heat.   To the blanc moon
Her office they prescribed, to the other five
Their planetary motions and aspects,
In sextile, square, and trine, and opposite,
Of noxious efficacy, and when to join   660
In synod unbenign, and taught the fixed
Their influence malignant when to shower,
Which of them rising with the sun, or falling,
Should prove tempestuous: To the winds they set
Their corners, when with bluster to confound   665
Sea, air, and shore, the thunder when to roll
With terror through the dark aerial hall.
Some say he bid his angels turn askance

651 ff. The changes in nature that were wrought by the loyal angels, at God's command, after the fall of man.

656. **blanc moon**: white(?) moon.   Cf. III:48.   The French word *blanc*.

668–78. Milton assumes that before the fall, the 'ecliptic,' or the sun's path, was in the same plane as the earth's equator, hence there were no seasons, but perpetual 'spring.'   After the fall, the plane of the sun's orbit and the plane of the earth's equator intersected at an angle 'twice ten degrees and more,' actually about twenty-three and one-half degrees.   Milton says that this was brought about in one of two ways. Either the sun remained as it was and the axis from pole to pole of the earth was tilted to such an angle with the sun's orbit; or the earth remained as it was and the orbit of the sun was tilted.   He then traces the

The poles of earth twice ten degrees and more
From the sun's axle; they with labor pushed
Oblique the centric globe: Some say the sun   670
Was bid turn reins from the equinoctial road
Like distant breadth to Taurus with the seven
Atlantic sisters, and the Spartan twins
Up to the tropic Crab; thence down amain   675
By Leo and the Virgin and the Scales,
As deep as Capricorn, to bring in change
Of seasons to each clime; else had the spring
Perpetual smiled on earth with vernant flowers,
Equal in days and nights, except to those   680
Beyond the polar circles; to them day
Had unbenighted shone, while the low sun
To recompense his distance, in their sight
Had rounded still the horizon, and not known
Or east or west, which had forbid the snow   685
From cold Estotiland, and south as far
Beneath Magellan.   At that tasted fruit
The sun, as from Thyestean banquet, turned
His course intended; else how had the world
Inhabited, though sinless, more than now,   690
Avoided pinching cold and scorching heat?
These changes in the heavens, though slow, produced
Like change on sea and land, sideral blast,
Vapor, and mist, and exhalation hot,
Corrupt and pestilent: Now from the north   695
Of Norumbega, and the Samoed shore
Bursting their brazen dungeon, armed with ice
And snow and hail and stormy gust and flaw,
Boreas and Caecias and Argestes loud
And Thrascias rend the woods and seas upturn;   700
With adverse blasts upturns them from the south
Notus and Afer black with thunderous clouds
From Sierra Leone; thwart of these as fierce

orbit of the sun through the zodiac after the change.   Taurus, the 'Atlantic Sisters' (the Pleiades), the Gemini (the 'Spartan twins,' 'Castor and Pollux'), the 'Tropic Crab,' Leo, 'The Virgin,' the Scales, and Capricorn constitute eight of the twelve signs or positions in the zodiac.

671. **the centric globe:** the earth, the center of the Ptolemaic system.

679. **vernant:** vernal, belonging to the spring of the year.

686. **Estotiland:** a fabulous island near the northeast part of North America.   A cold but richly endowed country, especially in precious metals.

687. **Magellan:** the Straits of Magellan at the southern tip of South America.

688. **Thyestean banquet:** the sun is said to have turned aside from a banquet that Atreus set before Thyestes consisting of the flesh of the latter's two sons.

696. **Norumbega:** Canada and the northeast states of this country.   **Samoed shore:** northeast shore of Siberia.

699–700. **Boreas ... Caecias ... Argestes ... Thrascias:** the north wind, the northeast wind, the north-west wind, the north-northwest wind, respectively.

702. **Notus and Afer:** the south wind and the southwest wind.

703. **Sierra Leone:** on the west coast of Africa.

Forth rush the Levant and the Ponent winds
Eurus and Zephyr with their lateral noise,   705
Sirocco, and Libecchio.   Thus began
Outrage from lifeless things; but discord first
Daughter of sin, among the irrational,
Death introduced through fierce antipathy:
Beast now with beast gan war, and fowl with fowl,   710
And fish with fish; to graze the herb all leaving,
Devoured each other; nor stood much in awe
Of man, but fled him, or with countenance grim
Glared on him passing: these were from without
The growing miseries, which Adam saw   715
Already in part, though hid in gloomiest shade,
To sorrow abandoned, but worse felt within,
And in a troubled sea of passion tossed,
Thus to disburden sought with sad complaint.
  'O miserable of happy! is this the end   720
Of this new glorious world, and me so late
The glory of that glory, who now become
Accursed of blessed, hide me from the face
Of God, whom to behold was then my height
Of happiness: yet well, if here would end   725
The misery, I deserved it, and would bear
My own deservings; but this will not serve;
All that I eat or drink, or shall beget,
Is propagated curse.   O voice once heard
Delightfully, "Increase and multiply,"   730
Now death to hear! for what can I increase
Or multiply, but curses on my head?
Who of all ages to succeed, but feeling
The evil on him brought by me, will curse
My head, "Ill fare our ancestor impure,   735
For this we may thank Adam;" but his thanks
Shall be the execration; so besides
Mine own that bide upon me, all from me
Shall with a fierce reflux on me redound,
On me as on their natural center light   740
Heavy, though in their place.   O fleeting joys
Of Paradise, dear bought with lasting woes!
Did I request thee, maker, from my clay
To mold me man, did I solicit thee
From darkness to promote me, or here place   745
In this delicious garden? as my will

704. **the Levant and the Ponent winds:** rising and setting of the sun; hence, east and west winds.

705. **Eurus and Zephyr:** the names of those winds.   **lateral noise:** accompanying sounds, i.e., of the blowing winds.

706. **Sirocco, and Libecchio:** these names are Italian, at the end of a list of classical names.

739. **redound:** flow back.

744 ff. This is the most important speech Adam makes so far as the main aim of the poem is concerned. He attempts 'to justify the ways of God to men,' and upon our credence of his words, extended or withheld, very largely depends the success or failure of the moral purpose of the poem.

Concurred not to my being, it were but right
And equal to reduce me to my dust,
Desirous to resign, and render back
All I received, unable to perform   750
Thy terms too hard, by which I was to hold
The good I sought not.   To the loss of that,
Sufficient penalty, why hast thou added
The sense of endless woes? inexplicable
Thy justice seems; yet to say truth, too late,   755
I thus contest; then should have been refused
Those terms whatever, when they were proposed:
Thou didst accept them; wilt thou enjoy the good,
Then cavil the conditions? and though God
Made thee without thy leave, what if thy son   760
Prove disobedient, and reproved, retort,
"Wherefore didst thou beget me?   I sought it not"
Wouldst thou admit for his contempt of thee
That proud excuse? yet him not thy election,
But natural necessity begot.   765
God made thee of choice his own, and of his own
To serve him, thy reward was of his grace,
Thy punishment then justly is at his will.
Be it so, for I submit, his doom is fair,
That dust I am, and shall to dust return: 770
O welcome hour whenever! why delays
His hand to execute what his decree
Fixed on this day? why do I overlive,
Why am I mocked with death, and lengthened out
To deathless pain? how gladly would I meet   775
Mortality my sentence, and be earth
Insensible, how glad would lay me down
As in my mother's lap? there I should rest
And sleep secure; his dreadful voice no more
Would thunder in my ears, no fear of worse   780
To me and to my offspring would torment me
With cruel expectation.   Yet one doubt
Pursues me still, lest all I cannot die,
Lest that pure breath of life, the spirit of man
Which God inspired, cannot together perish   785
With this corporeal clod; then in the grave,
Or in some other dismal place who knows
But I shall die a living death?   O thought
Horrid, if true! yet why? it was but breath
Of life that sinned; what dies but what had life   790
And sin? the body properly hath neither.
All of me then shall die: let this appease
The doubt, since human reach no further knows.

---

748. **equal**: fair, just.   769. **his doom is fair**: Adam accepts his situation as just.
771 ff. Adam longs for death and the end of his sufferings.

782 ff. Adam insists on the non-survival of the soul of bodily death.   A sect called the Mortalists held this belief in Milton's day and earlier.   These sentiments, expressed by Adam, are really Milton's own.

For though the Lord of all be infinite,
Is his wrath also? be it, man is not so,   795
But mortal doomed.   How can he exercise
Wrath without end on man whom death must end?
Can he make deathless death? that were to make
Strange contradiction, which to God himself
Impossible is held, as argument   800
Of weakness, not of power.   Will he, draw out,
For anger's sake, finite to infinite
In punished man, to satisfy his rigor
Satisfied never; that were to extend
His sentence beyond dust and nature's law,   805
By which all causes else according still
To the reception of their matter act,
Not to the extent of their own sphere.   But say
That death be not one stroke, as I supposed,
Bereaving sense, but endless misery   810
From this day onward, which I feel begun
Both in me, and without me, and so last
To perpetuity; ay me, that fear
Comes thundering back with dreadful revolution
On my defenseless head; both death and I   815
Am found eternal, and incorporate both,
Nor I on my part single, in me all
Posterity stands cursed: Fair patrimony
That I must leave ye, sons; O were I able
To waste it all myself, and leave ye none!   820
So disinherited how would ye bless
Me now your curse!   Ah, why should all mankind
For one man's fault thus guiltless be condemned,
If guiltless?   But from me what can proceed,
But all corrupt, both mind and will depraved,   825
Not to do only, but to will the same
With me? how can they then acquitted stand
In sight of God?   Him after all disputes
Forced I absolve: all my evasions vain,
And reasonings, though through mazes, lead me still   830
But to my own conviction: first and last
On me, me only, as the source and spring
Of all corruption, all the blame lights due;
So might the wrath.   Fond wish! couldst thou support
That burden heavier than the earth to bear   835
Than all the world much heavier, though divided

808 ff. Death may be a slow process of disintegration.   Note the extreme pessimism of the human pair's speeches from here on in the poem until help from heaven aids them to compose their minds and souls.

822 ff. The doctrine of original sin:

> 'In Adam's fall
> We sinned all.'

827. then: this word was inserted in 1674, and is lacking in the first edition.   Robert Bridges (*Milton's Prosody* [Oxford: University Press, 1921], p. 5) says 'then' was put in in 1674 to make the line a ten-syllable one.

With that bad woman?   Thus what thou desirest
And what thou fearest, alike destroys all hope
Of refuge, and concludes thee miserable
Beyond all past example and future, 840
To Satan only like both crime and doom.
O conscience, into what abyss of fears
And horrors hast thou driven me; out of which
I find no way, from deep to deeper plunged!'
  Thus Adam to himself lamented loud 845
Through the still night, not now, as ere man fell,
Wholesome and cool, and mild, but with black air
Accompanied, with damps and dreadful gloom,
Which to his evil conscience represented
All things with double terror: On the ground 850
Outstretched he lay, on the cold ground, and oft
Cursed his creation, death as oft accused
Of tardy execution, since denounced
The day of his offense.   'Why comes not death,'
Said he, 'with one thrice acceptable stroke 855
To end me?   Shall truth fail to keep her word,
Justice divine not hasten to be just?
But death comes not at call, justice divine
Mends not her slowest pace for prayers or cries.
O woods, O fountains, hillocks, dales and bowers, 860
With other echo late I taught your shades
To answer, and resound far other song.'
Whom thus afflicted when sad Eve beheld,
Desolate where she sat, approaching nigh,
Soft words to his fierce passion she assayed: 865
But her with stern regard he thus repelled.
 'Out of my sight, thou serpent, that name best
Befits thee with him leagued, thyself as false
And hateful; nothing wants, but that thy shape,
Like his, and color serpentine may show 870
Thy inward fraud, to warn all creatures from thee
Henceforth; lest that too heavenly form, pretended
To hellish falsehood, snare them.   But for thee
I had persisted happy, had not thy pride
And wandering vanity, when least was safe, 875
Rejected my forewarning, and disdained
Not to be trusted, longing to be seen
Though by the devil himself, him overweening
To overreach, but with the serpent meeting
Fooled and beguiled, by him thou, I by thee, 880
To trust thee from my side, imagined wise,

---

850 ff. Cf. Job's cursing under similar circumstances.

860–62. Adam had been a poet and had sung to all nature, and, like Orpheus, had taught nature to echo his song.

866 ff. This denunciation of Eve belongs with other famous attacks on woman.   It is a headlong, grim, one-sided, heedless, bitter denunciation of woman.   I read it as one of the most vividly personal utterances in all Milton's works.   It is the direct result of the whole disastrous affair with Mary Powell.

Constant, mature, proof against all assaults,
And understood not all was but a show
Rather than solid virtue, all but a rib
Crooked by nature, bent, as now appears,   885
More to the part sinister from me drawn,
Well if thrown out, as supernumerary
To my just number found.   O why did God,
Creator wise, that peopled highest heaven
With spirits masculine, create at last   890
This novelty on earth, this fair defect
Of nature, and not fill the world at once
With men as angels without feminine,
Or find some other way to generate
Mankind? this mischief had not then befallen,   895
And more that shall befall, innumerable
Disturbances on earth through female snares,
And strait conjunction with this sex: for either
He never shall find out fit mate, but such
As some misfortune brings him, or mistake,   900
Or whom he wishes most shall seldom gain
Through her perverseness, but shall see her gained
By a far worse, or if she love, withheld
By parents, or his happiest choice too late
Shall meet, already linked and wedlock-bound   905
To a fell adversary, his hate or shame:
Which infinite calamity shall cause
To human life, and household peace confound.'
    He added not, and from her turned, but Eve
Not so repulsed, with tears that ceased not flowing,   910
And tresses all disordered, at his feet
Fell humble, and embracing them, besought
His peace, and thus proceeded in her plaint.
    'Forsake me not thus, Adam, witness heaven
What love sincere, and reverence in my heart   915
I bear thee, and unwitting have offended,
Unhappily deceived; thy suppliant
I beg, and clasp thy knees; bereave me not,
Whereon I live, thy gentle looks, thy aid,
Thy counsel in this uttermost distress,   920
My only strength and stay: forlorn of thee,
Whither shall I betake me, where subsist?
While yet we live, scarce one short hour perhaps,
Between us two let there be peace, both joining,
As joined in injuries, one enmity   925
Against a foe by doom express assigned us,
That cruel serpent: On me exercise not
Thy hatred for this misery befallen,
On me already lost, me than thyself
More miserable; both have sinned, but thou   930

898 ff. Note how closely the remainder of Adam's speech portrays Milton's own personal experiences with women.

Against God only, I against God and thee,
And to the place of judgment will return,
There with my cries importune heaven, that all
The sentence from thy head removed may light
On me, sole cause to thee of all this woe,
Me me only just object of his ire.'   935
   She ended weeping, and her lowly plight,
Immovable till peace obtained from fault
Acknowledged and deplored, in Adam wrought
Commiseration; soon his heart relented   940
Towards her, his life so late and sole delight,
Now at his feet submissive in distress,
Creature so fair his reconcilement seeking,
His counsel whom she had displeased, his aid;
As one disarmed, his anger all he lost,   945
And thus with peaceful words upraised her soon.
   'Unwary, and too desirous, as before,   .
So now of what thou knowest not, who desirest
The punishment all on thyself; alas,
Bear thine own first, ill able to sustain   950
His full wrath whose thou feelest as yet least part,
And my displeasure bearest so ill.   If prayers
Could alter high decrees, I to that place
Would speed before thee, and be louder heard,
That on my head all might be visited,   955
Thy frailty and infirmer sex forgiven,
To me committed and by me exposed.
But rise, let us no more contend, nor blame
Each other, blamed enough elsewhere, but strive
In offices of love, how we may lighten   960
Each other's burden in our share of woe;
Since this day's death denounced, if aught I see,
Will prove no sudden, but a slow-paced evil,
A long day's dying to augment our pain,
And to our seed (O hapless seed!) derived.'   965
   To whom thus Eve, recovering heart, replied.
'Adam, by sad experiment I know
How little weight my words with thee can find,
Found so erroneous, thence by just event
Found so unfortunate; nevertheless,   970
Restored by thee, vile as I am, to place
Of new acceptance, hopeful to regain
Thy love, the sole contentment of my heart
Living or dying, from thee I will not hide
What thoughts in my unquiet breast are risen,   975
Tending to some relief of our extremes,
Or end, though sharp and sad, yet tolerable,
As in our evils, and of easier choice.

947 ff. Note how quickly following Eve's generosity in assuming all the blame Adam responds in like vein.   The famous reconcilement follows that has been likened to the reconcilement of Milton with his first wife as she sought to return to him.

If care of our descent perplex us most,
Which must be born to certain woe, devoured   980
By death at last, and miserable it is
To be to others cause of misery,
Our own begotten, and of our loins to bring
Into this cursed world a woeful race,
That after wretched life must be at last   985
Food for so foul a monster, in thy power
It lies, yet ere conception to prevent
The race unblest, to being yet unbegot.
Childless thou art, childless remain:
So death shall be deceived his glut, and with us two 990
Be forced to satisfy his ravenous maw.
But if thou judge it hard and difficult,
Conversing, looking, loving, to abstain
From love's due rites, nuptial embraces sweet,
And with desire to languish without hope,   995
Before the present object languishing
With like desire, which would be misery
And torment less than none of what we dread,
Then both ourselves and seed at once to free
From what we fear for both, let us make short,   1000
Let us seek death, or he not found, supply
With our own hands his office on ourselves;
Why stand we longer shivering under fears,
That show no end but death, and have the power,
Of many ways to die the shortest choosing,   1005
Destruction with destruction to destroy.'
     She ended here, or vehement despair
Broke off the rest; so much of death her thoughts
Had entertained, as dyed her cheeks with pale.
But Adam with such counsel nothing swayed,   1010
To better hopes his more attentive mind
Laboring had raised, and thus to Eve replied.
     'Eve, thy contempt of life and pleasure seems
To argue in thee something more sublime
And excellent than what thy mind contemns;   1015
But self-destruction therefore sought, refutes
That excellence thought in thee, and implies,
Not thy contempt, but anguish and regret
For loss of life and pleasure overloved.
Or if thou covet death, as utmost end   1020
Of misery, so thinking to evade
The penalty pronounced, doubt not but God
Hath wiselier armed his vengeful ire than so
To be forestalled; much more I fear lest death
So snatched will not exempt us from the pain   1025
We are by doom to pay; rather such acts
Of contumacy will provoke the highest

999 ff. Eve proposes suicide as the way out of their difficulties.
1013 ff. Adam rejects Eve's arguments for suicide.   1027. contumacy: willful disobedience.

To make death in us live: Then let us seek
Some safer resolution, which methinks
I have in view, calling to mind with heed   1030
Part of our sentence, that thy seed shall bruise
The serpent's head; piteous amends, unless
Be meant, whom I conjecture, our grand foe
Satan, who in the serpent hath contrived
Against us this deceit: to crush his head   1035
Would be revenge indeed; which will be lost
By death brought on ourselves, or childless days
Resolved, as thou proposest; so our foe
Shall scape his punishment ordained, and we
Instead shall double ours upon our heads.   1040
No more be mentioned then of violence
Against ourselves, and willful barrenness,
That cuts us off from hope, and savors only
Rancor and pride, impatience and despite,
Reluctance against God and his just yoke   1045
Laid on our necks.   Remember with what mild
And gracious temper he both heard and judged
Without wrath or reviling; we expected
Immediate dissolution, which we thought
Was meant by death that day, when lo, to thee   1050
Pains only in child-bearing were foretold,
And bringing forth, soon recompensed with joy,
Fruit of thy womb: On me the curse aslope
Glanced on the ground, with labor I must earn
My bread; what harm?   Idleness had been worse;   1055
My labor will sustain me; and lest cold
Or heat should injure us, his timely care
Hath unbesought provided, and his hands
Clothed us unworthy, pitying while he judged;
How much more, if we pray him, will his ear   1060
Be open, and his heart to pity incline,
And teach us further by what means to shun
The inclement seasons, rain, ice, hail and snow,
Which now the sky with various face begins
To show us in this mountain, while the winds   1065
Blow moist and keen, shattering the graceful locks
Of these fair spreading trees; which bids us seek
Some better shroud, some better warmth to cherish
Our limbs benumbed, ere this diurnal star
Leave cold the night, how we his gathered beams   1070
Reflected, may with matter sere foment,
Or by collision of two bodies grind
The air attrite to fire, as late the clouds
Justling or pushed with winds rude in their shock
Tine the slant lightning, whose thwart flame driven down   1075

1030 ff. Note that Adam only surmises a connection here between the serpent and Satan.
1069. **diurnal star:** day star, the sun.
1071. **sere:** dry.   Adam is suggesting various ways for making fire, something he had not needed before.
1073. **attrite:** rub together, abrade.

Kindles the gummy bark of fir or pine,
And sends a comfortable heat from far,
Which might supply the sun: such fire to use,
And what may else be remedy or cure
To evils which our own misdeeds have wrought,   1080
He will instruct us praying, and of grace
Beseeching him, so as we need not fear
To pass commodiously this life, sustained
By him with many comforts, till we end
In dust, our final rest and native home.   1085
What better can we do, than to the place
Repairing where he judged us, prostrate fall
Before him reverent, and there confess
Humbly our faults, and pardon beg, with tears
Watering the ground, and with our sighs the air   1090
Frequenting, sent from hearts contrite, in sign
Of sorrow unfeigned, and humiliation meek.
Undoubtedly he will relent and turn
From his displeasure; in whose look serene,
When angry most he seemed and most severe,   1095
What else but favor, grace, and mercy shone?'
    So spake our father penitent, nor Eve
Felt less remorse: they forthwith to the place
Repairing where he judged them prostrate fell
Before him reverent, and both confessed   1100
Humbly their faults, and pardon begged, with tears
Watering the ground, and with their sighs the air
Frequenting, sent from hearts contrite, in sign
Of sorrow unfeigned, and humiliation meek.

THE END OF THE TENTH BOOK

BOOK XI

THE ARGUMENT

The Son of God presents to his father the prayers of our first parents now repenting, and intercedes for them: God accepts them, but declares that they must no
longer abide in Paradise; sends Michael with a band of cherubim to dispossess
them; but first to reveal to Adam future things: Michael's coming down.   Adam
shows to Eve certain ominous signs; he discerns Michael's approach, goes out to
meet him: the angel denounces their departure.   Eve's lamentation.   Adam pleads,
but submits: The angel leads him up to a high hill, sets before him in vision what
shall happen till the flood.

Thus they in lowliest plight repentant stood
Praying, for from the mercy-seat above
Prevenient grace descending had removed
The stony from their hearts, and made new flesh
Regenerate grow instead, that sighs now breathed   5

1086 ff. and 1098 ff. Note the exact parallelism of these lines.

Unutterable, which the spirit of prayer
Inspired, and winged for heaven with speedier flight
Than loudest oratory: yet their port
Not of mean suitors, nor important less
Seemed their petition, than when the ancient pair   10
In fables old, less ancient yet than these,
Deucalion and chaste Pyrrha to restore
The race of mankind drowned, before the shrine
Of Themis stood devout.   To heaven their prayers
Flew up, nor missed the way, by envious winds   15
Blown vagabond or frustrate: in they passed
Dimensionless through heavenly doors; then clad
With incense, where the golden altar fumed,
By their great intercessor, came in sight
Before the father's throne: Them the glad Son   20
Presenting, thus to intercede began.
    'See father, what first fruits on earth are sprung
From thy implanted grace in man, these sighs
And prayers, which in this golden censer, mixed
With incense, I thy priest before thee bring,   25
Fruits of more pleasing savor from thy seed
Sown with contrition in his heart, than those
Which his own hand manuring all the trees
Of Paradise could have produced, ere fallen
From innocence.   Now therefore bend thine ear   30
To supplication, hear his sighs though mute;
Unskillful with what words to pray, let me
Interpret for him, me his advocate
And propitiation, all his works on me
Good or not good ingraft, my merit those   35
Shall perfect, and for these my death shall pay.
Accept me, and in me from these receive
The smell of peace toward mankind, let him live
Before thee reconciled, at least his days
Numbered, though sad, till death, his doom (which I   40
To mitigate thus plead, not to reverse)
To better life shall yield him, where with me
All my redeemed may dwell in joy and bliss,
Made one with me as I with thee am one.'
    To whom the father, without cloud, serene.   45
'All thy request for man, accepted Son,
Obtain, all thy request was my decree:
But longer in that Paradise to dwell,
The law I gave to nature him forbids:
Those pure immortal elements that know   50
No gross, no unharmonious mixture foul,
Eject him tainted now, and purge him off

8. **port**: bearing.

12. **Deucalion and chaste Pyrrha**: the names of the surviving man and woman in the Greek story of the flood.   Cf. Ovid, *Metamorphoses* I:260.

14. **Themis**: a Titaness, a form of the earth goddess of the law and arrangement of physical phenomena.

As a distemper, gross to air as gross,
And mortal food, as may dispose him best
For dissolution wrought by sin, that first   55
Distempered all things, and of incorrupt
Corrupted.   I at first with two fair gifts
Created him endowed, with happiness
And immortality: that fondly lost,
This other served but to eternize woe;   60
Till I provided death; so death becomes
His final remedy, and after life
Tried in sharp tribulation, and refined
By faith and faithful works, to second life,
Waked in the renovation of the just,   65
Resigns him up with heaven and earth renewed.
But let us call to synod all the blest
Through heaven's wide bounds; from them I will not hide
My judgments, how with mankind I proceed,
As how with peccant angels late they saw;   70
And in their state, though firm, stood more confirmed.'
    He ended, and the Son gave signal high
To the bright minister that watched, he blew
His trumpet, heard in Oreb since perhaps
When God descended, and perhaps once more   75
To sound at general doom.   The angelic blast
Filled all the regions: from their blissful bowers
Of amaranthine shade, fountain or spring,
By the waters of life, where'er they sat
In fellowships of joy: the sons of light   80
Hasted, resorting to the summons high,
And took their seats; till from his throne supreme
The almighty thus pronounced his sovereign will.
    'O sons, like one of us man is become
To know both good and evil, since his taste   85
Of that defended fruit; but let him boast
His knowledge of good lost, and evil got,
Happier, had it sufficed him to have known
Good by itself, and evil not at all.
He sorrows now, repents, and prays contrite,   90
My motions in him, longer than they move,
His heart I know, how variable and vain
Self-left.   Lest therefore his now bolder hand
Reach also of the tree of life, and eat,
And live forever, dream at least to live   95
Forever, to remove him I decree,
And send him from the garden forth to till
The ground whence he was taken, fitter soil.
    'Michael, this my behest have thou in charge,
Take to thee from among the cherubim   100
Thy choice of flaming warriors, lest the fiend

65. **Waked in the renovation of the just**: the saints at Judgment Day.
70. **peccant**: sinning.

Or in behalf of man, or to invade
Vacant possession some new trouble raise:
Haste thee, and from the Paradise of God
Without remorse drive out the sinful pair,   105
From hallowed ground the unholy, and denounce
To them and to their progeny from thence
Perpetual banishment.   Yet lest they faint
At the sad sentence rigorously urged,
For I behold them softened and with tears   110
Bewailing their excess, all terror hide.
If patiently thy bidding they obey,
Dismiss them not disconsolate; reveal
To Adam what shall come in future days,
As I shall thee enlighten, intermix   115
My covenant in the woman's seed renewed;
So send them forth, though sorrowing, yet in peace:
And on the east side of the garden place,
Where entrance up from Eden easiest climbs,
Cherubic watch, and of a sword the flame   120
Wide waving, all approach far off to fright,
And guard all passage to the tree of life:
Lest Paradise a receptacle prove
To spirits foul, and all my trees their prey,
With whose stolen fruit man once more to delude.'   125
    He ceased; and the archangelic power prepared
For swift descent, with him the cohort bright
Of watchful cherubim; four faces each
Had, like a double Janus, all their shape
Spangled with eyes more numerous than those   130
Of Argus, and more wakeful than to drowse,
Charmed with Arcadian pipe, the pastoral reed
Of Hermes, or his opiate rod.   Meanwhile
To resalute the world with sacred light
Leucothea waked, and with fresh dews embalmed   135
The earth, when Adam and first matron Eve
Had ended now their orisons, and found
Strength added from above, new hope to spring

113–15. God instructs Michael to provide a vision for Adam, an apocalypse or revelation.   It is interesting to note that Milton closes his poem as the Bible closes, with a vision, or dream, or revelation of 'that which is to come.'   The last half of this book and the whole of Book XII constitute Milton's *Book of Revelation*.

128–29. **four faces each had, like a double Janus:** the Roman god, Janus, from whom our month January derives, had two faces looking in opposite directions.   A double Janus would, therefore, have four faces.

130–33. **Argus:** the hundred-eyed monster set by Hera (Juno) to watch over Io.   Hermes (Mercury) lulled him to sleep with music ('Arcadian pipe, the pastoral reed') and killed him.

132. **Arcadian pipe:** the pipe (reed or flute) of Arcady, the ideal land of the pastoral poets.   **the pastoral reed:** the shepherd's pipe, which Hermes is said to have invented after inventing the lyre.

133. **opiate rod:** his staff or caduceus, a stick made of olive wood about which two serpents entwined. The rod was steeped in drugs of healing, and the caduceus today is used by the medical profession as a symbolic emblem of the whole profession.

135. **Leucothea:** the white or shining goddess, identified by the Romans with their goddess of the dawn.

137. **orisons:** prayers.

Out of despair, joy, but with fear yet linked;
Which thus to Eve his welcome words renewed.   140
　　'Eve, easily may faith admit, that all
The good which we enjoy, from heaven descends;
But that from us aught should ascend to heaven
So prevalent as to concern the mind
Of God high-blest, or to incline his will,   145
Hard to belief may seem; yet this will prayer,
Or one short sigh of human breath, upborne
Even to the seat of God.　For since I sought
By prayer the offended deity to appease,
Kneeled and before him humbled all my heart,   150
Methought I saw him placable and mild,
Bending his ear; persuasion in me grew
That I was heard with favor; peace returned
Home to my breast, and to my memory
His promise, that thy seed shall bruise our foe;   155
Which then not minded in dismay, yet now
Assures me that the bitterness of death
Is past, and we shall live.　Whence hail to thee,
Eve rightly called, mother of all mankind,
Mother of all things living, since by thee   160
Man is to live, and all things live for man.'
　　To whom thus Eve with sad demeanor meek.
'Ill worthy I such title should belong
To me transgressor, who for thee ordained
A help, became thy snare; to me reproach   165
Rather belongs, distrust and all dispraise:
But infinite in pardon was my judge,
That I who first brought death on all, am graced
The source of life; next favorable thou,
Who highly thus to entitle me vouchsafest,   170
Far other name deserving.　But the field
To labor calls us now with sweat imposed,
Though after sleepless night; for see the morn,
All unconcerned with our unrest, begins
Her rosy progress smiling; let us forth,   175
I never from thy side henceforth to stray,
Where'er our day's work lies, though now enjoined
Laborious, till day droop; while here we dwell,
What can be toilsome in these pleasant walks?
Here let us live, though in fallen state, content.'   180
　　So spake, so wished much-humbled Eve, but fate
Subscribed not; nature first gave signs, impressed
On bird, beast, air, air suddenly eclipsed
After short blush of morn; nigh in her sight
The bird of Jove, stooped from his airy tour,   185

148 ff. The power and worth of prayer is discovered by Adam.
182 ff. **nature first gave signs**: the garden itself begins to change.

185. **The bird of Jove**: the eagle.　　**stooped**: swooped down suddenly on his prey, a technical term from falconry.　　**tour**: either his circuit, or written for 'tower.'　Cf. II:635 and VII:441.

Two birds of gayest plume before him drove:
Down from a hill the beast that reigns in woods,
First hunter then, pursued a gentle brace,
Goodliest of all the forest, hart and hind;
Direct to the eastern gate was bent their flight.　　190
Adam observed, and with his eye the chase
Pursuing, not unmoved to Eve thus spake.
　　'O Eve, some further change awaits us nigh,
Which heaven by these mute signs in nature shows
Forerunners of his purpose, or to warn　　195
Us haply too secure of our discharge
From penalty, because from death released
Some days; how long, and what till then our life,
Who knows, or more than this, that we are dust,
And thither must return and be no more.　　200
Why else this double object in our sight
Of flight pursued in the air and o'er the ground
One way the selfsame hour? why in the east
Darkness ere day's mid-course, and morning light
More orient in yon western cloud that draws　　205
O'er the blue firmament a radiant white,
And slow descends, with something heavenly fraught.'
　　He erred not, for by this the heavenly bands
Down from a sky of jasper lighted now
In Paradise, and on a hill made halt,　　210
A glorious apparition, had not doubt
And carnal fear that day dimmed Adam's eye.
Not that more glorious, when the angels met
Jacob in Mahanaim, where he saw
The field pavilioned with his guardians bright;　　215
Nor that which on the flaming mount appeared
In Dothan, covered with a camp of fire,
Against the Syrian king, who to surprise
One man, assassin-like had levied war,
War unproclaimed.　The princely hierarch　　220
In their bright stand, there left his powers to seize
Possession of the garden; he alone,
To find where Adam sheltered, took his way,
Not unperceived of Adam, who to Eve,
While the great visitant approached, thus spake.　　225
　　'Eve, now expect great tidings, which perhaps
Of us will soon determine, or impose
New laws to be observed; for I descry
From yonder blazing cloud that veils the hill
One of the heavenly host, and by his gait　　230
None of the meanest, some great potentate
Or of the thrones above, such majesty

---

210. **halt:** in both first and second editions the word is printed 'alt.' Cf. VI:532. *OED* lists no occurrences from Milton of this old form, and states that apparently it was only part of the set phrase 'make alt' with variations.

230. **gait:** as usual, the old editions spell the word 'gate.'

Invests him coming; yet not terrible,
That I should fear, nor sociably mild,
As Raphael, that I should much confide,   235
But solemn and sublime, whom not to offend,
With reverence I must meet, and thou retire.'
He ended; and the archangel soon drew nigh,
Not in his shape celestial, but as man
Clad to meet man; over his lucid arms   240
A military vest of purple flowed
Livelier than Meliboean, or the grain
Of Sarra, worn by kings and heroes old
In time of truce; Iris had dipped the woof;
His starry helm unbuckled showed him prime   245
In manhood where youth ended; by his side
As in a glistering zodiac hung the sword,
Satan's dire dread, and in his hand the spear.
Adam bowed low, he kingly from his state
Inclined not, but his coming thus declared.   250
   'Adam, heaven's high behest no preface needs:
Sufficient that thy prayers are heard, and death,
Then due by sentence when thou didst transgress,
Defeated of his seizure many days
Given thee of grace, wherein thou mayest repent,   255
And one bad act with many deeds well done
Mayest cover: well may then thy Lord appeased
Redeem thee quite from death's rapacious claim;
But longer in this Paradise to dwell
Permits not; to remove thee I am come,   260
And send thee from the garden forth to till
The ground whence thou wast taken, fitter soil.'
   He added not, for Adam at the news
Heart-struck with chilling grip of sorrow stood,
That all his senses bound; Eve, who unseen   265
Yet all had heard, with audible lament
Discovered soon the place of her retire.
   'O unexpected stroke, worse than of death!
Must I thus leave thee Paradise? thus leave
Thee native soil, these happy walks and shades,   270
Fit haunt of gods? where I had hope to spend,
Quiet though sad, the respite of that day
That must be mortal to us both.   O flowers,
That never will in other climate grow,
My early visitation, and my last   275

240. **lucid:** shining.

241. **purple:** usually crimson or scarlet.   Cf. Phillips, *World of Words*, under 'purpura,' 'A Purple Garment, or Scarlet Robe.'

242. **Meliboean:** more vivid purple than any purple dye from Meliboea.

243. **Sarra:** Tyrian purple.

244. **Iris:** goddess of the rainbow.

247. **glistering zodiac:** shining glittering belt, studded with shining objects, as the belt of the zodiac in the heavens is studded with the twelve bright stars that are its signs.

At even, which I bred up with tender hand
From the first opening bud, and gave ye names,
Who now shall rear ye to the sun, or rank
Your tribes, and water from the ambrosial fount?
Thee lastly nuptial bower, by me adorned   280
With what to sight or smell was sweet; from thee
How shall I part, and whither wander down
Into a lower world, to this obscure
And wild, how shall we breathe in other air
Less pure, accustomed to immortal fruits?'   285
    Whom thus the angel interrupted mild.
'Lament not Eve, but patiently resign
What justly thou hast lost; nor set thy heart,
Thus overfond, on that which is not thine;
Thy going is not lonely, with thee goes   290
Thy husband, him to follow thou art bound;
Where he abides, think there thy native soil.'
    Adam by this from the cold sudden damp
Recovering, and his scattered spirits returned,
To Michael thus his humble words addressed.   295
    'Celestial, whether among the thrones, or named
Of them the highest, for such of shape may seem
Prince above princes, gently hast thou told
Thy message, which might else in telling wound,
And in performing end us; what besides   300
Of sorrow and dejection and despair
Our frailty can sustain, thy tidings bring,
Departure from this happy place, our sweet
Recess, and only consolation left
Familiar to our eyes, all places else   305
Inhospitable appear and desolate,
Nor knowing us nor known: and if by prayer
Incessant I could hope to change the will
Of him who all things can, I would not cease
To weary him with my assiduous cries: 310
But prayer against his absolute decree
No more avails than breath against the wind,
Blown stifling back on him that breathes it forth:
Therefore to his great bidding I submit.
This most afflicts me, that departing hence,   315
As from his face I shall be hid, deprived
His blessed countenance; here I could frequent,
With worship, place by place where he vouchsafed
Presence divine, and to my sons relate;
"On this mount he appeared, under this tree   320
Stood visible, among these pines his voice
I heard, here with him at this fountain talked:"
So many grateful altars I would rear
Of grassy turf, and pile up every stone
Of luster from the brook, in memory,   325
Or monument to ages, and thereon

Offer sweet smelling gums and fruits and flowers:
In yonder nether world where shall I seek
His bright appearances, or footstep trace?
For though I fled him angry, yet recalled   330
To life prolonged and promised race, I now
Gladly behold though but his utmost skirts
Of glory, and far off his steps adore.'
    To whom thus Michael with regard benign.
'Adam, thou knowest heaven his, and all the earth.   335
Not this rock only; his omnipresence fills
Land, sea, and air, and every kind that lives,
Fomented by his virtual power and warmed:
All the earth he gave thee to possess and rule,
No despicable gift; surmise not then   340
His presence to these narrow bounds confined
Of Paradise or Eden: this had been
Perhaps thy capital seat, from whence had spread
All generations, and had hither come
From all the ends of the earth, to celebrate   345
And reverence thee their great progenitor.
But this pre-eminence thou hast lost, brought down
To dwell on even ground now with thy sons:
Yet doubt not but in valley and in plain
God is as here, and will be found alike   350
Present, and of his presence many a sign
Still following thee, still compassing thee round
With goodness and paternal love, his face
Express, and of his steps the track divine.
Which that thou mayest believe, and be confirmed   355
Ere thou from hence depart, know I am sent
To show thee what shall come in future days
To thee and to thy offspring; good with bad
Expect to hear, supernal grace contending
With sinfulness of men; thereby to learn   360
True patience, and to temper joy with fear
And pious sorrow, equally inured
By moderation either state to bear,
Prosperous or adverse: so shalt thou lead
Safest thy life, and best prepared endure   365
Thy mortal passage when it comes.   Ascend
This hill; let Eve (for I have drenched her eyes)
Here sleep below while thou to foresight wakest,
As once thou sleptst, while she to life was formed.'
    To whom thus Adam gratefully replied.   370
'Ascend, I follow thee, safe guide, the path
Thou leadest me, and to the hand of heaven submit,
However chastening, to the evil turn
My obvious breast, arming to overcome
By suffering, and earn rest from labor won,   375
If so I may attain.'   So both ascend
In the visions of God: It was a hill

Of Paradise the highest, from whose top
The hemisphere of earth in clearest ken
Stretched out to the amplest reach of prospect lay.   380
Not higher that hill nor wider looking round,
Whereon for different cause the tempter set
Our second Adam in the wilderness,
To show him all earth's kingdoms and their glory.
His eye might there command wherever stood   385
City of old or modern fame, the seat
Of mightiest empire, from the destined walls
Of Cambalu, seat of Cathaian khan
And Samarkand by Oxus, Temir's throne,
To Paquin of Sinaean kings, and thence   390
To Agra and Lahor of great Mogul
Down to the golden Chersonese, or where
The Persian in Ecbatan sat, or since
In Hispahan, or where the Russian ksar
In Moscow, or the sultan in Bizance,   395
Turkestan-born; nor could his eye not ken
The empire of Negus to his utmost port
Ercoco and the less maritime kings
Mombasa, and Quiloa, and Melind,
And Sofala thought Ophir, to the realm   400
Of Congo, and Angola farthest south;
Or thence from Niger flood to Atlas mount
The kingdoms of Almansor, Fez and Sus,
Morocco and Algiers, and Tremisen;
On Europe thence, and where Rome was to sway   405

384 ff. The beginning of the grand apocalypse, or vision, with which the poem ends. For the geographical names, the reader is referred to Gilbert's *Geographical Dictionary of Milton.* In general, the vision is an epitome of the Biblical story from the expulsion from the garden to the beginnings of Christianity, the whole compressed into about 1000 lines of poetry (XI:450 ff.–XII:550). It opens with Michael's actually causing Adam to see below him on the plain many of the events that are told of in the *OT.* Then, to save time, Michael rapidly relates what is to happen, including the explanation of man's salvation, or the Christ's atonement for Adam's sin.

383–85. **Our second Adam ... His eye ...:** compare *PR* IV:25 ff.

388. **Cambalu, seat of Cathaian khan:** Peiping, seat of Chinese khan.

389. **Samarkand:** in central Russian Asia, about 100 miles from the river Oxus.   **Temir's throne:** the great Tamerlane.

390. **Paquin:** Pekin, Peiping.   **Sinaean:** Chinese.

391. **Agra and Lahor:** towns in India.   392. **Chersonese:** the peninsula of Malacca.

393. **Ecbatan:** cf. *PR* III:286; 'Ecbatana' in ancient Media.

394. **Hispahan:** capital of Persia at one time.

395. **Bizance:** Byzantium, Constantinople, Istanbul.   396. **Turkestan:** in central Asia.

397. **empire of Negus:** upper Ethiopia.

398. **Ercoco:** modern Arkeeko, a port on the Red Sea.

399. **Mombasa ... Quiloa ... Melind:** towns or regions on the east coast of Africa.

400. **Sofala:** on the same coast, farther south.   **Ophir:** mentioned in the Bible as the land of gold, *I Kings* 9:28.

401. **Congo, and Angola:** regions on the west coast of Africa.

402. **Niger flood to Atlas mount:** from the Niger River to the Atlas Mountains, in northwest Africa.

403. **Almansor, Fez and Sus:** part of the general region of Barbary.

404. **Morocco ... Algiers ... Tremisen:** in North Africa. Cf. I:584.

The world: in spirit perhaps he also saw
Rich Mexico the seat of Montezume,
And Cusco in Peru, the richer seat
Of Atabalipa, and yet unspoiled
Guiana, whose great city Geryon's sons   410
Call El Dorado: but to nobler sights
Michael from Adam's eyes the film removed
Which that false fruit that promised clearer sight
Had bred; then purged with euphrasy and rue
The visual nerve, for he had much to see;   415
And from the well of life three drops instilled.
So deep the power of these ingredients pierced,
Even to the inmost seat of mental sight,
That Adam now enforced to close his eyes,
Sunk down and all his spirits became entranced: 420
But him the gentle angel by the hand
Soon raised, and his attention thus recalled.
    'Adam, now ope thine eyes, and first behold
The effects which thy original crime hath wrought
In some to spring from thee, who never touched   425
The excepted tree, nor with the snake conspired,
Nor sinned thy sin, yet from that sin derive
Corruption to bring forth more violent deeds.'
    His eyes he opened, and beheld a field,
Part arable and tilth, whereon were sheaves   430
New reaped, the other part sheep-walks and folds;
In the midst an altar as the landmark stood
Rustic, of grassy sward; thither anon
A sweaty reaper from his tillage brought
First-fruits, the green ear, and the yellow sheaf,   435
Unculled, as came to hand; a shepherd next
More meek came with the firstlings of his flock
Choicest and best; then sacrificing, laid
The inwards and their fat, with incense strewed,
On the cleft wood, and all due rites performed.   440
His offering soon propitious fire from heaven
Consumed with nimble glance, and grateful steam;
The other's not, for his was not sincere;
Whereat he inly raged, and as they talked,
Smote him into the midriff with a stone   445
That beat out life; he fell, and deadly pale
Groaned out his soul with gushing blood effused.
Much at that sight was Adam in his heart
Dismayed, and thus in haste to the angel cried.
    'O Teacher, some great mischief hath befallen   450

407. **Montezume:** 'Motezume' in both first and second editions.
408. **Cusco:** former capital of Peru.   410. **Geryon's sons:** the Spanish.
411. **El Dorado:** literally 'the Golden,' the fabulous region somewhere in America where gold abounded.
414. **euphrasy and rue:** two plants of great medicinal virtue.
427. **sin:** omitted in second edition.   430. **arable and tilth:** tillable and tilled land.
430 ff. The story of Cain and Abel, *Genesis* 4.

To that meek man, who well had sacrificed;
Is piety thus and pure devotion paid?'
    To whom Michael thus, he also moved, replied.
'These two are brethren, Adam, and to come
Out of thy loins; the unjust the just hath slain,   455
For envy that his brother's offering found
From heaven acceptance; but the bloody fact
Will be avenged, and the other's faith approved
Lose no reward, though here thou see him die,
Rolling in dust and gore.'   To which our sire.   460
    'Alas, both for the deed and for the cause!
But have I now seen death?   Is this the way
I must return to native dust?   O sight
Of terror, foul and ugly to behold,
Horrid to think, how horrible to feel!'   465
    To whom thus Michael.   'Death thou hast seen
In his first shape on man; but many shapes
Of death, and many are the ways that lead
To his grim cave, all dismal; yet to sense
More terrible at the entrance than within.   470
Some, as thou sawest, by violent stroke shall die,
By fire, flood, famine, by intemperance more
In meats and drinks, which on the earth shall bring
Diseases dire, of which a monstrous crew
Before thee shall appear; that thou mayest know   475
What misery the inabstinence of Eve
Shall bring on men.'   Immediately a place
Before his eyes appeared, sad, noisome, dark,
A lazar-house it seemed, wherein were laid
Numbers of all diseased, all maladies   480
Of ghastly spasm, or racking torture, qualms
Of heart-sick agony, all feverous kinds,
Convulsions, epilepsies, fierce catarrhs,
Intestine stone and ulcer, colic pangs,
Demoniac phrenzy, moping melancholy   485
And moon-struck madness, pining atrophy,
Marasmus, and wide-wasting pestilence,
Dropsies, and asthmas, and joint-racking rheums.
Dire was the tossing, deep the groans, despair
Tended the sick busiest from couch to couch;   490
And over them triumphant death his dart
Shook, but delayed to strike, though oft invoked
With vows, as their chief good, and final hope.
Sight so deform what heart of rock could long
Dry-eyed behold?   Adam could not, but wept,   495
Though not of woman born; compassion quelled
His best of man, and gave him up to tears
A space, till firmer thoughts restrained excess,
And scarce recovering words his plaint renewed.

477 ff. The poetic depiction of the cave of death is a conventional one since the Middle Ages.
485–87. Not in first edition.

'O miserable mankind, to what fall   500
Degraded, to what wretched state reserved!
Better end here unborn.   Why is life given
To be thus wrested from us? rather why
Obtruded on us thus? who if we knew
What we receive, would either not accept   505
Life offered, or soon beg to lay it down,
Glad to be so dismissed in peace.   Can thus
The image of God in man created once
So goodly and erect, though faulty since,
To such unsightly sufferings be debased   510
Under inhuman pains?   Why should not man,
Retaining still divine similitude
In part, from such deformities be free,
And for his maker's image sake exempt?'
  'Their maker's image,' answered Michael, 'then   515
Forsook them, when themselves they vilified
To serve ungoverned appetite, and took
His image whom they served, a brutish vice,
Inductive mainly to the sin of Eve.
Therefore so abject is their punishment,   520
Disfiguring not God's likeness, but their own,
Or if his likeness, by themselves defaced
While they pervert pure nature's healthful rules
To loathsome sickness, worthily, since they
God's image did not reverence in themselves.'   525
  'I yield it just,' said Adam, 'and submit.
But is there yet no other way, besides
These painful passages, how we may come
To death, and mix with our connatural dust?'
  'There is,' said Michael, 'if thou well observe   530
The rule of not too much, by temperance taught
In what thou eatest and drinkest, seeking from thence
Due nourishment, not gluttonous delight,
Till many years over thy head return:
So mayest thou live, till like ripe fruit thou drop   535
Into thy mother's lap, or be with ease
Gathered, not harshly plucked, for death mature:
This is old age; but then thou must outlive
Thy youth, thy strength, thy beauty, which will change
To withered weak and gray; thy senses then   540
Obtuse, all taste of pleasure must forgo,
To what thou hast, and for the air of youth
Hopeful and cheerful, in thy blood will reign
A melancholy damp of cold and dry
To weigh thy spirits down, and last consume   545
The balm of life.'   To whom our ancestor.
  'Henceforth I fly not death, nor would prolong
Life much, bent rather how I may be quit
Fairest and easiest of this cumbrous charge,
Which I must keep till my appointed day   550

Of rendering up, and patiently attend
My dissolution.'   Michael replied,
  'Nor love thy life, nor hate; but what thou livest
Live well, how long or short permit to heaven:
And now prepare thee for another sight.'   555
  He looked and saw a spacious plain, whereon
Were tents of various hue; by some were herds
Of cattle grazing: others, whence the sound
Of instruments that made melodious chime
Was heard, of harp and organ; and who moved   560
Their stops and chords was seen: his volant touch
Instinct through all proportions low and high
Fled and pursued transverse the resonant fugue.
In other part stood one who at the forge
Laboring, two massy clods of iron and brass   565
Had melted (whether found where casual fire
Had wasted woods on mountain or in vale,
Down to the veins of earth, thence gliding hot
To some cave's mouth, or whether washed by stream
From underground) the liquid ore he drained   570
Into fit molds prepared; from which he formed
First his own tools; then, what might else be wrought
Fusil or graven in metal.   After these,
But on the hither side a different sort
From the high neighboring hills, which was their seat,   575
Down to the plain descended: by their guise
Just men they seemed, and all their study bent
To worship God aright, and know his works
Not hid, nor those things last which might preserve
Freedom and peace to men: they on the plain   580
Long had not walked, when from the tents behold
A bevy of fair women, richly gay
In gems and wanton dress; to the harp they sung
Soft amorous ditties, and in dance came on:
The men though grave, eyed them, and let their eyes   585
Rove without rein, till in the amorous net
Fast caught, they liked, and each his liking chose;
And now of love they treat till the evening star
Love's harbinger appeared; then all in heat
They light the nuptial torch, and bid invoke   590
Hymen, then first to marriage rites invoked;
With feast and music all the tents resound.
Such happy interview and fair event
Of love and youth not lost, songs, garlands, flowers,
And charming symphonies attached the heart   595
Of Adam, soon inclined to admit delight,
The bent of nature; which he thus expressed.
  'True opener of mine eyes, prime angel blest,
Much better seems this vision, and more hope

558 ff. The descendants of Cain.   Cf. *Genesis* 4:20–22.
573 ff. The descendants of Seth, and the events in *Genesis* 6:1, 2.

Of peaceful days portends, than those two past;   600
Those were of hate and death, or pain much worse,
Here nature seems fulfilled in all her ends.'
   To whom thus Michael. 'Judge not what is best
By pleasure, though to nature seeming meet,
Created, as thou art, to nobler end   605
Holy and pure, conformity divine.
Those tents thou sawest so pleasant, were the tents
Of wickedness, wherein shall dwell his race
Who slew his brother; studious they appear
Of arts that polish life, inventors rare,   610
Unmindful of their maker, though his spirit
Taught them, but they his gifts acknowledged none.
Yet they a beauteous offspring shall beget;
For that fair female troop thou sawest, that seemed
Of goddesses, so blithe, so smooth, so gay,   615
Yet empty of all good wherein consists
Woman's domestic honor and chief praise;
Bred only and completed to the taste
Of lustful appetence, to sing, to dance,
To dress, and troll the tongue, and roll the eye.   620
To these that sober race of men, whose lives
Religious titled them the sons of God,
Shall yield up all their virtue, all their fame
Ignobly, to the trains and to the smiles
Of these fair atheists, and now swim in joy,   625
(Erelong to swim at large) and laugh; for which
The world erelong a world of tears must weep.'
   To whom thus Adam of short joy bereft.
'O pity and shame, that they who to live well
Entered so fair, should turn aside to tread   630
Paths indirect, or in the midway faint!
But still I see the tenor of man's woe
Holds on the same, from woman to begin.'
   'From man's effeminate slackness it begins,'
Said the angel, 'who should better hold his place   635
By wisdom, and superior gifts received.
But now prepare thee for another scene.'
   He looked and saw wide territory spread
Before him, towns, and rural works between,
Cities of men with lofty gates and towers,   640
Concourse in arms, fierce faces threatening war,
Giants of mighty bone, and bold emprise;
Part wield their arms, part curb the foaming steed,
Single or in array of battle ranged
Both horse and foot, nor idly mustering stood;   645
One way a band select from forage drives
A herd of beeves, fair oxen and fair kine
From a fat meadow ground; or fleecy flock,
Ewes and their bleating lambs over the plain,
Their booty; scarce with life the shepherds fly,   650

But call in aid, which makes a bloody fray;
With cruel tournament the squadrons join;
Where cattle pastured late, now scattered lies
With carcasses and arms the ensanguined field
Deserted: Others to a city strong   655
Lay siege, encamped; by battery, scale, and mine,
Assaulting; others from the wall defend
With dart and javelin, stones and sulphurous fire;
On each hand slaughter and gigantic deeds.
In other part the sceptered heralds call   660
To council in the city gates: anon
Gray-headed men and grave, with warriors mixed,
Assemble, and harangues are heard, but soon
In factious opposition, till at last
Of middle age one rising, eminent   665
In wise deport, spake much of right and wrong,
Of justice, of religion, truth and peace,
And judgment from above: him old and young
Exploded and had seized with violent hands,
Had not a cloud descending snatched him thence   670
Unseen amid the throng: so violence
Proceeded, and oppression, and sword-law
Through all the plain, and refuge none was found.
Adam was all in tears, and to his guide
Lamenting turned full sad; 'O what are these,   675
Death's ministers, not men, who thus deal death
Inhumanly to men, and multiply
Ten thousandfold the sin of him who slew
His brother; for of whom such massacre
Make they but of their brethren, men of men?   680
But who was that just man, whom had not heaven
Rescued, had in his righteousness been lost?'
    To whom thus Michael.   'These are the product
Of those ill-mated marriages thou sawest:
Where good with bad were matched, who of themselves   685
Abhor to join; and by imprudence mixed,
Produce prodigious births of body or mind.
Such were these giants, men of high renown;
For in those days might only shall be admired,
And valor and heroic virtue called;   690
To overcome in battle, and subdue
Nations, and bring home spoils with infinite
Manslaughter, shall be held the highest pitch
Of human glory, and for glory done

---

651. **makes:** first edition reads 'tacks' which no editor has understood, Verity saying of it, 'perhaps a misprint. Milton never uses the word: it would scarcely give any sense here.' As a matter of fact, it should probably be retained here. Milton uses it in at least three forms in his prose. Cf. *OED* under 'tack,' *sb.* IV:10, 11. It means to hold one's own with, or to be even with, or to carry on without winning or losing, the last being about the meaning required here, as the fighting was seemingly endless.

691 ff. The offspring of the union of the 'sons of God' and the daughters of men, the giants, as in *Genesis* 6:1–8.

Of triumph, to be styled great conquerors,   695
Patrons of mankind, gods, and sons of gods,
Destroyers rightlier called and plagues of men.
Thus fame shall be achieved, renown on earth,
And what most merits fame in silence hid.
But he the seventh from thee, whom thou beheldest   700
The only righteous in a world perverse,
And therefore hated, therefore so beset
With foes for daring single to be just,
And utter odious truth, that God would come
To judge them with his saints: Him the most high   705
Rapt in a balmy cloud with winged steeds
Did, as thou sawest, receive, to walk with God
High in salvation and the climes of bliss,
Exempt from death; to show thee what reward
Awaits the good, the rest what punishment?   710
Which now direct thine eyes and soon behold.'
    He looked, and saw the face of things quite changed,
The brazen throat of war had ceased to roar,
All now was turned to jollity and game,
To luxury and riot, feast and dance,   715
Marrying or prostituting, as befell,
Rape or adultery, where passing fair
Allured them; thence from cups to civil broils.
At length a reverend sire among them came,
And of their doings great dislike declared,   720
And testified against their ways; he oft
Frequented their assemblies, whereso met,
Triumphs or festivals, and to them preached
Conversion and repentance, as to souls
In prison under judgments imminent: 725
But all in vain: which when he saw, he ceased
Contending, and removed his tents far off;
Then from the mountain hewing timber tall,
Began to build a vessel of huge bulk,
Measured by cubit, length, and breadth, and height,   730
Smeared round with pitch, and in the side a door
Contrived, and of provisions laid in large
For man and beast: when lo a wonder strange!
Of every beast, and bird, and insect small
Came sevens, and pairs, and entered in, as taught   735
Their order: last the sire, and his three sons
With their four wives; and God made fast the door.
Meanwhile the south wind rose, and with black wings
Wide hovering, all the clouds together drove
From under heaven; the hills to their supply   740
Vapor, and exhalation dusk and moist,

700. **the seventh from thee** ...: Enoch, *Genesis* 5.   719. **a reverend sire**: Noah.
726 ff. The story of Noah, the building of the ark, and the flood. Cf. *Genesis* 6 and 7.
735. **Came sevens, and pairs**: because in *Genesis* 6:20 the reading is 'two of every sort' and in *Genesis* 7:2, 'of every clean beast, thou shalt take by sevens ... of beasts that are not clean by two.'

Sent up amain; and now the thickened sky
Like a dark ceiling stood; down rushed the rain
Impetuous, and continued till the earth
No more was seen; the floating vessel swum   745
Uplifted; and secure with beaked prow
Rode tilting o'er the waves, all dwellings else
Flood overwhelmed, and them with all their pomp
Deep under water rolled; sea covered sea,
Sea without shore; and in their palaces   750
Where luxury late reigned, sea-monsters whelped
And stabled; of mankind, so numerous late,
All left, in one small bottom swum embarked.
How didst thou grieve then, Adam, to behold
The end of all thy offspring, end so sad,   755
Depopulation; thee another flood,
Of tears and sorrow a flood thee also drowned,
And sunk thee as thy sons; till gently reared
By the angel, on thy feet thou stoodest at last,
Though comfortless, as when a father mourns   760
His children, all in view destroyed at once;
And scarce to the angel utteredst thus thy plaint.
  'O visions ill foreseen! better had I
Lived ignorant of future, so had borne
My part of evil only, each day's lot   765
Enough to bear; those now, that were dispensed
The burden of many ages, on me light
At once, by my foreknowledge gaining birth
Abortive, to torment me ere their being,
With thought that they must be.   Let no man seek   770
Henceforth to be foretold what shall befall
Him or his children, evil he may be sure,
Which neither his foreknowing can prevent,
And he the future evil shall no less
In apprehension than in substance feel   775
Grievous to bear: but that care now is past,
Man is not whom to warn; those few escaped
Famine and anguish will at last consume
Wandering that watery desert: I had hope
When violence was ceased, and war on earth,   780
All would have then gone well, peace would have crowned
With length of happy days the race of man;
But I was far deceived; for now I see
Peace to corrupt no less than war to waste.
How comes it thus? unfold, celestial guide,   785
And whether here the race of man will end.'
To whom thus Michael.   'Those whom last thou sawest
In triumph and luxurious wealth, are they
First seen in acts of prowess eminent

751-52. The watery counterpart of *Isaiah* 13:19-21 and 34:11-15: 'And Babylon ... shall never be inhabited ... wild beasts of the islands shall cry in their desolate houses, and dragons in their pleasant palaces.'
787-839. Note the repetition in Michael's words of what Adam has already seen in vision.

And great exploits, but of true virtue void;   790
Who having spilt much blood, and done much waste
Subduing nations, and achieved thereby
Fame in the world, high titles, and rich prey,
Shall change their course to pleasure, ease, and sloth,
Surfeit, and lust, till wantonness and pride   795
Raise out of friendship hostile deeds in peace.
The conquered also, and enslaved by war
Shall with their freedom lost all virtue lose
And fear of God, from whom their piety feigned
In sharp contest of battle found no aid   800
Against invaders; therefore cooled in zeal
Thenceforth shall practice how to live secure,
Worldly or dissolute, on what their lords
Shall leave them to enjoy; for the earth shall bear
More than enough, that temperance may be tried: 805
So all shall turn degenerate, all depraved,
Justice and temperance, truth and faith forgot;
One man except, the only son of light
In a dark age, against example good,
Against allurement, custom, and a world   810
Offended; fearless of reproach and scorn,
Or violence, he of their wicked ways
Shall them admonish, and before them set
The paths of righteousness, how much more safe,
And full of peace, denouncing wrath to come   815
On their impenitence; and shall return
Of them derided, but of God observed
The one just man alive; by his command
Shall build a wondrous ark, as thou beheldest,
To save himself and household from amidst   820
A world devote to universal wrack.
No sooner he with them of man and beast
Select for life shall in the ark be lodged,
And sheltered round, but all the cataracts
Of heaven set open on the earth shall pour   825
Rain day and night, all fountains of the deep
Broke up, shall heave the ocean to usurp
Beyond all bounds, till inundation rise
Above the highest hills: then shall this mount
Of Paradise by might of waves be moved   830
Out of his place, pushed by the horned flood,
With all his verdure spoiled, and trees adrift
Down the great river to the opening gulf,
And there take root an island salt and bare,
The haunt of seals and orcs, and sea-mews' clang.   835
To teach thee that God attributes to place
No sanctity, if none be thither brought
By men who there frequent, or therein dwell.
And now what further shall ensue, behold.'

829-35. This end of the Garden of Eden is to be found in Persian literature.

He looked, and saw the ark hull on the flood,   840
Which now abated, for the clouds were fled,
Driven by a keen north-wind, that blowing dry
Wrinkled the face of deluge, as decayed;
And the clear sun on his wide watery glass
Gazed hot, and of the fresh wave largely drew,   845
As after thirst, which made their flowing shrink
From standing lake to tripping ebb, that stole
With soft foot towards the deep, who now had stopped
His sluices, as the heaven his windows shut.
The ark no more now floats, but seems on ground   850
Fast on the top of some high mountain fixed.
And now the tops of hills as rocks appear;
With clamor thence the rapid currents drive
Towards the retreating sea their furious tide.
Forthwith from out the ark a raven flies,   855
And after him, the surer messenger,
A dove sent forth once and again to spy
Green tree or ground whereon his foot may light;
The second time returning, in his bill
An olive leaf he brings, pacific sign: 860
Anon dry ground appears, and from his ark
The ancient sire descends with all his train;
Then with uplifted hands, and eyes devout,
Grateful to heaven, over his head beholds
A dewy cloud, and in the cloud a bow   865
Conspicuous with three listed colors gay,
Betokening peace from God, and covenant anew.
Whereat the heart of Adam erst so sad
Greatly rejoiced, and thus his joy broke forth,
    'O thou who future things canst represent   870
As present, heavenly instructor, I revive
At this last sight, assured that man shall live
With all the creatures, and their seed preserve.
Far less I now lament for one whole world
Of wicked sons destroyed, than I rejoice   875
For one man found so perfect and so just,
That God vouchsafes to raise another world
From him, and all his anger to forget.
But say, what mean those colored streaks in heaven,
Distended as the brow of God appeased,   880
Or serve they as a flowery verge to bind
The fluid skirts of that same watery cloud,
Lest it again dissolve and shower the earth?'
    To whom the archangel.   'Dextrously thou aimest;
So willingly doth God remit his ire,   885
Though late repenting him of man depraved,
Grieved at his heart, when looking down he saw
The whole earth filled with violence, and all flesh
Corrupting each their way; yet those removed.

866. **three listed colors gay**: three banded colors, bands side by side.

Such grace shall one just man find in his sight,   890
That he relents, not to blot out mankind,
And makes a covenant never to destroy
The earth again by flood, nor let the sea
Surpass his bounds, nor rain to drown the world
With man therein or beast; but when he brings   895
Over the earth a cloud, will therein set
His triple-colored bow, whereon to look
And call to mind his covenant: Day and night,
Seed time and harvest, heat and hoary frost
Shall hold their course, till fire purge all things new,   900
Both heaven and earth, wherein the just shall dwell.'

THE END OF THE ELEVENTH BOOK

BOOK XII

THE ARGUMENT

The angel Michael continues from the flood to relate what shall succeed; then,
in the mention of Abraham, comes by degrees to explain, who that seed of the
woman shall be, which was promised Adam and Eve in the fall; his incarnation,
death, resurrection, and ascension; the state of the Church till his second coming.
Adam greatly satisfied and recomforted by these relations and promises descends
the hill with Michael; wakens Eve, who all this while had slept, but with gentle
dreams composed to quietness of mind and submission.   Michael in either hand
leads them out of Paradise, the fiery sword waving behind them, and the cherubim
taking their stations to guard the place.

As one who in his journey baits at noon,
Though bent on speed, so here the archangel paused
Betwixt the world destroyed and world restored, —
If Adam aught perhaps might interpose;
Then with transition sweet new speech resumes.   5
    'Thus thou hast seen one world begin and end;
And man as from a second stock proceed.
Much thou hast yet to see, but I perceive
Thy mortal sight to fail; objects divine
Must needs impair and weary human sense: 10
Henceforth what is to come I will relate,
Thou therefore give due audience, and attend.
This second source of men, while yet but few;
And while the dread of judgment past remains
Fresh in their minds, fearing the deity,   15
With some regard to what is just and right
Shall lead their lives, and multiply apace,
Laboring the soil, and reaping plenteous crop,
Corn wine and oil; and from the herd or flock,

1. **baits**: Phillips, 'to stop to eat, drink, or take some refreshment on a journey.'   Cf. *SA* 1538.   But
the word is probably the same as *bate* from *abate*.   Cf. Webster, 'bait,' *intrans.*, 3.

Oft sacrificing bullock, lamb, or kid,   20
With large wine-offerings poured, and sacred feast,
Shall spend their days in joy unblamed, and dwell
Long time in peace by families and tribes
Under paternal rule; till one shall rise
Of proud ambitious heart, who not content   25
With fair equality, fraternal state,
Will arrogate dominion undeserved
Over his brethren, and quite dispossess
Concord and law of nature from the earth,
Hunting (and men not beasts shall be his game)   30
With war and hostile snare such as refuse
Subjection to his empire tyrannous:
A mighty hunter thence he shall be styled
Before the Lord, as in despite of heaven,
Or from heaven claiming second sovereignty;   35
And from rebellion shall derive his name,
Though of rebellion others he accuse.
He with a crew, whom like ambition joins
With him or under him to tyrannize,
Marching from Eden towards the west, shall find   40
The plain, wherein a black bituminous gurge
Boils out from under ground, the mouth of hell;
Of brick, and of that stuff they cast to build
A city and tower, whose top may reach to heaven;
And get themselves a name, lest far dispersed   45
In foreign lands their memory be lost
Regardless whether good or evil fame.
But God who oft descends to visit men
Unseen, and through their habitations walks
To mark their doings, them beholding soon,   50
Comes down to see their city, ere the tower
Obstruct heaven towers, and in derision sets
Upon their tongues a various spirit to rase
Quite out their native language, and instead
To sow a jangling noise of words unknown: 55
Forthwith a hideous gabble rises loud
Among the builders; each to other calls
Not understood, till hoarse, and all in rage,
As mocked they storm; great laughter was in heaven
And looking down, to see the hubbub strange   60
And hear the din; thus was the building left
Ridiculous, and the work confusion named.'
    Whereto thus Adam fatherly displeased.
'O execrable son so to aspire
Above his brethren, to himself assuming   65
Authority usurped, from God not given:

24 ff. The story of Nimrod; cf. *Genesis* 10:9 and Josephus, *Antiquities* I:iv:2.
41. **gurge:** swirl, eddy.
43 ff. The story of the tower of Babel; cf. *Genesis* 11:2–9.
59. **laughter was in heaven:** there are several derisive notes like this in the poem.

He gave us only over beast, fish, fowl
Dominion absolute; that right we hold
By his donation; but man over men
He made not lord; such title to himself 70
Reserving, human left from human free.
But this usurper his encroachment proud
Stays not on man; to God his tower intends
Siege and defiance: Wretched man! what food
Will he convey up thither to sustain 75
Himself and his rash army, where thin air
Above the clouds will pine his entrails gross,
And famish him of breath, if not of bread?'
   To whom thus Michael. 'Justly thou abhorrest
That son, who on the quiet state of men 80
Such trouble brought, affecting to subdue
Rational liberty; yet know withal,
Since thy original lapse, true liberty
Is lost, which always with right reason dwells
Twinned, and from her hath no dividual being: 85
Reason in man obscured, or not obeyed,
Immediately inordinate desires
And upstart passions catch the government
From reason, and to servitude reduce
Man till then free. Therefore since he permits 90
Within himself unworthy powers to reign
Over free reason, God in judgment just
Subjects him from without to violent lords;
Who oft as undeservedly enthrall
His outward freedom: Tyranny must be, 95
Though to the tyrant thereby no excuse.
Yet sometimes nations will decline so low
From virtue, which is reason, that no wrong,
But justice, and some fatal curse annexed
Deprives them of their outward liberty, 100
Their inward lost: Witness the irreverent son
Of him who built the ark, who for the shame
Done to his father, heard this heavy curse,
"Servant of servants," on his vicious race.
Thus will this latter, as the former world, 105
Still tend from bad to worse, till God at last
Wearied with their iniquities, withdraw
His presence from among them, and avert
His holy eyes; resolving from thenceforth
To leave them to their own polluted ways; 110
And one peculiar nation to select
From all the rest, of whom to be invoked,

71. **human left from human free:** toleration.

83–84. **true liberty is lost, which always with right reason dwells:** an important principle in Milton's thought.

85. **dividual:** divided, separate.

111. **one peculiar nation:** Israel.

A nation from one faithful man to spring: *abraham*
Him on this side Euphrates yet residing,
Bred up in idol worship; O that men   115
(Canst thou believe?) should be so stupid grown,
While yet the patriarch lived, who scaped the flood,
As to forsake the living God, and fall
To worship their own work in wood and stone
For gods! yet him God the most high vouchsafes   120
To call by vision from his father's house,
His kindred and false gods, into a land
Which he will show him, and from him will raise
A mighty nation, and upon him shower
His benediction so, that in his seed   125
All nations shall be blest; he straight obeys,
Not knowing to what land, yet firm believes:
I see him, but thou canst not, with what faith
He leaves his gods, his friends, and native soil
Ur of Chaldaea, passing now the ford   130
To Haran, after him a cumbrous train
Of herds and flocks, and numerous servitude;
Not wandering poor, but trusting all his wealth
With God, who called him, in a land unknown.
Canaan he now attains, I see his tents   135
Pitched about Sechem, and the neighboring plain
Of Moreh; there by promise he receives
Gift to his progeny of all that land;
From Hamath northward to the desert south
(Things by their names I call, though yet unnamed)   140
From Hermon east to the great western sea,
Mount Hermon, yonder sea, each place behold
In prospect, as I point them; on the shore
Mount Carmel; here the double-founted stream
Jordan, true limit eastward; but his sons   145
Shall dwell to Senir, that long ridge of hills.
This ponder, that all nations of the earth
Shall in his seed be blessed; by that seed
Is meant thy great deliverer, who shall bruise
The serpent's head; whereof to thee anon   150
Plainlier shall be revealed.   This patriarch blest,
Whom faithful Abraham due time shall call,
A son, and of his son a grandchild leaves,
Like him in faith, in wisdom, and renown; *Jacob*
The grandchild with twelve sons increased, departs   155
From Canaan, to a land hereafter called
Egypt, divided by the river Nile;
See where it flows, disgorging at seven mouths
Into the sea: to sojourn in that land
He comes invited by a younger son   160
In time of dearth, a son whose worthy deeds
Raise him to be the second in that realm

113. **one faithful man:** Abraham.   120 ff. The story of Abraham; cf. *Genesis* 12 ff.

Of Pharaoh: there he dies, and leaves his race
Growing into a nation, and now grown
Suspected to a sequent king, who seeks   165
To stop their overgrowth, as inmate guests
Too numerous; whence of guests he makes them slaves
Inhospitably, and kills their infant males:
Till by two brethren (those two brethren call
Moses and Aaron) sent from God to claim   170
His people from enthrallment, they return
With glory and spoil back to their promised land.
But first the lawless tyrant, who denies
To know their God, or message to regard,
Must be compelled by signs and judgments dire;   175
To blood unshed the rivers must be turned,
Frogs, lice and flies must all his palace fill
With loathed intrusion, and fill all the land;
His cattle must of rot and murrain die,
Botches and blains must all his flesh emboss,   180
And all his people; thunder mixed with hail,
Hail mixed with fire must rend the Egyptian sky
And wheel on the earth, devouring where it rolls;
What it devours not, herb, or fruit, or grain,
A darksome cloud of locusts swarming down   185
Must eat, and on the ground leave nothing green:
Darkness must overshadow all his bounds,
Palpable darkness, and blot out three days;
Last with one midnight stroke all the first-born
Of Egypt must lie dead.   Thus with ten wounds   190
The river-dragon tamed at length submits
To let his sojourners depart, and oft
Humbles his stubborn heart, but still as ice
More hardened after thaw, till in his rage
Pursuing whom he late dismissed, the sea   195
Swallows him with his host, but them lets pass
As on dry land between two crystal walls,
Awed by the rod of Moses so to stand
Divided, till his rescued gain their shore:
Such wondrous power God to his saint will lend,   200
Though present in his angel, who shall go
Before them in a cloud, and pillar of fire,
By day a cloud, by night a pillar of fire,
To guide them in their journey, and remove
Behind them, while the obdurate king pursues: 205
All night he will pursue, but his approach
Darkness defends between till morning watch;
Then through the fiery pillar and the cloud
God looking forth will trouble all his host
And craze their chariot-wheels: when by command   210
Moses once more his potent rod extends
Over the sea; the sea his rod obeys;
On their embattled ranks the waves return,

And overwhelm their war: the race elect
Safe towards Canaan from the shore advance   215
Through the wild desert, not the readiest way,
Lest entering on the Canaanite alarmed
War terrify them inexpert, and fear
Return them back to Egypt, choosing rather
Inglorious life with servitude; for life   220
To noble and ignoble is more sweet
Untrained in arms, where rashness leads not on.
This also shall they gain by their delay
In the wide wilderness, there they shall found
Their government, and their great senate choose   225
Through the twelve tribes, to rule by laws ordained:
God from the Mount of Sinai, whose gray top
Shall tremble, he descending, will himself
In thunder lightning and loud trumpet's sound
Ordain them laws; part such as appertain   230
To civil justice, part religious rites
Of sacrifice, informing them, by types
And shadows, of that destined seed to bruise
The serpent, by what means he shall achieve
Mankind's deliverance.   But the voice of God   235
To mortal ear is dreadful; they beseech
That Moses might report to them his will,
And terror cease; he grants what they besought
Instructed that to God is no access
Without mediator, whose high office now   240
Moses in figure bears, to introduce
One greater, of whose day he shall foretell,
And all the prophets in their age the times
Of great Messiah shall sing.   Thus laws and rites
Established, such delight hath God in men   245
Obedient to his will, that he vouchsafes
Among them to set up his tabernacle,
The holy one with mortal men to dwell:
By his prescript a sanctuary is framed
Of cedar, overlaid with gold, therein   250
An ark, and in the ark his testimony,
The records of his covenant, over these
A mercy-seat of gold between the wings
Of two bright cherubim, before him burn
Seven lamps as in a zodiac representing   255
The heavenly fires; over the tent a cloud
Shall rest by day, a fiery gleam by night,
Save when they journey, and at length they come,
Conducted by his angel to the land
Promised to Abraham and his seed: the rest   260
Were long to tell, how many battles fought,
How many kings destroyed, and kingdoms won,
Or how the sun shall in mid heaven stand still
A day entire, and night's due course adjourn,

263 ff. Joshua in Gibeon; cf. *Joshua* 10:12–13.

Man's voice commanding, "Sun in Gibeon stand,   265
And thou moon in the vale of Aialon,
Till Israel overcome;" so call the third
From Abraham, son of Isaac, and from him
His whole descent, who thus shall Canaan win.'
   Here Adam interposed. 'O sent from heaven,   270
Enlightener of my darkness, gracious things
Thou hast revealed, those chiefly which concern
Just Abraham and his seed: now first I find
Mine eyes' true opening, and my heart much eased,
Erewhile perplexed with thoughts what would become   275
Of me and all mankind; but now I see
His day, in whom all nations shall be blest
Favor unmerited by me, who sought
Forbidden knowledge by forbidden means.
This yet I apprehend not, why to those   280
Among whom God will deign to dwell on earth
So many and so various laws are given;
So many laws argue so many sins
Among them; how can God with such reside?'
   To whom thus Michael. 'Doubt not but that sin   285
Will reign among them, as of thee begot;
And therefore was law given them to evince
Their natural pravity, by stirring up
Sin against law to fight; that when they see
Law can discover sin, but not remove,   290
Save by those shadowy expiations weak,
The blood of bulls and goats, they may conclude
Some blood more precious must be paid for man,
Just for unjust, that in such righteousness
To them by faith imputed, they may find   295
Justification towards God, and peace
Of conscience, which the law by ceremonies
Cannot appease, nor man the moral part
Perform, and not performing cannot live.
So law appears imperfect, and but given   300
With purpose to resign them in full time
Up to a better covenant, disciplined
From shadowy types to truth, from flesh to spirit,
From imposition of strict laws, to free
Acceptance of large grace, from servile fear   305
To filial, works of law to works of faith.
And therefore shall not Moses, though of God
Highly beloved, being but the minister
Of law, his people into Canaan lead;
But Joshua whom the Gentiles Jesus call,   310
His name and office bearing, who shall quell
The adversary serpent, and bring back
Through the world's wilderness long wandered man
Safe to eternal Paradise of rest.

288. **pravity**: corruption.

Meanwhile they in their earthly Canaan placed   315
Long time shall dwell and prosper, but when sins
National interrupt their public peace,
Provoking God to raise them enemies:
From whom as oft he saves them penitent
By judges first, then under kings; of whom   320
The second, both for piety renowned
And puissant deeds, a promise shall receive
Irrevocable, that his regal throne
Forever shall endure; the like shall sing
All prophecy, that of the royal stock   325
Of David (so I name this king) shall rise
A son, the woman's seed to thee foretold,
Foretold to Abraham, as in whom shall trust
All nations, and to kings foretold, of kings
The last, for of his reign shall be no end.   330
But first a long succession must ensue,
And his next son for wealth and wisdom famed,
The clouded ark of God till then in tents
Wandering, shall in a glorious temple enshrine.
Such follow him, as shall be registered   335
Part good, part bad, of bad the longer scroll,
Whose foul idolatries, and other faults
Heaped to the popular sum, will so incense
God, as to leave them, and expose their land,
Their city, his temple, and his holy ark   340
With all his sacred things, a scorn and prey
To that proud city, whose high walls thou sawest
Left in confusion, Babylon thence called.
There in captivity he lets them dwell
The space of seventy years, then brings them back,   345
Remembering mercy, and his covenant sworn
To David, stablished as the days of heaven.
Returned from Babylon by leave of kings
Their lords, whom God disposed, the house of God
They first re-edify, and for a while   350
In mean estate live moderate, till grown
In wealth and multitude, factious they grow;
But first among the priests dissension springs,
Men who attend the altar, and should most
Endeavor peace: their strife pollution brings   355
Upon the temple itself: at last they seize
The scepter, and regard not David's sons,
Then lose it to a stranger, that the true
Anointed king Messiah might be born
Barred of his right; yet at his birth a star   360
Unseen before in heaven proclaims him come,
And guides the eastern sages, who inquire
His place, to offer incense, myrrh, and gold;
His place of birth a solemn angel tells

356 ff. Compare with *PR* I:240 ff.

To simple shepherds, keeping watch by night;   365
They gladly thither haste, and by a choir
Of squadroned angels hear his carol sung.
A virgin is his mother, but his sire
The power of the most high; he shall ascend
The throne hereditary, and bound his reign   370
With earth's wide bounds, his glory with the heavens.'
   He ceased, discerning Adam with such joy
Surcharged, as had like grief been dewed in tears,
Without the vent of words, which these he breathed.
   'O prophet of glad tidings, finisher   375
Of utmost hope! now clear I understand
What oft my steadiest thoughts have searched in vain,
Why our great expectation should be called
The seed of woman: Virgin mother, hail,
High in the love of heaven, yet from my loins   380
Thou shalt proceed, and from thy womb the Son
Of God most high; so God with man unites.
Needs must the serpent now his capital bruise
Expect with mortal pain: say where and when
Their fight, what stroke shall bruise the victor's heel.'   385
   To whom thus Michael. 'Dream not of their fight,
As of a duel, or the local wounds
Of head or heel: not therefore joins the Son
Manhood to godhead, with more strength to foil
Thy enemy; nor so is overcome   390
Satan, whose fall from heaven, a deadlier bruise,
Disabled not to give thee thy death's wound:
Which he, who comes thy Saviour, shall recure,
Not by destroying Satan, but his works
In thee and in thy seed: nor can this be,   395
But by fulfilling that which thou didst want,
Obedience to the law of God, imposed
On penalty of death, and suffering death,
The penalty to thy transgression due,
And due to theirs which out of thine will grow: 400
So only can high justice rest appaid.
The law of God exact he shall fulfill
Both by obedience and by love, though love
Alone fulfill the law; thy punishment
He shall endure by coming in the flesh   405
To a reproachful life and cursed death,
Proclaiming life to all who shall believe
In his redemption, and that his obedience
Imputed becomes theirs by faith, his merits
To save them, not their own, though legal works.   410
For this he shall live hated, be blasphemed,
Seized on by force, judged, and to death condemned
A shameful and accursed, nailed to the cross

   395 ff. Here is the real occasion for *Paradise Regained*. Only by fulfilling complete obedience to God can Satan be overcome.

By his own nation, slain for bringing life;
But to the cross he nails thy enemies,   415
The law that is against thee, and the sins
Of all mankind, with him there crucified,
Never to hurt them more who rightly trust
In this his satisfaction; so he dies,
But soon revives, death over him no power   420
Shall long usurp; ere the third dawning light
Return, the stars of morn shall see him rise
Out of his grave, fresh as the dawning light,
Thy ransom paid, which man from death redeems,
His death for man, as many as offered life   425
Neglect not, and the benefit embrace
By faith not void of works: this godlike act
Annuls thy doom, the death thou shouldst have died,
In sin forever lost from life; this act
Shall bruise the head of Satan, crush his strength   430
Defeating sin and death, his two main arms,
And fix far deeper in his head their stings
Than temporal death shall bruise the victor's heel,
Or theirs whom he redeems, a death like sleep,
A gentle wafting to immortal life.   435
Nor after resurrection shall he stay
Longer on earth than certain times to appear
To his disciples, men who in his life
Still followed him; to them shall leave in charge
To teach all nations what of him they learned   440
And his salvation, them who shall believe
Baptizing in the profluent stream, the sign
Of washing them from guilt of sin to life
Pure, and in mind prepared, if so befall,
For death, like that which the Redeemer died.   445
All nations they shall teach; for from that day
Not only to the sons of Abraham's loins
Salvation shall be preached, but to the sons
Of Abraham's faith wherever through the world;
So in his seed all nations shall be blest.   450
Then to the heaven of heavens he shall ascend
With victory, triumphing through the air
Over his foes and thine; there shall surprise
The serpent, prince of air, and drag in chains
Through all his realm, and there confounded leave;   455
Then enter into glory, and resume
His seat at God's right hand, exalted high
Above all names in heaven; and thence shall come,
When this world's dissolution shall be ripe,
With glory and power to judge both quick and dead,   460
To judge the unfaithful dead, but to reward
His faithful, and receive them into bliss,
Whether in heaven or earth, for then the earth
Shall be all Paradise, far happier place

Than this of Eden, and far happier days.'   465
   So spake the archangel Michael, then paused,
As at the world's great period; and our sire
Replete with joy and wonder thus replied.
   'O goodness infinite, goodness immense!
That all this good of evil shall produce,   470
And evil turn to good; more wonderful
Than that which by creation first brought forth
Light out of darkness! full of doubt I stand,
Whether I should repent me now of sin
By me done and occasioned, or rejoice   475
Much more, that much more good thereof shall spring,
To God more glory, more good will to men
From God, and over wrath grace shall abound.
But say, if our deliverer up to heaven
Must reascend, what will betide the few   480
His faithful, left among the unfaithful herd,
The enemies of truth; who then shall guide
His people, who defend? will they not deal
Worse with his followers than with him they dealt?'
   'Be sure they will,' said the angel; 'but from heaven   485
He to his own a comforter will send,
The promise of the father, who shall dwell
His spirit within them, and the law of faith
Working through love, upon their hearts shall write,
To guide them in all truth, and also arm   490
With spiritual armor, able to resist
Satan's assaults, and quench his fiery darts,
What man can do against them, not afraid,
Though to the death, against such cruelties
With inward consolations recompensed,   495
And oft supported so as shall amaze
Their proudest persecutors: for the spirit
Poured first on his apostles, whom he sends
To evangelize the nations, then on all
Baptized, shall them with wondrous gifts endue   500
To speak all tongues, and do all miracles,
As did their Lord before them. Thus they win
Great numbers of each nation to receive
With joy the tidings brought from heaven: at length
Their ministry performed, and race well run,   505
Their doctrine and their story written left,
They die; but in their room, as they forewarn,
Wolves shall succeed for teachers, grievous wolves,
Who all the sacred mysteries of heaven
To their own vile advantages shall turn   510
Of lucre and ambition, and the truth
With superstitions and traditions taint,
Left only in those written records pure,
Though not but by the spirit understood.
Then shall they seek to avail themselves of names,   515

Places and titles, and with these to join
Secular power, though feigning still to act
By spiritual, to themselves appropriating
The spirit of God, promised alike and given
To all believers; and from that pretense,   520
Spiritual laws by carnal power shall force
On every conscience; laws which none shall find
Left them enrolled, or what the spirit within
Shall on the heart engrave. What will they then
But force the spirit of grace itself, and bind   525
His consort liberty; what, but unbuild
His living temples, built by faith to stand,
Their own faith not another's: for on earth
Who against faith and conscience can be heard
Infallible? yet many will presume: 530
Whence heavy persecution shall arise
On all who in the worship persevere
Of spirit and truth; the rest, far greater part,
Well deem in outward rites and specious forms
Religion satisfied; truth shall retire   535
Bestuck with slanderous darts, and works of faith
Rarely be found: so shall the world go on,
To good malignant, to bad men benign,
Under her own weight groaning till the day
Appear of respiration to the just,   540
And vengeance to the wicked, at return
Of him so lately promised to thy aid
The woman's seed, obscurely then foretold,
Now amplier known thy Saviour and thy Lord,
Last in the clouds from heaven to be revealed   545
In glory of the father, to dissolve
Satan with his perverted world, then raise
From the conflagrant mass, purged and refined,
New heavens, new earth, ages of endless date
Founded in righteousness and peace and love   550
To bring forth fruits joy and eternal bliss.'
    He ended; and thus Adam last replied.
'How soon hath thy prediction, seer blest,
Measured this transient world, the race of time,
Till time stand fixed: beyond is all abyss,   555
Eternity, whose end no eye can reach.
Greatly instructed I shall hence depart,
Greatly in peace of thought, and have my fill
Of knowledge, what this vessel can contain;
Beyond which was my folly to aspire.   560
Henceforth I learn, that to obey is best,
And love with fear the only God, to walk
As in his presence, ever to observe
His providence, and on him sole depend,

534. **Well**: first edition reads 'Will' and most editors have used it, although second, third, and fourth editions read 'Well' and there is no choice so far as context is concerned. Either word can be used.

Merciful over all his works, with good   565
Still overcoming evil, and by small
Accomplishing great things, by things deemed weak
Subverting worldly strong, and worldly wise
By simply meek; that suffering for truth's sake
Is fortitude to highest victory,   570
And to the faithful death the gate of life;
Taught this by his example whom I now
Acknowledge my redeemer ever blest.'
   To whom thus also the angel last replied:
'This having learned, thou hast attained the sum   575
Of wisdom; hope no higher, though all the stars
Thou knewest by name, and all the ethereal powers,
All secrets of the deep, all nature's works,
Or works of God in heaven, air, earth, or sea,
And all the riches of this world enjoyedst,   580
And all the rule, one empire; only add
Deeds to thy knowledge answerable, add faith,
Add virtue, patience, temperance, add love,
By name to come called charity, the soul
Of all the rest: then wilt thou not be loath   585
To leave this Paradise, but shalt possess
A paradise within thee, happier far.
Let us descend now therefore from this top
Of speculation; for the hour precise
Exacts our parting hence; and see the guards,   590
By me encamped on yonder hill, expect
Their motion, at whose front a flaming sword,
In signal of remove, waves fiercely round;
We may no longer stay: go, waken Eve;
Her also I with gentle dreams have calmed   595
Portending good, and all her spirits composed
To meek submission: thou at season fit
Let her with thee partake what thou hast heard,
Chiefly what may concern her faith to know,
The great deliverance by her seed to come   600
(For by the woman's seed) on all mankind.
That ye may live, which will be many days,
Both in one faith unanimous though sad,
With cause for evils past, yet much more cheered
With meditation on the happy end.'   605
   He ended, and they both descend the hill;
Descended, Adam to the bower where Eve
Lay sleeping ran before, but found her waked;
And thus with words not sad she him received.
   'Whence thou returnest, and whither wentest, I know; 610
For God is also in sleep, and dreams advise,
Which he hath sent propitious, some great good
Presaging, since with sorrow and heart's distress
Wearied I fell asleep: but now lead on;
In me is no delay; with thee to go,   615

Is to stay here; without thee here to stay,
Is to go hence unwilling; thou to me
Art all things under heaven, all places thou,
Who for my willful crime art banished hence.
This further consolation yet secure   620
I carry hence; though all by me is lost,
Such favor I unworthy am vouchsafed,
By me the promised seed shall all restore.'
  So spake our mother Eve, and Adam heard
Well pleased, but answered not; for now too nigh   625
The archangel stood, and from the other hill
To their fixed station, all in bright array
The cherubim descended; on the ground
Gliding meteorous, as evening mist
Risen from a river o'er the marish glides,   630
And gathers ground fast at the laborer's heel
Homeward returning.   High in front advanced,
The brandished sword of God before them blazed
Fierce as a comet; which with torrid heat,
And vapor as the Libyan air adust,   635
Began to parch that temperate clime; whereat
In either hand the hastening angel caught
Our lingering parents, and to the eastern gate
Led them direct, and down the cliff as fast
To the subjected plain; then disappeared.   640
They looking back, all the eastern side beheld
Of Paradise, so late their happy seat,
Waved over by that flaming brand, the gate
With dreadful faces thronged and fiery arms:
Some natural tears they dropped, but wiped them soon;   645
The world was all before them, where to choose
Their place of rest, and providence their guide:
They hand in hand with wandering steps and slow,
Through Eden took their solitary way.

THE END

Paradise Regained
1640–1670

IN 1671, four years after the appearance in 1667 of *Paradise Lost*, appeared a volume containing *Paradise Regained* and *Samson Agonistes*.[1] We know little or nothing about the actual date of composition of either poem, not even which was written first. The story contained in Thomas Ellwood's autobiography[2] of how that priggish young Quaker upon finishing the reading of the manuscript of *Paradise Lost* suggested to Milton the idea of writing *Paradise Regained*, has been too readily accepted by some as the actual point of origin of this poem. Not a great deal of credence can be accorded to Ellwood's anecdote, except as an anecdote; and it is very doubtful that his remark to Milton had much to do with the creation of the poem.

The subject had been considered by Milton very early. He announced the poem's exact theme, probably unwittingly, about 1630, in the second stanza of *The Passion*, lines 13–14:

> 'Most perfect hero, tried in heaviest plight
> Of labors huge and hard, too hard for human wight.'

But he spent years deciding just which of the 'labors huge and hard' should constitute the subject of a poem. *Paradise Lost* apparently decided him. In the *Trinity College Manuscript* occur topics taken from the life of Christ as portrayed in the Gospels. 'Christ Born, Christ Bound, Christ Crucified, Christ Risen,' and *Christus Patiens* are listed as topics for literary treatment, the last definitely earmarked for a dramatic composition. In addition, the statement concerning fit material for literary treatment occurring in *The Reason of Church Government* (1641/42) must be considered. The theme of the poem, the Christ successfully withstanding temptation by Satan, thus reversing the effects of the fall of man brought about by Adam through Eve succumbing to the temptations of Satan, definitely connects *Paradise Regained* with *Paradise Lost* as a sort of continuation poem. And it is the brief epic announced in 1641/42.

Metrically, the poem is like *Paradise Lost*, being written in a pentameter blank verse. The student should read Milton's statement on *The Verse* written for the longer poem as he begins the study of the metrics of *Paradise Regained*.

The sources of the poem are more obvious than for many others of Milton's poems. The basic source is the account in the Gospels, Matthew and Luke especially, of the temptation of the Christ by Satan in the wilderness, after the forty-day fast. Professor Hughes has pointed out that Spenser's hero, Guyon, in the second book of the *Faerie Queene*, or the story of Guyon's temptation in the cave of Mammon, provided Milton with a model of the temptation of the Christ in *Paradise Regained*. Giles Fletcher's *Christ's Victory and Triumph* (1610), a seemingly much more direct subject, actually is much less of a genuine source for *Paradise Regained* than the second book of the *Faerie*

---

[1] The poems were licensed for publication on July 2, 1670, and entered in the *Stationers' Register* on September 20, 1670.

[2] *The History and Life of Thomas Ellwood*, Written by His Own Hand (London, 1906), pp. 121–23.

Queene. How many of the Continental dramatic and poetic treatments of the temptation Todd mentions were actually known to Milton is uncertain. None of them seems to have contributed directly to Milton's poem. Professor Hughes convincingly insists that the Christ of Milton's poem is in the direct line of the epic hero in Renaissance tradition from Boccaccio and Petrarch through Tasso.[1]

Paradise Regained is perhaps the most difficult for the reader to appreciate of all Milton's poems, though it is easy enough to understand. Many critics and readers have turned away from it in disappointment and even with disgust with what they have called its aridity. This poem is more responsible than any other for Pattison's statement that Milton's poetry as he grows older is marked by a progressive desiccation. But the poem has a good deal to offer to the student of Milton and to the student of the literature of the sixteenth and seventeenth centuries in England. The theme itself no longer particularly engages our attention directly; but the poem, judged and understood as a fulfillment of what the author set out to do in it, is at once striking and valuable. Study of it leads one gradually to understand Milton's indignation, as tradition has preserved the story, whenever someone compared *Paradise Regained* unfavorably with *Paradise Lost*. *Paradise Regained* lacks the embroidery of the longer poem, and concerns itself with a single episode or chain of episodes connected with a single major event in the life of Jesus. The poem deals only with the temptation of Jesus by Satan in the wilderness, and the very limitation of scope of this poem, as contrasted with the longer one, made the task Milton had assigned himself a much more difficult one. *Paradise Regained* is remarkable for its compression and economy of utterance. In reading it, we are constantly astonished at the degree of success Milton was able to attain in it, especially when we consider all elements in it, most of which seem able to contribute only to almost certain poetic failure.

Some critics have dismissed the poem on theological grounds; but surely a poet may be permitted his own theology. However, after three centuries, it is unlikely that the general attitude toward this poem will ever change materially. The poem belongs with all noble attempts by poets to deal with material that they could not wholly succeed in making poetic. *Paradise Regained* perhaps ranks higher poetically than the New Testament *Paraphrases* of Richard Baxter; and from any literary standpoint, meets the requirements of its canons better than most of the poetic treatments of Biblical subjects so numerous and popular in the seventeenth, eighteenth, and nineteenth centuries. But for most readers it will doubtless remain a sort of metrical tract. To say that it is as good or better than other works of its kind is apologetic criticism.

In it, Milton takes as his material the story of the temptation of Jesus by Satan as set forth in the Synoptic Gospels, Mark, Matthew, and Luke. (*Mark* 1:12–13; *Matthew* 4:1–11; *Luke* 4:1–13.) The order of events Milton principally followed is that found in Luke's account of the temptation.

> And Jesus being full of the Holy Ghost returned from Jordan, and was led by the Spirit into the wilderness, being forty days tempted of the devil. And in those days he did eat nothing: and when they were ended, he afterward hungered. And the devil said unto him, If thou be the Son of God, command this stone that it be made bread. And Jesus answered him, saying, It is written, That man shall not live by bread alone, but by every word of God. And the devil, taking him up into an high mountain, shewed unto him all the kingdoms of the world in a

---

[1] M. Y. Hughes, 'The Christ of *Paradise Regained* and the Renaissance Heroic Tradition,' *Studies in Philology*, vol. XXXV (1938), pp. 254–77.

moment of time. And the devil said unto him, All this power will I give thee, and the glory of them: for that is delivered unto me; and to whomsoever I will I give it. If thou therefore wilt worship me, all shall be thine. And Jesus answered and said unto him, Get thee behind me, Satan: for it is written, Thou shalt worship the Lord thy God, and him only shalt thou serve. And he brought him to Jerusalem, and set him on a pinnacle of the temple, and said unto him, If thou be the Son of God, cast thyself down from hence: For it is written, He shall give his angels charge over thee, to keep thee; And in their hands they shall bear thee up, lest at any time thou dash thy foot against a stone. And Jesus answering said unto him, It is said, Thou shalt not tempt the Lord thy God. And when the devil had ended all the temptation, he departed from him for a season.

In Matthew's account, when the temptation is over, the angels come and minister unto him. The three temptations, food or creature comforts, power or worldly glory, and 'casting himself down' or simple obedience to Satan, all resolve themselves into one: the temptation to fail in complete obedience to God. This is the substance of the poem, with a minimum of introductory, transitional, and explanatory material.

The poem contains only two characters, the Christ and Satan, and they are mouthpieces and personifications rather than persons. The Christ is God's 'official' champion, who as 'one greater Man' is to 'restore us' or to repair the ruin wrought by our first parents 'and the fruit of that forbidden tree.' Satan is no longer a fallen angel, but an experienced spirit of evil who feels the compulsion of God to enter into what he knows and feels is a hopeless contest with the Christ. When the two meet, 'the war, proclaimed of old in Eden between the serpent, and the seed of the serpent, and the seed of the woman (*Genesis* 3:15), now takes place; when that promised seed of the woman comes forth into the field (being initiated by baptism, and anointed by the Holy Ghost, unto the public office of his ministry) to fight with that old serpent, and at last to bruise his head.' [1] The result is a 'battle' in the form of a debate, the outcome of which is never in doubt. The Christ will overcome the Devil, in this instance, by refusing utterly to obey him, as this will be to obey God whose command is to disobey or to refuse to obey Satan.

The verse of the poem and its technical success have been accorded the highest praise by a few of the most sensitive and competent critics and poets since Milton's day; but on the whole, the praise has been for the technical excellence, and not for the complete poetic appeal of the lines. The lines will appeal most to the poet, and least to the person unable to appreciate easily exactly what Milton was doing with the meter and structure of the verse. Certainly the reader will not be carried along by the complete ensemble of the poetry as in many of his other poems. The austere economy of utterance, to which Milton rigidly held himself in this poem, is too much for most readers. It is perhaps not so much an arid as it is a too obviously technical accomplishment, the poet ultimately being unable to blend the angularities of the technique into the complete structure of the poem.

REFERENCES

Blakeney, E. H., *Paradise Regained*. London: Scholartis Press, 1932.

Masson, David, *Poetical Works*.

Newton, Thomas, *Paradise Regained*. London: J. and R. Tonson and S. Draper, 1752.

Todd, H. J., *Poetical Works*.

Verity, A. W., *The Cambridge Milton for Schools*.

Wyatt, A. J., *Paradise Regained*. London, n.d.

[1] John Lightfoot, *Horae Hebraicae et Talmudicae*, 1658–74, quoted from Robert Gandell; edition of the English translation (Oxford, 1859, 4 vols.), vol. II, p. 83.

Paradise Regained

(*1640–1670*)

A Poem in Four Books

This poem was first published in 1671 with *Samson Agonistes*, which it precedes. It was probably written over a long period of time, and not composed all at once at any particular time. But we know nothing of its date of composition. The second edition appeared in 1680, six years after Milton's death. The text of the second edition is of some importance to the textual editor; but the 1671 text offers only a few difficulties.

Metrically, the poem is much like *Paradise Lost*, being written in unrhymed pentameter throughout. The verse seems at first glance much stiffer than in the longer poem; but this characteristic is due as much to the less expansive nature of the material and its treatment as to the verse structure itself. The chief characteristics of the verse are its economy, its compression, and its lack of ornamentation.

THE FIRST BOOK

I who erewhile the happy garden sung,
By one man's disobedience lost, now sing
Recovered Paradise to all mankind,
By one man's firm obedience fully tried
Through all temptation, and the tempter foiled   5
In all his wiles, defeated and repulsed,
And Eden raised in the waste wilderness.
    Thou spirit who ledest this glorious eremite
Into the desert, his victorious field
Against the spiritual foe, and broughtest him thence   10
By proof the undoubted Son of God, inspire,
As thou art wont, my prompted song else mute,
And bear through height or depth of nature's bounds
With prosperous wing full summed to tell of deeds
Above heroic, though in secret done,   15
And unrecorded left through many an age,
Worthy to have not remained so long unsung.

1 ff. Having finished *PL*, Milton now turns to man's redemption through the obedience of Christ. Note that Milton insists that man was saved in exactly the same manner in which he was lost, namely, by Christ successfully resisting the temptations of Satan.

8. **eremite:** a hermit; indeed, the word from which *hermit* derived, a recluse.

14. **summed:** Phillips, 'in falconry, is when a hawk has her feathers, and is fit to be taken from the aerie or mew.' Hence, figuratively, 'full summed' is fully prepared.

Now had the great proclaimer with a voice
More awful than the sound of trumpet, cried
Repentance, and heaven's kingdom nigh at hand   20
To all baptized: to his great baptism flocked
With awe the regions round, and with them came
From Nazareth the son of Joseph deemed
To the flood Jordan, came as then obscure,
Unmarked, unknown; but him the Baptist soon   25
Descried, divinely warned, and witness bore
As to his worthier, and would have resigned
To him his heavenly office, nor was long
His witness unconfirmed: on him baptized
Heaven opened, and in likeness of a dove   30
The spirit descended, while the father's voice
From heaven pronounced him his beloved Son.
That heard the adversary, who roving still
About the world, at that assembly famed
Would not be last, and with the voice divine   35
Nigh thunderstruck, the exalted man, to whom
Such high attest was given, a while surveyed
With wonder, then with envy fraught and rage
Flies to his place, nor rests, but in mid air
To council summons all his mighty peers,   40
Within thick clouds and dark tenfold involved,
A gloomy consistory; and them amidst
With looks aghast and sad he thus bespake.
      'O ancient powers of air and this wide world,
For much more willingly I mention air,   45
This our old conquest, than remember hell
Our hated habitation; well ye know
How many ages, as the years of men,
This universe we have possessed, and ruled
In manner at our will the affairs of earth,   50
Since Adam and his facile consort Eve
Lost Paradise deceived by me, though since
With dread attending when that fatal wound
Shall be inflicted by the seed of Eve
Upon my head, long the decrees of heaven   55
Delay, for longest time to him is short;
And now too soon for us the circling hours
This dreaded time have compassed, wherein we
Must bide the stroke of that long threatened wound,
At least if so we can, and by the head   60
Broken be not intended all our power
To be infringed, our freedom and our being

18. **the great proclaimer:** John the Baptist.

18 ff. Woven together from the Gospel accounts of the baptism of Jesus and the forty days' temptation and fast in the wilderness.

39 ff. **mid air:** Satan, the adversary, now spends his time on earth. His abode is the middle air. See *Ephesians* 2:2; *PL* X:188–89, XII:454; and *PR* II:117.

42. **consistory:** council.

In this fair empire won of earth and air;
For this ill news I bring, the woman's seed
Destined to this, is late of woman born,   65
His birth to our just fear gave no small cause,
But his growth now to youth's full flower, displaying
All virtue, grace and wisdom to achieve
Things highest, greatest, multiplies my fear.
Before him a great prophet, to proclaim   70
His coming, is sent harbinger, who all
Invites, and in the consecrated stream
Pretends to wash off sin, and fit them so
Purified to receive him pure, or rather
To do him honor as their king; all come,   75
And he himself among them was baptized,
Not thence to be more pure, but to receive
The testimony of heaven, that who he is
Thenceforth the nations may not doubt; I saw
The prophet do him reverence, on him rising   80
Out of the water, heaven above the clouds
Unfold her crystal doors, thence on his head
A perfect dove descend, whate'er it meant,
And out of heaven the sovereign voice I heard,
"This is my Son beloved, in him am pleased."   85
His mother then is mortal, but his sire,
He who obtains the monarchy of heaven,
And what will he not do to advance his Son?
His first-begot we know, and sore have felt,
When his fierce thunder drove us to the deep;   90
Who this is we must learn, for man he seems
In all his lineaments, though in his face
The glimpses of his father's glory shine.
Ye see our danger on the utmost edge
Of hazard, which admits no long debate,   95
But must with something sudden be opposed,
Not force, but well couched fraud, well woven snares,
Ere in the head of nations he appear
Their king, their leader, and supreme on earth
I, when no other durst, sole undertook   100
The dismal expedition to find out
And ruin Adam, and the exploit performed
Successfully; a calmer voyage now
Will waft me; and the way found prosperous once
Induces best to hope of like success.'   105
  He ended, and his words impression left
Of much amazement to the infernal crew,
Distracted and surprised with deep dismay
At these sad tidings; but no time was then
For long indulgence to their fears or grief: 110
Unanimous they all commit the care
And management of this main enterprise

72. **consecrated stream**: the river Jordan.

To him their great dictator, whose attempt
At first against mankind so well had thrived
In Adam's overthrow, and led their march   115
From hell's deep-vaulted den to dwell in light,
Regents and potentates, and kings, yea gods
Of many a pleasant realm and province wide.
So to the coast of Jordan he directs
His easy steps; girded with snaky wiles,   120
Where he might likeliest find this new-declared,
This man of men, attested Son of God,
Temptation and all guile on him to try;
So to subvert whom he suspected raised
To end his reign on earth so long enjoyed: 125
But contrary unwitting he fulfilled
The purposed counsel preordained and fixed
Of the most high, who in full frequence bright
Of angels, thus to Gabriel smiling spake.
  'Gabriel this day by proof thou shalt behold,   130
Thou and all angels conversant on earth
With man or men's affairs, how I begin
To verify that solemn message late,
On which I sent thee to the Virgin pure
In Galilee, that she should bear a son   135
Great in renown, and called the Son of God;
Then toldest her doubting how these things could be
To her a virgin, that on her should come
The Holy Ghost, and the power of the highest
O'ershadow her: this man born and now upgrown,   140
To show him worthy of his birth divine
And high prediction, henceforth I expose
To Satan; let him tempt and now assay
His utmost subtilty, because he boasts
And vaunts of his great cunning to the throng   145
Of his apostasy; he might have learnt
Less overweening, since he failed in Job,
Whose constant perseverance overcame
Whate'er his cruel malice could invent.
He now shall know I can produce a man   150
Of female seed, far abler to resist
All his solicitations, and at length
All his vast force, and drive him back to hell,
Winning by conquest what the first man lost
By fallacy surprised.   But first I mean   155
To exercise him in the wilderness,
There he shall first lay down the rudiments
Of his great warfare, ere I send him forth
To conquer sin and death the two grand foes,
By humiliation and strong sufferance: 160

129. **Gabriel**: the reason for it being Gabriel to whom God here speaks appears in lines 133–34.
133 ff. The Annunciation.
144. **subtilty**: spelled in much more sensible fashion than our own commoner spelling of this word.

His weakness shall o'ercome satanic strength
And all the world, and mass of sinful flesh;
That all the angels and ethereal powers,
They now, and men hereafter may discern,
From what consummate virtue I have chose   165
This perfect man, by merit called my Son,
To earn salvation for the sons of men.'
    So spake the eternal father, and all heaven
Admiring stood a space, then into hymns
Burst forth, and in celestial measures moved,   170
Circling the throne and singing, while the hand
Sung with the voice, and this the argument.
    'Victory and triumph to the Son of God
Now entering his great duel, not of arms,
But to vanquish by wisdom hellish wiles.   175
The father knows the Son; therefore secure
Ventures his filial virtue, though untried,
Against whate'er may tempt, whate'er seduce,
Allure, or terrify, or undermine.
Be frustrate all ye stratagems of hell,   180
And devilish machinations come to nought.'
    So they in heaven their odes and vigils tuned:
Meanwhile the Son of God, who yet some days
Lodged in Bethabara where John baptized,
Musing and much revolving in his breast,   185
How best the mighty work he might begin
Of Saviour to mankind, and which way first
Publish his godlike office now mature,
One day forth walked alone, the spirit leading;
And his deep thoughts, the better to converse   190
With solitude, till far from track of men,
Thought following thought, and step by step led on,
He entered now the bordering desert wild,
And with dark shades and rocks environed round,
His holy meditations thus pursued.   195
    'O what a multitude of thoughts at once
Awakened in me swarm, while I consider
What from within I feel myself, and hear
What from without comes often to my ears,
Ill sorting with my present state compared.   200
When I was yet a child, no childish play
To me was pleasing, all my mind was set
Serious to learn and know, and thence to do
What might be public good; myself I thought
Born to that end, born to promote all truth,   205
All righteous things: therefore above my years,
The law of God I read, and found it sweet,
Made it my whole delight, and in it grew
To such perfection, that ere yet my age

165. **chose**: the obsolete form of the past participle.
201 ff. This sounds like an autobiographical passage from Milton's own memory, ending with line 207.

Had measured twice six years, at our great feast   210
I went into the temple, there to hear
The teachers of our law, and to propose
What might improve my knowledge or their own;
And was admired by all, yet this not all
To which my spirit aspired, victorious deeds   215
Flamed in my heart, heroic acts, one while
To rescue Israel from the Roman yoke,
Then to subdue and quell o'er all the earth
Brute violence and proud tyrannic power,
Till truth were freed, and equity restored: 220
Yet hold it more humane, more heavenly first
By winning words to conquer willing hearts,
And make persuasion do the work of fear;
At least to try, and teach the erring soul
Not willfully misdoing, but unware   225
Misled; the stubborn only to subdue.
These growing thoughts my mother soon perceiving
By words at times cast forth inly rejoiced,
And said to me apart, "high are thy thoughts
O Son, but nourish them and let them soar   230
To what height sacred virtue and true worth
Can raise them, though above example high;
By matchless deeds express thy matchless sire.
For know, thou art no son of mortal man,
Though men esteem thee low of parentage,   235
Thy father is the eternal king, who rules
All heaven and earth, angels and sons of men,
A messenger from God foretold thy birth
Conceived in me a virgin, he foretold
Thou shouldst be great and sit on David's throne,   240
And of thy kingdom there should be no end.
At thy nativity a glorious choir
Of angels in the fields of Bethlehem sung
To shepherds watching at their folds by night,
And told them the Messiah now was born,   245
Where they might see him, and to thee they came;
Directed to the manger where thou layest,
For in the inn was left no better room:
A star, not seen before in heaven appearing
Guided the wise men thither from the east,   250
To honor thee with incense, myrrh, and gold,
By whose bright course led on they found the place,
Affirming it thy star new graven in heaven,
By which they knew thee king of Israel born.
Just Simeon and prophetic Anna, warned   255
By vision, found thee in the temple, and spake

214 ff. The personal note again, for this reads like Milton's ideas for great literary subjects, and ambitions for the revolution in England.

230 ff. Another paraphrase of passages from Gospel verses.

240 ff. Compare with *PL* XII:356 ff.

Before the altar and the vested priest,
Like things of thee to all that present stood."
This having heard, straight I again revolved
The law and prophets, searching what was writ   260
Concerning the Messiah, to our scribes
Known partly, and soon found of whom they spake
I am; this chiefly, that my way must lie
Through many a hard assay even to the death,
Ere I the promised kingdom can attain,   265
Or work redemption for mankind, whose sins'
Full weight must be transferred upon my head.
Yet neither thus disheartened or dismayed,
The time prefixed I waited, when behold
The Baptist, (of whose birth I oft had heard,   270
Not knew by sight) now come, who was to come
Before Messiah and his way prepare.
I as all others to his baptism came,
Which I believed was from above; but he
Straight knew me, and with loudest voice proclaimed   275
Me him (for it was shown him so from heaven)
Me him whose harbinger he was; and first
Refused on me his baptism to confer,
As much his greater, and was hardly won;
But as I rose out of the laving stream,   280
Heaven opened her eternal doors, from whence
The spirit descended on me like a dove,
And last the sum of all, my father's voice,
Audibly heard from heaven, pronounced me his,
Me his beloved Son, in whom alone   285
He was well pleased: by which I knew the time
Now full, that I no more should live obscure,
But openly begin, as best becomes
The authority which I derived from heaven.
And now by some strong motion I am led   290
Into this wilderness, to what intent
I learn not yet, perhaps I need not know;
For what concerns my knowledge God reveals.'
    So spake our morning star then in his rise,
And looking round on every side beheld   295
A pathless desert, dusk with horrid shades;
The way he came not having marked, return
Was difficult, by human steps untrod;
And he still on was led, but with such thoughts
Accompanied of things past and to come   300
Lodged in his breast, as well might recommend
Such solitude before choicest society.
Full forty days he passed, whether on hill
Sometimes, anon in shady vale, each night
Under the covert of some ancient oak,   305

259 ff. Another summary of the life of Jesus up to and immediately after his baptism.
302. An Alexandrine line, apparently.

Or cedar, to defend him from the dew,
Or harbored in one cave, is not revealed;
Nor tasted human food, nor hunger felt
Till those days ended, hungered then at last
Among wild beasts: they at his sight grew mild,   310
Nor sleeping him nor waking harmed, his walk
The fiery serpent fled, and noxious worm,
The lion and fierce tiger glared aloof.
But now an aged man in rural weeds,
Following, as seemed, the quest of some stray ewe,   315
Or withered sticks to gather; which might serve
Against a winter's day when winds blow keen,
To warm him wet returned from field at eve,
He saw approach, who first with curious eye
Perused him, then with words thus uttered spake.   320
    'Sir, what ill chance hath brought thee to this place
So far from path or road of men, who pass
In troop or caravan, for single none
Durst ever, who returned, and dropped not here
His carcass, pined with hunger and with drought?   325
I ask the rather, and the more admire,
For that to me thou seemest the man, whom late
Our new baptizing prophet at the ford
Of Jordan honored so, and called thee Son
Of God; I saw and heard, for we sometimes   330
Who dwell this wild, constrained by want, come forth
To town or village nigh (nighest is far)
Where aught we hear, and curious are to hear,
What happens new; fame also finds us out.'
    To whom the Son of God. 'Who brought me hither   335
Will bring me hence, no other guide I seek.'
    'By miracle he may,' replied the swain,
'What other way I see not, for we here
Live on tough roots and stubs, to thirst inured
More than the camel, and to drink go far,   340
Men to much misery and hardship born;
But if thou be the Son of God, command
That out of these hard stones be made thee bread;
So shalt thou save thyself and us relieve
With food, whereof we wretched seldom taste.'   345
    He ended, and the Son of God replied.
'Thinkest thou such force in bread? is it not written
(For I discern thee other than thou seemest)
Man lives not by bread only, but each word
Proceeding from the mouth of God; who fed   350
Our fathers here with manna; in the mount
Moses was forty days, nor eat nor drank,
And forty days Eliah without food

314. **an aged man in rural weeds**: symbolic, perhaps, of Satan's inability now to adopt young disguises.
352. **eat**: past tense, as frequently in this form.
353. **Eliah**: Elijah; cf. *I Kings* 19.

Wandered this barren waste, the same I now:
Why dost thou then suggest to me distrust,   355
Knowing who I am, as I know who thou art?'
　　Whom thus answered the archfiend now undisguised.
''Tis true, I am that spirit unfortunate,
Who leagued with millions more in rash revolt
Kept not my happy station, but was driven   360
With them from bliss to the bottomless deep,
Yet to that hideous place not so confined
By rigor unconniving, but that oft
Leaving my dolorous prison I enjoy
Large liberty to round this globe of earth,   365
Or range in the air, nor from the heaven of heavens
Hath he excluded my resort sometimes.
I came among the sons of God, when he
Gave up into my hands Uzzean Job
To prove him, and illustrate his high worth;   370
And when to all his angels he proposed
To draw the proud king Ahab into fraud
That he might fall in Ramoth, they demurring,
I undertook that office, and the tongues
Of all his flattering prophets glibbed with lies   375
To his destruction, as I had in charge.
For what he bids I do; though I have lost
Much luster of my native brightness, lost
To be beloved of God, I have not lost
To love, at least contemplate and admire   380
What I see excellent in good, or fair,
Or virtuous, I should so have lost all sense.
What can be then less in me than desire
To see thee and approach thee, whom I know
Declared the Son of God, to hear attent   385
Thy wisdom, and behold thy godlike deeds?
Men generally think me much a foe
To all mankind: why should I? they to me
Never did wrong or violence, by them
I lost not what I lost, rather by them   390
I gained what I have gained, and with them dwell
Copartner in these regions of the world,
If not disposer; lend them oft my aid,
Oft my advice by presages and signs,
And answers, oracles, portents and dreams,   395
Whereby they may direct their future life.
Envy they say excites me, thus to gain
Companions of my misery and woe.
At first it may be; but long since with woe
Nearer acquainted, now I feel by proof,   400
That fellowship in pain divides not smart,
Nor lightens aught each man's peculiar load.

369. **Uzzean Job:** cf. *Job* 1:1, 'there was a man in the land of Uz whose name was Job.'
372-73. **Ahab ... Ramoth:** cf. *I Kings* 22:19-22.　　　385. **attent:** attentively.

Small consolation then, were man adjoined:
This wounds me most (what can it less) that man,
Man fallen shall be restored, I never more.'   405
    To whom our Saviour sternly thus replied.
'Deservedly thou grievest, composed of lies
From the beginning, and in lies wilt end;
Who boastest release from hell, and leave to come
Into the heaven of heavens; thou comest indeed,   410
As a poor miserable captive thrall,
Comes to the place where he before had sat
Among the prime in splendor, now deposed,
Ejected, emptied, gazed, unpitied, shunned,
A spectacle of ruin or of scorn   415
To all the host of heaven; the happy place
Imparts to thee no happiness, no joy,
Rather inflames thy torment, representing
Lost bliss, to thee no more communicable,
So never more in hell than when in heaven.   420
But thou art serviceable to heaven's king.
Wilt thou impute to obedience what thy fear
Extorts, or pleasure to do ill excites?
What but thy malice moved thee to misdeem
Of righteous Job, then cruelly to afflict him   425
With all inflictions, but his patience won?
The other service was thy chosen task,
To be a liar in four hundred mouths;
For lying is thy sustenance, thy food.
Yet thou pretendest to truth; all oracles   430
By thee are given, and what confessed more true
Among the nations? that hath been thy craft,
By mixing somewhat true to vent more lies.
But what have been thy answers, what but dark
Ambiguous and with double sense deluding,   435
Which they who asked have seldom understood,
And not well understood as good not known?
Whoever by consulting at thy shrine
Returned the wiser, or the more instruct
To fly or follow what concerned him most,   440
And run not sooner to his fatal snare?
For God hath justly given the nations up
To thy delusions; justly, since they fell
Idolatrous, but when his purpose is
Among them to declare his providence   445
To thee not known, whence hast thou then thy truth,
But from him or his angels president
In every province, who themselves disdaining
To approach thy temples, give thee in command
What to the smallest tittle thou shalt say   450
To thy adorers; thou with trembling fear,
Or like a fawning parasite obeyest;
Then to thyself ascribest the truth foretold.

428. **a liar in four hundred mouths:** the false prophets in *I Kings* 22:6, 22.

But this thy glory shall be soon retrenched;
No more shalt thou by oracling abuse   455
The Gentiles; henceforth oracles are ceased,
And thou no more with pomp and sacrifice
Shalt be inquired at Delphos or elsewhere,
At least in vain, for they shall find thee mute.
God hath now sent his living oracle   460
Into the world, to teach his final will,
And sends his spirit of truth henceforth to dwell
In pious hearts, an inward oracle
To all truth requisite for men to know.'
    So spake our Saviour; but the subtle fiend,   465
Though inly stung with anger and disdain,
Dissembled, and this answer smooth returned.
    'Sharply thou hast insisted on rebuke,
And urged me hard with doings, which not will
But misery hath wrested from me; where   470
Easily canst thou find one miserable,
And not enforced ofttimes to part from truth;
If it may stand him more in stead to lie,
Say and unsay, feign, flatter, or abjure?
But thou art placed above me, thou art Lord;   475
From thee I can and must submiss endure
Check or reproof, and glad to scape so quit.
Hard are the ways of truth, and rough to walk,
Smooth on the tongue discoursed, pleasing to the ear,
And tunable as sylvan pipe or song;   480
What wonder then if I delight to hear
Her dictates from thy mouth? most men admire
Virtue, who follow not her lore: permit me
To hear thee when I come (since no man comes)
And talk at least, though I despair to attain.   485
Thy father, who is holy, wise and pure,
Suffers the hypocrite or atheous priest
To tread his sacred courts, and minister
About his altar, handling holy things,
Praying or vowing, and vouchsafed his voice   490
To Balaam reprobate, a prophet yet
Inspired; disdain not such access to me.'
    To whom our Saviour with unaltered brow.
'Thy coming hither, though I know thy scope,
I bid not or forbid; do as thou findest   495
Permission from above; thou canst not more.'
    He added not; and Satan bowing low
His gray dissimulation, disappeared
Into thin air diffused: for now began
Night with her sullen wing to double-shade   500
The desert, fowls in their clay nests were couched;
And now wild beasts came forth the woods to roam.

THE END OF THE FIRST BOOK

456. **henceforth oracles are ceased:** cf. *Nat. Ode* 173, 'the oracles are dumb.'

THE SECOND BOOK

Meanwhile the new-baptized, who yet remained
At Jordan with the Baptist, and had seen
Him whom they heard so late expressly called
Jesus Messiah Son of God declared,
And on that high authority had believed,   5
And with him talked, and with him lodged, I mean
Andrew and Simon, famous after known
With others though in holy writ not named,
Now missing him their joy so lately found,
So lately found, and so abruptly gone,   10
Began to doubt, and doubted many days,
And as the days increased, increased their doubt:
Sometimes they thought he might be only shown,
And for a time caught up to God, as once
Moses was in the mount, and missing long;   15
And the great Thisbite who on fiery wheels
Rode up to heaven, yet once again to come.
Therefore as those young prophets then with care
Sought lost Eliah, so in each place these
Nigh to Bethabara; in Jericho   20
The city of palms, Aenon, and Salem old,
Machaerus and each town or city walled
On this side the broad lake Gennesaret,
Or in Perea, but returned in vain.
Then on the bank of Jordan, by a creek: 25
Where winds with reeds, and osiers whispering play
Plain fishermen, no greater men them call,
Close in a cottage low together got
Their unexpected loss and plaints outbreathed.
'Alas, from what high hope to what relapse   30
Unlooked for are we fallen, our eyes beheld
Messiah certainly now come, so long
Expected of our fathers; we have heard
His words, his wisdom full of grace and truth,
"Now, now, for sure, deliverance is at hand,   35
The kingdom shall to Israel be restored:"
Thus we rejoiced, but soon our joy is turned
Into perplexity and new amaze:
For whither is he gone, what accident
Hath rapt him from us? will he now retire   40
After appearance, and again prolong
Our expectation? God of Israel,
Send thy Messiah forth, the time is come;

7. **Andrew and Simon**: two of the disciples of Jesus.

16. **the great Thisbite**: cf. *II Kings* 2:11; Elijah, who was caught up to heaven in a fiery chariot. Also cf. *Pr. Bomb.* 1:7–8, and *The Passion* 36:37.

19. **Eliah**: Elijah.

20 ff. The names are chiefly those of Palestinian towns.

23. **the broad lake Gennesaret**: the Sea of Galilee in northern Palestine.

Behold the kings of the earth how they oppress
Thy chosen, to what height their power unjust   45
They have exalted, and behind them cast
All fear of thee, arise and vindicate
Thy glory, free thy people from their yoke,
But let us wait; thus far he hath performed,
Sent his anointed, and to us revealed him,   50
By his great prophet, pointed at and shown,
In public, and with him we have conversed;
Let us be glad of this, and all our fears
Lay on his providence; he will not fail
Nor will withdraw him now, nor will recall,   55
Mock us with his blest sight, then snatch him hence,
Soon we shall see our hope, our joy return.'
    Thus they out of their plaints new hope resume
To find whom at the first they found unsought:
But to his mother Mary, when she saw   60
Others returned from baptism, not her son,
Nor left at Jordan, tidings of him none;
Within her breast, though calm; her breast though pure,
Motherly cares and fears got head, and raised
Some troubled thoughts, which she in sighs thus clad.   65
    'O what avails me now that honor high
To have conceived of God, or that salute
"Hail highly favored, among women blest;"
While I to sorrows am no less advanced,
And fears as eminent, above the lot   70
Of other women, by the birth I bore,
In such a season born when scarce a shed
Could be obtained to shelter him or me
From the bleak air; a stable was our warmth,
A manger his, yet soon enforced to fly   75
Thence into Egypt, till the murderous king
Were dead, who sought his life, and missing filled
With infant blood the streets of Bethlehem;
From Egypt home returned, in Nazareth
Hath been our dwelling many years, his life   80
Private, unactive, calm, contemplative,
Little suspicious to any king; but now
Full grown to man, acknowledged, as I hear,
By John the Baptist, and in public shown,
Son owned from heaven by his father's voice;   85
I looked for some great change; to honor? no,
But trouble, as old Simeon plain foretold,
That to the fall and rising he should be
Of many in Israel, and to a sign
Spoken against, that through my very soul   90
A sword shall pierce, this is my favored lot,
My exaltation to afflictions high;
Afflicted I may be, it seems, and blest;

74 ff. Paraphrasing Scripture again, chiefly to tell what had happened before the poem opens.

I will not argue that, nor will repine.
But where delays he now? some great intent   95
Conceals him: when twelve years he scarce had seen,
I lost him, but so found, as well I saw
He could not lose himself; but went about
His father's business; what he meant I mused,
Since understand; much more his absence now   100
Thus long to some great purpose he obscures.
But I to wait with patience am inured;
My heart hath been a storehouse long of things
And sayings laid up, portending strange events.'
    Thus Mary pondering oft, and oft to mind   105
Recalling what remarkably had passed
Since first her salutation heard, with thoughts
Meekly composed awaited the fulfilling:
The while her son tracing the desert wild,
Sole but with holiest meditations fed,   110
Into himself descended, and at once
All his great work to come before him set;
How to begin, how to accomplish best
His end of being on earth, and mission high:
For Satan with sly preface to return   115
Had left him vacant, and with speed was gone
Up to the middle region of thick air,
Where all his potentates in council sat;
There without sign of boast, or sign of joy,
Solicitous and blank he thus began.   120
    'Princes, heaven's ancient sons, ethereal thrones,
Demonian spirits now, from the element
Each of his reign allotted, rightlier called,
Powers of fire, air, water, and earth beneath,
So may we hold our place and these mild seats   125
Without new trouble; such an enemy
Is risen to invade us, who no less
Threatens than our expulsion down to hell;
I, as I undertook, and with the vote
Consenting in full frequence was empowered,   130
Have found him, viewed him, tasted him, but find
Far other labor to be undergone
Than when I dealt with Adam first of men,
Though Adam by his wife's allurement fell,
However to this man inferior far,   135
If he be man by mother's side at least,
With more than human gifts from heaven adorned,
Perfections absolute, graces divine,
And amplitude of mind to greatest deeds.
Therefore I am returned, lest confidence   140
Of my success with Eve in Paradise
Deceive ye to persuasion over-sure
Of like succeeding here; I summon all

120. **blank:** Phillips, 'pale and wan, that is, out of countenance.' White.

Rather to be in readiness, with hand
Or counsel to assist; lest I who erst   145
Thought none my equal, now be overmatched.'
    So spake the old serpent doubting, and from all
With clamor was assured their utmost aid
At his command; when from amidst them rose
Belial the dissolutest spirit that fell,   150
The sensualest, and after Asmodai
The fleshliest incubus, and thus advised.
    'Set women in his eye and in his walk,
Among daughters of men the fairest found;
Many are in each region passing fair   155
As the noon sky; more like to goddesses
Than mortal creatures, graceful and discreet,
Expert in amorous arts, enchanting tongues
Persuasive, virgin majesty with mild
And sweet allayed, yet terrible to approach,   160
Skilled to retire, and in retiring draw
Hearts after them tangled in amorous nets.
Such object hath the power to soften and tame
Severest temper, smooth the ruggedest brow,
Enerve, and with voluptuous hope dissolve,   165
Draw out with credulous desire, and lead
At will the manliest, resolutest breast,
As the magnetic hardest iron draws.
Women, when nothing else, beguiled the heart
Of wisest Solomon, and made him build,   170
And made him bow to the gods of his wives.'
    To whom quick answer Satan thus returned.
'Belial, in much uneven scale thou weighest
All others by thyself; because of old
Thou thyself dotest on womankind, admiring   175
Their shape, their color, and attractive grace,
None are, thou thinkest, but taken with such toys.
Before the flood thou with thy lusty crew,
False titled sons of God, roaming the earth
Cast wanton eyes on the daughters of men,   180
And coupled with them, and begot a race.
Have we not seen, or by relation heard,
In courts and regal chambers how thou lurkest,
In wood or grove by mossy fountain side,
In valley or green meadow to waylay   185
Some beauty rare, Calisto, Clymene,
Daphne, or Semele, Antiopa,

150. **Belial:** the name means 'worthlessness.'

151. **Asmodai:** Asmodeus, in book of *Tobit*, a lustful, satyr-like demon.   Cf. *PL* IV:168–71, VI:365.

152. **incubus:** in Latin, the nightmare.

153 ff. Jesus is to be tempted as were the 'sons of God' (*PL* XI:622) by the 'bevy of fair women' (*PL* XI:582).   This passage is very similar to *PL* XI:581–95 and 614–27.

186–88. **Calisto . . . Syrinx:** all names of women, famous in ancient legends, seduced by gods masquerading in human shapes.   For any or all cf. Ovid, *Metamorphoses*.

Or Amymone, Syrinx, many more
Too long, then layest thy scapes on names adored,
Apollo, Neptune, Jupiter, or Pan,   190
Satyr, or Faun, or Sylvan?   But these haunts
Delight not all; among the sons of men,
How many have with a smile made small account
Of beauty and her lures, easily scorned
All her assaults, on worthier things intent?   195
Remember that Pellean conqueror,
A youth, how all the beauties of the east
He slightly viewed, and slightly overpassed;
How he surnamed of Africa dismissed
In his prime youth the fair Iberian maid.   200
For Solomon he lived at ease, and full
Of honor, wealth, high fare, aimed not beyond
Higher design than to enjoy his state;
Thence to the bait of women lay exposed;
But he whom we attempt is wiser far   205
Than Solomon, of more exalted mind,
Made and set wholly on the accomplishment
Of greatest things; what woman will you find,
Though of this age the wonder and the fame,
On whom his leisure will vouchsafe an eye   210
Of fond desire? or should she confident,
As sitting queen adored on beauty's throne,
Descend with all her winning charms begirt
To enamor, as the zone of Venus once
Wrought that effect on Jove, so fables tell;   215
How would one look from his majestic brow
Seated as on the top of virtue's hill,
Discountenance her despised, and put to rout
All her array; her female pride deject,
Or turn to reverent awe? for beauty stands   220
In the admiration only of weak minds
Led captive; cease to admire, and all her plumes
Fall flat and shrink into a trivial toy,
At every sudden slighting quite abashed:
Therefore with manlier objects we must try   225
His constancy, with such as have more show
Of worth, of honor, glory, and popular praise;
Rocks whereon greatest men have oftest wrecked;
Or that which only seems to satisfy
Lawful desires of nature, not beyond;   230
And now I know he hungers where no food
Is to be found, in the wild wilderness;
The rest commit to me, I shall let pass

196. **that Pellean conqueror**: Alexander the Great.

199. **he surnamed of Africa**: Scipio Africanus.   The story is told in Burton's *Anatomy of Melancholy*
III:2, from Livy, XXVI:50.

210. **vouchsafe**: in some modern editions, 'vouchsafed,' for no apparent reason.

214. **the zone of Venus**: the girdle of Venus.

No advantage, and his strength as oft assay.'
  He ceased, and heard their grant in loud acclaim;   235
Then forthwith to him takes a chosen band
Of spirits likest to himself in guile
To be at hand, and at his beck appear,
If cause were to unfold some active scene
Of various persons each to know his part;   240
Then to the desert takes with these his flight;
Where still from shade to shade the Son of God
After forty days' fasting had remained,
Now hungering first, and to himself thus said.
  'Where will this end? four times ten days I have passed   245
Wandering this woody maze, and human food
Nor tasted, nor had appetite; that fast
To virtue I impute not, or count part
Of what I suffer here; if nature need not,
Or God support nature without repast   250
Though needing, what praise is it to endure?
But now I feel I hunger, which declares,
Nature hath need of what she asks; yet God
Can satisfy that need some other way,
Though hunger still remain: so it remain   255
Without this body's wasting, I content me,
And from the sting of famine fear no harm,
Nor mind it, fed with better thoughts that feed
Me hungering more to do my father's will.'
  It was the hour of night, when thus the Son   260
Communed in silent walk, then laid him down
Under the hospitable covert nigh
Of trees thick interwoven; there he slept,
And dreamed, as appetite is wont to dream,
Of meats and drinks, nature's refreshment sweet;   265
Him thought, he by the brook of Cherith stood
And saw the ravens with their horny beaks
Food to Elijah bringing even and morn,
Though ravenous, taught to abstain from what they brought:
He saw the prophet also how he fled   270
Into the desert, and how there he slept
Under a juniper; then how awaked,
He found his supper on the coals prepared,
And by the angel was bid rise and eat,
And eat the second time after repose,   275
The strength whereof sufficed him forty days;
Sometimes that with Elijah he partook,
Or as a guest with Daniel at his pulse.
Thus wore out night, and now the herald lark
Left his ground nest, high towering to descry   280
The morn's approach, and greet her with his song:

266. **Cherith:** a brook in Palestine.

278. **pulse:** Phillips, 'a general name for all those sorts of grain that are contained in cods (pods), husks, or shells; as beans, peas, vetches, &c.'

As lightly from his grassy couch uprose
Our Saviour, and found all was but a dream,
Fasting he went to sleep, and fasting waked.
Up to a hill anon his steps he reared,   285
From whose high top to ken the prospect round,
If cottage were in view, sheepcote or herd;
But cottage, herd or sheepcote none he saw,
Only in a bottom saw a pleasant grove,
With chant of tuneful birds resounding loud;   290
Thither he bent his way, determined there
To rest at noon, and entered soon the shade
High roofed and walks beneath, and alleys brown
That opened in the midst a woody scene,
Nature's own work it seemed (nature taught art)   295
And to a superstitious eye the haunt
Of wood gods and wood nymphs; he viewed it round,
When suddenly a man before him stood,
Not rustic as before, but seemlier clad,
As one in city, or court, or palace bred,   300
And with fair speech these words to him addressed.
      'With granted leave officious I return,
But much more wonder that the Son of God
In this wild solitude so long should bide
Of all things destitute, and well I know,   305
Not without hunger.   Others of some note,
As story tells, have trod this wilderness;
The fugitive bond-woman with her son
Outcast Nebaioth, yet found he relief
By a providing angel; all the race   310
Of Israel here had famished, had not God
Rained from heaven manna, and that prophet **bold**
Native of Thebez wandering here was fed
Twice by a voice inviting him to eat.
Of thee these forty days none hath regard,   315
Forty and more deserted here indeed.'
      To whom thus Jesus; 'what concludest thou hence?
They all had need, I as thou seest have none.'
      'How hast thou hunger then?' Satan replied,
'Tell me if food were now before thee set,   320
Wouldst thou not eat?'   'Thereafter as I like
The giver,' answered Jesus.   'Why should that
Cause thy refusal,' said the subtle fiend,
'Hast thou not right to all created things,
Owe not all creatures by just right to thee   325
Duty and service, nor to stay till bid,
But tender all their power? nor mention I

293. **brown**: dark.   298. **a man before him stood**: Satan in disguise.

309. **Nebaioth**: Ishmael's son, *Genesis* 25:13.   **found he relief**: first, second, third editions read
'he,' but 1705 edition changed to 'here' and retained in most editions after that and defended as correct
reading.   But Milton printed 'he.'

312-13. **prophet bold native of Thebez**: Elijah of Thisbe.

Meats by the law unclean, or offered first
To idols, those young Daniel could refuse;
Nor proffered by an enemy, though who   330
Would scruple that, with want oppressed? behold
Nature ashamed, or better to express,
Troubled that thou shouldst hunger, hath purveyed
From all the elements her choicest store
To treat thee as beseems, and as her Lord   335
With honor, only deign to sit and eat.'
   He spake no dream, for as his words had end,
Our Saviour lifting up his eyes beheld
In ample space under the broadest shade
A table richly spread, in regal mode,   340
With dishes piled, and meats of noblest sort
And savor, beasts of chase, or fowl of game,
In pastry built, or from the spit, or boiled,
Grisamber-steamed; all fish from sea or shore,
Freshet, or purling brook, of shell or fin,   345
And exquisitest name, for which was drained
Pontus and Lucrine bay, and Afric coast.
Alas how simple, to these cates compared,
Was that crude apple that diverted Eve!
And at a stately sideboard by the wine   350
That fragrant smell diffused, in order stood
Tall stripling youths rich clad, of fairer hue
Than Ganymed or Hylas, distant more
Under the trees now tripped, now solemn stood
Nymphs of Diana's train, and naiades   355
With fruits and flowers from Amalthea's horn,
And ladies of the Hesperides, that seemed
Fairer than feigned of old, or fabled since
Of fairy damsels met in forest wide
By knights of Logres, or of Lyonnesse,   360
Lancelot or Pelleas, or Pellenore,
And all the while harmonious airs were heard
Of chiming strings, or charming pipes and winds
Of gentlest gale Arabian odors fanned
From their soft wings, and Flora's earliest smells.   365

340 ff. The feast is set forth in rich and vivid contrast to the surrounding bleakness.

344. **Grisamber-steamed**: a perfume used in cookery.   Ambergris.

347. **Pontus**: the Black Sea.   **Lucrine bay**: near Naples, famous for its oysters.

348. **cates**: delicacies.

353. **Ganymed or Hylas**: the first, Jove's cup-bearer, and the second, a youth attending Hercules.

355. **Diana's train**: Diana, virgin goddess of the hunt, was attended by a train of nymphs.
naiades: nymphs of streams and rivers.

356. **Amalthea's horn**: the Cretan nymph who nursed Jove, and to whose horn he gave the power of pouring out fruit and flowers.

357. **ladies of the Hesperides**: daughters of Hesperus, keepers of the garden of the golden apples.

360. **knights of Logres, or of Lyonnesse**: the first, a name for Britain, and the second for part of Cornwall, used in medieval and later romances of chivalry.

361. **Lancelot or Pelleas, or Pellenore**: names of knights.   365. **Flora**: goddess of flowers.

Such was the splendor, and the tempter now
His invitation earnestly renewed.
  'What doubts the Son of God to sit and eat?
These are not fruits forbidden, no interdict
Defends the touching of these viands pure,   370
Their taste no knowledge works, at least of evil,
But life preserves, destroys life's enemy,
Hunger, with sweet restorative delight.
All these are spirits of air, and woods, and springs,
Thy gentle ministers, who come to pay   375
Thee homage, and acknowledge thee their Lord:
What doubtest thou Son of God? sit down and eat.'
  To whom thus Jesus temperately replied:
'Saidst thou not that to all things I had right?
And who withholds my power that right to use?   380
Shall I receive by gift what of my own,
When and where likes me best, I can command?
I can at will, doubt not, as soon as thou,
Command a table in this wilderness,
And call swift flights of angels ministrant   385
Arrayed in glory on my cup to attend:
Why shouldst thou then obtrude this diligence,
In vain, where no acceptance it can find,
And with my hunger what hast thou to do?
Thy pompous delicacies I contemn,   390
And count thy specious gifts no gifts but guiles.'
  To whom thus answered Satan malcontent:
'That I have also power to give thou seest,
If of that power I bring thee voluntary
What I might have bestowed on whom I pleased,   395
And rather opportunely in this place
Chose to impart to thy apparent need,
Why shouldst thou not accept it? but I see
What I can do or offer is suspect;
Of these things others quickly will dispose   400
Whose pains have earned the far fet spoil.'   With that
Both table and provision vanished quite
With sound of harpies' wings, and talons heard;
Only the importune tempter still remained,
And with these words his temptation pursued.   405
  'By hunger, that each other creature tames,
Thou art not to be harmed, therefore not moved;
Thy temperance invincible besides,
For no allurement yields to appetite,
And all thy heart is set on high designs,   410
High actions; but wherewith to be achieved?
Great acts require great means of enterprise,
Thou art unknown, unfriended, low of birth,
A carpenter thy father known, thyself
Bred up in poverty and straits at home;   415

401. **far fet**: far-fetched, 'fet' being the old past participle.

Lost in a desert here and hunger-bit:
Which way or from what hope dost thou aspire
To greatness? whence authority derivest,
What followers, what retinue canst thou gain,
Or at thy heels the dizzy multitude,   420
Longer than thou canst feed them on thy cost?
Money brings honor, friends, conquest, and realms;
What raised Antipater the Edomite,
And his son Herod placed on Judah's throne;
(Thy throne) but gold that got him puissant friends?   425
Therefore, if at great things thou wouldst arrive,
Get riches first, get wealth, and treasure heap,
Not difficult, if thou hearken to me,
Riches are mine, fortune is in my hand;
They whom I favor thrive in wealth amain,   430
While virtue, valor, wisdom sit in want.'
    To whom thus Jesus patiently replied;
'Yet wealth without these three is impotent,
To gain dominion or to keep it gained.
Witness those ancient empires of the earth,   435
In height of all their flowing wealth dissolved:
But men endued with these have oft attained
In lowest poverty to highest deeds;
Gideon and Jephtha, and the shepherd lad,
Whose offspring on the throne of Judah sat   440
So many ages, and shall yet regain
That seat, and reign in Israel without end.
Among the heathen, (for throughout the world
To me is not unknown what hath been done
Worthy of memorial) canst thou not remember   445
Quintius, Fabricius, Curius, Regulus?
For I esteem those names of men so poor
Who could do mighty things, and could contemn
Riches though offered from the hand of kings.
And what in me seems wanting, but that I   450
May also in this poverty as soon
Accomplish what they did, perhaps and more?
Extol not riches then, the toil of fools,
The wise man's cumbrance if not snare, more apt
To slacken virtue, and abate her edge,   455
Than prompt her to do aught may merit praise.
What if with like aversion I reject
Riches and realms; yet not for that a crown,
Golden in show, is but a wreath of thorns,
Brings dangers, troubles, cares, and sleepless nights   460

423. **Antipater the Edomite:** a man with great riches who apparently bought 'Judah's throne' for his son Herod from Mark Antony.

439. **Gideon and Jephtha, and the shepherd lad:** the first, the hero who delivered Israel from the Midianites (*Judges* 6–8:35), the second, a judge of Israel for six years (*Judges* 11 and 12), and the last, David, King of Israel.

446. **Quintius . . . :** four renowned heroes and leaders of the ancient Romans.

To him who wears the regal diadem,
When on his shoulders each man's burden lies;
For therein stands the office of a king,
His honor, virtue, merit and chief praise,
That for the public all this weight he bears.   465
Yet he who reigns within himself, and rules
Passions, desires, and fears, is more a king;
Which every wise and virtuous man attains:
And who attains not, ill aspires to rule
Cities of men, or headstrong multitudes,   470
Subject himself to anarchy within,
Or lawless passions in him which he serves.
But to guide nations in the way of truth
By saving doctrine, and from error lead
To know, and knowing worship God aright,   475
Is yet more kingly, this attracts the soul,
Governs the inner man, the nobler part,
That other o'er the body only reigns,
And oft by force, which to a generous mind
So reigning can be no sincere delight.   480
Besides to give a kingdom hath been thought
Greater and nobler done, and to lay down
Far more magnanimous, than to assume.
Riches are needless then, both for themselves,
And for thy reason why they should be sought,   485
To gain a scepter, oftest better missed.'

THE END OF THE SECOND BOOK

THE THIRD BOOK

So spake the Son of God, and Satan stood
A while as mute confounded what to say,
What to reply, confuted and convinced
Of his weak arguing, and fallacious drift;
At length collecting all his serpent wiles,   5
With soothing words renewed, him thus accosts.
  'I see thou knowest what is of use to know,
What best to say canst say, to do canst do;
Thy actions to thy words accord, thy words
To thy large heart give utterance due, thy heart   10
Contains of good, wise, just, the perfect shape.
Should kings and nations from thy mouth consult,
Thy counsel would be as the oracle
Urim and Thummim, those oraculous gems
On Aaron's breast: or tongue of seers old   15

---

14. **Urim and Thummim**: sacred objects of some sort worn in or on the priest's costume. Their exact nature, origin, and use are not known. Milton here makes them part of the priest's breastplate as decorations of precious stones. Cf. *PL* III:596–98.

Infallible; or wert thou sought to deeds
That might require the array of war, thy skill
Of conduct would be such, that all the world
Could not sustain thy prowess, or subsist
In battle, though against thy few in arms.   20
These godlike virtues wherefore dost thou hide?
Affecting private life, or more obscure
In savage wilderness, wherefore deprive
All earth her wonder at thy acts, thyself
The fame and glory, glory the reward   25
That sole excites to high attempts the flame
Of most erected spirits, most tempered pure
Ethereal, who all pleasures else despise,
All treasures and all gain esteem as dross,
And dignities and powers all but the highest?   30
Thy years are ripe, and overripe, the son
Of Macedonian Philip had ere these
Won Asia and the throne of Cyrus held
At his dispose, young Scipio had brought down
The Carthaginian pride, young Pompey quelled   35
The Pontic king and in triumph had rode.
Yet years, and to ripe years judgment mature,
Quench not the thirst of glory, but augment.
Great Julius, whom now all the world admires
The more he grew in years, the more inflamed   40
With glory, wept that he had lived so long
Inglorious: but thou yet are not too late.'
    To whom our Saviour calmly thus replied.
'Thou neither dost persuade me to seek wealth
For empire's sake, nor empire to affect   45
For glory's sake by all thy argument.
For what is glory but the blaze of fame,
The people's praise, if always praise unmixed?
And what the people but a herd confused,
A miscellaneous rabble, who extol   50
Things vulgar, and well weighed, scarce worth the praise.
They praise and they admire they know not what;
And know not whom, but as one leads the other;
And what delight to be by such extolled,
To live upon their tongues and be their talk,   55
Of whom to be dispraised were no small praise?
His lot who dares be singularly good.
The intelligent among them and the wise
Are few, and glory scarce of few is raised.

32. **Macedonian Philip:** conqueror of Macedonia and father of Alexander the Great.
33. **throne of Cyrus:** the great king of Persia.
34. **young Scipio:** who drove the Carthaginian out of Spain.
35. **young Pompey:** the elder Pompey.
36. **The Pontic king:** Mithridates.   39. **Great Julius:** Julius Caesar.
49. **what the people . . . :** Milton held about this attitude towards the common people, especially in government and in matters of taste and discernment.

This is true glory and renown, when God   60
Looking on the earth, with approbation marks
The just man, and divulges him through heaven
To all his angels, who with true applause
Recount his praises; thus he did to Job,
When to extend his fame through heaven and earth,   65
As thou to thy reproach mayest well remember,
He asked thee, "hast thou seen my servant Job?"
Famous he was in heaven, on earth less known;
Where glory is false glory, attributed
To things not glorious, men not worthy of fame.   70
They err who count it glorious to subdue
By conquest far and wide, to overrun
Large countries, and in field great battles win,
Great cities by assault: what do these worthies,
But rob and spoil, burn, slaughter, and enslave   75
Peaceable nations, neighboring, or remote,
Made captive, yet deserving freedom more
Than those their conquerors, who leave behind
Nothing but ruin wheresoe'er they rove,
And all the flourishing works of peace destroy,   80
Then swell with pride, and must be titled gods,
Great benefactors of mankind, deliverers,
Worshiped with temple, priest and sacrifice;
One is the son of Jove, of Mars the other,
Till conqueror death discover them scarce men,   85
Rolling in brutish vices, and deformed,
Violent or shameful death their due reward.
But if there be in glory aught of good,
It may by means far different be attained
Without ambition, war, or violence;   90
By deeds of peace, by wisdom eminent,
By patience, temperance; I mention still
Him whom thy wrongs with saintly patience borne,
Made famous in a land and times obscure;
Who names not now with honor patient Job?   95
Poor Socrates (who next more memorable?)
By what he taught and suffered for so doing,
For truth's sake suffering death unjust, lives now
Equal in fame to proudest conquerors.
Yet if for fame and glory aught be done,   100
Aught suffered; if young African for fame
His wasted country freed from Punic rage,
The deed becomes unpraised, the man at least,
And loses, though but verbal, his reward.
Shall I seek glory then, as vain men seek   105
Oft not deserved?   I seek not mine, but his
Who sent me, and thereby witness whence I am.'

96. **Socrates**: the Greek philosopher who was 'executed' by popular vote.
101. **young African**: the Scipio of line 34.
102. **Punic**: Carthaginian.

To whom the tempter murmuring thus replied.
'Think not so slight of glory; therein least
Resembling thy great father: he seeks glory,   110
And for his glory all things made, all things
Orders and governs, nor content in heaven
By all his angels glorified, requires
Glory from men, from all men good or bad,
Wise or unwise, no difference, no exemption;   115
Above all sacrifice, or hallowed gift
Glory he requires, and glory he receives
Promiscuous from all nations, Jew, or Greek,
Or barbarous, nor exception hath declared;
From us his foes pronounced glory he exacts.'   120
To whom our Saviour fervently replied.
'And reason; since his word all things produced,
Though chiefly not for glory as prime end,
But to show forth his goodness, and impart
His good communicable to every soul   125
Freely; of whom what could he less expect
Than glory and benediction, that is thanks,
The slightest, easiest, readiest recompense
From them who could return him nothing else,
And not returning that would likeliest render   130
Contempt instead, dishonor, obloquy?
Hard recompense, unsuitable return
For so much good, so much beneficence.
But why should man seek glory? who of his own
Hath nothing, and to whom nothing belongs   135
But condemnation, ignominy, and shame?
Who for so many benefits received
Turned recreant to God, ingrate and false,
And so of all true good himself despoiled,
Yet, sacrilegious, to himself would take   140
That which to God alone of right belongs;
Yet so much bounty is in God, such grace,
That who advance his glory, not their own,
Them he himself to glory will advance.'
So spake the Son of God; and here again   145
Satan had not to answer, but stood struck
With guilt of his own sin, for he himself
Insatiable of glory had lost all,
Yet of another plea bethought him soon.
'Of glory as thou wilt,' said he, 'so deem,   150
Worth or not worth the seeking, let it pass:
But to a kingdom thou art born, ordained
To sit upon thy father David's throne;
By mother's side thy father, though thy right
Be now in powerful hands, that will not part   155
Easily from possession won with arms;

138. **recreant:** Phillips, '(old word) a faint-hearted, or cowardly fellow.'   A deserter.
153. **thy father David's throne:** the throne of Israel.

Judaea now and all the promised land
Reduced a province under Roman yoke,
Obeys Tiberius; nor is always ruled
With temperate sway; oft have they violated   160
The temple, oft the law with foul affronts,
Abominations rather, as did once
Antiochus: and thinkest thou to regain
Thy right in sitting still or thus retiring?
So did not Macheabus: he indeed   165
Retired unto the desert, but with arms;
And o'er a mighty king so oft prevailed,
That by strong hand his family obtained,
Though priests, the crown, and David's throne usurped,
With Modin and her suburbs once content.   170
If kingdom move thee not, let move thee zeal,
And duty; zeal and duty are not slow;
But on occasion's forelock watchful wait.
They themselves rather are occasion best,
Zeal of thy father's house, duty to free   175
Thy country from her heathen servitude;
So shalt thou best fulfill, best verify
The prophets old, who sung thy endless reign,
The happier reign the sooner it begins,
Reign then; what canst thou better do the while?'   180
    To whom our Saviour answer thus returned.
'All things are best fulfilled in their due time,
And time there is for all things, truth hath said:
If of my reign prophetic writ hath told,
That it shall never end, so when begin   185
The father in his purpose hath decreed,
He in whose hand all times and seasons roll.
What if he hath decreed that I shall first
Be tried in humble state, and things adverse,
By tribulations, injuries, insults,   190
Contempts, and scorns, and snares, and violence,
Suffering, abstaining, quietly expecting
Without distrust or doubt, that he may know
What I can suffer, how obey? who best
Can suffer, best can do; best reign, who first   195
Well hath obeyed; just trial ere I merit
My exaltation without change or end.
But what concerns it thee when I begin
My everlasting kingdom, why art thou
Solicitous, what moves thy inquisition?   200
Knowest thou not that my rising is thy fall,
And my promotion will be thy destruction?'
    To whom the tempter inly racked replied.

159. **Tiberius:** the Roman emperor then reigning.
163. **Antiochus:** a Roman procurator of Palestine, guilty of every atrocity; cf. *I Maccabees* 1:20–25.
165. **Machabeus:** the founder of one of the most heroic periods in Jewish history, beginning 166 B.C.
170. **Modin:** a town in Palestine.

'Let that come when it comes; all hope is lost
Of my reception into grace; what worse?   205
For where no hope is left, is left no fear;
If there be worse, the expectation more
Of worse torments me than the feeling can.
I would be at the worst; worst is my port,
My harbor and my ultimate repose,   210
The end I would attain, my final good.
My error was my error, and my crime
My crime; whatever for itself condemned,
And will alike be punished; whether thou
Reign or reign not; though to that gentle brow   215
Willingly I could fly, and hope thy reign,
From that placid aspect and meek regard,
Rather than aggravate my evil state,
Would stand between me and thy father's ire,
(Whose ire I dread more than the fire of hell)   220
A shelter and a kind of shading cool
Interposition, as a summer's cloud.
If I then to the worst that can be haste,
Why move thy feet so slow to what is best,
Happiest both to thyself and all the world,   225
That thou who worthiest art shouldst be their king?
Perhaps thou lingerest in deep thoughts detained
Of the enterprise so hazardous and high;
No wonder, for though in thee be united
What of perfection can in man be found,   230
Or human nature can receive, consider
Thy life hath yet been private, most part spent
At home, scarce viewed the Galilean towns,
And once a year Jerusalem, few days'
Short sojourn; and what thence couldst thou observe?   235
The world thou hast not seen, much less her glory,
Empires, and monarchs, and their radiant courts,
Best school of best experience, quickest in sight
In all things that to greatest actions lead.
The wisest, unexperienced, will be ever   240
Timorous and loath, with novice modesty,
(As he who seeking asses found a kingdom)
Irresolute, unhardy, unadventurous:
But I will bring thee where thou soon shalt quit
Those rudiments, and see before thine eyes   245
The monarchies of the earth, their pomp and state,
Sufficient introduction to inform
Thee, of thyself so apt, in regal arts,
And regal mysteries; that thou mayest know
How best their opposition to withstand.'   250
    With that (such power was given him then) he took
The Son of God up to a mountain high.
It was a mountain at whose verdant feet

242. Referring to Saul, first king of Israel.   Compare *I Samuel* 9:3.

A spacious plain outstretched in circuit wide
Lay pleasant; from his side two rivers flowed,   255
The one winding, the other straight and left between
Fair champaign with less rivers interveined,
Then meeting joined their tribute to the sea:
Fertile of corn the glebe, of oil and wine,
With herds the pasture thronged, with flocks the hills,   260
Huge cities and high towered, that well might seem
The seats of mightiest monarchs, and so large
The prospect was, that here and there was room
For barren desert fountainless and dry.
To this high mountaintop the tempter brought   265
Our Saviour, and new train of words began.
    'Well have we speeded, and o'er hill and dale,
Forest and field, and flood, temples and towers
Cut shorter many a league; here thou beholdest
Assyria and her empire's ancient bounds,   270
Araxes and the Caspian lake, thence on
As far as Indus east, Euphrates west,
And oft beyond; to south the Persian bay,
And inaccessible the Arabian drought:
Here Nineveh, of length within her wall   275
Several days' journey, built by Ninus old,
Of that first golden monarchy the seat,
And seat of Salmanassar, whose success
Israel in long captivity still mourns;
There Babylon the wonder of all tongues,   280
As ancient, but rebuilt by him who twice
Judah and all thy father David's house
Led captive, and Jerusalem laid waste,
Till Cyrus set them free; Persepolis
His city there thou seest, and Bactra there;   285
Ecbatana her structure vast there shows,
And Hecatompylos her hundred gates,
There Susa by Choaspes, amber stream,

259. **glebe**: soil, land.

269 ff. The first prospect is to the east.   The whole episode is much like that in *PL* XI:376–411.

271. **Araxes**: a river in Armenia.

274. **Arabian drought**: the Desert of Arabia.

275. **Nineveh**: an ancient city, on the Tigris, said to have been sixty miles in circuit, totally destroyed, as the Biblical *Jonah* records, by the Medes *ca.* 600 B.C.

278. **Salmanassar**: Shalmaneser, who conquered the northern kingdom of Israel (Samaria) *ca.* 725 B.C.

280 ff. **Babylon**: the great Assyrian city on the Euphrates River in Mesopotamia.   Milton made Nimrod the founder of it, *PL* XII:24–44.   Rebuilt by 'Nebuchadnezzar,' the Biblical conqueror of Jerusalem.

284. **Cyrus**: the great Persian king who allowed the Jews to return from captivity.
     Persepolis: an ancient Persian city, Cyrus's capital.

285. **Bactra**: another ancient city of the Persians.

286. **Ecbatana**: a stronghold of the Medes, captured by Cyrus.

287. **Hecatompylos**: another ancient city in Persia.

288. **Susa by Choaspes**: a Persian city on the Choaspes River, the water of which, boiled, was carried by Cyrus, for drinking purposes, on his campaigns.   Cf. Herodotus.

The drink of none but kings; of later fame
Built by Emathian, or by Parthian hands, 290
The great Seleucia, Nisibis, and there
Artaxata, Teredon, Ctesiphon,
Turning with easy eye thou mayest behold.
All these the Parthian, now some ages past,
By great Arsaces led, who founded first 295
That empire, under his dominion holds
From the luxurious kings of Antioch won.
And just in time thou comest to have a view
Of his great power; for now the Parthian king
In Ctesiphon hath gathered all his host 300
Against the Scythian, whose incursions wild
Have wasted Sogdiana; to her aid
He marches now in haste; see, though from far,
His thousands, in what martial equipage
They issue forth, steel bows, and shafts their arms 305
Of equal dread in flight, or in pursuit;
All horsemen, in which fight they most excel;
See how in warlike muster they appear,
In rhombs and wedges, and half-moons, and wings.'
 He looked and saw what numbers numberless 310
The city gates outpoured, light armed troops
In coats of mail and military pride;
In mail their horses clad, yet fleet and strong,
Prancing their riders bore, the flower and choice
Of many provinces from bound to bound; 315
From Arachosia, from Candahor east,
And Margiana to the Hyrcanian cliffs
Of Caucasus, and dark Iberian dales,
From Atropatia and the neighboring plains
Of Adiabene, Media, and the south 320
Of Susiana to Balsara's haven.
He saw them in their forms of battle ranged,
How quick they wheeled, and flying behind them shot
Sharp sleet of arrowy showers against the face
Of their pursuers, and overcame by flight; 325

291. **The great Seleucia, Nisibis:** the first, a city near Bagdad; the second, a city on the Tigris River.

292. **Artaxata, Teredon, Ctesiphon:** three ancient cities in Mesopotamia.

295. **great Arsaces:** flourished about 250 B.C.

297. **Antioch:** a city in Syria on the Orontes River, the capital of the Seleucids.

301. **Scythian:** a savage, unknown people to the north.

302. **Sogdiana:** an old province of the Persian Empire.

309. **rhombs:** phalanxes.

316. **Arachosia . . . Candahor:** the first, Afghanistan; the second, Candahor, a province of the first.

317. **Margiana:** modern Khorasan.   **Hyrcanian cliffs:** near the Caspian Sea.

318. **dark Iberian dales:** in modern Georgia, the country between the Black Sea and the Caspian. Strabo accounts for the darkness.

319. **Atropatia:** part of Media.

320. **Adiabene, Media:** Median names.

321. **Balsara's haven:** Basra.

The field all iron cast a gleaming brown,
Nor wanted clouds of foot, nor on each horn,
Cuirassiers all in steel for standing fight;
Chariots or elephants indorsed with towers
Of archers, nor of laboring pioneers   330
A multitude with spades and axes armed
To lay hills plain, fell woods, or valleys fill,
Or where plain was raise hill, or overlay
With bridges rivers proud, as with a yoke;
Mules after these, camels and dromedaries,   335
And wagons fraught with utensils of war.
Such forces met not, nor so wide a camp,
When Agrican with all his northern powers
Besieged Albracca, as romances tell;
The city of Gallaphrone, from thence to win   340
The fairest of her sex Angelica
His daughter, sought by many prowessed knights,
Both paynim, and the peers of Charlemain.
Such and so numerous was their chivalry;
At sight whereof the fiend yet more presumed,   345
And to our Saviour thus his words renewed.
    'That thou mayest know I seek not to engage
Thy virtue, and not every way secure
On no slight grounds thy safety; hear, and mark
To what end I have brought thee hither and shown   350
All this fair sight; thy kingdom though foretold
By prophet or by angel, unless thou
Endeavor, as thy father David did,
Thou never shalt obtain; prediction still
In all things, and all men, supposes means,   355
Without means used, what it predicts revokes.
But say thou wert possessed of David's throne
By free consent of all, none opposite,
Samaritan or Jew; how couldst thou hope
Long to enjoy it quiet and secure,   360
Between two such enclosing enemies
Roman and Parthian? therefore one of these
Thou must make sure thy own, the Parthian first
By my advice, as nearer and of late
Found able by invasion to annoy   365
Thy country, and captive lead away her kings

---

329. **elephants indorsed with towers**: with 'towers' mounted on their backs.

330. **nor of . . . pioneers**: 'nor [wanted]'; pioneers are modern sappers or engineers.

338. **Agrican**: King of Tartary, who attacked 'Gallaphrone' (l. 340), King of China.

339. **Albracca**: cf. the story of the siege in Boiardo, *Orlando Innamorato* 1:10.

342. **prowessed**: possessed of prowess, distinguished bravery.

344. **chivalry**: force of mounted men, principally knights.

362. **Roman and Parthian**: Satan proposes that Jesus shall make himself a military conqueror, like David, beginning by subduing the 'Parthian' (the Orient in general), then by subduing the 'Roman' (the West).

Antigonus, and old Hyrcanus bound,
Mauger the Roman: it shall be my task
To render thee the Parthian at dispose;
Choose which thou wilt by conquest or by league.   370
By him thou shalt regain, without him not,
That which alone can truly reinstall thee
In David's royal seat, his true successor,
Deliverance of thy brethren, those ten tribes
Whose offspring in his territory yet serve   375
In Habor, and among the Medes dispersed,
Ten sons of Jacob, two of Joseph lost
Thus long from Israel; serving as of old
Their fathers in the land of Egypt served,
This offer sets before thee to deliver.   380
These if from servitude thou shalt restore
To their inheritance, then, nor till then,
Thou on the throne of David in full glory,
From Egypt to Euphrates and beyond
Shalt reign, and Rome or Caesar not need fear.'   385
    To whom our Saviour answered thus unmoved.
'Much ostentation vain of fleshly arm,
And fragile arms, much instrument of war
Long in preparing, soon to nothing brought,
Before mine eyes thou hast set; and in my ear   390
Vented much policy, and projects deep
Of enemies, of aids, battles and leagues,
Plausible to the world, to me worth naught.
Means I must use thou sayest, prediction else
Will unpredict and fail me of the throne: 395
My time I told thee, (and that time for thee
Were better farthest off) is not yet come;
When that comes think not thou to find me slack
On my part aught endeavoring, or to need
Thy politic maxims, or that cumbersome   400
Luggage of war there shown me, argument
Of human weakness rather than of strength.
My brethren, as thou callest them; those ten tribes
I must deliver, if I mean to reign
David's true heir, and his full scepter sway   405
To just extent over all Israel's sons;
But whence to thee this zeal, where was it then
For Israel, or for David, or his throne,
When thou stoodest up his tempter to the pride
Of numbering Israel, which cost the lives   410
Of threescore and ten thousand Israelites
By three days' pestilence? such was thy zeal
To Israel then, the same that now to me.
As for those captive tribes, themselves were they

367 ff. **Antigonus, and old Hyrcanus**: two of 'her' (Palestine's) kings who had been seized by the 'Parthian' in spite of ('mauger') the 'Roman.'
376. **Habor:** a Biblical name, denoting a region, but known today only as the name of a river.

Who wrought their own captivity, fell off   415
From God to worship calves, the deities
Of Egypt, Baal next and Ashtaroth,
And all the idolatries of heathen round,
Besides their other worse than heathenish crimes;
Nor in the land of their captivity   420
Humbled themselves, or penitent besought
The God of their forefathers; but so died
Impenitent, and left a race behind
Like to themselves, distinguishable scarce
From Gentiles, but by circumcision vain,   425
And God with idols in their worship joined.
Should I of these the liberty regard,
Who freed, as to their ancient patrimony,
Unhumbled, unrepentant, unreformed,
Headlong would follow; and to their gods perhaps   430
Of Bethel and of Dan? no, let them serve
Their enemies, who serve idols with God.
Yet he at length, time to himself best known,
Remembering Abraham by some wondrous call
May bring them back repentant and sincere,   435
And at their passing cleave the Assyrian flood,
While to their native land with joy they haste,
As the Red Sea and Jordan once he cleft,
When to the promised land their fathers passed;
To his due time and providence I leave them.'   440
   So spake Israel's true king, and to the fiend
Made answer meet, that made void all his wiles.
So fares it when with truth falsehood contends.

THE END OF THE THIRD BOOK

THE FOURTH BOOK

Perplexed and troubled at his bad success
The tempter stood, nor had what to reply,
Discovered in his fraud, thrown from his hope,
So oft, and the persuasive rhetoric
That sleeked his tongue, and won so much on Eve,   5
So little here, nay lost; but Eve was Eve,
This far his over-match, who self-deceived
And rash, beforehand had no better weighed
The strength he was to cope with, or his own:
But as a man who had been matchless held   10
In cunning, overreached where least he thought,
To salve his credit, and for very spite
Still will be tempting him who foils him still,

417. **Baal ... Ashtaroth:** male and female deities of the Biblical Canaanites.
431. **Bethel and Dan:** towns in Palestine.

And never cease, though to his shame the more;
Or as a swarm of flies in vintage time,   15
About the wine press where sweet must is poured,
Beat off, returns as oft with humming sound;
Or surging waves against a solid rock,
Though all to shivers dashed, the assault renew,
Vain battery, and in froth or bubbles end;   20
So Satan, whom repulse upon repulse
Met ever; and to shameful silence brought,
Yet gives not o'er though desperate of success,
And his vain importunity pursues.
He brought our Saviour to the western side   25
Of that high mountain, whence he might behold
Another plain, long but in breadth not wide;
Washed by the southern sea, and on the north
To equal length backed with a ridge of hills
That screened the fruits of the earth and seats of men   30
From cold septentrion blasts, thence in the midst
Divided by a river, of whose banks
On each side an imperial city stood,
With towers and temples proudly elevate
On seven small hills, with palaces adorned,   35
Porches and theaters, baths, aqueducts,
Statues and trophies, and triumphal arcs,
Gardens and groves presented to his eyes
Above the height of mountains interposed.
By what strange parallax or optic skill   40
Of vision multiplied through air, or glass
Of telescope, were curious to inquire:
And now the tempter thus his silence broke.
    'The city which thou seest no other deem
Than great and glorious Rome, queen of the earth   45
So far renowned, and with the spoils enriched
Of nations; there the capitol thou seest
Above the rest lifting his stately head
On the Tarpeian rock, her citadel
Impregnable, and there Mount Palatine   50
The imperial palace, compass huge, and high
The structure, skill of noblest architects,
With gilded battlements, conspicuous far,
Turrets and terraces, and glittering spires.
Many a fair edifice besides, more like   55
Houses of gods (so well I have disposed

16. **must:** new wine, direct from the press.

31. **septentrion:** northern, literally 'seven plow oxen,' meaning the seven stars about the Great (pole star) or Little Bear in the northern sky.

32. **of:** Masson printed 'off,' but surely the construction is 'on each side of whose banks an imperial city stood.'

33 ff. Description of Rome. Satan has tried, in order, sumptuous banqueting to cater to hunger, temporal power with its appeal to patriotism, and now supreme riches, to tempt Christ.

40. **parallax:** the apparent displacement of an object as seen from two different points.

My airy microscope) thou mayest behold
Outside and inside both, pillars and roofs
Carved work, the hand of famed artificers
In cedar, marble, ivory or gold.   60
Thence to the gates cast round thine eye, and see
What conflux issuing forth, or entering in,
Praetors, proconsuls to their provinces
Hasting or on return, in robes of state;
Lictors and rods the ensigns of their power,   65
Legions and cohorts, turms of horse and wings:
Or embassies from regions far remote
In various habits on the Appian road,
Or on the Aemilian, some from farthest south,
Syene, and where the shadow both way falls,   70
Meroë Nilotic isle, and more to west,
The realm of Bocchus to the Blackmoor sea;
From the Asian kings and Parthian among these,
From India and the golden Chersonese,
And utmost Indian isle Taprobane,   75
Dusk faces with white silken turbans wreathed:
From Gallia, Gades, and the British west,
Germans and Scythians, and Sarmatians north
Beyond Danubius to the Tauric pool.
All nations now to Rome obedience pay,   80
To Rome's great emperor, whose wide domain
In ample territory, wealth and power,
Civility of manners, arts, and arms,
And long renown thou justly mayest prefer
Before the Parthian; these two thrones except,   85
The rest are barbarous, and scarce worth the sight,
Shared among petty kings too far removed;
These having shown thee, I have shown thee all
The kingdoms of the world, and all their glory.
This emperor hath no son, and now is old,   90
Old, and lascivious, and from Rome retired
To Capreae an island small but strong

57. **microscope:** 'a certain instrument whereby the full proportion of the smallest things may be discerned.' — Phillips.

62. **conflux:** flowing together; hence, 'mingling.'   66. **turms:** troops.

68. **Appian road:** one of the main roads to and from Rome, running south from Rome.

69. **Aemilian:** another road, running north from Rome. Compare *Sonnet II*.

70. **Syene:** modern Assouan, a frontier town in southern Egypt.   **the shadow both way falls:** at or near the equator, the sun is directly overhead at noon and directly east and west before and after.

71. **Meroë Nilotic isle:** one of the most famous islands in the upper Nile.

72. **realm of Bocchus:** roughly, modern Morocco.
Blackmoor sea: the sea near the land of the Moors.

74. **Chersonese:** cf. *PL* XI:392, east of India.

75. **Taprobane:** Ceylon, but perhaps Sumatra.   77. **Gallia, Gades:** France, Cadiz (Spain).

78. **Sarmatians:** a people living north of the Black Sea.

79. **Danubius to the Tauric pool:** Danube to the Sea of Azof in Russia.

90. **This emperor:** Tiberius.   92. **Capreae:** Capri.

On the Campanian shore, with purpose there
His horrid lusts in private to enjoy,
Committing to a wicked favorite   95
All public cares, and yet of him suspicious,
Hated of all, and hating; with what ease
Endued with regal virtues as thou art,
Appearing, and beginning noble deeds,
Mightest thou expel this monster from his throne   100
Now made a sty, and, in his place ascending
A victor people free from servile yoke?
And with my help thou mayest; to me the power
Is given, and by that right I give it thee.
Aim therefore at no less than all the world,   105
Aim at the highest, without the highest attained
Will be for thee no sitting, or not long
On David's throne, be prophesied what will.'
  To whom the Son of God unmoved replied.
'Nor doth this grandeur and majestic show   110
Of luxury, though called magnificence,
More than of arms before, allure mine eye,
Much less my mind; though thou shouldst add to tell
Their sumptuous gluttonies, and gorgeous feasts
On citron tables or Atlantic stone;   115
(For I have also heard, perhaps have read)
Their wines of Setia, Cales, and Falerne,
Chios and Crete, and how they quaff in gold,
Crystal and myrrhine cups embossed with gems
And studs of pearl, to me shouldst tell who thirst   120
And hunger still: then embassies thou showest
From nations far and nigh; what honor that,
But tedious waste of time to sit and hear
So many hollow compliments and lies,
Outlandish flatteries? then proceedest to talk   125
Of the emperor, how easily subdued,
How gloriously; I shall, thou sayest, expel
A brutish monster: what if I withal
Expel a devil who first made him such?
Let his tormentor conscience find him out,   130
For him I was not sent, nor yet to free
That people victor once, now vile and base,
Deservedly made vassal, who once just,
Frugal, and mild, and temperate, conquered well,
But govern ill the nations under yoke,   135
Peeling their provinces, exhausted all

115. **citron tables or Atlantic stone**: tables of lemon wood or of marble.

117–18. **wines of Setia, Cales, and Falerne, Chios and Crete**: the first three are famous old Campanian vintages, set forth in Pliny, *Natural History* XIV. The latter two are Greek vintages.

119. **Crystal and myrrhine cups**: rock crystal, perhaps glass; and the second, made of the stone or material called *murrha* by the Romans. Littleton (1693) and Phillips (1706), 'a precious stone having the color of Myrrh, and the smell of sweet ointment.'

120–21. Irony.

By lust and rapine; first ambitious grown
Of triumph that insulting vanity;
Then cruel, by their sports to blood inured
Of fighting beasts, and men to beasts exposed,   140
Luxurious by their wealth, and greedier still,
And from the daily scene effeminate.
What wise and valiant man would seek to free
These thus degenerate, by themselves enslaved,
Or could of inward slaves make outward free?   145
Know therefore when my season comes to sit
On David's throne, it shall be like a tree
Spreading and overshadowing all the earth,
Or as a stone that shall to pieces dash
All monarchies besides throughout the world,   150
And of my kingdom there shall be no end:
Means there shall be to this, but what the means,
Is not for thee to know, nor me to tell.'
    To whom the tempter impudent replied.
'I see all offers made by me how slight   155
Thou valuest, because offered, and rejectest:
Nothing will please the difficult and nice,
Or nothing more than still to contradict:
On the other side know also thou, that I
On what I offer set as high esteem,   160
Nor what I part with mean to give for naught;
All these which in a moment thou beholdest,
The kingdoms of the world to thee I give;
For given to me, I give to whom I please,
No trifle; yet with this reserve, not else,   165
On this condition, if thou wilt fall down,
And worship me as thy superior lord,
Easily done, and hold them all of me;
For what can less so great a gift deserve?'
    Whom thus our Saviour answered with disdain.   170
'I never liked thy talk, thy offers less,
Now both abhor, since thou hast dared to utter
The abominable terms, impious condition;
But I endure the time, till which expired,
Thou hast permission on me.   It is written   175
The first of all commandments.   "Thou shalt worship
The Lord thy God, and only him shalt serve;"
And darest thou to the Son of God propound
To worship thee accursed, now more accursed
For this attempt bolder than that on Eve,   180
And more blasphemous? which expect to rue.
The kingdoms of the world to thee were given,
Permitted rather, and by thee usurped,
Other donation none thou canst produce:
If given, by whom but by the king of kings,   185

154 ff. Satan having made all his offers, including the supreme temptation in lines 167–68, and all being
rejected, the grand debate begins.

God over all supreme? if given to thee,
By thee how fairly is the giver now
Repaid?   But gratitude in thee is lost
Long since.   Wert thou so void of fear or shame,
As offer them to me the Son of God,   190
To me my own, on such abhorred pact,
That I fall down and worship thee as God?
Get thee behind me; plain thou now appearest
That evil one, Satan forever damned.'
   To whom the fiend, with fear abashed replied.   195
'Be not so sore offended, Son of God;
Though sons of God both angels are and men,
If I to try whether in higher sort
Than these thou bearest that title, have proposed
What both from men and angels I receive,   200
Tetrarchs of fire, air, flood, and on the earth
Nations besides from all the quartered winds,
God of this world invoked and world beneath;
Who then thou art, whose coming is foretold
To me most fatal, me it most concerns.   205
The trial hath endamaged thee no way,
Rather more honor left and more esteem;
Me naught advantaged, missing what I aimed,
Therefore let pass, as they are transitory,
The kingdoms of this world; I shall no more   210
Advise thee, gain them as thou canst, or not.
And thou thyself seemest otherwise inclined
Than to a worldly crown, addicted more
To contemplation and profound dispute,
As by that early action may be judged,   215
When slipping from thy mother's eye thou wentest
Alone into the temple; there wast found
Among the gravest rabbis disputant '
On points and questions fitting Moses' chair,
Teaching, not taught; the childhood shows the man,   220
As morning shows the day.   Be famous then
By wisdom; as thy empire must extend,
So let extend thy mind o'er all the world,
In knowledge, all things in it comprehend,
All knowledge is not couched in Moses' law,   225
The Pentateuch or what the prophets wrote,
The Gentiles also know, and write, and teach
To admiration, led by nature's light;
And with the Gentiles much thou must converse,
Ruling them by persuasion as thou meanest,   230
Without their learning how wilt thou with them,
Or they with thee hold conversation meet?
How wilt thou reason with them, how refute
Their idolisms, traditions, paradoxes?
Error by his own arms is best evinced.   235

201. **Tetrarchs:** quarter sub-rulers of the four elements.   235. **evinced:** overcome.

Look once more ere we leave this specular mount
Westward, much nearer by southwest, behold
Where on the Aegean shore a city stands
Built nobly, pure the air, and light the soil,
Athens the eye of Greece, mother of arts   240
And eloquence, native to famous wits
Or hospitable, in her sweet recess,
City or suburban, studious walks and shades;
See there the olive grove of Academe,
Plato's retirement, where the Attic bird   245
Trills her thick-warbled notes the summer long,
There flowery hill Hymettus with the sound
Of bees' industrious murmur oft invites
To studious musing; there Ilissus rolls
His whispering stream; within the walls then view   250
The schools of ancient sages; his who bred
Great Alexander to subdue the world,
Lyceum there, and painted Stoa next:
There thou shalt hear and learn the secret power
Of harmony in tones and numbers hit   255
By voice or hand, and various-measured verse,
Aeolian charms and Dorian lyric odes,
And his who gave them breath, but higher sung,
Blind Melesigenes thence Homer called,
Whose poem Phoebus challenged for his own.   260
Thence what the lofty grave tragedians taught
In chorus or iambic, teachers best
Of moral prudence, with delight received
In brief sententious precepts, while they treat
Of fate, and chance, and change in human life;   265
High actions, and high passions best describing:
Thence to the famous orators repair,
Those ancient, whose resistless eloquence
Wielded at will that fierce democracy,
Shook the arsenal and fulmined over Greece,   270
To Macedon, and Artaxerxes' throne;
To sage philosophy next lend thine ear,
From heaven descended to the low-roofed house
Of Socrates, see there his tenement,
Whom well inspired the oracle pronounced   275
Wisest of men; from whose mouth issued forth
Mellifluous streams that watered all the schools
Of academics old and new, with those

236. **this specular mount:** sight-aiding mountain.
245. **Attic bird:** the nightingale. Compare Sophocles, *Oed. Col.* 671.
247. **Hymettus:** famous hill near Athens, famous for its honey.   249. **Ilissus:** a river.
251–52. **his who bred Great Alexander:** Aristotle was Alexander's tutor.
253. **painted Stoa:** a portico; resort of the group taking their name from it, the Stoics.
260. **Phoebus:** Apollo.
261. **the lofty grave tragedians:** Aeschylus, Sophocles, Euripides.
270. **fulmined over Greece:** cf. Aristophanes, *Acharnenses* 523.

Surnamed Peripatetics, and the sect
Epicurean, and the Stoic severe;   280
These here revolve, or, as thou likest, at home,
Till time mature thee to a kingdom's weight;
These rules will render thee a king complete
Within thyself, much more with empire joined.'
   To whom our Saviour sagely thus replied.   285
'Think not but that I know these things, or think
I know them not; not therefore am I short
Of knowing what I ought: he who receives
Light from above, from the fountain of light,
No other doctrine needs, though granted true;   290
But these are false, or little else but dreams,
Conjectures, fancies, built on nothing firm.
The first and wisest of them all professed
To know this only, that he nothing knew;
The next to fabling fell and smooth conceits,   295
A third sort doubted all things, though plain sense;
Others in virtue placed felicity,
But virtue joined with riches and long life,
In corporal pleasure he, and careless ease,
The Stoic last in philosophic pride,   300
By him called virtue; and his virtuous man,
Wise, perfect in himself, and all possessing
Equal to God, oft shames not to prefer,
As fearing God nor man, contemning all
Wealth, pleasure, pain or torment, death and life,   305
Which when he lists, he leaves, or boasts he can,
For all his tedious talk is but vain boast,
Or subtle shifts conviction to evade.
Alas what can they teach, and not mislead;
Ignorant of themselves, of God much more,   310
And how the world began, and how man fell
Degraded by himself, on grace depending?
Much of the soul they talk, but all awry,
And in themselves seek virtue, and to themselves
All glory arrogate, to God give none,   315
Rather accuse him under usual names,
Fortune and fate, as one regardless quite
Of mortal things.   Who therefore seeks in these
True wisdom, finds her not, or by delusion
Far worse, her false resemblance only meets,   320
An empty cloud.   However many books
Wise men have said are wearisome; who reads
Incessantly, and to his reading brings not
A spirit and judgment equal or superior,
(And what he brings, what needs he elsewhere seek)   325

279. **Peripatetics:** the Aristotelians.

321 ff. Not so much an attack on studies, as on fruitless studies.   The whole speech is reminiscent of the book of *Ecclesiastes*.   But it is too easy to forget that Satan has tempted Christ with 'the contemplative life,' and Christ must reject it.   Cf. lines 369–70.

Uncertain and unsettled still remains,
Deep versed in books and shallow in himself,
Crude or intoxicate, collecting toys,
And trifles for choice matters, worth a sponge;
As children gathering pebbles on the shore.   330
Or if I would delight my private hours
With music or with poem, where so soon
As in our native language can I find
That solace?   All our law and story strewed
With hymns, our psalms with artful terms inscribed,   335
Our Hebrew songs and harps in Babylon,
That pleased so well our victor's ear, declare
That rather Greece from us these arts derived;
Ill imitated, while they loudest sing
The vices of their deities, and their own   340
In fable, hymn, or song, so personating
Their gods ridiculous, and themselves past shame.
Remove their swelling epithets thick laid
As varnish on a harlot's cheek, the rest,
Thin sown with aught of profit or delight,   345
Will far be found unworthy to compare
With Sion's songs, to all true tastes excelling,
Where God is praised aright, and godlike men,
The holiest of holies, and his saints;
Such are from God inspired, not such from thee;   350
Unless where moral virtue is expressed
By light of nature not in all quite lost.
Their orators thou then extollest, as those
The top of eloquence, statists indeed,
And lovers of their country, as may seem;   355
But herein to our prophets far beneath,
As men divinely taught, and better teaching
The solid rules of civil government
In their majestic unaffected style
Than all the oratory of Greece and Rome.   360
In them is plainest taught, and easiest learnt,
What makes a nation happy, and keeps it so,
What ruins kingdoms, and lays cities flat;
These only with our law best form a king.'
    So spake the Son of God; but Satan now   365
Quite at a loss, for all his darts were spent,
Thus to our Saviour with stern brow replied.
    'Since neither wealth, nor honor, arms nor arts,
Kingdom nor empire pleases thee, nor aught
By me proposed in life contemplative,   370
Or active, tended on by glory, or fame,
What dost thou in this world? the wilderness
For thee is fittest place, I found thee there,
And thither will return thee, yet remember
What I foretell thee, soon thou shalt have cause   375
To wish thou never hadst rejected thus

Nicely or cautiously my offered aid,
Which would have set thee in short time with ease
On David's throne; or throne of all the world,
Now at full age, fullness of time, thy season, 380
When prophecies of thee are best fulfilled.
Now contrary, if I read aught in heaven,
Or heaven write aught of fate, by what the stars
Voluminous, or single characters,
In their conjunction met, give me to spell, 385
Sorrows, and labors, opposition, hate,
Attends thee, scorns, reproaches, injuries,
Violence and stripes, and lastly cruel death,
A kingdom they portend thee, but what kingdom,
Real or allegoric I discern not, 390
Nor when, eternal sure, as without end,
Without beginning; for no date prefixed
Directs me in the starry rubric set.'
 So saying he took (for still he knew his power
Not yet expired) and to the wilderness 395
Brought back the Son of God, and left him there,
Feigning to disappear. Darkness now rose,
As daylight sunk, and brought in louring night
Her shadowy offspring unsubstantial both,
Privation mere of light and absent day. 400
Our Saviour meek and with untroubled mind
After his airy jaunt, though hurried sore,
Hungry and cold betook him to his rest,
Wherever, under some concourse of shades
Whose branching arms thick intertwined might shield 405
From dews and damps of night his sheltered head,
But sheltered slept in vain, for at his head
The tempter watched, and soon with ugly dreams
Disturbed his sleep; and either tropic now
'Gan thunder, and both ends of heaven, the clouds 410
From many a horrid rift abortive poured
Fierce rain with lightning mixed, water with fire
In ruin reconciled: nor slept the winds
Within their stony caves, but rushed abroad
From the four hinges of the world, and fell 415
On the vexed wilderness, whose tallest pines,
Though rooted deep as high, and sturdiest oaks
Bowed their stiff necks, laden with stormy blasts,
Or torn up sheer: ill wast thou shrouded then,
O patient Son of God, yet only stoodest 420
Unshaken; nor yet stayed the terror there,
Infernal ghosts, and hellish furies, round,
Environed thee, some howled, some yelled, some shrieked,
Some bent at thee their fiery darts, while thou
Sattest unappalled in calm and sinless peace. 425
Thus passed the night so foul till morning fair

409. **tropic:** each side of the heavens.

Came forth with pilgrim steps in amice gray;
Who with her radiant finger stilled the roar
Of thunder, chased the clouds, and laid the winds,
And grisly specters, which the fiend had raised   430
To tempt the Son of God with terrors dire.
And now the sun with more effectual beams
Had cheered the face of earth, and dried the wet
From drooping plant, or dropping tree; the birds
Who all things now behold more fresh and green,   435
After a night of storm so ruinous,
Cleared up their choicest notes in bush and spray
To gratulate the sweet return of morn;
Nor yet amidst this joy and brightest morn
Was absent, after all his mischief done,   440
The prince of darkness, glad would also seem
Of this fair change, and to our Saviour came,
Yet with no new device, they all were spent,
Rather by this his last affront resolved,
Desperate of better course, to vent his rage,   445
And mad despite to be so oft repelled.
Him walking on a sunny hill he found,
Backed on the north and west by a thick wood,
Out of the wood he starts in wonted shape;
And in a careless mood thus to him said.   450
    'Fair morning yet betides thee Son of God,
After a dismal night; I heard the wrack
As earth and sky would mingle; but myself
Was distant; and these flaws, though mortals fear them
As dangerous to the pillared frame of heaven,   455
Or to the earth's dark basis underneath,
Are to the main as inconsiderable,
And harmless, if not wholesome, as a sneeze
To man's less universe, and soon are gone;
Yet as being ofttimes noxious where they light   460
On man, beast, plant, wasteful and turbulent,
Like turbulencies in the affairs of men,
Over whose heads they roar, and seem to point,
They oft fore-signify and threaten ill:
This tempest at this desert most was bent;   465
Of men at thee, for only thou here dwellest.
Did I not tell thee, if thou didst reject
The perfect season offered with my aid
To win thy destined seat, but wilt prolong
All to the push of fate, pursue thy way   470
Of gaining David's throne no man knows when,
For both the when and how is nowhere told,
Thou shalt be what thou art ordained, no doubt;
For angels have proclaimed it, but concealing
The time and means: each act is rightliest done,   475
Not when it must, but when it may be best.

427. amice: fur, hence soft.

If thou observe not this, be sure to find,
What I foretold thee, many a hard assay
Of dangers, and adversities and pains,
Ere thou of Israel's scepter get fast hold;   480
Whereof this ominous night that closed thee round,
So many terrors, voices, prodigies
May warn thee, as a sure foregoing sign.'
　　So talked he, while the Son of God went on
And stayed not, but in brief him answered thus.   485
　　'Me worse than wet thou findest not; other harm
Those terrors which thou speakest of, did me none;
I never feared they could, though noising loud
And threatening nigh; what they can do as signs
Betokening, or ill boding, I contemn   490
As false portents, not sent from God, but thee;
Who knowing I shall reign past thy preventing,
Obtrudest thy offered aid, that I accepting
At least might seem to hold all power of thee,
Ambitious spirit, and wouldst be thought my God,   495
And stormest refused, thinking to terrify
Me to thy will; desist, thou art discerned
And toilest in vain, nor me in vain molest.'
　　To whom the fiend now swollen with rage replied:
'Then hear, O son of David, virgin-born;   500
For Son of God to me is yet in doubt,'
Of the Messiah I have heard foretold
By all the prophets; of thy birth at length
Announced by Gabriel with the first I knew,
And of the angelic song in Bethlehem field,   505
On thy birthnight, that sung thee Saviour born.
From that time seldom have I ceased to eye
Thy infancy, thy childhood, and thy youth,
Thy manhood last, though yet in private bred;
Till at the ford of Jordan whither all   510
Flocked to the Baptist, I among the rest,
Though not to be baptized, by voice from heaven
Heard thee pronounced the Son of God beloved.
Thenceforth I thought thee worth my nearer view
And narrower scrutiny, that I might learn   515
In what degree or meaning thou art called
The Son of God, which bears no single sense;
The son of God I also am, or was,
And if I was, I am; relation stands;
All men are sons of God; yet thee I thought   520
In some respect far higher so declared.
Therefore I watched thy footsteps from that hour,
And followed thee still on to this waste wild;
Where by all best conjectures I collect
Thou art to be my fatal enemy.   525
Good reason then, if I beforehand seek
To understand my adversary, who

And what he is; his wisdom, power, intent,
By parle, or composition, truce, or league
To win him, or win from him what I can.   530
And opportunity I here have had
To try thee, sift thee, and confess have found thee
Proof against all temptation as a rock
Of adamant, and as a center, firm
To the utmost of mere man both wise and good,   535
Not more; for honors, riches, kingdoms, glory
Have been before contemned, and may again:
Therefore to know what more thou art than man,
Worth naming Son of God by voice from heaven,
Another method I must now begin.'   540
    So saying he caught him up, and without wing
Of hippogrif bore through the air sublime
Over the wilderness and o'er the plain;
Till underneath them fair Jerusalem,
The holy city lifted high her towers,   545
And higher yet the glorious temple reared
Her pile, far off appearing like a mount
Of alabaster, topped with golden spires:
There on the highest pinnacle he set
The Son of God; and added thus in scorn: 550
    'There stand, if thou wilt stand; to stand upright
Will ask thee skill; I to thy father's house
Have brought thee, and highest placed, highest is best,
Now show thy progeny; if not to stand,
Cast thyself down; safely if Son of God: 555
For it is written, "He will give command
Concerning thee to his angels, in their hands
They shall uplift thee, lest at any time
Thou chance to dash thy foot against a stone."'
    To whom thus Jesus: 'Also it is written,   560
"Tempt not the Lord thy God,"' he said and stood.
But Satan smitten with amazement fell
As when earth's son Antaeus (to compare
Small things with greatest) in Irassa strove
With Jove's Alcides, and oft foiled still rose,   565
Receiving from his mother earth new strength,
Fresh from his fall, and fiercer grapple joined,
Throttled at length in the air, expired and fell;
So after many a foil the tempter proud,
Renewing fresh assaults, amidst his pride   570
Fell whence he stood to see his victor fall.
And as that Theban monster that proposed
Her riddle, and him, who solved it not, devoured;
That once found out and solved, for grief and spite
Cast herself headlong from the Ismenian steep,   575

529. **parle:** parley.   542. **hippogrif:** a fabulous flying dragon.
563 ff. A favorite story, told by Ovid, *Metamorphoses* IX.
572. The Sphinx connected with Oedipus.

So struck with dread and anguish fell the fiend,
And to his crew, that sat consulting, brought
Joyless triumphals of his hoped success,
Ruin, and desperation, and dismay,
Who durst so proudly tempt the Son of God.   580
So Satan fell and straight a fiery globe
Of angels on full sail of wing flew nigh,
Who on their plumy vanes received him soft
From his uneasy station, and upbore
As on a floating couch through the blithe air,   585
Then in a flowery valley set him down
On a green bank, and set before him spread
A table of celestial food, divine,
Ambrosial, fruits fetched from the tree of life,
And from the fount of life ambrosial drink,   590
That soon refreshed him wearied, and repaired
What hunger, if aught hunger had impaired,
Or thirst, and as he fed, angelic choirs
Sung heavenly anthems of his victory
Over temptation, and the tempter proud.   595
    'True image of the father whether throned
In the bosom of bliss, and light of light
Conceiving or remote from heaven, enshrined
In fleshly tabernacle, and human form,
Wandering the wilderness, whatever place,   600
Habit, or state, or motion, still expressing
The Son of God, with godlike force endued
Against the attempter of thy father's throne,
And thief of Paradise; him long of old
Thou didst debel, and down from heaven cast   605
With all his army, now thou hast avenged
Supplanted Adam, and by vanquishing
Temptation, hast regained lost Paradise,
And frustrated the conquest fraudulent:
He never more henceforth will dare set foot   610
In Paradise to tempt; his snares are broke:
For though that seat of earthly bliss be failed,
A fairer Paradise is founded now
For Adam and his chosen sons, whom thou
A Saviour art come down to reinstall.   615
Where they shall dwell secure, when time shall be
Of tempter and temptation without fear.
But thou, infernal serpent, shalt not long
Rule in the clouds; like an autumnal star
Or lightning thou shalt fall from heaven trod down   620
Under his feet: for proof, ere this thou feelest
Thy wound, yet not thy last and deadliest wound
By this repulse received, and holdest in hell

581. **globe**: ring, group, circle.
583. **vanes**: as in *PL*, Milton printed 'vans,' as have all editors here.
605. **debel**: conquer.

No triumph; in all her gates Abaddon rues
Thy bold attempt; hereafter learn with awe   625
To dread the Son of God: he all unarmed
Shall chase thee with the terror of his voice
From thy demoniac holds, possession foul,
Thee and thy legions, yelling they shall fly,
And beg to hide them in a herd of swine,   630
Lest he command them down into the deep
Bound, and to torment sent before their time.
Hail Son of the most high, heir of both worlds,
Queller of Satan, on thy glorious work
Now enter, and begin to save mankind.'   635
  Thus they the Son of God our Saviour meek
Sung victor, and from heavenly feast refreshed
Brought on his way with joy; he unobserved
Home to his mother's house private returned.

THE END

624. **Abaddon**: hell.

Samson Agonistes
1640–1670

THE second poem, contained in the 1671 volume in which *Paradise Regained* was the first, was *Samson Agonistes*. We know nothing of its date of composition, being as ignorant of it as of the actual date of *Paradise Regained*.

With the exception of the choruses and some lines in Samson's monologues, the meter of the poem is blank verse in the same pentameter (five feet) rhythms used in the other two long poems. But the verse is peculiar, being unlike anything else in the language. As one approaches it for the first time, some of it seems to be completely anarchic, and for over two centuries, no satisfactory account of its metrics existed. About fifty years ago, Robert Bridges began to expound his theories of the metrics of much of Milton's poetry, and in 1921 published his much-revised observations in final form. His discussion of the metrics of *Samson Agonistes* probably represents the ultimate point to which an analysis of its metrics can be developed. But, though Bridges' work was sound and better grounded than any other analysis of the verse ever made, it is not only incomplete, but perhaps more difficult to understand than the cadences he attempted to describe. The verse of *Samson Agonistes* has never yielded all its secrets to metricists, and probably never will, as it contains elements in its unusual cadences that conform to no known metrical system. There is a haunting and pervading beauty in the verses that the reader inevitably comes to feel arises from the manipulation of the harmonics of the verse. But the secret of that beauty and its laws still belongs to Milton. The verse of this poem is certainly a development of that employed in the other two long poems; but the laws of this development have been impossible to discover.

The sources of *Samson Agonistes* are few in number and easy of access. The main source is the book of *Judges* in the Old Testament, chapters 13–16. Milton used almost every detail found in the Biblical story of Samson at some point or other, often retaining the language itself of the 1611 version. Verity says truly that the best introduction to the reading of this poem and to its study is 'to master the contents of *Judges* 13–16.' However, in the action itself of Milton's poem, only the catastrophe has been taken direct from Scripture. All other parts of the dramatic machinery by which the catastrophe is developed are Milton's own invention, although most of the elements he used are to be found in different circumstances in Scripture. He may also have drawn a little from the eighth chapter of Josephus' *Antiquities of the Jews*; and from George Sandys' *Relation of a Journey* (1615), Milton may have taken the description of the palace of the Philistines. He seems to have taken nothing from the then well-known *History of Samson* written by the most popular English poet of the century, Francis Quarles (1592–1644), that had appeared in 1632. Todd mentions an Italian play by Alessandro Roselli, *La Rappresentatione di Sansone*, published at Florence in 1554, as well as an anonymous French play, *Tragedie nouvelle de Samson le fort*, of 1622. Another possibility as a source was Ziegler's tragedy of *Samson*, published at Augsburg in 1547. But Milton seems not to have used any of these.   The claims made a generation ago for Vondel's *Samson*, of 1660, seem much less plausible and important as the years go by.

Milton had thought over the idea of a poem on Samson for many years before he finally printed *Samson Agonistes*.   As early as 1641, in *The Reason of Church Government*, he had briefly developed the story of Samson as a political allegory.[1]   In the *Trinity College Manuscript* there are entries of topics with Samson as the central figure, *Samson purso-phorus* or *Hybristes*, or *Samson marriing* (*sic*, for marrying), or in *Rameth Lechi, Jud. 15, Dagonalia*.   The last was definitely the title of a drama that was never written.   *Samson Agonistes* was the only tragedy Milton ever finished; and, as he carefully explained in the Preface, it is not in a conventional dramatic form.

The action that takes place in the poem is drawn strictly from verses 21–30 of *Judges 16*.

> But the Philistines took him, and put out his eyes, and brought him down to Gaza, and bound him with fetters of brass; and he did grind [corn] in the prison house.   Howbeit the hair of his head began to grow again after he was shaven.   [Milton's action begins at this point.] Then the lords of the Philistines gathered themselves together for to offer a great sacrifice unto Dagon their god, and to rejoice: for they said, 'Our god hath delivered Samson our enemy into our hand.'   And when the people saw him, they praised their god: for they said, 'Our god hath delivered into our hands our enemy, and the destroyer of our country, which slew many of us.'   And it came to pass, when their hearts were merry, that they said, 'Call for Samson, that he may make us sport.'   And they called for Samson out of the prison house; and he made them sport: and they set him between the pillars.   And Samson said unto the lad that held him by the hand, 'Suffer me that I may feel the pillars whereupon the house standeth, that I may lean upon them.'   Now the house was full of men and women; and all the lords of the Philistines were there; and there were upon the roof about three thousand men and women, that beheld while Samson made sport.   And Samson called unto the Lord, and said, 'O Lord God, remember me, I pray thee, and strengthen me, I pray thee, only this once, O God, that I may be at once avenged of the Philistines for my two eyes.'   And Samson took hold of the two middle pillars upon which the house stood, and on which it was borne up, of the one with his right hand, and of the other with his left.   And Samson said, 'Let me die with the Philistines.'   And he bowed himself with all his might; and the house fell upon the lords, and upon all the people that were therein.   So the dead which he slew at his death were more than they which he slew in his life.

Milton took this action and made it the main action of his poem; but he used it according to classical Greek dramatic principles.   Strictly preserving the unities of time and place, all the action of the poem actually takes place at one spot and almost entirely through the central character.   The drama is the subjective tragedy of Samson, the man, and his final triumph over his enemies as he dies.   But we learn of this triumph only indirectly, as it must take place off stage, although Samson is before us on the stage until the last three hundred lines of the poem.   Actually, as in a Greek tragedy, Samson does nothing while on the stage, except to make up his mind.   He is the complete protagonist of the plot.

Milton has taken many liberties with the details of the Biblical story in this passive tragic action.   He brings directly to Samson five different persons and a chorus of Hebrews.   The first person to approach him is his father, Manoa, who has made up his mind to ransom Samson from the Philistines even if it costs him his fortune.   The second person is Delilah, the wife who betrayed Samson to the Philistines.   Samson rejects her advances, insisting that she is an enemy.   Next comes Harapha, the giant, a character Milton has interpolated for this occasion, as he was not in the Biblical story of Samson

---

[1] See E. M. Clark, 'Milton's Earlier Samson,' *University of Texas Studies in English*, vol. VII (1927), pp. 144–54.

at all, although he is mentioned in *II Samuel* 21:16. He too is an enemy, and Samson unsuccessfully tries to goad him into personal combat. Two other persons of little consequence, one hostile to Samson, the public officer, and the Hebrew messenger, complete the number of persons actually appearing in the poem. The chorus, a projection of Samson's own mind and consciousness, as well as the conventional sustainer of the protagonist found in many Greek tragedies, with Manoa, more than offsets the machinations and disturbances caused by the persons hostile to Samson. With this Biblical material and within the canons of the best Greek tragedies, Milton worked out his tragic poem.

For the modern reader, *Samson Agonistes* is probably the most difficult to read, study, and understand of all Milton's poems. John Churton Collins said that this was because:

> it is an attempt to transplant Attic tragedy in its most perfect form, in the form that is to say which it assumes in the drama of Sophocles, into English literature. On these dramas therefore it is modelled, reproducing with exact fidelity their structure, their diction, their tone and spirit, animated throughout with the same ethical purpose, and evolving itself under the same metaphysical conditions.[1]

Collins was one of the most outspoken admirers of the poem who ever discussed it. He states further:

> [it is] magnificent drama, a drama from which the unlearned reader will gain a better idea of the masterpieces of the Greek stage than he could derive from any translation however faithful, a drama which no scholar would hesitate to pronounce as not unworthy of comparison with the great originals themselves.[2]

Goethe said after rereading it that he knew of scarcely any other work that had been composed so entirely in the spirit of the ancients. Coleridge called it 'the finest imitation of ancient Greek drama that ever had been or ever would be written.' Many other equally laudatory statements concerning it could be drawn from other writers. Professor Parker, the latest scholar to deal with *Samson Agonistes*, points out that Milton has used not one, but many of the great Greek tragedies as models for *Samson*. His final estimate of Milton's drama is that 'he almost excels the models at their mighty art.' The same writer concludes, after quoting Matthew Arnold's statement that *Samson Agonistes* 'is great with all the greatness of Milton,' with these two sentences:

> It is more than an imitation of Attic drama, in the same sense that the *Aeneid* is more than an imitation of Homer. It is, I think, so truly an individual work of art, despite all its debts to the past, that we are justified now in adding the name of John Milton to the brief catalogue of 'Tragic Poets unequall'd yet by any...'[3]

For the reader innocent of Greek and with no direct knowledge of Greek tragedy, the above quotations, as one begins the study of the poem, only serve to discourage the attempt, and to such a reader can mean little, as they must be taken entirely on faith. It is obvious that with the great decline of Greek study in the past generation, the number of new readers attracted to this poem will not tend to increase.

Perhaps today the best approach to the poem is through an attempt to see how it was a part of Milton's plans and ambitions. His heroic plans for a national literature, written by himself, as set forth in 1641, were consummated in the appearance of the 1671 volume containing *Paradise Regained* and *Samson Agonistes*. He had produced his great epic work of 'highest hope and hardest attempting... whereof the two poems of Homer,

[1] J. C. Collins, *Samson Agonistes* (Oxford: Clarendon Press [1935]), pp. 7–8.   [2] *Ibid.*, p. 8.
[3] W. R. Parker, *Milton's Debt to Greek Tragedy in Samson Agonistes* (Baltimore: Johns Hopkins Press, 1937), p. 250.

and those other two of Virgil and Tasso are a diffuse... model,' which was *Paradise Lost*. He now offers *Paradise Regained* as an 'epic form whereof... the book of Job [is] a brief model,' and then prints *Samson Agonistes* as an example of 'those dramatic constitutions wherein Sophocles and Euripides reign.' Thus, by offering examples in both the 'diffuse' and 'brief' epic, of a definite nature, and in a 'dramatic constitution' modeled after Sophocles and Euripides, Milton resolves his original dilemma posed by himself to himself in 1641. The full quotation from which the preceding fragmentary citations are taken raises the question as to 'whether that Epic form... or whether those Dramatic Constitutions... shall be found more doctrinal and exemplary to a nation.' In *Paradise Lost*, *Paradise Regained*, and *Samson Agonistes*, he has tried to give an answer to his question, not by answering the 'whether' directly, but by providing an example of each that use of them might settle the issue.

Today we are scarcely in an age that finds much that is 'doctrinal or exemplary to a nation' in either the type of epic Milton loved or in the only type of drama which he admired as such. Consequently, we can scarcely judge the worth of the dramatic example he produced, so far as its value to mankind is concerned. Mankind today does not read *Samson Agonistes*, and even if it did, it has no moral values at all, in Milton's sense of having them, by which to judge it. Our age has lost all grasp of any values attaching to self-assigned tasks 'of highest hope and hardest attempting' on any national scale.

In order to understand the poem the reader must pay a good deal of attention to Milton's own introduction to it, especially to the statement that 'division into act and scene referring chiefly to the stage (to which this work never was intended) is here omitted.' In other words, we cannot judge *Samson Agonistes* as an English drama; for us, it remains what we find it on the printed page, namely, a poem only about three hundred lines shorter than the 'brief epic' *Paradise Regained* and without division into parts of any kind. As if he had himself realized the relatively greater difficulty of the poem, Milton provided it with an introduction, 'Of That Sort of Dramatic Poem Which is Called Tragedy,' and in addition supplied it with a three-hundred-word 'Argument' or prose synopsis.

The title, *Samson Agonistes*, means 'Samson the champion.' The word 'Agonistes' literally means in the Greek an amateur athlete who competed in the public games. The title might be translated 'Samson the wrestler,' the blind contester at the public games of the Philistines in the poem. It is interesting to note that, as Professor Parker has pointed out, in Milton's day the word *agonize* [1] is defined as meaning 'to play the champion' or 'to play the champion or valiant combatant.' Milton's plans to use Samson as the hero of a literary work go back to the entries in the *Trinity College Manuscript*. We find him therein, as Moody says, looking at

> five phases of Samson's history, as is indicated by the note: 'Samson Pursophorus, or Hybristes, or Samson Marrying, or Ramath-Lechi, Judges XV, Dagonalia, Judges XVI.' Samson Pursophorus, or the Bearer of the Firebrand, would have dealt with the hero's exploit of firing the corn; Samson Hybristes, or the Violent, with his bearing away of the gates of Gaza, or some similar action of disdain for his Philistine foes; Samson Marrying, with his earlier life, and his marriage with the woman of Timnath; Ramath-Lechi, with his slaughter of the Philistines at Lehi; Dagonalia, with his destruction of the temple and his death.

It has become almost conventional to point to *Samson Agonistes* as the last poetry we possess from Milton's now almost senile pen. Whenever they have accepted a date late in Milton's life for its composition, editors, commentators, and students have a

[1] Cf. Edward Phillips' *New World of Words*, 1658 *et seq.*

difficult time in reconciling this senility with the obviously more virile pen found in this poem than in *Paradise Regained*. It is high time to consider how little we actually know of the compositional dates of these poems and to forget most of what has been said about such dates, because all of it has been based on the assumption that the date of publication indicates the late date of composition of these poems. Perhaps the date when they were finished is relatively near the date of their public appearance; but in the same year in which these two poems, *Paradise Regained* and *Samson Agonistes*, were licensed for printing, namely, 1670, appeared the prose *History of Britain*. Now we know that at least the first four books out of a total of six in that work had been completed by 1650, but it went unpublished for twenty years. In much the same fashion, perhaps not only *Paradise Regained* and *Samson Agonistes*, but probably other subjects contained in the *Trinity College Manuscript* list, had been experimented with and perhaps completed; but in their author's opinion were unfit for publication. The two poems we are considering seem more likely to have been largely composed in their general outlines at almost any time after 1640, and slowly brought to completion between 1650 and 1670, their date of publication.

Samson Agonistes has been so persistently seized on as autobiographical that it is refreshing to find the fullest treatment of it we have ever had, namely that by Professor Parker, almost completely ignoring the autobiographical parallels in the poem. This is wise because in the past they have been overplayed. That is, throughout the history of Milton criticism and scholarship, none of his longer poems, early or late, has yielded much to the attacks of those who wish to make them reflect greatly the events, public or private, that were taking place during the times of their composition. Thus, *Paradise Lost* has yielded almost nothing to the seekers of symbolic or allegorical use of the revolutionary events taking place during its composition. In the same way, the autobiographical parallels in *Samson Agonistes*, regardless of how striking they seem, are much more accidental than real. Not a one of them can be completely trusted, and, as always with autobiographical passages in Milton's more serious poems, we should remember his own warning contained in the *Pro Populo*:

> One is not to regard what the poet says; but what person in the play speaks, and what that person says; for different persons are introduced, sometimes good, sometimes bad; sometimes wise men, sometimes fools; and such words are put into their mouths, as it is most proper for them to speak; not such as the poet would speak, if he were to speak in his own person.[1]

Milton intended *Samson Agonistes* to be an example of 'those dramatic constitutions wherein Sophocles and Euripides reign' that would be found 'doctrinal and exemplary to a nation.'[2] Moreover, he held that 'tragedy, as it was anciently composed, hath ever been held the gravest, moralest, and most profitable of all other poems.' With this conception of its purpose, with the great Greek tragedies as models, with Aristotle's critical pronouncements as guides, he thereupon set out to 'vindicate tragedy from the small esteem, or rather infamy, which in the account of many it undergoes at this day.' The result is *Samson Agonistes*. In the foreword, Milton explained that all deviations from the Greek pattern derived from the Italian tragedy. He says 'the ancients and Italians are rather followed, as of much more authority and fame.'

Although it was *Paradise Regained*, or a 'brief epic,' that Milton said was best exemplified by the book of *Job*, so far as the action goes, *Samson Agonistes* is much more like *Job*

---

[1] *Col.* VII:307.   [2] *Reason of Church Government, Col.* III:1:237.

than is *Paradise Regained*. In it as in *Job*, the various characters come to and talk with the protagonist and hero of the theme of the tragedy. But this Job-like action takes place in a Greek tragic form.

Samson Agonistes is usually cited as final proof that Milton lacked dramatic sense and could not develop dramatic character as Shakespeare could. So almost universal has been this cry that it is taken as a fact. Perhaps it is a fact. But there is another and more basic aspect of *Samson Agonistes* that must be considered before Milton's dramatic capacities can be adequately discussed. Milton definitely set out to write *Samson Agonistes* 'according to ancient rule and best example.' There is no dramatic suspense or character development in Greek tragedy in any modern sense. The tragic poet took a well-known and traditional story; the audience knew exactly what was going to happen and to whom it must happen; and the tragedy was judged solely on the success or failure of the formal manner of presentation.

Can it be that Milton's apparent lack of dramatic sense and capacity for character development, contrasting so sharply with Shakespeare's possession of such qualities, is due to his insistence on writing drama or tragedy only in the ancient manner, and hence making it impossible or at least unprofitable to compare him with Shakespeare? Have generations of critics simply failed to see in Milton's few attempts at drama that he was protesting against the form taken by the drama of his day, and that we really know nothing about his dramatic capacities as compared with Shakespeare's because he persistently refused to write the same kind of drama as Shakespeare wrote? Certainly wherever in his works we find him dealing with dramatic themes or with any theme in a dramatic fashion, we find him dealing with them or presenting them in an Attic rather than in a current manner 'which by all judicious hath been counted absurd and . . . to gratify the people.' Milton was certainly no rabble-gratifier. His so-called lack of a dramatic sense is apparently more due to his failure to subscribe to the drama of his age than anything else. He tried in his own work to produce examples of classical drama, perhaps chiefly because his artistic taste and training demanded it.

REFERENCES

Bridges, Robert, *Milton's Prosody*.
Chambers, E. K., *Samson Agonistes*. London, 1897.
Collins, J. C., *Samson Agonistes*. London, 1883. Frequently reprinted.
Hanford, J. H., 'Samson Agonistes and Milton in Old Age,' *University of Michigan Publications, Language and Literature*, vol. I (1925), pp. 167–89.
Masson, David, *Poetical Works*.
Newton, Thomas, *Paradise Regained and Poems*. London, 1752.
Parker, W. R., *Milton's Debt to Greek Tragedy in Samson Agonistes*. Baltimore: Johns Hopkins Press, 1937.
Percivall, H. M., *Samson Agonistes*. London, 1890.
Todd, H. J., *Poetical Works*.
Verity, A. W., *The Cambridge Milton for Schools*.
Wyatt, A. J., *Samson Agonistes*. London, n.d.

Samson Agonistes

(1640–1670)

A Dramatic Poem

Aristot. Poet. cap. 6.   Τραγωδία μίμησις πράξεως σπουδαίας, &c. — Tragoedia est imitatio actionis seriae, &c.   Per misericordiam et metum perficiens talium affectuum lustrationem.

OF THAT SORT OF DRAMATIC POEM WHICH IS CALLED TRAGEDY

Tragedy, as it was anciently composed, hath been ever held the gravest, moralest, and most profitable of all other poems: therefore said by Aristotle to be of power by raising pity and fear, or terror, to purge the mind of those and such like passions, that is to temper and reduce them to just measure with a kind of delight, stirred up by reading or seeing those passions well imitated.   Nor is nature wanting in her own effects to make good his assertion: for so in physic things of melancholic hue and quality are used against melancholy, sour against sour, salt to remove salt humors. Hence philosophers and other gravest writers, as Cicero, Plutarch and others, frequently cite out of tragic poets, both to adorn and illustrate their discourse.   The apostle Paul himself thought it not unworthy to insert a verse of Euripides into the text of Holy Scripture, 1 Cor. 15.33. and Paraeus commenting on the *Revelation*, divides the whole book as a tragedy, into acts distinguished each by a chorus of heavenly harpings and songs between.   Heretofore men in highest dignity have labored not a little to be thought able to compose a tragedy.   Of that honor Dionysius the elder was no less ambitious, than before of his attaining to the tyranny. Augustus Caesar also had begun his *Ajax*, but unable to please his own judgment with what he had begun, left it unfinished.   Seneca the philosopher is by some thought the author of those tragedies (at least the best of them) that go under that name. Gregory Nazianzen a father of the church, thought it not unbeseeming the sanctity of his person to write a tragedy, which he entitled, *Christ Suffering*.   This is mentioned to vindicate tragedy from the small esteem, or rather infamy, which in the account of many it undergoes at this day with other common interludes; happening through the poet's error of intermixing comic stuff with tragic sadness and gravity; or introducing trivial and vulgar persons, which by all judicious hath been counted absurd; and brought in without discretion, corruptly to gratify the people.   And though ancient tragedy use no prologue, yet using sometimes, in case of self-defence, or explanation, that which Martial calls an epistle; in behalf of this tragedy coming forth after the ancient manner, much different from what among us passes for best, thus much beforehand may be epistled; that chorus is here introduced after the Greek manner, not ancient only but modern, and still in use among the Italians. In the modelling therefore of this poem, with good reason, the ancients and Italians are rather followed, as of much more authority and fame.   The measure of verse used in the chorus is of all sorts, called by the Greeks *Monostrophic*, or rather *Apolelymenon*, without regard had to strophe, antistrophe or epode, which were a kind of stanzas framed only for the music, then used with the chorus that sung; not essential to the poem, and therefore not material; or being divided into stanzas or pauses, they may be called *Allaeostropha*.   Division into act and scene referring chiefly to the stage (to which this work never was intended) is here omitted.

It suffices if the whole drama be found not produced beyond the fifth act.   Of the style and uniformity, and that commonly called the plot, whether intricate or explicit, which is nothing indeed but such economy, or disposition of the fable as may stand best with verisimilitude and decorum; they only will best judge who are not unacquainted with Aeschylus, Sophocles, and Euripides, the three tragic poets unequalled yet by any, and the best rule to all who endeavor to write tragedy. The circumscription of time wherein the whole drama begins and ends, is according to ancient rule, and best example, within the space of 24 hours.

THE ARGUMENT

Samson made captive, blind, and now in the prison at Gaza, there to labor as in a common workhouse, on a festival day, in the general cessation from labor, comes forth into the open air, to a place nigh, somewhat retired there to sit a while and bemoan his condition. Where he happens at length to be visited by certain friends and equals of his tribe, which make the chorus, who seek to comfort him what they can; then by his old father Manoa, who endeavors the like, and withal tells him his purpose to procure his liberty by ransom; lastly, that this feast was proclaimed by the Philistines as a day of thanksgiving for their deliverance from the hands of Samson, which yet more troubles him. Manoa then departs to prosecute his endeavor with the Philistian lords for Samson's redemption; who in the meanwhile is visited by other persons; and lastly by a public officer to require his coming to the feast before the lords and people, to play or show his strength in their presence; he at first refuses, dismissing the public officer with absolute denial to come; at length persuaded inwardly that this was from God, he yields to go along with him, who came now the second time with great threatenings to fetch him; the chorus yet remaining on the place, Manoa returns full of joyful hope, to procure erelong his son's deliverance: in the midst of which discourse an Ebrew comes in haste confusedly at first; and afterwards more distinctly relating the catastrophe, what Samson had done to the Philistines, and by accident to himself; wherewith the Tragedy ends.

THE PERSONS

SAMSON

MANOA, *the father of Samson*	*Public Officer*
DALILA, *his wife*	*Messenger*
HARAPHA of Gath	*Chorus of Danites*

(The abbreviations of characters' names are Milton's.)

The Scene before the Prison in Gaza

Sams. A little onward lend thy guiding hand
To these dark steps, a little further on;
For yonder bank hath choice of sun or shade,
There I am wont to sit, when any chance
Relieves me from my task of servile toil,   5
Daily in the common prison else enjoined me,
Where I a prisoner chained, scarce freely draw
The air imprisoned also, close and damp,
Unwholesome draught: but here I feel amends,
The breath of heaven fresh blowing, pure and sweet,   10
With day-spring born; here leave me to respire.
This day a solemn feast the people hold
To Dagon their sea-idol, and forbid

11. **respire:** breathe.   13. **Dagon:** god of the Philistines, supposedly a fish god.

Laborious works, unwillingly this rest
Their superstition yields me; hence with leave 15
Retiring from the popular noise, I seek
This unfrequented place to find some ease,
Ease to the body some, none to the mind
From restless thoughts, that like a deadly swarm
Of hornets armed, no sooner found alone, 20
But rush upon me thronging, and present
Times past, what once I was, and what am now.
O wherefore was my birth from heaven foretold
Twice by an angel, who at last in sight
Of both my parents all in flames ascended 25
From off the altar, where an offering burned,
As in a fiery column charioting
His godlike presence, and from some great act
Or benefit revealed to Abraham's race?
Why was my breeding ordered and prescribed 30
As of a person separate to God,
Designed for great exploits; if I must die
Betrayed, captived, and both my eyes put out,
Made of my enemies the scorn and gaze;
To grind in brazen fetters under task 35
With this heaven-gifted strength?   O glorious strength
Put to the labor of a beast, debased
Lower than bond-slave!   Promise was that I
Should Israel from Philistian yoke deliver;
Ask for this great deliverer now, and find him 40
Eyeless in Gaza at the mill with slaves,
Himself in bonds under Philistian yoke;
Yet stay, let me not rashly call in doubt
Divine prediction; what if all foretold
Had been fulfilled but through mine own default, 45
Whom have I to complain of but myself?
Who this high gift of strength committed to me,
In what part lodged, how easily bereft me,
Under the seal of silence could not keep,
But weakly to a woman must reveal it, 50
O'ercome with importunity and tears.
O impotence of mind, in body strong!
But what is strength without a double share
Of wisdom, vast, unwieldy, burdensome,
Proudly secure, yet liable to fall 55
By weakest subtleties, not made to rule,
But to subserve where wisdom bears command.
God, when he gave me strength, to show withal
How slight the gift was, hung it in my hair.
But peace, I must not quarrel with the will 60
Of highest dispensation, which herein
Haply had ends above my reach to know:
Suffices that to me strength is my bane,

22 ff. Cf. *Judges* 13:3 ff.

And proves the source of all my miseries;
So many, and so huge, that each apart   65
Would ask a life to wail, but chief of all,
O loss of sight, of thee I most complain!
Blind among enemies, O worse than chains,
Dungeon, or beggary, or decrepit age!
Light the prime work of God to me is extinct,   70
And all her various objects of delight
Annulled, which might in part my grief have eased,
Inferior to the vilest now become
Of man or worm; the vilest here excel me,
They creep, yet see, I dark in light exposed   75
To daily fraud, contempt, abuse, and wrong,
Within doors, or without, still as a fool,
In power of others, never in my own;
Scarce half I seem to live, dead more than half.
O dark, dark, dark, amid the blaze of noon,   80
Irrecoverably dark, total eclipse
Without all hope of day!
O first created beam, and thou great word,
'Let there be light, and light was over all;'
Why am I thus bereaved thy prime decree?   85
The sun to me is dark
And silent as the moon,
When she deserts the night
Hid in her vacant interlunar cave.
Since light so necessary is to life,   90
And almost life itself, if it be true
That light is in the soul,
She all in every part; why was the sight
To such a tender ball as the eye confined?
So obvious and so easy to be quenched,   95
And not as feeling through all parts diffused,
That she might look at will through every pore?
Then had I not been thus exiled from light;
As in the land of darkness yet in light,
To live a life half dead, a living death,   100
And buried; but O yet more miserable!
Myself, my sepulcher, a moving grave,
Buried, yet not exempt
By privilege of death and burial
From worst of other evils, pains and wrongs,   105
But made hereby obnoxious more
To all the miseries of life,
Life in captivity
Among inhuman foes.
But who are these? for with joint pace I hear   110
The tread of many feet steering this way;
Perhaps my enemies who come to stare
At my affliction, and perhaps to insult,
Their daily practice to afflict me more.

   Chor. This, this is he; softly a while,   115
Let us not break in upon him;
O change beyond report, thought, or belief!
See how he lies at random, carelessly diffused,
With languished head unpropped,
As one past hope, abandoned,   120
And by himself given over;
In slavish habit, ill-fitted weeds
O'er worn and soiled;
Or do my eyes misrepresent? Can this be he,
That heroic, that renowned,   125
Irresistible Samson? whom unarmed
No strength of man, or fiercest wild beast could withstand;
Who tore the lion, as the lion tears the kid,
Ran on embattled armies clad in iron,
And weaponless himself,   130
Made arms ridiculous, useless the forgery
Of brazen shield and spear, the hammered cuirass,
Chalybean tempered steel, and frock of mail
Adamantean proof;
But safest he who stood aloof,   135
When insupportably his foot advanced,
In scorn of their proud arms and warlike tools,
Spurned them to death by troops. The bold Ascalonite
Fled from his lion ramp, old warriors turned
Their plated backs under his heel;   140
Or groveling soiled their crested helmets in the dust.
Then with what trivial weapon came to hand,
The jaw of a dead ass, his sword of bone,
A thousand foreskins fell, the flower of Palestine
In Ramath-lechi famous to this day: 145
Then by main force pulled up, and on his shoulders bore
The gates of Azza, post, and massy bar
Up to the hill by Hebron, seat of giants old,
No journey of a sabbath day, and loaded so;
Like whom the Gentiles feign to bear up heaven.   150
Which shall I first bewail,
Thy bondage or lost sight,
Prison within prison
Inseparably dark?
Thou art become (O worst imprisonment!)   155
The dungeon of thyself; thy soul
(Which men enjoying sight oft without cause complain)
Imprisoned now indeed,
In real darkness of the body dwells,
Shut up from outward light   160
To incorporate with gloomy night;

133. **Chalybean tempered steel**: tempered by the Chalybes, a people famous in antiquity for their iron-work. They lived in Asia Minor.

138. **The bold Ascalonite**: cf. *Judges* 14:19.   141 ff. Cf. *I Samuel* 18:25.

147. **Azza**: for Gaza, the town of the Philistines.

For inward light alas
Puts forth no visual beam.
O mirror of our fickle state,
Since man on earth unparalleled!   165
The rarer thy example stands,
By how much from the top of wondrous glory,
Strongest of mortal men,
To lowest pitch of abject fortune thou art fallen.
For him I reckon not in high estate   170
Whom long descent of birth
Or the sphere of fortune raises;
But thee whose strength, while virtue was her mate,
Might have subdued the earth,
Universally crowned with highest praises.   175
   Sam. I hear the sound of words, their sense the air
Dissolves unjointed ere it reach my ear.
    Chor. He speaks, let us draw nigh. Matchless in might,
The glory late of Israel, now the grief;
We come thy friends and neighbors not unknown   180
From Eshtaol and Zora's fruitful vale
To visit or bewail thee, or if better,
Counsel or consolation we may bring,
Salve to thy sores, apt words have power to swage
The tumors of a troubled mind,   185
And are as balm to festered wounds.
   Sam. Your coming, friends, revives me, for I learn
Now of my own experience, not by talk,
How counterfeit a coin they are who 'friends'
Bear in their superscription (of the most   190
I would be understood) in prosperous days
They swarm, but in adverse withdraw their head
Not to be found, though sought. Ye see, O friends,
How many evils have enclosed me round;
Yet that which was the worst now least afflicts me,   195
Blindness, for had I sight, confused with shame,
How could I once look up, or heave the head,
Who like a foolish pilot have shipwrecked,
My vessel trusted to me from above,
Gloriously rigged; and for a word, a tear,   200
Fool, have divulged the secret gift of God
To a deceitful woman: tell me friends,
Am I not sung and proverbed for a fool
In every street, do they not say, 'how well
Are come upon him his deserts'? yet why?   205
Immeasurable strength they might behold
In me, of wisdom nothing more than mean;
This with the other should, at least, have paired,
These two proportioned ill drove me transverse.
   Chor. Tax not divine disposal, wisest men   210
Have erred, and by bad women been deceived;

181. **Eshtaol and Zora:** two towns in Palestine.

And shall again, pretend they ne'er so wise.
Deject not then so overmuch thyself,
Who hast of sorrow thy full load besides;
Yet truth to say, I oft have heard men wonder   215
Why thou shouldst wed Philistian women rather
Than of thine own tribe fairer, or as fair,
At least of thy own nation, and as noble.
   Sam. The first I saw at Timna, and she pleased
Me, not my parents, that I sought to wed,   220
The daughter of an infidel: they knew not
That what I motioned was of God; I knew
From intimate impulse, and therefore urged
The marriage on; that by occasion hence
I might begin Israel's deliverance,   225
The work to which I was divinely called;
She proving false, the next I took to wife
(O that I never had! fond wish too late)
Was in the vale of Sorec, Dalila,
That specious monster, my accomplished snare.   230
I thought it lawful from my former act,
And the same end; still watching to oppress
Israel's oppressors: of what now I suffer
She was not the prime cause, but I myself,
Who vanquished with a peal of words (O weakness!)   235
Gave up my fort of silence to a woman.
   Chor. In seeking just occasion to provoke
The Philistine, thy country's enemy,
Thou never wast remiss, I bear thee witness:
Yet Israel still serves with all his sons.   240
   Sam. That fault I take not on me, but transfer
On Israel's governors, and heads of tribes,
Who seeing those great acts which God had done
Singly by me against their conquerors
Acknowledged not, or not at all considered   245
Deliverance offered: I on the other side
Used no ambition to commend my deeds,
The deeds themselves, though mute, spoke loud the doer;
But they persisted deaf, and would not seem
To count them things worth notice, till at length   250
Their lords the Philistines with gathered powers
Entered Judea seeking me, who then
Safe to the rock of Etham was retired,
Not flying, but forecasting in what place
To set upon them, what advantaged best;   255
Meanwhile the men of Judah to prevent
The harass of their land, beset me round;
I willingly on some conditions came
Into their hands, and they as gladly yield me
To the uncircumcised a welcome prey,   260
Bound with two cords; but cords to me were threads
Touched with the flame: on their whole host I flew

Unarmed, and with a trivial weapon felled
Their choicest youth; they only lived who fled.
Had Judah that day joined, or one whole tribe,   265
They had by this possessed the towers of Gath,
And lorded over them whom now they serve;
But what more oft in nations grown corrupt,
And by their vices brought to servitude,
Than to love bondage more than liberty,   270
Bondage with ease than strenuous liberty,
And to despise, or envy, or suspect
Whom God hath of his special favor raised
As their deliverer; if he aught begin,
How frequent to desert him, and at last   275
To heap ingratitude on worthiest deeds?
   Cho. Thy words to my remembrance bring
How Succoth and the fort of Penuel
Their great deliverer contemned,
The matchless Gideon in pursuit   280
Of Madian and her vanquished kings:
And how ungrateful Ephraim
Had dealt with Jephtha, who by argument,
Not worse than by his shield and spear
Defended Israel from the Ammonite,   285
Had not his prowess quelled their pride
In that sore battle when so many died
Without reprieve adjudged to death,
For want of well pronouncing Shibboleth.
   Sam. Of such examples add me to the roll,   290
Me easily indeed mine may neglect,
But God's proposed deliverance not so.
   Chor. Just are the ways of God,
And justifiable to men;
Unless there be who think not God at all,   295
If any be, they walk obscure;
For of such doctrine never was there school,
But the heart of the fool,
And no man therein doctor but himself.
   Yet more there be who doubt his ways not just,   300
As to his own edicts, found contradicting,
Then give the reins to wandering thought,
Regardless of his glory's diminution;
Till by their own perplexities involved
They ravel more, still less resolved,   305
But never find self-satisfying solution.
   As if they would confine the interminable,
And tie him to his own prescript,
Who made our laws to bind us, not himself,
And hath full right to exempt   310
Whomso it pleases him by choice
From national obstriction, without taint

278. **Succoth and the fort of Penuel:** cf. *Judges* 8:8 ff.

Of sin, or legal debt;
For with his own laws he can best dispense.
   He would not else who never wanted means, 315
Nor in respect of the enemy just cause
To set his people free,
Have prompted this heroic Nazarite,
Against his vow of strictest purity,
To seek in marriage that fallacious bride, 320
Unclean, unchaste.
   Down reason then, at least vain reasonings down,
Though reason here aver
That moral verdict quits her of unclean:
Unchaste was subsequent, her stain not his. 325
   But see here comes thy reverend sire
With careful step, locks white as down,
Old Manoa: advise
Forthwith how thou oughtest to receive him.
   Sam. Ay me, another inward grief awaked, 330
With mention of that name renews the assault.
   Man. Brethren and men of Dan, for such ye seem,
Though in this uncouth place; if old respect,
As I suppose, towards your once gloried friend,
My son now captive, hither hath informed 335
Your younger feet, while mine cast back with age
Came lagging after; say if he be here.
   Chor. As signal now in low dejected state,
As erst in highest, behold him where he lies.
   Man. O miserable change! is this the man, 340
That invincible Samson, far renowned,
The dread of Israel's foes, who with a strength
Equivalent to angels' walked their streets,
None offering fight; who single combatant
Dueled their armies ranked in proud array, 345
Himself an army, now unequal match
To save himself against a coward armed
At one spear's length. O ever failing trust
In mortal strength! and oh what not in man
Deceivable and vain! Nay what thing good 350
Prayed for, but often proves our woe, our bane?
I prayed for children, and thought barrenness
In wedlock a reproach; I gained a son,
And such a son as all men hailed me happy;
Who would be now a father in my stead? 355

---

318. **heroic Nazarite**: a 'Nazarite' was separated or consecrated to the service of God by certain vows, which swore him to abstinence from wine, from cutting his hair, and from contact with the dead. In addition, Samson was a 'hero' or fighting champion of his people. Cf. *Numbers* 6:1–21.

333. **uncouth place**: as usual, 'strange place,' but note how the word here partakes of its present meaning of 'awkward' or 'uncivilized.'

345. **Dueled their armies**: a 'duel' is between two and only two combatants. The meaning here is that Samson, one combatant, fought the entire army of the Philistines, the other combatant.

351. **bane**: originally, 'murderer,' now 'ruin.'

O wherefore did God grant me my request,
And as a blessing with such pomp adorned?
Why are his gifts desirable, to tempt
Our earnest prayers, then given with solemn hand
As graces, draw a scorpion's tail behind?   360
For this did the angel twice descend? for this
Ordained thy nurture holy, as of a plant;
Select, and sacred, glorious for a while,
The miracle of men: then in an hour
Ensnared, assaulted, overcome, led bound,   365
Thy foes' derision, captive, poor, and blind
Into a dungeon thrust, to work with slaves?
Alas methinks whom God hath chosen once
To worthiest deeds, if he through frailty err,
He should not so o'erwhelm, and as a thrall   370
Subject him to so foul indignities,
Be it but for honor's sake of former deeds.
    Sam. Appoint not heavenly disposition, father,
Nothing of all these evils hath befallen me
But justly; I myself have brought them on,   375
Sole author I, sole cause: if aught seem vile,
As vile hath been my folly, who have profaned
The mystery of God given me under pledge
Of vow, and have betrayed it to a woman,
A Canaanite, my faithless enemy.   380
This well I knew, nor was at all surprised,
But warned by oft experience: did not she
Of Timna first betray me, and reveal
The secret wrested from me in her height
Of nuptial love professed, carrying it straight   385
To them who had corrupted her, my spies,
And rivals? In this other was there found
More faith? who also in her prime of love,
Spousal embraces, vitiated with gold,
Though offered only, by the scent conceived   390
Her spurious first born; treason against me?
Thrice she assayed with flattering prayers and sighs,
And amorous reproaches to win from me
My capital secret, in what part my strength
Lay stored, in what part summed, that she might know: 395
Thrice I deluded her, and turned to sport
Her importunity, each time perceiving
How openly, and with what impudence
She purposed to betray me, and (which was worse
Than undissembled hate) with what contempt   400
She sought to make me traitor to myself;
Yet the fourth time, when mustering all her wiles,

   390. The meaning is that Dalila 'conceived' her first-born 'child,' treason against Samson, merely by smelling the gold offered her by the Philistines.

   392. **Thrice she assayed:** three times she tried; cf. *Judges* 16:6–14.

   394. **capital secret:** a pun, 'capital' meaning a 'great' secret, and also involving his 'head.'

With blandished parleys, feminine assaults,
Tongue batteries, she surceased not day nor night
To storm me overwatched, and wearied out.   405
At times when men seek most repose and rest,
I yielded, and unlocked her all my heart,
Who with a grain of manhood well resolved
Might easily have shook off all her snares:
But foul effeminacy held me yoked   410
Her bond-slave; O indignity, O blot
To honor and religion! servile mind
Rewarded well with servile punishment!
The base degree to which I now am fallen,
These rags, this grinding, is not yet so base   415
As was my former servitude, ignoble,
Unmanly, ignominious, infamous,
True slavery, and that blindness worse than this,
That saw not how degenerately I served.
    Man. I cannot praise thy marriage choices, son,   420
Rather approved them not; but thou didst plead
Divine impulsion prompting how thou mightest
Find some occasion to infest our foes.
I state not that; this I am sure; our foes
Found soon occasion thereby to make thee   425
Their captive, and their triumph; thou the sooner
Temptation foundest, or over potent charms
To violate the sacred trust of silence
Deposited within thee; which to have kept
Tacit, was in thy power; true; and thou bearest   430
Enough, and more the burden of that fault;
Bitterly hast thou paid, and still art paying
That rigid score.   A worse thing yet remains,
This day the Philistines a popular feast
Here celebrate in Gaza; and proclaim   435
Great pomp, and sacrifice, and praises loud
To Dagon, as their god who hath delivered
Thee Samson bound and blind into their hands,
Them out of thine, who slewest them many a slain.
So Dagon shall be magnified, and God,   440
Besides whom is no god, compared with idols,
Disglorified, blasphemed, and had in scorn
By the idolatrous rout amidst their wine;
Which to have come to pass by means of thee,
Samson, of all thy sufferings think the heaviest,   445
Of all reproach the most with shame that ever
Could have befallen thee and thy father's house.
    Sam. Father, I do acknowledge and confess
That I this honor, I this pomp have brought
To Dagon, and advanced his praises high   450

433 ff. **A worse thing yet remains:** the poem now changes to a 'present evil' from the recital of Samson's past troubles, and the 'popular feast' is likewise a consequence of Samson's sin. The Philistines are to celebrate his captivity and degradation.

Among the heathen round; to God have brought
Dishonor, obloquy, and oped the mouths
Of idolists, and atheists; have brought scandal
To Israel, diffidence of God, and doubt
In feeble hearts, propense enough before   455
To waver, or fall off and join with idols:
Which is my chief affliction, shame and sorrow,
The anguish of my soul, that suffers not
Mine eye to harbor sleep, or thoughts to rest.
This only hope relieves me, that the strife   460
With me hath end; all the contest is now
'Twixt God and Dagon; Dagon hath presumed,
Me overthrown, to enter lists with God,
His deity comparing and preferring
Before the God of Abraham.   He, be sure,   465
Will not connive, or linger, thus provoked,
But will arise and his great name assert:
Dagon must stoop, and shall erelong receive
Such a discomfit, as shall quite despoil him
Of all these boasted trophies won on me,   470
And with confusion blank his worshipers.
     Man. With cause this hope relieves thee, and these words
I as a prophecy receive: for God,
Nothing more certain, will not long defer
To vindicate the glory of his name   475
Against all competition, nor will long
Endure it, doubtful whether God be Lord,
Or Dagon.   But for thee what shall be done?
Thou must not in the meanwhile here forgot
Lie in this miserable loathsome plight   480
Neglected.   I already have made way
To some Philistian lords, with whom to treat
About thy ransom: well they may by this
Have satisfied their utmost of revenge
By pains and slaveries, worse than death inflicted   485
On thee, who now no more canst do them harm.
     Sam. Spare that proposal, father, spare the trouble
Of that solicitation; let me here,
As I deserve, pay on my punishment;
And expiate, if possible, my crime,   490
Shameful garrulity.   To have revealed
Secrets of men, the secrets of a friend,
How heinous had the fact been, how deserving
Contempt, and scorn of all, to be excluded
All friendship, and avoided as a blab,   495
The mark of fool set on his front?
But I God's counsel have not kept, his holy secret
Presumptuously have published, impiously,
Weakly at least, and shamefully: A sin
That Gentiles in their parables condemn   500

455. **propense enough:** ready enough.

To their abyss and horrid pains confined.
   Man. Be penitent and for thy fault contrite,
But act not in thy own affliction, son,
Repent the sin, but if the punishment
Thou canst avoid, self-preservation bids;   505
Or the execution leave to high disposal,
And let another hand, not thine, exact
Thy penal forfeit from thyself; perhaps
God will relent, and quit thee all his debt;
Whoever more approves and more accepts   510
(Best pleased with humble and filial submission)
Him who imploring mercy sues for life,
Than who self-rigorous chooses death as due;
Which argues over-just, and self-displeased
For self-offense, more than for God offended.   515
Reject not then what offered means, who knows
But God hath set before us, to return thee
Home to thy country and his sacred house,
Where thou mayest bring thy offerings, to avert
His further ire, with prayers and vows renewed.   520
   Sam. His pardon I implore; but as for life,
To what end should I seek it? when in strength
All mortals I excelled, and great in hopes
With youthful courage and magnanimous thoughts
Of birth from heaven foretold and high exploits,   525
Full of divine instinct, after some proof
Of acts indeed heroic, far beyond
The sons of Anak, famous now and blazed,
Fearless of danger, like a petty god
I walked about admired of all and dreaded   530
On hostile ground, none daring my affront.
Then swollen with pride into the snare I fell
Of fair fallacious looks, venereal trains,
Softened with pleasure and voluptuous life;
At length to lay my head and hallowed pledge   535
Of all my strength in the lascivious lap
Of a deceitful concubine who shore me
Like a tame wether, all my precious fleece,
Then turned me out ridiculous, despoiled,
Shaven, and disarmed among my enemies.   540
   Chor. Desire of wine and all delicious drinks,
Which many a famous warrior overturns,
Thou couldst repress, nor did the dancing ruby
Sparkling, out-poured, the flavor, or the smell,
Or taste that cheers the heart of gods and men,   545
Allure thee from the cool crystalline stream.
   Sam. Wherever fountain or fresh current flowed
Against the eastern ray, translucent, pure,

528. **sons of Anak:** Anak and his descendants were giants. Cf. *Numbers* 13:33.
533. **venereal trains:** artifices of love.
547 ff. Samson, as a Nazarite, drank no wine.

With touch ethereal of heaven's fiery rod
I drank, from the clear milky juice allaying   550
Thirst, and refreshed; nor envied them the grape
Whose heads that turbulent liquor fills with fumes.
   Chor. O madness, to think use of strongest wines
And strongest drinks our chief support of health,
When God with these forbidden made choice to rear   555
His mighty champion, strong above compare,
Whose drink was only from the liquid brook.
   Sam. But what availed this temperance, not complete
Against another object more enticing?
What boots it at one gate to make defense,   560
And at another to let in the foe
Effeminately vanquished? by which means,
Now blind, disheartened, shamed, dishonored, quelled,
To what can I be useful, wherein serve
My nation, and the work from heaven imposed,   565
But to sit idle on the household hearth,
A burdenous drone; to visitants a gaze,
Or pitied object, these redundant locks
Robustious to no purpose clustering down,
Vain monument of strength; till length of years   570
And sedentary numbness craze my limbs
To a contemptible old age obscure.
Here rather let me drudge and earn my bread,
Till vermin or the draff of servile food
Consume me, and oft-invocated death   575
Hasten the welcome end of all my pains.
   Man. Wilt thou then serve the Philistines with that gift
Which was expressly given thee to annoy them?
Better at home lie bed-rid, not only idle,
Inglorious, unemployed, with age outworn.   580
But God who caused a fountain at thy prayer
From the dry ground to spring, thy thirst to allay
After the brunt of battle, can as easy
Cause light again within thy eyes to spring,
Wherewith to serve him better than thou hast;   585
And I persuade me so; why else this strength
Miraculous yet remaining in those locks?
His might continues in thee not for naught,
Nor shall his wondrous gifts be frustrate thus.
   Sam. All otherwise to me my thoughts portend,   590
That these dark orbs no more shall treat with light,
Nor the other light of life continue long,
But yield to double darkness nigh at hand:
So much I feel my genial spirits droop,
My hopes all flat, nature within me seems   595
In all her functions weary of herself;
My race of glory run, and race of shame,

549. **heaven's fiery rod**: the rod of Moses; cf. *Exodus* 17.
574. **draff**: dregs, lees, husks, refuse.   581–83. Cf. *Judges* 15:9.

And I shall shortly be with them that rest.
   Man. Believe not these suggestions which proceed
From anguish of the mind and humors black,   600
That mingle with thy fancy. I however
Must not omit a father's timely care
To prosecute the means of thy deliverance
By ransom or how else: meanwhile be calm,
And healing words from these thy friends admit.   605
   Sam. O that torment should not be confined
To the body's wounds and sores
With maladies innumerable
In heart, head, breast, and reins;
But must secret passage find   610
To the inmost mind,
There exercise all his fierce accidents,
And on her purest spirits prey,
As on entrails, joints, and limbs,
With answerable pains, but more intense,   615
Though void of corporal sense.
   My griefs not only pain me
As a lingering disease,
But finding no redress, ferment and rage,
Nor less than wounds immedicable   620
Rankle, and fester, and gangrene,
To black mortification.
Thoughts my tormentors armed with deadly stings
Mangle my apprehensive tenderest parts,
Exasperate, exulcerate, and raise   625
Dire inflammation which no cooling herb
Or medicinal liquor can assuage,
Nor breath of vernal air from snowy Alp.
Sleep hath forsook and given me o'er
To death's benumbing opium as my only cure.   630
Thence faintings, swoonings of despair,
And sense of heaven's desertion.
   I was his nursling once and choice delight,
His destined from the womb,
Promised by heavenly message twice descending.   635
Under his special eye
Abstemious I grew up and thrived amain;
He led me on to mightiest deeds,
Above the nerve of mortal arm
Against the uncircumcised, our enemies.   640
But now hath cast me off as never known,
And to those cruel enemies,
Whom I by his appointment had provoked,
Left me all helpless with the irreparable loss
Of sight, reserved alive to be repeated   645
The subject of their cruelty, or scorn.
Nor am I in the list of them that hope;
Hopeless are all my evils, all remediless;

This one prayer yet remains, might I be heard,
No long petition, speedy death,   650
The close of all my miseries, and the balm.
    Chor. Many are the sayings of the wise
In ancient and in modern books enrolled;
Extolling patience as the truest fortitude;
And to the bearing well of all calamities,   655
All chances incident to man's frail life
Consolatories writ
With studied argument, and much persuasion sought
Lenient of grief and anxious thought,
But with the afflicted in his pangs their sound   660
Little prevails, or rather seems a tune,
Harsh, and of dissonant mood from his complaint,
Unless he feel within
Some source of consolation from above;
Secret refreshings, that repair his strength,   665
And fainting spirits uphold.
    God of our fathers, what is man!
That thou towards him with hand so various,
Or might I say contrarious,
Temperest thy providence through his short course,   670
Not evenly, as thou rulest
The angelic orders and inferior creatures mute,
Irrational and brute.
Nor do I name of men the common rout,
That wandering loose about   675
Grow up and perish, as the summer fly,
Heads without name no more remembered,
But such as thou hast solemnly elected,
With gifts and graces eminently adorned
To some great work, thy glory,   680
And people's safety, which in part they effect:
Yet toward these thus dignified, thou oft
Amidst their height of noon,
Changest thy countenance, and thy hand with no regard
Of highest favors past   685
From thee on them, or them to thee of service.
    Nor only dost degrade them, or remit
To life obscured, which were a fair dismission,
But throwest them lower than thou didst exalt them high,
Unseemly falls in human eye,   690
Too grievous for the trespass or omission,
Oft leavest them to the hostile sword
Of heathen and profane, their carcasses
To dogs and fowls a prey, or else captived;
Or to the unjust tribunals, under change of times,   695
And condemnation of the ingrateful multitude.
If these they scape, perhaps in poverty
With sickness and disease thou bowest them down,
Painful diseases and deformed,

In crude old age;   700
Though not disordinate, yet causeless suffering
The punishment of dissolute days, in fine,
Just or unjust, alike seem miserable,
For oft alike, both come to evil end.
    So deal not with this once thy glorious champion,   705
The image of thy strength, and mighty minister.
What do I beg? how hast thou dealt already?
Behold him in this state calamitous, and turn
His labors, for thou canst, to peaceful end.
    But who is this, what thing of sea or land?   710
Female of sex it seems,
That so bedecked, ornate, and gay,
Comes this way sailing
Like a stately ship
Of Tarsus, bound for the isles   715
Of Javan or Gadire
With all her bravery on, and tackle trim,
Sails filled, and streamers waving,
Courted by all the winds that hold them play,
An amber scent of odorous perfume   720
Her harbinger, a damsel train behind;
Some rich Philistian matron she may seem,
And now at nearer view, no other certain
Than Dalila thy wife.
    Sam. My wife, my traitress, let her not come near me.   725
    Chor. Yet on she moves, now stands and eyes thee fixed,
About to have spoke, but now, with head declined
Like a fair flower surcharged with dew, she weeps
And words addressed seem into tears dissolved,
Wetting the borders of her silken veil: 730
But now again she makes address to speak.
    Dal. With doubtful feet and wavering resolution
I came, still dreading thy displeasure, Samson,
Which to have merited, without excuse,
I cannot but acknowledge; yet if tears   735
May expiate (though the fact more evil drew
In the perverse event than I foresaw)
My penance hath not slackened, though my pardon
No way assured.   But conjugal affection
Prevailing over fear, and timorous doubt   740
Hath led me on desirous to behold
Once more thy face, and know of thy estate.
If aught in my ability may serve
To lighten what thou sufferest, and appease

710–31. Contrast the pomp and circumstance of Dalila seeking forgiveness with the humiliation and uncontrollable grief of Eve under similar conditions, *PL* X:910 ff.

714–15. **ship of Tarsus:** cf. *Isaiah* 2:16 and *Ezekiel* 27:25. Tarsus is the Tarshish of Scripture, a seaport.

715–16. **isles of Javan:** the isles of Greece.   **Gadire:** Latin Gades, modern Cadiz; cf. *PR* IV:77.
720. **An amber scent:** ambergris.

Thy mind with what amends is in my power,   745
Though late, yet in some part to recompense
My rash but more unfortunate misdeed.
　　Sam. Out, out hyaena; these are thy wonted arts,
And arts of every woman false like thee,
To break all faith, all vows, deceive, betray,   750
Then as repentant to submit, beseech,
And reconcilement move with feigned remorse,
Confess, and promise wonders in her change,
Not truly penitent, but chief to try
Her husband, how far urged his patience bears,   755
His virtue or weakness which way to assail:
Then with more cautious and instructed skill
Again transgresses, and again submits;
That wisest and best men full oft beguiled
With goodness principled not to reject   760
The penitent, but ever to forgive,
Are drawn to wear out miserable days,
Entangled with a poisonous bosom snake,
If not by quick destruction soon cut off
As I by thee, to ages an example.   765
　　Dal. Yet hear me Samson; not that I endeavor
To lessen or extenuate my offense,
But that on the other side if it be weighed
By itself, with aggravations not surcharged,
Or else with just allowance counterpoised,   770
I may, if possible, thy pardon find
The easier towards me, or thy hatred less.
First granting, as I do, it was a weakness
In me, but incident to all our sex,
Curiosity, inquisitive, importune   775
Of secrets, then with like infirmity
To publish them, both common female faults:
Was it not weakness also to make known
For importunity, that is for naught,
Wherein consisted all thy strength and safety?   780
To what I did thou showedst me first the way.
But I to enemies revealed, and should not.
Nor shouldst thou have trusted that to woman's frailty
Ere I to thee, thou to thyself wast cruel.
Let weakness then with weakness come to parle   785
So near related, or the same of kind,
Thine forgive mine; that men may censure thine
The gentler, if severely thou exact not
More strength from me, than in thyself was found.
And what if love, which thou interpretest hate,   790
The jealousy of love, powerful of sway
In human hearts, nor less in mine towards thee,
Caused what I did?　I saw thee mutable

---

　748. **hyaena:** Pliny, *Natural History* VIII:44, and elsewhere, cites many instances of the hyena's cunning and evil, treacherous ways.

Of fancy, feared lest one day thou wouldst leave me
As her at Timna, sought by all means therefore
How to endear, and hold thee to me firmest: 795
No better way I saw than by importuning
To learn thy secrets, get into my power
Thy key of strength and safety: thou wilt say,
'Why then revealed?' I was assured by those   800
Who tempted me, that nothing was designed
Against thee but safe custody, and hold:
That made for me, I knew that liberty
Would draw thee forth to perilous enterprises,
While I at home sat full of cares and fears   805
Wailing thy absence in my widowed bed;
Here I should still enjoy thee day and night
Mine and love's prisoner, not the Philistines',
Whole to myself, unhazarded abroad,
Fearless at home of partners in my love.   810
These reasons in love's law have passed for good,
Though fond and reasonless to some perhaps;
And love hath oft, well meaning, wrought much woe,
Yet always pity or pardon hath obtained.
Be not unlike all others, not austere   815
As thou art strong, inflexible as steel.
If thou in strength all mortals dost exceed,
In uncompassionate anger do not so.
    Sam. How cunningly the sorceress displays
Her own transgressions, to upbraid me mine?   820
That malice not repentance brought thee hither,
By this appears: I gave, thou sayest, the example,
I led the way; bitter reproach, but true,
I to myself was false ere thou to me,
Such pardon therefore as I give my folly,   825
Take to thy wicked deed: which when thou seest
Impartial, self-severe, inexorable,
Thou wilt renounce thy seeking, and much rather
Confess it feigned, weakness is thy excuse,
And I believe it, weakness to resist   830
Philistian gold: if weakness may excuse,
What murderer, what traitor, parricide,
Incestuous, sacrilegious, but may plead it?
All wickedness is weakness: that plea therefore
With God or man will gain thee no remission.   835
But love constrained thee; call it furious rage
To satisfy thy lust: Love seeks to have love;
My love how couldst thou hope, who tookest the way
To raise in me inexpiable hate,
Knowing, as needs I must, by thee betrayed?   840
In vain thou strivest to cover shame with shame,
Or by evasions thy crime uncoverest more.
    Dal. Since thou determinest weakness for no plea
In man or woman, though to thy own condemning,

Hear what assaults I had, what snares besides,   845
What sieges girt me round, ere I consented;
Which might have awed the best resolved of men,
The constantest to have yielded without blame.
It was not gold, as to my charge thou layest,
That wrought with me: thou knowest the magistrates   850
And princes of my country came in person,
Solicited, commanded, threatened, urged,
Adjured by all the bonds of civil duty
And of religion, pressed how just it was,
How honorable, how glorious to entrap   855
A common enemy, who had destroyed
Such numbers of our nation: and the priest
Was not behind, but ever at my ear,
Preaching how meritorious with the gods
It would be to ensnare an irreligious   860
Dishonorer of Dagon: what had I
To oppose against such powerful arguments?
Only my love of thee held long debate;
And combated in silence all these reasons
With hard contest: at length that grounded maxim   865
So rife and celebrated in the mouths
Of wisest men; that to the public good
Private respects must yield; with grave authority
Took full possession of me and prevailed;
Virtue, as I thought, truth, duty so enjoining.   870
    Sam. I thought where all thy circling wiles would end;
In feigned religion, smooth hypocrisy.
But had thy love, still odiously pretended,
Been, as it ought, sincere, it would have taught thee
Far other reasonings, brought forth other deeds.   875
I before all the daughters of my tribe
And of my nation chose thee from among
My enemies, loved thee, as too well thou knewest,
Too well, unbosomed all my secrets to thee,
Not out of levity, but overpowered   880
By thy request, who could deny thee nothing;
Yet now am judged an enemy.   Why then
Didst thou at first receive me for thy husband?
Then, as since then, thy country's foe professed:
Being once a wife, for me thou wast to leave   885
Parents and country; nor was I their subject,
Nor under their protection but my own,
Thou mine, not theirs: if aught against my life
Thy country sought of thee, it sought unjustly,
Against the law of nature, law of nations,   890
No more thy country, but an impious crew
Of men conspiring to uphold their state
By worse than hostile deeds, violating the ends
For which our country is a name so dear;
Not therefore to be obeyed.   But zeal moved thee;   895

To please thy gods thou didst it; gods unable
To acquit themselves and prosecute their foes
But by ungodly deeds, the contradiction
Of their own deity, gods cannot be:
Less therefore to be pleased, obeyed, or feared,   900
These false pretexts and varnished colors failing,
Bare in thy guilt how foul must thou appear?
   Dal. In argument with men a woman ever
Goes by the worse, whatever be her cause.
   Sam. For want of words no doubt, or lack of breath,   905
Witness when I was worried with thy peals.
   Dal. I was a fool, too rash, and quite mistaken
In what I thought would have succeeded best.
Let me obtain forgiveness of thee, Samson,
Afford me place to show what recompense   910
Towards thee I intend for what I have misdone,
Misguided; only what remains past cure
Bear not too sensibly, nor still insist
To afflict thyself in vain: though sight be lost,
Life yet hath many solaces, enjoyed   915
Where other senses want not their delights
At home in leisure and domestic ease,
Exempt from many a care and chance to which
Eyesight exposes daily men abroad.
I to the lords will intercede, not doubting   920
Their favorable ear, that I may fetch thee
From forth this loathsome prison-house, to abide
With me, where my redoubled love and care
With nursing diligence, to me glad office,
May ever tend about thee to old age   925
With all things grateful cheered, and so supplied,
That what by me thou hast lost thou least shalt miss.
   Sams. No, no, of my condition take no care;
It fits not; thou and I long since are twain;
Nor think me so unwary or accursed   930
To bring my feet again into the snare
Where once I have been caught; I know thy trains
Though dearly to my cost, thy gins, and toils;
Thy fair enchanted cup, and warbling charms
No more on me have power, their force is nulled,   935
So much of adder's wisdom I have learned
To fence my ear against thy sorceries.
If in my flower of youth and strength, when all men
Loved, honored, feared me, thou alone could hate me
Thy husband, slight me, sell me, and forgo me;   940
How wouldst thou use me now, blind, and thereby
Deceivable, in most things as a child
Helpless, thence easily contemned, and scorned,
And last neglected? How wouldst thou insult
When I must live uxorious to thy will   945
In perfect thralldom, how again betray me,

Bearing my words and doings to the lords
To gloss upon, and censuring, frown or smile?
This jail I count the house of liberty
To thine whose doors my feet shall never enter.   950
    Dal. Let me approach at least, and touch thy hand.
    Sam. Not for thy life, lest fierce remembrance wake
My sudden rage to tear thee joint by joint.
At distance I forgive thee, go with that;
Bewail thy falsehood, and the pious works   955
It hath brought forth to make thee memorable
Among illustrious women, faithful wives;
Cherish thy hastened widowhood with the gold
Of matrimonial treason: so farewell.
    Dal. I see thou art implacable, more deaf   960
To prayers, than winds and seas, yet winds to seas
Are reconciled at length, and sea to shore:
Thy anger, unappeasable, still rages,
Eternal tempest never to be calmed.
Why do I humble thus myself, and suing   965
For peace, reap nothing but repulse and hate?
Bid go with evil omen and the brand
Of infamy upon my name denounced?
To mix with thy concernments I desist
Henceforth, nor too much disapprove my own.   970
Fame if not double-faced is double-mouthed,
And with contrary blast proclaims most deeds,
On both his wings, one black, the other white,
Bears greatest names in his wild airy flight.
My name perhaps among the circumcised   975
In Dan, in Judah, and the bordering tribes,
To all posterity may stand defamed,
With malediction mentioned, and the blot
Of falsehood most unconjugal traduced.
But in my country where I most desire,   980
In Ecron, Gaza, Asdod, and in Gath
I shall be named among the famousest
Of women, sung at solemn festivals,
Living and dead recorded, who to save
Her country from a fierce destroyer, chose   985
Above the faith of wedlock bands, my tomb
With odors visited and annual flowers.
Not less renowned than in Mount Ephraim,
Jael, who with inhospitable guile
Smote Sisera sleeping through the temples nailed.   990
Nor shall I count it heinous to enjoy
The public marks of honor and reward
Conferred upon me, for the piety
Which to my country I was judged to have shown.
At this whoever envies or repines   995

981. **Ecron, Gaza, Asdod, and in Gath:** four of the five chief towns of the Philistines.
988 ff. Cf. *Judges* 4:5 ff.

I leave him to his lot, and like my own.
    Chor. She's gone, a manifest serpent by her sting
Discovered in the end, till now concealed.
    Sam. So let her go, God sent her to debase me,
And aggravate my folly who committed   1000
To such a viper his most sacred trust
Of secrecy, my safety, and my life.
    Chor. Yet beauty, though injurious, hath strange power,
After offense returning, to regain
Love once possessed, nor can be easily   1005
Repulsed, without much inward passion felt
And secret sting of amorous remorse.
    Sam. Love-quarrels oft in pleasing concord end,
Not wedlock-treachery endangering life.
    Chor. It is not virtue, wisdom, valor, wit,   1010
Strength, comeliness of shape, or amplest merit
That woman's love can win or long inherit;
But what it is, hard is to say,
Harder to hit,
(Which way soever men refer it)   1015
Much like thy riddle, Samson, in one day
Or seven, though one should musing sit;
    If any of these or all, the Timnian bride
Had not so soon preferred
Thy paranymph, worthless to thee compared,   1020
Successor in thy bed,
Nor both so loosely disallied
Their nuptials, nor this last so treacherously
Had shorn the fatal harvest of thy head.
Is it for that such outward ornament   1025
Was lavished on their sex, that inward gifts
Were left for haste unfinished, judgment scant,
Capacity not raised to apprehend
Or value what is best
In choice, but oftest to affect the wrong?   1030
Or was too much of self-love mixed,
Of constancy no root infixed,
That either they love nothing, or not long?
    Whate'er it be, to wisest men and best
Seeming at first all heavenly under virgin veil,   1035
Soft, modest, meek, demure,
Once joined, the contrary she proves, a thorn
Intestine, far within defensive arms
A cleaving mischief, in his way to virtue
Adverse and turbulent, or by her charms   1040
Draws him awry enslaved
With dotage, and his sense depraved
To folly and shameful deeds which ruin ends.
What pilot so expert but needs must wreck
Embarked with such a steers-mate at the helm?   1045

1016. **thy riddle:** cf. *Judges* 16:12–14.   1020. **paranymph:** friend of the bridegroom.

Favored of heaven who finds
One virtuous rarely found,
That in domestic good combines:
Happy that house! his way to peace is smooth:
But virtue which breaks through all opposition,   1050
And all temptation can remove,
Most shines and most is acceptable above.
    Therefore God's universal law
Gave to the man despotic power
Over his female in due awe,   1055
Nor from that right to part an hour,
Smile she or lour:
So shall he least confusion draw
On his whole life, not swayed
By female usurpation, nor dismayed.   1060
    But had we best retire, I see a storm?
    Sam. Fair days have oft contracted wind and rain.
    Chor. But this another kind of tempest brings.
    Sam. Be less abstruse, my riddling days are past.
    Chor. Look now for no enchanting voice, nor fear   1065
The bait of honeyed words; a rougher tongue
Draws hitherward, I know him by his stride,
The giant Harapha of Gath, his look
Haughty as is his pile high-built and proud.
Comes he in peace? what wind hath blown him hither   1070
I less conjecture than when first I saw
The sumptuous Dalila floating this way:
His habit carries peace, his brow defiance.
    Sam. Or peace or not, alike to me he comes.
    Chor. His fraught we soon shall know, he now arrives.   1075
    Har. I come not Samson, to condole thy chance,
As these perhaps, yet wish it had not been,
Though for no friendly intent.   I am of Gath,
Men call me Harapha, of stock renowned
As Og or Anak and the Emins old   1080

1068. **Harapha of Gath:** this name has baffled many commentators, due to the fact that the *AV* translated the Hebrew of *II Samuel* 21:16 (*harapha*) as 'the giant.'   The Hebrew word appears to be a noun with its definite article; but no one knows exactly what the word *harapha* means.   In the *AV*, the words *rapha* and *raphaim*, occurring in other verses, are translated respectively as *giant* and *giants*; but the original editions of the *AV* put *Rapha* or *Raphaim* as proper names in the margin.   The Greek of *II Samuel* 21:16 reads 'the Rapha.'   Biblical commentators have assumed that the word means *giant*.   Professor Parker has pointed out (*London Times Literary Supplement*, 1937, p. 12) that the name occurs in Phillips, and is said to mean a medicine.   But Phillips has '*Heb.* a medicine' in parentheses and intended this to indicate from which of the two possible Hebrew roots the word came.   He took it as a proper name, as did most of Milton's contemporaries.   See G. Diodati, *Annotations* (London, 1648), p. 193; and Edward Leigh, *Critica Sacra* (London, 1642), pp. 492–93.   In the edition of 1650 (p. 233), Leigh explicitly states that Harapha was the parent of the giants mentioned elsewhere in the *OT*.   For a modern scholarly treatment, see Brown, Driver, and Briggs, *Hebrew and English Lexicon* (New York, 1907), p. 952, where the word is treated as a proper name of unknown origin or exact meaning, but certainly meaning a parent in *II Samuel*.

   1069. **pile:** bulk.   1075. **fraught:** freight, import; hence, intention.

   1080. **Og or Anak and the Emins:** Og, King of Bashan; cf. *Deuteronomy* 3:11.   Anak, cf. line 528, cf. *Joshua* 15:13 and *Numbers* 13:33, a giant.   The Emins was the name of a race of giants; cf. *Deuteronomy* 2:10.   'Kiriathaim' was the name of their town; cf. *Genesis* 14:5.

That Kiriathaim held, thou knowest me now
If thou at all art known.   Much I have heard
Of thy prodigious might and feats performed
Incredible to me, in this displeased,
That I was never present on the place   1085
Of those encounters, where we might have tried
Each other's force in camp or listed field:
And now am come to see of whom such noise
Hath walked about, and each limb to survey,
If thy appearance answer loud report.   1090
   Sam. The way to know were not to see but taste.
   Har. Dost thou already single me? I thought
Gyves and the mill had tamed thee; O that fortune
Had brought me to the field where thou art famed
To have wrought such wonders with an ass's jaw;   1095
I should have forced thee soon wish other arms,
Or left thy carcass where the ass lay thrown:
So had the glory of prowess been recovered
To Palestine, won by a Philistine
From the unforeskinned race, of whom thou bearest   1100
The highest name for valiant acts, that honor
Certain to have won by mortal duel from thee,
I lose, prevented by thy eyes put out.
   Sam. Boast not of what thou wouldst have done, but do
What then thou wouldst, thou seest it in thy hand.   1105
   Har. To combat with a blind man I disdain,
And thou hast need much washing to be touched.
   Sam. Such usage as your honorable lords
Afford me assassinated and betrayed,
Who durst not with their whole united powers   1110
In fight withstand me single and unarmed,
Nor in the house with chamber ambushes
Close-banded durst attack me, no not sleeping,
Till they had hired a woman with their gold
Breaking her marriage faith to circumvent me.   1115
Therefore without feigned shifts let be assigned
Some narrow place enclosed, where sight may give thee,
Or rather flight, no great advantage on me;
Then put on all thy gorgeous arms, thy helmet
And brigandine of brass, thy broad habergeon,   1120
Vant-brace and greaves, and gauntlet, add thy spear
A weaver's beam, and seven-times-folded shield,

1092–93. Obviously the semicolon in 1092 and the interrogation point in 1093 in some, not all, 1671 copies (others, representing an earlier state, have a semicolon in both lines) should be interchanged.   The 1680 edition puts an interrogation point after 'me' in 1092 and a period after 'thee' in 1093.   The text and notes in the Columbia edition are inadequate.

1093. **Gyves:** fetters.   1119 ff. Articles of fighting apparel.

1120. **brigandine:** coat of mail.   **habergeon:** armor for the neck and shoulders.

1121. **Vant-brace:** armor for the forearm.   **greaves:** armor for the legs.

1122. **weaver's beam:** Goliath's spear was described as a weaver's beam for size. Cf. *I Samuel* 17:7. **seven-times-folded shield:** made of seven thicknesses or folds of leather or metal.

I only with an oaken staff will meet thee,
And raise such outcries on thy clattered iron,
Which long shall not withhold me from thy head,   1125
That in a little time while breath remains thee,
Thou oft shalt wish thyself at Gath to boast
Again in safety what thou wouldst have done
To Samson, but shalt never see Gath more.
   Har. Thou durst not thus disparage glorious arms   1130
Which greatest heroes have in battle worn,
Their ornament and safety, had not spells
And black enchantments, some magician's art
Armed thee or charmed thee strong, which thou from heaven
Feignedst at thy birth was given thee in thy hair,   1135
Where strength can least abide, though all thy hairs
Were bristles ranged like those that ridge the back
Of chafed wild boars, or ruffled porcupines.
   Sam. I know no spells, use no forbidden arts;
My trust is in the living God who gave me   1140
At my nativity this strength, diffused
No less through all my sinews, joints and bones,
Than thine, while I preserved these locks unshorn,
The pledge of my unviolated vow.
For proof hereof, if Dagon be thy god,   1145
Go to his temple, invocate his aid
With solemnest devotion, spread before him
How highly it concerns his glory now
To frustrate and dissolve these magic spells,
Which I to be the power of Israel's God   1150
Avow, and challenge Dagon to the test,
Offering to combat thee his champion bold,
With the utmost of his godhead seconded:
Then thou shalt see, or rather to thy sorrow
Soon feel, whose God is strongest, thine or mine.   1155
   Har. Presume not on thy God, whate'er he be,
Thee he regards not, owns not, hath cut off
Quite from his people, and delivered up
Into thy enemies' hand, permitted them
To put out both thine eyes, and fettered send thee   1160
Into the common prison, there to grind
Among the slaves and asses thy comrades,
As good for nothing else, no better service
With those thy boisterous locks, no worthy match
For valor to assail, nor by the sword   1165
Of noble warrior, so to stain his honor,
But by the barber's razor best subdued.
   Sam. All these indignities, for such they are
From thine, these evils I deserve and more,
Acknowledge them from God inflicted on me   1170
Justly, yet despair not of his final pardon
Whose ear is ever open; and his eye
Gracious to readmit the suppliant;

In confidence whereof I once again
Defy thee to the trial of mortal fight,   1175
By combat to decide whose god is God,
Thine or whom I with Israel's sons adore.
    Har. Fair honor that thou dost thy God, in trusting
He will accept thee to defend his cause,
A murderer, a revolter, and a robber.   1180
    Sam. Tongue-doughty giant, how dost thou prove me these?
    Har. Is not thy nation subject to our lords?
Their magistrates confessed it, when they took thee
As a league-breaker and delivered bound
Into our hands: for hadst thou not committed   1185
Notorious murder on those thirty men
At Ascalon, who never did thee harm,
Then like a robber strippedst them of their robes?
The Philistines, when thou hadst broke the league,
Went up with armed powers thee only seeking,   1190
To others did no violence nor spoil.
    Sam. Among the daughters of the Philistines
I chose a wife, which argued me no foe;
And in your city held my nuptial feast:
But your ill-meaning politician lords,   1195
Under pretense of bridal friends and guests,
Appointed to await me thirty spies,
Who threatening cruel death constrained the bride
To wring from me and tell to them my secret,
That solved the riddle which I had proposed.   1200
When I perceived all set on enmity,
As on my enemies, wherever chanced,
I used hostility, and took their spoil
To pay my underminers in their coin.
My nation was subjected to your lords.   1205
It was the force of conquest; force with force
Is well ejected when the conquered can.
But I a private person, whom my country
As a league-breaker gave up bound, presumed
Single rebellion and did hostile acts.   1210
I was no private but a person raised
With strength sufficient and command from heaven
To free my country; if their servile minds
Me their deliverer sent would not receive,
But to their masters gave me up for nought,   1215
The unworthier they; whence to this day they serve.
I was to do my part from heaven assigned,
And had performed it if my known offense
Had not disabled me, not all your force:
These shifts refuted, answer thy appellant   1220
Though by his blindness maimed for high attempts,

1186–87. **those thirty men at Ascalon:** cf. *Judges* 14:19.
1197. **thirty spies:** cf. *Judges* 14:11, as in line 386.
1220. **thy appellant:** thy appealer.

Who now defies thee thrice to single fight,
As a petty enterprise of small enforce.
    Har. With thee a man condemned, a slave enrolled,
Due by the law to capital punishment?   1225
To fight with thee no man of arms will deign.
    Sam. Camest thou for this, vain boaster, to survey me,
To descant on my strength, and give thy verdict?
Come nearer, part not hence so slight informed;
But take good heed my hand survey not thee.   1230
    Har. O Baal-zebub! can my ears unused
Hear these dishonors, and not render death?
    Sam. No man withholds thee, nothing from thy hand
Fear I incurable; bring up thy van,
My heels are fettered, but my fist is free.   1235
    Har. This insolence other kind of answer fits.
    Sams. Go baffled coward, lest I run upon thee,
Though in these chains, bulk without spirit vast,
And with one buffet lay thy structure low,
Or swing thee in the air, then dash thee down   1240
To the hazard of thy brains and shattered sides.
    Har. By Astaroth erelong thou shalt lament
These braveries in irons laden on thee.
    Chor. His giantship is gone somewhat crestfallen,
Stalking with less unconscionable strides,   1245
And lower looks, but in a sultry chafe.
    Sam. I dread him not, nor all his giant brood,
Though fame divulge him father of five sons
All of gigantic size, Goliah chief.
    Chor. He will directly to the lords, I fear,   1250
And with malicious counsel stir them up
Some way or other yet further to afflict thee.
    Sam. He must allege some cause, and offered fight
Will not dare mention, lest a question rise
Whether he durst accept the offer or not,   1255
And that he durst not plain enough appeared.
Much more affliction than already felt
They cannot well impose, nor I sustain;
If they intend advantage of my labors
The work of many hands, which earns my keeping   1260
With no small profit daily to my owners.
But come what will, my deadliest foe will prove
My speediest friend, by death to rid me hence,
The worst that he can give, to me the best.
Yet so it may fall out, because their end   1265
Is hate, not help to me, it may with mine
Draw their own ruin who attempt the deed.
    Chor. O how comely it is and how reviving
To the spirits of just men long oppressed!

1231. **Baal-zebub:** a chief god of the Philistines.
1242. **Astaroth:** a female deity of the Philistines; actually, a plural.
1247-49. Cf. *II Samuel* 22:15-22.   1249. **Goliah:** Goliath, the giant slain by David.

When God into the hands of their deliverer 1270
Puts invincible might
To quell the mighty of the earth, the oppressor,
The brute and boisterous force of violent men
Hardy and industrious to support
Tyrannic power, but raging to pursue 1275
The righteous and all such as honor truth;
He all their ammunition
And feats of war defeats
With plain heroic magnitude of mind
And celestial vigor armed, 1280
Their armories and magazines contemns,
Renders them useless, while
With winged expedition
Swift as the lightning glance he executes
His errand on the wicked, who surprised 1285
Lose their defense distracted and amazed.
   But patience is more oft the exercise
Of saints, the trial of their fortitude,
Making them each his own deliverer,
And victor over all 1290
That tyranny or fortune can inflict,
Either of these is in thy lot,
Samson, with might endued
Above the sons of men; but sight bereaved
May chance to number thee with those 1295
Whom patience finally must crown.
This idol's day hath been to thee no day of rest,
  Laboring thy mind
More than the working day thy hands,
And yet perhaps more trouble is behind. 1300
For I descry this way
Some other tending, in his hand
A scepter or quaint staff he bears,
Comes on amain, speed in his look.
By his habit I discern him now 1305
A public officer, and now at hand.
His message will be short and voluble.
   Off. Ebrews, the prisoner Samson here I seek.
   Chor. His manacles remark him, there he sits.
   Off. Samson, to thee our lords thus bid me say; 1310
This day to Dagon is a solemn feast,
With sacrifices, triumph, pomp, and games;
Thy strength they know surpassing human rate,
And now some public proof thereof require
To honor this great feast, and great assembly; 1315
Rise therefore with all speed and come along,
Where I will see thee heartened and fresh clad
To appear as fits before the illustrious lords.
   Sam. Thou knowest I am an Ebrew, therefore tell them,
Our law forbids at their religious rites 1320

My presence; for that cause I cannot come.
    Off. This answer, be assured, will not content them.
    Sam. Have they not sword-players, and every sort
Of gymnic artists, wrestlers, riders, runners,
Jugglers and dancers, antics, mummers, mimics,   1325
But they must pick me out with shackles tired,
And over-labored at their public mill,
To make them sport with blind activity?
Do they not seek occasion of new quarrels
On my refusal to distress me more,   1330
Or make a game of my calamities?
Return the way thou camest, I will not come.
    Off. Regard thyself, this will offend them highly.
    Sam. Myself? my conscience and internal peace.
Can they think me so broken, so debased   1335
With corporal servitude, that my mind ever
Will condescend to such absurd commands?
Although their drudge, to be their fool or jester,
And in my midst of sorrow and heart-grief
To show them feats, and play before their god,   1340
The worst of all indignities, yet on me
Joined with extreme contempt? I will not come.
    Off. My message was imposed on me with speed,
Brooks no delay: is this thy resolution?
    Sam. So take it with what speed thy message needs.   1345
    Off. I am sorry what this stoutness will produce.
    Sa. Perhaps thou shalt have cause to sorrow indeed.
    Chor. Consider, Samson; matters now are strained
Up to the height, whether to hold or break;
He's gone, and who knows how he may report   1350
Thy words by adding fuel to the flame?
Expect another message more imperious,
More lordly thundering than thou well wilt bear.
    Sam. Shall I abuse this consecrated gift
Of strength, again returning with my hair   1355
After my great transgression, so requite
Favor renewed, and add a greater sin
By prostituting holy things to idols;
A Nazarite in place abominable
Vaunting my strength in honor to their Dagon?   1360
Besides, how vile, contemptible, ridiculous,
What act more execrably unclean, profane?
    Chor. Yet with this strength thou servest the Philistines,
Idolatrous, uncircumcised, unclean.
    Sam. Not in their idol-worship, but by labor   1365
Honest and lawful to deserve my food
Of those who have me in their civil power.
    Chor. Where the heart joins not, outward acts defile not.
    Sam. Where outward force constrains, the sentence holds
But who constrains me to the temple of Dagon,   1370

1359. **A Nazarite**: a man consecrated to God.

Not dragging? the Philistian lords command.
Commands are no constraints.   If I obey them,
I do it freely; venturing to displease
God for the fear of man, and man prefer,
Set God behind: which in his jealousy   1375
Shall never, unrepented, find forgiveness.
Yet that he may dispense with me or thee
Present in temples at idolatrous rites
For some important cause, thou needest not doubt.
   Chor. How thou wilt here come off surmounts my reach.   1380
   Sam. Be of good courage, I begin to feel
Some rousing motions in me which dispose
To something extraordinary my thoughts.
I with this messenger will go along,
Nothing to do, be sure, that may dishonor   1385
Our Law, or stain my vow of Nazarite.
If there be aught of presage in the mind,
This day will be remarkable in my life
By some great act, or of my days the last.
   Chor. In time thou hast resolved, the man returns.   1390
   Off. Samson, this second message from our lords
To thee I am bid say.   Art thou our slave,
Our captive, at the public mill our drudge,
And darest thou at our sending and command
Dispute thy coming? come without delay;   1395
Or we shall find such engines to assail
And hamper thee, as thou shalt come of force,
Though thou wert firmlier fastened than a rock.
   Sam. I could be well content to try their art,
Which to no few of them would prove pernicious.   1400
Yet knowing their advantages too many,
Because they shall not trail me through their streets
Like a wild beast, I am content to go.
Masters' commands come with a power resistless
To such as owe them absolute subjection;   1405
And for a life who will not change his purpose?
(So mutable are all the ways of men)
Yet this be sure, in nothing to comply
Scandalous or forbidden in our Law.
   Off. I praise thy resolution, doff these links: 1410
By this compliance thou wilt win the lords
To favor, and perhaps to set thee free.
   Sam. Brethren farewell, your company along
I will not wish, lest it perhaps offend them
To see me girt with friends; and how the sight   1415
Of me as of a common enemy,
So dreaded once, may now exasperate them
I know not.   Lords are lordliest in their wine;
And the well-feasted priest then soonest fired
With zeal, if aught religion seem concerned: 1420
No less the people on their holy-days

Impetuous, insolent, unquenchable;
Happen what may, of me expect to hear
Nothing dishonorable, impure, unworthy
Our God, our Law, my nation, or myself,   1425
The last of me or no I cannot warrant.
   Chor. Go, and the Holy One
Of Israel be thy guide
To what may serve his glory best, and spread his name
Great among the heathen round: 1430
Send thee the angel of thy birth, to stand
Fast by thy side, who from thy father's field
Rode up in flames after his message told
Of thy conception, and be now a shield
Of fire; that spirit that first rushed on thee   1435
In the camp of Dan
Be efficacious in thee now at need.
For never was from heaven imparted
Measure of strength so great to mortal seed,
As in thy wondrous actions hath been seen.   1440
But wherefore comes old Manoa in such haste
With youthful steps? much livelier than erewhile
He seems: supposing here to find his son,
Or of him bringing to us some glad news?
   Man. Peace with you brethren; my inducement hither   1445
Was not at present here to find my son,
By order of the lords new parted hence
To come and play before them at their feast.
I heard all as I came, the city rings
And numbers thither flock, I had no will,   1450
Lest I should see him forced to things unseemly.
But that which moved my coming now, was chiefly
To give ye part with me what hope I have
With good success to work his liberty.
   Chor. That hope would much rejoice us to partake   1455
With thee; say reverend sire, we thirst to hear.
   Man. I have attempted one by one the lords
Either at home, or through the high street passing,
With supplication prone and father's tears
To accept of ransom for my son their prisoner,   1460
Some much averse I found and wondrous harsh,
Contemptuous, proud, set on revenge and spite;
That part most reverenced Dagon and his priests,
Others more moderate seeming, but their aim
Private reward, for which both God and state   1465
They easily would set to sale, a third
More generous far and civil, who confessed
They had enough revenged, having reduced
Their foe to misery beneath their fears,
The rest was magnanimity to remit,   1470
If some convenient ransom were proposed.
What noise or shout was that? it tore the sky.

Chor. Doubtless the people shouting to behold
Their once great dread, captive, and blind before them,
Or at some proof of strength before them shown.
    Man. His ransom, if my whole inheritance 1475
May compass it, shall willingly be paid
And numbered down: much rather I shall choose
To live the poorest in my tribe, than richest,
And he in that calamitous prison left.
No, I am fixed not to part hence without him. 1480
For his redemption all my patrimony,
If need be, I am ready to forgo
And quit: not wanting him, I shall want nothing.
    Chor. Fathers are wont to lay up for their sons, 1485
Thou for thy son art bent to lay out all;
Sons wont to nurse their parents in old age,
Thou in old age carest how to nurse thy son
Made older than thy age through eyesight lost.
    Man. It shall be my delight to tend his eyes, 1490
And view him sitting in his house, ennobled
With all those high exploits by him achieved,
And on his shoulders waving down those locks,
That of a nation armed the strength contained:
And I persuade me God hath not permitted 1495
His strength again to grow up with his hair
Garrisoned round about him like a camp
Of faithful soldiery, were not his purpose
To use him further yet in some great service,
Not to sit idle with so great a gift 1500
Useless, and thence ridiculous about him.
And since his strength with eyesight was not lost,
God will restore him eyesight to his strength.
    Chor. Thy hopes are not ill founded nor seem vain
Of his delivery, and thy joy thereon 1505
Conceived, agreeable to a father's love,
In both which we, as next participate.
    Man. I know your friendly minds, and — O what noise!
Mercy of Heaven what hideous noise was that!
Horribly loud unlike the former shout. 1510
    Chor. Noise call you it or universal groan
As if the whole inhabitation perished,
Blood, death, and deathful deeds are in that noise,
Ruin, destruction at the utmost point.
    Man. Of ruin indeed methought I heard the noise, 1515
Oh it continues, they have slain my son.
    Chor. Thy son is rather slaying them, that outcry
From slaughter of one foe could not ascend.
    Man. Some dismal accident it needs must be;
What shall we do, stay here or run and see? 1520
    Chor. Best keep together here, lest running thither
We unawares run into danger's mouth.

1481 ff. Note the puns.

This evil on the Philistines is fallen,
From whom could else a general cry be heard?
The sufferers then will scarce molest us here,   1525
From other hands we need not much to fear.
What if his eyesight (for to Israel's God
Nothing is hard) by miracle restored,
He now be dealing dole among his foes,
And over heaps of slaughtered walk his way?   1530
    Man. That were a joy presumptuous to be thought.
    Chor. Yet God hath wrought things as incredible
For his people of old; what hinders now?
    Man. He can I know, but doubt to think he will;
Yet hope would fain subscribe, and tempts belief.   1535
A little stay will bring some notice hither.
    Chor. Of good or bad so great, of bad the sooner;
For evil news rides post, while good news baits.
And to our wish I see one hither speeding,
An Ebrew, as I guess, and of our tribe.   1540
    Messenger. O whither shall I run, or which way fly
The sight of this so horrid spectacle
Which erst my eyes beheld and yet behold;
For dire imagination still pursues me.
But providence or instinct of nature seems,   1545
Or reason though disturbed, and scarce consulted
To have guided me aright, I know not how,
To thee first reverend Manoa, and to these
My countrymen, whom here I knew remaining,
As at some distance from the place of horror,   1550
So in the sad event too much concerned.
    Man. The accident was loud, and here before thee
With rueful cry, yet what it was we hear not,
No preface needs, thou seest we long to know.
    Mess. It would burst forth, but I recover breath   1555
And sense distract, to know well what I utter.
    Man. Tell us the sum, the circumstance defer.
    Mess. Gaza yet stands, but all her sons are fallen,
All in a moment overwhelmed and fallen.
    Man. Sad, but thou knowest to Israelites not saddest   1560
The desolation of a hostile city.
    Mess. Feed on that first, there may in grief be surfeit.
    Man. Relate by whom.
    Mess.   By Samson.
    Man.   That still lessens
The sorrow, and converts it nigh to joy.
    Mess. Ah Manoa I refrain, too suddenly   1565
To utter what will come at last too soon;
Lest evil tidings with too rude irruption
Hitting thy aged ear should pierce too deep.
    Man. Suspense in news is torture, speak them out.

1538. **baits:** travels slowly. Cf. *PL* XII:1.
1567. **irruption:** not the same meaning as *eruption*; a bursting in.

Mess. Then take the worst in brief, Samson is dead.　　　　1570
　Man. The worst indeed, O all my hopes defeated
To free him hence! but death who sets all free
Hath paid his ransom now and full discharge.
What windy joy this day had I conceived
Hopeful of his delivery, which now proves　　　　　　　　1575
Abortive as the first-born bloom of spring
Nipped with the lagging rear of winter's frost.
Yet ere I give the reins to grief, say first,
How died he? death to life is crown or shame.
All by him fell thou sayest, by whom fell he,　　　　　1580
What glorious hand gave Samson his death's wound?
　Mess. Unwounded of his enemies he fell.
　Man. Wearied with slaughter then or how? explain.
　Mess. By his own hands.
　Man.　　　　　　　　　Self-violence?　What cause
Brought him so soon at variance with himself　　　　　1585
Among his foes?
　Mess.　　　　Inevitable cause
At once both to destroy and be destroyed;
The edifice where all were met to see him
Upon their heads and on his own he pulled.
　Man. O lastly over-strong against thyself!　　　　1590
A dreadful way thou tookest to thy revenge.
More than enough we know; but while things yet
Are in confusion, give us if thou canst,
Eye-witness of what first or last was done,
Relation more particular and distinct.　　　　　　　1595
　Mess. Occasions drew me early to this city,
And as the gates I entered with sunrise,
The morning trumpets festival proclaimed
Through each high street: little I had dispatched
When all abroad was rumored that this day　　　　　1600
Samson should be brought forth to show the people
Proof of his mighty strength in feats and games;
I sorrowed at his captive state, but minded
Not to be absent at that spectacle.
The building was a spacious theater　　　　　　　　1605
Half round on two main pillars vaulted high,
With seats where all the lords and each degree
Of sort, might sit in order to behold,
The other side was open, where the throng
On banks and scaffolds under sky might stand;　　　1610
I among these aloof obscurely stood
The feast and noon grew high, and sacrifice
Had filled their hearts with mirth, high cheer, and wine,
When to their sports they turned.　Immediately
Was Samson as a public servant brought,　　　　　1615
In their state livery clad; before him pipes
And timbrels, on each side went armed guards,
Both horse and foot before him and behind

Archers, and slingers, cataphracts and spears.
At sight of him the people with a shout   1620
Rifted the air clamoring their god with praise,
Who had made their dreadful enemy their thrall.
He patient but undaunted where they led him,
Came to the place, and what was set before him
Which without help of eye, might be assayed,   1625
To heave, pull, draw, or break, he still performed
All with incredible, stupendous force,
None daring to appear antagonist.
At length for intermission sake they led him
Between the pillars; he his guide requested   1630
(For so from such as nearer stood we heard)
As overtired to let him lean a while
With both his arms on those two massy pillars
That to the arched roof gave main support.
He unsuspicious led him; which when Samson   1635
Felt in his arms, with head a while inclined,
And eyes fast fixed he stood, as one who prayed,
Or some great matter in his mind revolved.
At last with head erect thus cried aloud,
'Hitherto, lords, what your commands imposed   1640
I have performed, as reason was, obeying,
Not without wonder or delight beheld.
Now of my own accord such other trial
I mean to show you of my strength, yet greater;
As with amaze shall strike all who behold.'   1645
Thus uttered, straining all his nerves he bowed,
As with the force of winds and waters pent,
When mountains tremble, those two massy pillars
With horrible convulsion to and fro,
He tugged, he shook, till down they came and drew   1650
The whole roof after them, with burst of thunder
Upon the heads of all who sat beneath,
Lords, ladies, captains, counselors, or priests,
Their choice nobility and flower, not only
Of this but each Philistian city round   1655
Met from all parts to solemnize this feast.
Samson with these immixed, inevitably
Pulled down the same destruction on himself;
The vulgar only scaped who stood without.
    Chor. O dearly bought revenge, yet glorious!   1660
Living or dying thou hast fulfilled
The work for which thou wast foretold
To Israel, and now liest victorious
Among thy slain self-killed
Not willingly, but tangled in the fold,   1665
Of dire necessity, whose law in death conjoined
Thee with thy slaughtered foes in number more
Than all thy life had slain before.

1619. **cataphracts:** cavalry with both men and horses armored.

Semichor. While their hearts were jocund and sublime,
Drunk with idolatry, drunk with wine.
And fat regorged of bulls and goats, 1670
Chanting their idol, and preferring
Before our living dread who dwells
In Silo his bright sanctuary:
Among them he a spirit of frenzy sent,
Who hurt their minds, 1675
And urged them on with mad desire
To call in haste for their destroyer;
They only set on sport and play
Unwittingly importuned
Their own destruction to come speedy upon them. 1680
So fond are mortal men
Fallen into wrath divine,
As their own ruin on themselves to invite,
Insensate left, or to sense reprobate,
And with blindness internal struck. 1685
Semichor. But he though blind of sight,
Despised and thought extinguished quite,
With inward eyes illuminated
His fiery virtue roused
From under ashes into sudden flame, 1690
And as an evening dragon came,
Assailant on the perched roosts,
And nests in order ranged
Of tame villatic fowl; but as an eagle
His cloudless thunder bolted on their heads. 1695
So virtue given for lost,
Depressed, and overthrown, as seemed,
Like that self-begotten bird
In the Arabian woods embossed,
That no second knows nor third, 1700
And lay erewhile a holocaust,
From out her ashy womb now teemed,
Revives, reflourishes, then vigorous most
When most unactive deemed,
And though her body die, her fame survives, 1705
A secular bird ages of lives.
Man. Come, come, no time for lamentation now,
Nor much more cause, Samson hath quit himself
Like Samson, and heroicly hath finished 1710
A life heroic, on his enemies
Fully revenged, hath left them years of mourning,
And lamentation to the sons of Caphtor
Through all Philistian bounds. To Israel
Honor hath left, and freedom, let but them 1715

1695. **villatic fowl**: barnyard fowl.   1699–1700. The phoenix bird.
1700. **embossed**: Phillips: 'imbossed. To imboss a deer is to chase her into the thickets.' From the Italian *imboscare*, 'to take cover or shelter in a wood, as a deer does.'
1713. **sons of Caphtor**: the Philistines.

Find courage to lay hold on this occasion,
To himself and father's house eternal fame;
And which is best and happiest yet, all this
With God not parted from him, as was feared,
But favoring and assisting to the end.   1720
Nothing is here for tears, nothing to wail
Or knock the breast, no weakness, no contempt,
Dispraise, or blame, nothing but well and fair,
And what may quiet us in a death so noble.
Let us go find the body where it lies   1725
Soaked in his enemies' blood, and from the stream
With lavers pure and cleansing herbs wash off
The clotted gore.   I with what speed the while
(Gaza is not in plight to say us nay)
Will send for all my kindred, all my friends   1730
To fetch him hence and solemnly attend
With silent obsequy and funeral train
Home to his father's house: there will I build him
A monument, and plant it round with shade
Of laurel ever green, and branching palm,   1735
With all his trophies hung, and acts enrolled
In copious legend, or sweet lyric song.
Thither shall all the valiant youth resort,
And from his memory inflame their breasts
To matchless valor, and adventures high: 1740
The virgins also shall on feastful days
Visit his tomb with flowers, only bewailing
His lot unfortunate in nuptial choice,
From whence captivity and loss of eyes.
  Chor. All is best, though we oft doubt,   1745
What the unsearchable dispose
Of highest wisdom brings about,
And ever best found in the close.
Oft he seems to hide his face,
But unexpectedly returns   1750
And to his faithful champion hath in place
Bore witness gloriously; whence Gaza mourns
And all that band them to resist
His uncontrollable intent,
His servants he with new acquist   1755
Of true experience from this great event
With peace and consolation hath dismissed,
And calm of mind all passion spent.

THE END

Italian, Latin, and Greek Poems
and Translations

The Italian Sonnets
1630?

IN THE 1645 *Poems*, Milton included five sonnets and a canzone in Italian, printing them again in 1673. The reader is referred to the general introduction to the sonnets (pages 121–24) for an account of the place of these poems among Milton's sonnets and in his poetic development. These Italian poems have been translated several times, notably by Cowper, Strutt, Langthorne, Masson, Pattison, Moody, Smart, and in the Columbia Milton. The translation used here is that by Moody, with a few revisions which take into account the discoveries of Smart. Moody intended to furnish a line-for-line rendering, in an irregular meter, without rhyme.

REFERENCE

Smart, J. S., *The Sonnets of Milton.*

II

(1630?)

This sonnet was first printed in the 1645 *Poems*, and reprinted in 1673. With the other Italian sonnets, it is part of the record of Milton's first love, and from these Italian poems, much can be learned of the person addressed in them. The opening lines of this poem state that the bright name of the lady addressed honors the vale of Reno, and the 'nobil varco' or 'famous ford.' The district in which these places are located is one of the regions into which Italy was divided by Augustus, and is called Emilia, from the Via Emilia. Milton mentions this great highway in *Paradise Regained* IV:69. Martial mentioned the region frequently by the name Emilia, and Leandro Alberti described it at length. The 'nobil varco' or 'famous ford' is, of course, the most famous ford in the world, the one where Julius Caesar crossed the Rubicon. The vale of the Reno is northwest of the

Rubicon, but both are in the same general region; indeed, in his *Geographicum* (1627), Ferrari speaks of the Rubicon as 'fluvius Aemiliae.'

The 'hidden name' of the person addressed, especially the beloved lady, was a favorite device of the Italians. Gandolfo Porrino, for instance, in one poem discloses the name of his lady as being Lucia without, however, coming closer to the name than addressing her as the light ('luce') which beneficently showers its blessing on the earth, on mankind, and also shows the path to heaven. The name of Milton's lady lay concealed for centuries; and its presence was first suspected by J. S. Smart, whose *Sonnets of Milton* appeared in 1921.[1]

Donna leggiadra il cui bel nome honora		Lady gay and gracious, whose fair name honors
L'herbosa val di Reno, e il nobil varco,		The grassy vale of Reno, and the famous ford,
Bene è colui d'ogni valore scarco		Surely that man is empty of all worth
Qual tuo spirto gentil non innamora,		Whom thy gentle spirit doth not enamor,
Che dolcemente mostra si di fuora	5	Thy spirit, that sweetly manifests itself,
De sui atti soavi giamai parco,		Never niggard of delightful actions,
E i don', che son d'amor saette ed arco.		Nor of those gifts, Love's arrows and his bow,
La onde l'alta tua virtu s'infiora.		Wherewith thy virtue high enflowers itself.
Quando tu vaga parli, o lieta canti		When thou speakest in thy beauty, or singest in thy joy,
Che mover possa duro alpestre legno,	10	Sounds that might move the firm trees from the mountains,
Guardi ciascun a gli occhi, ed a gli orecchi		Let whoso finds himself unworthy of thy service
L'entrata, chi di te si truova indegno;		Guard well the gateway of his sight and hearing;
Gratia sola di su gli vaglia, inanti		Grace from above avail him
Che'l disio amoroso al cuor s'invecchi.		Ere amorous desire lodge in his heart.

III

(1630?)

This sonnet was printed in the 1645 *Poems* and again in 1673. It is perhaps the freshest and most original of the Italian sonnets. It is a love poem in which Milton compares his cultivation of his love in a strange tongue, Italian, to the youthful shepherdess tending a beautiful but alien plant far from its native soil.

Qual in colle aspro, al imbrunir di sera		As on a rough hillside, at dusk of evening,
L'avezza giovinetta pastorella		A little shepherd girl, as she is wont,
Va bagnando l'herbetta strana e bella		Goes watering some fair flower that moves her wonder,
Che mal si spande a disusata spera		A stranger in that clime, ill flourishing
Fuor di sua natia alma primavera,	5	Far from the comfort of its native springtime,
Cosi amor meco insu la lingua snella		Even so doth Love upon my eager tongue
Desta il fior novo di strania favella,		Rear the new flower of a foreign speech,
Mentre io di te, vezzosamente altera,		While I of thee, haughty and gracious one,

[1] See pp. 137-44.

Canto, dal mio buon popol non inteso

   E'l bel Tamigi cangio col bell Arno.   10

   Amor lo volse, ed io a l'altrui peso

Seppi ch'amor cosa mai volse indarno.

   Deh! foss'il mio cuor lento e'l duro seno

   A chi pianta dal ciel si buon terreno.

Sing, of my own good folk not compre-
hended,
And change fair Thames for the fair Arno.
Love willed it, and at others' cost
I learned that Love wills nought in vain.
Ah, that my slow heart and rude breast might
  be
As kind a soil to Him who plants from
  Heaven.

Canzone

(1630?)

This poem was printed in the 1645 *Poems* and again in 1673. The name indicated, in Italian, the words of a song unaccompanied by any instrument, just as 'sonnetto' meant a song to be accompanied by a stringed instrument. The form never was used much in England, unlike the sonnet form; but its structure and form suggested much of the metrical basis of Spenser's *Epithalamion* and *Prothalamion*, and of *Lycidas*. This *Canzone* is perhaps the best of Milton's poems in Italian. Camerini, an Italian critic, describes it as most beautiful, if not entirely without faults, 'vaghissima, se non al tutto irreprensibile.' This statement was quoted with approval by Carducci, who further stated that some of Milton's lines would not seem out of place in Dante or Petrarch, although the sonnets, not this *Canzone*, are frequently hard and labored, and unidiomatic.

Ridonsi donne e giovani amorosi
M'accostandosi attorno, e 'perche scrivi,
Perche tu scrivi in lingua ignota e strana
Verseggiando d'amor, e come t'osi?
Dinne, se la tua speme sia mai vana,   5
E de pensieri lo miglior t'arrivi;'
Cosi mi van burlando, 'altri rivi
Altri lidi t'aspettan, & altre onde
Nelle cui verdi sponde
Spuntati ad hor, ad hor a la tua chioma   10
L'immortal guiderdon d'eterne frondi
Perche alle spalle tue soverchia soma?'
  Canzon dirotti, e tu per me rispondi
'Dice mia donna, e'l suo dir e il mio cuore,
"Questa e lingua di cui si vanta amore."'   15

The ladies and young lovers laugh at me,
Standing in circle round me, and 'Why write,
Why write thus in a language strange, un-
known,
Versifying of love? How dost thou dare it?
Speak, as thou wilt have thy hope not vain,
And of thy thoughts the best betide thee.'
So they go mocking at me: 'Other rivers,
Other shores await thee, other waters,
On whose green banks
Now, even now, grows for thy hair
The immortal guerdon of unfading fronds.
Why on thy shoulders the superfluous load?'
  Canzone, I will tell thee, and do thou make
answer:
'My Lady saith, and her speech is my heart,
"This is Love's language, of which Love is
boastful."'

IV

(1630?)

This poem was printed in the 1645 *Poems* and again in 1673. Addressed to Diodati, the friend of his youth, this poem is most interesting to the student of Milton as in it he wishes to retract the opinion once expressed to the same person that the maidens of England, with golden hair and rosy cheeks, are the most beautiful. In *Elegy I* he merely praises them, but no one of them individually moves him. But in this Italian sonnet, he confesses that Love has now caught his heart in his meshes, not with tresses of gold and rosy cheeks, but with a dark, alien, Italian beauty.

Diodati, e te'l diro con maraviglia,
  Quel ritroso io ch'amor spreggiar solea
  E de suoi lacci spesso mi ridea
  Gia caddi, ov'huom dabben talhor s'impiglia.
Ne treccie d'oro, ne guancia vermiglia   5
  M'abbaglian si, ma sotto nova idea
  Pellegrina bellezza che'l cuor bea,
  Portamenti alti honesti, e nelle ciglia
Quel sereno fulgor d'amabil nero,
  Parole adorne di lingua piu d'una,   10
  E'l cantar che di mezzo l'hemispero
Traviar ben puo la faticosa luna,
  E degli occhi suoi auventa si gran fuoco
  Che l'incerar gli orecchi mi fia poco.

Diodati (I tell it thee with wonder)
That stubborn I, who did disparage love,
And often mocked his wiles, have fallen already
Where worthiest men sometimes ensnare themselves.
Nor golden tresses nor a rosy cheek
Undo me thus, but under novel guise
A type of foreign beauty steeps my heart,
A high and modest port, and in the eyebrows
The quiet splendor of a lovely darkness,
Rich words, and more than from a single language,
And song that from her middle hemisphere
Might draw the moon o'ertoiled;
And from her eyes proceeds so strong a fire,
To stop my ears with wax would help me little.

V

(1630?)

This poem was printed in the 1645 *Poems* and again in 1673. Addressed to 'his lady' in conventional fashion, this is said to be the poorest of the Italian sonnets, and, as Smart says of it, 'one of the few pieces by Milton which we might wish he had condemned to disappear after they had remained unpublished for the Horatian term.' The only defense that can be offered for the poem is its conventionality.

Per certo i bei vostr'occhi, donna mia
  Esser non puo che non sian lo mio sole
  Si mi percuoton forte, come ei suole
  Per l'arene di Libia chi s'invia,

In truth, your beauteous eyes, my Lady,
Cannot be other than my sun;
So sore they smite me, as he smiteth
The traveler in the sands of Libia;

V:2. **sian**: printed 'fian' in 1673.

Mentre un caldo vapor (ne senti pria) 5
 Da quel lato si spinge ove mi duole,
 Che forse amanti nelle lor parole
 Chiaman sospir; io non so che si sia:
Parte rinchiusa, e turbida si cela
 Scosso mi il petto, e poi n'uscendo poco 10
 Quivi d'attorno o s'agghiaccia, o s'ingiela;
Ma quanto a gli occhi giunge a trovar loco
 Tutte le notti a me suol far piovose
 Finche mia alba rivien colma di rose.

From that side where I feel my pain, out-
    gushes
A burning vapor, never felt before,
Which mayhap lovers in their language
Call sighs; for me, I know not what it be.
A part within lurks pent and turbid,
Shaking my breast; a part forth-issuing
Congeals and freezes in the air about;
But whatso findeth passage to my eyes
Is wont to darken all my nights with rain,
Till thou return, my day-spring crowned
    with roses.

VI

(1630?)

This poem was printed in the 1645 *Poems* and again in 1673. Above every other poem Milton ever wrote in other languages than English, this sonnet should have been written in English, not so much for what it would have contributed to English poetry as for what it would have contributed to succeeding generations' understanding of the poet. Instead, therefore, of it being the most quoted set of verses about Milton's youthful nature and ambitions, it is virtually neglected by all students of him, and is literally unknown to most of his readers. Compare with *Elegy VII*.

Giovane piano, e semplicetto amante
 Poi che fuggir me stesso in dubbio sono,
 Madonna a voi del mio cuor l'humil dono
 Faro divoto; io certo a prove tante
L'hebbi fedele, intrepido, costante, 5
 Di pensieri leggiadro, accorto, e buono;
 Quando rugge il gran mondo, e scocca il
    tuono,
 S'arma di se, e d'intero diamante,
Tanto cel forse, e d'invidia sicuro,
 Di timori, e speranze al popol use 10
 Quanto d'ingegno, e d'alto valor vago,
E di cetra sonora, e delle muse:
 Sol troverete in tal parte men duro
 Ove amor mise l'insanabil ago.

A young, and meek, and simple lover,
Perplexed how I shall flee from my own self,
Lady, the humble offering of my heart
To you I dedicate: be sure, in many trials
I found it faithful, constant, valorous,
Gracious of thought, discreet, and good.
When the great sky roars, or bursts the
    thunder,
With itself it arms itself, with entire ada-
    mant,
As heedless of all violence or spite,
Of vulgar hopes and fears,
As 'tis in love with noble gifts and worth,
With the sonorous lyre, and with the Muses.
In one sole part thou'lt find it not so strong,
Where Love set his incurable sting.

V:10. Smart (*Sonnets of Milton*, p. 154) says the first clause is 'almost certainly a printer's error for *sotto il mio petto.*'
VI:8. e: lacking in 1673 edition, but present in 1645.

The Latin Poems

MILTON printed his Latin poems in two parts. He called the first part, containing seven elegies, *Elegiarum Liber*, or Book of Elegies; and the second part, containing ten pieces in various non-elegiac meters and eleven epigrams, *Sylvarum Liber*, or Book of Sylvae. The elegy has come to mean in English almost entirely a sad song or poem lamenting a death or other unfortunate event or circumstance. But it meant something other than this to Milton. He means by it both a poem expressing a tender or gentle passion or emotion, such as grief or love, and a poem in a definite meter made up of a hexameter line (six feet) followed by a pentameter (five feet). Thus, Milton means by the elegy that form of verse written in alternate hexameters and pentameters that is not heroic, iambic, or lyric in the classical sense. It may express any tender, plaintive, or even melancholic emotion. He says of it:

> For light elegy is the care of many gods, and calls to its numbers whom it will; Bacchus [god of wine and revelry] comes, and Erato [the muse of amatory verse], Ceres [the earth goddess of growing things, hence of fertility], and Venus [the goddess of love], and tender stripling Amor [Cupid, the god of love] with his rosy mother [Venus]. Such poets [as the elegiac] therefore, have a right to generous feasts and to stew full often in old wine.[1]

The elegy may be mournful, but it need not be.[2] His conception of the elegy was derived partly from the ancient classics, particularly the Greek of Mimnermus through later writers and the Romans, especially Ovid, and partly from the current use of the elegy in the Renaissance. Milton wrote elegies that were metrical epistles, such as *I*, *IV*, and *VI*; laments or epitaphs, such as *II* and *III*; and one on the coming of spring and another on a passing love affair.

The other type of Latin poetry which he called the 'sylva' was, according to Littleton's *Latin Dictionary* (1693),[3] 'a work or writing made or ruffled up in haste.' That is, the *Sylvarum Liber* is a book of Latin miscellanies. It contains poems in various meters, other than the elegiac, and on various subjects.

In writing Latin verse, Milton was only following the regular practice of all educated men of his time. Throughout the western world, all boys who attended grammar school and all young men who attended college had to do exercises in Latin verse and prose in imitation and paraphrase of classical models, just as earlier, students in all Europe had

---

[1] *Elegy VI*, 49–54.

[2] See *Apology, Col.* III:1:341:24.

[3] This was the dictionary that made use of Milton's manuscript thesaurus or lexicon, mentioned by Phillips. The editors of this dictionary acknowledge on the title page of the 1693 and subsequent editions that they have made use of a 'large manuscript in three volumes of Mr. John Milton.' No other vestige of Milton's Latin thesaurus remains so far as is known.

used theological models for Latin exercises. The tradition that the educated man wrote Latin verse was well established long before Milton's day.

His Latin poetry is essentially the poetry of his youth. It is much more illuminating than the early English verse in studying his youthful interests and development, his early friendships, and most intimate thoughts and aspirations. Most of the Latin poems were written within a period of fifteen years, and almost all of them within twenty years, or between 1626 and 1646. Milton probably began writing poems in Latin almost as early as in English, perhaps even before he wrote any in English, although none survives from any time before 1626. An unusual fact about the Latin poetry is that no manuscript copy of any of it, except the *Ode to John Rouse*, has survived. Milton either kept no manuscript copies of his Latin poetry as he did of his English verse, or else every manuscript copy he kept has been lost or destroyed. The *Ode* was sent to John Rouse and preserved by him, not by Milton. There is no Latin verse in the *Trinity College Manuscript*. Most of the Latin poems, having been written by 1645, were printed in the volume of *Poems* Milton published in that year. Every Latin poem he ever wrote, except the two Salmasius pieces, more lampoons than poetry, was included in the 1673 volume, and no other Latin poems have been surely identified as Milton's since his lifetime, although from time to time various Latin poems have been attributed to him. But there is no proof that any Latin poem Milton himself failed to print actually was written by him.

The Latin poems were principally written during two different times or periods. Most of them were written within three years, 1626–29, while he was at Cambridge. Then for some years Milton apparently wrote no Latin poetry whatever. The Italian journey, however, gave rise, directly or indirectly, to the two longest poems he ever wrote in Latin, *Mansus* and the *Epitaphium Damonis*, probably both written in 1639 and 1640; to the three short poems addressed to Leonora, whom he heard sing in Rome; and to the *Scazontes* addressed to Salsillo of Rome. After these, he wrote Latin poetry sparingly, seeing fit to publish only two more with his other poems, *Ad Patrem*, and the *Ode to John Rouse*. The epigrammatic pieces in one or two of his Latin prose works finished his efforts in Latin verse.

Milton was chiefly influenced in his Latin poems by the lighter poems of Ovid, Virgil, and Horace, which were his chief delight as a young man, and important to him in the order named. He was long under the spell of Ovid, whose *Amores* he imitated and adapted in his own elegiac verse. Of the Greeks, his favorites were Homer and Euripides; but he read many others, as his own copy of Pindar, which survives, testifies. A thorough and exhaustive study of his early reading and literary interests as expressed in his Latin poems has yet to be made. Professor Hanford has surpassed Masson in his account of Milton's youth;[1] but a close, detailed study of the Latin poems and the readings from which they grew is still lacking.[2]

Not many readers today can judge Milton's Latin poetry as such, but must read it only in translation. It is, therefore, of greater value to most readers today for the autobiographical content and its contribution to the understanding of his development as a poet than for its own sake. Those few students who can read it as Latin or neo-Latin poetry

---

[1] J. H. Hanford, 'The Youth of Milton,' *University of Michigan Publications in Language and Literature*, vol. I (1925), pp. 89–163.

[2] But see Walter MacKellar, *The Latin Poems of John Milton*. This is a most useful work that is, however, principally concerned with an account of the poems themselves, with translation and notes. Also E. K. Rand, 'Milton in Rustication,' *Studies in Philology*, vol. XIX (1922), pp. 109–35.

will find, as a number of competent critics have pointed out, that it ranks with the best neo-Latin verse ever written.

Milton's own attitude towards it is reflected in the statement on the title pages of both 1645 and 1673 editions: 'Poemata.   Quorum pleraque intra annum aetatis vigesimum con- scripsit.'   This may be translated: 'Poems, most of which were written before the twen- tieth year of his age.'   That is, he judged all his Latin poems as the poems of his youth. The statement he appended to *Elegy VII* is equally clear in saying that these Latin poems were the poems of his youth, now well behind him.   Both of these statements are contained in the 1645 edition.   The 1673 edition repeats them and adds the more explicit statement of the youthfulness of the poems in the first stanza of the *Ode to John Rouse*.

Milton's Latin poems are presented here in the same order and general arrangement in which he printed them.   The text is that of the edition of 1673, except for the two pieces connected with Salmasius which are not found in that edition, and for which the text in the two prose pieces of 1658 and 1654 respectively have been used.   Moody's transla- tion as revised in 1924 by Professor Rand is retained with a few necessary modifications, and the few poems which he failed to translate are translated.   The encomiums and com- mendatory verses addressed to Milton are omitted.

REFERENCES

Hanford, J. H., *Handbook* (third edition, 1939), pp. 133–38.
MacKellar, Walter, *The Latin Poems of John Milton*.   New Haven: Yale University Press, 1930.
Masson, David, *Poetical Works of John Milton*.
Todd, H. J., *Poetical Works*.
Warton, Thomas, *Poems . . . by John Milton*, pp. 409–574.

Elegiarum Liber Primus — First Book of Elegies

<table>
<tr><td>

Elegia Prima

AD CAROLUM DIODATUM

(*1626*)

</td><td>

Elegy I

TO CHARLES DICDATI

(*1626*)

</td></tr>
</table>

This verse-letter marks the occasion of Milton's rustication from college during his second academic year, 1625–26, owing to a dispute with his tutor, William Chappell (see introductory biography).   It is addressed to his bosom friend Charles Diodati, to whom also the sixth Latin *Elegy* and the Italian *Sonnet IV* are addressed, and in whose memory the *Epitaphium Damonis* was written.   Diodati was the son of an Italian father, a physician settled in London, and an English mother.   Milton's acquaintance with him, begun at Saint Paul's School, continued after Diodati went up to Oxford, two years before Milton went to Cambridge.   When the present epistle was written, Diodati had taken his first degree, and was visiting in the neighborhood of Chester.

The chief interest of the elegy, besides the light it throws on the incident of Milton's rustication and his feeling toward his college, lies in the account which he gives of his pastimes during this period of enforced vacation.   The enthusiastic account of his theater-going is especially noteworthy, though ambiguity exists throughout the passage as to whether actual stage representations or merely the reading of drama is meant, an ambiguity which is increased by the fact that the illustrations seem drawn equally from Roman comedy and Greek tragedy, and from the contemporary drama of England.   He also recounts his walks in the streets and parks of London, with a youthful zest and freshness doubly delightful in a character like his.   His praise of the girls whom he encounters, though couched in the conventional language of pseudo-classic poetry, is thoroughly youthful and gay; even here, however, there is a touch of strenuousness at the end, nonetheless earnest for being half-playfully uttered.

Tandem, chare, tuae mihi pervenere tabellae,
   Pertulit et voces nuncia charta tuas,
Pertulit occiduâ Devae Cestrensis ab orâ
   Vergivium prono quà petit amne salum.
Multùm crede juvat terras aluisse remotas 5
   Pectus amans nostri, tamque fidele caput,
Quòdque mihi lepidum tellus longinqua sodalem
   Debet, at unde brevi reddere jussa velit.
Me tenet urbs refluâ quam Thamesis alluit undâ,
   Meque nec invitum patria dulcis habet. 10
Jam nec arundiferum mihi cura revisere Camum,
   Nec dudum vetiti me laris angit amor.
Nuda nec arva placent, umbrasque negantia molles,
   Quàm male Phoebicolis convenit ille locus!
Nec duri libet usque minas perferre magistri
   Caeteraque ingenio non subeunda meo. 16
Si sit hoc exilium patrios adiisse penates,
   Et vacuum curis otia grata sequi,
Non ego vel profugi nomen, sortemve recuso,
   Laetus et exilii conditione fruor. 20
O utinam vates nunquam graviora tulisset
   Ille Tomitano flebilis exul agro;
Non tunc Jonio quicquam cessisset Homero
   Neve foret victo laus tibi prima Maro.
Tempora nam licet hîc placidis dare libera Musis, 25
   Et totum rapiunt me mea vita libri.
Excipit hinc fessum sinuosi pompa theatri,
   Et vocat ad plausus garrula scena suos.
Seu catus auditur senior, seu prodigus haeres,

At last, dear friend, your letter has reached me; the missive paper bears me your words from the western shore of the Dee, by Chester, where that river goes down swiftly to the Irish Sea.   Much joy it gives me to think that a far-off country keeps well for me so dear a head as yours, and a heart that loves me; and that this distant region owes me my merry mate, aye, and will soon repay him at my prayers.   That city which Thames washes with her tidal wave keeps me fast, nor does my pleasant birthplace detain me against my will.   I have no wish to go back to reedy Cam; I feel no homesickness for that forbidden college room of mine.   The bare fields there, niggard of pleasant shade, do not please me.   How ill does that place suit with poets!   I have no fancy to endure forever my stern master's threats or those other actions at which my nature rebelled.   If this is 'exile,' to live under my fathers' roof and be free to use my leisure pleasantly, I will not repudiate either the name of outcast or his lot, but will in all happiness enjoy this state of exile.   Oh would that Ovid, sad exile in the fields of Thrace, had never suffered a worse lot!   Then he would have yielded not a whit even to Ionian Homer, nor would the first praise be thine, Virgil, for he would have vanquished thee.

I have time free now to give to the tranquil Muses.   My books, my very life, claim me wholly.   When I am weary, the pomp of the theater with its sweeping pall awaits me, and the garrulous stage invites me to its own applause.   Sometimes the cautious old man holds the scene, or the prodigal heir, or the

Seu procus, aut positâ casside miles adest,
Sive decennali foecundus lite patronus   31
    Detonat inculto barbara verba foro,
Saepe vafer gnato succurrit servus amanti,
    Et nasum rigidi fallit ubique patris;
Saepe novos illic virgo mirata calores   35
    Quid sit amor nescit, dum quoque nescit,
        amat.
Sive cruentatum furiosa Tragoedia sceptrum
    Quassat, et effusis crinibus ora rotat,
Et dolet, et specto, juvat et spectasse do-
        lendo,
    Interdum et lacrymis dulcis amaror inest:
Seu puer infelix indelibata reliquit   41
    Gaudia, et abrupto flendus amore cadit,
Seu ferus è tenebris iterat Styga criminis
        ultor
    Conscia funereo pectora torre movens,
Seu maeret Pelopeia domus, seu nobilis Ili,   45
    Aut luit incestos aula Creontis avos.
Sed neque sub tecto semper nec in urbe late-
        mus,
    Irrita nec nobis tempora veris eunt.
Nos quoque lucus habet vicinâ consitus
        ulmo
    Atque suburbani nobilis umbra loci.   50
Saepius hic blandas spirantia sidera flam-
        mas
    Virgineos videas praeteriisse choros.
Ah quoties dignae stupui miracula formae
    Quae possit senium vel reparare Jovis;   54
Ah quoties vidi superantia lumina gemmas,
    Atque faces quotquot volvit uterque polus;
Collaque bis vivi Pelopis quae brachia vin-
        cant,
    Quaeque fluit puro nectare tincta via,
Et decus eximium frontis, tremulosque capil-
        los,
    Aurea quae fallax retia tendit Amor.   60
Pellacesque genas, ad quas hyacinthina sordet
    Purpura, et ipse tui floris, Adoni, rubor.
Cedite laudatae toties Heroides olim,
    Et quaecunque vagum cepit amica Jovem.
Cedite Achaemeniae turritâ fronte puellae,   65
    Et quot Susa colunt, Memnoniamque
        Ninon.
Vos etiam Danaae fasces submittite nymphae,
    Et vos Iliacae, Romuleaeque nurus.
Nec Pompeianas Tarpëia Musa columnas
    Jactet, et Ausoniis plena theatra stolis.   70
Gloria virginibus debetur prima Britannis,

wooer, or the soldier with his helmet laid aside; or the lawyer, pregnant with a ten-years' suit, thunders barbarous words before an ignorant court. The wily servant helps his young master in his love-scrapes, and tricks the stern father under his very nose; and the girl, wondering at the new ardors that fill her, knows not what love is, and while she knows not, loves. Then frenzied Tragedy shakes her bloody scepter, and rolls her eyes under her disheveled hair. I suffer and yet I gaze, and find it good to suffer and gaze. A sweet bitterness now and then mingles with my tears as I see some hapless boy leave all his joys untasted and fall lamentable for the rending of his love; or when the fierce avenger of crime recrosses Styx out of the shades, and terrifies conscious breasts with baleful torch; or when the house of Pelops mourns, or mourns the noble house of Ilus; or when the hall of Creon atones for the incest of its ancestors.

But I do not stay indoors always, nor even in town; I do not let the spring slip by unused. I visit the neighboring park, thickset with elms or the noble shade of some suburban place. There often one may see the virgin bands go past, stars that breathe alluring flames. Ah, how many times have I stood stupefied before the miracle of some gracious form, such as might give old Jove his youth again! Ah, how many times have I seen eyes brighter than gems, brighter than all the fires that roll about either pole, necks whiter than the arms of Pelops, twice called to life, or the Milky Way that flows with pure nectar! And exquisite grace of brow, and floating locks, golden nets which Love casts deceivingly, inviting cheeks, to which the purple of the hyacinth, yea, even the blush of thy flower, Adonis, is dull! Yield, ye Heröides so praised of yore, and all ye loves that snared gadding Jove! Yield, ye Persian damsels with your turreted brows; and all ye who dwell in Susa, in Memnonian Nineveh! Even ye, maidens of Danaüs, lower the fasces; and ye Trojan brides, and ye of the race of Romulus! Let not the poet who lived by the Tarpeian rock [Ovid] boast the dames of Pompey's porch, nor the theater full of Roman stoles. To the virgins of Britain first

Extera sat tibi sit foemina posse sequi.
Tuque urbs Dardaniis Londinum structa
    colonis
Turrigerum latè conspicienda caput,
Tu nimium felix intra tua moenia claudis 75
    Quicquid formosi pendulus orbis habet.
Non tibi tot caelo scintillant astra sereno
    Endymioneae turba ministra deae,
Quot tibi conspicuae formáque auróque
    puellae
Per medias radiant turba videnda vias,   80
Creditur huc geminis venisse invecta colum-
    bis
    Alma pharetrigero milite cincta Venus,
Huic Cnidon, et riguas Simoentis flumine
    valles,
    Huic Paphon, et roseam posthabitura
    Cypron.
Ast ego, dum pueri sinit indulgentia caeci, 85
    Moenia quàm subitò linquere fausta paro;
Et vitare procul malefidae infamia Circes
    Atria, divini Molyos usus ope.
Stat quoque juncosas Cami remeare paludes,
    Atque iterum raucae murmur adire Scholae.
Interea fidi parvum cape munus amici,   91
    Paucaque in alternos verba coacta modos.

glory is due; suffice it, foreign woman, that thou canst follow them! And thou city of London, built by Dardanian colonists, thy towered head conspicuous far and wide, thou, too happy, enclosest with thy walls whatever beauty the pendulous Earth owns. Not so many stars twinkle over thee in the clear night sky, ministrant troops of Endymion's goddess, as through thy highways throng troops of girls, bright with beauty and with gold, drawing all eyes with their radiance. Men say that hither blessed Venus came, escorted by her quivered soldier-boy, drawn by twin doves, willing to love London more than Cnidos, or the vales watered by the stream of Simöis, or Paphos, or rosy Cyprus.

But for my part, while the blind boy grants me immunity, I make ready to leave these fortunate walls as quickly as I may; and avoid far off the evil halls of Circe the deceiver, using the help of moly, that heavenly plant. It has been arranged for me to go back to the bulrush swamps of Cam, and to the raucous murmur of the school. Meanwhile take this poor gift of a faithful friend, these few words constrained into the measure of elegy.

Elegia Secunda

Anno aetatis 17

IN OBITUM PRAECONIS
ACADEMICI CANTABRIGIENSIS

(*1626*)

Elegy II

In his 17th year

ON THE DEATH OF THE
UNIVERSITY BEADLE

(*1626*)

The person to whose memory this elegy is addressed, Richard Ridding, M.A., of Saint John's College, Cambridge, died in the autumn of 1626, near the beginning of Milton's third year at the University. Three persons at Cambridge bear the title of Esquire Bedel (Latin *praeco*, herald or crier). Their duties are, to bear the mace before the Chancellor on solemn occasions, and to give summons. The office is one of considerable dignity, and has a life tenure. The opening lines of the elegy have a suspicion of humor in them, but it is safe to say that Milton's tribute was meant in all seriousness. At any rate, the passing away of a picturesque figure from the University life gave the young Latinist too good an opportunity for versifying to be neglected. The date heading, *anno aetatis 17*, is here and elsewhere misleading; Milton was, in the autumn of 1626, near the end of his eighteenth year.

Te, qui conspicuus baculo fulgente solebas
　Palladium toties ore ciere gregem,
Ultima praeconum praeconem te quoque saeva
　Mors rapit, officio nec favet ipsa suo.
Candidiora licet fuerint tibi tempora plumis
　Sub quibus accipimus delituisse Jovem,　6
O dignus tamen Haemonio juvenescere succo,
　Dignus in Aesonios vivere posse dies,
Dignus quem Stygiis medicâ revocaret ab undis
　Arte Coronides, saepe rogante deâ.　10
Tu si jussus eras acies accire togatas,
　Et celer à Phoebo nuntius ire tuo,
Talis in Iliacâ stabat Cyllenius aulâ
　Alipes, aethereâ missus ab arce Patris.
Talis et Eurybates ante ora furentis Achillei
　Rettulit Atridae jussa severa ducis.　16
Magna sepulchrorum regina, satelles Averni
　Saeva nimis Musis, Palladi saeva nimis,
Quin illos rapias qui pondus inutile terrae,
　Turba quidem est telis ista petenda tuis.　20
Vestibus hunc igitur pullis Academia luge,
　Et madeant lacrymis nigra feretra tuis.
Fundat et ipsa modos querebunda Elegéia tristes,
　Personet et totis naenia moesta scholis.

As beadle, you were wont, standing conspicuous with your shining staff, to assemble the flock of Pallas: but now Death, the ultimate beadle, savagely arrests you, too, beadle, and shows no favor even to his own office. 'Tis true, the locks of your temples were whiter than the swan-plumes under which Jove is storied to have hid, but O, you deserved to grow young again like Aeson, with the simples drawn by Medea from the flowers of Haemonvale! [Aesculapius], son of Coronis, heeding the goddess's prayers importunate, should have called you back with his healing art from the Stygian waves. Whenever you were ordered to go as a swift herald from your Apollo [the vice-chancellor of the university] and bring together the togaed hosts, you stood like wing-foot Hermes in the Trojan halls, sent from the ethereal citadel of his Father; or like the herald Eurybates, when before the stormy face of Achilles he delivered the stern demands of King Agamemnon. O thou great queen of sepulchers, handmaid of Avernus, too harsh to the Muses and the arts of Pallas, why shouldst thou not seize instead some human clod, some useless weight of earth? Against such rabble thy arrows might better be aimed. O Academe, grieve in mourning vestment for this good man, and bedew his dark bier with thy tears. Let complaining Elegy pour out her sad strains, and let a mournful dirge ring through all the schools.

Elegia Tertia

Anno aetatis 17

In Obitum Praesulis Wintoniensis

(*1626*)

Elegy III

In his 17th year

On the Death of Dr. Andrewes, Bishop of Winchester

(*1626*)

The subject of this elegy, Dr. Launcelot Andrewes, died in September, 1626, at the close of the second long vacation of Milton's academic course. He was a fit subject for eulogy at the hands of young Cantabrigians, because he not only was a Cambridge man, but had at one time been Master of Pembroke Hall. The tone of the elegy affords a curious contrast to Milton's later utterances, in his anti-episcopal pamphlets, concerning this same bishop.

Moestus eram, et tacitus nullo comitante
    sedebam,
  Haerebantque animo tristia plura meo,
Protinus en subiit funestae cladis imago
  Fecit in Angliaco quam Libitina solo;
Dum procerum ingressa est splendentes mar-
    more turres   5
  Dira sepulchrali mors metuenda face;
Pulsavitque auro gravidos et jaspide muros,
  Nec metuit satrapum sternere falce greges.
Tunc memini clarique ducis, fratrisque ve-
    rendi
  Intempestivis ossa cremata rogis.   10
Et memini heroum quos vidit ad aethera
    raptos,
  Flevit et amissos Belgia tota duces.
At te praecipuè luxi dignissime praesul,
  Wintoniaeque olim gloria magna tuae;
Delicui fletu, et tristi sic ore querebar,   15
  'Mors fera Tartareo diva secunda Jovi,
Nonne satis quod sylva tuas persentiat iras,
  Et quod in herbosos jus tibi detur agros,
Quodque afflata tuo marcescant lilia tabo,
  Et crocus, et pulchrae Cypridi sacra rosa, 20
Nec sinis ut semper fluvio contermina quercus
  Miretur lapsus praetereuntis aquae?
Et tibi succumbit liquido quae plurima coelo
  Evehitur pennis quamlibet augur avis,
Et quae mille nigris errant animalia sylvis, 25
  Et quod alunt mutum Proteos antra pecus.
Invida, tanta tibi cum sit concessa potestas;
  Quid juvat humanâ tingere caede manus?
Nobileque in pectus certas acuisse sagittas, 29
  Semideamque animam sede fugâsse suâ?'
Talia dum lacrymans alto sub pectore volvo,
  Roscidus occiduis Hesperus exit aquis,
Et Tartessiaco submerserat aequore currum
  Phoebus, ab Eöo littore mensus iter.
Nec mora, membra cavo posui refovenda
    cubili,   35
  Considerant oculos noxque soporque meos.
Cum mihi visus eram lato spatiarier agro,
  Heu nequit ingenium visa referre meum.
Illic puniceâ radiabant omnia luce,
  Ut matutino cum juga sole rubent.   40

Sad and silent I sat, comradeless; and many griefs clung about my soul. Then suddenly, behold, there arose before me an image of the deadly plague which Libitina spread on English soil, when dire Death, fearful with his sepulchral torch, entered the glorious marble towers of the great, shook the walls heavy with jasper and gold, and feared not to lay low with his scythe the host of princes. Then I thought on that illustrious duke [Duke Christian of Brunswick, a victim of the War of the Palatinate] and his worshiped brother-in-arms, whose bones were consumed on untimely pyres; and I thought on those heroes whom all Belgia saw snatched away to the skies — saw, and wept her lost leaders. But for you chiefly I grieved, good Bishop, once the great glory of your Winchester. I melted in tears, and with sad lip thus complained: 'Cruel Death, second among gods to Tartarean Jove, is it then not enough that the woods should feel thy wrath, and that power should be given thee over the green things of the fields? That, touched by thy pestilent breath, the lily withers, and the crocus, and the rose sacred to beautiful Cypris? Thou dost not permit the oak to stand forever by the stream, looking at the slipping-by of the water. To thee succumb the birds, as many as are borne on wings through the liquid sky, even the birds, though they give augury; and all the thousand animals that roam the dark forests; and the dumb herd that the caves of Proteus shelter. Envious! When so much power has been granted thee, what does it pleasure thee to steep thy hands in human slaughter, sharpen thy certain arrows to pierce a noble breast, and drive from its tenement a soul half-divine?'

While thus with tears I brooded in the depth of my heart, dewy Hesperus rose from the western waters; for Phoebus, having measured out his journey from the shores of dawn, had submerged his chariot in the seas beyond Spain. Forthwith I laid my limbs upon my pliant bed to be refreshed by sleep. Night and slumber had closed my eyes, when suddenly I seemed to be walking in a wide field. Alas, I have no gift to tell what I saw! There all things shone with a purpureal light, as when the mountaintops are flushed

Ac veluti cum pandit opes Thaumantia proles,
  Vestitu nituit multicolore solum.
Non dea tam variis ornavit floribus hortos
  Alcinoi, Zephyro Chloris amata levi.
Flumina vernantes lambunt argentea cam-
    pos,   45
  Ditior Hesperio flavet arena Tago.
Serpit odoriferas per opes levis aura Favoni,
  Aura sub innumeris humida nata rosis.
Talis in extremis terrae Gangetidis oris
  Luciferi regis fingitur esse domus.   50
Ipse racemiferis dum densas vitibus umbras
  Et pellucentes miror ubique locos,
Ecce mihi subitò Praesul Wintonius astat,
  Sidereum nitido fulsit in ore jubar;
Vestis ad auratos defluxit candida talos, 55
  Infula divinum cinxerat alba caput.
Dumque senex tali incedit venerandus amictu,
  Intremuit laeto florea terra sono.
Agmina gemmatis plaudunt caelestia pennis,
  Pura triumphali personat aethra tubâ. 60
Quisque novum amplexu comitem cantuque
    salutat,
  Hosque aliquis placido misit ab ore sonos;
'Nate veni, et patrii felix cape gaudia regni,
  Semper ab hinc duro, nate, labore vaca.'
Dixit, et aligerae tetigerunt nablia turmae, 65
  At mihi cum tenebris aurea pulsa quies.
Flebam turbatos Cephaleiâ pellice somnos,
  Talia contingant somnia saepe mihi.

with the morning sun; and the earth gleamed with a vestment of many colors, even as when Iris scatters her wealth abroad. Not with so various flowers did Chloris, goddess loved of light Zephyr, adorn the gardens of King Alcinoüs. Silver streams laved the green champaign; the sand shone richer than Hesperian Tagus. Through the odorous leafage breathed the light breath of Favonius, rising humid from under bowers of roses. Such a place men fable the home of the King of Light to be, far on the shores beyond Ganges. As I stood wondering at the dense shadows of the clustered vines and the radiance of these places everywhere, behold, suddenly before me stood Winchester's bishop! His face shone with glory like the stars; down to his golden sandals his robe flowed all candid; a white fillet encircled his saintly head. As the old man, thus venerably clad, walked on, the flowery earth trembled with joyful sound; hosts of angels clapped their jeweled wings, and through the air rang out a clear, triumphal horn. Each angel saluted his new comrade with embrace and song; and from the placid lips of One came these words: 'Come, son, enjoy the gladness of thy father's realm; rest henceforth from thy hard labors.' As He spoke, the winged choirs touched their psalteries. But from me my golden rest fled with the darkness, and I was left weeping that the Dawn, paramour of Cephalus, had stirred my sleep. May the like dreams come to me often again!

Elegia Quarta

Anno aetatis 18

AD THOMAM JUNIUM PRAECEPTOREM SUUM,
APUD MERCATORES ANGLICOS HAMBURGAE
AGENTES, PASTORIS MUNERE FUNGENTEM

(1625–27)

Elegy IV

In his 18th year

TO HIS TUTOR, THOMAS YOUNG,
CHAPLAIN TO THE ENGLISH MERCHANTS
AT HAMBURG

(1625–27)

Thomas Young, a young Scotch divine who had come to England in the wake of King James, had been Milton's domestic tutor. About 1620, Young accepted a position abroad as minister of a Protestant church supported by the English merchants resident at Hamburg in Germany. A Latin prose-letter from Milton to Young exists, dated March 26,

1625 (*Fam. Ep. 1*). The present verse-letter, written in 1625 or 1627, some years after Young's departure, shows by its tone of tenderness and solicitude that, in spite of his dilatoriness in writing, Milton still cherished a sincere affection for his former tutor. He compares his love for Young to that of Alcibiades for Socrates, and plainly states his debt to him for initiation into the delights of classical literature.

The prophecy with which the epistle closes, that Young would soon see his native shores again, was fulfilled. He received a living at Stowmarket, Suffolk, and held it uninterruptedly until the close of his life in 1655. When the Long Parliament met to inaugurate a new state of things in the church, Young came forward with the famous pamphlet against Bishop Hall and his defense of Episcopacy. This pamphlet was signed *Smectymnuus*, a name made up from the initials of Young and the four other ministers who had collaborated in the production; it was the first of the remarkable series of Smectymnuan pamphlets to which Milton contributed. After Milton's break with the Presbyterians, and his embroilment in the divorce controversy, his intimacy with Young probably ceased.

Curre per immensum subitò mea littera
    pontum,
I, pete Teutonicos laeve per aequor agros,
Segnes rumpe moras, et nil, precor, obstet
    eunti,
Et festinantis nil remoretur iter.
Ipse ego Sicanio fraenantem carcere ventos   5
    Aeolon, et virides sollicitabo Deos;
Caeruleamque suis comitatam Dorida nym-
    phis,
Ut tibi dent placidam per sua regna viam.
At tu, si poteris, celeres tibi sume jugales,
    Vecta quibus Colchis fugit ab ore viri.   10
Aut queis Triptolemus Scythicas devenit in
    oras
Gratus Eleusinâ missus ab urbe puer.
Atque ubi Germanas flavere videbis arenas
    Ditis ad Hamburgae moenia flecte gradum,
Dicitur occiso quae ducere nomen ab Hamâ,
    Cimbrica quem fertur clava dedisse neci. 16
Vivit ibi antiquae clarus pietatis honore
    Praesul Christicolas pascere doctus oves;
Ille quidem est animae plusquam pars altera
    nostrae,
Dimidio vitae vivere cogor ego.   20
Hei mihi quot pelagi, quot montes interjecti
    Me faciunt aliâ parte carere mei!
Charior ille mihi quam tu doctissime Graiûm
    Cliniadi, pronepos qui Telamonis erat. 24
Quámque Stagirites generoso magnus alumno,
    Quem peperit Lybico Chaonis alma Jovi.
Qualis Amyntorides, qualis Philyrëius heros
    Myrmidonum regi, talis et ille mihi.

Run through the great sea, my letter; go, over the smooth waters seek the shores of Germany. Tarry not; let nothing, I pray, stand in the way of your going; let nothing impair your haste. I myself will pray to Aeolus, who chains the winds in his Sicilian cave, and to all the green-haired gods, and to cerulean Doris with her nymphs, that they give you a quiet way through their realms. But do you, if possible, get for yourself that swift dragon-team, wherewith Medea fled from the face of her husband; or that with which the boy Triptolemus came into Scythia, a welcome messenger from Eleusis. And when you shall see the German sands gleam, turn your course to the walls of wealthy Hamburg, which takes its name, they say, from Hama, slain by the club of the Danish giant. There a priest of honored fame for ancient piety dwells, skilled to pasture the flocks of Christ. He is the other half of my soul, yea, more; without him I am forced to live a half-life. Ah me, how many seas, how many mountains, interpose to part me from my other self! Dearer he is to me than wert thou, Socrates, wisest of Greeks, to Alcibiades, who had Telamon for ancestor; dearer than the great Stagyrite to his high-born pupil Alexander, whom kindly Olympias of Chaonia bore to Lybian Jove. As to the king of the Myrmidons was Phoenix, the son of Amyntor, or Chiron, son of nymph Philyra, such is this man to me. I followed his foot-

Primus ego Aonios illo praeeunte recessus
    Lustrabam, et bifidi sacra vireta jugi,   30
Pieriosque hausi latices, Clioque favente,
    Castalio sparsi laeta ter ora mero.
Flammeus at signum ter viderat arietis
    Aethon,
    Induxitque auro lanea terga novo,   34
Bisque novo terram sparsisti Chlori senilem
    Gramine, bisque tuas abstulit Auster opes:
Necdum ejus licuit mihi lumina pascere vultu,
    Aut linguae dulces aure bibisse sonos.
Vade igitur, cursuque Eurum praeverte sono-
    rum,
    Quàm sit opus monitis res docet, ipsa vides.
Invenies dulci cum conjuge forte sedentem, 41
    Mulcentem gremio pignora chara suo,
Forsitan aut veterum praelarga volumina
    patrum
    Versantem, aut veri biblia sacra Dei.
Caelestive animas saturantem rore tenellas,
    Grande salutiferae religionis opus.   46
Utque solet, multam, sit dicere cura salutem,
    Dicere quam decuit, si modo adesset,
    herum.
Haec quoque paulum oculos in humum defixa
    modestos,
    Verba verecundo sis memor ore loqui: 50
'Haec tibi, si teneris vacat inter praelia
    Musis
    Mittit ab Angliaco littore fida manus.
Accipe sinceram, quamvis sit sera, salutem;
    Fiat et hoc ipso gratior illa tibi.
Sera quidem, sed vera fuit, quam casta recepit
    Icaris a lento Penelopeia viro.   56
Ast ego quid volui manifestum tollere cri-
    men,
    Ipse quod ex omni parte levare nequit.
Arguitur tardus meritò, noxamque fatetur,
    Et pudet officium deseruisse suum.   60
Tu modò da veniam fasso, veniamque roganti,
    Crimina diminui, quae patuere, solent.
Non ferus in pavidos rictus diducit hiantes,
    Vulnifico pronos nec rapit ungue leo.
Saepe sarissiferi crudelia pectora Thracis 65
    Supplicis ad moestas deliceure preces.

steps when I first wandered through the hollows of the Aonian mount, and through the sacred groves of the twice cloven hill; with him I first drank the waters of the Pierian spring, and under favor of Clio wet my happy lips thrice with wine of Castaly. But flame-clad Aethon, the sun-hero, had three times seen the sign of the ram, and clothed the woolly back with new gold; and twice, O Flora, thou hadst sprinkled the old earth with new verdure, and twice had Auster, the south wind, stolen away thy wealth, nor yet was it granted mine eyes to feast upon this man's face, or mine ears to drink in the sweet tones of his voice.

Go, then, and outstrip in your flight the sonorous east wind. What need there is of admonition, occasion teaches and you yourself can see. Perchance you will come upon him as he sits with his sweet wife, fondling in his breast the dear pledges of their love; or perchance as he turns the massive tomes of the ancient Fathers, or the sacred books of the true God; or as he sprinkles with heavenly dew the souls not yet grown strong in faith — great work of healing religion. Take care to give him fair greeting, as is wont, and to say what it would beseem your master to say if he were there. Remember, fixing your modest eyes a while on the ground, to speak these words, shyly: 'These verses — if there is time in the midst of battles for the gentle Muses — a faithful hand sends thee from the English shore. Accept his heartfelt greeting, late though it be. Aye, let it come all the welcomer for that. Late indeed, but true, was that greeting which chaste Penelope, daughter of Icarius, received from her tardy husband. But why should I seek to clear away a patent fault which my master can in no wise extenuate? Justly he is proved dilatory, and confesses the wrong; he is ashamed to have put off the performance of such a duty. Grant grace to a sinner confessed, a sinner pleading. Wrongs revealed lose half their weight. The wild beast does not open his yawning jaws upon a trembling victim; the lion will not wound with his claw those who lie prone. The cruel hearts of pike-bearing Thracians have often melted at the mournful cry of a suppliant; hands stretched

Extensaeque manus avertunt fulminis ictus,
  Placat et iratos hostia parva Deos.
Jamque diu scripsisse tibi fuit impetus illi,
  Neve moras ultra ducere passus Amor.   70
Nam vaga Fama refert, heu nuntia vera
  malorum!
  In tibi finitimis bella tumere locis,
Teque tuàmque urbem truculento milite
  cingi,
  Et jam Saxonicos arma parasse duces.
Te circum latè campos populatur Enyo,   75
  Et sata carne virûm jam cruor arva rigat.
Germanisque suum concessit Thracia Mar-
  tem,
  Illuc Odrysios Mars pater egit equos.
Perpetuóque comans jam deflorescit oliva,
  Fugit et aerisonam Diva perosa tubam,   80
Fugit io terris, et jam non ultima virgo
  Creditur ad superas justa volasse domos.
Te tamen intereà belli circumsonat horror,
  Vivis et ignoto solus inópsque solo;
Et, tibi quam patrii non exhibuere penates   85
  Sede peregrinâ quaeris egenus opem.
Patria dura parens, et saxis saevior albis
  Spumea quae pulsat littoris unda tui,
Siccine te decet innocuos exponere faetus;
  Siccine in externam ferrea cogis humum,   90
Et sinis ut terris quaerant alimenta remotis
  Quos tibi prospiciens miserat ipse Deus,
Et qui laeta ferunt de caelo nuntia, quique
  Quae via post cineres ducat ad astra, do-
  cent?
Digna quidem Stygiis quae vivas clausa tene-
  bris,   95
  Aeternâque animae digna perire fame!
Haud aliter vates terrae Thesbitidis olim
  Pressit inassueto devia tesqua pede,
Desertasque Arabum salebras, dum regis
  Achabi
  Effugit atque tuas, Sidoni dira, manus.   100
Talis et horrisono laceratus membra flagello,
  Paulus ab Aemathiâ pellitur urbe Cilix.
Piscosaeque ipsum Gergessae civis Jesum
  Finibus ingratus jussit abire suis.
At tu sume animos, nec spes cadat anxia
  curis   105
Nec tua concutiat decolor ossa metus.
Sis etenim quamvis fulgentibus obsitus armis,
  Intententque tibi millia tela necem,
At nullis vel inerme latus violabitur armis,
  Deque tuo cuspis nulla cruore bibet.   110

out in appeal avert the lightning-stroke, and a little offering placates the anger of Gods.

'For a long time now he has been moved to write thee, and now at last Love would not suffer more delay; for vague Rumor alas, true messenger of ill! says that thy neighborhood is big with wars, that thou and thy city are girt about with truculent soldiery, and that the Saxon chiefs are already in arms. About thee far and wide Enyo the war goddess lays waste the fields, and blood drenches the ground sown with the bodies of men. Mars deserts his Thrace for Germany, and thither drives his Odrysian horses. The olive, always green, now withers; and the Goddess who hates the trumpet's brazen clang has fled. Look! she has fled from earth, and already the Maid of Justice, not waiting till the end, is thought to have flown to the celestial realms. Meanwhile about thee sounds the horror of war, where thou livest alone and poor in a strange land. Thou must needs seek in foreign parts the sustenance which thy fatherland denies thee. Fatherland, stern parent, harsher than the white rocks beaten by the foam of your shore, does it beseem you so to expose your innocent offspring, so to drive them out, O heart of iron! into a strange land? Those whom God in his providence sent to thee, bearing good tidings from Heaven, to teach the way to the stars after the body is ashes, will you force these to seek their food in distant regions? If so, you are worthy to live forever shut in the darkness of death, and to perish with the eternal hunger of the soul! Thus did Elijah the Tishbite of old tread with unaccustomed foot the devious desert ways and the rough wastes of Araby, when he fled from out the hands of King Ahab and of thee, dire Jezebel. Thus, his limbs torn by the harsh-crackling scourge, was Cilician Paul driven from the city of Macedon; and thus even Jesus himself was bidden by the citizens, ungrateful souls! to depart from the shores of fishy Gergessa.

'But do thou take heart; let not care or worry steal thy hope, nor ashen fear invade thy bones. For though thou art girt about by gleaming arms, and though a thousand arrows threaten death, no weapon shall touch thy naked side, nor from thy blood shall any

Namque eris ipse Dei radiante sub aegide
   tutus,
   Ille tibi custos, et pugil ille tibi;
Ille Sionaeae qui tot sub moenibus arcis
   Assyrios fudit nocte silente viros;   114
Inque fugam vertit quos in Samaritidas oras
   Misit ab antiquis prisca Damascus agris,
Terruit et densas pavido cum rege cohortes,
   Aere dum vacuo buccina clara sonat,
Cornea pulvereum dum verberat ungula
   campum,   119
   Currus arenosam dum quatit actus humum,
Auditurque hinnitus equorum ad bella ruen-
   tûm,
   Et strepitus ferri, murmuraque alta virûm.
Et tu (quod superest miseris) sperare me-
   mento,
   Et tua magnanimo pectore vince mala.   124
Nec dubites quandoque frui melioribus annis,
   Atque iterum patrios posse videre lares.'

javelin drink. For thou shalt be safe under the radiant aegis of God. He shall be thy keeper and thy champion; He who, under the walls of Jerusalem, citadel of Zion, overwhelmed so many Assyrian men in the silence of night, and put to flight those whom primeval Damascus had sent from her ancient fields into Samaria. He terrified the dense cohorts and made the king to quake, when on the silence shrilled the clear trumpet, when horny hoofs smote the dust of the field and the chariot in its flight shook the sands, and there was heard the neighing of horses rushing to war, and the clash of iron, and the swelling roar of men. Remember to hope, for that is what is left to the wretched. Surmount thy misfortunes great-heartedly. And doubt not that better times will come, and that once more thou mayst see thine old home.'

Elegia Quinta

Anno aetatis 20

IN ADVENTUM VERIS

(1628–29?)

Elegy V

In his 20th year

ON THE COMING OF SPRING

(1628–29?)

This poem throws light upon Milton's youthful character. The influence of Ovid, everywhere latent and in many places explicitly acknowledged in the Latin poems, is here most evident. The quite pagan fervor and abandon of the entire poem is remarkable. The opening sentence of the second paragraph (lines 25–26), it will be seen, was afterwards transferred almost bodily to the *Sonnet to the Nightingale*. It is interesting to compare lines 1–24, concerning the power of the spring to unloose the fountains of poetic inspiration, with Milton's statement to Phillips, many years after, that his vein 'never flowed freely but from the autumnal equinox to the vernal.' Lines 17–20 either anticipate or echo *Vacation Exercise* (1628), lines 34–36.

In se perpetuo Tempus revolubile gyro
   Jam revocat Zephyros vere tepente novos.
Induiturque brevem Tellus reparata juventam,
   Jamque soluta gelu dulce virescit humus.
Fallor? an et nobis redeunt in carmina vires,   5
   Ingeniumque mihi munere veris adest?
Munere veris adest, iterumque vigescit ab illo
   (Quis putet) atque aliquod jam sibi poscit
   opus.
Castalis ante oculos, bifidumque cacumen
   oberrat,

Time, revolving in perpetual gyre, now as the spring grows tepid calls back new Zephyrs. Earth refreshened puts on brief youth, and the ground loosened by thaws grows gently green. Do I mistake? Doth not also my strength in song return? At the spring's gift is not inspiration here? At the spring's gift 'tis here! Again it gathers strength therefrom (who could believe it?) and looks about for some noble task. Castaly sways before my eyes, and the twice-cloven peak of Parnassus;

Et mihi Pirenen somnia nocte ferunt.   10
Concitaque arcano fervent mihi pectora
    motu,
Et furor, et sonitus me sacer intùs agit.
Delius ipse venit, video Penëide lauro
Implicitos crines, Delius ipse venit.
Jam mihi mens liquidi raptatur in ardua
    coeli,   15
Perque vagas nubes corpore liber eo.
Perque umbras, perque antra feror penetralia
    vatum,
Et mihi fana patent interiora Deûm.
Intuiturque animus toto quid agatur Olympo,
Nec fugiunt oculos Tartara caeca meos.   20
Quid tam grande sonat distento spiritus
    ore?
Quid parit haec rabies, quid sacer iste
    furor?
Ver mihi, quod dedit ingenium, cantabitur
    illo;
Profuerint isto reddita dona modo.   24
Jam Philomela tuos foliis adoperta novellis
Instituis modulos, dum silet omne nemus.
Urbe ego, tu sylvâ simul incipiamus utrique,
Et simul adventum veris uterque canat.
Veris io rediere vices, celebremus honores
Veris, et hoc subeat Musa perennis opus. 30
Jam sol Aethiopas fugiens Tithoniaque arva,
Flectit ad Arctöas aurea lora plagas.
Est breve noctis iter, brevis est mora noctis
    opacae
Horrida cum tenebris exulat illa suis.   34
Jamque Lycaonius plaustrum caeleste Boötes
Non longâ sequitur fessus ut ante viâ,
Nunc etiam solitas circum Jovis atria toto
Excubias agitant sidera rara polo.
Nam dolus, et caedes, et vis cum nocte reces-
    sit,
Neve Giganteum Dii timuere scelus.   40
Forte aliquis scopuli recubans in vertice
    pastor,
Roscida cum primo sole rubescit humus,
'Hac,' ait, 'hac certè caruisti nocte puellâ
Phoebe tuâ, celeres quae retineret equos.'
Laeta suas repetit sylvas, pharetramque
    resumit   45
Cynthia, luciferas ut videt alta rotas,
Et tenues ponens radios gaudere videtur
Officium fieri tam breve fratris ope.
'Desere,' Phoebus ait, 'thalamos Aurora
    seniles,

and the dreams of night bring to me Pirene, the Corinthian spring. My breast is moved with mysterious fervors; madness and divine tumult inly stir me. Delian Apollo himself comes (I see his locks bound with Daphne's laurel), Delian Apollo himself comes. Now my spirit is rapt into the skyey steeps, and freed from the flesh I walk through the wandering clouds; through the shades I go, and the caverns, inmost prophetic sanctuaries; and the inner fanes of the gods lie open to me. My soul sees all that comes to pass in Olympus, and the darks of Hades escape not my vision. What lofty song does my soul intend, as it stands with lips apart? what does this madness bring to birth, this sacred fury? The spring, the spring which gave me dower of genius, my genius will celebrate. Thus her gifts repaid shall profit her.

Now, Philomel, in thy bower of new leaves, thou beginnest thy modulations, while all the woods are still. Thou in the forest and I in the town, let us begin together, and together chant the coming on of spring. Sing ho! spring now hath her turn again! let us celebrate the glory of spring, let the undying Muse take up her task. For now the sun, fleeing from the Ethiop strand and the orient fields of Tithonus, turns to the north his golden reins. The journey of night grows brief; brief is the tarrying of murky night, she goes to exile with her horrid shades. Now Boötes, keeper of Lycaon's child, no more follows the heavenly wain wearily, in a long pathway as before; now even the wonted watches of the stars about the courts of Jove are sparsely set throughout the firmament. For, along with night, bloodshed and fraud and violence retreat; nor do the gods fear any longer the villainy of their giant foes. Perchance some shepherd, lying on a summit of rock, as he sees the dewy earth reddening with dawn, says, 'Surely this night, O Phoebus, thou hast lacked loving arms to hold thee back, thee and thy swift horses.' Cynthia, when from her high station she beholds the sun's bright wheels, seems to rejoice that by her brother's aid her task has been shortened, and, laying by her faint rays, joyously goes back to her forest and her quiver.

'O Aurora,' Phoebus cries, 'leave the

Quid juvat effoeto procubuisse toro?   50
Te manet Aeolides viridi venator in herba,
   Surge, tuos ignes altus Hymettus habet.'
Flava verecundo dea crimen in ore fatetur,
   Et matutinos ocyus urget equos.
Exuit invisam Tellus rediviva senectam,   55
   Et cupit amplexus Phoebe subire tuos;
Et cupit, et digna est, quid enim formosius
     illâ,
   Pandit ut omniferos luxuriosa sinus,
Atque Arabum spirat messes, et ab ore ve-
     nusto
   Mitia cum Paphiis fundit amoma rosis.   60
Ecce coronatur sacro frons ardua luco,
   Cingit ut Idaeam pinea turris Opim;
Et vario madidos intexit flore capillos,
   Floribus et visa est posse placere suis.
Floribus effusos ut erat redimita capillos   65
   Tenario placuit diva Sicana Deo.
Aspice Phoebe tibi faciles hortantur amores,
   Mellitasque movent flamina verna preces.
Cinnameâ Zephyrus leve plaudit odorifer
     alâ,
   Blanditiasque tibi ferre videntur aves.   70
Nec sine dote tuos temeraria quaerit amores
   Terra, nec optatos poscit egena toros,
Alma salutiferum medicos tibi gramen in
     usus
   Praebet, et hinc titulos adjuvat ipsa tuos.
Quòd si te pretium, si te fulgentia tangunt   75
   Munera, (muneribus saepe coemptus amor)
Illa tibi ostentat quascunque sub aequore
     vasto,
   Et superinjectis montibus abdit opes.
Ah quoties cum tu clivoso fessus Olympo
   In vespertinas praecipitaris aquas,   80
'Cur te,' inquit, 'cursu languentem Phoebe
     diurno
   Hesperiis recipit caerula mater aquis?
Quid tibi cum Tethy? quid cum Tartesside
     lymphâ,
   Dia quid immundo perluis ora salo?
Frigora Phoebe meâ melius captabis in
     umbrâ,   85
   Huc ades, ardentes imbue rore comas.
Mollior egelidâ veniet tibi somnus in herbâ,
   Huc ades, et gremio lumina pone meo.
Quáque jaces circum mulcebit lene susur-
     rans
   Aura per humentes corpora fusa rosas.   90
Nec me (crede mihi) terrent Semelëia fata,

couch of old Tithonus! what does that chilly bed avail thee? Cephalus the hunter waits for thee in the grassy nook. Arise! Thy flame is waiting thee on high Hymettus!' With shy, averted face, the bright goddess confesses her fault, and more swiftly urges on the horses of morning. Earth, revivified, casts off her hated age, and longs for thy embraces, O Apollo! longs for them, and deserves them. For what more beautiful than she, when she bares her rich breast, breathing of the harvests of Araby, and when upon her lovely lips the balsams of the Orient mingle with the roses of Paphos? Lo! she encircles her high brow with sacred trees, as the tower of pines that crowns the goddess Ops on Ida; and flowers many-hued she weaves in her dew-drenched hair, in hope of pleasing her lover, as that Sicilian goddess, Proserpine, when she had bound her loose locks with flowers, pleased Taenarian Dis. Look hither, Apollo; willing love awaits thee; the spring winds are full of honeyed supplication. Odorous Zephyr lightly claps his cinnamon-scented wings, and the very birds seem to bear thee blandishments. Nor does Earth, overbold, come empty-handed to seek thy love, nor is she poor who asks the bridals of her longing. The kindly goddess brings thee wholesome herbs for medicine, whereby she may help thy fame as healer. If riches, if shining gifts, will win thee (and love is still purchased with gifts), she lays before thee all the treasures hidden under the mighty sea or under the roots of the hills. Ah, ever and again, when thou, wearied by the steep sky, hast cast thyself into the vesperine waters, she cries, 'Oh, why! Apollo, must it be the cerulean ocean-mother who receives thee when thou comest to the west weary from thy day's course? What is Tethys to thee? What to thee the Hesperian tide? Why wilt thou bathe thy divine face in impure brine? A better coolness, Apollo, thou mayst find in my shade. Come hither, dip thy hot locks in my dew. A softer sleep shall come to thee in the cool grass. Come hither, and lay thy glories in my breast. Where thou liest a gently whispering breeze will soothe our bodies as we sink relaxed in dewy roses. Believe me, I fear not Semele's fate; I fear not thy chariot, nor

Nec Phaëtonteo fumidus axis equo;
Cum tu Phoebe tuo sapientius uteris igni,
  Huc ades et gremio lumina pone meo.'
Sic Tellus lasciva suos suspirat amores;   95
  Matris in exemplum caetera turba ruunt.
Nunc etenim toto currit vagus orbe Cupido,
  Languentesque fovet solis ab igne faces.
Insonuere novis lethalia cornua nervis,
  Triste micant ferro tela corusca novo.   100
Jamque vel invictam tentat superasse Dianam,
  Quaeque sedet sacro Vesta pudica foco.
Ipsa senescentem reparat Venus annua formam,
  Atque iterum tepido creditur orta mari.
Marmoreas juvenes clamant *Hymenaee* per
    urbes,   105
  Litus *io Hymen*, et cava saxa sonant.
Cultior ille venit tunicâque decentior aptâ,
  Puniceum redolet vestis odora crocum.
Egrediturque frequens ad amoeni gaudia veris
  Virgineos auro cincta puella sinus.   110
Votum est cuique suum, votum est tamen
    omnibus unum,
  Ut sibi quem cupiat, det Cytherea virum.
Nunc quoque septenâ modulatur arundine
    pastor,
  Et sua quae jungat carmina Phyllis habet.
Navita nocturno placat sua sidera cantu,   115
  Delphinasque leves ad vada summa vocat.
Jupiter ipse alto cum conjuge ludit Olympo,
  Convocat et famulos ad sua festa Deos.
Nunc etiam Satyri cum sera crepuscula sur-
    gunt,
  Pervolitant celeri florea rura choro,   120
Sylvanusque suâ cyparissi fronde revinctus,
  Semicaperque deus, semideusque caper.
Quaeque sub arboribus Dryades latuere ve-
    tustis
  Per juga, per solos expatiantur agros.
Per sata luxuriat fruticetaque Maenalius Pan,
  Vix Cybele mater, vix sibi tuta Ceres,   126
Atque aliquam cupidus praedatur Oreada
    Faunus,
  Consulit in trepidos dum sibi nympha pedes.
Jamque latet, latitansque cupit male tecta
    videri,
  Et fugit, et fugiens pervelit ipsa capi. 130
Dii quoque non dubitant caelo praeponere
    sylvas,
  Et sua quisque sibi numina lucus habet.
Et sua quisque diu sibi numina lucus habeto,
  Nec vos arboreâ dii precor ite domo.

the smoking axle of the car that Phaethon would drive. If thou wilt use thy fires right wisely, Apollo, come hither, and lay thy glories in my breast!'

Thus amorously breathes the wanton Earth, and all the rout of her children follow headlong after her example. For now over the whole world Cupid wanders, and at the fire of the sun rekindles his torch. On the lethal horns of his bow sounds a new string; new tips shine baleful on his bright arrows. Now he attempts to conquer even unconquered Diana, even the pure Vestal as she sits by the sacred hearth. Venus herself, in her yearly fashion, purges all signs of age from her form, and seems once more just risen from the warm sea. Through the marble walls of cities the young men cry *Hymenaeus!* the shores and hollow rocks give back the cry *Io, Hymen!* Hymen himself comes in gala attire, handsome in his neat tunic, his fragrant vestment breathing the scent of the purple crocus. In crowds the girls go out with gold-cinctured breasts to take the pleasure of the pleasant spring. Each has her special prayer, yet every one the same, that Cytherea may give her the man on whom her heart is set.

Now, too, the shepherd pipes on his seven reeds, and Phyllis has a song to match. The sailor prays the favor of his stars with nightly song; the sprightly dolphins come to the surface of the waves to listen. Jove himself and his spouse make merry on high Olympus; he invites even the menial deities to his high feast. And now, when the late twilight falls, fleet bands of satyrs skim over the blossomy fields; and with them Sylvanus, crowned with frond of cypress, god half-goat and goat half-god. The Dryads who hide amid old trees now roam abroad over the ridges, over the lonely fields. Through tilth and covert riots Maenalian Pan; mother Cybele and Ceres are scarce safe from him. Wanton Faunus stalks some Oread, while the nymph flies with startled feet. Now she hides, and, covered not too well, hopes to be seen in her hiding; she flees, but as she flees could wish that she were caught. The gods desert the sky for the woods of earth; each grove has its deity.

Long may each grove have its deity! Gods, desert not, I pray, your homes amid the trees.

Te referant miseris te Jupiter aurea terris   135

Saecla, quid ad nimbos aspera tela redis?

Tu saltem lentè rapidos age Phoebe jugales

Quà potes, et sensim tempora veris eant.

Brumaque productas tardè ferat hispida
noctes,

Ingruat et nostro serior umbra polo.   140

O Jove, may the golden ages bring thee back, back to this wretched earth. Why dost thou return to the clouds, thy savage armories? At least do thou, Phoebus, curb as much as may be thy rapid team, and let the days of spring pass slowly. Let it be long ere rough winter brings us its tedious nights; let the shades fall later than their wont about our pole!

Elegia Sexta

(*1629*)

AD CAROLUM DIODATUM
RURI COMMORANTEM.

Qui cum Idibus Decemb. scripsisset, et sua carmina excusari postulasset si solito minus essent bona, quod inter lautitias quibus erat ab amicis exceptus, haud satis felicem operam Musis dare se posse affirmabat, hunc habuit responsum.

Elegy VI

(*1629*)

(*To Charles Diodati, who, sending the author some verses from the country at Christmas-time, asked him to excuse their mediocrity on the ground that they were composed amid the distractions of the festival season.*)

The above note, given in the original editions, explains the purport of the elegy. The verse-letter of Diodati's, here referred to, was written on the thirteenth of December, 1629, and Milton's reply was probably sent soon after Christmas. It is of extreme autobiographic interest, for two reasons. It contains a noble statement of Milton's poetic creed, at a time when he felt with almost equal intensity the softer and the sterner sides of the poet's vocation; and it gives an account of the *Hymn on the Nativity*, just completed, or perhaps still under way. The picture of Christmas merrymaking in an English country-house gains a peculiar charm from the queer medium of seventeenth-century Latin in which it is conveyed.

Mitto tibi sanam non pleno ventre salutem,

Quâ tu distento forte carere potes.

At tua quid nostram prolectat Musa camoe-
nam,

Nec sinit optatas posse sequi tenebras?

Carmine scire velis quám te redamémque
colámque,   5

Crede mihi vix hoc carmine scire queas.

Nam neque noster amor modulis includitur
arctis,

Nec venit ad claudos integer ipse pedes.

Quàm bene solennes epulas, hilaremque
Decembrim

Festaque coelifugam quae coluere Deum,   10

Deliciasque refers, hiberni gaudia ruris,

Unsurfeited with feasting, I send you a good-health, for which your full stomach may give you need. Why do you tempt me to write verses by sending me yours? Why will you not allow my Muse to stay in the shadow she loves? You desire me to tell in verse how much I love and cherish you? Believe me, that is a thing you can scarcely hope to learn in verse of mine; my love cannot be held in the strict bonds of meter, nor comes it whole and unimpaired to feet that limp.

How well you tell of your high feastings, of your December merriment, and all the gaieties that celebrate the coming of the heavenly One to earth! [1] How well you tell

---

[1] A double reference is intended, to Christ and to Saturn; the Roman Saturnalia was celebrated in December.

Haustaque per lepidos Gallica musta focos.
Quid quereris refugam vino dapibusque
    poesin?
Carmen amat Bacchum, carmina Bacchus
    amat.
Nec puduit Phoebum virides gestasse corym-
    bos,   15
Atque hederam lauro praeposuisse suae.
Saepius Aoniis clamavit collibus *Euoe*
Mista Thyonêo turba novena choro.
Naso Corallaeis mala carmina misit ab agris:
Non illic epulae non sata vitis erat.   20
Quid nisi vina, rosasque racemiferumque
    Lyaeum
Cantavit brevibus Tëia Musa modis,
Pindaricosque inflat numeros Teumesius Evan,
Et redolet sumptum pagina quaeque merum.
Dum gravis everso currus crepat axe supinus,
Et volat Eléo pulvere fuscus eques.   26
Quadrimoque madens lyricen Romanus Iaccho
Dulce canit Glyceran, flavicomamque
    Chloen.
Jam quoque lauta tibi generoso mensa paratu,
Mentis alit vires, ingeniumque fovet.   30
Massica foecundam despumant pocula venam,
Fundis et ex ipso condita metra cado.
Addimus his artes, fusumque per intima
    Phoebum
Corda, favent uni Bacchus, Apollo, Ceres.
Scilicet haud mirum tam dulcia carmina per te
Numine composito tres peperisse Deos.   36
Nunc quoque Thressa tibi caelato barbitos
    auro
Insonat argutâ molliter icta manu;
Auditurque chelys suspensa tapetia circum,
Virgineos tremulâ quae regat arte pedes.   40
Illa tuas saltem teneant spectacula Musas,
Et revocent, quantum crapula pellit iners.
Crede mihi dum psallit ebur, comitataque
    plectrum
Implet odoratos festa chorea tholos,
Percipies tacitum per pectora serpere Phoe-
    bum,   45
Quale repentinus permeat ossa calor,
Perque puellares oculos digitumque sonantem
Irruet in totos lapsa Thalia sinus.
Namque Elegía levis multorum cura deorum
    est,
Et vocat ad numeros quemlibet illa suos;   50
Liber adest elegis, Eratoque, Ceresque, Ve-
    nusque,

of the joys of winter in the country, and of the French must quaffed by the jolly fireside! But why do you complain that poetry is a runaway from wining and dining? Song loves Bacchus, and Bacchus loves song. Apollo was not ashamed to wear the green clusters; nay, even to put the ivy of the wine-god above his own laurel. Many a time the nine Muses have mixed with the Bacchic chorus crying *Evoe* on the Heliconian hills. Those verses which Ovid sent from the fields of Thrace were bad, because there were no feasts there and no vineyards. What but roses and the grape-laden vine did Anacreon sing in those tiny staves of his? Teumesian Bacchus inspired Pindar's strain; each page of his breathes ardor from the drained cup, as he sings of the crash of the heavy chariot over-turned, and the rider flying by, dark with the dust of the Elean racecourse. The Roman lyrist drank first of the four-year-old vintage, ere he sang so sweetly of Glycera and blonde-haired Chloe. The sinews of thy genius, too, draw strength from the nobly laden table. Your Massic cups foam with a rich vein of song; you pour bottled verses straight from the jar. To this, add art, and Apollo pene-trant within the inmost chambers of your heart; small wonder that such delightful verses come from you, since three gods in accord, Bacchus, Apollo, and Ceres, brought them to birth.

For you, too, the Thracian lute, gold-embossed, sounds now, gently touched by a master hand. In tapestried rooms is heard the lyre, swaying with its quivering measures the feet of young girls in the dance. Let such gracious sights as this hold your Muse at gaze, and let them call back all the inspiration that dull surfeit drives away. Trust me, when the ivory keys of the virginal leap under the player's fingers, and the crowd of dancers fills the perfumed chambers, you will feel the spirit of song stealing into your heart, pene-trating your very bones with a sudden glow. From the eyes and fingers of the girlish player, Thalia will slip into your breast and possess it all.

For light elegy is the care of many gods, and calls to its numbers whom it will; Bac-chus comes, and Erato, Ceres and Venus, and

Et cum purpureâ matre tenellus Amor.
Talibus inde licent convivia larga poetis,
   Saepius et veteri commaduisse mero.
At qui bella refert, et adulto sub Jove
     coelum,   55
   Heroasque pios, semideosque duces,
Et nunc sancta canit superum consulta de-
     orum,
   Nunc latrata fero regna profunda cane,
Ille quidem parcè Samii pro more magistri
   Vivat, et innocuos praebeat herba cibos; 60
Stet prope fagineo pellucida lympha catillo,
   Sobriaque è puro pocula fonte bibat.
Additur huic scelerisque vacans, et casta
     juventus,
   Et rigidi mores, et sine labe manus.
Qualis veste nitens sacrâ, et lustralibus undis
   Surgis ad infensos augur iture Deos.   66
Hoc ritu vixisse ferunt post rapta sagacem
   Lumina Tiresian, Ogygiumque Linon,
Et lare devoto profugum Calchanta, se-
     nemque
   Orpheon edomitis sola per antra feris; 70
Sic dapis exiguus, sic rivi potor Homerus
   Dulichium vexit per freta longa virum,
Et per monstrificam Perseiae Phoebados
     aulam,
   Et vada foemineis insidiosa sonis,
Perque tuas rex ime domos, ubi sanguine
     nigro   75
   Dicitur umbrarum detinuisse greges.
Diis etenim sacer est vates, divûmque sacer-
     dos,
   Spirat et occultum pectus, et ora Jovem.
At tu si quid agam, scitabere (si modò
     saltem
   Esse putas tanti noscere siquid agam) 80
Paciferum canimus caelesti semine regem,
   Faustaque sacratis saecula pacta libris,
Vagitumque Dei, et stabulantem paupere
     tecto
   Qui suprema suo cum patre regna colit.
Stelliparumque polum, modulantesque aethere
     turmas,   85
   Et subitò elisos ad sua fana Deos.
Dona quidem dedimus Christi natalibus illa
   Illa sub auroram lux mihi prima tulit.
Te quoque pressa manent patriis meditata
     cicutis,
   Tu mihi, cui recitem, judicis instar eris. 90

tender stripling Love with his rosy mother. Such poets, therefore, have a right to generous feasts and to stew full often in ancient wine. But the poet who will tell of wars, and of Heaven under adult Jove, and of pious heroes, and leaders half-divine, singing now the holy counsels of the gods above, and now the realms profound where Cerberus howls, such a poet must live sparely, after the manner of Pythagoras, the Samian teacher. Herbs must furnish him his innocent food; let clear water in a beechen cup stand at his side, and let his drink be sober draughts from the pure spring. His youth must be chaste and void of offense; his manners strict, his hands without stain. He shall be like a priest shining in sacred vestment, washed with lustral waters, who goes up to make augury before the offended gods. In this wise, they say, the sage Tiresias lived, after his eyes were darkened; and Theban Linus, and Calchas, who fled from his doomed hearth, and Orpheus, roaming in old age through lonely caverns, quelling the wild beasts with his music. So, a spare eater and a drinker of water, Homer carried Odysseus through the long courses of the sea, through the hall of monster-making Circe, and past the shoals insidious with women's song; and through thy realms, nethermost king, where they say he held with a spell of black blood the troops of the shades. Yea, for the bard is sacred to the gods; he is their priest; mysteriously from his lips and his breast he breathes Jove.

But if you will know what I am doing, I will tell you, if indeed you think my doings worth your concern. I am singing the King of Heaven, bringer of peace, and the fortunate days promised by the Holy Book; the crying of the infant God, and the stabling under a poor roof of Him who rules with His father the realms above; the star-creating heavens, the hymning of angels in the air, and the gods suddenly shattered in their own fanes. This poem I made as a birthday gift for Christ; the first light of Christmas dawn brought me the theme.

And other strains which I have piped musingly on my native reed await you; you, when I recite them to you, will be my judge.

Elegia Septima

Anno aetatis undevigesimo

(*1627–28*)

Elegy VII

In his nineteenth year

(*1627–28*)

This elegy constitutes a personal confession of an unusually intimate kind, a confession of 'love at first sight' for a girl whom the poet encountered by chance in some public place in London. See *Sonnets IV, V,* and *VI.* Though conceived in a tone of whimsical extravagance and with the conventional sentimental machinery of the pseudo-classic poet, it indubitably records a real experience which is significant for an understanding of Milton's character. The unusual form of the date attached, in which the ordinal is put in place of the numeral, seems to imply that the poem was written before his nineteenth year was completed, i.e., some time between May 1 and December 9, 1627, or 1628. The postscript which follows the poem probably is to be taken with this elegy alone, though from the manner in which it is printed in the original editions, it may be taken to have a general application to the entire seven.

Nondum blanda tuas leges Amathusia nôram,
   Et Paphio vacuum pectus ab igne fuit.
Saepe cupidineas, puerilia tela, sagittas,
   Atque tuum sprevi maxime, numen, Amor.
'Tu puer imbelles' dixi 'transfige colum-
      bas,   5
   Conveniunt tenero mollia bella duci.
Aut de passeribus tumidos age, parve, tri-
      umphos,
   Haec sunt militiae digna trophaea tuae:
In genus humanum quid inania dirigis arma?
   Non valet in fortes ista pharetra viros.'
Non tulit hoc Cyprius, (neque enim Deus ullus
      ad iras   11
   Promptior) et duplici jam ferus igne calet.
Ver erat, et summae radians per culmina
      villae
   Attulerat primam lux tibi Maie diem:
At mihi adhuc refugam quaerebant lumina
      noctem   15
   Nec matutinum sustinuere jubar.
Astat Amor lecto, pictis Amor impiger alis,
   Prodidit astantem mota pharetra Deum:
Prodidit et facies, et dulce minantis ocelli,
   Et quicquid puero, dignum et Amore
      fuit.   20
Talis in aeterno juvenis Sigeius Olympo
   Miscet amatori pocula plena Jovi;
Aut qui formosas pellexit ad oscula nymphas
   Thiodamantaeus Naiade raptus Hylas; 24
Addideratque iras, sed et has decuisse putares,

I did not yet know thy laws, bland Aphrodite, and my heart was still free from Paphian fire. Often I spoke scorn of Cupid's arrows, those boyish darts, and chiefly scoffed, Love, at thy divinity. 'Thou boy,' said I, 'go shoot peaceful doves; only languid battles suit so delicate a chieftain. Or make a swelling triumph, child, over a conquest of sparrows. These are trophies worthy of thy warfare. Why take up thy silly arms against mankind? That quiver of thine avails not against strong men.' The Cyprian boy could not endure this (there is no god swifter to anger), and at my words the savage burned with a double fire.

It was spring, and shining over the roofs of the town, dawn had brought the May Day; but my eyes were turned toward retreating night, and could not endure the radiance of morning. Suddenly Love stood by my bed, Love with painted wings for speed. The swaying quiver betrayed the god where he stood; his countenance betrayed him, and the sweet menace of his eyes, and whatever else about him was boyish and lovely. So Ganymede, the Trojan lad, looks, as he brims the cups of amorous Jove in ever-during Olympus; or the boy who lured the beautiful nymphs to his kisses, Hylas, son of Thiodamas, the water-maiden's prey. Wrath was on him, but you would have deemed it an added grace;

Addideratque truces, nec sine felle minas.
Et 'Miser exemplo sapuisses tutiùs,' inquit,
  'Nunc mea quid possit dextera testis eris.
Inter et expertos vires numerabere nostras,
  Et faciam vero per tua damna fidem.   30
Ipse ego si nescis strato Pythone superbum
  Edomui Phoebum, cessit et ille mihi;
Et quoties meminit Peneidos, ipse fatetur
  Certiùs et graviùs tela nocere mea.   34
Me nequit adductum curvare peritiùs arcum,
  Qui post terga solet vincere Parthus
     eques.
Cydoniusque mihi cedit venator, et ille
  Inscius uxori qui necis author erat.
Est etiam nobis ingens quoque victus Orion,
  Herculeaeque manus, Herculeusque comes.
Jupiter ipse licet sua fulmina torqueat in
     me,   41
  Haerebunt lateri spicula nostra Jovis.
Caetera quae dubitas meliùs mea tela doce-
     bunt,
  Et tua non leviter corda petenda mihi.   44
Nec te stulte tuae poterunt defendere Musae,
  Nec tibi Phoebaeus porriget anguis opem.'
Dixit, et aurato quatiens mucrone sagittam,
  Evolat in tepidos Cypridos ille sinus.
At mihi risuro tonuit ferus ore minaci,
  Et mihi de puero non metus ullus erat,   50
Et modò quà nostri spatiantur in urbe
     Quirites
  Et modò villarum proxima rura placent.
Turba frequens, faciéque simillima turba
     dearum
  Splendida per medias itque reditque vias.
Auctaque luce dies gemino fulgore corus-
     cat,   55
  Fallor? an et radios hinc quoque Phoebus
     habet.
Haec ego non fugi spectacula grata severus,
  Impetus et quò me fert juvenilis, agor.
Lumina luminibus malè providus obvia misi
  Neve oculos potui continuisse meos.   60
Unam forte aliis supereminuisse notabam,
  Principium nostri lux erat illa mali.
Sic Venus optaret mortalibus ipsa videri,
  Sic regina Deûm conspicienda fuit.   64
Hanc memor objecit nobis malus ille Cupido,

and he spoke words of threatening cruelty, full of spite. 'Wretch,' he said, 'thou hadst been wiser to learn my power by the spectacle of others' pain; now thou shalt in thine own person prove what my arm can do. Thou shalt be numbered among those who have felt my might; thy pangs shall strengthen men's belief in me. Perhaps thou art ignorant that I, even I, subdued Apollo, made haughty by his victory over Python; to me that great god had to yield. Whene'er he thinks on Daphne, he confesses that my darts carry surer and deadlier harm than his own. The Parthian horseman, who conquers as he flees, draws not his bow more skillfully than I. The Cydonian hunter yields the palm to me, and Cephalus, who slew his wife unwittingly. Huge Orion I overcame, and the strong hand of Hercules, and Hercules's friend. Jove himself may turn his thunderbolts against me, but before they strike, my arrows have pierced the side of Jove. If thou still doubtest, my weapons will teach thee the rest better than words, my weapons, with which not lightly shall I seek thy heart. Deem not, fool, that thy Muses can succor thee, nor that the serpent of Apollo the healer can give thee any aid!' So he spake, and, shaking his arrow with the golden tip, he flew away into the warm breast of his mother Cypris. But I smiled derisively at his fierce threats, and had not the slightest fear of the boy.

And now I took my pleasure, sometimes in the city parks, where our citizens promenade, sometimes at neighboring country-places. Crowds of girls, with faces like to the faces of goddesses, came and went radiantly through the walks; the day brightened with a double splendor. Surely, the sun himself stole his beams from their faces. I was not stern with myself; I did not flee from the gracious spectacle, but let myself be led wherever youthful impulse directed. Rashly I sent my gaze to meet theirs; I could not control my eyes. Then by chance I noted one supreme above the others, and the light of her eyes was the beginning of my ills. She looked as Venus might wish to seem to mortals; lovely to behold as the queen of the gods was she. That rascal Cupid, harboring his

Solus et hos nobis texuit antè dolos.
Nec procul ipse vafer latuit, multaeque sa-
    gittae,
    Et facis a tergo grande pependit onus.
Nec mora, nunc ciliis haesit, nunc virginis
    ori,
    Insilit hinc labiis, insidet inde genis: 70
Et quascunque agilis partes jaculator ober-
    rat,
    Hei mihi, mille locis pectus inerme ferit.
Protinus insoliti subierunt corda furores,
    Uror amans intùs, flammaque totus eram.
Interea misero quae jam mihi sola placebat,
    Ablata est oculis non reditura meis.   76
Ast ego progredior tacitè querebundus, et
    excors,
    Et dubius volui saepe referre pedem.
Findor, et haec remanet, sequitur pars altera
    votum,
    Raptaque tàm subitò gaudia flere juvat.   80
Sic dolet amissum proles Junonia coelum,
    Inter Lemniacos praecipitata focos.
Talis et abreptum solem respexit, ad Orcum
    Vectus ab attonitis Amphiaraus equis.   84
Quid faciam infelix, et luctu victus, amores
    Nec licet inceptos ponere, neve sequi.
O utinam spectare semel mihi detur amatos
    Vultus, et coràm tristia verba loqui!
Forsitan et duro non est adamante creata,
    Forte nec ad nostras surdeat illa preces.   90
Crede mihi nullus sic infeliciter arsit,
    Ponar in exemplo primus et unus ego.
Parce precor teneri cum sis Deus ales amoris,
    Pugnent officio nec tua facta tuo.
Jam tuus O certè est mihi formidabilis
    arcus,
                               95
    Nate deâ, jaculis nec minus igne potens:
Et tua fumabunt nostris altaria donis,
    Solus et in superis tu mihi summus eris.
Deme meos tandem, verùm nec deme furores,
    Nescio cur, miser est suaviter omnis amans:
Tu modo da facilis, posthaec mea siqua futura
    est,   101
    Cuspis amaturos figat ut una duos.

grudge, had thrown her in my path; all alone, he had woven this plot against me. Not far off the sly god was hiding; his torch and many arrows hung as a great load from his back. Not a moment did he lose. Now he clung to her eyelids, now to her virgin face; thence he hopped upon her lips, and occupied her cheeks; and wherever the nimble archer went, ah, me! from a thousand points of vantage he struck my defenseless breast. Suddenly unwonted furies assailed my heart; I burned inly with love, I was all flame. Meanwhile she who was my only delight in misery disappeared, never to be given to my eyes again.

I started on, full of mute complaining, stupefied. Often I stood in doubt whether to go on or turn back. My being was divided, my body remained behind, but my thoughts went after her. I found relief in weeping for the joy so suddenly snatched from me. Such was the grief of Juno's offspring Vulcan, for the heaven he had lost, when he was shot down the sky to the hearths of Lemnos; thus Amphiaraus borne down to Orcus by his thunderstricken horses, gazed back from the abyss at the vanishing light of the sun. What shall I do, wretch that I am, and overcome by grief? I cannot take up my love or lay it by. O, may it be granted me to see her loved countenance again and to speak sadly with her face to face! Perhaps she is not all made of adamant, mayhap she would not be deaf to my prayers. Surely no one ever suffered more in Love's flame. I may stand first, a prime exemplar of love-sorrows. Spare me, I pray, since love is tender, and thou art its winged god! Let not thy deeds refute thy office. Now, ah, now at last thy bow is fearful to me, thou goddess-born, whose arrows are potent as fire! Henceforth thine altars shall smoke with my gifts; among all the gods thou shalt be for me single and supreme. Take away, then, my tortures, nay, take them not away! I know not why it is, loving is such sweet wretchedness. Only grant thou leniently, that if hereafter any maiden is my destiny, the two hearts fated to love may be pinned together by a single shaft.

Haec ego mente olim laevâ, studioque supino
  Nequitiae posui vana trophaea meae.
Scilicet abreptum sic me malus impulit error,
  Indocilisque aetas prava magistra fuit.
Donec Socraticos umbrosa Academia rivos 5
  Praebuit, admissum dedocuitque jugum.
Protinus extinctis ex illo tempore flammis,
  Cincta rigent multo pectora nostra gelu.
Unde suis frigus metuit puer ipse sagittis,
  Et Diomedéam vim timet ipsa Venus. 10

These vain trophies of my idleness I set up in time past, in unbalanced mood and with lax endeavor. Vicious error hurried me astray, and my untaught years were an ill mistress to me; until the shady Academe [i.e., Plato's philosophy] offered me its Socratic streams, and loosened from my neck the yoke to which I had submitted. At once all these youthful flames became extinct, and since then my breast is rigid with accumulated ice; whence Cupid himself fears freezing for his arrows, and Venus dreads my Diomedean strength.

[Epigrammata]

[Epigrams]

The short pieces which follow were originally printed without the general title Epigrams, under which they appear in modern editions, but were included under the title Elegies, as being written in elegiac meter. The four epigrams on the Gunpowder Plot are heavy and tasteless. The epigrams on Leonora Baroni are interesting autobiographically. It has been plausibly conjectured that Milton heard this famous singer at the concert which he speaks of attending at the palace of Cardinal Francesco Barberini, during his first visit to Rome, October and November, 1638. The Baroni were originally a Neapolitan family, but they had settled in Rome about a year before Milton's visit. Of Leonora, Bayle's *Dictionary*, quoted by Masson, says that she was 'one of the finest voices in the world,' and that 'an infinity of *beaux esprits* made verses in her praise.'

IN PRODITIONEM BOMBARDICAM
(*1626–30*)

Cum simul in regem nuper satrapasque Britan-
    nos
Ausus es infandum perfide Fauxe nefas,
Fallor? an et mitis voluisti ex parte videri,
  Et pensare malâ cum pietate scelus;
Scilicet hos alti missurus ad atria caeli, 5
  Sulphureo curru flammivolisque rotis.
Qualiter ille feris caput inviolabile Parcis
  Liquit Jördanios turbine raptus agros.

ON THE GUNPOWDER PLOT
(*1626–30*)

When, perfidious Faux, you attempted your late unspeakable crime against the King and the British lords, do I mistake you, or did you really want to show a partial mildness and compensate your crime with a false piety? Doubtless you intended to send them to the high courts of Heaven in a chariot of sulphurous smoke and wheeling flame, even as Elijah, that head inviolable by the fierce Parcae, was snatched away in a whirlwind from the fields of Jordan.

IN EANDEM
(1626–30)

Siccine tentasti caelo donâsse Jâcobum
  Quae septemgemino Belua monte lates?
Ni meliora tuum poterit dare munera numen,
  Parce precor donis insidiosa tuis.
Ille quidem sine te consortia serus adivit   5
  Astra, nec inferni pulveris usus ope.
Sic potiùs foedos in caelum pelle cucullos,
  Et quot habet brutos Roma profana Deos,
Namque hac aut aliâ nisi quemque adjuveris arte,
  Crede mihi caeli vix bene scandet iter.   10

ON THE SAME
(1626–30)

O Beast acrouch on the seven hills, did you attempt thus to send King James to Heaven? Unless your divinity has power to bestow better largess, forbear, I pray, your insidious gifts. Without the aid of your infernal powder he has gone, timely late, to the companionable stars. Do you rather blow skyward your base cowls, and all the brute gods profane Rome worships; for unless you aid them thus or somehow else, they will hardly, believe me, clamber up the hard road to Heaven.

IN EANDEM
(1626–30)

Purgatorem animae derisit Iäcobus ignem,
  Et sine quo superûm non adeunda domus.
Frenduit hoc trinâ monstrum Latiale coronâ
  Movit et horrificum cornua dena minax.
Et 'Nec inultus' ait 'temnes mea sacra Britanne,   5
  Supplicium spretâ religione dabis.
Et si stelligeras unquam penetraveris arces,
  Non nisi per flammas triste patebit iter.'
O quàm funesto cecinisti proxima vero,
  Verbaque ponderibus vix caritura suis!   10
Nam prope Tartareo sublime rotatus ab igni
  Ibat ad aethereas umbra perusta plagas.

ON THE SAME
(1626–30)

King James laughed at those purgatorial fires through which, forsooth, the soul must approach its supernal home. At this the triple-crowned Latin monster gnashed its teeth, and moved its ten horns in horrid threat, saying: 'Man of Britain, thou shalt not mock my mysteries unpunished; thou shalt pay for despising my religion; and if ever thou enterest the starry dome of Heaven, only through flame shall the sorry way lie open.' O how near the awful truth did you speak! A little more, and the words had not lacked their weight. For almost he went, rolled high by Tartarean fire, a burnt shade, to the upper shores.

IN EANDEM
(1626–30)

Quem modò Roma suis devoverat impia diris,
  Et Styge damnarât Taenarioque sinu,
Hunc vice mutatâ jam tollere gestit ad astra,
  Et cupit ad superos evehere usque Deos.

ON THE SAME
(1626–30)

Him whom impious Rome had vowed to her own Furies, whom she had damned to Styx and the Taenarian gulf, him, contrary-wise, she now longs to send to the stars, and seeks to exalt him to the gods on high.

IN INVENTOREM BOMBARDAE
(1626–30)

Japetionidem laudavit caeca vetustas,
  Qui tulit aetheream solis ab axe facem;
At mihi major erit, qui lurida creditur arma,
  Et trifidum fulmen surripuisse Jovi.

ON THE INVENTOR OF GUNPOWDER
(1626–30)

Blind antiquity praised Prometheus, who brought the heavenly torch from the sun; but for me he shall be greater who stole from Jove his lurid arms and three-forked thunderbolt.

AD LEONORAM ROMAE CANENTEM

(1638–39)

Angelus unicuique suus (sic credite gentes)
    Obtigit aethereis ales ab ordinibus.
Quid mirum? Leonora tibi si gloria major,
    Nam tua praesentem vox sonat ipsa Deum.
Aut Deus, aut vacui certè mens tertia coeli   5
    Per tua secretò guttura serpit agens;
Serpit agens, facilisque docet mortalia corda
    Sensim immortali assuescere posse sono.
Quòd si cuncta quidem Deus est, per cunctaque
        fusus,
    In te unâ loquitur, caetera mutus habet.   10

TO LEONORA, SINGING AT ROME

(1638–39)

To every man his angel is allotted (believe it, ye people!), his winged angel from the ethereal hierarchies. What wonder, Leonora, if a greater glory be yours? For your very voice sounds the present God. Either God Himself, or surely at least the third Mind emptying Heaven of itself, thrills mysteriously through your throat; thrills, suavely accustoming mortal hearts by tender degrees to immortal sounds. Yea, if all things be God, and He be transfused through all, yet in you alone He speaks, the rest He possesses in silence.

AD EANDEM

(1638–39)

Altera Torquatum cepit Leonora poëtam,
    Cuius ab insano cessit amore furens.
Ah miser ille tuo quantò feliciùs aevo
    Perditus, et propter te Leonora foret!
Et te Pieriâ sensisset voce canentem   5
    Aurea maternae fila movere lyrae,
Quamvis Dircaeo torsisset lumina Pentheo
    Saevior, aut totus desipuisset iners,
Tu tamen errantes caecâ vertigine sensus
    Voce eadem poteras composuisse tuâ;   10
Et poteras aegro spirans sub corde quietem
    Flexanimo cantu restituisse sibi.

TO THE SAME

(1638–39)

Another Leonora captivated Torquato, the poet, who went mad for love of her. Ah, poor fellow, how much happier had he been to lose his wits in this your day, and on your dear account, hearing you sing with Pierian voice, and wake the golden strings of your mother's lyre! Though he rolled his eyes more fiercely than Pentheus, and raved to swooning, you could have soothed his blind and reeling senses with your voice; and breathing quiet into his sick breast, restored him to himself with your soul-moving song.

AD EANDEM

(1638–39)

Credula quid liquidam Sirena Neapoli jactas,
    Claraque Parthenopes fana Achelöiados,
Littoreamque tuâ defunctam Naiada ripâ
    Corpore Chalcidico sacra dedisse rogo?
Illa quidem vivitque, et amoenâ Tibridis undâ
    Mutavit rauci murmura Pausilipi.   6
Illic Romulidûm studiis ornata secundis,
    Atque homines cantu detinet atque Deos.

TO THE SAME

(1638–39)

Why, O credulous Naples, do you boast of the renowned fanes of the Siren Parthenope, daughter of Achelous; why do you boast of having given Chalcidian funeral to the shore-nymph when she was found dead on your coasts? Behold, she lives; she has but changed the murmurs of hoarse Posilipo for the pleasant wave of Tiber. There, adorned by the love and favor of the Romans, she holds both men and gods with her singing.

APOLOGUS DE RUSTICO ET HERO

(1645?–73?)

Rusticus ex malo sapidissima poma quotan-
    nis
  Legit, et urbano lecta dedit Domino:
Hic incredibili fructûs dulcedine captus
  Malum ipsam in proprias transtulit areolas.
Hactenus illa ferax, sed longo debilis aevo, 5
  Mota solo assueto, protinùs aret iners.
Quod tandem ut patuit Domino, spe lusus
    inani,
  Damnavit celeres in sua damna manus.
Atque ait, 'Heu quantò satius fuit illa Coloni
  (Parva licet) grato dona tulisse animo! 10
Possem ego avaritiam froenare, gulamque
    voracem:
  Nunc periere mihi et foetus et ipse parens.'

A TALE OF A FARMER AND HIS LORD

(1645?–73?)

Every year a farmer harvested the best apples from a tree and gave them to his lord in the city. The latter, greatly taken with the unbelievable sweetness of the fruit, transplanted the tree itself to his own gardens. Although fruitful until now, the tree, grown weak from old age, thus removed from its accustomed soil, forthwith withered and died. When this became known to the lord, feeling deceived by his fond desire, he damned his hands because they were so quick to work against themselves. And he said, 'Alas, it would have been better to have accepted gratefully what my farmer sent me, little as it was. I might have bridled my greed and my consuming appetite. Now I have lost both the fruit and the tree itself that bore it.'

Sylvarum Liber
Poems in Various Meters

In Obitum Procancellarii Medici

Anno aetatis 16

(1626)

On the Death of the Vice-Chancellor, a Physician

In his 16th year

(1626)

The personage here celebrated in Horatian verse was John Gostlin, M.D., twice Vice-Chancellor of the University of Cambridge, whose death occurred in October, 1626, at the beginning of Milton's third academic year. The verses are devoid of the personal accent, except at the close, where we may perhaps detect a strain of warmer feeling breaking through the tone of exaggerated eulogy conventionally accepted as the proper one for such academic verse-tributes.

Parere fati discite legibus,
Manusque Parcae jam date supplices,
  Qui pendulum telluris orbem
    Iäpeti colitis nepotes.
Vos si relicto mors vaga Taenaro   5
Semel vocârit flebilis, heu morae
  Tentantur incassùm dolique;

Children of Iapetus, who inhabit the pendulous orb of earth, learn to obey the laws of fate, and raise hands of humble supplication to the Parcae. If once wandering Death coming from Tartarus calls you, alas, with woeful voice, in vain shall you resort to stratagem and delay. Everyone must go through the

Per tenebras Stygis ire certum est.
Si destinatam pellere dextera
Mortem valeret, non ferus Hercules   10
    Nessi venenatus cruore
        Aemathiâ jacuisset Oetâ.
Nec fraude turpi Palladis invidae
Vidisset occisum Ilion Hectora, aut
    Quem larva Pelidis peremit   15
        Ense Locro, Jove lacrymante.
Si triste Fatum verba Hecatëia
Fugare possint, Telegoni parens
    Vixisset infamis, potentique
        Aegiali soror usa virgâ.   20
Numenque trinum fallere si queant
Artes medentûm, ignotaque gramina,
    Non gnarus herbarum Machaon
        Eurypyli cecidisset hastâ.
Laesisset et nec te Philyreie   25
Sagitta echidnae perlita sanguine,
    Nec tela te fulmenque avitum
        Caese puer genitricis alvo.
Tuque O alumno major Apolline,
Gentis togatae cui regimen datum,   30
    Frondosa quem nunc Cirrha luget,
        Et mediis Helicon in undis,
Jam praefuisses Palladio gregi
Laetus, superstes, nec sine gloria,
    Nec puppe lustrasses Charontis   35
        Horribiles barathri recessus.
At fila rupit Persephone tua
Irata, cum te viderit artibus
    Succoque pollenti tot atris
        Faucibus eripuisse mortis.   40
Colende praeses, membra precor tua
Molli quiescant cespite, et ex tuo
    Crescant rosae, calthaeque busto,
        Purpureoque hyacinthus ore.
Sit mite de te judicium Aeaci,   45
Subrideatque Aetnaea Proserpina,
    Interque felices perennis
        Elysio spatiere campo.

shades of Styx.   If strength of arm availed to ward off destined death, fierce Hercules would not have fallen on Macedonian Oeta, poisoned by the blood of Nessus; nor would Ilion have seen Hector slain through the base guile of envious Pallas; nor Sarpedon, whom the phantom of Achilles slew with the Locrian sword, while Jove shed tears.   If words of witchcraft could forestall Fate, wicked Circe, parent of Telegonus, would have lived on, and the sister of Absyrtus, Medea, would still wield her potent wand.   If arts of medicine and knowledge of mysterious plants could thwart the triple goddesses, Machaon, the son of Aesculapius, with all his skill in herbs, would not have fallen before the spear of Eurypylus; nor would the arrow of Hercules, smeared with the blood of Hydra, have undone thee, Chiron; nor wouldst thou, Aesculapius, cut at thy birth from thy mother's womb, have perished by the bolts of thy grandfather's thunder.

And if lore in medicine availed, you, Vice-Chancellor, to whom was given direction over the gowned throng of the schools, and who were more learned than your nurseling Apollo, would not now be mourned by the leafy city of Cirrha at Parnassus' foot, nor by Helicon sitting amid its springs.   You would still survive glad and honored to have charge over Pallas's flock.   You would not have gone in Charon's boat to visit the awful abyss.   But Persephone slit the thread of your life, angry when she saw how many lives you snatched from the black jaws of death by the art of your potent medicines.   Loved master, I pray that your limbs may rest quiet beneath the gentle sod, and that from your grave roses may spring, and marigold, and the purple-mouthed hyacinth.   May Aeacus pronounce judgment mildly on you, and Proserpina, maid of Aetna, give you a smile, and may you walk forever in the Elysian fields among the blessed.

In Quintum Novembris

Anno aetatis 17

(*1626–28*)

On the Fifth of November [Anniversary of the Gunpowder Plot]

In his 17th year

(*1626–28*)

The Gunpowder Plot, with the accessories which popular bigotry and ignorance accumulated around it, was long a favorite subject for academic versifying. The most elaborate effort in this kind is the *Locustae*, or *Apollyonists*, of Phineas Fletcher, a Cambridge University poet whose work had a traceable influence upon Milton's later production. After Fletcher's *Locustae*, the present poem, written in 1626, for the twenty-first anniversary of Guy Fawkes's Day, is perhaps the most notable. It is a very youthful performance, turgid in style and unrestrained in its vituperation of Catholicism, but it has certain Miltonic qualities notwithstanding, oddly distorted by the double convention of matter and of manner to which the young poet is here subjected.

Jam pius extremâ veniens Iäcobus ab arcto
Teucrigenas populos, latéque patentia regna
Albionum tenuit, jamque inviolabile foedus
Sceptra Caledoniis conjunxerat Anglica Scotis:
Pacificusque novo felix divesque sedebat   5
In solio, occultique doli securus et hostis:
Cum ferus ignifluo regnans Acheronte tyrannus,
Eumenidum pater, aethereo vagus exul Olympo,
Forte per immensum terrarum erraverat orbem,   9
Dinumerans sceleris socios, vernasque fideles,
Participes regni post funera moesta futuros;
Hic tempestates medio ciet aëre diras,
Illic unanimes odium struit inter amicos,
Armat et invictas in mutua viscera gentes;
Regnaque olivifera vertit florentia pace,   15
Et quoscunque videt purae virtutis amantes,
Hos cupit adjicere imperio, fraudumque magister
Tentat inaccessum sceleri corrumpere pectus,
Insidiasque locat tacitas, cassesque latentes
Tendit, ut incautos rapiat, seu Caspia tigris
Insequitur trepidam deserta per avia praedam   21
Nocte sub illuni, et somno nictantibus astris.
Talibus infestat populos Summanus et urbes
Cinctus caeruleae fumanti turbine flammae.

Good King James, coming from the far north, had begun his rule over the descendants of Trojan Brut and the broad realms of Albion, and inviolable treaty had joined the scepters of England and Scotland. Rich, happy, and at peace, he was sitting on his new throne, recking naught of open enemies or secret guile. But the fierce tyrant who rules over Acheron's fiery flood, the father of the Eumenides, the restless outcast from Heaven, was wandering through the stretches of the world, numbering his associates in evil and his faithful slaves, sharers after death in his sad realms. Here he rouses dire tempests in mid-air; there he puts hatred between loving friends. He incites invincible nations to turn the sword against each other's breast, and lays waste kingdoms that bloom with the olive of peace. Whomever he sees in love with purity and virtue, he longs to subdue to his rule; and he tries with all his master-arts of fraud to corrupt hearts into which evil has no entrance. He lays silent plots, stretches hidden snares, to seize the incautious; like the Caspian tiger, who follows his timid prey through pathless wilds under a moonless sky where the stars blink drowsily. With no worse destruction does Summanus, the Etruscan thunder-god, come upon the cities and the peoples, wreathed in a whirlwind of smoke and blue flame.

Jamque fluentisonis albentia rupibus arva 25
Apparent, et terra Deo dilecta marino,
Cui nomen dederat quondam Neptunia proles
Amphitryoniaden qui non dubitavit atrocem
Aequore tranato furiali poscere bello,
Ante expugnatae crudelia saecula Troiae. 30
  At simul hanc opibusque et festâ pace
        beatam
Aspicit, et pingues donis Cerealibus agros,
Quodque magis doluit, venerantem numina
        veri
Sancta Dei populum, tandem suspiria rupit
Tartareos ignes et luridum olentia sulphur. 35
Qualia Trinacriâ trux ab Jove clausus in Aetna
Efflat tabifico monstrosus ab ore Typhoeus.
Ignescunt oculi, stridetque adamantinus ordo
Dentis, ut armorum fragor, ictaque cuspide
        cuspis.
Atque 'Pererrato solum hoc lacrymabile
        mundo   40
Inveni,' dixit; 'gens haec mihi sola rebellis,
Contemtrixque jugi, nostrâque potentior arte.
Illa tamen, mea si quicquam tentamina pos-
        sunt,
Non feret hoc impune diu, non ibit inulta,'
Hactenus; et piceis liquido natat aëre pen-
        nis;   45
Quà volat, adversi praecursant agmine venti,
Densantur nubes, et crebra tonitrua fulgent.
  Jamque pruinosas velox superaverat Alpes,
Et tenet Ausoniae fines, à parte sinistrâ
Nimbifer Appenninus erat, priscique Sa-
        bini,   50
Dextra veneficiis infamis Hetruria, nec non
Te furtiva Tibris Thetidi videt oscula dantem;
Hinc Mavortigenae consistit in arce Quirini.
Reddiderant dubiam jam sera crepuscula
        lucem,
Cum circumgreditur totam Tricoronifer ur-
        bem,   55
Panificosque deos portat, scapulisque viro-
        rum
Evehitur, praeeunt submisso poplite reges,
Et mendicantum series longissima fratrum;
Cereaque in manibus gestant funalia caeci,
Cimmeriis nati in tenebris, vitamque tra-
        hentes.   60
Templa dein multis subeunt lucentia taedis
(Vesper erat sacer iste Petro) fremitusque
        canentum
Saepe tholos implet vacuos, et inane locorum.

And now, in his flight, Satan sees appear the fields girdled by white wave-beaten cliffs, the land loved by the sea-god, named of old from Neptune's son Albion, who feared not to cross the sea and give furious battle to fierce Hercules, before the cruel cycles of defeated Troy. He gazes on this land, happy in wealth and festal peace, and on the fields rich laden with grain, and — what irks him more — on a people worshiping the holy power of the true God. At the sight he breaks forth in sighs that flame with hellish fire and reek with lurid sulphur, such sighs as the fell monster Typhoeus, shut up in Trinacrian Aetna by Jupiter, breathes from his pestilential mouth. His eyes blaze and the adamant row of his grinding teeth sounds like the clashing of arms and the shock of spear against spear. 'This,' he says, 'is the one lamentable sight I have seen in my wanderings through the world. This people alone is rebellious against me, scorning my yoke and stronger than my arts. They shall not long do so with impunity, if my efforts are of any avail; this land shall not go unpunished for long, or long escape my vengeance.' And as he ceases to speak, his pitchy wings swim through the liquid air. Wherever he flies, rush contrary winds in hosts, clouds gather, and lightning flashes thick.

Now his swift flight had carried him beyond the rimy Alps to the borders of Italy. On his left hand were the ancient land of the Sabines and the cloud-wrapped Apennine; on his right Etruria, ill-famed for its poisoners. Thee too, Tiber, he saw, giving furtive kisses to Thetis. Soon he stood on the citadel of Mars's son Quirinus, in the dubious twilight. Through the great city the Triple-Crowned Sovereign was going in procession, borne on the shoulders of men, and carrying the gods of bread. Kings bowed the knee before him; long lines of begging brothers bore in their hands wax tapers, blind souls all, born and bred in Cimmerian darkness! Soon they entered the temples which shone with their many torches (it was the Holy Eve of Peter), and the voices of the singers filled the hollow domes and empty spaces with noise like the

Qualiter exululat Bromius, Bromiique caterva,
Orgia cantantes in Echionio Aracyntho,   65
Dum tremit attonitus vitreis Asopus in undis,
Et procul ipse cavâ responsat rupe Cithaeron.
His igitur tandem solenni more peractis,
Nox senis amplexus Erebi taciturna reliquit,
Praecipitesque impellit equos stimulante
    flagello,   70
Captum oculis Typhlonta, Melanchaetemque
    ferocem,
Atque Acherontaeo prognatam patre Siopen
Torpidam, et hirsutis horrentem Phrica
    capillis.
Interea regum domitor, Phlegetontius
    haeres
  Ingreditur thalamos (neque enim secretus
    adulter   75
Producit steriles molli sine pellice noctes)
At vix compositos somnus claudebat ocellos,
Cum niger umbrarum dominus, rectorque
    silentum,
Praedatorque hominum falsâ sub imagine
    tectus
Astitit, assumptis micuerunt tempora canis,
Barba sinus promissa tegit, cineracea longo 81
Syrmate verrit humum vestis, pendetque
    cucullus
Vertice de raso, et ne quicquam desit ad artes,
Cannabeo lumbos constrinxit fune salaces.
Tarda fenestratis figens vestigia calceis.   85
Talis uti fama est, vastâ Franciscus eremo
Tetra vagabatur solus per lustra ferarum,
Sylvestrique tulit genti pia verba salutis
Impius, atque lupos domuit, Libycosque
    leones.
  Subdolus at tali Serpens velatus amictu   90
Solvit in has fallax ora execrantia voces;
'Dormis, nate? Etiamne tuos sopor opprimit
    artus?
Immemor O fidei, pecorumque oblite tuorum!
Dum cathedram venerande tuam, diademaque
    triplex   94
Ridet Hyperboreo gens barbara nata sub axe,
Dumque pharetrati spernunt tua jura Britanni:
Surge, age, surge piger, Latius quem Caesar
    adorat,
Cui reserata patet convexi janua caeli,
Turgentes animos, et fastus frange procaces,
Sacrilegique sciant, tua quid maledictio
    possit,   100
Et quid Apostolicae possit custodia clavis; .

howling of Bacchus and his crew, when they
hymn their orgies on Theban Aracynthus,
while Asopus trembles astonished in his
glassy waves, and even Cithaeron afar off
answers from his hollow cliff.

When at last these rites of customary pomp
were done, Night left silently the arms of old
Erebus, and with flaying whip, drove her
four horses headlong across the sky, Blind-
Eyes, and fierce Black-Hair, and sullen Silence
born of hell, and Shudder wrapped in her
streaming mane.

Meanwhile the subduer of kings and heir
of Phlegethon entered his bridal chamber
(for the secret adulterer prolongs no sterile
nights *sans* a gentle mistress at his side); but
scarcely had sleep sealed his eyes when the
black lord of the shades, ruler of the silences
and preyer upon men, stood in a false shape
at his bedside. His temples shone with
show of snowy hair; a long beard covered his
breast; his ashen vestment swept the ground
in a long train. From his shaven head hung
a cowl; and as a last touch of art, he had
bound his salt loins with a rope of hemp, and
moved his latticed sandals in slow steps.
Such a figure was Francis the eremite, when
he wandered, as they tell, alone, through the
dark haunts of wild beasts, subduing wolves
and Libyan lions, and bearing to the forest
people, impiously, the pious words of salvation.

Thus deceitfully clad, the false Serpent
opened his execrable lips and spake: 'Dost
thou sleep, my son? Does slumber oppress
even thy limbs? O unmindful of the Faith,
and forgetful of thy flock! Canst thou sleep
while a barbarous people by the North Pole
laugh at thy throne and thy triple diadem,
thou whom all should venerate? Canst thou
sleep while the quiver-bearing Britons spurn
thy laws? Come, arise! arise! thou slothful
one, whom the Holy Roman Caesar adores,
and to whom the gate of the vaulted sky lies
all unbarred. Break their pride and shameless insolence! Let their sacrilegious eyes see
what thy malediction can do, and what the
custody of the apostolic key. Take thought

Et memor Hesperiae disjectam ulciscere
  classem,
Mersaque Iberorum lato vexilla profundo,
Sanctorumque cruci tot corpora fixa pro-
  brosae,
Thermodoontéa nuper regnante puella.   105
At tu si tenero mavis torpescere lecto
Crescentesque negas hosti contundere vires,
Tyrrhenum implebit numeroso milite pontum,
Signaque Aventino ponet fulgentia colle:
Relliquias veterum franget, flammisque cre-
  mabit,   110
Sacraque calcabit pedibus tua colla profanis,
Cujus gaudebant soleïs dare basia reges.
Nec tamen hunc bellis et aperto Marte
  lacesses,
Irritus ille labor, tu callidus utere fraude,
Quaelibet haereticis disponere retia fas est; 115
Jamque ad consilium extremis rex magnus ab
  oris
Patricios vocat, et procerum de stirpe creatos,
Grandaevosque patres trabeâ, canisque ve-
  rendos;
Hos tu membratim poteris conspergere in
  auras,   119
Atque dare in cineres, nitrati pulveris igne
Aedibus injecto, quà convenere, sub imis.
Protinus ipse igitur quoscunque habet Anglia
  fidos
Propositi, factique mone, quisquámne tuorum
Audebit summi non jussa facessere Papae.
Perculsosque metu subito, casúmque stu-
  pentes   125
Invadat vel Gallus atrox, vel saevus Iberus.
Saecula sic illic tandem Mariana redibunt,
Tuque in belligeros iterum dominaberis
  Anglos.
Et nequid timeas, divos divasque secundas
Accipe, quotque tuis celebrantur numina
  fastis.'   130
Dixit et adscitos ponens malefidus amictus
Fugit ad infandam, regnum illaetabile, Lethen.
  Jam rosea Eoas pandens Tithonia portas
Vestit inauratas redeunti lumine terras;
Maestaque adhuc nigri deplorans funera
  nati   135
Irrigat ambrosiis montana cacumina guttis;
Cum somnos pepulit stellatae janitor aulae
Nocturnos visus, et somnia grata revolvens.
  Est locus aeternâ septus caligine noctis,
Vasta ruinosi quondam fundamina tecti,

to avenge the scattered armada of Spain, the
Iberian standards overwhelmed in the broad
deep, and all the bodies of thy saints who
died on the ignominious cross during the late
reign of the Amazonian queen.[1] If thou
preferrest to drowse in thy soft bed and refuse
to crush the growing strength of the enemy,
he will soon fill the Tyrrhenian Sea with his
ships, and plant his shining standards on the
Aventine hill. He will break the relics of
old saints and burn them with fire. He will
plant his profane heel on thy sacred neck,
thou whose sandals kings once rejoiced to
kiss. But do not assault him with open war;
that would be labor lost. Rather use cunning
and fraud; it is righteous to set any kind of
trap for heretics. Just now their king calls
from far and wide his great men to council,
his lords and commons, and aged bishops
venerable with robe and snowy hair. These
thou canst blow limb from limb, their ashes
thou canst scatter to the wind, by placing
nitrous-powder beneath the building where
they convene. Straightway therefore do
thou admonish of the proposed deed all those
in England who are still faithful. Who of
thy servants will dare to refuse obedience to
his sovereign Pope? Then, when the nation is
seized with panic terror and stupefied by the
catastrophe, let either the fierce Gaul or the
savage Spaniard invade them, and the days of
Queen Mary will at last return. Once more
thou shalt rule over the martial English.
And, that thou mayest put away all fear, I
tell thee that all the gods and goddesses, as
many deities as thy church-calendar celebrates, favor the plan.' So speaking, the
traitor laid aside the dress he had assumed,
and fled to the joyless realms of Lethe.

Now rosy dawn, opening the eastern gates,
gilded the earth with returning light. Sorrowing for the death of her black son, Memnon, she sprinkled the mountaintops with
ambrosial tears. The porter of the starry
halls drove away sleep, and rolled back the
pleasant dreams and visions of the night.

There is a place girt eternally with the
darkness of night, the vast foundations of a

[1] The reference is to the persecution of the Catholics
under Elizabeth.

Nunc torvi spelunca phoni, prodotaeque
    bilinguis   141
Effera quos uno peperit discordia partu.
Hic inter caementa jacent praeruptaque saxa,
Ossa inhumata virûm, et trajecta cadavera
    ferro;
Hic dolus intortis semper sedet ater ocellis,
Jurgiaque, et stimulis armata calumnia
    fauces.   146
Et furor, atque viae moriendi mille videntur
Et timor, exanguisque locum circumvolat
    horror,
Perpetuoque leves per muta silentia manes,
Exululat tellus et sanguine conscia stag-
    nat.   150
Ipsi etiam pavidi latitant penetralibus antri
Et phonos, et prodotes, nulloque sequente per
    antrum
Antrum horrens, scopulosum, atrum feralibus
    umbris
Diffugiunt sontes, et retrò lumina vortunt,
Hos pugiles Romae per saecula longa
    fideles   155
Evocat antistes Babylonius, atque ita fatur.
'Finibus occiduis circumfusum incolit aequor
Gens exosa mihi, prudens natura negavit
Indignam penitus nostro conjungere mundo:
Illuc, sic jubeo, celeri contendite gressu, 160
Tartareoque leves difflentur pulvere in auras
Et rex et pariter satrapae, scelerata propago
Et quotquot fidei caluere cupidine verae
Consilii socios adhibete, operisque minis-
    tros.'
Finierat, rigidi cupidè paruere gemelli. 165
  Interea longo flectens curvamine coelos
Despicit aethereâ dominus qui fulgurat arce,
Vanaque perversae ridet conamina turbae,
Atque sui causam populi volet ipse tueri.
  Esse ferunt spatium, quà distat ab Aside
    terra   170
Fertilis Europe, et spectat Mareotidas undas;
Hic turris posita est Titanidos ardua famae
Aerea, lata, sonans, rutilis vicinior astris
Quàm superimpositum vel Athos vel Pelion
    Ossae
Mille fores aditusque patent, totidemque
    fenestrae,   175
Amplaque per tenues translucent atria muros;
Excitat hic varios plebs agglomerata susurros;
Qualiter instrepitant circum mulctralia
    bombis

building long since given to ruin, now the cave of fierce Murder and double-tongued Treachery, whom the hag Discord brought forth at one birth. Here amid heaps of rubble and broken stones lie the unburied bones of men, corpses impaled on steel. Here forever sits Craft, black, with distorted eyes; and Contention; and Calumny with viper jaws; and Fury; and Fear; and a thousand types of death. Pale Horror flies about the place. Perpetually through the silences howl the insubstantial ghosts. The conscious earth is soaked with blood. In the inmost recesses of the cavern Murder and Treachery lurk and tremble, and though no one pursues them, on they go through the cavern, the gruesome, rocky cavern, black with lethal shades; guiltily they flee, ever casting looks behind.

These champions of Rome, faithful through long ages, the Babylonish priest calls together, and addresses thus: 'On the western confines of the world dwells a people hateful to me; their land is sea-girt, for scrupulous Nature has not held it worthy to be joined closely to our world. Thither, I command you, hasten quickly. As many men as you find burning with desire of the true faith, take them to you as helpers and associates; then, with hell-powder blow the king and his chiefs, vile race that they are, into thin air.' He ended, and the harsh twins [Murder and Treachery] obeyed him eagerly.

Meantime the Lord, who moveth the heavens in a wide circle and lighteneth from the ethereal citadel, looks down, and smiles at the vain plottings of the erring crowd, and will himself safeguard his people's cause.

Men tell of a place, midway between fertile Europe and the Asian land, looking toward the waters of Lake Maeotis. Here is placed the tower of Rumor, daughter of the Titan Earth. Of brass is the great tower, broad and resonant, nearer the ruddy stars than Ossa piled high with Pelion or Athos. A thousand doors and entrances stand open, and a thousand windows. Through the thin beaten walls gleam the ample courts within. Here crowds of people make a various whispering, like the buzzing of swarms of flies about the milk pails or through the wattles of the

Agmina muscarum, aut texto per ovilia
      junco,   179
Dum Canis aestivum coeli petit ardua culmen
Ipsa quidem summâ sedet ultrix matris in
      arce,
Auribus innumeris cinctum caput eminet olli,
Queis sonitum exiguum trahit, atque levis-
      sima captat
Murmura, ab extremis patuli confinibus orbis.
Nec tot Aristoride servator inique juvencae
Isidos, immiti volvebas lumina vultu,   186
Lumina non unquam tacito nutantia somno,
Lumina subjectas late spectantia terras.
Istis illa solet loca luce carentia saepe
Perlustrare, etiam radianti impervia soli. 190
Millenisque loquax auditaque visaque linguis
Cuilibet effundit temeraria, veráque mendax
Nunc minuit, modò confictis sermonibus
      auget.
Sed tamen a nostro meruisti carmine laudes
Fama, bonum quo non aliud veracius ullum,
Nobis digna cani, nec te memorasse pige-
      bit   196
Carmine tam longo, servati scilicet Angli
Officiis vaga diva tuis, tibi reddimus aequa.
Te Deus aeternos motu qui temperat ignes,
Fulmine praemisso alloquitur, terrâque tre-
      mente: 200
'Fama siles? an te latet impia Papistarum
Conjurata cohors in meque meosque Britan-
      nos,
Et nova sceptrigero caedes meditata Iäcobo:'
Nec plura, illa statim sensit mandata
      Tonantis,
Et satis antè fugax stridentes induit alas, 205
Induit et variis exilia corpora plumis;
Dextra tubam gestat Temesaeo ex aere sono-
      ram.
Nec mora jam pennis cedentes remigat auras,
Atque parum est cursu celeres praevertere
      nubes,
Jam ventos, jam solis equos post terga reli-
      quit: 210
Et primò Angliacas solito de more per urbes
Ambiguas voces, incertaque murmura spargit,
Mox arguta dolos, et detestabile vulgat
Proditionis opus, nec non facta horrida dictu,
Authoresque addit sceleris, nec garrula cae-
      cis   215
Insidiis loca structa silet; stupuere relatis,
Et pariter juvenes, pariter tremuere puellae,

sheepcotes, when the Dog Star climbs to the summit of the summer sky. Throned at the top of her citadel sits Rumor herself, avenger of her mother, Earth; about her head grow innumerable ears, by whose aid she gathers in the slightest sound, the lightest murmur, from the ends of the broad earth. More eyes she has than thou, Argus, Arestor's son, unjust keeper of the cow Io, eyes that never close in sleep, but continually look abroad over the lands beneath; with them she is wont to search through places void of light, impervious even to the sun's rays. With a thousand tongues she pours out in uncon-sidering speech to any chance comer all that she sees or hears, now deceitfully making less the truth, now swelling it with imagined fabrications.

But, for all that, O Rumor, thou hast merited well at our hands, by reason of one good deed, than which there was never a truer. Thou art worthy to be praised in my song; I shall not be reproached for the length of my celebration of thee. For through thy offices, uncertain goddess, the English were saved, and we should render thee fit recom-pense. God, who tempers with motion the eternal fires, sent forth His thunderbolt, and while the earth shook therewith, thus spake to thee: 'Rumor, art thou silent? Markest thou not the impious brood of Papists con-spired against me and my Britains, or the novel murder meditated against King James?' No more He spake, but straightway she heeds the mandates of the Thunderer; and, swift before, now she puts on strident wings, puts on a light body feathered with motley plum-age, and in her right hand takes a horn of sounding brass. She tarries not. Her wings oar the yielding atmosphere. 'Tis not enough for her to pass in flight the driving clouds; she leaves the winds behind now, and now the horses of the Sun. First, as is her wont, she scatters vague whispers, uncertain rumors, through the English cities; then with clear voice publishes the designs of the enemy and his detestable work of guile; she reveals the facts in all their horror and adds in her garrulity the very authors of the crime and the place prepared for hidden treachery. At her tale young men stand stupefied, maidens

Effaetique senes pariter, tantaeque ruinae
Sensus ad aetatem subitò penetraverat om-
  nem
Attamen interea populi miserescit ab alto   220
Aethereus pater, et crudelibus obstitit ausis
Papicolûm; capti poenas raptantur ad acres;
At pia thura Deo, et grati solvuntur hono-
  res;
Compita laeta focis genialibus omnia fumant;
Turba choros juvenilis agit: Quintoque
  Novembris   225
Nulla dies toto occurrit celebratior anno.

tremble, and weak old men; the sense of the awful ruin to come overwhelms all ages equally. But meanwhile the Heavenly Father pities this people from on high, and frustrates the daring cruelty of the Pope-worshipers. The plotters are captured and dragged to torture. Incense and honors are offered to God in gratitude; the merry crossroads smoke with genial bonfires. The throngs of young men dance. No day in all the year is more celebrated than the Fifth of November.

In Obitum Praesulis Eliensis

Anno aetatis 17

(*1626*)

On the Death of the Bishop of Ely

In his 17th year

(*1626*)

This poem is parallel, in every respect except that of verse-form, with *Elegy III* on the death of Dr. Lancelot Andrewes, Bishop of Winchester. Dr. Nicholas Felton, Bishop of Ely, was likewise a Cambridge man, and had likewise been Master of Pembroke. His death occurred in October, 1626. No connection of a personal sort is known to have existed between Dr. Felton and Milton, though the tone of the poem might seem to imply such a connection. The concluding verses, in spite of their somewhat conventional phrasing, are premonitory of Milton's power to suggest the vastness of cosmic space.

Adhuc madentes rore squalebant genae,
  Et sicca nondum lumina;
Adhuc liquentis imbre turgebant salis,
  Quem nuper effudi pius,
Dum maesta charo justa persolvi rogo   5
  Wintoniensis praesulis.
Cum centilinguis Fama (proh semper mali
  Cladisque vera nuntia)
Spargit per urbes divitis Britanniae,
  Populosque Neptuno satos,   10
Cessisse morti, et ferreis sororibus
  Te generis humani decus,
Qui rex sacrorum illâ fuisti in insulâ
  Quae nomen Anguillae tenet.
Tunc inquietum pectus irâ protinus   15
  Ebulliebat fervidâ,
Tumulis potentem saepe devovens deam:
  Nec vota Naso in Ibida
Concepit alto diriora pectore,

My cheeks were still damp and stained, and my swollen eyes not yet dry from the salt tears I had shed in doing my sad duty over the precious bier of Winchester's bishop, when hundred tongued Rumor (O, always true messenger of evil and disaster!) spread through the cities of rich Britain and among the people sprung from Neptune, the news that you, who were chief pontiff of religion in the isle that bears the name of Ely, had yielded to Death and the dire Sisters. Then straightway ire boiled in my unquiet breast, and often I cursed the potent goddess of the grave, with curses more savage than Ovid conjured up against Ibis. More sparingly did

Graiusque vates parciùs   20
Turpem Lycambis execratus est dolum,
    Sponsamque Neobolen suam.
At ecce diras ipse dum fundo graves,
    Et imprecor neci necem,
Audisse tales videor attonitus sonos   25
    Leni, sub aurâ, flamine:
'Caecos furores pone, pone vitream
    Bilemque et irritas minas,
Quid temerè violas non nocenda numina,
    Subitoque ad iras percita.   30
Non est, ut arbitraris elusus miser,
    Mors atra Noctis filia,
Erebóve patre creta, sive Erinnye,
    Vastóve nata sub Chao:
Ast illa caelo missa stellato, Dei   35
    Messes ubique colligit;
Animasque mole carneâ reconditas
    In lucem et auras evocat:
Ut cum fugaces excitant Horae diem
    Themidos Jovisque filiae;   40
Et sempiterni ducit ad vultus patris;
    At justa raptat impios
Sub regna furvi luctuosa Tartari,
    Sedesque subterraneas
Hanc ut vocantem laetus audivi, citò   45
    Foedum reliqui carcerem,
Volatilesque faustus inter milites
    Ad astra sublimis feror:
Vates ut olim raptus ad coelum senex
    Auriga currus ignei,   50
Non me Boötis terruere lucidi
    Sarraca tarda frigore, aut
Formidolosi Scorpionis brachia,
    Non ensis Orion tuus.
Praetervolavi fulgidi solis globum,   55
    Longéque sub pedibus deam
Vidi triformem, dum coercebat suos
    Fraenis dracones aureis.
Erraticorum siderum per ordines,
    Per lacteas vehor plagas,   60
Velocitatem saepe miratus novam,
    Donec nitentes ad fores
Ventum est Olympi, et regiam chrystalli-
    nam, et
    Stratum smaragdis atrium.
Sed hic tacebo, nam quis effari queat   65
    Oriundus humano patre
Amoenitates illius loci, mihi
    Sat est in aeternum frui.'

the Grecian bard Archilochus curse the treachery of Lycambes, and Neobule, his own betrothed. But lo, while I was pouring forth heavy curses and was calling down destruction upon the Destroyer, methought I heard astonied these words, borne by a gentle breath beneath the breeze: 'Quench thy blind wrath; quench thy gleaming bile and thy unavailing threats. Why dost thou rashly violate the powers which cannot be harmed, but which may be moved to sudden wrath? Death is not, as thou deemest, poor deluded soul, the dark daughter of Night, born of Erebus or Erinys in the vasts of Chaos. No, she is sent from starry heaven to reap everywhere the fields of God. Souls hidden under the weight of flesh she calls into the air and the light, even as the fleet Hours, daughters of Themis and Jove, bring forth day from night. And these souls she leads before the face of the Sempiternal Father; but the souls of the impious she justly hurries away to the mournful realms of savage Hell, and the subterranean abodes. When I heard her voice calling me I rejoiced; straightway I left my foul prison of flesh, and in the midst of winged soldiery was borne in blessedness to the stars, as of old the aged prophet was rapt to heaven charioted in fire. The wain of bright Boötes, slow with cold, did not appall me, nor the arms of the fearful Scorpion, nor thy sword, Orion. I sped past the globe of the fulgid sun; far beneath my feet I saw the tri-form goddess of the moon tugging at the golden reins of her dragons. Through the ranks of the erratic stars, and the milky stretches of space, I was borne, wondering at the novel speed of my flight, until I came to the glittering portals of Olympus, and the palace of crystal, and the courts paved with jasper and malachite. But here I will be silent, for who born of mortal father can tell the pleasures of that place? It is enough for me to enjoy it forever.'

Naturam non Pati Senium

(*1628*)

That Nature is not Subject to Old Age

(*1628*)

It is probable, from a letter (*Fam. Ep. 3*) written by Milton to Alexander Gill, his former master at Saint Paul's School, that this piece was composed to oblige a Fellow of Christ's College, who was called upon to furnish some verse of the kind for the commencement exercises of 1628. Milton says: 'A certain Fellow of our college, who had to act as Respondent in the philosophical disputation at this Commencement, chanced to entrust to my puerility the composition of the verses required by the annual custom to be written on the questions in dispute, being himself already long past the age for trifles of that sort, and more intent on serious things.' The 'Respondent in the philosophical disputation' was a person chosen from among the candidates for the Master's degree, to uphold a given thesis, and defend it against the attacks of two opponents, similarly chosen. He was required to furnish a kind of poetical illustration of his thesis, to be distributed among the audience before the disputation began. The question here dealt with, that of the ultimate decay or eternal youthfulness of Nature, was a popular one in the seventeenth century, philosophic thought being about equally divided upon it. Milton's verses are a vigorous poetic protest against the theory of degeneracy, conceived with a fervor of conviction and a strength of imagery which gives the trifle a permanent significance. Milton was at the end of his fourth academic year at the time of writing, and hence in the twentieth year of his age. The poem may have been printed by the University in 1628, and thus have the distinction of being the first poem of Milton's to be printed.

Heu quàm perpetuis erroribus acta fatiscit
Avia mens hominum, tenebrisque immersa
    profundis
Oedipodioniam volvit sub pectore noctem!
Quae vesana suis metiri facta deorum
Audet, et incisas leges adamenta perenni   5
Assimilare suis, nulloque solubile saeclo
Consilium fati perituris alligat horis.
  Ergóne marcescet sulcantibus obsita rugis
Naturae facies, et rerum publica mater
Omniparum contracta uterum sterilescet ab
    aevo?   10
Et se fassa senem malè certis passibus ibit
Sidereum tremebunda caput? num tetra
    vetustas
Annorumque aeterna fames, squalorque situs-
    que
Sidera vexabunt? an et insatiabile tempus
Esuriet caelum, rapietque in viscera patrem?
Heu, potuitne suas imprudens Jupiter arces 16
Hoc contra munîsse nefas, et temporis isto
Exemisse malo, gyrosque dedisse perennes?
Ergo erit ut quandoque sono dilapsa tremendo

Ah, how man's roving mind is driven and wearied by perpetual error, involved in profound shade and night such as blind Oedipus knew! Foolishly he dares to measure the deeds of the gods by his own, to his own laws he likens those laws graven on eternal adamant; and the will of Fate, never to be changed or undone, he links with his own perishable days. Shall the face of Nature wither, and be furrowed with wrinkles? Shall the universal Mother grow sterile with age, and her all-creating womb shrivel to nothingness? Shall she go stricken with eld, her steps uncertain, her starry head palsied? Shall the hideousness of age, and filth, and wasting, and the eternal famine of the years, vex the stars? Shall insatiable Time eat up the sky and devour his own father? Alas, could not improvident Jove have warded off this evil from the orbs of Heaven, made them exempt from this sickness of Time, and given them perpetual revolutions? 'Tis true, then, that a day will come when with fearful

Convexi tabulata ruant, atque obvius ictu   20
Stridat uterque polus, superâque ut Olympius
    aulâ
Decidat, horribilisque retectâ Gorgone Pallas.
Qualis in Aegaeam proles Junonia Lemnon
Deturbata sacro cecidit de limine caeli.   24
Tu quoque Phoebe tui casus imitabere nati
Praecipiti curru, subitáque ferere ruinâ
Pronus, et extinctâ fumabit lampade Nereus,
Et dabit attonito feralia sibila ponto.
Tunc etiam aërei divulsis sedibus Haemi
Dissultabit apex, imoque allisa barathro   30
Terrebunt Stygium dejecta Ceraunia Ditem
In superos quibus usus erat, fraternaque bella.

    At pater omnipotens fundatis fortius astris
Consuluit rerum summae, certoque peregit
Pondere fatorum lances, atque ordine
    summo   35
Singula perpetuum jussit servare tenorem.
Volvitur hinc lapsu mundi rota prima diurno;
Raptat et ambitos sociâ vertigine caelos.
Tardior haud solito Saturnus, et acer ut olim
Fulmineum rutilat cristatâ casside Mavors.
Floridus aeternùm Phoebus juvenile corus-
    cat,   41
Nec fovet effoetas loca per declivia terras
Devexo temone Deus; sed semper amicâ
Luce potens eadem currit per signa rotarum,
Surgit odoratis pariter formosus ab Indis   45
Aethereum pecus albenti qui cogit Olympo
Mane vocans, et serus agens in pascua coeli,
Temporis et gemino dispertit regna colore.
Fulget, obitque vices alterno Delia cornu,
Caeruleumque ignem paribus complectitur
    ulnis.   50
Nec variant elementa fidem, solitóque
    fragore
Lurida perculsas jaculantur fulmina rupes.
Nec per inane furit leviori murmure Corus,
Stringit et armiferos aequali horrore Gelonos
Trux Aquilo, spiratque hyemem, nimbosque
    volutat.   55
Utque solet, Siculi diverberat ima Pelori
Rex maris, et raucâ circumstrepit aequora
    conchâ
Oceani Tubicen, nec vastâ mole minorem

sound the floor of Heaven shall be broken up, when either pole shall shriek against the stroke, as Olympian Jove falls from his supernal dwelling, and dread Pallas, with the Gorgon uncovered on her shield; even as Vulcan, thrown from Heaven's brink, fell down to Aegean Lemnos. Thou too, O Sun-god, shalt imitate the calamity of thy son Phaethon and fall headlong from thy chariot, borne down in sudden ruin, and with thy quenched lamp the Ocean shall smoke and give forth deathly hisses from his waves. Then, torn from its foundation, the airy summit of Mt. Haemus shall topple down; the Ceraunian mountains once used as missiles in the fratricidal wars of the gods shall crash into the lowest gulf, and terrify Stygian Dis.

Nay, not so. The omnipotent Father, planning for his universe, has more strongly established the stars. The scales of Fate He has balanced with surer weights. He has commanded all things in the great order to preserve unendingly their even way. Wherefore, the first wheel of the Universe [the Primum Mobile] rolls diurnal, and communicates its dizzy motion to the spheres within. Saturn goes no slower than his wont, and eager as of old fulminates red-crested Mars. Florid Phoebus shines ever young, nor does he deflect his team down declivities of sky to warm abandoned places of the earth; but always through the same zodiacal signs he goes charioting, strong with friendly light. The morning and the evening star rise lovely as of yore from the odorous East, shepherding their ethereal flocks on the blanching plains of heaven; in the morning they call home the stars, in the evening lead them out to pasture; disparting the realms of time with twin variety of light. As of old the moon shines through the changing phases of her horns, clasping with the same arms her cerulean fire. The elements, too, keep faith. With the same old crash the lurid lightning smites the cliffs. With undiminished roar Caurus rages through the void, and savage Aquilo flings its same horror of snow and storm against the martial Scythians. The Sea-king still lashes the bases of Sicilian Pelorus; the trumpeter of ocean still sounds his hoarse conch over the waters. With the same vast

Aegaeona ferunt dorso Balearica cete.
Sed neque Terra tibi saecli vigor ille vetusti
Priscus abest, servatque suum Narcissus
      odorem,   61
Et puer ille suum tenet et puer ille decorem
Phoebe tuusque et Cypri tuus, nec ditior olim
Terra datum sceleri celavit montibus aurum
Conscia, vel sub aquis gemmas. Sic denique
      in aevum   65
Ibit cunctarum series justissima rerum,
Donec flamma orbem populabitur ultima, latè
Circumplexa polos, et vasti culmina caeli;
Ingentique rogo flagrabit machina mundi.

weight giant Aegaeon, they tell, bestrides the back of the Balearic whale. Nor from thee, Earth, does thy ancient vigor fade. The narcissus keeps its odor; the flower of thy boy, O Apollo, is still beautiful, and of thine, Aphrodite. Rich as of old, Earth still guiltily hides the sinful gold in her mountains, and the gems beneath her waves.

So, in fine, the just round of things shall go forever, until the last conflagration lays all waste, envelopes the poles, and wraps the summits of the mighty sky, and as on a huge pyre blazes the frame of the world.

De Idea Platonica Quemadmodum Aristoteles Intellexit

(1628–29)

On the Platonic Idea as It Was Understood by Aristotle

(1628–29)

This is probably also an academic exercise, written on some occasion similar to the foregoing. It is an attempt to burlesque Aristotle's interpretation, too rigid and physical, of the Platonic doctrine of Ideas or Archetypes. Milton speaks not in his own person, but in the person of a literal-minded Aristotelian, who demands loudly to know where the archetype of man can be found, in the heavens above or the earth beneath. The manner of refutation here adopted is unexpectedly genial and humorous.

Dicite sacrorum praesides nemorum deae,
Tuque O noveni perbeata numinis
Memoria mater, quaeque in immenso procul
Antro recumbis otiosa Aeternitas,
Monumenta servans, et ratas leges Jovis,   5
Caelique fastos atque ephemeridas Deûm,
Quis ille primus cuius ex imagine
Natura solers finxit humanum genus,
Aeternus, incorruptus, aequaevus polo,
Unusque et universus, exemplar Dei?   10
Haud ille Palladis gemellus innubae
Interna proles insidet menti Jovis;
Sed quamlibet natura sit communior,
Tamen seorsùs extat ad morem unius,
Et, mira, certo stringitur spatio loci;   15
Seu sempiternus ille siderum comes
Caeli pererrat ordines decemplicis,
Citimúmve terris incolit Lunae globum:
Sive inter animas corpus adituras sedens
Obliviosas torpet ad Lethes aquas: 20

Ye goddesses who guard the sacred grove, and thou, O Memory, happy mother of the nine-fold deity; and Eternity, lazily recumbent far off in thy great cavern, guarding the laws and ordinance of Jove and keeping the chronicles and feast-calendars of Heaven, tell me, who was that first Being, eternal, incorruptible, coeval with the sky, that one and universal Being, exemplar of God, after whose image cunning nature patterned humankind? It surely does not lurk unborn in the brain of Jove, a twin to virgin Pallas. Though its nature is common to many, yet, wonderful to tell, it exists apart after the manner of an individual, and has a local habitation. Perchance as comrade to the sempiternal stars it wanders through the ten spheres of heaven, and inhabits the globe of the Moon, nearest to earth. Perchance it sits drowsing by the oblivious waters of Lethe, among the spirits that wait to enter some living body and be

Sive in remotâ forte terrarum plagâ
Incedit ingens hominis archetypus gigas,
Et [d]iis tremendus erigit celsum caput
Atlante maior portitore siderum.
Non cui profundum caecitas lumen dedit   25
Dircaeus augur vidit hunc alto sinu;
Non hunc silenti nocte Plëiones nepos
Vatum sagaci praepes ostendit choro;
Non hunc sacerdos novit Assyrius, licet
Longos vetusti commemoret atavos Nini,   30
Priscumque Belon, inclytumque Osiridem.
Non ille trino gloriosus nomine
Ter magnus Hermes (ut sit arcani sciens)
Talem reliquit Isidis cultoribus.
At tu perenne ruris Academi decus   35
(Haec monstra si tu primus induxti scholis)
Jam jam poëtas urbis exules tuae
Revocabis, ipse fabulator maximus,
Aut institutor ipse migrabis foras·

born. Or in some remote region of the world does this archetype of man walk about as a huge giant, lifting its high head to frighten the gods, taller than Atlas the star-bearer? No, the seer Tiresias, to whom blindness gave but added depth of vision, never saw it in his dreams. Winged Mercury never showed it to the wise band of seers, as he taught them in the silent night. The Assyrian priest, though he knew the long ancestry of ancient Ninus, knew old Belus and renowned Osiris, never heard of such a creature. Not even Hermes Trismegistus, trine and glorious name, though he knew many secret things, told aught of this to the worshipers of Isis.

Ah, Plato, unfading glory of the Academe, if you were the first to bring such monsters as this into the schools, you really ought to call back the poets whom you exiled from your republic, for you are the greatest fabler of them all. Bring them in, or else you, the founder, must go out!

Ad Patrem

(1635?–45?)

To My Father

(1635?–45?)

This poem may have been written, if we trust lines 83 and 101–10, after the return from Italy, after the attack on Milton by the Halls, and after the vicious responses to the Divorce Tracts. It may even have been written expressly for the 1645 *Poems*, or at least in connection with the appearance of that volume, as the poet's father would have been called on to defer the expenses of its publication. It is at once an earnest avowal of indebtedness and an eloquent plea for the right to continue in the service of song. A very persuasive turn is given to the plea by the poet's declaration that the whole course of his father's conduct towards him has tended to develop in him the longing for high ideal aims; and that, moreover, his father's love of musical composition is only another form of the Muse's service. Milton's intellectual pride and exultant sense of power comes out strikingly as the poem draws toward its close.

Nunc mea Pierios cupiam per pectora fontes
Irriguas torquere vias, totumque per ora
Volvere laxatum gemino de vertice rivum;
Ut tenues oblita sonos audacibus alis   4
Surgat in officium venerandi Musa parentis.
Hoc utcunque tibi gratum pater optime carmen

Now may the Pierian fountains pour their waters through my heart, and the stream that falls from the twin peaks of Parnassus roll all its flood upon my lips. My Muse will put by her trivial strain, and rise on audacious wings to praise the parent whom I venerate. I know not how welcome, best of fathers, this

Exiguum meditatur opus, nec novimus ipsi
Aptiùs à nobis quae possint munera donis
Respondere tuis, quamvis nec maxima pos-
sint   9
Respondere tuis, nedum ut par gratia donis
Esse queat, vacuis quae redditur arida verbis.
Sed tamen haec nostros ostendit pagina census,
Et quod habemus opum chartâ numeravimus
istâ,
Quae mihi sunt nullae, nisi quas dedit aurea
Clio
Quas mihi semoto somni peperere sub an-
tro,   15
Et nemoris laureta sacri Parnassides umbrae.
  Nec tu vatis opus divinum despice carmen,
Quo nihil aethereos ortus, et semina caeli,
Nil magis humanam commendat origine men-
tem,
Sancta Prometheáe retinens vestigia flam-
mae.   20
Carmen amant superi, tremebundaque Tartara
carmen
Ima ciere valet, divosque ligare profundos,
Et triplici duros Manes adamante coercet.
Carmine sepositi retegunt arcana futuri
Phoebades, et tremulae pallentes ora Sibyl-
lae;   25
Carmina sacrificus sollennes pangit ad aras
Aurea seu sternit motantem cornua taurum;
Seu cùm fata sagax fumantibus abdita fibris
Consulit, et tepidis Parcam scrutatur in
extis.
Nos etiam patrium tunc cum repetemus Olym-
pum,   30
Aeternaeque morae stabunt immobilis aevi,
Ibimus auratis per caeli templa coronis,
Dulcia suaviloquo sociantes carmina plectro,
Astra quibus, geminique poli convexa sona-
bunt.   34
Spiritus et rapidos qui circinat igneus orbes,
Nunc quoque sidereis intercinit ipse choreis
Immortale melos, et inenarrabile carmen;
Torrida dum rutilus compescit sibila serpens,
Demissoque ferox gladio mansuescit Orion;
Stellarum nec sentit onus Maurusius Atlas.
Carmina regales epulas ornare solebant,   41
Cum nondum luxus, vastaeque immensa
vorago
Nota gulae, et modico spumabat coena Lyaeo.
Tum de more sedens festa ad convivia vates
Aesculeâ intonsos redimitus ab arbore crines,

song will be, this slender work that I meditate for you; but I know no better gift with
which to repay your gifts. Gifts the greatest
would be too little to repay you, much less
can the mere arid return of words hope to
equal your kindness. But still this page can
set forth my account; on this sheet I have
summed up my wealth, which is nothing except what golden Clio gave me, and what
dreams have brought me in sequestered caverns, and the laurels of the sacred wood, the
shady places of Parnassus.

Do not, my father, hold in disesteem the
work of the bard, divine song, than which
nothing more clearly shows man's ethereal
beginning, and heavenly seed, and the high
origin of his mind. For in song linger holy
traces of that fire which Prometheus stole.
The gods love song. It has strength to compel the trembling deeps of Tartarus, to bind
the lower gods, and chain the cruel shades
with triple adamant. Song reveals the
secrets of the distant future, spoken by
Apollo's priestesses and by the pallid lips of
quivering Sibyls. The sacrificer makes verse
before the solemn altars, whether he strikes
the tossing head of the bull between its gilded
horns, or knowingly consults the destinies
hidden in the fuming flesh, and reads fate from
the entrails still warm with life. We too,
when we return to our native Heaven, and
when the changeless eras of eternity are ours,
shall go through the skyey temples crowned
with gold, matching sweet hymns to the soft
beat of the plectrum; the stars and the deeps
of the twin poles shall ring with them. And
even now that fiery spirit who flies round the
swift orbs, himself sings amid the starry
chorus an immortal melody a song ineffable,
while the ruddy serpent-constellation Ophiuchus stills his hot hissing, and fierce Orion,
lowering his sword, grows gentle, and Mauri-
tanian Atlas feels no longer the weight of the
stars.

Poetry was wont to adorn the feasts of
kings, in the old days when luxury and the
vast abyss of the greedy maw were not yet
known, but when the table sparkled with
seemly and moderate wine. Then, according
to the good custom, the bard, seated at the
convivial board, his unshorn locks bound

Heroumque actus, imitandaque gesta cane-
    bat,   46
Et chaos, et positi latè fundamina mundi,
Reptantesque deos, et alentes numina glandes,
Et nondum Aetneo quaesitum fulmen ab
    antro.
Denique quid vocis modulamen inane juvabit,
Verborum sensusque vacans, numerique lo-
    quacis?   51
Silvestres decet iste choros, non Orphea can-
    tus,
Qui tenuit fluvios et quercubus addidit aures
Carmine, non citharâ, simulacraque functa
    canendo
Compulit in lacrymas; habet has à carmine
    laudes.   55
  Nec tu perge precor sacras contemnere
    Musas,
Nec vanas inopesque puta, quarum ipse peri-
    tus
Munere, mille sonos numeros componis ad
    aptos,
Millibus et vocem modulis variare canoram
Doctus, Arionii meritò sis nominis haeres. 60
Nunc tibi quid mirum, si me genuisse poëtam
Contigerit, charo si tam propè sanguine juncti
Cognatas artes, studiumque affine sequamur:
Ipse volens Phoebus se dispertire duobus,
Altera dona mihi, dedit altera dona parenti,
Dividuumque Deum genitorque puerque tene-
    mus.   66
  Tu tamen ut simules teneras odisse ca-
    moenas,
Non odisse reor, neque enim, pater, ire jube-
    bas
Quà via lata patet, quà pronior area lucri,
Certaque condendi fulget spes aurea nummi:
Nec rapis ad leges, malè custoditaque gen-
    tis   71
Jura, nec insulsis damnas clamoribus aures.
Sed magis excultam cupiens ditescere mentem,
Me procul urbano strepitu, secessibus altis
Abductum Aoniae jucunda per otia ripae 75
Phoebaeo lateri comitem sinis ire beatum.
Officium chari taceo commune parentis,
Me poscunt majora, tuo pater optime sumptu
Cum mihi Romuleae patuit facundia linguae,
Et Latii veneres, et quae Jovis ora dece-
    bant   80
Grandia magniloquis elata vocabula Graiis,
Addere suasisti quos jactat Gallia flores,

with oak leaves, used to chant the exploits
of heroes and their emulable deeds; and
chaos, and the broad-laid foundations of the
world; and the infant gods crawling to find
their acorn food; and the thunderbolt not yet
brought from the cavern of Aetna. And what
does mere music avail without words, tune
vacant of sense and eloquent numbers? That
will do for the sylvan chorus of the birds, but
not for Orpheus; 'twas with his singing
voice, not with the sound of his cithara, that
he held back rivers, gave ears to the oaks, and
drove the ghosts of the dead to tears. From
song he has the praise for these marvels.

Do not, father, I pray, go on contemning
the sacred Muses. Do not think them vain
and poor, by whose grace you yourself are
skilled to fit a thousand sounds to tune and
rhythm, and varying your clear voice through
a thousand modulations, may be by right of
knowledge heir to Arion's name. If it has
been your lot to beget me a poet, why should
you think it strange that, close-joined as we
are by the dear tie of blood, we pursue kindred
arts and studies? Phoebus wished to divide
himself, and gave one half himself to me and
the other half to you. Father and son, we
share between us the god.

But for all your pretense of hatred against
poetry I do not believe that you hate it. For
you did not command me, father, to go where
the way lies open broad, and there is freer
field for earning lucre; where the hope of gain
shines golden and sure. Nor did you drag me
to the bar, to grope among the nation's ill-
guarded laws, nor damn my ears to the insipid
clamor of pleaders. Nay, rather you wished
to enrich still more my mind, already well-
nurtured, and led me far from the city uproar
into high retirement, and permitted me to
enjoy happy leisure by the Aonian stream,
and to walk a glad companion at Apollo's
side.

I will say nothing of the common love and
duty due to a dear parent; your claims on me
are higher. When, at your cost, dear father,
I had mastered the tongue of Romulus and
seen all the graces of it, and had learned the
noble idiom of the magniloquent Greeks, fit
for the great mouth of Jove himself, you persuaded me to add to these the flowers which

Et quam degeneri novus Italus ore loquelam
Fundit, barbaricos testatus voce tumultus,
Quaeque Palaestinus loquitur mysteria vates.
Denique quicquid habet coelum, subjectaque
    coelo   86
Terra parens, terraeque et coelo interfluus aer,
Quicquid et unda tegit, pontique agitabile
    marmor,
Per te nosse licet, per te, si nosse libebit.
Dimotáque venit spectanda scientia nube,   90
Nudaque conspicuos inclinat ad oscula vultus,
Ni fugisse velim, ni sit libâsse molestum.
    I nunc, confer opes quisquis malesanus
      avitas
Austriaci gazas, Perüanaque regna praeoptas.
Quae potuit majora pater tribuisse, vel ipse
Jupiter, excepto, donâsset ut omnia, coelo? 96
Non potiora dedit, quamvis et tuta fuissent,
Publica qui juveni commisit lumina nato
Atque Hyperionios currus, et fraena diei,
Et circum undantem radiatâ luce tiaram.   100
Ergo ego jam doctae pars quamlibet ima
    catervae
Victrices hederas inter, laurosque sedebo,
Jamque nec obscurus populo miscebor inerti,
Vitabuntque oculos vestigia nostra profanos.
Este procul vigiles curae, procul este que-
    relae,   105
Invidiaeque acies transverso tortilis hirquo,
Saeva nec anguiferos extende Calumnia rictus;
In me triste nihil faedissima turba potestis,
Nec vestri sum juris ego; securaque tutus
Pectora, vipereo gradiar sublimis ab ictu.   110
    At tibi, chare pater, postquam non aequa
      merenti
Posse referre datur, nec dona rependere factis,
Sit memorâsse satis, repetitaque munera
    grato
Percensere animo, fidaeque reponere menti.
    Et vos, O nostri, juvenilia carmina, lusus,
Si modo perpetuos sperare audebitis an-
    nos,   116
Et domini superesse rogo, lucemque tueri,
Nec spisso rapient oblivia nigra sub Orco,
Forsitan has laudes, decantatumque parentis
Nomen, ad exemplum, sero servabitis
    aevo.   120

France boasts; and the speech which the modern Italian pours from his degenerate lips, bearing witness in every accent of the barbarian tumults; and the language in which the singers of Palestine speak their mysteries. Afterwards, whatever the sky holds, or mother earth under the sky, or the air of heaven between; whatever the wave hides, or the restless marble of the sea, of all this through you I am enabled to learn, through you, if I care to learn. From the parted cloud comes Science, naked and lovely, and bends her entrancing face to my kisses; unless I wish to flee, unless I find it irksome to taste her lips.

Go, gather wealth, ye dull minds that care for the old treasures of Austria, and of the Peruvian realm. What greater gift than learning could my father have given me, or Jove himself, unless he had given me all but his very sky? Not more potent, though more dangerous, was the gift of him who entrusted to his son the general light, and the chariot of Hyperion, and the reins of day, and the tiara of undulating radiance. Therefore, since I am a part, though the humblest, of the gifted throng, I shall sit among the victor's ivy and laurel. I shall not mix obscurely with the dull rabble; my footsteps shall be far from profane eyes. Let wakeful Care avaunt, and Complaint, and Envy with her crooked leer. Fierce Calumny, open not thy poisonous jaws! Varlets, ye have no power of evil over me; I am not under your law. With secure breast I shall walk, lifted high above your viper stroke.

But as for you, dear father, since it is not granted me to render justice to your desert, or equal your gifts with my deeds, let it suffice that I remember, that in all gratitude I count over my blessings, and hold them faithfully in mind.

And ye, my boyish verses, pastime of my youth, perchance if ye dare to hope for immortality, dare to look upon the light after your master is dead, and are not snatched away to crowded Orcus and its dark oblivion, perchance these praises which I sing in the name of my father will last as an example for the age to come.

Psalm CXIV

(1634)

Psalm 114

(1634)

This psalm translation is probably, indeed, all but certainly, that referred to in the *Fam. Epist. 5*, dated December 4, 1634, and addressed to Alexander Gill, the younger. It is not known from what version of the *Psalm*, Hebrew, Greek, Latin, or English, Milton constructed this metrical translation or paraphrase. This is *Psalm 114* in the Hebrew, *113* in the Greek *Septuagint*, *113* in the Roman Catholic *Vulgate*, and *114* in the English version of 1611. The English of the 1611 version, Milton's favorite English version, follows.

Ἰσραὴλ ὅτε παῖδες, ὅτ᾽ ἀγλαὰ φῦλ᾽ Ἰακώβου
Αἰγύπτιον λίπε δῆμον, ἀπεχθέα, βαρβαρό-
    φωνον,
Δὴ τότε μοῦνον ἔην ὅσιον γένος υἷες Ἰούδα·
Ἐν δὲ Θεὸς λαοῖσι μέγα κρείων βασίλευεν.   4
Εἶδε καὶ ἐντροπάδην φύγαδ᾽ ἐρρώησε θάλασσα
Κύματι εἰλυμένη ῥοθίῳ, ὁ δ᾽ ἄρ ἐστυφελίχθη
Ἱρὸς Ἰορδάνης ποτὶ ἀργυροειδέα πηγήν·
Ἐκ δ᾽ ὄρεα σκαρθμοῖσιν ἀπειρέσια κλονέοντο,
Ὡς κριοὶ σφριγόωντες εὔτραφερῷ ἐν ἀλωῇ·
Βαιότεραι δ᾽ ἅμα πᾶσαι ἀνασκίρτησαν ἐρί-
    πναι,   10
Οἷα παραὶ σύριγγι φίλῃ ὑπὸ μητέρι ἄρνες.
Τίπτε σύγ᾽, αἰνὰ θάλασσα, πέλωρ φύγαδ᾽
    ἐρρώησας;
Κύματι εἰλυμένη ῥοθίῳ; τί δ᾽ ἄρ᾽ ἐστυφελί-
    χθης
Ἱρὸς Ἰορδάνη, ποτὶ ἀργυροειδέα πηγήν;   14
Τίπτ᾽, ὄρεα, σκαρθμοῖσιν ἀπειρέσια κλονέεσθε,
Ὡς κριοὶ σφριγόωντες εὔτραφερῷ ἐν ἀλωῇ;
Βαιότεραι τί δ᾽ ἄρ᾽ ὕμμες ἀνασκιρτήσατ᾽ ἐρί-
    πναι,
Οἷα παραὶ σύριγγι φίλῃ ὑπὸ μητέρι ἄρνες;
Σείεο γαῖα τρέουσα Θεὸν μεγάλ᾽ ἐκτυπέοντα,
Γαῖα, Θεὸν τρείουσ᾽ ὕπατον σέβας Ἰσσακίδαο,
Ὅς τε καὶ ἐκ σπιλάδων ποταμοὺς χέε μορμύρον-
    τας,   21
Κρήνην τ᾽ ἀέναον πέτρης ἀπὸ δακρυοέσσης.

[When Israel went out of Egypt, the house of Jacob from a people of strange language;
    Judah was his sanctuary, and Israel his dominion.
 The sea saw it, and fled: Jordan was driven back.
The mountains skipped like rams, and the little hills like lambs.
What ailed thee, O thou sea, that thou fleddest? thou Jordan, that thou wast driven back?
Ye mountains, that ye skipped like rams; and ye little hills, like lambs?
Tremble, thou earth, at the presence of the Lord, at the presence of the God of Jacob;
 Which turned the rock into a standing water, the flint into a fountain of waters.]

Philosophus ad regem quendam qui eum ignotum et in[son]tem inter reos forte captum inscius damnaverat τὴν ἐπὶ θανάτῳ πορευόμενος, haec subito misit.

A philosopher, who, though innocent, was found among the guilty, and, being unrecognized, was therefore condemned to death, on his way to execution, suddenly sent this message to a king.

(*1642–45*)   (Perhaps connected with *Sonnet VIII*)

'Ω ἄνα, εἰ ὀλέσῃς με τὸν ἔννομον, οὐδέ τιν'
   ἀνδρῶν
Δεινὸν ὅλως δράσαντα, σοφώτατον ἴσθι κάρη-
   νον
Ῥηϊδιῶς ἀφέλοιο, τὸ δ' ὕστερον αὖθι νοήσεις,
Μαψιδίως δ' ἄρ' ἔπειτα τεὸν πρὸς θυμὸν ὀδύρῃ,
Τοῖον δ' ἐκ πόλιος περιώνυμον ἄλκαρ ὀλέσσας.

If you kill me, O King, a law-abiding citizen who has done no man any wrong, you will be recklessly cutting off a most learned head; later on, you will realize what you have done; but in vain you will grieve to your own heart because you destroyed such a famous defense of your city.

In Effigiei ejus Sculptorem

(*1645*)

'Αμαθεῖ γεγράφθαι χειρὶ τήνδε μὲν εἰκόνα
Φαίης τάχ' ἄν, πρὸς εἶδος αὐτοφυὲς βλέπων·
Τὸν δ' ἐκτυπωτὸν οὐκ ἐπιγνόντες φίλοι
Γελᾶτε φαύλου δυσμίμημα ζωγράφου.

On the Engraver of His Picture

(*1645*)

Perhaps you would say this portrait was done by a tyro, if you looked at the real shape and figure; but since the man portrayed here is unknown to you, you are only smiling at the inept copy by a poor engraver.

Ad Salsillum Poetam Romanum Aegrotantem.   Scazontes

(*1638–39*)

Choliambics, To Salsillo, a Roman Poet, in His Illness

(*1638–39*)

The person addressed in these verses, Giovanni Salzilli, Milton probably met in Rome. His poetry has long been forgotten.   He was a member of the literary society called L'Accadèmia dei Fantastici, or Academy of the Fantastics; and his poems were mostly written as contributions to this club.   That he was one of Milton's Roman acquaintances we should know, without the testimony of the present composition, by his commendatory verses prefixed to the Latin poems.   These verses are in the usual fulsome strain, exalting Milton above Homer, Virgil, and Tasso.   In the opening lines, Milton alludes jestingly to the kind of meter he has chosen to use, scazons, or 'limping measure,' in which a spondee or trochee is inserted instead of the expected iambus in the last foot of each line.

O Musa gressum quae volens trahis claudum,
Vulcanioque tarda gaudes incessu,
Nec sentis illud in loco minus gratum,
Quàm cùm decentes flava Dëiope suras
Alternat aureum ante Junonis lectum,   5
Adesdum et haec s'is verba pauca Salsillo
Refer, camoena nostra cui tantum est cordi,
Quamque ille magnis praetulit immeritò divis.
Haec ergo alumnus ille Londini Milto,
Diebus hisce qui suum linquens nidum   10
Polique tractum, (pessimus ubi ventorum,
Insanientis impotensque pulmonis
Pernix anhela sub Jove exercet flabra)
Venit feraces Itali soli ad glebas,
Visum superbâ cognitas urbes famâ   15
Virosque doctaeque indolem juventutis,
Tibi optat idem hic fausta multa Salsille,
Habitumque fesso corpori penitùs sanum;
Cui nunc profunda bilis infestat renes,
Praecordiisque fixa damnosùm spirat.   20
Nec id pepercit impia quòd tu Romano
Tam cultus ore Lesbium condis melos.
O dulce divûm munus, O salus Hebes
Germana! Tuque Phoebe morborum terror
Pythone caeso, sive tu magis Paean   25
Libenter audis, hic tuus sacerdos est.
Querceta Fauni, vosque rore vinoso
Colles benigni, mitis Evandri sedes,
Siquid salubre vallibus frondet vestris,
Levamen aegro ferte certatim vati.   30
Sic ille charis redditus rursùm Musis
Vicina dulci prata mulcebit cantu.
Ipse inter atros emirabitur lucos
Numa, ubi beatum degit otium aeternum,
Suam reclivis semper Aegeriam spectans.   35
Tumidusque et ipse Tibris hinc delinitus
Spei favebit annuae colonorum:
Nec in sepulchris ibit obsessum reges
Nimiùm sinistro laxus irruens loro:
Sed fraena melius temperabit undarum,   40
Adusque curvi salsa regna Portumni.

O Muse, who hast elected to drag a club-foot after thee, who rejoicest to go slowly limping like Vulcan, and esteemest thyself no less engaging so than is blonde-haired Deiope when she moves her trim ankles in the dance before the golden couch of Juno, come, prithee, and bear these few words to Salsillo, who is so partial to my poetry that he puts me, all unworthy as I am, before the divine singers of old. Say that the man whom he praises sends him these verses; London-bred Milton, who a while ago left his nest and his accustomed tract of sky, where the worst of wild winds fills the sky from its ungovernable lungs with fleet and panting blasts, and came to the fruitful glebe of Italy, to see its proud cities, its noble men, and its gifted youth. Now he sends thee greeting, Salsillo, and much health to thy afflicted body. Surfeit of bile infests thy reins, and spreads sickness through thy organs; it is too impious to spare thee, for all the polished Lesbian song that thou pourest from thy Roman mouth.

O Health, sweetest gift of the gods, sister of Hebe! and thou Apollo (or Paean, if thou lovest that name better), thou who didst slay Python and art the terror of disease, behold, this is a priest of thine! O ye oaken groves of Faunus, and ye Roman hills gracious with the dew of the grape, ye seats of mild Evander, if any healing simple grows in your valleys, hasten, strive each to be first in bringing alleviation to your sick poet. Then, restored once more to the dear Muses, he will charm the near fields with sweet song. Numa himself, where he reclines under the dark trees in a blissful eternity of ease, and gazes forever at his Egeria, will wonder. Swollen Tiber, soothed by the music, will spare the crop on which the farmer has set his hope of the year. He will cease to rush on with his left rein too loose, to overwhelm the very kings in their sepulchers; but he will temper his waves, till they reach the salt realms of Portumnus, god of the curving harbor.

Mansus

(1639)

Joannes Baptista Mansus Marchio Villensis vir ingenii laude, tum literarum studio, nec non et bellica virtute apud Italos clarus in primis est. Ad quem Torquati Tassi Dialogus extat de Amicitia scriptus; erat enim Tassi amicissimus; ab quo etiam inter Campaniae principes celebratur, in illo poemate cui titulus GERUSALEMME CONQUISTATA, lib. 20.

> *Fra cavalier magnanimi, è cortesi*
> *Risplende il Manso....*

Is authorem Neapoli commorantem summa benevolentia prosecutus est, multaque ei detulit humanitatis officia. Ad hunc itaque hospes ille antequam ab ea urbe discederet, ut ne ingratum se ostenderet, hoc carmen misit.

Manso

(1639)

Giovanni Battista Manso, Marquis of Villa, is a man of the highest repute in Italy, for genius, scholarship, and military accomplishments. Torquato Tasso addressed to him his Dialogue on Friendship; he was a dear friend of that poet, and is mentioned among the princes of Campania in the poem entitled GERUSALEMME CONQUISTATA, book xx:

> *Among magnanimous and courteous knights*
> *Shines Manso.*

During the present author's stay at Naples, he was indebted to this nobleman for many offices of kindness and courtesy. After leaving the city, therefore, he sent the following verses to his host, in token of gratitude.

The above headnote, prefixed to the poem for the edition of 1645, leaves only a few additional words of explanation to be given. Milton owed his introduction to Manso, as he tells us in the *Defensio Secunda*, to an eremite friar with whom he fell in on the way from Rome to Naples, in November, 1638. Born in 1561, the marquis was now verging upon his eightieth year, and was one of the very few munificent private patrons of art and letters still alive in Italy. He had sheltered Tasso, in 1588, when the poet was wandering friendless and distracted over Italy, and published affectionate personal memoirs of that poet after his death. He had stood in the same relation of friendship and helpfulness to Marini, upon whose shoulders Tasso's mantle fell. At Marini's death, in 1625, he had taken charge of his burial and erected a monument in his honor. A man so intimately connected with the glories of Italian poetry could not but be interesting to Milton. We have abundant evidence that the interest was returned. Milton himself says: 'As long as I staid in Naples, I found him truly most friendly to me, he himself acting as my guide through the different parts of the city and the palace of the viceroy, and coming himself more than once to my inn to visit me; and at my going away he seriously excused himself to me in that, though he wished to have shown me greater attention, he had not been able to do so in that city, because I would not be more close in the matter of religion.' The complimentary epigram which Manso gave to his young English guest, and which the latter prefixed to his Latin poems, rather bluntly excludes his religious convictions from eulogy: 'If, as thy mind, form, bearing, face, and morals, so also thy creed were, thou wouldst be not an Angle but an angel.'

In the *Epitaphium Damonis* there is a description of the wrought or painted cups which Manso gave his guest as a keepsake:

'I dreamed of showing thee the two cups which Manso gave me, Manso, not the least glory of the Neapolitan shore. They are wonders of art, even as the giver is wonderful. About them is wrought a double brede; in the midst rolls the Red Sea, and spring scatters its odors; along the far coasts of Araby the trees drop balsam.... In another place is the mighty stretch of sky, where Olympus lies open to view.'

The poem to Manso is one of singular elegance, and occasionally of high beauty. Autobiographically the most interesting passage is that in which the poet states his intention of writing an epic upon King Arthur; by which announcement he makes a tacit claim to be included in the list of those poets whom Manso has befriended. The concluding passage, in which Milton longs for such a patron and friend as Manso had been to Tasso and Marini, is conceived in a strain of surprising humility and dependence, rising, however, at the end, into confident exultation.

The exact date of the poem cannot be fixed. It was composed either in Italy, after Milton left Naples, or in England, soon after his return.

Haec quoque Manse tuae meditantur carmina
    laudi
Pierides, tibi Manse choro notissime Phoebi,
Quandoquidem ille alium haud aequo est
    dignatus honore,
Post Galli cineres, et Mecaenatis Hetrusci.
Tu quoque si nostrae tantùm valet aura Ca-
    moenae,   5
Victrices hederas inter, laurosque sedebis.
Te pridem magno felix concordia Tasso
Junxit, et aeternis inscripsit nomina chartis.
Mox tibi dulciloquum non inscia Musa Mari-
    num   9
Tradidit, ille tuum dici se gaudet alumnum,
Dum canit Assyrios divûm prolixus amores;
Mollis et Ausonias stupefecit carmine nym-
    phas.
Ille itidem moriens tibi soli debita vates
Ossa tibi soli, supremaque vota reliquit.
Nec manes pietas tua chara fefellit amici,   15
Vidimus arridentem operoso ex aere poetam.
Nec satis hoc visum est in utrumque, et nec
    pia cessant
Officia in tumulo, cupis integros rapere Orco,
Quà potes, atque avidas Parcarum eludere
    leges: 19
Amborum genus, et variâ sub sorte peractam
Describis vitam, moresque, et dona Minervae;
Aemulus illius Mycalen qui natus ad altam
Rettulit Aeolii vitam facundus Homeri.
Ergo ego te Cliûs et magni nomine Phoebi
Manse pater, jubeo longum salvere per
    aevum   25
Missus Hyperboreo juvenis peregrinus ab axe.
Nec tu longinquam bonus aspernabere musam,
Quae nuper gelidâ vix enutrita sub Arcto
Imprudens Italas ausa est volitare per urbes.
Nos etiam in nostro modulantes flumine
    cygnos   30
Credimus obscuras noctis sensisse per umbras,

These verses too, Manso, the Muses intend in praise of you, who are already so well-known to Apollo's choir, and honored by the god above any man since Gallus died and Tuscan Maecenas. If the breath of my song avails, you too shall sit among the victor's laurels and ivy.

First, a happy friendship joined you with great Tasso, and wrote both your names on eternal scrolls. Next, the Muse, knowing your worth, gave to you sweet-tongued Marini; he rejoiced to be called your fosterling while he sang in copious strains the Assyrian loves of the gods, and enthralled the Italian nymphs with his soft accents. When the poet died, he who had owed you his life gave into your care, to yours alone, his bones and deathbed wishes. Your dear piety was true even to the ghost of your friend, as that monument tells in which he still smiles at us from the wrought bronze. Even this did not satisfy you; your kindly offices did not cease at the tomb. You longed to save both your poet friends from Orcus, and, so much as lay in you, to cheat the avid laws of the Parcae. And so you told the ancestry of both, their character, their gifts of mind, the various fortune of their lives, emulous of him who was born on high Mycale, fluent Herodotus, chronicler of Aeolian Homer. Therefore, sire, in the name of Clio and of mighty Phoebus, I, who come a wandering youth from the Hyperborean realms, send you greeting and long life. You, who are so kind, will not scorn a stranger's Muse, who, nourished sparely in the frozen north, lately dared a venturesome flight through the cities of Italy.[1] I too, methinks, have heard, through the obscure shades of night, the swans singing in my river at home, where

---

[1] The reference is to the Latin verses contributed by Milton to the Italian academies.

Quà Thamesis late puris argenteus urnis
Oceani glaucos perfundit gurgite crines.
Quin et in has quondam pervenit Tityrus
    oras.
Sed neque nos genus incultum, nec inutile
    Phoebo   35
Quà plaga septeno mundi sulcata Trione
Brumalem patitur longâ sub nocte Boöten.
Nos etiam colimus Phoebum, nos munera
    Phoebo,
Flaventes spicas, et lutea mala canistris,
Halantemque crocum (perhibet nisi vana
    vetustas)   40
Misimus, et lectas Druidum de gente choreas.
(Gens Druides antiqua sacris operata deorum
Heroum laudes imitandaque gesta canebant)
Hinc quoties festo cingunt altaria cantu
Delo in herbosâ Graiae de more puellae   45
Carminibus laetis memorant Corinëida Loxo,
Fatidicamque Upin, cum flavicomâ Hecaërge
Nuda Caledonio variatas pectora fuco.
Fortunate senex, ergo quacunque per orbem
Torquati decus, et nomen celebrabitur in-
    gens,   50
Claraque perpetui succrescet fama Marini,
Tu quoque in ora frequens venies plausumque
    virorum,
Et parili carpes iter immortale volatu.
Dicetur tum sponte tuos habitâsse penates
Cynthius, et famulas venisse ad limina Musas:
At non sponte domum tamen idem, et regis
    adivit   56
Rura Pheretiadae coelo fugitivus Apollo;
Ille licet magnum Alciden susceperat hospes;
Tantùm ubi clamosos placuit vitare bubulcos,
Nobile mansueti cessit Chironis in antrum,
Irriguos inter saltus frondosaque tecta   61
Peneium prope rivum: ibi saepe sub ilice
    nigrâ
Ad citharae strepitum blandâ prece victus
    amici
Exilii duros lenibat voce labores.
Tum neque ripa suo, barathro nec fixa sub
    imo,   65
Saxa stetere loco, nutat Trachinia rupes,
Nec sentit solitas, immania pondera, silvas,
Emotaeque suis properant de collibus orni,
Mulcenturque novo maculosi carmine lynces.
Diis dilecte senex, te Jupiter aequus opor-
    tet   70
Nascentem, et miti lustrarit lumine Phoebus,

argent Thames, bending above her clear urns,
lets her glaucous locks stream wide into the
ocean. What do I say? did not Chaucer himself, our Tityrus, come once to these shores?

In truth, we who endure the long nights
under wintry Boötes and that region of the
firmament over which wheels the sevenfold
wain, are no untaught race, useless to Apollo.
We, too, worship him; of old we sent him
gifts to his own island, sent him yellowing
ears of grain, and baskets of golden apples,
and odorous crocus-flowers (unless the
ancient record lies). These we sent, borne
by a chosen band of Druids, an ancient race,
skilled in the sacred rites of the gods, and
singers of the noble deeds of heroes. Often,
in memory of this pilgrimage, the Greek
girls circle the altars in grassy Delos, as is
their gracious wont, and in glad songs commemorate Loxo, daughter of Corineus, and
prophetic Upis, and Hecaërge of the yellow
hair, Druid maids, whose nude breasts were
stained with Caledonian woad.

Fortunate old man! wherever through the
world the mighty name of Tasso is celebrated
with honor, wherever the imperishable
fame of Marini spreads, you too shall be on
the lips of men for praise; you shall fly side
by side with these poets on their immortal
way. It shall be said that of his own accord
Cynthian Apollo dwelt in your house, and
that the Muses came as familiars to your
threshold. When Apollo came a heavenly
fugitive to the fields of King Admetus, it was
not of his own free accord, though Admetus
had been host to great Alcides. And when
he wished to be rid for a while of the shouting plowmen, he went to that far-famed
cave of the gentle centaur Chiron, amid irriguous slopes and roofs of shade, near to the
river Peneius. Often there under the dark
ilex, at his friend's request, he took his cither
and sang to lighten the harsh labors of his
exile. Then neither the banks of the stream
nor the rocks in the chasm stood quiet. The
Trachinian cliff swayed, no longer feeling
the mighty weight of its forests. The ash-
trees from the mountains drew near, and the
spotted lynxes, softened at the new song.

Old man loved of the gods! Surely Jupiter
and Phoebus and the grandson of Atlas must

Atlantisque nepos; neque enim nisi charus ab
    ortu
Diis superis poterit magno favisse poetae.
Hinc longaeva tibi lento sub flore senectus
Vernat, et Aesonios lucratur vivida fusos,   75
Nondum deciduos servans tibi frontis ho-
    nores,
Ingeniumque vigens, et adultum mentis
    acumen.
O mihi si mea sors talem concedat amicum
Phoebaeos decorâsse viros qui tam bene nôrit,
Si quando indigenas revocabo in carmina
    reges,   80
Arturumque etiam sub terris bella moventem;
Aut dicam invictae sociali foedere mensae,
Magnanimos Heroas, et (O modo spiritus
    adsit)
Frangam Saxonicas Britonum sub Marte
    phalanges.
Tandem ubi non tacitae permensus tempora
    vitae,   85
Annorumque satur cineri sua jura relinquam,
Ille mihi lecto madidis astaret ocellis,
Astanti sat erit si dicam 'Sim tibi curae';
Ille meos artus liventi morte solutos
Curaret parvâ componi molliter urnâ.   90
Forsitan et nostros ducat de marmore vultus,
Nectens aut Paphiâ myrti aut Parnasside
    lauri
Fronde comas, at ego securâ pace quiescam.
Tum quoque, si qua fides, si praemia certa
    bonorum,
Ipse ego caelicolûm semotus in aethera di-
    vûm,   95
Quò labor et mens pura vehunt, atque ignea
    virtus
Secreti haec aliquâ mundi de parte videbo
(Quantum fata sinunt) et totâ mente serenùm
Ridens purpureo suffundar lumine vultus
Et simul aethereo plaudam mihi laetus
    Olympo.   100

have poured upon you mildest radiance at your birth; for no man, unless he were dear from his cradle to the gods above, could have had the fortune to befriend a great poet. This is why your age keeps green with clinging blossoms and covers the stretch that the fates span for Aeson; late blossoms fade not from it; this is why your head preserves so long its locks unfallen, your nature its vigor, and your mind the keenness of its prime. Oh, may Fate give me such a friend, a man who knows so well how to honor the sons of Phoebus, if ever I shall recall in song the kings of my native land, and Arthur, who carried war even into fairyland. Or I shall tell of those great-hearted champions bound in the invincible society of the Round Table, and (O may the spirit be in me!) I shall break the Saxon phalanxes with British war. Then, when I have lived the measure of my life, not in inglorious silence, and, sated with years, shall give the urn its rights, my patron will stand with wet eyes at my bedside. As he stands there, I shall only say, 'Have me in thy care.' He will place my limbs, loosened in death, softly in their humble grave; and perhaps he will carve my face in marble, and bind my sculptured brows with Paphian myrtle or with the laurel of Parnassus, and I shall rest in peace. Then, if faith means aught, if there is any reward for the righteous, I shall stand among the ethereal deities in Paradise, whither labor, and a pure mind, and righteousness that burneth as a flame, carry the souls of men: from some corner of the secret world, the fates permitting, I shall look down and behold all this; my soul shall smile, my serene face shall be suffused with purpureal light, and glad at heart I shall clap my hands in the air of Heaven.

Epitaphium Damonis

(1640)

On the Death of Damon

(1640)

Milton's intimacy with Charles Diodati continued after they had both left college, and ripened into a friendship of a very pure and exalted kind, as is proved by the letters which passed between them, while one was at Horton and the other in the north of England engaged in the study of medicine. Charles Diodati, according to the register of Saint Anne's, was buried at Blackfriars, on August 27, 1638. Milton probably did not hear of his bereavement until he reached Geneva, in June, 1639, when Diodati had been dead almost a year, carried off, within a fortnight of his sister, apparently by some epidemic which swept over that region of Blackfriars where the two had taken lodgings. The elegy which follows was written, if we are to take literally the passage beginning 'Twice the ear had grown green on the stalk' (l. 9), about two years after Diodati's death, i.e., in the autumn of 1640.

Aside from the rare beauty and passion of the poem in its Latin form, it has much autobiographic interest. The life which the two friends led together is treated in much more explicit detail than is the case in *Lycidas*, and without the fiction necessary there. Diodati's medical studies, their talks and walks in the country about Horton, Milton's own experiences in Italy and his poetic ambitions, all come in for a treatment which is unusually concrete in spite of the pastoral disguise. Of pre-eminent interest is the passage concerning the great epic poem on the legendary history of Britain which Milton has already under way, and his decision to write in English instead of Latin. It would be pleasant to know whether the shepherds and shepherdesses who figure in the threnody are actual friends of Milton and Diodati, disguised according to the pastoral convention; in the case of Chloris 'from the stream of Chelmer' (l. 90), at least, a real person seems to be indicated.

ARGUMENTUM

Thyrsis et Damon ejusdem viciniae pastores, eadem studia sequuti a pueritia amici erant, ut qui plurimum. Thyrsis animi causa profectus peregrè de obitu Damonis nuncium accepit. Domum postea reversus, et rem ita esse comperto, se, suamque solitudinem hoc carmine deplorat. Damonis autem sub persona hîc intelligitur Carolus Deodatus ex urbe Hetruriae Luca paterno genere oriundus, caetera Anglus; ingenio, doctrina, clarissimisque caeteris virtutibus, dum viveret, juvenis egregius.

Himerides nymphae (nam vos et Daphnin et
    Hylan,
Et plorata diu meministis fata Bionis)
Dicite Sicelicum Thamesina per oppida carmen:
Quas miser effudit voces, quae murmura
    Thyrsis,

ARGUMENT

Thyrsis and Damon, shepherds dwelling in the same region and pursuing the same studies, were close friends from boyhood. Thyrsis, while traveling abroad for the improvement of his mind, receives news of Damon's death. Returning after a time and finding it true, he deplores himself and his solitude in the following poem. By Damon is to be understood Charles Diodati, connected through his father's family with the Tuscan city of Lucca; in other respects an Englishman: a youth distinguished, during his short life, for unusual talents, learning, and virtue.

Nymphs of Sicily's pastoral song, who forget not Daphnis or Hylas or the long lamented fate of Bion, repeat these Sicilian verses through the cities of Thames; these words which forlorn Thyrsis poured out in grief for Damon's taking-off before his time.

Et quibus assiduis exercuit antra querelis,   5
Fluminaque, fontesque vagos, nemorumque
    recessus,
Dum sibi praereptum queritur Damona, neque
    altam
Luctibus exemit noctem loca sola pererrans.
Et jam bis viridi surgebat culmus arista,   9
Et totidem flavas numerabant horrea messes,
Ex quo summa dies tulerat Damona sub um-
    bras,
Nec dum aderat Thyrsis; pastorem scilicet
    illum
Dulcis amor Musae Thusca retinebat in urbe.
Ast ubi mens expleta domum, pecorisque
    relicti   14
Cura vocat, simul assuetâ sedítque sub ulmo,
Tum verò amissum tum denique sentit ami-
    cum,
Coepit et immensum sic exonerare dolorem.
  'Ite domum impasti, domino jam non
    vacat, agni.
Hei mihi! quae terris, quae dicam numina
    coelo,   19
Postquam te immiti rapuerunt funere Damon;
Siccine nos linquis, tua sic sine nomine virtus
Ibit, et obscuris numero sociabitur umbris?
At non ille, animas virgâ qui dividit aureâ,
Ista velit, dignumque tui te ducat in agmen,
Ignavumque procul vecus arceat omne si-
    lentum.   25
  'Ite domum impasti, domino jam non
    vacat, agni.
Quicquid erit, certè nisi me lupus antè videbit,
Indeplorato non comminuere sepulchro,
Constabitque tuus tibi honos, longúmque
    vigebit
Inter pastores: Illi tibi vota secundo   30
Solvere post Daphnin, post Daphnin dicere
    laudes
Gaudebunt, dum rura Pales, dum Faunus
    amabit:
Si quid id est, priscamque fidem coluisse,
    piúmque,
Palladiásque artes, sociúmque habuisse ca-
    norum.
  'Ite domum impasti, domino jam non
    vacat, agni.   35
Haec tibi certa manent, tibi erunt haec praemia
    Damon,
At mihi quid tandem fiet modò? quis mihi
    fidus

He filled the caves with his murmured complaint, the rivers, the purling springs, and the depths of the woods; deep into the night he prolonged his sobs, as he wandered in lonely ways. Twice now the ear had grown green on the stalk, and twice had the yellow harvests been gathered into barns, since the fatal day which bore Damon to the shades, and Thyrsis absent. For love of the sweet Muse kept that shepherd in the far-off city of Tuscany. But when a mind replete, and anxiety for the flock he had left behind, called him home, he sat down beneath the accustomed elm; and then, ah, then at last he felt the loss of his friend, and thus he sought to lighten his overwhelming grief in speech:

'Go to your folds unfed, my lambs; your master has no time for you. Ah me! what powers shall I name on earth or in heaven, now that they have seized thee, Damon, in a cruel death? Dost thou leave us so? Shall thy virtue thus go hence without a name, and be merged with shades obscure? Ah, no; he who marshals dead souls with his golden wand, wills it not so; he will lead thee apart into a company worthy thy fellowship, and banish far off the base herd of the voiceless.

'Go to your folds unfed, my lambs; your master has no time for you. Be sure, whatever comes, unless the wolf's eye see me first, thou shalt not crumble in the tomb unwept. Thy honors shall be established, and long be kept green among shepherds. To thee, next after Daphnis, they shall rejoice to discharge their vows and of thee, next after Daphnis, to speak praises, so long as Pales and Faunus love the fields, if it means aught for a man to have been faithful like them of old, and pious, and learned in the arts of Pallas, and to have had a poet for his friend.

'Go to your folds unfed, my lambs; your master has no time for you. These rewards, Damon, are thine for certain. But me, what will become of me? What faithful comrade

Haerebit lateri comes, ut tu saepe solebas
Frigoribus duris, et per loca foeta pruinis,
Aut rapido sub sole, siti morientibus herbis?
Sive opus in magnos fuit eminùs ire leones   41
Aut avidos terrere lupos praesepibus altis;
Quis fando sopire diem, cantuque solebit?
     'Ite domum impasti, domino jam non
          vacat, agni.
Pectora cui credam? quis me lenire docebit   45
Mordaces curas, quis longam fallere noctem
Dulcibus alloquiis, grato cùm sibilat igni
Molle pirum, et nucibus strepitat focus, at
          malus auster
Miscet cuncta foris, et desuper intonat ulmo.
     'Ite domum impasti, domino jam non
          vacat, agni.   50
Aut aestate, dies medio dum vertitur axe,
Cum Pan aesculeâ somnum capit abditus
          umbrâ,
Et repetunt sub aquis sibi nota sedilia nym-
          phae.
Pastoresque latent, stertit sub sepe colonus,
Quis mihi blanditiásque tuas, quis tum mihi
          risus,   55
Cecropiosque sales referet, cultosque lepores?
     'Ite domum impasti, domino jam non
          vacat, agni.
At jam solus agros, jam pascua solus oberro,
Sicubi ramosae densantur vallibus umbrae,
Hic serum expecto, supra caput imber et
          Eurus   60
Triste sonant, fractaeque agitata crepuscula
          silvae.
     'Ite domum impasti, domino jam non
          vacat, agni.
Heu quam culta mihi priùs arva procacibus
          herbis
Involvuntur, et ipsa situ seges alta fatiscit!
Innuba neglecto marcescit et uva racemo,   65
Nec myrteta juvant; ovium quoque taedet, at
          illae
Moerent, inque suum convertunt ora magis-
          trum.
     'Ite domum impasti, domino jam non
          vacat, agni.
Tityrus ad corylos vocat, Alphesiboeus ad
          ornos,
Ad salices Aegon, ad flumina pulcher Amyn-
          tas,   70
"Hic gelidi fontes, hîc illita gramina musco,

will cling to my side, as thou didst, when through the bitter cold of the frost-filled countrysides we went to frighten the hungry wolves from the folds, or when we must needs go afar under the steep sun, where the herbs were dying of thirst, to hunt the great lions? Who will solace my day with talk and with singing?

'Go to your folds unfed, my lambs; your master has no time for you. To whom shall I entrust my heart? Who will teach me to assuage my eating cares? Who will cheat the long night with sweet converse, when the mellow pears hiss before the cheery fire, and nuts pop on the hearth, and outside the wild wind makes chaos, storming through the elm-tops?

'Go to your folds unfed, my lambs; your master has no time for you. Or in summer, when the sun is in the zenith at noon, when Pan slumbers deep-hidden in the oak-shade and the nymphs seek their accustomed nooks under the waters, when the shepherds are all quiet and the boor snores under the hedge, who will bring me thy blandishments, thy laughter, thy wit, thy graceful learning?

'Go to your folds unfed, my lambs; your master has no time for you. Now I wander alone through the fields and pastures, all alone now; where the shadows of the branches thicken in the valley, I wait the evening; over my head the wind and the rain-cloud make a mourning sound, and the forest twilight is all astir with gleams and shadows.

'Go to your folds unfed, my lambs; your master has no time for you. Alas, how my fields, once well-tended, are overgrown with weeds! The high corn cracks open with blight; the grape-clusters hang withered, unmarried to the elm. My myrtles please me not: I am weary of my sheep as well, but they turn their mournful eyes upon their master.

'Go to your folds unfed, my lambs; your master has no time for you. Tityrus calls to the hazels, Alphesiboeus to the ash-trees, Aegon to the willows; to the rivers beautiful Amyntas calls: "Here," they cry, "are cool fountains, here the sward is soft with moss,

Hic Zephyri, hîc placidas interstrepit arbu-
 tus undas;"
Ista canunt surdo, frutices ego nactus abibam.
 'Ite domum impasti, domino jam non
  vacat, agni.
Mopsus ad haec, nam me redeuntem forte
  notârat   75
(Et callebat avium linguas, et sidera Mop-
 sus)
"Thyrsi quid hoc?" dixit, "quae te coquit
 improba bilis?
Aut te perdit amor, aut te malè fascinat
 astrum,
Saturni grave saepe fuit pastoribus astrum,
Intimaque obliquo figit praecordia plumbo."
 'Ite domum impasti, domino jam non
  vacat, agni.   81
Mirantur nymphae, et "quid te Thyrsi fu-
 turum est?
Quid tibi vis?" aiunt, "non haec solet esse
 juventae
Nubila frons, oculique truces, vultusque
 severi,
Illa choros, lususque leves, et semper amorem
Jure petit, bis ille miser qui serus amavit." 86
 'Ite domum impasti, domino jam non
  vacat, agni.
Venit Hyas, Dryopéque, et filia Baucidis
 Aegle
Docta modos, citharaeque sciens, sed perdita
 fastu,
Venit Idumanii Chloris vicina fluenti;   90
Nil me blanditiae, nil me solantia verba,
Nil me, si quid adest, movet, aut spes ulla
 futuri.
 'Ite domum impasti, domino jam non
  vacat, agni.
Hei mihi quam similes ludunt per prata
 juvenci,
Omnes unanimi secum sibi lege sodales, 95
Nec magis hunc alio quisquam secernit ami-
 cum
De grege, sic densi veniunt ad pabula thoes,
Inque vicem hirsuti paribus junguntur ona-
 gri:
Lex eadem pelagi, deserto in littore Proteus
Agmina phocarum numerat, vilisque volu-
 crum   100
Passer habet semper quicum sit, et omnia
 circum
Farra libens volitet, serò sua tecta revisens,

here are gentle winds, here the arbutus murmurs to the placid stream." They sing to a
deaf ear; I plunge into the bushes and leave
them.

'Go to your folds unfed, my lambs; your
master has no time for you. Mopsus chances
to see me returning (skilled in the stars and in
the speech of birds is Mopsus), and adds his
voice to theirs. "What ails thee, Thyrsis,"
he says, "what shameful fit of spleen torments
thee? Either love wastes thee, or some star
has cast on thee a baleful charm: Saturn's star
has oft been bitter to shepherds, and with his
slant dart of lead has pierced their inmost
hearts."

'Go to your folds unfed, my lambs; your
master has no time for you. The nymphs
gaze at me astonished, and "Thyrsis," they
say, "what is in store for thee? what wilt
thou? This cloudy brow, these threatening
eyes, this gloomy face, these belong not to
youth. Youth cares for dancing and gaiety,
and follows after love as its right; twice
wretched is he who loves late."

'Go to your folds unfed, my lambs; your
master has no time for you. Hyas comes, and
Dryope; Aegle comes, daughter of Baucis,
skilled in numbers and the lyre, and deadly
proud withal; Chloris comes, from the stream
of Chelmer hard by: their blandishments,
their soothing words, are nothing to me.
Nothing in the present pleasures me, nor have
I any hope for the future.

'Go to your folds unfed, my lambs; your
master has no time for you. Ah me! how
like one another are the herds at sport in the
fields, all companions of like feeling under a
single law! No one of them seeks out a
separate friend from the herd. Even so the
jackals come in crowds to feed, and in varying
turn the shaggy zebras pair. The same law
rules on the seas, where on the desert shore
Proteus numbers his drove of sea-calves.
Even the sparrow, humblest of birds, has
always a mate, with whom he flies in happy
freedom to every heap of corn, returning late

Quem si sors letho objecit, seu milvus adunco
Fata tulit rostro, seu stravit arundine fossor,
Protinus ille alium socio petit inde volatu.
Nos durum genus, et diris exercita fatis 106
Gens homines aliena animis, et pectore
    discors,
Vix sibi quisque parem de millibus invenit
    unum,
Aut si sors dederit tandem non aspera votis,
Illum inopina dies quâ non speraveris horâ
Surripit, aeternum linquens in saecula dam-
    num. 111
   'Ite domum impasti, domino jam non
    vacat, agni.
Heu quis me ignotas traxit vagus error in oras
Ire per aëreas rupes, Alpemque nivosam! 114
Ecquid erat tanti Romam vidisse sepultam?
Quamvis illa foret, qualem dum viseret olim,
Tityrus ipse suas et oves et rura reliquit;
Ut te tam dulci possem caruisse sodale,
Possem tot maria alta, tot interponere
    montes, 119
Tot silvas, tot saxa tibi, fluviosque sonantes.
Ah certè extremùm licuisset tangere dextram,
Et bene compositos placidè morientis ocellos,
Et dixisse "Vale, nostri memor ibis ad astra."
   'Ite domum impasti, domino jam non
    vacat, agni.
Quamquam etiam vestri nunquam meminisse
    pigebit 125
Pastores Thusci, Musis operata juventus,
Hic Charis, atque Lepos; et Thuscus tu quoque
    Damon,
Antiquâ genus unde petis Lucumonis ab urbe.
O ego quantus eram, gelidi cum stratus ad
    Arni
Murmura, populeumque nemus, quà mollior
    herba, 130
Carpere nunc violas, nunc summas carpere
    myrtos,
Et potui Lycidae certantem audire Menalcam.
Ipse etiam tentare ausus sum, nec puto mul-
    tùm
Displicui, nam sunt et apud me munera vestra
Fiscellae; calathique et cerea vincla cicutae,
Quin et nostra suas docuerunt nomina fa-
    gos 136
Et Datis, et Francinus, erant et vocibus ambo
Et studiis noti, Lydorum sanguinis ambo.
   'Ite domum impasti, domino jam non va-
    cat, agni.

to his own nest; yet, if this mate dies, or a curve-beaked falcon slays it, or the ditcher pierces it with his arrow, straight he flutters off to find another. But we men are a hard race, driven by a ruthless fate, alien mind from mind, heart from heart discordant. Hardly out of a thousand does a man find one congenial spirit; or, if fortune sends one, at last relenting at our prayers, yet, in an hour when we least expect it, he is snatched from us, leaving eternal loss behind.

'Go to your folds unfed, my lambs; your master has no time for you. Alas, what restless fancy drew me to foreign shores, across the skyey precipices of the snow-clad Alps? What was there so precious in the sight of buried Rome (even if she had been as she was when Tityrus of old left his sheep and his fields to see her) that I could part from my sweet companion, could put between him and me so many deep seas, so many mountains and forests, so many rocks and sounding rivers? Ah, if I had stayed, I could at least have touched his hand at the last, closed his dying eyes, and said, "Farewell, do not forget me as thou goest to the stars."

'Go to your folds unfed, my lambs; your master has no time for you. Yet, for all, I shall never be loath to keep you in my mind, Tuscan shepherds, youths devoted to the Muses; with you dwell Grace and Pleasantness. Thou, too, Damon, wert a Tuscan; thou tracest thy lineage from Lucca, ancient city of Lucumo. Oh, how mighty was I, when I lay stretched by cool murmuring Arno, on softest grass in the poplar grove, and could now pluck violets, and now sprigs of myrtle, while I listened to Menalcas contending with Lycidas in song. I myself dared to enter the strife, and I think I did not much displease; for I have the gifts you gave me in reward, rush-baskets, and osier-plaits, and waxen reed-stops. Nay, Datis and Francinus, both of them famous scholars and singers, and both of Tuscan blood, taught my name in song to their native beeches.

'Go to your folds unfed, my lambs; your master has no time for you. Such strains as

Haec mihi tum laeto dictabat roscida luna, 140
Dum solus teneros claudebam cratibus hoedos.
Ah quoties dixi, cùm te cinis ater habebat,
"Nunc canit, aut lepori nunc tendit retia
  Damon,
Vimina nunc texit, varios sibi quod sit in
  usus;"
Et quae tum facili sperabam mente futura 145
Arripui voto levis, et praesentia finxi,
"Heus bone numquid agis? nisi te quid forte
  retardat,
Imus? et argutâ paulùm recubamus in umbra,
Aut ad aquas Colni, aut ubi jugera Cassi-
  belauni?
Tu mihi percurres medicos, tua gramina,
  succos,   150
Helleborúmque, humilésque crocos, foli-
  úmque hyacinthi,
Quasque habet ista palus herbas, artesque
  medentûm,"
Ah pereant herbae, pereant artesque me-
  dentûm
Gramina, postquam ipsi nil profecere ma-
  gistro.
Ipse etiam, nam nescio quid mihi grande
  sonabat   155
Fistula, ab undecimâ jam lux est altera nocte,
Et tum forte novis admôram labra cicutis,
Dissiluere tamen rupta compage, nec ultra
Ferre graves potuere sonos, dubito quoque ne
  sim
Turgidulus, tamen et referam, vos cedite
  sylvae.   160
  'Ite domum impasti, domino jam non
    vacat, agni.
Ipse ego Dardanias Rutupina per aequora
  puppes
Dicam, et Pandrasidos regnum vetus Ino-
  geniae,
Brennùmque Arviragúmque duces, priscùmque
  Belinum,
Et tandem Armoricos Britonum sub lege
  colonos;   165
Tum gravidam Arturo fatali fraude Jögernen
Mendaces vultus, assumptáque Gorloïs arma,
Merlini dolus. O mihi tum si vita supersit,
Tu procul annosa pendebis fistula pinu
Multùm oblita mihi, aut patriis mutata
  camoenis   170
Brittonicum strides, quid enim? omnia non
  licet uni

these the moist moon used to whisper to my
glad ear while all alone I was shutting my
kids in the wattled close.   Ah, how many
times I said, aye even when the urn was holding thy ashes, "Now Damon is singing, or
setting traps for the hare.   Now he is plaiting
osiers for his various uses."   With easy mind
I hoped, and lightly I fitted the future to my
wish, picturing it all present before my eyes.
"Heigh, friend," I would say, "art thou busy?
If nothing is to hinder, shall we go lie and
chat a bit in the shade, by the waters of
Colne [1] or on the heights of Cassebelaunus? [2]
Thou shalt tell over to me thy herbs and medicines, hellebore, and the lowly crocus, and
hyacinth-leaf; thou shalt tell me what simples
are to be found in such and such a pond, and
reveal to me all the arts of healing."   Ah,
perish the simples!   Perish the arts of healing!   They could not profit their master!
And as for me, 'tis eleven nights and a day
now since I, ah, I know not what large strain
my pipe was trying to sound.   I was accustoming my lips to new reeds perhaps: suddenly the fastening burst; the reeds flew
asunder, unable to endure longer the grave
sounds to which I racked them.   I know not,
perhaps I am overbold; still, I will tell about
it.   Give way, my woodland song, to a
sterner theme.

  'Go to your folds unfed, my lambs; your
master has no time for you.   I am about to
sing of the Trojan ships that passed along our
Kentish coast, and the old realm of Imogene,
daughter of Pandrasus and the chiefs Brennus
and Arviragus and old Belinus, and the colonists who settled at last in Armorica under
British laws.   Then I shall tell of Igraine,
pregnant with Arthur through the fatal wiz-
ardry of Merlin, who gave to Uther Pendragon the face and the armor of her husband
Gorloïs.   Oh then, if life is granted me, thou,
my shepherd-pipe, shalt hang neglected on
the gnarled pine, or be changed to shrill forth
the strains of my native land, and the cry of
Britons in battle.   Native strains, do I say?

---

[1] A river flowing past Horton.
[2] Near St. Albans, in Herts.

Non sperâsse uni licet omnia, mi satis ampla
Merces, et mihi grande decus (sim ignotus in
    aevum
Tum licet, externo penitúsque inglorius orbi)
Si me flava comas legat Usa, et potor Alauni,
Vorticibúsque frequens Abra, et nemus omne
    Treantae,   176
Et Thamesis meus ante omnes, et fusca metallis
Tamara, et extremis me discant Orcades undis.
  'Ite domum impasti, domino jam non
    vacat, agni.
Haec tibi servabam lentâ sub cortice lauri, 180
Haec, et plura simul, tum quae mihi pocula
    Mansus,
Mansus Chalcidicae non ultima gloria ripae
Bina dedit, mirum artis opus, mirandus et
    ipse,
Et circùm gemino caelaverat argumento:
In medio rubri maris unda, et odoriferum
    ver   185
Littora longa Arabum, et sudantes balsama
    sylvae,
Has inter Phoenix divina avis, unica terris
Caeruleùm fulgens diversicoloribus alis
Auroram vitreis surgentem respicit undis.
Parte alia polus omnipatens, et magnus
    Olympus,   190
Quis putet? hic quoque Amor, pictaeque in
    nube pharetrae,
Arma corusca faces, et spicula tincta pyropo;
Nec tenues animas, pectúsque ignobile vulgi
Hinc ferit, at circùm flammantia lumina tor-
    quens
Semper in erectum spargit sua tela per
    orbes   195
Impiger, et pronos nunquam collimat ad
    ictus,
Hinc mentes ardere sacrae, formaeque deorum.
  'Tu quoque in his, nec ne fallit spes lubrica
    Damon,
Tu quoque in his certè es, nam quò tua dulcis
    abiret
Sanctáque simplicitas, nam quò tua candida
    virtus?   200
Nec te Lethaeo fas quaesivisse sub Orco,
Nec tibi conveniunt lacrymae, nec flebimus
    ultrà,
Ite procul lacrymae, purum colit aethera
    Damon,
Aethera purus habet, pluvium pede reppulit
    arcum;

Yea, one man cannot hope to accomplish all things. It will be sufficient reward and honor for me, even though I remain forever unknown and inglorious among the other nations of the world, if only blond-haired Ouse shall read me, and he who drinks of Alanwater, and the whirling Humber, and the woods of Trent; above all, if my Thames shall sing my songs, and Tamur mineral-stained and the far-off wave-beaten Orkneys.

'Go to your folds unfed, my lambs; your master has no time for you. All these plans and dreams I was keeping for thee, under the clinging laurel-bark, these and more besides. I dreamed of showing thee the two cups which Manso gave me, Manso, not the least glory of the Neapolitan shore. They are wonders of art, even as the giver is wonderful. About them is wrought a double brede; in the midst the Red Sea rolls, and spring scatters its odors; along the far coasts of Araby the trees drop balsam. Among the trees Phoenix, divine bird, unique on earth, blazes cerulean with multi-colored wings, while he watches the morning rise over the vitreous waters. In another place is the mighty stretch of sky where Olympus lies open to view. Yes, and Love is there, too; in clouds his quiver is pictured, his shining arms, his torch, his arrows tipped with fiery bronze. But he does not aim upon our earth at light minds, at the herd of vulgar souls. No; he rolls his flaming eyes and steadfastly sends his arrows upward through the orbs of heaven, never aiming a downward stroke. Under his fire the souls of the blessed burn, and the bodies of the gods.

'The gods! Thou art among them, Damon, unless elusive hope deceives me; among them thou surely art. For whither should thy sweet and holy simplicity go? Whither thy righteousness and candor? 'Twould be sin to seek thee in Lethean Orcus. Tears are not for thee; I shall weep no more. Go hence, lamentation! Damon the pure dwells in skies of purity. Beneath his feet he has spurned the rainbow. Among hero-souls

Heroúmque animas inter, divósque perennes,
Aethereos haurit latices et gaudia potat   206
Ore sacro.   Quin tu coeli post jura recepta
Dexter ades,   placidúsque fave quicunque
    vocaris,
Seu tu noster eris Damon, sive aequior audis
Diodotus, quo te divino nomine cuncti   210
Coelicolae nôrint, sylvísque vocabere Damon.
Quòd tibi purpureus pudor, et sine labe
    juventus
Grata fuit, quòd nulla tori libata voluptas,
En etiam tibi virginei servantur honores;
Ipse caput nitidum cinctus rutilante co-
    rona,   215
Letáque frondentis gestans umbracula palmae
Aeternum perages immortales hymenaeos;
Cantus ubi, choreisque furit lyra mista
    beatis,
Festa Sionaeo bacchantur et orgìa thyrso.'

and deathless divinities he drinks the draught of Paradise; he sips joy with his sacred lips. Now that thou possessest the rights of Heaven, O my friend, stand at my right hand, show me thy gentle favor, however I call upon thee, whether by the old name of Damon that our woods heard, or whether Diodotus please thee better, the divine name Gift-of-God, by which the heavenly people know thee.   Because thy cheek kept its rosy blush and thy youth its stainlessness, because thou knewest not the joy of marriage, lo, for thy virginal spirit virginal honors are reserved. Thy bright head crowned with light, and glad palms in thy hand, thou dost ever act and act again the immortal nuptials, there where singing is, and the lyre mixes madly with the chorals beatific, and the wild orgies rage under the thyrsus of Sion.'

Ad Joannem Rousium

OXONIENSIS ACADEMIAE
BIBLIOTHECARIUM

(Jan. 23, 1646)

De libro Poematum amisso, quem ille sibi denuo mitti postulabat, ut cum aliis nostris in Bibliotheca publica reponeret, Ode.

To John Rouse

LIBRARIAN OF THE UNIVERSITY OF
OXFORD

(Jan. 23, 1646)

On a book of poems, which he (the Librarian of Oxford) lately asked to be sent to him, in order that he might place it with the author's other works in the public library, and which was lost on the journey.   An Ode.

In 1646, John Rouse, Librarian of the Bodleian, applied to Milton for copies of all the works which he had published, in order that a complete set might be deposited in the library.   Milton accordingly sent his 1645 volume of English and Latin poems ('double book in a single binding'), together with the eleven prose pamphlets written between 1641 and 1644.   The pamphlets arrived safely, but the volume of poems was lost or stolen on the journey.   Rouse then applied for another copy, which Milton sent, accompanying it with the following half-serious ode, addressed to the lost book.   The references in it to the troubled state of England were rendered particularly pertinent by the fact that, at the time of writing, Oxford was the headquarters of the Cavalier army, and all academic routine had been broken up.   Milton looks forward, rather wistfully and wearily, to the time when the Muses of learning shall be recalled to their old abodes, and the 'harpy pest' of royal soldiery be driven away.   He sees in the placing of his own books in the care of a sedulous scholar, and in the shadow of a great library, an earnest of the time when 'a distant generation, an age of sounder hearts, will render fairer judgment on all things.'   To get the full force of the passage, we must remember that Milton had just come to the end of the divorce controversy, which had exhausted him with its passion and bitterness.

STROPHE I

Gemelle cultu simplici gaudens liber,
Fronde licet geminâ,
Munditiéque nitens non operosâ,
Quam manus attulit
Juvenilis olim,   5
Sedula tamen haud nimii poetae;
Dum vagus Ausonias nunc per umbras
Nunc Britannica per vireta lusit
Insons populi, barbitóque devius
Indulsit patrio, mox itidem pectine Daunio
Longinquum intonuit melos   11
Vicinis, et humum vix tetigit pede;

ANTISTROPHE

Quis te, parve liber, quis te fratribus
Subduxit reliquis dolo,
Cum tu missus ab urbe,   15
Docto jugiter obsecrante amico,
Illustre tendebas iter
Thamesis ad incunabula
Caerulei patris,
Fontes ubi limpidi   20
Aonidum, thyasusque sacer
Orbi notus per immensos
Temporum lapsus redeunte coelo,
Celeberque futurus in aevum;

STROPHE 2

Modò quis deus, aut editus deo   25
Pristinam gentis miseratus indolem
(Si satis noxas luimus priores
Mollique luxu degener otium)
Tollat nefandos civium tumultus,
Almaque revocet studia sanctus   30
Et relegatas sine sede Musas
Jam penè totis finibus Angligenûm;
Immundasque volucres
Unguibus imminentes
Figat Apollineâ pharetrâ,   35
Phinéamque abigat pestem procul amne Pe-
          gaséo.

ANTISTROPHE

Quin tu, libelle, nuntii licet malâ
Fide, vel oscitantiâ
Semel erraveris agmine fratrum,
Seu quis te teneat specus,   40
Seu qua te latebra, forsan unde vili
Callo teréris institoris insulsi,
Laetare felix, en iterum tibi

STROPHE I

Double book in a single binding, crowned mayhap with double laurel, bright with un-studied adornment lavished in time past by my boyish hand, a sedulous hand, but not yet overmuch a poet's, while I played through Italy's forest-shade or over the green fields of England, in those days when, still innocent of my nation's troubles, I touched my native lute, or played with Italian quill a far-brought melody to those about me, my feet scarce touching the earth for elation,

ANTISTROPHE

Who filched thee, little book, from thy mates, when at my learned friend's repeated instance thou tookest thy way from the great city to the cradle of blue Thames, where the limpid fountains of the Muses are, and where ring the sacred shouts of the Bacchic dance which shall be heard and held famous forever, as long as the sky rolls through the immense cycles of Time?

STROPHE II

Ah, what god or demi-god will take pity on the pristine worth of our English race (if we have enough atoned for our past faults, and our soft degenerate ease) and take from us this curse of civil strife, call back with holy voice the kindly studies of the Muses who have been thrust from their old abodes and driven almost quite from English ground, transfix with Apollo's dart the unclean birds whose claws threaten us, and drive away the whole harpy pest far from the waters of Hippocrene?

ANTISTROPHE

Thou, little book, though by the perfidy or carelessness of my messenger thou wert stolen from the number of thy mates, to be thrown into some cave or den, where per-haps thou art rubbed by a stupid huckster's sordid palm, yet be glad: lo! the bright hope

Spes nova fulget posse profundam
Fugere Lethen, vehique superam   45
In Jovis aulam remige pennâ;

STROPHE 3

Nam te Roüsius sui
Optat peculî, numeróque justo
Sibi pollicitum queritur abesse,
Rogatque venias ille cujus inclyta   50
Sunt data virûm monumenta curae:
Téque adytis etiam sacris
Voluit reponi quibus et ipse praesidet
Aeternorum operum custos fidelis,
Quaestorque gazae nobilioris,   55
Quàm cui praefuit Iön
Clarus Erechtheides
Opulenta dei per templa parentis
Fulvosque tripodas, donaque Delphica
Iön Actaea genitus Creusâ.   60

ANTISTROPHE

Ergo tu visere lucos
Musarum ibis amoenos,
Diamque Phoebi rursus ibis in domum
Oxoniâ quam valle colit
Delo posthabitâ,   65
Bifidóque Parnassi jugo:
Ibis honestus,
Postquam egregiam tu quoque sortem
Nactus abis, dextri prece sollicitatus amici.
Illic legéris inter alta nomina   70
Authorum, Graiae simul et Latinae
Antiqua gentis lumina, et verum decus.

EPODOS

Vos tandem haud vacui mei labores,
Quicquid hoc sterile fudit ingenium,
Jam serò placidam sperare jubeo   75
Perfunctam invidiâ requiem, sedesque beatas
Quas bonus Hermes
Et tutela dabit solers Roüsi,
Quò neque lingua procax vulgi penetrabit,
        atque longè
Turba legentum prava facesset;   80
At ultimi nepotes,
Et cordatior aetas
Judicia rebus aequiora forsitan
Adhibebit integro sinu.
Tum livore sepulto,   85
Si quid meremur sana posteritas sciet
Roüsio favente.

may again be thine to escape oblivion, and
be lifted on oaring wings to the courts of
Jove:

STROPHE III

For Rouse, he into whose care are given the
mighty monuments of departed minds, desires
thee to be of his flock; he complains that thou
art lacking from the full number promised
him, and asks that thou be sent. Thee too he
will place in the sacred inner places over
which he presides; faithful guardian he of
works eternal, and custodian of nobler
treasures than those shining tripods and
Delphic offerings of which Ion, famous son
of Apollo and the Attic maid Creusa, had
custody in the rich temple of his father.

ANTISTROPHE

Therefore thou shalt go to look upon the
pleasant groves of the Muses; thou shalt enter
the divine house of Apollo where he dwells
in the vale of Oxford, preferring that habitation to Delos and to cloven-peaked Parnassus.
Thou shalt go with honor, at the solicitation
of a propitious friend, who reserves for thee
no common destiny. Thou shalt be read
among the lofty names of Greek and Latin
authors, ancient lights of the people and their
true glory.

EPODOS

You then, my labors, were not vain, whatever this poor genius of mine has put forth.
I bid you look forward to a time when envy
shall have worn itself out, and you shall enjoy quiet rest in those blessed abiding-places
which good Hermes and the watchful tutelage
of Rouse shall give you, where the prattling
tongue of the vulgar shall not penetrate, and
the crowd of silly readers keep far off. A distant generation, an age of sounder hearts, perhaps will render fairer judgment on all things;
and then, when all spite and rancor is buried,
Posterity will be able to see with clear eyes
whether any merit is mine by Rouse's
favor.

Ode tribus constat strophis, totidémque antistrophis unâ demum epodo clausis, quas, tametsi omnes nec versuum numero, nec certis ubique colis exactè respondeant, ita tamen secuimus, commodè legendi potius, quam ad antiquos concinendi modos rationem spectantes. Alioquin hoc genus rectiùs fortasse dici monostrophicum debuerat. Metra partim sunt κατὰ σχέσιν, partim ἀπολελυμένα. Phaleucia quae sunt, spondaeum tertio loco bis admittunt, quod idem in secundo loco Catullus ad libitum fecit.

The ode is made up of three strophes, the same number of antistrophes, and ends with one epode. Although the strophes and antistrophes do not correspond either in the number of verses, or exactly everywhere with fixed, unvarying cola, yet we have so divided them intending that they may be conveniently read rather than that they may be chanted according to the ancient measures. Otherwise, it would have been more proper perhaps to call this sort of writing 'monostrophic.' The meters are partly κατὰ σχέσια, 'in correlation, responsive,' and partly ἀπολελυμένα, 'free from such restraint of correlation.' The Phalaecian verses twice admit a spondee in the third foot, and Catullus admits one at will in the second foot.

In Salmasii Hundredam

(From the First Defense, 1651)

Quis expedivit Salmasio suam *Hundredam*,
Picámque docuit verba nostra conari?
Magister artis venter, et Jacobaei
Centum, exulantis viscera marsupii regis.
Quòd si dolosi spes refulserit nummi,   5
Ipse Antichristi qui modò primatum Papae
Minatus uno est dissipare sufflatu,
Cantabit ultrò Cardinalitium melos.

On Salmasius' Hundred

Who provided Salmasius his hundred, and taught the magpie to try to use our words? His master of arts, his belly, and a hundred jacobuses, or the viscera of the exiled king's money-bag. If there shines the hope of treacherous coin, he who the primacy of the pope as antichrist promised to dissipate with a breath, even he will sing a tune to a cardinal.

In Salmasium

(From the Second Defense, 1654)

Gaudete scombri, et quicquid est piscium salo,
Qui frigidâ hyeme incolitis algentes freta,
Vestrûm misertus ille Salmasius eques
Bonus amicire nuditatem cogitat;
Chartaeque largus apparat papyrinos   5
Vobis cucullos praeferentes Claudii
Insignia nomenque et decus Salmasii,
Gestetis ut per omne cetarium forum
Equitis clientes, scriniis mungentium
Cubito virorum, et capsulis gratissimos.   10

On Salmasius

Rejoice herrings and other fish that in winter live in cold waters, for that miserable knight, Salmasius, liberal of paper, is sad about you; he will prepare clothes to cover you that will bear the insignia of Claude Saumaise, and through your fishy ways you may all wear these paper clothes, as clients of a knight, and this will be valuable to those who wipe their noses on their sleeves.

Cf. note by Professor William Abbott Oldfather suggesting the deletion of 'est' in line 1, and transposing last two words in line 8, 'Pro Ioanne Miltono Poeta Populum Anglicanum Iterum Defendente,' *Philological Quarterly* XIX (1940), 88–89.

Miscellaneous English Metrical Pieces and the Psalm Paraphrases

---

From *Of Reformation Touching Church Discipline in England,* 1641

Dante, *Inferno* XIX:115

Ah Constantine, of how much ill was cause
Not thy conversion, but those rich domains
That the first wealthy pope received of thee.

Petrarch, *Sonnet* 108

Founded in chaste and humble poverty,
'Gainst them that raised thee dost thou lift thy horn,
Impudent whore, where hast thou placed thy hope?
In thy adulterers, or thy illgot wealth?
Another Constantine comes not in haste.   5

Ariosto, *Orl. Fur.* XXXIV:73 and 80

And to be short, at last his guide him brings
Into a goodly valley, where he sees
A mighty mass of things strangely confused,
Things that on earth were lost, or were abused.

Then passed he to a flowery mountain green,   5
Which once smelt sweet, now stinks as odiously;
This was that gift (if you the truth will have)
That Constantine to good Sylvestro gave.

From *The Reason of Church Government,* 1641/2

When I die, let the earth be rolled in flames.
— Said by Tiberius.

From *The Apology for Smectymnuus,* 1642

Horace, *Sat.* I:1:24

laughing to teach the truth
What hinders? as some teachers give to boys
Junkets and knacks, that they may learn apace.

Horace, *Sat.* I:10:14
> Jesting decides great things
> Stronglier, and better oft than earnest can.

Sophocles, *Electra* 624
> Tis you that say it, not I, you do the deeds,
> And your ungodly deeds find me the words.

From *Areopagitica*, 1644

Euripides, *Supplices* 438
> This is true Liberty when freeborn men
> Having to advise the public may speak free,
> Which he who can, and will, deserves high praise,
> Who neither can nor will, may hold his peace;
> What can be juster in a state than this?   5

From *Tetrachordon*, 1645

Horace, *Epist.* I:16:40
> Whom do we count a good man, whom but he
> Who keeps the laws and statutes of the senate,
> Who judges in great suits and controversies,
> Whose witness and opinion wins the cause;
> But his own house, and the whole neighborhood   5
> Sees his foul inside through his whited skin.

On the New Forcers of Conscience Under the Long Parliament
(*1645–46*)

This poem occurs in the *Manuscript* and was first printed in 1673. It is taken out of its regular order and placed as it is here because of its topical appeal. It seems to be an experiment in a sonnet-like form with a double sestet.

> Because you have thrown off your prelate lord,
>   And with stiff vows renounced his liturgy
>   To seize the widowed whore plurality
>   From them whose sin ye envied, not abhorred,
> Dare ye for this adjure the civil sword   5
>   To force our consciences that Christ set free,
>   And ride us with a classic hierarchy
>   Taught ye by mere A. S. and Rutherford?

Men whose life, learning, faith and pure intent
  Would have been held in high esteem with Paul   10
  Must now be named and printed heretics
By shallow Edwards and Scotch what-d'-ye-call:
  But we do hope to find out all your tricks,
  Your plots and packing worse than those of Trent,
    That so the Parliament   15
May with their wholesome and preventive shears
Clip your phylacteries, though bank your ears,
    And succor our just fears
When they shall read this clearly in your charge
New presbyter is but old priest writ large.   20

From *The Tenure of Kings and Magistrates*, 1649

Seneca, *Her. Fur.* 922

There can be slain
No sacrifice to God more acceptable
Than an unjust and wicked king.

From *The History of Britain*, 1670

Translated from Geoffrey of Monmouth's Latin

Goddess of shades, and huntress, who at will
Walkest on the rolling sphere, and through the deep,
On thy third reign the earth look now, and tell
What land, what seat of rest thou biddest me seek,
What certain seat, where I may worship thee   5
For aye, with temples vowed, and virgin choirs.

Brutus, far to the west, in the ocean wide
Beyond the realm of Gaul, a land there lies,
Sea-girt it lies, where giants dwelt of old,
Now void, it fits thy people; thither bend
Thy course, there shalt thou find a lasting seat,   5
There to thy sons another Troy shall rise,
And kings be born of thee, whose dreaded might
Shall awe the world, and conquer nations bold.

Translated from Matthew of Westminster

Low in a mead of kine under a thorn,
Of head bereft lieth poor Kenelm king-born.

The Psalm Paraphrases

THE first two of these paraphrases are probably the earliest of Milton's verse that has been preserved. In 1648 and in 1653 he tried his hand again at psalm paraphrases, probably with the intent of producing them for a new hymnal. But Milton could do nothing in any way remarkable with the form, and his paraphrases are today only curiosities.

A Paraphrase on Psalm CXIV

(1620–25)

This and the following Psalm were done by the author when fifteen years old.

When the blest seed of Terah's faithful son,
After long toil their liberty had won,
And passed from Pharian fields to Canaan land,
Led by the strength of the almighty's hand,
Jehovah's wonders were in Israel shown,   5
His praise and glory was in Israel known.
That saw the troubled sea, and shivering fled,
And sought to hide his froth-becurled head
Low in the earth, Jordan's clear streams recoil,
As a faint host that hath received the foil.   10
The high, huge-bellied mountains skip like rams
Amongst their ewes, the little hills like lambs.
Why fled the ocean?   And why skipped the mountains?
Why turned Jordan toward his crystal fountains?
Shake earth, and at the presence be aghast   15
Of him that ever was, and aye shall last,
That glassy floods from rugged rocks can crush,
And make soft rills from fiery flint-stones gush.

Psalm CXXXVI

Let us with a gladsome mind
Praise the Lord, for he is kind.
            For his mercies aye endure,
            Ever faithful, ever sure.

Let us blaze his name abroad,   5
For of gods he is the God;
    For his, &c.

O let us his praises tell,
Who doth the wrathful tyrants quell.   10
    For his, &c.

Who with his miracles doth make
Amazed heaven and earth to shake.
    For his, &c.   15

Who by his wisdom did create
The painted heavens so full of state.
    For his, &c.   19

Who did the solid earth ordain
To rise above the watery plain.
    For his, &c.

Who by his all-commanding might,   25
Did fill the new-made world with light.
    For his, &c.

And caused the golden-tressed sun,
All the day long his course to run.   30
    For his, &c.

The horned moon to shine by night,
Amongst her spangled sisters bright.
    For his, &c.   35

He with his thunder-clasping hand,
Smote the first-born of Egypt land.
    For his, &c.   39

And in despite of Pharaoh fell,
He brought from thence his Israel.
    For his, &c.

The ruddy waves he cleft in twain,   45
Of the Erythraean main.
    For his, &c.

The floods stood still like walls of glass,
While the Hebrew bands did pass.   50
    For his, &c.

But full soon they did devour
The tawny king with all his power.
    For his, &c.   55

His chosen people he did bless
In the wasteful wilderness.
     For his, &c.   59

In bloody battle he brought down
Kings of prowess and renown.
     For his, &c.

He foiled bold Seon and his host,   65
That ruled the Amorrean coast.
     For his, &c.

And large-limbed Og he did subdue,
With all his overhardy crew.   70
     For his, &c.

And to his servant Israel,
He gave their land therein to dwell.
     For his, &c.   75

He hath with a piteous eye
Beheld us in our misery.
     For his, &c.   79

And freed us from the slavery
Of the invading enemy.
     For his, &c.

All living creatures he doth feed,   85
And with full hand supplies their need.
     For his, &c.

Let us therefore warble forth
His mighty majesty and worth.
     For his, &c.   90

That his mansion hath on high
Above the reach of mortal eye.
     For his mercies aye endure,
     Ever faithful, ever sure.   95

Nine of the Psalms Done into Meter,

Wherein all but what is in a different character, are the
very words of the text, translated from the original.
April, 1648.   J. M.

(The marginal words are Milton's notes, some being translations of Hebrew
words, and others more exact translations.)

PSALM LXXX

1 Thou shepherd that dost Israel *keep*
  Give ear *in time of need,*
Who leadest like a flock of sheep
  Thy loved Joseph's seed,
That sittest between the cherubs *bright*   5
  Between their wings outspread
Shine forth, *and from thy cloud give light,*
  And on our foes thy dread

2 In Ephraim's view and Benjamin's,
  And in Manasseh's sight   10
Awake * thy strength, come, and *be seen*   * *Gnorera.*
  To save us *by thy might.*

3 Turn us again, *thy grace divine*
  To us O God *vouchsafe;*
Cause thou thy face on us to shine   15
  And then we shall be safe.

4 Lord God of hosts, how long wilt thou,
  How long wilt thou declare
Thy *smoking wrath, *and angry brow*   * *Gnashanta.*
  Against thy people's prayer.   20

5 Thou feedest them with the bread of tears,
  Their bread with tears they eat,
And makst them *largely drink the tears   * *Shalish.*
  Wherewith their cheeks are wet.

6 A strife thou makest us *and a prey*   25
  To every neighbor foe,
Among themselves they *laugh, they *play,
  And *flouts at us they throw   * *Jilgnagu.*

7 Return us, *and thy grace divine,*
  O God of hosts *vouchsafe*   30
Cause thou thy face on us to shine,
  And then we shall be safe.

8 A vine from Egypt thou hast brought,
  Thy free love made it thine,
And drovest out nations *proud and haut*   35
  To plant this *lovely* vine.

9 Thou didst prepare for it a place
  And root it deep and fast
That it *began to grow apace,*
  And filled the land *at last.*   40

10 With her *green* shade that covered *all,*
    The hills were *overspread*
Her boughs as *high as* cedars tall
    Advanced their lofty head.

11 Her branches *on the western side*   45
    Down to the sea she sent,
And *upward* to that river *wide*
    Her other branches *went.*

12 Why hast thou laid her hedges low
    And broken down her fence,   50
That all may pluck her, as they go,
    With rudest violence?

13 The *tusked* boar out of the wood
    Upturns it by the roots,
Wild beasts there browse, and make their food   55
    Her grapes and tender shoots.

14 Return now, God of hosts, look down
    From heaven, thy seat divine,
Behold *us, but without a frown,*
    And visit this *thy* vine.   60

15 Visit this vine, which thy right hand
    Hath set, and planted *long,*
And the young branch, that for thyself
    Thou hast made firm and strong.

16 But now it is consumed with fire,   65
    And cut *with axes* down,
They perish at thy dreadful ire,
    At thy rebuke and frown.

17 Upon the man of thy right hand
    Let thy *good* hand be *laid,*   70
Upon the son of man, whom thou
    Strong for thyself hast made.

18 So shall we not go back from thee
    To ways of sin and shame,
Quicken us thou, then *gladly* we   75
    Shall call upon thy name.

[19] Return us, *and thy grace divine*
    Lord God of hosts *vouchsafe,*
Cause thou thy face on us to shine,
    And then we shall be safe.   80

PSALM LXXXI

1 To God our strength sing loud, *and clear*
    Sing loud to God *our king,*
To Jacob's God, *that all may hear*
    Loud acclamations ring.

2 Prepare a hymn, prepare a song   5
    The timbrel hither bring
The *cheerful* psaltery bring along
    And harp *with* pleasant *string,*

3 Blow, *as is wont*, in the new moon
   With trumpets' *lofty sound*,   10
The appointed time, the day whereon
   Our solemn feast *comes round*.

4 This was a statute *given of old*
   For Israel *to observe*
A law of Jacob's God, *to hold*   15
   From whence they might not swerve.

5 This he a testimony ordained
   In Joseph, *not to change*,
When as he passed through Egypt land;
   The tongue I heard, was strange.   20

6 From burden, *and from slavish toil*
   I set his shoulder free;
His hands from pots, *and miry soil*
   Delivered were *by me*.

7 When trouble did thee sore assail,   25
   On me then didst thou call,
And I to free thee *did not fail*,
   And led thee out of thrall.
I answered thee in * thunder deep   * *Be Sether ragnam.*
   With clouds encompassed round;   30
I tried thee at the water *steep*
   Of Meriba *renowned*.

8 Hear O my people, *hearken well*,
   I testify to thee
Thou ancient stock of Israel,   35
   If thou wilt list to me,

9 Throughout the land of thy abode
   No alien god shall be
Nor shalt thou to a foreign god
   In honor bend thy knee.   40

10 I am the Lord thy God which brought
   Thee out of Egypt land
Ask large enough, and I, *besought*,
   Will grant thy full demand.

11 And yet my people would not *hear*,   45
   Nor hearken to my voice;
And Israel *whom I loved so dear*
   Misliked me for his choice.

12 Then did I leave them to their will
   And to their wandering mind;   50
Their own conceits they followed still
   Their own devices blind.

13 Oh that my people would *be wise*
   To serve me *all their days*,
And oh that Israel would *advise*   55
   To walk my *righteous* ways.

14 Then would I soon bring down their foes
   That now so proudly rise,
And turn my hand against *all those*
   That are their enemies.   60

15 Who hate the Lord should *then be fain*
   To bow to him and bend,
But *they, his people, should remain,*
   Their time should have no end.
16 And he would feed them *from the shock*   65
   With flour of finest wheat,
And satisfy them from the rock
   With honey *for their meat.*

PSALM LXXXII

1 God in the * great * assembly stands   * *Bagnadath-el.*
   Of kings and lordly states,
† Among the gods † on both his hands   † *Bekerev.*
   He judges and debates.
2 How long will ye * pervert the right   * *Tishphetu*   5
   With * judgment false and wrong   *gnavel.*
Favoring the wicked *by your might.*
   Who thence grow bold and strong
3 * Regard the * weak and fatherless   * *Shiphtu-dal.*
   * Dispatch the * poor man's cause,   10
And † raise the man in deep distress
   By † just and equal laws.   † *Hatzdiku.*
4 Defend the poor and desolate,
   And rescue from the hands
Of wicked men the low estate   15
   Of him *that help demands.*
5 They know not nor will understand,
   In darkness they walk on
The earth's foundations all are * moved
   And * out of order gone.   * *Jimmotu.* 20
6 I said that ye were gods, yea all
   The sons of God most high
7 But ye shall die like men, and fall
   As other princes *die.*
8 Rise God, * judge thou the earth in might,   25
   This *wicked* earth * redress,   * *Shiphta.*
For thou art he who shalt by right
   The nations all possess.

PSALM LXXXIII

1 Be not thou silent *now at length*
   O God hold not thy peace,
Sit thou not still O God of *strength*
   We cry and do not cease.
2 For lo thy *furious* foes *now* * swell   5
   And * storm outrageously,   * *Jehemajun.*
And they that hate thee *proud and fell*
   Exalt their heads full high.

3 Against thy people they † contrive   † *Jagnarimu.*
       † Their plots and counsels deep,   † *Sod.* 10
    *Them to ensnare they chiefly strive   * *Jithjagnatsugnal.*
    *Whom thou dost hide and keep.   * *Tsephuneca.*
4 'Come let us cut them off' say they,
    'Till they no nation be
  That Israel's name forever may   15
    Be lost in memory.'
5 For they consult † with all their might,   † *Lev jachdau.*
    And all as one in mind
  Themselves against thee they unite
    And in firm union bind.   20
6 The tents of Edom, and the brood
    Of *scornful* Ishmael,
  Moab, with them of Hagar's blood
    That in the desert dwell,
7 Gebal and Ammon *there conspire,*   25
    And *hateful* Amalec,
  The Philistines, and they of Tyre
    Whose bounds the sea doth check.
8 With them *great* Asshur also bands
    And doth confirm the knot,   30
  All these have lent their armed hands
    To aid the sons of Lot.
9 Do to them as to Midian *bold*
    That wasted all the coast
  To Sisera, and as *is told*   35
    Thou didst to Jabin's *host,*
  When at the brook of Kishon *old*
    They were repulsed and slain,
10 At Endor quite cut off, and rolled
    As dung upon the plain.   40
11 As Zeb and Oreb evil sped
    So let their princes speed
  As Zeba, and Zalmunna *bled*
    So let their princes *bleed.*
12 *For they amidst their pride* have said   45
    'By right now shall we seize
  God's houses, and *will now invade*
    † Their stately palaces.'   † *Neoth Elohim*
                                      bears both.
13 My God, oh make them as a wheel
    No quiet let them find,   50
  Giddy and *restless* let *them reel*
    Like stubble from the wind.
14 *As when* an *aged* wood takes fire
    Which on a sudden strays,
  The *greedy* flame runs higher and higher   55
    Till all the mountains blaze,
15 So with thy whirlwind them pursue,
    And with thy tempest chase;
16 And till they *yield thee honor due;   * *They seek thy*
    Lord fill with shame their face.   *name,* Heb. 60

17 Ashamed and troubled let them be,
    Troubled and shamed forever,
  Ever confounded, and so die
    With shame, *and scape it never.*
18 Then shall they know that thou whose name   65
    Jehovah is alone,
  Art the most high, *and thou the same*
    O'er all the earth *art one.*

PSALM LXXXIV

1 How lovely are thy dwellings fair!
    O Lord of hosts, how dear
  The *pleasant* tabernacles are!
    Where thou dost dwell so near.
2 My soul doth long and almost die   5
    Thy courts O Lord to see,
  My heart and flesh aloud do cry,
    O living God, for thee.
3 There even the sparrow *freed from wrong*
    Hath found a house of *rest*,   10
  The swallow there, to lay her young
    Hath built her *brooding* nest,
  Even *by* thy altars Lord of hosts
    They find their safe abode,
  And home they fly from round the coasts   15
    Toward thee, my king, my God.
4 Happy, who in thy house reside
    Where thee they ever praise,
5 Happy, whose strength in thee doth bide,
    And in their hearts thy ways.   20
6 They pass through Baca's *thirsty* vale,
    That dry and barren ground
  As through a fruitful watery dale
    Where springs and showers abound.
7 They journey on from strength to strength   25
    With joy and gladsome cheer
  Till all before *our* God *at length*
    In Sion do appear.
8 Lord God of hosts hear *now* my prayer
    O Jacob's God give ear,   30
9 Thou God our shield look on the face
    Of thy anointed *dear*.
10 For one day in thy courts *to be*
    Is better, *and more blest*
  Than *in the joys of vanity*,   35
    A thousand days *at best*.
  I in the temple of my God
    Had rather keep a door,
  Than dwell in tents, *and rich abode*
    With sin *forevermore*.   40

11 For God the Lord both sun and shield
    Gives grace and glory *bright*,
No good from them shall be withheld
    Whose ways are just and right.
12 Lord *God* of hosts *that reignest on high*,   45
    That man is *truly* blest,
Who *only* on thee doth rely,
    And in thee only rest.

PSALM LXXXV

1 Thy land to favor graciously
    Thou hast not Lord been slack,
Thou hast from *hard* captivity
    Returned Jacob back.
2 The iniquity thou didst forgive   5
    That wrought thy people woe,
And all their sin, *that did thee grieve*
    Hast hid *where none shall know*.
3 Thine anger all thou hadst removed,
    And *calmly* didst return   10
From thy † fierce wrath which we had proved   † Heb. *The burning*
    Far worse than fire to burn.   *heat of thy wrath.*
4 God of our saving health and peace,
    Turn us, and us restore,
Thine indignation cause to cease   15
    Toward us, *and chide no more*.
5 Wilt thou be angry without end,
    Forever angry thus
Wilt thou thy frowning ire extend
    From age to age on us?   20
6 Wilt thou not * turn, and *hear our voice*   * Heb. *Turn*
    And thus again * revive,   *to quicken us.*
That so thy people may rejoice
    By thee preserved alive.
7 Cause us to see thy goodness Lord,   25
    To us thy mercy shew
Thy saving health to us afford
    And life in us renew.
8 *And now* what God the Lord will speak
    I will *go straight and* hear,   30
For to his people he speaks peace
    And to his saints *full dear*,
To his dear saints he will speak peace,
    But let them nevermore
Return to folly, *but surcease*   35
    To trespass as before.
9 Surely to such as do him fear
    Salvation is at hand
And glory shall *erelong appear*
    To dwell within our land.   40

10 Mercy and Truth *that long were missed*
    Now *joyfully* are met
  Sweet Peace and Righteousness have kissed
    And hand in hand are set.
11 Truth from the earth *like to a flower*   45
    Shall bud and blossom *then,*
  And justice from her heavenly bower
    Look down *on mortal men.*
12 The Lord will also then bestow
    Whatever thing is good   50
  Our land shall forth in plenty throw
    Her fruits *to be our food.*
13 Before him righteousness shall go
    His royal harbinger,
  Then * will he come, and not be slow   * Heb. *He will set* 55
    His footsteps cannot err.   *his steps to the way.*

PSALM LXXXVI

1 Thy *gracious* ear, O Lord, incline,
    O hear me *I thee pray,*
  For I am poor, and almost pine
    With need, *and sad decay.*
2 Preserve my soul, for † I have trod   † Heb. *I am good,* 5
    Thy ways, and love the just,   *loving, a doer of*
  Save thou thy servant O my God   *good and holy*
    Who *still* in thee doth trust.   *things.*
3 Pity me Lord for daily thee
    I call; 4 Oh make rejoice   10
  Thy servant's soul; for Lord to thee
    I lift my soul *and voice,*
5 For thou art good, thou Lord art prone
    To pardon, thou to all
  Art full of mercy, thou *alone*   15
    To them that on thee call.
6 Unto my supplication Lord
    Give ear, and to the cry
  Of my *incessant* prayers afford
    Thy hearing graciously.   20
7 I in the day of my distress
    Will call on thee *for aid;*
  For thou wilt *grant* me *free access*
    And answer, *what I prayed.*
8 Like thee among the gods is none   25
    O Lord, nor any works
  Of all that other gods have done
    Like to thy *glorious* works.
9 The nations all whom thou hast made
    Shall come, *and all shall frame*   30
  To bow them low before thee Lord
    And glorify thy name.

10 For great thou art, and wonders great
   By thy strong hand are done,
Thou *in thy everlasting seat*   35
   Remainest God alone.
11 Teach me O Lord thy way *most right*,
   I in thy truth will bide,
To fear thy name my heart unite
   So shall it never slide   40
12 Thee will I praise O Lord my God
   Thee honor, and adore
With my whole heart, and blaze abroad
   Thy name forevermore.
13 For great thy mercy is toward me,   45
   And thou hast freed my soul
Even from the lowest hell set free
   From deepest darkness foul.
14 O God the proud against me rise
   And violent men are met   50
To seek my life, and in their eyes
   No fear of thee have set.
15 But thou Lord art the God most mild
   Readiest thy grace to shew,
Slow to be angry, and *art styled*   55
   Most merciful, most true.
16 Oh turn to me *thy face at length*,
   And me have mercy on,
Unto thy servant give thy strength,
   And save thy handmaid's son.   60
17 Some sign of good to me afford,
   And let my foes *then* see
And be ashamed, because thou Lord
   Dost help and comfort me.

PSALM LXXXVII

1 Among the holy mountains *high*
   Is his foundation fast,
There seated in his sanctuary,
   His temple there is placed.
2 Sion's *fair* gates the Lord loves more   5
   Than all the dwellings *fair*
Of Jacob's *land, though there be store,*
   And all within his care.
3 City of God, most glorious things
   Of thee *abroad* are spoke;   10
I mention Egypt, *where proud kings*
   Did our forefathers yoke,
4 I mention Babel to my friends,
   Philistia *full of scorn*,
And Tyre with Ethiop's *utmost ends*,   15
   Lo this man there was born:

5 But *twice that praise shall in our ear*
    Be said of Sion *last*
  This and this man was born in her,
    High God shall fix her fast.   20
6 The Lord shall write it in a scroll
    That ne'er shall be outworn
  When he the nations doth enroll
    That this man there was born.
7 Both they who sing, and they who dance   25
    With sacred songs are there,
  In thee *fresh brooks, and soft streams glance*
    And all my fountains *clear.*

PSALM LXXXVIII

1 Lord God that dost me save and keep,
    All day to thee I cry;
  And all night long, before thee *weep*
    Before thee *prostrate lie.*
2 Into thy presence let my prayer   5
    With sighs devout ascend
  And to my cries, that *ceaseless are,*
    Thine ear with favor bend.
3 For cloyed with woes and trouble store
    Surcharged my soul doth lie,   10
  My life *at death's uncheerful door*
    Unto the grave draws nigh.
4 Reckoned I am with them that pass
    Down to the *dismal* pit
  I am a * man, but weak alas   * Heb. *A man without* 15
    And for that name unfit.   *manly strength.*
5 From life discharged and parted quite
    Among the dead *to sleep,*
  And like the slain *in bloody fight*
    That in the grave lie *deep,*   20
  Whom thou rememberest no more,
    Dost nevermore regard,
  Them from thy hand delivered o'er
    Death's hideous house hath barred.
6 Thou in the lowest pit *profound*   25
    Hast set me *all forlorn,*
  Where thickest darkness *hovers round,*
    In horrid deeps *to mourn.*
7 Thy wrath *from which no shelter saves*
    Full sore doth press on me;   30
  * Thou breakest upon me all thy waves,   * *The* Hebr.
    * And all thy waves break me.   *bears both.*
8 Thou dost my friends from me estrange,
    And makest me odious,
  Me to them odious, *for they change,*   35
    And I here pent up thus.

9 Through sorrow, and affliction great
   Mine eye grows dim and dead,
  Lord all the day I thee entreat,
   My hands to thee I spread.   40
10 Wilt thou do wonders on the dead,
   Shall the deceased arise
  And praise thee *from their loathsome bed*
   With pale and hollow eyes?
11 Shall they thy loving kindness tell   45
   On whom the grave *hath hold*,
  Or they *who* in perdition *dwell*
   Thy faithfulness *unfold*?
12 In darkness can thy mighty *hand*
   Or wondrous acts be known,   50
  Thy justice in the *gloomy* land
   Of *dark* oblivion?
13 But I to thee O Lord do cry
   Ere yet my life be spent,
  And *up to thee* my prayer *doth hie*   55
   Each morn, and thee prevent.
14 Why wilt thou Lord my soul forsake,
   And hide thy face from me,
15 That am already bruised, and † shake   † *Heb. Prae*
   With terror sent from thee;   *concussione.* 60
  Bruised, and afflicted and *so low*
   As ready to expire,
  While I thy terrors undergo
   Astonished with thine ire.
16 Thy fierce wrath over me doth flow   65
   Thy threatenings cut me through.
17 All day they round about me go,
   Like waves they me pursue.
18 Lover and friend thou hast removed
   And severed from me far.   70
  They *fly me now* whom I have loved,
   And as in darkness are.

Psalm I

(Done into verse, 1653)

Blessed is the man who hath not walked astray
In counsel of the wicked, and in the way
Of sinners hath not stood, and in the seat
Of scorners hath not sat.   But in the great
Jehovah's law is ever his delight,   5
And in his law he studies day and night.
He shall be as a tree which planted grows
By watery streams, and in his season knows
To yield his fruit, and his leaf shall not fall,
And what he takes in hand shall prosper all.   10
Not so the wicked, but as chaff which fanned
The wind drives, so the wicked shall not stand
In judgment, or abide their trial then,
Nor sinners in the assembly of just men.
For the Lord knows the upright way of the just,   15
And the way of bad men to ruin must.

Psalm II

(Done Aug. 8, 1653.   Terzetti)

Why do the Gentiles tumult, and the nations
  Muse a vain thing, the kings of the earth upstand
  With power, and princes in their congregations
Lay deep their plots together through each land,
  Against the Lord and his Messiah dear   5
  'Let us break off,' say they, 'by strength of hand
Their bonds, and cast from us, no more to wear,
  Their twisted cords:' he who in heaven doth dwell
  Shall laugh, the Lord shall scoff them, then severe
Speak to them in his wrath, and in his fell   10
  And fierce ire trouble them; 'but I' saith he
  'Anointed have my king (though ye rebel)
On Sion my holy hill.'   A firm decree
  I will declare; the Lord to me hath said
  'Thou art my Son I have begotten thee   15
This day; ask of me, and the grant is made;
  As thy possession I on thee bestow
  The heathen, and as thy conquest to be swayed
Earth's utmost bounds: them shalt thou bring full low
  With iron scepter bruised, and them disperse   20
  Like to a potter's vessel shivered so.'
And now be wise at length ye kings averse
  Be taught ye judges of the earth; with fear
  Jehovah serve, and let your joy converse

With trembling; kiss the Son lest he appear   25
    In anger and ye perish in the way
If once his wrath take fire like fuel sere.
Happy all those who have in him their stay

Psalm III

(Aug. 9, 1653)

When he fled from Absalom

Lord how many are my foes
            How many those
   That in arms against me rise
         Many are they
  That of my life distrustfully thus say,   5
'No help for him in God there lies.'
But thou Lord art my shield my glory,
            Thee through my story
   The exalter of my head I count
         Aloud I cried   10
  Unto Jehovah, he full soon replied
And heard me from his holy mount.
I lay and slept, I waked again,
         For my sustain
   Was the Lord.   Of many millions   15
         The populous rout
  I fear not though encamping round about
They pitch against me their pavilions.
Rise Lord, save me my God for thou
            Hast smote ere now   20
   On the cheekbone all my foes,
         Of men abhorred
  Hast broke the teeth.   This help was from the Lord
Thy blessing on thy people flows.

Psalm IV

(Aug. 10, 1653)

Answer me when I call
God of my righteousness
In straits and in distress
Thou didst me disenthrall
And set at large; now spare,   5
    Now pity me, and hear my earnest prayer.
Great ones how long will ye
My glory have in scorn
How long be thus forborne
Still to love vanity,   10
To love, to seek, to prize

Things false and vain and nothing else but lies?
Yet know the Lord hath chose
Chose to himself apart
The good and meek of heart
(For whom to choose he knows)   15
Jehovah from on high
    Will hear my voice what time to him I cry.
Be awed, and do not sin,
Speak to your hearts alone,
Upon your beds, each one,   20
And be at peace within.
Offer the offerings just
    Of righteousness and in Jehovah trust.
Many there be that say   25
'Who yet will show us good?'
Talking like this world's brood;
But Lord, thus let me pray,
On us lift up the light
    Lift up the favor of thy countenance bright.   30
Into my heart more joy
And gladness thou hast put
Than when a year of glut
Their stores doth overcloy
And from their plenteous grounds   35
    With vast increase their corn and wine abounds
In peace at once will I
Both lay me down and sleep
For thou alone dost keep
Me safe where'er I lie   40
As in a rocky cell
    Thou Lord alone in safety makst me dwell.

Psalm V

(Aug. 12, 1653)

Jehovah to my words give ear
    My meditation weigh
    The voice of my complaining hear
My king and God for unto thee I pray.
    Jehovah thou my early voice   5
        Shalt in the morning hear
    In the morning I to thee with choice
Will rank my prayers, and watch till thou appear.
    For thou art not a God that takes
        In wickedness delight   10
    Evil with thee no biding makes
Fools or madmen stand not within thy sight.
    All workers of iniquity

          Thou hatest; and them unblest
          Thou wilt destroy that speak a lie   15
The bloody and guileful man doth God detest.
          But I will in thy mercies dear
           Thy numerous mercies go
          Into thy house; I in thy fear
Will towards thy holy temple worship low   20
          Lord lead me in thy righteousness
           Lead me because of those
          That do observe if I transgress
Set thy ways right before, where my step goes.
          For in his faltering mouth unstable   25
           No word is firm or sooth
          Their inside, troubles miserable;
An open grave their throat, their tongue they smooth.
          God, find them guilty, let them fall
           By their own counsels quelled;   30
          Push them in their rebellions all
Still on; for against thee they have rebelled;
          Then all who trust in thee shall bring
           Their joy, while thou from blame
          Defendest them, they shall ever sing   35
And shall triumph in thee, who love thy name.
          For thou Jehovah wilt be found
           To bless the just man still,
          As with a shield thou wilt surround
Him with thy lasting favor and good will.   40

Psalm VI

(Aug. 13, 1653)

Lord in thy anger do not reprehend me
    Nor in thy hot displeasure me correct;
Pity me Lord for I am much deject
    Am very weak and faint; heal and amend me,
For all my bones, that even with anguish ache,   5
    Are troubled, yea my soul is troubled sore
And thou O Lord how long? turn Lord, restore
    My soul, O save me for thy goodness' sake
For in death no remembrance is of thee;
    Who in the grave can celebrate thy praise?   10
Wearied I am with sighing out my days,
    Nightly my couch I make a kind of sea;
My bed I water with my tears; mine eye
    Through grief consumes, is waxen old and dark
In the midst of all mine enemies that mark.   15
    Depart all ye that work iniquity,
Depart from me, for the voice of my weeping
    The Lord hath heard, the Lord hath heard my prayer
My supplication with acceptance fair
    The Lord will own, and have me in his keeping.   20

Mine enemies shall all be blank and dashed
   With much confusion; then grow red with shame,
They shall return in haste the way they came
   And in a moment shall be quite abashed.

Psalm VII

(Aug. 14, 1653)

Upon the words of Chush the Benjamite against him

Lord my God to thee I fly
Save me and secure me under
Thy protection while I cry,
Lest as a lion (and no wonder)
He haste to tear my soul asunder   5
Tearing and no rescue nigh.

Lord my God if I have thought
Or done this, if wickedness
Be in my hands, if I have wrought
Ill to him that meant me peace,   10
Or to him have rendered less,
And not freed my foe for naught;

Let the enemy pursue my soul
And overtake it, let him tread
My life down to the earth and roll   15
In the dust my glory dead,
In the dust and there outspread
Lodge it with dishonor foul.

Rise Jehovah in thine ire
Rouse thyself amidst the rage   20
Of my foes that urge like fire;
And wake for me, their fury assuage;
Judgment here thou didst engage
And command which I desire.

So the assemblies of each nation   25
Will surround thee, seeking right,
Thence to thy glorious habitation
Return on high and in their sight.
Jehovah judgeth most upright
All people from the world's foundation.   30

Judge me Lord, be judge in this
According to my righteousness,
And the innocence which is
Upon me: cause at length to cease
Of evil men the wickedness   35
And their power that do amiss.

But the just establish fast,
Since thou art the just God that tries
Hearts and reins.   On God is cast
My defense, and in him lies   40
In him who both just and wise
Saves the upright of heart at last.

God is a just judge and severe,
And God is every day offended;
If the unjust will not forbear,   45
His sword he whets, his bow hath bended
Already, and for him intended
The tools of death, that waits him near.

(His arrows purposely made he
For them that persecute.)   Behold   50
He travails big with vanity,
Trouble he hath conceived of old
As in a womb, and from that mold
Hath at length brought forth a lie.

He digged a pit, and delved it deep,   55
And fell into the pit he made,
His mischief that due course doth keep,
Turns on his head, and his ill trade
Of violence will undelayed
Fall on his crown with ruin steep.   60

Then will I Jehovah's praise
According to his justice raise
And sing the name and deity
Of Jehovah the most high.

Psalm VIII

(*Aug. 14, 1653*)

O Jehovah our Lord how wondrous great
   And glorious is thy name through all the earth?
So as above the heavens thy praise to set
   Out of the tender mouths of latest birth,

Out of the mouths of babes and sucklings thou   5
   Hast founded strength because of all thy foes
To stint the enemy, and slack the avenger's brow
   That bends his rage thy providence to oppose

When I behold thy heavens, thy fingers' art,
   The moon and stars which thou so bright hast set,   10
In the pure firmament, then saith my heart,
   O what is man that thou rememberest yet,

And thinkest upon him; or of man begot
   That him thou visitest and of him art found;
Scarce to be less than gods, thou madest his lot,   15
   With honor and with state thou hast him crowned.

O'er the works of thy hand thou madest him lord,
   Thou hast put all under his lordly feet,
All flocks, and herds, by thy commanding word,
   All beasts that in the field or forest meet.   20

Fowl of the heavens, and fish that through the wet
   Sea-paths in shoals do slide.   And know no dearth.
O Jehovah our Lord how wondrous great
   And glorious is thy name through all the earth.

INDEX OF TITLES AND FIRST LINES

(The apparent discrepancy between the page given to some titles and that of the first lines of the same poems is due to the length of some headnotes. The titles are in italic type.)